D1450965

DATE			

JUL   1996

BAKER & TAYLOR

Dickens and Thackeray

Dickens and Thackeray

Punishment and Forgiveness

John R. Reed

OHIO UNIVERSITY PRESS

ATHENS

Ohio University Press, Athens, Ohio 45701

99   98   97   96   95   5   4   3   2   1

Ohio University Press books are printed on acid-free paper ∞

Library of Congress Cataloging-in-Publication Data

Reed, John Robert, 1938–
    Dickens and Thackeray : punishment and forgiveness / John R. Reed.
        p.   cm.
    Includes bibliographical references and index.
    ISBN 0–8214–1117–9
    1. Dickens, Charles, 1812–1870—Political and social views.
2. Punishment in literature.   3. Thackeray, William Makepeace,
1811–1863—Political and social views.   4. Literature and society—
England—History—19th century.   5. English fiction—19th century—
History and criticism.   6. Thackeray, William Makepeace, 1811–1863—
Ethics.   7. Dickens, Charles, 1812–1870—Ethics.   8. Forgiveness in
literature.   I. Title.
PR4592.P76R44   1995
823′.809353—dc20
                                                            94-40416
                                                            CIP

For Ruth

Table of Contents

Acknowledgements

Some of the contents of this study appeared elsewhere in different form. Material from chapter 2 appeared in "Learning to Punish: Victorian Children's Literature," *Bucknell Review: Culture and Education in Victorian England,* ed. Patrick Scott and Pauline Fletcher (Lewisburg: Bucknell University Press, 1990), 99–107. Material on Dickens appeared in "Authorized Punishment in Dickens's Fiction," *Studies in the Novel,* 24, No. 2 (Summer 1992), 112–30. And general materials appeared in "Paying Up: The Last Judgment and Forgiveness of Debt," *Victorian Literature and Culture,* 20, ed. John Maynard and Adrienne Auslander Munich (New York: AMS Press, 1993), 55–68.

Preface

Punishment and forgiveness seem essential to the human condition. It would be difficult to find any human society in which some form of punishment is not employed to discipline its members and some form of forgiveness or pardon is not allowed for those who have broken its rules. But if these two rudimentary actions are ubiquitous, they are certainly not uniform, varying not only through history, but from one religion, nation, or community to another.[1]

It is important to make some elementary distinctions about what we mean by punishment and forgiveness. In *Punishment and Desert,* for example, John Kleinig writes that "'Punishment' . . . properly applies only to those legal sanctions in which the offender is exposed to moral condemnation; otherwise he is more appropriately spoken of as being penalized."[2] A rule-breaker may be a good man, but he can be penalized for breaking the rule, even if the rule itself is considered by many as immoral. Punishment thus has more than a simple disciplining function, for it also seeks to instruct and acculturate its object. Moreover, punishment is generally connected directly to a specific order of offense, and this connection often evokes an attempt to determine the level of desert the offender has accumulated. In a sense, the violator acquires a debt to his community that he must redeem through physical pain, deprivation, or other forms of hurt. Unlike entitlement and liability, which are associated with institutions and contracts, desert is specifically allied with a willing agent. "Desert claims," says Kleinig, "rely on the valuation of characteristics possessed or things done by the subject," and these valuations are often relative and slippery (61). They can never be precise. If a wrongdoer is assumed to be a free and willing agent, punishment, too, assumes such freedom. Again, Kleinig writes that "only those conditions specifying that punishment is an *activity of some responsible agent or agency,* whereby it *deliberately* acts to impose on a moral agent because it believes that agent to have committed some wrong, can be said to be conceptually necessary to a significant, nonmetaphorical use of the word" (42). In his important book *Punishment and Responsibility,* H. L. A. Hart deals with the complicated nature of legal judgment under the doctrine of *mens rea,* which is allied to the notion of free will insofar as it takes into consideration the state of mind of the person accused of a crime.[3]

Punishment is a morally charged term, but it is here necessary to make an additional distinction. Sir Walter Moberly states that the most important question about punishment is—Is it deserved?[4] Not all punishment is just. If a person who has committed no wrong is nonetheless made to suffer, he or she suffers an unjust punishment, or, as Kleinig would say, penalty. Human justice often errs and the innocent are often punished, but this is not the true rudimentary sense of the term "punishment," which requires wrongdoing. Only genuine offenders can be punished. Of course, the degree of relationship between desert and punishment can vary from the most corrupt and careless individual or institutional action up to the flawless judgment of an all-knowing divinity.

A. C. Ewing held as one fundamental assumption of his book *The Morality of Punishment* (1929) that "in Ethics it is possible for us to have real knowledge of what is good and right," and much thinking about punishment begins with a similar outlook.[5] However this may be, there is no doubt that in human society punishment has been viewed in many different ways, with different purposes. The ancient *lex talionis* required an eye for an eye and a tooth for a tooth—as precise a form of desert as possible. This is a form of retributive punishment: suffering designed as a form of blame for a transgression of some rule or law. Retributive punishment can be impersonal or vindictive, merely correcting through suffering, or taking delight in the infliction of pain as a form of vengeance. Hegel, for example, saw punishment as an annulment of crime, a turning crime back on itself. But, Moberly indicates, "Punishment never *is* itself the intrinsic retribution of wrong; it never can itself undo wrong" (200). It is simply a sign for the cancellation of the crime.

R. A. Duff distinguishes between two classes of punishment. Retributivists consider punishment justified as an intrinsic response to an offense, whereas consequentialists see punishment in terms of its contingent benefits.[6] The Utilitarian attitude toward punishment, beginning with Jeremy Bentham, is an example of this latter attitude. Punishment does not function to avenge crime, but to prevent it. Punishment becomes distributive and exemplary—those who deserve punishment receive it to correct their future behavior, and at the same time their being punished serves as an example to others not to commit the same crime and deserve the same punishment. R. A. Duff comments, however, that deterrence cannot be the only objective of punishment; punishment must be proportional to a moral wrong as well (153).

For Bentham, a non-Christian, forgiveness is a virtue only when justice has done its work (Moberly 50). But most of Western culture is influenced morally by the teachings of Christianity. Duff asks if the Christian faith's requirement to forgive those who trespass against us should not reasonably be the spirit of our treatment of others (65). He urges that our critical response in judging others should be informed by a humility about the values by which we judge ourselves (72). Thus, in both the moral and legal systems that characterize Western culture, the urge to punish is tempered by the adjuration to forgive. Again a distinction must be made between pardoning and forgiving an offense. Nigel Walker remarks that "Forgiveness does not seem to have degrees."[7] Forgiveness occurs when a victim's resentment is reduced to nil, not merely lessened. To pardon is to free the offender from punishment, but that does not mean the offender is forgiven for the injury. To forgive is to remit all debt for the injury, but that does not mean the offender will escape punishment for the forgiven injury. Hence the victim of an assault may forgive the attacker, but legal authorities might punish the attacker anyway. "Forgiveness" is a word in a moral lexicon, "pardon" in a legal one.[8] "Punishment" appears in both.

There has been a great deal of discussion about punishment and justice in the last two centuries and it remains a lively topic.[9] Much recent discussion goes over old ground, but some of it seeks to offer new remedies. Kleinig is one recent writer who suggests a variation on a scheme proposed in the nineteenth century—establishing a scale of wrongdoing with appropriate punishments for each degree (125). Walter Kaufmann, writing out of a moral and philosophical rather than legal tradition, recommends the outright abolition of guilt and institutionalized justice. He argues that most people in modern times suffer from decidophobia, the dread of autonomy.[10] The road to autonomy is blocked by guilt and justice. Kaufmann lists the stages of justice as (1) conforming to custom, (2) constituting the sum of the virtues, (3) standing for a particular virtue, and (4) representing the quality of punishments and distributions. The fifth stage of justice, he says, is the death of retributive justice, and the next should be the death of distributive justice as well, because modern scepticism has led both to the death of justice and to doubt about natural law. Kaufmann prefers responsibility to guilt, and recommends a new integrity of the individual. The autonomous individual forgives him or herself, he says, while cautioning that not all who forgive themselves are autonomous (125). It will come as no surprise to anyone who knows of Walter Kaufmann's contribution to scholarship that this remedy for the human race sounds a good deal like existential philosophy, and that Kaufmann's examples of autonomous individuals of the past include Socrates, Nietzsche, and Goethe.

Punishment is one mode of trying to internalize in another person values that we as a community embrace. Yet punishment can be viewed in two distinctly different modes, that of the agency of justice and that of the person punished. Elaine Scarry writes that "Moments in the Old Testament where punishment is rendered because of doubt are to a large extent paradigmatic of all other moments of punishment: that is, immoral behavior or disobedience or cruelty are extreme forms of doubt, extreme failures of belief, the failure to absorb into oneself and to embody in one's acts and attitudes a concept of God."[11] But, as the history of punishment and human justice indicates, this is not a simple endeavor. One reason is precisely that there is an external and an internal way of perceiving pain and suffering. Scarry instructs us that it is next to impossible to experience in our own imagination the pain—especially the bodily pain—of another human being. That is why novels and other narratives become necessary to sensitize us to anguish not our own. According to Scarry, "the fact that the very word 'pain' has its etymological home in *'poena'* or 'punishment' reminds us that even the elementary act of naming this most interior of events entails an immediate mental somersault out of the body into the external social circumstances that can be pictured as having caused the hurt" (16).

In the equation of punishment and forgiveness, by far the greater degree of attention has been given to punishment. Perhaps that is because forgiveness seems such a relatively simple, unproblematic concept. Ewing, for example, writing in the tradition of ethics and law, supposes that "It might be said that there is rarely any difficulty in reconciling the duty of forgiveness and the duty of punishment" (31). The duty of forgiveness! Would this expression appear anywhere today in the secular discourse on justice? John Rawls' impressive *A Theory of Justice,* in proposing a justice of fairness, discusses duty at length and necessarily canvasses notions of punishment, but the word forgiveness scarcely shows itself.[12] And it is for this reason necessary for us to recover the strikingly important role forgiveness played in Western culture only a few decades ago.

Whatever scheme of guilt, reparation, punishment, and forgiveness we may construct in the future, we have a good idea of what that scheme has been for the last hundred years or so. And that scheme has ancient roots. Concern with punishment and forgiveness is solidly embedded in Western culture and has a peculiar cast because it is so profoundly influenced by Christianity as well as by the Hebraic tradition. In choosing this polarity, therefore, I go as deeply as it may be possible to go into the cultural bases of our belief and behavior. But my purpose in treating punishment and forgiveness as themes is not philosophical but aesthetic, for what I hope to show is the way strongly held beliefs about what punishment and forgiveness involve determine the ways in which stories can be told. I have chosen two of the most prominent novelists of their day, who have shown staying power into our own and who, while sharing certain rudimentary moral convictions, are nevertheless sufficiently unlike to permit them to tell their stories in markedly different ways. In pursuing this enterprise I am obviously reasserting what some feel to be a discredited humanistic approach to literature; that is, I believe literary texts are not merely part of a network of "texts" divorced from a generative human intellect and spirit, but that they are the expressions of unique imaginative sources with their own imaginative methods.

We have been celebrating theory long enough for reactions to have set in, and thus objections are increasingly being raised against new formalisms and new anarchies. Without taking a position "against theory," or advocating a cessation of the advancement of theoretical positions, this study explores certain underlying assumptions affecting the creation of texts. Borrowing a gesture from Marxist approaches, it locates a base from which a superstructure emerges, but the base I examine is moral rather than economic. Many practicing critics may have lost their faith in literary texts as vehicles for message, but there can be little doubt that many texts, especially before the twentieth century, were intended to bear such messages. We need not fall back into the black hole of intentionality, asserting that all meaning must be linked to an author's conscious design, but it may nonetheless be unwise to ignore either an author's stated intentions and the evidences which bear those intentions out, or signs of less self-conscious processes shaping literary works. For Dickens, the narrator of a novel enjoys the role of Fate, Providence, or some other directing power, who can so arrange the distribution of justice that the novel's moral pattern will not easily be mistaken. Like providence, the narrator may use vile agents to carry out punishments that no official scheme of justice would endorse. He can also arrange the events of his plot and their ordering so that a fundamental moral order will prevail.

Because I wish to preserve some sense of distance between author and narrative without abandoning the concept of a real author altogether, I have drawn upon some terms and ideas employed in narratology. Thus it seems useful to me to distinguish between the real Dickens and Thackeray, the men who conceived and wrote novels, and an implied author who is the organizing agency for a given narrative, though not to be confused with the narrative voice that conveys the matter of the text to the reader. Similarly, literary criticism has recently turned its attention toward the role of audiences in the interpretation of texts and I have tried here to demonstrate how both Dickens and Thackeray had high expectations about their readers' participation in their endeavor, though these two authors manifested their expectations in very different ways.

Inevitably this study is repetitive, because I hope to show the constants underlying the apparently various surfaces of literary texts and to demonstrate the recurring narrative strategies these authors used to convey an unvarying message without violating certain self-imposed sanctions. One method of doing this is through redundancy itself. Susan Rubin Suleiman has studied redundancy as a feature of propagandistic writing. She observes, "In the *roman è thèse,* where a single 'correct' reading is required (or more exactly, is posited as a desired effect), we can expect that there will be a considerable amount of redundancy."[13] I am arguing here that where an implicit message serves as the foundation of a narrative, a similar redundancy will be in play. Repeated, mirrored, and parodied expressions or events accumulating through a text reinforce, either subtly or boldly, its underlying assumptions. Perhaps I may be forgiven for employing the device of redundancy that worked so well for the authors under discussion. I try to quote numerous passages from their works that indicate that the language of punishment and forgiveness is theirs, not something I have superimposed upon them.

I have avoided examining only one major text—*The Mystery of Edwin Drood.* It was tempting to approach that text with Dickens' pattern of treating punishment and forgiveness in mind, but ultimately I felt that a need to project some ending for the narrative might corrupt an analysis of what is there, and so I avoided the novel altogether.

In what follows, I offer a brief examination of how Victorians saw punishment and forgiveness in representative aspects of society, and then proceed to examine in detail the works of Dickens and Thackeray.

NOTES

1. In *Plato and Punishment* (Berkeley: University of California Press, 1981), Mary Margaret Mackenzie shows some similarities and many differences between classical Greek and modern views of punishment. For example, in Homer, what might be called punishment is a matter of individual activity and is characterized by a sense of liability but not necessarily blame, a curious notion for the twentieth century (86). Of course, Greek thinking allowed for retributive punishment by the gods, and there was institutional punishment exacted by monarchs. Plato's approach to punishment is founded on the chief moral assumption "that vice has evil consequences, whereas virtue produces good" (146). Centuries later Dickens would root his moral narratives on a similar belief.

2. John Kleinig, *Punishment and Desert* (The Hague: Martinus Nijhoff, 1973), 28. Subsequent references appear in the text.

3. H. L. A. Hart, *Punishment and Responsibility: Essays in the Philosophy of Law* (New York: Oxford University Press, 1968), 200ff.

4. Sir Walter Moberly, *The Ethics of Punishment* (Hamden, CT: Archon Books, 1968), 78. Subsequent references appear in the text.

5. A. C. Ewing, *The Morality of Punishment with Some Suggestions for a General Theory of Ethics* (Montclair, NJ: Patterson Smith, 1970) [Originally published 1929], 6. Subsequent references appear in the text.

6. R. A. Duff, *Trials and Punishments* (Cambridge: Cambridge University Press, 1986), 3–4. Subsequent references appear in the text.

7. Nigel Walker, *Why Punish?* (Oxford: Oxford University Press, 1991), 14. Subsequent references appear in the text.

8. Walker says, "Forgiveness is an attitude: mercy is an action" (115).

9. In addition to works already mentioned, some other works attending to punishment as a moral or legal issue include A. von Hirsch's *Doing Justice: The Choice of Punishments: Report of the Committee for the Study of Incarceration* (New York: Hill and Wang, 1976), J. F. Gibbs' *Crime, Punishment and Deterrence* (Amsterdam: Elsevier, 1975), C. L. Ten's *Crime, Guilt and Punishment* (Oxford: Clarendon Press, 1987), and Nigel Walker's *Punishment, Danger and Stigma* (Oxford: Basil Blackwell, 1980). An interesting debate carried out with great courtesy also considers the far less popular issue of mercy. See Jeffrie G. Murphy and Jean Hampton, *Forgiveness and Mercy* (Cambridge: Cambridge University Press, 1988).

10. Walter Kaufmann, *Without Guilt and Justice: From Decidophobia to Autonomy* (New York: Delta Books, 1975), 3. Subsequent references appear in the text.

11. Elaine Scarry, *The Body in Pain: The Making and Unmaking of the World* (New York: Oxford University Press, 1985), 202). Subsequent references appear in the text.

12. John Rawls, *A Theory of Justice* (Cambridge: The Belknap Press of Harvard University Press, 1971), passim.

13. Susan Rubin Suleiman, *Authoritarian Fictions: The Ideological Novel As a Literary Genre* (New York: Columbia University Press, 1983), 150.

PART ONE

The Context

ONE

Attitudes Toward Punishment and Forgiveness in Moral Texts of the Victorian Period

VICTORIAN SOCIETY was overwhelmingly Christian in its "official" culture and therefore punishment and forgiveness played important roles in the moral lives of its citizenry whether willingly or not. But, although Christianity emphasizes forgiveness over punishment, Victorian society made only token efforts to follow that course in its institutions, no matter how much its benign forms of propaganda encouraged charity and mercy.

According to Nietzsche, Christianity is the weakling's way of assuming power, and it often carries with it a bad conscience about the methods used. The *ressentiment* of the underdog rankles long after it has provided the energy and wiliness to supplant the healthy but unselfconscious master race. As a consequence, it becomes necessary for good Christians to deny the lust for power by proclaiming their humility and their unworthiness in the eyes of God, or to identify themselves as merely instruments of God's providential purpose. But this denial, this hypocrisy, has its revenge in removing the natural world as a source of pleasure and delight from the true Christian, whose attention should be directed elsewhere. Therefore, what was natural and a source of renewal for the master race becomes a source of discontent for the Christian, for whom nature is unnatural, requiring the dominating power of the spirit. This attitude, in turn, begets a pernicious dualism setting body and soul at odds. Disease—physical, psychological, or moral—is the inevitable result. Punishment and self-punishment become inevitable accessories of Christianity, whereas something like self-forgiveness characterizes the master race.

This is an interesting narrative but most readers today have sense enough to distrust any account that begins with the phrase "According to Nietzsche," and this account is no exception, though Nietzsche's approach to the question of moral superiority is helpful in understanding how human beings, at least in the last few hundred years, have dealt with matters of authority and responsibility. In the present study I shall be concerned with the way in which one culture viewed the task of establishing moral and other rules and how it enforced those rules or excused their violation. In order to understand these matters I shall have to examine theological, ethical, legal, and educational attitudes.

Because religious belief underlay so much of Victorian thought and action, it is probably best to begin with the moral and theological situation. That faith was mainly protestant, and, in the period I am considering, significantly influenced by the Evangelical movement. This faith was founded primarily on Scripture; therefore a natural beginning for a discussion of punishment and forgiveness is the Bible. But the Bible offers an inconsistent message, or array of messages over which theologians and scholars have quarreled for centuries. Take Original Sin. If humankind begins life already fallen, must we assume that it already requires or deserves punishment or is a probationary mercy allowed? Must it be washed clean by conversion or baptism? This avenue of thought runs from the solution of predestination to that of universal divine forgiveness. Or consider the intent of God's punishment in the Old Testament. Does he punish with absolute justice? If so, how explain the many acts of mercy toward sinners? Does he follow some *lex talionis* of his own? If so, why does he often punish whole peoples for the offenses of one or a few individuals?[1] And what of the New Testament? Does Christ's image of a loving God replace the Old Testament judge? Does Paul take Christ's teaching too far when he states a new ethical code of love, asking his followers not to take revenge, but to forgive their enemies? Paul argued that this was a practical approach because the true way to change the heart from bad to good was through acceptance and forgiveness, not condemnation and punishment.

The trouble with the Bible is, of course, that it is such a complex document, assembled over such a long period of time, that selective reference can be used to support any number of competing and even contradictory arguments. It is no surprise, then, that nineteenth-century England, so intent upon reviving the Christian message, should be a hotbed of theological controversy. Prominent among the many disputes was the very significant issue of punishment in the afterlife, arguably the most important form of punishment that a Christian can consider. Rowland Williams was put on trial for his paper in *Essays and Reviews* denying the existence of eternal punishment.[2] F. D. Maurice's unorthodox views on the subject in *Theological Essays* got him fired from King's College. Maurice did not deny that there was a heaven and a hell but explained that they were not conceivable in spatial and temporal terms.[3] He argued that eternity in relation to God has nothing to do with time or duration, hence eternity in reference to life or to punishment also has nothing to do with time or duration.[4] Moreover, God did not assign humans to either one. Eternal life is to do God's will and become the servant of His love towards one's fellows, and to be filled by the love of self-sacrifice and hence set free from selfishness. Eternal death is having one's own way, being left alone by God. "What is Perdition but a loss?" Maurice asked. "What is eternal damnation, but the loss of a good which God had revealed to His creatures, of which He had put them in possession?" (Maurice 345). Dante, he said, had understood this loss as suffering. "The loss of intellectual life, of the vision of God, is with him the infinite horror of hell. Men are in eternal misery, because they are still covetous, proud, loveless" (345). Maurice objected to the use of eternal punishment as a means of coercing people to abandon sin. Humankind should learn instead to fear sin rather than punishment. Maurice went further and shocked his orthodox colleagues by maintaining the possibility of conversion after death. As Torben Christensen concludes, "The apocatastasis, the restitution of all things in God, appears to be the necessary outcome of Maurice's eschatological teaching" (288). But Maurice's critics were wrong to equate his views with Universalism (certain salvation of all humanity), though obviously his hopes for the Final Judgment tended that way.

> For Maurice, as for Newman, the significance of eschatology was that it spoke of the final consummation of the relationship with God, in which man existed in his present life. Heaven was the acknowledgement of, and growth into, that relationship. Hell was the failure to recognize and live in terms of it; it was the failure to recognize where the true fulfilment of human nature was to be found.[5]

For Maurice Judgment Day did not involve the analogy of a judge dispensing punishment and reward, but the parallel legal analogy of a judge who seeks out the truth. Speaking of this concept in Scripture, Maurice said: "Everywhere the idea is kept before us of judgment, in its fullest, largest, most natural sense, as importing discrimination or discovery" (226).

Like Maurice, James Hinton declared that "Sinning is damnation: self-indulgence is to be cast into hell."[6] Thus damnation is not a future event but an eternal process. Admitting that he did not know what happens at the death of the body, Hinton nonetheless felt that that event could not be the end of an individual's probation for eternity. W. R. Greg carried this admission of ignorance further, suggesting that we do not know enough about good and evil in men to understand just reward and punishment, and that although we can prove man's determination to believe in an afterlife, we cannot prove the existence of such a hereafter.[7]

Geoffrey Rowell says that the debate on hell and the afterlife was largely concentrated between 1830 and 1880 and that views were notably modified over the years (17).[8] He gives as one example Bishop Samuel Wilberforce's preaching of everlasting punishment at the beginning of the century and his son's later espousal of Universalism (3). Rowell offers a series of articles in *The Nineteenth Century* in 1877 under the title "A Modern 'Symposium'" as another illustration of growing doubts about an afterlife. These articles were in response to a positivist paper by Frederic Harrison, but not even High Anglican or Catholic respondents mentioned hell. Still, there were many who adhered to the concept of eternal punishment, among them John Henry Newman in such works as *The Dream of Gerontius* and *A Grammar of Assent*.[9] In 1866 Edward Henry Bickersteth's long theological poem *Yesterday, To-Day, and For Ever* appeared, which included a vivid account of the Last Judgment, including the sufferings of Satan. Even the mild-natured William Allingham recorded the following exchange in his diary: "Thornton Hunt is dead—Leigh Hunt was saying one day, what a fine thing it would be if a subscription could be made *to abolish Hell;* but I remarked 'Decidedly a bad investment, that would be!'—which grieved Hunt considerably.' "[10] In 1884 Allingham noted that Tennyson "spoke of Eternal Punishment as an obsolete belief." Allingham replied that the Bible seems to endorse it to which Tennyson responded that it is not a right translation, then asked Allingham if he had read Farrar's book, remarking that "here he proves from original sources that no such doctrine existed in the early days of Christianity" (328). The book Tennyson refers to is F. W. Farrar's *Eternal Hope* (1878), which argued, as did Maurice, that hell was a state of the spirit not a habitation and suggested that the individual soul's fate was not irrevocably sealed at death, positions that called forth an orthodox response from Pusey, *What is of Faith as to Everlasting Punishment?* (1880) (Rowell 139ff.). Gladstone, who expressed concern over meliorating books like *Eternal Hope,* felt that this unfortunate tendency to minimize the "terrors of the Lord" began with Mivart's *The Happiness of Hell*.[11] However, he credited Farrar with a belief in eternal punishment that he himself could endorse. "Punishment may be considered as a judgment from without, but it is also a natural growth from within, and is the consequence, in the way of natural growth, which sin deliberately persisted in of itself brings about" (120). Gladstone would have been pleased with the Reverend John Warton's account in *Death-Bed Scenes and Pastoral Conversations* of his attempt to rescue the soul of one Mr. Marsden. Marsden is a nonbeliever who has ruined his health with drink and now is slowly dying. He does not want Warton's ministrations but the cleric persists. At one point Marsden says he does not want to listen to Warton's arguments because he has made up his mind. Warton's response is classic.

> "Made up to do what?" I demanded eagerly. "To die in your sins? without repentance; without prayer; without a tear; without asking for pardon; without calling upon your Saviour to intercede for your soul; without beseeching the Holy Spirit to purify and sanctify it, before it quits your body to appear before its Judge? Is it this to which your mind is made up? Then it is made up to dwell with everlasting burnings; in lakes of fire and brimstone which will never be quenched; with gnawing worms, with stinging scorpions, with furious devils, exulting in torments which they will inflict upon you."[12]

Later Warton admits that such graphic images of pain may not be literally true, but are necessary representations for the limited human imagination to appreciate suffering. When Marsden objects to the idea of eternal punishment for offenses in temporal existence, Warton assures him that, just as eternal glory would have followed from a virtuous life, so eternal punishment is not an unjust consequence of sin. The sinner who has refused to be taught his errors in this life will discover in the next the meaning of Christ's sacrifice. God will then say to the lost creature: "Your punishment will force this conviction upon you, and the conviction shall be a part of your punishment. Your reward should have been eternal, however short your life, if you had loved and feared me; your punishment shall be eternal, because you have hated and despised me" (62).

Thomas Arnold, whose creed was somewhat gentler than Warton's, nonetheless could conceive of an unforgiveable state of sin which closely approximates Marsden's condition as Warton presents it. That state is occasioned by the sin of blasphemy against the Holy Spirit, the condemnation of Christianity "because its spirit is pure and meek and self-denying, and [the sinner] is lustful, and revengeful, and selfish. . . ." Such a sinner speaks not only against Christ but against the Holy Ghost; "he has chosen to love evil and hate good, and if good triumph he must be for ever miserable."[13] One argument against God's eternal punishment was that it would involve condemning the greater part of humanity. There were, of course, many responses to this charge, but Henry Thornton offers a mild one. If you believe that God can punish one offender justly, then you must assume that all such offenders will be punished, whether many or few. The truly just and virtuous may constitute a very small minority after all, as the example of Noah and his family seems to suggest, since they alone were saved in their generation.[14]

J. Arthur Hoyles lists three mutually exclusive theories of punishment in the afterlife. One is that such punishment is an eternal torment. Objections to this theory are that it does not allow for degrees of culpability and that it makes no provision for repentance and amendment. A second theory is that of complete destruction of the sinful, which, however, overlooks the immortality of the soul. Punishment as a refining power is the third theory, which, in Roman Catholicism, led to the concept of Purgatory, approved by Pope Gregory at the beginning of the seventh century A.D. (Hoyles 84–89). All three of these theories were current in nineteenth-century England, though outside the Catholic Church the first predominated. One need only recall Dante's *Inferno* to realize that there are answers to the claim that the theory fails to allow for degrees of culpability, since the degree of suffering may be scaled to the degree of offense. Many still adhered to the venerable tradition represented by Thomas à Kempis' *Of The Imitation of Christ* which asserted: "There is no sin but shall have its own proper torment." This popular text declared: "In what things a man hath sinned, in the same shall he be the more grievously punished."[15] So a glutton will starve, a slothful person be prodded, and so forth. In his sermon "The Terror of the Day of Judgment as Arising from its Justice," Edward Bouverie Pusey acknowledged that there would be a division of the faithful and the sinful on the last day and that there would be degrees of joy and suffering to all according to their deserts.[16] And his was not an unusual position, one text supporting it being Christ's declaration that in his Father's house there were many mansions (John 14:2).

Disputants in Victorian England got well past the simple image of a sea of fire forever tormenting naked souls. As we have seen, Maurice and others supported the notion that amendment might occur after death. If the human soul is immortal, time is not its centrally determining factor. However, Maurice and those who thought like him were overlooking one of the most familiar images of human existence—that it is a probationary period during which our behavior determines our station in the afterlife. According to this scheme, human death is the end of the race. Beyond that finish line our individual merits will be calculated. I have purposely used a sporting metaphor; the most common metaphors were with systems of legal justice. God sits in judgment like a king or a judge, dividing the worthy from the unworthy. Pusey pointed out that the terror of the Day of Judgment is precisely that it *is* a judgment, that it is, in large part, an expression of God's displeasure (16). In his sermon "Sin and Judgment," R. W. Church acknowledged that we must be guarded in what we say about the punishment of sin, knowing as little as we do, but this did not prevent him from making certain assertions. He accepted life as a test.

> It is, as it seems to me, that the future is viewed in immediate and exclusive relation to this life as a life of probation, a life given for obedience and duty, and inextricably connected with it. To this life succeeds judgment; and judgment is always spoken of as if it were something complete and final. There is no perspective disclosed beyond the doom which follows it. The curtain falls; the drama seems played out: it is as if we were to understand that all is henceforth over.[17]

And he accepted judgment as an appropriate termination of the trial of life. "Whatever may be the measures and differences of sin, we cannot misunderstand about retribution, absolute, as terrible as words can describe it, on sin which has not been forgiven" (106). God, he says,

> has told us that He will judge and punish the wicked. Nothing can be more plain and certain in the whole Gospel than that the punishment of unforgiven sin will be something infinitely more awful than we have faculties to conceive. He has *not* told us how He means to deal with all the infinite and inscrutable problems, as we call them, arising out of human sin. Shall we persist in asking? (115)

Church's purpose is not to stress God's punishment, however, but to urge ready repentance on the part of his audience. He ends his sermon with the question: Can we not trust to God's mercy? (124).

But why is any concept of eternal punishment needed? Basically because the operation of justice is not always evident in human existence. We may be preached at day in and day out that God works in mysterious ways his objects to achieve, and that we can trust to providential accomplishment of justice. But our daily experience gives us scant proof of this promise. We see the wicked triumph and the good fail and disappear. We see poverty and pain and we acknowledge the steady injustice of our own lot. Why then should we follow "rules" or "laws" that prevent us from satisfying our desires and achieving our aims? Fear of a higher power is the first step toward addressing this attitude. James Fitzjames Stephen allowed that you cannot persuade the mass of men unless you can threaten them. Religion therefore requires the power of coercion that resides in such concepts as the Last Judgment.[18] One of the most mordant modern fables caricaturing the theory of a wrathful God is H. G. Wells' *The Island of Dr. Moreau* (1896). Prendick has arrived at Moreau's island by mistake. While there, he discovers that Moreau is transforming animals into human-like creatures and giving them laws to obey. They have a strong tendency, however, to regress to their animal natures. When Moreau is killed by one of his experimental animals, Prendick is left alone with the increasingly brutish creatures. He needs some form of mastery to control them. Here is the scene as he and his faithful Dog Man confront the others.

> None about the fire attempted to salute me. Most of them disregarded me—ostentatiously. I looked round for the Hyaena-Swine, but he was not there. Altogether, perhaps, twenty of the Beast Folk squatted, staring into the fire or talking to one another.
>
> "He is dead, he is dead, the Master is dead,' said the voice of the Ape Man to the right of me. 'The House of Pain—there *is* no House of Pain."
>
> "He is not dead," said I, in a loud voice. "Even now he watches us."
>
> This startled them. Twenty pairs of eyes regarded me.
>
> "The House of Pain is gone," said I. "It will come again. The Master you cannot see. Yet even now he listens above you."
>
> "True, true!" said the Dog Man.
>
> They were staggered at my assurance. An animal may be ferocious and cunning enough, but it takes a real man to tell a lie. "The Man with the Bandaged Arm speaks a strange thing," said one of the Beast folk.
>
> "I tell you it is so," I said. "The Master and the House of Pain will come again. Woe be to him who breaks the Law!"[19]

Fear of an unseen Being above us who can strike at any time requires some degree of reinforcement. The many narratives of strange providential retribution represent attempts to do just that. Many preachers sought to provide a much more mundane class of evidence for such providential justice. Charles Kingsley preached more than one sermon on this theme. In a sermon entitled "Retribution" on the text "Be sure your sin will find you out" (Numbers 32:23), Kingsley remarked that there is no mention of the next life in this passage because it is meant to show that every man's sins will inevitably come home to him in this world. Look in your own heart and you will see that most of your sorrows are your own fault, he says. Sin does not succeed, except perhaps in a material way, but finds out the sinner in his or her heart.[20] Kingsley elaborated the here-and-now nature of this retribution in his sermon "Blessing and Cursing."

> Let us take home, I say, the awful belief, that every wrong act of ours does of itself sow the seeds of its own punishment; and that those seeds will assuredly bear fruit, now, here in this life. Let us believe that God's judgments, though they will culminate, no doubt, hereafter in one great day and 'one divine far-off event, to which the whole creation moves,' are yet about our path and about our bed, now, here, in this life. Let us believe, that if we are to prepare to meet our God, we must do it now, here in this life, yea and all day long; for he is not far off from any one of us, seeing that in him we live, and move, and have our being; and can never go from his presence, never flee from his spirit. Let us believe that God's good laws, and God's good order, are in themselves and of themselves, the curse and punishment of every sin of ours; and that Ash-Wednesday, returning year after year, whether we be glad or sorry, good or evil, bears witness to that most awful and yet most blessed fact. (268)

Human experience does not invariably show justice worked out in this way and hence a stronger deterrent to sin becomes necessary. What could be more terrifying than the concept of suffering extended beyond this life and guaranteed in the next? As we shall see later, religion came to share the language of commercial exchange in illustrating how an ill-spent life accumulates a debt of sin that must be redeemed (at high interest) hereafter. All of which brings us back to Nietzsche, according to whom the truly strong simply take what they want. They are natural masters. The weak and slavish must therefore employ a ruse to restrain the strong and to enhance their own authority. To do this they create the fable of a deity stronger than any human whose authority extends back before human life began and onward beyond its end. According to this scenario, the Victorians lived in an atmosphere inevitably tainted with the need for various forms of punishment both material and subjective. But a society based upon proliferating punishments also requires the meek emollient of forgiveness.

I shall speak in greater detail about theories of legal punishment later, but at this point we should take a preliminary look at the motives that lead men to employ punishment and to construct laws whose violation occasions such punishments. At the primitive level, punishment may be nothing more than a form of retaliation. If you break my window, I break yours. The danger with this pattern is splendidly, if comically, illustrated by those Laurel and Hardy episodes when such a pattern of destructive retaliation, beginning with something as trivial as the inadvertent damaging of a shrub, may escalate rapidly to the trashing of vehicles and the virtual demolition of houses. This is also the basis of the feud—injury responding to injury.[21] These private combats, however, may be hazardous for the larger community in which they take place and so it becomes necessary to establish a rule or a law to contain violence. Some adjudicating authority must arise to administer justice—a Solomon, let us say, who is admired for his wisdom, or a Charlemagne, who is admired for his power. The *lex talionis* is a version of the feud halted at its first step, hence preventing the explosion into dangerous violence. The punishment is *equivalent* to the offense. But there are crimes for which an equivalent punishment is impossible. If my neighbor destroys three of my cows, but has no cows of his or her own, what punishment can be employed? The neighbor may own a great deal of real property or an abundance of gold. Very well, then he or she can be made to *compensate* me for my injury. These uses of punishment are *retributive*. An offense gets what it deserves.

A second form of punishment does not seek to repay an offense; its intent is to prevent repetitions of the transgression by the guilty party or by any other member of the community. This is *exemplary* punishment, which does not require the same rigorous justice assumed in retributive punishment. If five pickpockets are arrested at a fair, one may be executed as an example to others not to engage in picking pockets. Theoretically, the point is made and the law can afford to be lenient and let the others off with lesser sentences.

Yet another and perhaps more curious approach to punishment aims at *reform, rehabilitation, or redemption* of the offender; it can be utilitarian or deeply rooted in moral values. Its constraints may range from simple deprivation to extreme physical pain, all in the interest of bringing the offender to a consciousness of the offense and of what behavior is necessary to live in liberty and comfort. In essence, it is a crude form of behavior modification.

In the Old Testament there is a great deal of retributive and exemplary punishment. It is generally a means of healing some breach between God and his people. The people must be brought back to a right way of thinking and behaving. Because that right way is ultimately good for them, God's punishments may often be seen as rehabilitative, or therapeutic, as well.[22] But set against this pattern of punishment is a scriptural emphasis upon God's mercy. In the nineteenth century many commentators on the Bible contrasted the benevolence of the New Testament with the punitive character of the Old Testament, though it is not difficult to find many instances in the Old Testament stressing God's mercy, especially in the Psalms.

Another trait of nineteenth-century thinking was connecting economics with punishment and reward. Max Weber long ago demonstrated the relationship be-

tween protestant faith and economic ambition.[23] Boyd Hilton has pointed out
that the language of finance is shared with religion in the use of such words as
"redeem," "forgive," and even "convert."[24] There are many scriptural passages
that encourage this shared vocabulary; one of the most familiar is part of the
Lord's Prayer: "And forgive us our debts as we forgive our debtors" (Matthew
6:12). Here is Henry Thornton's explication of the passage.

> By the word 'debts' is here evidently meant 'trespasses' or sins; for
> the word 'trespasses' is used in the same prayer, instead of 'debts,' in
> another part of Scripture. By our trespasses, we may be said to become
> debtors to God; for we incur a penalty proportioned to the sins which
> we commit. Now the debts, which we thus incur, we cannot pay.
> There is no hope that we shall ever pay them; for the future obedience
> of our whole lives, even if it should be perfect, can never cancel the
> trespasses, which are past; just as the paying regularly all our future
> debts can never cancel a debt which is already standing out against us.
> We are, therefore, taught, in this prayer, to implore a free forgiveness;
> and we are in it likened to debtors who have nothing to pay; and who,
> therefore, can only ask a free discharge. We are enabled by other parts
> of Scripture to know on what ground it is that we obtain this pardon of
> our sins. That we ought to pray for pardon is all that we are here
> taught. The more particular doctrine of the manner of that pardon was
> to be divulged and explained when Christ should have paid the ransom
> of His death. (69–70)

Thornton was concerned particularly with our debt to God. John Ruskin tried
to explain to his young friends at Winnington Hall how the passage applies to
our fellow human beings. Forgiveness is an active power of delivering or releas-
ing from guilt, he says, then observes that the Lord's Prayer says nothing about
forgiving sin as respects us. "Note the distinction in Luke: forgive us our sins, as
we forgive—those who are *indebted* to us. In Matthew it is 'debts' in both cases.
You know that 'Sin' is especially an act against God. But debt may be to man.
You can remit—or release a debt, cannot you. Quite a different thing from pardoning an offense." Ruskin goes on to stress that forgiving people all their debts
means "'regarding the person exactly as you would have regarded them had
they *never* sinned, erred, or been in debt to you.' Anything *less* than this is no
forgiveness. It is the *Blotting out* of sin and its memory."[25]

From Coleridge on, there was a growing discontent with the balance-sheet
approach to rewards and punishments regarding God and his judgments upon
man, and, as Ruskin's position suggests, there was a comparable reluctance to
apply this religious double-entry method to fellow humans.[26] But throughout the
century the severer forms of religion retained that image. Late in the century the
great Baptist preacher Charles Haddon Spurgeon published a work entitled *The
Cheque book of the Bank of Faith*. There were many other passages in the Bible to

justify this attitude. Matthew 6: 19–21, for example, urges us not to lay up treasures on earth, but to accumulate them in heaven where moths and rust will not
corrupt them. Many preachers encouraged their flocks to invest in heavenly rewards by divesting themselves of some portion of their earthly treasures in the
form of charity or tithes to the church. But the general trend of religious feeling
during the century was toward a loving God, not one who, like a wizened ac-
countant, kept a running tab of our offenses and good works. As we shall see, this
latter attitude was much abused in the fiction of the age. Speaking of one perverse form of this spiritual accounting, Elizabeth Jay says: "The effort to maintain a favourable spiritual bank balance by acts of gratuitous self-punishment
provides the common denominator in characters otherwise as diverse as Mrs.
Clennam, Miss Clack, Mrs. Prime and Mrs. Bolton, Christina Pontifex and Mr.
Bulstrode."[27]

There is obviously a strong connection between justice and mercy or pardon
and between punishment and forgiveness. But to understand their dynamic and
some of the hypocrisies and confusions that might arise out of that dynamic we
must glance briefly at some root expectations of nineteenth-century Christianity. As I tried to show in *Victorian Will*, one essential for a good Christian was to
free himself from self-will through a willing subjection to God's will.[28] Self-
forgetfulness and humility are primary achievements. "Humbleness is peculiar to
Christianity," F. W. Robertson instructed an Oxford congregation. "Goodness is
admired and taught in all religions. But to be good, and feel that your good is
nothing; to advance and become more conscious of pollution; to ripen in all excellence, and like corn to bend the head when full of ripe bursting grain—that is
Christianity."[29] Sometimes God must do us the favor of bringing us to that condition of humility. To be humble we must first be contrite. As Charles Kingsley
pointed out, the word *contrite* means literally "crushed to powder." Kingsley
went on to say that God may bring sorrow on those who sin, but He wants thereby to redeem, not to destroy them.

> Yes. He will make short work at times with men's spirits. He grinds
> hearts to powder, that they may be broken and contrite before him:
> but only that he may heal them; that out of the broken fragments of the
> hard, proud, self-deceiving heart of stone, he may create a new and
> harder heart of flesh, human and gentle, humble and simple. And then
> he will return and have mercy. He will show that he will not contend
> for ever. He will show that he does not wish our spirits to fail before
> him, but to grow and flourish before him to everlasting life. He will
> create the fruit of the lips, and give us cause to thank him in spirit and
> in truth. (307)

Robertson frames the same notion in a kindlier way when he explains: "Trial is
not the mark of an angry God; it is the evidence of deepest parental love" (33).
Kingsley is almost joyful about the benefits of suffering. "Happy, thrice happy

are they who have walked through the valley of the shadow of death, and found it the path which leads to everlasting life."[30] He reminds his audience that Christ too was made perfect by suffering. Pusey observes that "The severity of God, awful as it is, has a side of love." To wound here, he says, may be to spare forever.

> The sinner is any how the object of God's special care, in that He adapts His severe chastening to his transgressions and his ills. To be neglected, over-looked, passed over, might imply, that God knew the soul to be dross and refuse, from which the refiner's fire could extract no gold. Prosperous, unchastened wickedness would be a token of damnation. The most awful severity of God accompanying the sinner to his last breath, were a token of love, that God had not abandoned him. (17)

The Reverend John Warton used a related argument with a reluctant parishioner who was suffering great pain and anger after her husband abandoned her and she underwent the agony of a miscarriage. First Warton managed to convince Martha Bilson, a servant woman, that she had put herself in the way of this pain because the result of changing service to a household where she made a better wage had led to her meeting with the young man she married to such unfortunate ends. So it was her greed and ambition that brought on this rebuke that will now allow her to improve her moral being, though she will likely remain a physical invalid for the rest of her life. In a characteristically evangelical mode, the minister stresses the significance of the death bed and draws a stark contrast. The pious and Christian Mrs. Clayton dies quickly and peacefully at an advanced age, whereas Martha Bilson's mother develops a protracted illness. Speaking of Mrs. Clayton's death the Reverend Warton says: "That was a comfortable sight, as you have justly mentioned; and it should suggest a useful reflection to us all, and should teach us to be always prepared; that we may not stand in need of a lingering and painful disease to warn and prepare us to make ready for death. Did you make this reflection, Martha?" (77)[31]

James Hinton wrote an entire book to justify the role of pain in human life. If we knew all of God's plan, he said, we would feel joy, not sorrow in pain. The thesis of his work was "that things which we have inevitably called evil may yet be truly good."[32] Hinton connected this acceptance of pain with providential justice. In *Philosophy and Religion,* he wrote: "Nature obeys the man who acts right, for he takes part with God. In right action Nature has her origin and her existence; to right action she owes an absolute allegiance. Hence it is, sin works its own punishment: there is no deception, no defect, no error in Nature's justice; each wrong, however it may seem for a time to succeed, is fully avenged."[33]

Martin Tupper presents the same idea more graphically in his poem "Of Good in Things Evil."

Pain and sin are convicts, and toil in their fetters for good;
The weapons of evil are turned against itself, fighting under better banners:
The leech delighteth in stinging, and the wicked loveth to do harm,
But the wise Physician of the Universe useth that ill tendency for health.[34]

These are statements of the familiar providential message reasserted so many times during the century, and vigorously by Thomas Carlyle who declared in *Past and Present:* "The law of Fact is that Justice must and will be done."[35] And again: "Nature's Laws, I must repeat, are eternal: her small still voice, speaking from the inmost heart of us, shall not, under terrible penalties, be disregarded" (145). Robertson's version of this position runs: "There is a law in this world that sin and sorrow shall be joined together" (*Human Race,* 235). R. W. Dale offered his version of this complex relationship as follows:

> Conscience, even apart from revelation, menaces the guilty with retribution; and revelation confirms the menace. There are some who maintain that the penalty cannot be escaped; that the Eternal Law is automatic and inflexible; that whatever a man deserves to suffer, he will suffer. But even though we recoil from the appalling doctrine which enthrones a rigid Justice over the moral universe and denies to Mercy all authority and power, it is certain that the penalties which are due to wrong-doing cannot be wholly averted by any human forgiveness of the wrong-doer.[36]

Even without overt pain or sorrow, we feel the bite of our own conscience which makes us yearn for peace. That peace comes when we blame ourselves and therefore have hope to mend. To blame oneself, of course, is not enough. Repentance will save any soul alive, Kingsley announced confidently, but mere remorse will not (*Good News,* 95). The message of absolution, Kingsley says, is "that there is continual forgiveness for those who really confess and repent" (*Works,* 21:385). Then he recommends the Christian course of behavior.

> Only let us remember to ask for pardon and to ask for peace, that we may use them as the collect bids us;—To ask for pardon, not merely that we may escape punishment; not even to escape punishment at all, if punishment be wholesome for us, as it often is: but that we may be cleansed from our sins; that we may not be left to our own weakness and our own bad habits, to grow more and more useless, more and more unhappy day by day, but that we may be cleansed from them; and grow purer, nobler, juster, stronger, more worthy of our place in God's kingdom, as our years roll by. (*Works,* 21, 386)

Another essential of the good Christian is to forgive penitent offenders. But here too complications arise. F. W. Robertson wrote a thoughtful sermon on

"Christian Forgiveness," delivered at midcentury (Brighton, March 28, 1852). Since Robertson was a popular liberal churchman, I shall use his views as representative of a large segment of the middle class. Elsewhere, in a different sermon, Robertson asserts: "Christianity is a revelation of Divine forgiveness—a requirement thereupon that we should forgive each other."[37] Christ is the chief model of forgiveness and all of humankind is obliged to imitate his charity. The sermon "Christian Forgiveness" instructs us on its proper application. Robertson begins by noting that "Christian forgiveness is not the natural growth of the heart," but must be cultivated (*Human Race,* 204). Rabbinical law called for enduring an offense three times before executing revenge. Peter asked Christ if forgiving seven times was sufficient, but Christ replied that we must forgive transgressions seventy times seven times. In short, "Christianity is a spirit, not a set of rules" (205). We will be forgiven if we confess our transgression and repent. Robertson also addresses the daily expectation of the Christian ethic. Much of human vindictiveness arises out of false pride, a refusal to admit error. But "the plain Christian rule is, the man who has done wrong has no right to consider consequences. Have you wronged; repair. Have you erred; apologize" (207). We must ignore our worldly honor in favor of Christian honor. "The first noblest attitude of man is innocence; the second noblest, apology. The manliness of saying 'I have done wrong, forgive me,' is as high above that of the mere man of honor as the brilliancy of heaven's son transcends the glitter of an earthly lamp" (208).

Robertson uses the parable of the unjust steward to register the important qualification that all forgiveness is provisional. If God forgives us, he expects us to do the same in our turn. Forgiveness implies favor and remission of punishment. You may be in favor and yet be punished or be excused punishment though not in favor. Robertson concludes of God's forgiveness that salvation is love and an unforgiving, vindictive heart puts itself in hell. This picture of Christian forgiveness obviously connects smoothly with F. D. Maurice's views about punishment in the afterlife and with the heavily promoted message of Christian love, as represented, for example, by Arthur Penrhyn Stanley's sermon "The Two Great Commandments," in which Stanley declares the primacy of Christ's injunction to love God and to love your neighbor as yourself. "This is the root of all Christian charity, of all Christian forgiveness, of all Christian justice, of all Christian toleration."[38] Robertson concludes that "The Gospel is built on unlimited forgiveness" (210). But that forgiveness is premised on the transgressor's acknowledgment of fault. In another sermon, Robertson explains that forgiveness and absolution are not the same, but that absolution is the authoritative declaration of forgiveness. Its first use is to save the transgressor from remorse.[39] John Warton's version of this provisional character of God's forgiveness is adapted to Martha Bilson's uneducated condition. He says to this young woman, still wishing to see her husband punished for his behavior, "you ask God, in the Lord's prayer, to forgive *you your* trespasses against himself, only on the condition that *you* forgive others *their* trespasses against you; and Jesus said to us all, 'when ye pray, forgive, that ye may be forgiven'" (69–70).

By now it should be apparent that divine and human forgiveness are not simple matters. To summarize so far, Christianity requires forgiveness; it is a principal virtue. But divine and, by extension, human forgiveness are provisional. The forgiven must act likewise and be forgiving. Moreover, to be forgiven, one must first acknowledge fault. There are further refinements and Robertson explored them in a sermon on "The Prodigal and His Brother." This parable, Robertson says, teaches the alienation of the human heart from its divine father—the going away of the son from the father. It also teaches the unsatisfying nature of human happiness. And most certainly it teaches the readiness of forgiveness to the truly repentant. Moreover, that forgiveness is forthcoming before repentance takes the form of virtuous behavior. It is a forgiveness granted while a man "is yet afar off" (*Human Race,* 280). This means that for forgiveness a sinner does not have to have achieved virtue, but only to have discovered that he desires it.

The parable brings up another problem with forgiveness in the person of the virtuous son who has never offended and who therefore complains that his father has never made such a fuss about him. He stands for the good Christian perplexed by the mystery of God's dealings. The prodigal may be said to have accumulated a debt of sin which is forgiven him entirely by his father, who lifts him up to his original position. Is this fair to the steady Christian who has never strayed? Robertson claims that the virtuous person will enjoy peace in his heart. Though the heart rewon to salvation may feel rapture, the religious man too should feel joy and thank God for the happiness of others (283). However, although the prodigal may be forgiven his sins, he cannot avert their natural consequences. "When we have lived long a life of sin, do we think that repentance and forgiveness will obliterate all the traces of sin upon the character?" Robertson asks, and then answers his own question. "Be sure that every sin pays its price: 'Whatsoever a man soweth, that shall he also reap'" (285).

In "The Three Crosses of Calvary," Robertson cautions against presuming on a late repentance to wash away sin. One of Christ's companions was the unrepentant thief who signifies the unlikelihood of late repentance. But the good thief offers an example that such a thing *can* happen. Moreover, as with the prodigal son, it is total forgiveness— "up to that time he had done nothing to make himself meet for glory, after his conversion he could do nothing; and yet, forgiven and redeemed upon the cross, he passed straight to Paradise" (122). So, as Robertson puts it elsewhere, "Peace is enjoyed by those who have been in covenant with God, as it were, during all their lifetime; and peace is attainable by those who have only received his forgiveness late" (227).

In "Joseph's Forgiveness of His Brethren," Robertson adds another dimension to Christian forgiveness. When he was dying, Joseph's father sent Joseph's brothers to ask his forgiveness because he understood the duty of apology, the acknowledgment of transgression. They themselves were motivated by a fear of revenge. Forgiveness is not merely a moral but also a religious duty. In the Old Testament it was a duty for a Jew to forgive one of his faith who apologized. After Christ, we must consider all men our brothers and thus potentially deserving of our forgiveness. The example of Joseph's mercy demonstrates that Christ did not invent forgiveness; he simply emphasized its central role in the new faith. What is significant about Joseph's forgiveness is his conscious rejection of the role of avenger. "Am I in the place of God?" he asks (36). Joseph rejects vengeance sincerely, but there is an insidious cold-blooded version of this rejection that actually conceals a vindictive heart, forgoing vengeance only because it assumes that punishment will be effected by some other agent, perhaps God. Joseph forgave because he understood how good can come out of evil. And so he forgot the injury. It is possible to forgive and not forget, but the best forgiveness forgets the offense.

This last assertion in Robertson's sermon raises a new problem, for it seems to suggest that there are many degrees or grades of forgiveness. A passage from "Christian Forgiveness" illustrates this quandary.

> God forgave David. He suffered retribution without wrath. Yes, and it may be that although forgiving a man we cannot receive him as before, with perfect, hearty, entire forgiveness. He has forfeited a right to friendship, and is refused admission to your home. You have no rankling feeling. You would do him a service. But you have no foolish, weak sentiment which would let off the criminal or break down boundaries (210).

But if we have truly forgiven, can we still remember the offense and act on it by shunning the person forgiven, or is Robertson here confusing forgiveness with pardon? I shall take up this distinction later in a different context but mention it here simply to indicate that even an intelligent specialist in the subject like Robertson found some areas of it difficult to resolve.

If there is some obscurity remaining in the effect upon others of our granting forgiveness, there is some also on the effect in ourselves. It is our Christian duty to be selfless and humble and to forgive the penitent. But consider how these traits seem to come into conflict in this passage from "Joseph's Forgiveness of His Brethren."

> I say not that there is no such thing as the duty of redressing wrongs, especialy those of others. There is a keen sense of wrong, a mighty demand of the heart for justice, which cannot be put aside. And he who cannot feel indignation against wrong cannot, in a manly way, forgive injury. But I say, the only revenge which is essentially Christian is that of retaliating by forgiveness. And he who has ever tasted

that Godlike feeling of forbearance when insulted; of speaking well of one who has slandered him (pleasure all the more exquisite if the slanderer does not know it); of doing service in requital of an injury: he, and only he, can know how it is possible for our frail Humanity, by abnegating the place of God the avenger, to occupy the place of God the absolver. (37)

Robertson's tone here suggests just the opposite of that humility he elsewhere recommends, for it presents an exultation in the triumph of virtue. Clearly self-aggrandizement is not what Robertson wishes to foster, but the joy of forgiveness could easily slide into pharisiacal self-satisfaction.

Henry Thornton, in his *A Family Commentary upon the Sermon on the Mount*, cautions that one who forgives but does not forget an offense is not living according to Christ's injunction. Some may profess to forgive and forget but nonetheless show that they transgress Christ's rule through uncharitableness, and "even they who confer some favour on the person who has injured them, may not be clear of the sin in question; since the very pride of superiority may lead a man to confer a favour on him from whom an injury has been experienced. To receive a favour from an enemy is a better proof of a forgiving spirit than to bestow it" (18). An additional test of the forgiving spirit requires that we forgive not only the offender who is generally condemned and defamed for his actions but also one who has offended us in such a manner "that the world takes part with him rather than with us: and when the offender seems to suffer no punishment, or inconvenience of any kind, for his offence. If we can forgive freely in cases of this kind, it is a strong mark of our having attained to a truly forgiving spirit" (81).

To prevent such self-satisfaction, Robertson and others, from strict Calvinists to Roman Catholics, emphasized man's sinful and weak nature. In a sermon on "The Pharisee and the Publican," Robertson stressed the importance of recognizing one's own sinfulness and of being penitent for it (*Human Race,* 38). C. H. Spurgeon reiterates the message that "Holy Scripture tells us that man by nature is *dead* in trespasses and sins."[40] Spurgeon also insisted that those saved from sin were saved through free grace alone, but this was a sectarian view. Throughout his very popular *Family Prayers,* the evangelical Henry Thornton stressed time and again that men are weak, sinful, fallen beings who need constant grace and pardon from God. R. W. Dale very simply declared that "The Christian gospel assumes that men have sinned; that though some are worse and some better than others, all have sinned and need the divine forgiveness" (179). John Cummings in *The Daily Life; or Precepts and Prescriptions for Christian Living* wrote that man should recognize himself as the fallen remains of pristine magnificence and thus be humbled by his sins.[41] Robertson presents the same idea in "The Peace of God" when he contrasts the faith available to Adam and Eve and that available to all who came after the fall.

Man's religion then was the religion of spontaneous innocence; the only religion left open to man now, the only religion possible, is the religion of penitence. It is this, my brethren, which makes the Gospel from first to last to bear the character of a system of cure. It is not a work of improvement for a nature which is already good, it is a work of remedy for a nature which has become diseased. (*Human Race,* 223)

Dale again, inverting an Arnoldian expression, says that there is in mankind a power that makes for unrighteousness and this is what it means to be a fallen race.

If we are all so imperfect and must constantly be watchful of our own corrupt nature, how can we presume to judge others? The answer, generally, is that we cannot, as Robertson pointed out indirectly in his description of Joseph refusing to play the judge and avenge a wrong done to him. But Robertson is more explicit in his sermon "Guilt of Judging—Contemptuousness," where he advises his audience not to pass judgment lightly on those who hold values different from themselves. Paul taught his followers not to judge others and not to acknowledge judgment by others, for we are accountable to God, not to man. All too often those who do judge their fellow men are the least capable of true judgment.

Are those who judge others wiser than their brethren? Are they free from human frailty? Are they the meek, the learned, the holy, and the wise? or are they not generally the self-instructed, the weakest of both sexes, the impetuous, the talkative, who presume to judge on the authority, perhaps, of some minister, who is to them as a pope? "Who art thou that judgest another man's servant? to his own master he standeth or falleth." (*Human Race,* 106)[42]

Matthew 7:1 instructs: "Judge not lest ye be judged," and surely this is one of the most familiar cautionary passages in the Bible. During the nineteenth century in England it was repeated in many forms. This poem by Adelaide Proctor is only one example of the way it found popular expression.

JUDGE NOT

Judge not; the workings of his brain
And of his heart thou canst not see;
What looks to thy dim eyes a stain,
In God's pure light may only be
A scar, brought from some well-won field,
Where thou wouldst only faint and yield.

> The look, the air, that frets thy sight,
> May be a token, that below
> The soul has closed in deadly fight
> With some infernal fiery foe,
> Whose glance would scorch thy smiling grace,
> And cast thee shuddering on thy face!
>
> The fall thou darest to despise—
> Maybe the angel's slackened hand
> Has suffered it, that he may rise
> And take a firmer, surer stand;
> Or, trusting less to earthly things,
> May henceforth learn to use his wings.
>
> And judge none lost; but wait and see,
> With hopeful pity, not disdain;
> The depth of the abyss may be
> The measure of the height of pain
> And love and glory that may raise
> This soul to God in after days![43]

The old standby *Of the Imitation of Christ* warns against rash judgment. Thomas à Kempis says: "Turn thine eyes unto thyself, and beware thou judge not the deeds of other men. In judging of others a man laboureth in vain, often erreth, and easily sinneth; but in judging and discussing of himself, he always laboureth fruitfully" (23).

If we can know so little about the mystery of the individual, how do we ever come to pass judgment and thereby create the moral climate in which forgiveness can operate? Moreover, if we cannot know what motives prompted a wicked act, can we know what motivates apparently virtuous behavior such as apology and good works? In his commentary on Matthew 7:1,2, Henry Thornton offers a way around the prohibition on judgment, explaining that Christ was not forbidding the passing of judgment on the wickedness of the world, but had in mind certain kinds of punishment, such as those that are rash or hasty, those that are partial, and those that are harsh or severe (108). But even if it is permitted to judge evil in this world, the true Christian cannot *execute* justice. Christ unmistakably said that his followers must not resist evil. "There must be such a spirit in my followers, that however great may be the ill-treatment which they receive, they must be willing quietly to suffer it; as much so as if, when a man were to smite thee on the right cheek, thou wert to turn to him the other also. Revenge is utterly excluded out of my code. The law of My Kingdom is that of the free forgiveness of each other" (51).[44] If a good person may possibly judge others but not punish, all that is available to him is the opportunity to endure insult and injury and to forgive them. As we shall see, this dilemma plays an important part in the way Victorian novelists constructed their stories and their characters.

One reason that men were cautioned not to judge and execute justice rashly was God's interdiction: "Vengeance is mine." But if God was the custodian of justice, he was also the dispenser of mercy. To nineteenth-century commentators no act of mercy was greater than the sacrifice of Christ on the cross. The Atonement was God's universal act of forgiveness for mankind's ingrained sin; it made humans capable of salvation again. Boyd Hilton writes that in the first half of the nineteenth century in England there does seem to have been a dominant mode of thought, "An amalgam of enlightenment rationalism and evangelical eschatology, and its core or 'hinge' was the Christian doctrine of the Atonement" (3). What the Atonement signified for evangelicals was the opening of the way to forgiveness for anyone who embraces the opportunity. This is a genuine departure from the Calvinist belief in predestination and election. But, as the century progressed, even this modified view yielded to a broader interpretation. Unitarians, for example, did not recognize the divinity of Christ, thus discounting his death as God's opening through him of the path to human expiation. But even Trinitarians modified their views. Hilton says that by the 1870s the Atonement was widely seen as a supremely noble but essentially symbolic gesture by the Son of God, and a case of willing self-sacrifice, a means of demonstrating love for man and not a literal redemption (296). Frederick Robertson was one clergyman who stressed the Atonement as an example of glorious suffering and as manifesting part of the great law of the universe—death for life, death of one for the life of many (*Human Race,* 157–58). Others maintained well into the century that the Atonement was the central concept of Christianity.[45] Albert Barnes took great pains to establish a connection between God's and man's government by way of the Atonement. Christ's atoning sacrifice was necessary, according to Barnes, because man had violated God's law and the penalty was incurred. Only the Atonement could remove the difficulties in the way of pardon. One argument runs that "it is impossible for an offender by his future good conduct to repair the errors of the past, or to accumulate so much merit as to be a compensation or an offset for his former sins"; hence some other positive action equivalent to the original "error" is required to clear the slate (202). *"The atonement is something substituted in the place of the penalty of the law, which will answer the same ends as the punishment of the offender himself would.* It is *instead* of the punishment" (244). It secures reconciliation between God and man. Man's racial sin is both forgiven and forgotten. Barnes speculates that the earth, as a theater of revolt against the government of God, "is illustrating in scenes of sorrow the effect of a violation of the Divine laws" (270). The Atonement may thus illustrate to other worlds the character of God in his salvation of the guilty.

For Barnes and others like him the Atonement is the one device to make possible God's forgiveness for man's original sin and the extension of His grace to individual sinners. Barnes goes on to suggest that human governments are fallible because they lack something like atonement. He yearns for some solution to that problem.

> If it were possible to institute an arrangement which would secure a proper expression of the majesty and honour of the law and the interests of justice, and, at the same time, make it proper to indulge the benevolent feelings of the heart; that would send forth all who are pardoned, however guilty they may have been, thoroughly reformed, prepared to take their places in the community as industrious and honest men, securing their good behaviour in all time to come, it is obvious that an object would be accomplished which never has been secured in the administration of justice. (76)

Barnes' naive assumption that all human justice is likely to be uniform, magisterial, and honorable aside, there are many objections to likening human to divine justice. R. W. Dale, writing later in the century, explained that there is a substantial and inescapable difference between human and divine government. It is illegitimate, he says, reversing the direction of Barnes' argument, to contend that because a good man does not require an "atonement" before he forgives, God can require none. The simple fact is, he says, that "*we* never forgive sin; we cannot forgive it. We may dismiss the just resentment which had been provoked by cruel wrong. We may love the doer of the wrong with an undiminished affection. But to forgive his sin is beyond our authority and power" (243). This is what Ruskin taught the girls of Winnington Hall. Humans may forgive other humans the injuries they cause, but only God can forgive sin.

This perception is monumentally important in shaping the way we view the moral universe. Christ's role is, from a strict point of view, to redeem men through his death. A milder way of viewing Christ's purpose, represented by Maurice, Robertson, and others, was to teach the new religion and to validate its lessons in the actions of His own life. He becomes our principal model for behavior. The next step beyond that is to see Him as no more than a man, but the very best kind of man. But oh how these varying attitudes toward the Atonement change our pictures of punishment and forgiveness. In the most severe reading, God's justice *requires* Christ's death in order to reinstitute humans in God's grace and make them capable of forgiveness. In the milder version, Christ represents the fulfillment of the revelation of a new religion of love and mercy. In the most liberal version, Christ is a man who transcended the grim myth of the Old Testament, based largely on injunction, threat, and punishment, offering instead a humane philosophy of brotherhood. In the first, all are depraved and can be saved only by agencies beyond their own power. In the next, the model of salvation is extended to all who can imitate it and therefore save themselves. In the last, each individual must discover his or her own way to make the principles of brotherhood work in his or her own historical context. In each case, the matter of human justice and of who is allowed to punish is complicated. In the first case, only God should punish and can forgive sin. In the next, God discourages punishment altogether in favor of forgiveness and endurance. In the last, no human is so free from error that he or she may arrogate the execution of justice. All are equally adrift in a world of suffering and confusion and should sympathize with one another and forgive.

There was obviously an increasingly benign view of religious faith and man's relationship to his maker during the nineteenth century. Some have attributed this melioration to the revival of religious feeling manifested in Evangelicalism. But the spirit may have been more general than that. In any case, one way to ensure the continued mollification of moral feeling was to see to it that the younger generation embibed the necessary Christian spirit. This, of course, is done through the various processes of education. It is also the model of God as Father and human as child that provides one of the justifications for judgment and punishment in this world. Once again F. W. Robertson offers a way of understanding how a religion of forgiveness can be reconciled with the practice of punishment. In his sermon "The Law Our Schoolmaster," Robertson explains that God treats the world as schoolmasters should treat children. There are two stages in world and individual development—pupilage and faith. The first requires law. Law to the Jews was a system of checks and restraints designed to control transgressors and was thus not applicable to the righteous person. Law is a schoolmaster to rule those who cannot rule themselves. In the stage of pupilage, then,

> "it would be madness to relax from restraint. Imagine a governor amidst a population of convicts trusting to high principle. Imagine a parent having no fixed hours, no rules, no *law* in his household, no punishment for evil! There is a morbid feeling against punishment; but it is God's system. Men have often false notions about personal liberty and personal dignity. They are trying the principle of faith when the stage has not yet come to have done with law. (*Human Race,* 64)

Restraint teaches us about the inward force of evil that we must resist and the need for obedience to a higher will. It helps us form habits of faith until we achieve self-command and can lay aside the law.

There are some unexamined assumptions in Robertson's sermon that I shall touch on briefly. One is that it is possible to discover an unambiguous set of instructions for living that we may safely recognize as the Law. Another is that that set of instructions is right for all persons. If the Law remains ambiguous to any great degree, it will require interpretation, and with interpretation comes variation and even caprice, so that any given reading of the Law might be considered arbitrary. If the Law, or its interpretation, is arbitrary, then there is no sound reason why any given individual should submit to it, and the process of habituation to it is nothing more than indoctrination. The "good" person is, by definition, one who has successfully internalized the set of rules which his or her society approves. From this point of view, education is simply a form of coercion designed to make citizens their own policemen. When you have internalized the Law, you may safely be released into your own custody. But this is not the same as laying aside the Law. Quite to the contrary, it is the triumph of the Law over all other alternative patterns of behavior. Many Victorians openly admitted this connection, but believed that discipline and coercion were essential to instilling the "truth" in human hearts. Kingsley felt that humans needed help in self-discipline, just as soldiers do, for their own good. J. F. Stephen argued against J. S. Mill's concept of liberty, saying that it was only through coercion that people could be brought to behave properly, and a Baptist like Spurgeon simply felt that humans remained too weak and sinful ever to trust themselves and must always lean upon Christ.

Robertson struggled to avoid declaring the truth or the Law to be self-evident. Time and again he declared Christianity a religion of spirit, not of rules. But, if that is the case, how could we ever be sure of the disciplines and restraints that must be employed to help along our errant brethren toward faith? Let me quote at length another passage from one of Robertson's sermons that tries to face this problem but which quickly drifts from practical issues to abstract principles.

> We have come to think that education may be maintained by mere laws of love instead of discipline, and that public punishment may be abolished. We say that these things are contrary to the Gospel; and here, doubtless, there is an underlying truth; it is true that there may be a severity in education which defeats itself, it is true that love and tenderness may do more than severity; but yet under a system of mere love and tenderness no character can acquire manliness or firmness. When you have once got rid of the idea of public punishment, then, by degrees, you will also get rid of the idea of sin: where is it written in the Word of God that the sword of His minister is to be borne in vain? In this world of groaning and of anguish, tell us where it is that the law which links suffering to sin has ceased to act? Nay, so long as there is evil, so long will there be penalty; and woe to that man who attempts to contradict the eternal system of God; so long as the spirit of evil is in the world, so long must human punishment remain to bear its testimony that the God of the universe is a righteous God. This is what we have to feel: sin, live according to the lusts of the flesh, and you will become the children of God's wrath; live after the Spirit, the higher nature that is in you, and then the law hath hold on you no longer. (*Human Race,* 126–27)

We wish to bring our children up to value a faith based upon love and forgiveness. But to do this, we must chasten them. From the beginning to the end of the century, new views about how to instill "correct" values in children were emerging. We shall touch on a few manifestations of this changing attitude toward education to punishment and forgiveness in the next chapter.

Despite intelligent attempts to deal with the complexities involved in the concepts and actions of punishment and forgiveness, from the simplest individual instances to the monumental instance of a Last Judgment, moral commentators during the nineteenth century in England could rarely escape the presuppositions of the Christian faith, presuppositions that regularly assumed the human possession of a law of righteousness and at least a gross certainty of good and evil. Therefore, although many writers urged caution in passing judgment on others, and promoted humility and self-judgment instead, few moralists found it possible to avoid assigning a central place for punishment—whether natural, providential, or individual—in their schemes of human experience. Later we shall see that social institutions were even less able to privilege forgiveness over punishment, though this aim remained prominent in the imaginative literature of the time. But if punishment could not be displaced as a tool of social control, literature could work to modify its role while promoting gentler sentiments, and this process began early with literature for children. As Robertson suggested in the passage quoted above, love is best, but a sublunary world requires some degree of severity to instill moral firmness.

NOTES

1. J. Arthur Hoyles, *Punishment in the Bible* (London: Epworth Press, 1986), 37, 13. Subsequent references in the text.

2. James Fitzjames Stephen defended Rowland Williams in the heresy trial for his contribution to *Essays and Reviews* (1860), and wrote a book about it entitled *Defense of the Reverend Rowland Williams* (1862). See K. J. M. Smith, *James Fitzjames Stephen: Portrait of a Victorian Rationalist* (Cambridge: Cambridge University Press, 1988), 220.

3. Torben Christensen, *The Divine Order: A Study in F. D. Maurice's Theology* (Leiden: E. J. Brill, 1973), 278, 275. Subsequent references in the text.

4. Frederick Denison Maurice, *Theological Essays* (Cambridge: Macmillan and Co., 1853), 341. Subsequent references in the text.

5. Geoffrey Rowell. *Hell and the Victorians: A Study of the Nineteenth-Century Theological Controversies Concerning Eternal Punishment and the Future Life* (Oxford: Clarendon Press, 1974), 89. Michael Wheeler observes that for Victorians the question of hell turned on the notion of hope. For Newman, for example, a suicide loses all hope whereas Frederick W. Farrar's "eternal hope" embraces even

the worst of sinners (*Death and the Future Life in Victorian Literature and Theology* [Cambridge: Cambridge University Press, 1990], 191).

6. James Hinton, *Man and His Dwelling Place* (New York: D. Appleton and Co., 1872), 95–96. Subsequent references in the text.

7. W. R. Greg, *The Creed of Christendom: Its Foundations Contrasted with Its Superstructure* (Toronto: Rose-Belford Publishing Co., 1878 [Originally published 1852], 368 and 373). Subsequent references in the text.

8. Michael Wheeler notes that the major debate within the Anglican church regarding hell and everlasting punishment occurred during the 1870s and focused on the Athanasian creed (192ff.).

9. Michael Wheeler has a chapter on Newman's *The Dream of Gerontion*, in *Death and the Future Life*, where he explains that part of Gerontius' pain is in the fear of eternal punishment, which Newman described as the turning point between Christianity and pantheism (395). Rowell says that, in contrast to his brother Charles' belief in eternal punishment, J. H. Newman was critical of it and said that the expression "guilt ought to be punished: should be replaced by "guilt deserves to be punished" (58). Thomas Vargish also examines Newman's peculiar view of eternal punishment and reactions against it in *Newman: The Contemplation of Mind* (Oxford: The Clarendon Press, 1970), 111ff.

10. William Allingham, *A Diary, 1824–1889*, ed. H. Allingham and D. Radford, intro. John Julius Norwich (New York: Penguin Books, 1985), 226. Subsequent references in the text.

11. William Ewart Gladstone, *Correspondence on Church and Religion*, 2 vols., selected and arranged by D. C. Lathbury (New York: The Macmillan Co., 1910, 2:123. Subsequent references in the text.

12. The Reverend John Warton, *Death-Bed Scenes and Pastoral Conversations*, 3 vols. (London: John Murray, 1830), 2:17–18.

13. Thomas Arnold, *The Miscellaneous Works* (New York: D. Appleton & Co, 1846), 158.

14. Henry Thornton, *Family Prayers: To Which Is Added, A Family Commentary upon The Sermon On The Mount* (New York: Swords, Stanford & Co., 1837), 125ff.

15. Thomas à Kempis, *Of the Imitation of Christ* (London: Oxford University Press, 1947), 53.

16. Edward Bouverie Pusey, *Sermons for the Church's Seasons from Advent to Trinity* (New York: E. P. Dutton & Co, 1883), 18.

17. R. W. Church, *Human Life and Its Conditions: Sermons Preached Before the University of Oxford in 1876–1878 with Three Ordination Sermons* (London: Macmillan and Co., 1878), 105. Subsequent references in the text.

18. James Fitzjames Stephen, *Liberty, Equality, Fraternity* (London: Smith, Elder, and Co., 1873), 116, 122.

19. H. G. Wells, *The Island of Dr. Moreau* (New York: Penguin, 1988), 125.

20. Charles Kingsley, *Village Sermons*, and *Town and Country Sermons*, vol. 21 of *The Works of Charles Kingsley*, 29 vols. (Hildesheim: George Olms Verlagsbuch-

handlung, 1969). (Originally published in London by Macmillan and Co., 1884), 56–57. Subsequent references in the text.

21. A classic depiction of the character of the blood feud occurs in Mark Twain's *Huckleberry Finn*. For a modern urban account of how such feuds begin, see Sydney Lea's poem, "The Feud" in *The Floating Candles* (Urbana: University of Illinois Press, 1982), 31–45.

22. See Chapter 3 of Hoyles.

23. Max Weber, *The Protestant Ethic and the Spirit of Capitalism*, trans. Talbot Parsons (New York: Scribners, 1958 [Originally published 1920]).

24. Boyd Hilton, *The Age of Atonement: The Influence of Evangelicalism on Social and Economic Thought, 1795–1865* (Oxford: Clarendon Press, 1988), 127.

25. John Ruskin, *The Winnington Letters: John Ruskin's Correspondence with Margaret Alexis Bell and the Children at Winnington Hall,* ed. Van Akin Burd (Cambridge: The Belknap Press of Harvard University Press, 1969), 240. Ruskin reasserts this last point on page 245.

26. Geoffrey Rowell says that Coleridge had no respect for crude notions about eternal punishment. He disliked the idea of a belief in hell being tied to a balance sheet of rewards and punishments, but admitted the role of rewards in Christian morality (67–68). See John R. Reed, "Paying Up: The Last Judgment and Forgiveness of Debts," in *Victorian Literature and Culture,* 20, ed. John Maynard and Adrienne Auslander Munich (New York: AMS Press, 1993), 55–68, for an examination of the debt metaphor and the Last Judgment.

27. Elizabeth Jay, *The Religion of the Heart: Anglican Evangelicalism and the Nineteenth-Century Novel* (Oxford: The Clarendon Press, 1979), 181–82.

28. John R. Reed, *Victorian Will* (Athens: Ohio University Press, 1989), see especially Chapter 3.

29. Frederick W. Robertson, *"The Human Race" and Other Sermons Preached at Cheltenham, Oxford, and Brighton* (New York: Harper & Brothers, 1881), 34. Though humbleness is the subject of this sermon, its language reveals an all-too-evident pride in that humility. Subsequent references in the text.

30. Kingsley, *The Good News of God: Sermons* [Originally published 1885], *Works,* 24:92.

31. Geoffrey Rowell discusses the large part that death-bed scenes played in Evangelical religion, including the suggestion that children should have experience of real deathbed scenes (7ff.). He calls attention to F. W. Robertson's aversion to the evangelical love of deathbed scenes (75). Elizabeth Jay also notes the central importance of the presentation of deathbed scenes in evangelical biography. "Death is not seen as an interim state on the way to final union with, or alienation from, God, but as a climax in itself. Judgement is awarded on earth rather than waiting for the final Judgement Seat. Reprobates endure the agonies of hell actually on their death-beds" (155). Michael Wheeler discusses the importance of deathbeds in his first chapter.

32. James Hinton, *The Mystery of Pain : A Book for the Sorrowful* (New York:

Mitchell Kennerley, 1914 [Originally published 1866], 16, 6. Subsequent references in the text.

33. *Philosophy and Religion: Selections from the Manuscripts of the Late James Hinton,* ed. Caroline Haddon (London: Kegan Paul, Trench and Co., 1881), 74.

34. Martin Tupper, *Proverbial Philosophy: In Four Series* (London: E. Moxon, Son and Co., n.d.), 54.

35. Thomas Carlyle, *Past and Present,* ed. Richard D. Altick (Boston: Houghton Mifflin Company, 1965), 19. Subsequent references in the text.

36. R. W. Dale, *Christian Doctrine: A Series of Discourses* (New York: A. C. Armstrong and Son, 1895), 246. Subsequent references in the text.

37. F. W. Robertson, *Sermons on Bible Subjects* (London: J. M. Dent and Co., 1906), 31.

38. Arthur Penrhyn Stanley, *Addresses and Sermons Delivered at St. Andrews in 1872, 1875 and 1877* (London: Macmillan and Co., 1877), 173.

39. F. W. Robertson, *Sermons on St. Paul's Epistles to the Corinthians: Delivered at Trinity Chapel, Brighton* (Boston: Ticknor and Fields, 1866), 281–82.

40. Charles Haddon Spurgeon, *Sermons, Sixth Series* (New York: Sheldon and Co., 1865), 187.

41. John Cummings, *The Daily Life; or Precepts and Prescriptions for Christian Living* (Boston: John P. Jewett and Co., 1855), 52–53.

42. Many years before, Bishop Joseph Butler had urged similar restraint in judgment.

"No one ever did a designed injury to another, but at the same time he did a much greater to himself. If therefore we would consider things justly, such an one is, according to the natural course of our affections, an object of compassion, as well as of displeasure: and to be affected really in this manner, I say really, in opposition to show and pretence, argues the true greatness of mind" (*Sermons,* vol. 2 of *The Works of the Right Reverend Father in God Joseph Butler, D.C. L., Late Lord Bishop of Durham,* with preface by Samuel Halifax, 2 vols. [Oxford: The Clarendon Press, 1874], 115).

43. Adelaide Proctor, *The Complete Poetical Works,* intro. Charles Dickens (New York: Thomas Y. Crowell and Co., n.d.), 11–12.

44. Bishop Butler got around this dilemma by explaining that, although goodwill toward our fellow man is our duty and another's guilt or injuriousness does not dispense with it, we nonetheless may fulfill both our social and our moral obligations of goodwill and punishment of wrong. He gives as an example the execution of a convicted felon. "What justifies public executions is, not that the guilt or demerit of the criminal dispenses with the obligation of good-will, neither would this justify any severity; but that his life is inconsistent with the quiet and happiness of the world" (110).

45. Albert Barnes, *The Atonement, in its Relations to Law and Moral Government* (Philadelphia: Parry & Mcmillan, 1860), 9. Subsequent references in the text.

TWO

Education

IF CULTURE is the text each member of a community must learn to interpret, punishment is one of its most obvious grammars for neophytes. Education is a premiere form of social management, and modern societies are generally aware of the degree to which their populations are aculturated through organized public education. Introducing young people to an institutional culture involves the delineation of values, which in turn requires an explanation of approval and blame. Accordingly, one important purpose of education is to teach the consequences of wrongdoing. For example, children must be made to appreciate the significance of intentionally inflicted pain. Different cultures have different methods of punishment, and their educational schemes have different ways of applying those methods to their citizens. Most modern educational systems forgo physical punishment; they employ systems that withhold privilege or encourage obedience and approved performance through a hierarchy of rewards. In the United States these rewards are generally material; in Japan, they are psychological.

England at the beginning of the nineteenth century offers an interesting cultural moment when ideas about punishment were changing, thereby calling for a revision of values. The bloody code of capital punishment—so notorious in the eighteenth century—was being replaced with more "humane" forms of punishment, and the concept of rehabilitation was emerging as a new objective. During these years some reform movements had material successes, notably reform of prisons and of the penal code. Other reforms were instrumental in altering attitudes toward wrongdoing in the culture at large. One of these was the reform in education.

During the early nineteenth century, several educational changes occurred. The universities were reformed, the proliferating public schools offered new morally grounded models for training youths, and opportunities were extended

30

to the laboring and poorer classes. Evangelicalism affirmed the value of literacy, and the Sunday School movement it promoted encouraged the teaching of secular and religious subjects in a moral context. Philanthropic organizations encouraged the creation of "ragged schools" (rudimentary charitable establishments) and the improvement of the "national" schools (supervised by the Church of England). One consequence of this emphasis upon education was a larger reading public, especially among the young. In what follows, I shall examine some ways in which the growing body of literature written specifically for young people, or utilized in their education, treated the subject of punishment. All the works I discuss were very popular in their own day and remained so for many years after. These works represent actual practices of their time and served as handbooks for the instruction of parents and children, in the process institutionalizing new values and methods for dealing with misconduct.

Gillian Avery asserts that there is a clear increase in the savagery of child punishment as one moves backward from Victorian to Georgian times, and this pattern parallels actual legal practice.[1] Physical means of correction such as flogging are mentioned regularly, but so are other forms of threat and humiliation. A notorious and often cited example occurs in Mrs. Sherwood's famous children's tale *The History of the Fairchild Family* (1818). When the Fairchild children quarrel among themselves, their father immediately disciplines them by whipping their hands and making them stand in a corner unfed through the morning. But this is not all. To emphasize the enormity of sibling conflict, the father later takes them to gaze upon the remains of a hanged man.

> Just between [the house] and the wood stood a gibbet, on which the body of a man hung in chains: it had not yet fallen to pieces, although it had hung there some years. The body had on a blue coat, a silk handkerchief round the neck, with shoes and stockings, and every other part of the dress still entire: but the face of the corpse was so shocking, that the children could not look at it.[2]

This, Mr. Fairchild says, is the final outcome of one brother's hatred for another. He explains that, left to its own selfish and resentful nature, the human heart inclines to such barbarities. Only dependence upon God and the example of Christ can spare man from such consequences of his depravity.

Mrs. Sherwood modified her position as she grew older, so that with the publication of Part IV of *The History of Henry Milner* in 1837 she has Henry's guardian explain his changed attitudes regarding the Millenium and eternal punishment. Now he feels that after death all men will be given a chance to purge their sins through suffering so that they may be admitted to the New Jerusalem.[3] This was an advanced position for Mrs. Sherwood's day and quite a departure from orthodox thinking. As we saw in Chapter 1, the question of what happens in the afterlife was still warmly disputed past mid-century. Mrs. Sherwood had believed as late as 1829 that only the saints (Evangelicals) would survive the Millenium; later she softened this extreme position.

At first Evangelicals denounced fiction as a pernicious mode of entertainment, but soon they themselves discovered its power for conveying moral messages. Legh Richmond disapproved of fiction, but utilized a rigid narrative form in his extremely popular *The Dairyman's Daughter.* And it was not long before the Religious Tract Society (RTS) and the Society for the Promotion of Christian Knowledge (SPCK) were consciously trying to provide religiously oriented children's fiction to replace romances and fairy tales.[4] Much of the evangelically inspired literature for children emphasized human depravity and the need to trust in divine providence and its scheme of retribution and redemption. As we saw in Chapter 1, the popular evangelical text *Family Prayers* by Henry Thornton emphasized human sinfulness and the need for utter dependence upon God for grace and pardon. This passage from the prayer for the "Twenty-Sixth Morning" is a mild example.

> Thou art infinitely great and glorious! Before Thee, the angels veil their faces; and the heavens are not pure in Thy sight! We are weak, and helpless; sinful, and corrupt; exposed to dangers on every side, and in continual need of Thy gracious assistance. O Lord, preserve us through this day. By Thee we have been protected during the night. Continue to us Thy wonted care; and guard, we pray Thee, both our bodies and our souls from every kind of evil.[5]

Elizabeth Jay writes that because of this stern conviction of human depravity, "The Evangelical attempt to curb and oppress the natural vitality of childhood became a favorite theme for critical novelists" (140). Writing in 1869, Charlotte Yonge classified this subgenre of children's fiction as the Sunday story or religious fiction, crediting Hannah More's Cheap Repository Tracts as perhaps the earliest version and noting Mrs. Sherwood's tales among the most popular and effective in "inculcating a kind of Calvinistic piety."[6] The stories produced by the Religious Tract Society, she said, emphasized sudden conversion and early death. Some of these stories she considered well done but concluded: "the mixture of sentimentality with religion, the direful judgments brought on the unconverted, and the prominence given to feeling and conscious piety, are all undesirable" (309). By the time Yonge wrote, a new atmosphere was available to writers of children's books who wanted to emphasize religion. Yonge herself was a contributor to this mode. Her own model for a religious book was Alessandro Manzoni's adult novel *I Promessi Sposi,* which she praised for "drawing out the poetry of all that is good, enlisting the sympathies on behalf of purity, faith and forgiveness, and making vice hateful and despicable" (310). What children were to learn from religion in the later part of the century differed considerably from what they were taught at its beginning. Mrs. Favell Lee Mortimer wrote an instruction manual for children and teachers of children entitled *Peep of Day*. It provided simple explanations about body, soul, world, events in Christ's life, and so forth in a manner understandable for young children. But throughout, the book emphasizes human mortality. In Lesson IV on the soul Mortimer writes, "Your body will decay: it will turn to dust; but your soul will live for ever: it will never decay."[7] Lesson XXXIX on the death of Judas declares:

> It was very wicked in Judas to hang himself instead of praying to God to forgive him.
>   Where did Judas' soul go when he died?"
>   It went to hell, and to Satan. Judas is in the wicked place now; and Jesus will judge him at the last day, and say, Depart, thou cursed. (103)

Describing the Judgment Day to infants, Mortimer has her instructor persona say that those who do not love God will be put in a lake of fire called hell to gnash their teeth and weep and wail forever. One day God will burn up the world she says, adding several graphic details before making her point. Even though the material world will be consumed in time, "The wicked will not be able to escape from God. They will burn for ever and ever" (138). Of course, the book teaches gentler lessons as well, insisting that Jesus always forgives those who truly repent, a lesson illustrated by the examples of the sinful woman who begged Christ for forgiveness and of Simon, the rich man who felt he needed none (62ff.). But as a work designed for the youngest order of children, *Peep of Day* is rather grim fare.

Even this emphasis on death, exemplified by the constant use of deathbed scenes in evangelical literature, was gradually transformed over the years. From being a reminder of our sinfulness and the ever-imminent snatching of our soul to judgment, deathbed scenes became emblematic of innocence in the figure of a sweet, appealing, loving child who cannot survive in a world that oppresses or misunderstands him or her.[8] This tradition of the childhood deathbed scene was prominent in more aesthetically acceptable fiction as well. Little Nell and Paul Dombey are notable examples, but such deaths occur in a wide range of novels addressed to different audiences, such as Florence Montgomery's *Misunderstood* (1869) and Horatia Ewing's *The Story of a Short Life* (1885). In Montgomery's novel, young Humphrey Duncombe's father misinterprets the boy's behavior and makes his displeasure known. His disapproval weighs so heavily on Humphrey that it contributes to his death. Humphrey is actually a good boy characterized by a devoted love for his dead mother. His death is depicted as practically sacramental. For Humphrey to die seems more a reward than a punishment, since, as the author observes, his nature is too fine for this world and is more suitable for heaven. The use of death scenes for pious ends could, of course, be carried to extreme. Charlotte Yonge disliked Frederick Farrar's *Eric,* in which some exaggerated scenes of this kind occur, calling it "that morbid dismal tale . . . which we hope no mother or boy ever reads, since it really can answer no purpose but to make them unhappy and suspicious, besides that it enforces by numerous telling examples that the sure reward of virtue is a fatal accident" (454).

As most historians of children and their literature seem to agree, attitudes toward children in England grew gentler as the nineteenth century progressed.[9] In his sermon of 1879 entitled "The Children's Creed," Dean Stanley offered the following as a major list of what children should be taught. They should learn that God is goodness and justice; that his rules for the government of the world are His will and wish for us; that "even sickness and pain, are for our good, and we must trust that He has some good reason for it, perhaps to make us strong and brave and healthy."[10] In addition, children should be taught to imitate Christ and to understand that there is something in all humans, called the voice of God or the spirit of God, that distinguishes right from wrong; in fact, this spirit functions as conscience, reinforcing the moral scheme impressed upon children in their earliest education. Finally, children should be taught to love one another.

Another body of early juvenile literature was less concerned with intimidating children into accepting their culture's moral code than with providing pragmatic formulas for successful adaptation to that culture. One of the most enduring children's stories of this kind was Thomas Day's *Sandford and Merton* (1783–89). Day, though a religious man, took a materialist approach to punishment. On the whole, his story is more about avoiding the consequences of unwise behavior than about the need to punish. He argues for a *reasonable* life. Nonetheless, punishment must be addressed in a world arranged according to moral values. The first specific reference to punishment in Day's story describes how an ill-tempered tailor in India is immediately punished by the elephant he injures.[11] The stories of "The Good-Natured Little Boy" and "The Ill-Natured Little Boy," provide a version of the industrious and idle apprentice syndrome. One boy performs a series of spontaneous good deeds and is rewarded for them the same day. The other commits a series of offenses which result in retributively similar injuries. Punishment is quick, certain, and appropriate to the wrong committed. This is an organic pattern of justice, based as much upon good sense as upon moral law. Mr. Barlow, the mentor for Sandford and Merton, explains that a sensible man will behave well to all around him, since he never knows when he may need help himself. The last extended treatment of punishment as such occurs when little Tommy Merton (the pampered, upper-class child) wants to punish a cat that has killed his pet robin. Mr. Barlow says: You can't punish him if you haven't disciplined him. The disciplining takes the form of some painful behavior modification for the cat, but this pain is viewed as education, not punishment. Tommy also wants to punish the rabbits that have killed his newly planted trees, but Mr. Barlow suggests that the wise move is not to avenge oneself upon the rabbits for what is natural in them (seeking nourishment), but to protect the trees instead. Here practical sense is offered as a countermeasure to a sheerly retributive impulse. When Day's day was past, Charlotte Yonge summed him up by saying that he "is best known as the author of 'Sandford and Merton,' once a child's classic standing next to 'Robinson Crusoe,' and really containing much that is very charming, though mixed with much queer unsatisfactory stuff of the theorist author" (237). Charles Dickens was not so forgiving and presented Mr. Barlow as the embodiment of boredom, relentlessly turning everything—from burlesque to panorama to dinner conversation—into moral instruction. Dickens claimed that his own ignorance of the natural world resulted from his loathing for Mr. Barlow's relentless expositions on the subject. He despised Harry Sandford, who appeared to him no more than a "hypocritical young prig," and said that he would rather follow the example of the wicked Master Mash than imitate Harry.[12] For Dickens, Day's book represented precisely what children's literature should not be—humorless instruction. But Day's influence was still strong enough to call forth a full-length parody by F. C. Burnand, entitled *The New History of Sandford and Merton,* as late as 1872.[13]

Day's story emphasizes a due subordination to the existing social order and patience in the face of human hardships, but also suggests that reasonable people can achieve a great measure of contentment through virtuous and frugal behavior. Maria Edgeworth, influenced by Day's work, also emphasized acceptance of social roles and the use of reason over outright punishment as the chief means of dealing with wrongdoing among children, as did other writers like Hannah More and Mrs. Trimmer. Time and again in *Practical Education* (1798, 1801), Maria Edgeworth and her father insist: "To prevent, we cannot too often repeat it, is better than to punish, without humouring children; that is to say, without yielding to their caprices, or to their *will.*"[14] They warn that those who think they have conquered obstinacy in young people through bodily pain have really only suppressed the disease for a time, and will find it break out again when restraint is removed. The Edgeworths argue that punishment as vengeance is outdated and that a more enlightened attitude sees punishment as working toward the general happiness of all society. "In fact," they claim, "severity is seldom necessary in a well-conducted education. The smallest possible degree of pain, which can in any case produce the required effect, is indisputably the just measure of the punishment which ought to be inflicted in any given case" (235–36). Influenced by Day, the Edgeworths also insist that whatever punishment is used, it must be immediate. They stress the importance of instilling early on the importance of reputation in children, teaching them to connect the relationship between their past and present selves so that they understand the values of integrity and distrust. The wisest course is to find preventatives for defects in manners, temper, and understanding in children and thereby replace punishment with hope, which is the source of "Courage, generosity, industry, perseverance, all the magic of talents, all the powers of genius, all the virtues that appear spontaneous in great minds . . ." (254). Charlotte Yonge had little admiration for Mr. Edgeworth's educational writings, claiming that his statement that children should be taught nothing that they cannot understand was destructive of sound educational principles and that the man must have been "singularly deficient either in imagination or sense of beauty" (302). But she appreciated Maria's genius and praised the *Parent's Assistant, Popular Tales,* and *Early Lessons* as containing fine work, though she had some reservations about Edgeworth's approach.

> "Principles," as she calls them—by which is meant religious faith producing obedience to moral precepts—are taken for granted; and the good sense, honour, and expediency of life is the theme. It is a high-minded expediency, the best side of Epicureanism. Honesty *is* the best policy, but policy it always is: success is always the object and the reward, but it is not a showy, gaudy gratification of vanity, although it may be of pride. (303)

Despite her criticism, Yonge seems sorry that Edgeworth's writings have gone out of fashion. Children today, she says, find them too dry. "Is it the natural impatience of the last generation's fashions, or is it that they are too much used to sentiment, rapid incident, and broad fun, to appreciate quiet detail?" (304–5).

If evangelical writings emphasized physical and emotional chastisement to correct childish misbehavior, and rationalists preferred reason to both of these, another school of thought considered direct pain a useful and commonsensical device for simple training. As with Day's "educated" cat, Captain Frederick Marryat's characters must learn correct behavior through physical suffering. Corporal punishment is both discipline and punishment. The education of young Johnny Easy in *Mr. Midshipman Easy* (1836) is a clear example. Like Day's Tommy Merton, young Jack Easy has been spoiled by his family and become so dangerously ungovernable that finally the family agrees to send him to school, but to one where flogging is not permitted. Dr. Middleton, the family medical advisor who takes Johnny to the school, asks how Mr. Bonnycastle, the master of the school, can manage without flogging. The educator replies, "I can produce more effect by one caning than twenty floggings."[15] He has not abandoned corporal punishment, but refined it, he explains to Dr. Middleton.

> "Look at that cub, doctor, sitting there more like a brute than a reasonable being; do you imagine that I could ever lick it into shape without strong measures? At the same time, allow me to say that I consider my system by far the best. At the public schools, punishment is no check; it is so trifling that it is derided: with me punishment is punishment in the true sense of the word, and the consequence is that it is much more seldom resorted to." (20)

Fear and love, he says, are the two strongest impulses in human nature, but appeal to the former never fails. He puts his method to use immediately with little

Johnny, striking him with his cane each time the boy refuses to do as he is told. When he has thus wrenched compliance from the child, he sends him supperless to bed to "facilitate" his studies the next day. Marryat intrudes at this point to approve Mr. Bonnycastle's method. "Pain and hunger alone," he observes, "will tame brutes, and the same remedy must be applied to conquer those passions in man which assimilate him with brutes" (24). He adds that while Johnny's family sleeps confident that he is not being birched, Johnny himself is already "so far advanced in knowledge as to have a tolerable comprehension of the *mystery of the cane*" (25). Marryat approves physical punishment but advises that it be used sparingly. Later in the novel, Jack himself fights a shipboard bully to protect a young midshipman and rebels against the institutionalized brutality of the navy.

Corporal punishment remained an important element in the Victorian attitude toward children and became a notorious shared experience of boys who attended the English public schools. Much has been written about the use of caning to discipline boys at private and public schools. Dr. Thomas Arnold, who wished to minimize the practice, nonetheless defended it. Corporal punishment, he observed, is said to be degrading, but that is a foolish position based upon the mistaken notions of aristocratic personal honor and dignity and upon the popular demand for independence. Punishment inflicted by a parent or master for the purpose of correction is not degrading, nor is it more degrading for being physical. In any case, that form of punishment was confined to boys under fifteen. Boys of the higher forms were controlled by moral persuasion.

> The beau-ideal of school discipline with regard to young boys would appear to be this—that whilst corporal punishment was retained on principle as fitly answering to, and marking the naturally inferior state of, boyhood, morally and intellectually, and therefore as conveying no peculiar degradation to persons in such a state, we should cherish and encourage to the utmost all attempts made by the several boys as individuals to escape from the natural punishment of their age by rising above its naturally low tone of principle.[16]

Arnold's very severe view of young boys is echoed by Frederick Robertson when he describes that time when the child passes into the man. "We call that period boyhood—the most unruly, the most selfish, the most ungovernable of all epoches of human existence."[17] Arthur Stanley, who had studied under Arnold and written his biography, might have sympathized with this view of boyhood, but himself offered a far different view of children. Little children, he said, give an idea of what man was meant to be. "No doubt there are bad children—naughty children; and even in good children, there is something which may become very bad. Still, in children there is an innocence, a lightness of heart, an ignorance of evil, a joyousness, and a simplicity, which ought to be refreshing to every one" (Humphrey 106). This is very different from being told that you are born in sin and

emerge into the world weighted with damnation, under the immediate obligation to put yourself at the mercy of a judging God.

Arnold's was just one voice among many on this subject, which remained a
lively one well into the twentieth century, as a work like George Orwell's
"Such, Such Were the Joys" indicates.[18] Arnold spoke of discipline in the public
schools, but others supported his moral position more generally. Frederick Robertson put the case directly in a passage already quoted on page 25 of this study
when he declared that "under a system of mere love and tenderness no character
can acquire manliness or firmness" (126). In a world governed by the righteous
Law of God, retribution is guaranteed for offenders and thus the human practice
of punishing is a correct mode of behavior because it imitates God's own practice. But this justification assumes two very important givens—that there actually exists such a providential pattern and that the sinful can been seen to suffer
from their offenses in this world. Once these assumptions are challenged, new
grounds of defense for punishment must be found.

If an emphasis upon physical pain as a consequence of wrongdoing remained a
significant element of introducing children to Victorian culture, new and subtler
features were equally significant. Early moralistic children's fiction sought to
make inherently wicked children obey the strictures of religion and thus become
good citizens. More secular writers wanted to employ logic in achieving similar
results. But a characteristic tendency in the Victorian years was to teach children
to punish themselves. This approach was assisted by the growing belief that children came into this world fallen but not evil. In fact, a familiar figure in the
literature of the middle years of the century is the pure child who succeeds in
converting wayward adults, a reversal of the Georgian pattern of benevolent
adult disciplining child. There are numerous examples of the good effects of self-
incrimination in Victorian literature. A whole genre developed in the public
school novel, from Thomas Hughes' *Tom Brown's Schooldays* (1857) and Frederick
W. Farrar's *Eric, or Little By Little* (1858), clear to the end of the century. But in
the interests of brevity, I would like to glance at a special category of tales that
utilize the natural world as their instructive library.

Mary Howitt's popular *Sketches of Natural History* (1834) was inspired by a
sympathy for animals and a positive view of children, but was, in the early
nineteenth-century manner, more informational than moralistic. Mrs. Gatty, one
of the most popular moral educators of the Victorian period, reversed the equation, offering a skeleton of natural history to carry the weight of a substantial
moral lesson. Mrs. Gatty's *Parables From Nature* first appeared in 1855 and continued through five series until 1871. Each parable was designed to help the juvenile audience learn how to become a part of society. "The Law of Authority and
Obedience" uses a community of bees to demonstrate that social order requires
hierarchical structures where some guide and some labor. A group of bees, dis-
contented because they do not see the justice of one bee being queen when they
were all created equal, sets out to found a republic where all are working bees.
But they cannot agree on rudiments of social life and finally must return to the

order of the hive. "Training and Restraining" criticizes the desire for individual freedom. The Wind convinces flowers in a garden that the poles and strings that support them and the careful pruning with which they have been tended are the offensive tyrannies of gardeners. The flowers liberate themselves and are promptly devastated by wind and rain so that most must be scrapped by the gardener. The lesson is clear to the young mistress of the house:

> "now, at last, I quite understand what you have so often said about the necessity of training, and restraint, and culture, for us as well as for flowers, in a fallen world. The wind has torn away these poor things from their fastenings, and they are growing wild whichever way they please. I know I should once have argued, that if it were their natural mode of growing it must therefore be the best. But I cannot say so, now that I see the result. They are doing whatever they like, unrestrained; and the end is, that my beautiful GARDEN is turned into a WILDERNESS."[19]

One recognizes here a kinship with Matthew Arnold's more complex indictment of doing as one likes in *Culture and Anarchy*.

"The Law of the Wood" inculcates the necessity of mutual accommodation by showing that the spruce trees who wish to proliferate without consideration for their neighbors are the first to be singled out by the woodsman's axe. "Kicking" is the story of a lively colt that doesn't wish to be ridden and thinks that it is serving itself by kicking and therefore discouraging riders until one day he throws and injures a young girl; he is severely disciplined by his master, a discipline that is a kindness too, for Firefly, the colt, comes to feel guilt for injuring his young mistress and learns that submission is not bad. "Animals under man—servants under masters—children under parents—wives under husbands—men under authorities—nations under rulers—all under God,—it is the same with all:—in obedience of will is the only true peace" (268).

Mrs. Gatty's nature parables were popular, but the most striking work of this kind was Charles Kingsley's *Water-babies* (1863). This children's story traces the growth of young Tom the chimney sweep's soul after his "husk" has been purged in a stream (i.e., he drowns). Living in a pond and protected by water fairies, Tom learns about the ways of nature, which are remarkably anthropomorphic. The important turn of events for our present purpose is Tom's encounter with Mrs. Bedonebyasyoudid, who explains why Tom is punished in kind for tormenting water creatures even though he did not realize that he was doing wrong.

> "And so, if you do not know that things are wrong, that is no reason why you should not be punished for them; though not as much, not as much, my little man" (and the lady looked very kindly, after all), "as if you did know."
>
> "Well, you are a little hard on a poor lad," said Tom.

"Not at all; I am the best friend you ever had in all your life. But I will tell you; I cannot help punishing people when they do wrong. I like it no more than they do; I am often very, very sorry for them, poor things: but I cannot help it. If I tried not to do it, I should do it all the same. For I work by machinery, just like an engine; and am full of wheels and springs inside; and am wound up very carefully, so that I cannot help going."[20]

Those who don't listen to Mrs. Doasyouwouldbedoneby, she says, must inevitably answer to her.

This is a modernized version of the law of cause and effect, otherwise known as natural punishment; it assumes as Thomas Carlyle and George Eliot did in their different ways that we sow the seeds of our own destinies. For the one, whatever punishment we receive is what we deserve; for the other, it is the result of invariant consequence. But the significant distinction in Kingsley's scheme, at least insofar as it applies to children, is that this process is natural and does not require external authority to make it happen. Nature itself offers the opportunity for therapeutic punishment for those who can perceive it. Kingsley openly rejects corporal punishment. When Mrs. Bedonebyasyoudid does not flog or browbeat Tom after an offense, Kingsley remarks, "But perhaps the way of beating, and hurrying, and frightening, and questioning, was not the way that the child should go; for it is not even the way in which a colt should go if you want to break it in and make it a quiet serviceable horse" (215–16). Mrs. Gatty's Firefly might disagree. But what is clear here is that Kingsley does not merely use episodes from nature to illustrate a moral, he *trusts* nature as a foundation of morality because it literally embodies the divine purpose. Poetic justice governs this world. The crows who kill one of their kind for refusing to steal grouses' eggs die when they consume a dog's carcass laced with strychnine. Grimes, the master who had abused Tom when he was a chimney sweep, suffers the Dantean punishment in his afterlife of being immovably fixed in a chimney. Kingsley, avid fisherman that he was, could not resist interjecting that the best way to cure a salmon poacher is to put him under water for twenty-four hours.

Kingsley said that the doctrine of his book was "your soul makes your body, just as a snail makes his shell" (86). What we become, in his scheme, is the consequence of our own actions. But the significantly Victorian version of this model is that we develop over time and learn from our past acts in what amounts to an evolutionary pattern, and Kingsley makes overt references both to evolution and devolution in his tale. The burden now is on the individual, even the individual child, to learn from natural events and internalize those values. No religious faith is necessary in *Water-babies;* the morality is pragmatically designed for social coexistence. Of course Kingsley stresses the existence of a higher power, but he insists that we learn God's purpose by looking at the world around us and into our own heart.

Two widely separated articles from the *Quarterly Review* indicate the direction and dimension of the change represented by *Water-babies*. In an article on children's fiction in 1842, Elizabeth Eastlake complained about the increasing appeal in juvenile literature "solely to reason" in the infant.[21] She associated this trend with American juvenile literature that, she said, revealed the calculating character of Americans. A quarter of a century later, a similar review article by Bennett G. Johns deplored the heavily religious approach of Mrs. Sherwood's *The Fairchild Family,* whose purpose, he said, was to impress on the minds of children "their own utter, entire, unmitigated, constant wickedness in thought, word, and action; their love for wickedness, and their fitness for hell to which they are all most surely and infallibly doomed, and to which they must go unless God specially saves them."[22] The author championed a more enlightened position, assuming that "the conscience of a child, taught fairly to love what is pure, brave and true, is tenderly alive to a sense of every injustice as a departure from his own high standard" (62).

Of course that high standard was instilled by adult authorities, but, projected on the juvenile population, it revealed a new perspective on society as a world in which children (and adults) are not "corrected" by physical punishment, but encouraged to "good" behavior by imitating a "natural" code in which wickedness, being unnatural, injures itself, and in which education can transform misguided souls into worthy citizens who have learned to edit their own worst inclinations. As adult society increasingly endorsed the model of an integral, self-directed individuality, it displayed for its children a paradigm in which childhood itself became the model of redemptive self-correction in a developmental scheme. The soul of the State makes the body of the State, just as a snail makes his shell. Matthew Arnold in his post-Hegelian manner believed that the State could be the population's own best self; similarly, the child, in learning to aspire to his or her own best self through introspection, could contribute to that evolving, progressing, and developing political entity.

In nineteenth-century children's literature, retribution for offenses was generally very direct. It could be punishment administered by a character for violations of the gentlemanly code, as in *Mr. Midshipman Easy* when Tartar is shot in a duel by Jack's Sicilian friend for having been verbally abusive to Jack, or it could be the kind of large-scale providential retribution characteristic of Kingsley's *Westward Ho!* which became a model for an entire class of boy's books to follow.[23] J. S. Bratton notes that in girls' books of the time, wicked children are always punished. Speaking of Charlotte Yonge, Bratton says: "In her stories retribution for wrongdoing may be death, perhaps the death of an innocent child, which brings the evildoer to agonized repentance in several books" (177).

The nineteenth century experienced a radical transformation in its way of perceiving blame and punishment. One major feature of that transformation involved the realization that human nature, like external nature and its various species, is not fixed but mutable. That being so, it seemed reasonable to assume that it was mutable toward good and that, when institutions were not employing educative and other rehabilitative schemes to effect that change, individuals could be doing it for themselves. At one simple level this is the positive doctrine of self-help, but at a far more rudimentary and intimate level, this training for participation in a progressive world alterable for the better starts in the nursery when young children begin to learn the new plot by which they are to shape their lives. But if children's literature could cross the boundary from punishment to love with only minor hesitations and impediments, the attempt to make this journey in the real world of human transgression and justice was not so easy. Chapter 3 explores the assumptions, efforts, and consequences involved in the Victorian program for reforming its system of justice.

NOTES

1. Gillian Avery, *Nineteenth-Century Children: Heroes and Heroines in English Children's Stories 1780-1900* (London: Hodder and Stoughton, 1965), 204ff.

2. Mary Sherwood, *The History of the Fairchild Family,* preface by Barry Westburg (New York: Garland Publishing, Inc., 1977), 57.

3. This narrative is summarized in Elizabeth Jay's *The Religion of the Heart: Anglican Evangelicalism and the Nineteenth-Century Novel* (Oxford: The Clarendon Press, 1979), 83.

4. J. S. Bratton, *The Impact of Victorian Children's Fiction* (Totowa, NJ: Barnes & Noble Books, 1981), 38. See also Jay for the Evangelicals' approach to fiction.

5. Henry Thornton, *Family Papers: To Which Is Added, A Family Commentary Upon The Sermon On The Mount* (New York: Swords, Stanford, & Co., 1837), 67.

6. Charlotte Yonge, "Children's Literature of the Last Century. 2. Didactic Fiction," *Macmillan's Magazine* 20 (August 1869), 308. Subsequent references appear in the text.

7. Favell Lee Mortimer, *The Peep of Day: Or, A Series of the Earliest Religious Instruction the Infant Mind is Capable of Receiving; with Verses Illustrative of the Subjects* (Boston: American Tract Society, n.d.), 24. Subsequent references appear in the text.

8. Elizabeth Jay remarks: "Perhaps the one truly distinguishing feature of the Evangelical biography is the care devoted to the presentation of the death-bed scene" (154). Jay examines the fascination with deathbed scenes in some detail, mentioning the publishing phenomena that accompanied that fascination.

"Enterprising publishers were not long in recognizing the market that existed for series of death-bed scenes culled from biographies and such appetizing titles as *Death-Bed Triumphs of Eminent Christians* appeared. Confronted with the evidence of a man like Henry Nevinson, who recalled that in his grandfather's house in the 1860s *The Family Sepulchre* was one of the few books considered acceptable Sunday reading for the children, it is relevant to inquire how familiarity with this tradition affected the presentation of such scenes in the novel" (161–62).

9. F. M. L. Thompson's conclusion about trends in the treatment of children during the nineteenth century is concise. "The only change in upbringing that can be discerned with any confidence is a trend towards less frequent and less harsh use of beating, strappings, and beltings over the course of the century, and the partial substitution of verbal correction and non-corporal punishments" (*The Rise of Respectable Society: A Social History of Victorian Britain 1830-1900* [Cambridge: Harvard University Press, 1988], 134). Claudia Nelson's *Boys will be Girls: The Feminine Ethic and British Children's Fiction, 1857-1917* (New Brunswick: Rutgers University Press, 1991) argues that the male protagonists of many early Victorian children's stories were already presented according to feminine concepts of worthiness, hence unlike the rougher types commonly associated with active boyhood.

10. Frances A. Humphrey, *Dean Stanley with the Children* (Boston: D. Lothrop and Co., 1884), 159–60. Subsequent references appear in the text.

11. Thomas Day, *The History of Sandford and Merton* (London: Darton and Hodge, n.d.), 3.

12. Charles Dickens, "Mr. Barlow," *The Uncommercial Traveller and Reprinted Pieces* (New York: Oxford University Press, 1964), 339–40.

13. See Avery, 20ff.

14. Maria Edgeworth and Richard Lovell Edgeworth, *Practical Education,* 2 vols., intro. Gina Luria (New York: Garland Publishing Inc., 1974), 1:162.

15. Captain Frederick Marryat, *Mr. Midshipman Easy,* intro. David Hannay (London: Macmillan and Co., Ltd., 1932), 19.

16. Thomas Arnold, *The Miscellaneous Works* (New York: D. Appleton & Co., 1846), 359.

17. Frederick W. Robertson, *"The Human Race"* and *Other Sermons Preached at Cheltenham, Oxford, and Brighton* (New York: Harper & Brothers, 1881), 25. Far from considering children essentially innocent, Thomas Arnold assumed that youthful innocence was really fragile inexperience and that a school's function was to hasten boys from childhood to manhood, thereby making them wise rather than ignorant and responsible rather than wild as soon as possible. See *Thomas Arnold on Education: A Selection from His Writings,* intro. T. W. Bamford (Cambridge: Cambridge University Press, 1970), especially page 80.

18. There are many books dealing with the public schools. Edward C. Mack's two volumes, *Public Schools and British Opinion 1780-1860* (New York: Columbia University Press, 1939) and *Public Schools and British Opinion Since 1860* (New York: Columbia University Press, 1941) are classics, exhaustively examin-

ing responses to the schools. See also John R. Reed's *Old School Ties: The Public Schools in British Literature* (Syracuse: Syracuse University Press, 1964), for the role of the public schools in literature.

19. Mrs. [Margaret Scott] Gatty, *Parables From Nature* (London: J. M. Dent, n.d.), 38–39. Subsequent references appear in the text.

20. Charles Kingsley, *The Water-babies* (Ann Arbor: University Microfilms, Inc., 1966), 196–97. Subsequent references appear in the text.

21. Elizabeth Eastlake, "Children's Fiction," *Quarterly Review* 71 (December 1842), 62–63. Subsequent references appear in the text.

22. Bennett G. Johns, "Children's Fiction," *Quarterly Review* 122 (January 1867), 73. Subsequent references appear in the text.

23. See Bratton for a discussion of boys' books. See also E. S. Turner, *Boys Will Be Boys* (London: Michael Joseph, 1957), Patrick Howarth, *Play Up and Play the Game: The Heroes of Popular Fiction* (London: Methuen, 1973), and Louis James, "Tom Brown's Imperialist Sons," *Victorian Studies* 18 (1973), 89–99, for various accounts of boys' literature in the latter part of the nineteenth century with comments on changing models of manliness.

THREE

Legal Punishment

DICKENS AND THACKERAY matured in a period when ideas about legal systems and procedures were undergoing important review. Michael Ignatieff has described in detail the rise of the penitentiary in England and Michel Foucault has offered a reading of the changing perception about the nature and purpose of imprisonment. Many scholars have contributed to the recording of the gradual "humanization" of the old "bloody code," which depended heavily upon execution and later transportation for the discouragement of crime.[1] Both civil and criminal laws were being reformed, though in some cases the reforms seemed less satisfactory than what they replaced. The solitary system of prison confinement, for example, might have been superior to hanging, but relatively few criminals were hanged, whereas all convicted offenders from petty thieves to murderers were at least temporarily liable to solitary confinement, which many critics claimed was an excessive harshness capable of driving people insane. The New Poor Law was notoriously crueler than what it replaced, converting a form of relief into a punitive institution. These and other reforms—some only recommended, some tried only briefly, and some that succeeded—were proposed by two especially eager constituencies: religious, generally Evangelical enthusiasts represented by men like John Howard, and rationalist political theorists represented by men like Jeremy Bentham. Both groups sought to replace retribution with rehabilitation, though from widely different assumptions. One set hoped to touch the conscience of offenders and win them back to a Christian life, the other sought to train offenders' minds to the appreciation of a better moral order.[2] For both camps men were malleable beings capable of improvement. The schemes for that improvement varied considerably, but the basic hope of rehabilitation was behind them all.

The penitentiary system was a successful reform in the sense that it gained acceptance and became institutionalized and systematized over the century. One of its advocates, Joseph Adshead, who described various enormities at Newgate, Bridewell, and Coldbath Fields, among other prisons, rejected the silent system, respectfully disagreeing with Dickens' approval of that method, and recommended the example of the model prison at Pentonville that had been opened December 21, 1842, a few years before the appearance of Adshead's *Prisons and Prisoners* (1845). This prison followed the separate system, which Adshead considered more humane and moral than solitary confinement, which he viewed as primarily a means of punishment, not reformation.[3] The Pentonville experiment seemed to work well, satisfying the need to remove criminals from the streets, yet treating them humanely. Confinement in a penitentiary could conveniently be viewed either as retributive punishment or as an opportunity for rehabilitation. But measured by its ability to deter crime, the penitentiary was no more effective than other methods. Michael Ignatieff argues that the system continued to receive support because it satisfied a larger social need.

> It had appeal because the reformers succeeded in presenting it as a response, not merely to crime, but to the whole social crisis of a period, and as part of a larger strategy of political, social, and legal reform designed to reestabish order on a new foundation. As a result, while criticized for its functional shortcomings, the penitentiary continued to command support because it was seen as an element of a larger vision of order that by the 1840s commanded the reflexive assent of the propertied and powerful. (210)

To some degree this reordering of society was a response to the increased criminalization of behavior that had developed in the eighteenth century, presumably as a gesture by the propertied classes to extend their advantages and to control labor. By extending game laws and making it illegal to take firewood and deadfall from private lands, the propertied classes increasingly criminalized the customs of the poor. Many communities refused to consider some of their practices as crimes. This was especially true when they involved means of subsistence, as with many of the transgressions enumerated in the game laws.[4]

Nineteenth-century reformers proposed to maintain legal punishment as an exemplary control over criminal behavior, but also hoped to democratize that punishment by making it a means of recalling individuals to productive and salutary roles in society. Views differed widely, but one of the great impulses of the age, whether prompted by fear, hope, or compassion, was to reenlist the wayward in the positive improvements of the community at large. Clive Emsley writes that "The gospel of work was central to Victorian ideology; instilling habits of work and morality on the convict who was perceived, very often, to have taken the short step from idleness to crime was regarded as being beneficial both to society and to the offender" (247). More broadly, Martin J. Wiener states that building middle-class character was seen as a major function of the law (53).

Legal punishment was viewed in a variety of ways. Some argued strictly for retributive justice—one version or another of the *lex talionis*. Others argued for exemplary justice; without recommending punishment as an apt desert for a given offense, it was nonetheless recommended as a warning to potential offenders. Still others saw punishment as purgative or hygienic—the isolation or expulsion of a diseased agent from the community. Many regarded punishment chiefly as a means of moral rehabilitation. In most cases, though, what influenced those who took an interest in the penal system was the establishment of social order through some form of painful or constraining discipline.[5] A great irony of prison reform is that prisons at the turn of the eighteenth century allowed prisoners a good deal more personal freedom than they would later be allotted. Prisons were certainly not wholesome places, but if you possessed money or influence you could have things pretty much your own way. That would all disappear as the rigorously organized cellular system of the penitentiary established itself. But this removal of personal freedom was designed as a benefit. As the first great proponent of prison reform, John Howard, pointed out, the prisons of his time were morally and physically repulsive places where prisoners were treated as less than human. Moved by evangelical fervor, Howard insisted on the need to view prisoners as fellow men in a society universally inclined to sin (Ignatieff 56). Confinement in prison should not foster degeneracy, but combat it. This function could be viewed at the elementary level of physical well-being.

> Since disease in institutions had moral as well as physical causes, hygienic rituals were designed to fulfill disciplinary functions. To teach the poor to be clean, it was necessary to teach them to be godly, tractable, and self-disciplined. Hartleian assumptions led the doctors to be confident that once the bodies of the poor were subjected to regulation, their minds would acquire a taste for order. (Ignatieff 61)

When put into practice in the prisons, medical examinations could be the first step in rebuilding character. Just as modern behavior modification often calls for an initial humbling or breaking of the spirit—some form of abasement—so the humiliating experience of being stripped and examined, then shaved and bathed, could instill a primary sense of powerlessness in prisoners.

Reform movements were often consciously reacting not merely to inequality of justice and squalid physical conditions but to the brutality of the old system. Many scholars have described the abuses of the Bloody Code, but as Clive Emsley explains, much capital legislation in the eighteenth century defined offenses in a narrow way for narrowly perceived circumstances and were not designed for general application or institutional codification (203).[6] Moreover, as we have seen in the case of children's literature, recourse to physical violence was far more acceptable as a mode of correction before 1800 than it was in the decades following. Emsley says: "A degree of physical punishment meted out to dependants seems to have been accepted, or at least tolerated across social groups during the eighteenth century and well into the nineteenth; thus masters beat their servants, husbands their wives, and parents their children (40). But if reformers sought to eliminate extremes of brutality, by far the greater number still called for severe punishments, whether physical or mental. As Edward Cox wrote in 1877 in a guide for judges and magistrates: "Punishment means pain—bodily or mental pain—and there is no punishment that does not involve the conception of pain inflicted in some form upon the subject."[7] He reasoned that the severity of punishment must be increased to the point where it operates to deter the criminal from thinking he is gaining an advantage by crime (14). He acknowledged philanthropists' complaints against the death sentence, but insisted that no lesser penalty had been found sufficiently deterrent to the highest crime, murder. Late in the century a distinguished member of the legal profession could recommend extending the range of capital punishment. Mr. Serjeant William Ballantine, a good friend of Dickens, wrote, "The punishment of death is still continued, and is thought to be sufficient to intimidate brutal offenders, and of one thing I have no doubt, that there is no example of a criminal under a capital sentence, who would not with joy exchange the penalty for any other form of punishment known to law." Ballantine then suggested that death be an optional judgment on criminals who cruelly injured others, especially police officers in the fulfillment of their duties.[8] Ballantine also called for the revival of transportation as a punishment.

Prison reform demands some attention to the character of those to be reformed, namely those prosecuted and imprisoned. John Bender, following upon some suggestions of Foucault, has argued that fiction of the eighteeenth century anticipates changes from the eighteenth-century prison to the nineteenth-century penitentiary because the penitentiaries assumed novelistic ideas of character and re-presented the sensible world in order to alter motivation, and thereby reconstruct the fictions of human identity.[9] Newgate and older prisons were designed for temporary detention, not for confinement, and were therefore arranged on a domestic pattern. These prisons neither told stories nor assigned roles. The new penitentiaries banished chance and fortune in favor of concrete human planning. The aim of the new penitentiary was thus to manipulate identity by recomposing the fictions on which it was founded. Although Bender's claim for the novel as forbear of the new way of perceiving—and therefore of shaping—identity may be extreme, there seems little reason to dispute that a new perception of identity and of the ways of transforming it were shared by novelists and reformers.

Some attempt was under way as well to understand the specifically criminal identity. Clive Emsley writes that "[t]hroughout the period 1750 to 1900 most experts and commentators went out of their way to deny any relationship between low wages, poverty, and the bulk of crime. The main causes of crime were given as moral weakness, luxury, idleness, corrupting literature, parental neglect and lack of education . . ." (49–50). Nonetheless, medical notions of heredity and other scientific ideas began to affect these assumptions. By the end of the century Cesare Lombroso's semiotics of the criminal could be taken as seriously as William Combe's phrenology had been at the beginning of the century. In *Reconstructing the Criminal*, Martin J. Wiener traces the changing attitude toward the criminal during the nineteenth century, from a figure expressing fundamental character defects stemming from the failure to deny wayward impulses or to make long-term calculations about self-interest, to a figure largely the product of determining social, economic, and hereditary forces with little opportunity for the exercise of a conscious will (46, 160). A scientific approach replaced the older moral outlook.

Some efforts to define criminality were categorical. Thomas Plint, like many other commentators on the subject, argued in *Crime in England, Its Relation, Character, and Extent as developed from 1801 to 1848* (1851) that there existed a separate criminal class, not identifiable with the lower classes, but professional in nature.[10] Recent studies—notably George Rudé's *Criminal and Victim: Crime and Society in Early Nineteenth-Century England* (1985), conclude that although there were certainly professional criminals, there is no evidence to support a case for a definable criminal class in Victorian England. Rudé says that the lurid picture of the Victorian underworld that J. J. Tobias drew, following Dickens, is exaggerated, since even notorious Victorian neighborhoods such as St. Giles were past their prime by the 1840s.[11]

Many nineteenth-century observers recognized the existence of professional criminals without defining them as a separate class. Edward Cox said that the professional criminal does not consider his activity a sin or a crime but merely a business. "Penal servitude should be inflexibly awarded to a convict of this class [meaning category], the object of such a punishment being to restrain him for the longest possible period from the exercise of his nefarious calling and to make it more difficult for him to follow it after his release" (136). Yet despite attempts by Plint and others to break the association, crime was overwhelmingly identified with the lower classes. Plint's own list showed that most crimes were against property and noted, reasonably, that more such crimes occurred in heavily populated urban centers. Rudé's modern assessment confirms Plint's findings on this point. In his study of nineteenth-century Sussex, Gloucestershire, and Middlesex, Rudé found larceny to be the chief category of crime in all three counties, though with different emphases. Money, valuables, and materials from the workplace were more likely targets for larceny in Gloucestershire than in Sussex, where food, clothing, and household goods ranked after money. London had some unusual variations, such as stealing pint pots from public houses and stripping lead from buildings (23, 11, 31).

Rudé establishes three categories of crime: acquisitive crime, social or survival crime, and protest crime (78). All three categories are likely to include a large number of lower-class individuals, especially the second and third categories. Sussex listed three types of offenders: gentleman, yeoman, and laborer, the last group accounting for by far the greater number of crimes. Of course in examining Victorian records we must keep in mind that there were ideological reasons for bringing to trial and convicting lower-class citizens, while only reprimanding or excusing members of higher classes. Magistrates, lawyers, and judges were gentlemen themselves and hence more likely to sympathize with the foibles of their order. Moreover, as I have already noted, some of the crimes for which common folk were punished were relatively recent consequences of propertied gentlemen enclosing land to which they then claimed exclusive right. Thus poaching was a common crime in Gloucestershire, while rioting over enclosures and the killing and maiming of cattle were familiar there and in Sussex. Men, sometimes very prominent men, made great financial hauls through criminal behavior, but though many of them were punished, they were regarded as white-collar offenders and never considered part of the criminal class (Emsley 129).

The detection of crime was not well organized until long after Peel's Metropolitan Police Act of 1829, and through much of the century the burden of apprehension and prosecution fell upon the victim him or herself, a condition that discouraged bringing complaints because of the cost and effort involved.[12] Occasional serious cases might require the intervention of the government as prosecutor or as financial guarantor, but, "[a]s late as the mid–nineteenth century no public official was responsible for ensuring that even the most serious offences were prosecuted" (Hay and Snyder 22–23). Businessmen and property owners could afford to form protective associations for the apprehension and prosecution of persons who committed crimes against them, but no such organization was easily available to common folks. When the police began to take on the function of prosecutors, chances were that the felons they charged were from the lower orders. Better policing did not mean better justice for the many, though Clive Emsley notes that the increasing role of the police as prosecutors might actually have brought them closer to the working classes, helping to foster police legitimacy (150). Even if domesticating the working class was one function of the new police, it is worth remembering that the police were generally considered beneficial by the working class (194).

While reformers were trying to change the nature of the prisons, little was yet being done—though the problem was recognized—to make punishments themselves equitable. Martin J. Wiener writes that "Perhaps the most persistent motor pushing Victorian penal policy was the imperative to remove elements of uncertainty and variability from punishment" (103). But such an imperative was far more easily felt than achieved. At the end of the Regency there were still two hundred capital crimes on the books, though legal and lay communities were reluctant to exercise the full severity of the law. Rudé gives examples of the apparent capriciousness of justice from early in the century.

> At the Gloucester Lent Assizes that year [1820], John Roberts, a glover,
> was transported for life for stealing four £1 notes from the person of

John Hall of Bishop's Cleeve. Meanwhile, at the London Assizes the same sentence was passed on three young pickpockets: on John Furzman, 16, who stole a handkerchief worth 2s, from George Douglas Woodfall of Westminster; on William Whaley, 16, for stealing a handkerchief (3s.) from John Barry in Bishopsgate Street; and on William Harwood, aged 14, who stole an even cheaper handkerchief, valued at 1s., from Daniel Deacon in Barbican. (Yet, though an improvement on the sentence of death, the absurdity of this life-sentence on a 14-year-old boy becomes all the more evident when we learn that in the same session, the same presiding judge—the City Recorder—fined Joseph Henry Howell, a boy of the same age, 1s. and discharged him after finding him guilty of stealing a £5 note from his master, John Tucker, a cloth-dresser in the City of London!). (107)

Rudé concludes that criminal law was largely an expression of class patronage. Law mediated to the advantage of the ruling class, but through legal forms. Massive changes in the system came about to accommodate the needs and objectives of those rapidly becoming the new rulers of England at the end of the eighteenth and beginning of the nineteenth centuries. Since not only criminal law but all law may be viewed as a ruling-class instrument for the control and guidance of the population at large, I would like to glance briefly at a few different and out-of-the-way areas of legal restraint.

During the first half of the nineteenth century, when infanticide was a capital offense, officials and citizens were unlikely to find mothers guilty of this crime. "The last woman to be executed for murdering her child under twelve months old was Rebecca Smith of Wiltshire in 1849."[13] From then on the Home Secretary invariably reprieved mothers convicted of such crimes. Pardon for such a crime seems strange in a society where all classes might be supposed to regard it as especially abominable. However, as Lionel Rose's detailed study of infanticide shows, there were many reasons for this leniency. To begin with, the ability to deal with medical evidence was primitive. Moreover, coroners, elected for life by ratepayers, were usually themselves ignorant of medical matters. The prosecution had to prove that the child had lived separated from its mother, a difficult detail at this time. In addition, circumstances often made the cause of death problematic. Many children died on washing day. Children were sometimes smothered because they slept in the same bed with their parents, who were sometimes narcotized by drink. Also, the very ignorance of young mothers might cause a child's death. The "privy defence," for example, argued that the child had been accidentally discharged into a privy under natural circumstances with the mother not fully understanding what had happened (Rose 73). Aside from all of these reasons, however, is a simpler and starker explanation for the pardon extended to these women. In the early part of the century infant life was held cheap. Infant death was common, and, when births could be threatening to economic welfare, they were considered seriously unwelcome. Reform of the laws surrounding the birth, death, and selling, or "farming" of infants became serious around mid-century, and then partly because of the enhanced self-image of the medical profession. Lionel Rose comments: "The death of 'surplus' or unwanted babies was a biological necessity at a time when birth control was scarcely understood, and it is only as the birth rate fell at the very end of the last century that the value of infant life correspondingly rose" (187).

Infanticide, to us a hideous crime, appears to change its value with changing social needs. One recalls the ancient Greek practice of exposing unwanted infants to the elements. The law in Victorian England remained basically lenient and merciful to women who may have been responsible for the deaths of their own infants, though it became increasingly rigorous in establishing means to protect children who passed into the dangerous hands of others. It does not seem entirely clear to what extent middle-class values about infanticide were absorbed by the lower classes, but the laws instituted by middle-class ideology certainly impinged upon their lives.[14]

Infanticide may seem a marginal crime in the overall panoply of criminal action, and so may suicide. But there are some interesting connections between the two crimes. It might at first appear that a principal difference is in the area of punishment. A mother found guilty of murdering her infant can be executed, imprisoned, or pardoned, but you cannot so punish or excuse a successful suicide, who in a sense has preempted all of these reactions. Nonetheless, legal determination of guilt for the crime of suicide could have important consequences, and Victorian juries were generally reluctant to bring a verdict of *felo de se*, perhaps because they wished to avoid those consequences, which, at the practical level, could involve forfeiture of goods to the crown or loss of life insurance.[15] But just as important or even more important to many people was the question of burial. Before 1823 suicides were buried in the public highway; after that year burial had to take place in a burial ground, but no religious rites in a consecrated burial ground could be obtained for a *felo de se* until the Burial Act of 1880. And until 1882, on the coroner's orders, police were required to bury the body of a *felo de se* privately between the hours of nine and twelve at night (Andersen 221).

Inquests were not popular with rate payers, so many suicides and infanticides might not have been investigated, though pressure to pursue suicides was strong. Very likely a class difference existed here as elsewhere in the law, with suicide among the upper and professional classes being under-registered. Similarly, class might easily determine the view one took of this offense. For the middle class a female suicide would generally be regarded as a sinner, but for the working class as a victim.

As with infanticide, attitudes toward suicide changed over the century as law began to be perceived as a means of individual rehabilitation as well as of social discipline. The new crime of attempted suicide gave authorities the opportunity for counselling, usually conducted by a prison chaplain (Anderson 263).[16] The primary function of the law regarding attempted suicides was therefore not to punish the individual but to provide time for recovery and counselling. Part of this increased attention to rehabilitation followed from the growing belief in the medical community that suicide was an insane act and that sanity was directly linked to physical condition.[17] The identifying of mental functions with the brain made it easier to consider the person attempting suicide as a victim of a physical malady. This connection between bodily circumstances and mental control had long been assumed in regard to women. "In the case of a woman, lactation and recent childbirth, as well as pregnancy, 'delayed menstruation,' and the menopause, were all regarded as likely to precipitate suicide" (Andersen 224).

In general, suicide thus moved from being a crime committed by a reasoning individual with the power to choose his or her fate to an offense committed by a being not fully in command of his or her will. Tending away from the punishment of successful suicides through loss of goods and insurance to survivors or exclusion from Christian burial, the law inclined more toward the treatment of attempted suicides to help them become suitable members of the community. In Victorian times public welfare, decency, and order seemed to require suppression of attempted suicides. And yet there is no definite reason why a society cannot accommodate suicide to its culture. Just as ancient Greeks considered infanticide a legitimate practice in certain circumstances, the Romans endorsed suicide under appropriate conditions.[18] The Victorian aversion to suicide was rooted in its brand of Christian morality. It was a sin to take one's life, and for the prevailing morality of the time much sin was equatable with crime. As suicide came to be viewed more as an irresponsible act, it was considered less in terms of punishment and more in terms of utility. But whether sin, crime, or imprudence, suicide remained an anomalous act, and the most consistent pressure exerted by society was to bring the individual into conformity with its codes, at first by moral and physical coercion and threat, later by education and behavior modification. As Jacques Donzelot has pointed out in *The Policing of Families* (1979), social work and education gradually replaced repressive punishment during the nineteenth century. By penetrating the family through welcome (or unwelcome) services, the values of the prevailing authorities could be instilled in the minds of individuals so that they would begin to police themselves.

Infanticide and suicide are crimes toward which feelings changed over the century, as scientific information and moral expectations altered. In general, the movement from the eighteenth century into the twentieth was ameliorative. Punishment was inflected away from revenge and duty, and toward mercy and care. But another form of law designed to extend mercy was curiously inflected in the opposite direction, a phenomenon directly relatable to the capitalist ethos developing during the nineteenth century. The Poor Law was established to help the impoverished to survive. For a long while it was administered at the parish level. But the old system created abuses in the eyes of the authorities—notably the use of outdoor relief (contributing to the welfare of families living in their own quarters, not in a workhouse) and the economic distortion of the labor market (relief could supplement low wages, for example, and thus depress the wage scale artificially). The New Poor Law of 1834 was designed to correct these and other abuses, but, as Derek Fraser observes, both outdoor relief and distortion of the labor market continued after the 1834 law.[19] The real impetus behind the law was a moral one, seeking to convert idle persons into industrious, and thus useful members of the community. The education of pauper children was a high priority, rescuing the young from poverty by giving them rudimentary education and some industrial training while at the same time establishing habits of usefulness, industry, and virtue valuable in a free market economy.[20] In 1873 education became a mandatory condition of outdoor relief.

Reform of the Poor Law shared many aims with other reform activities in the early part of the century. A great emphasis fell on moral rehabilitation and education, driven by an ideology that valued economic efficiency and personal discipline. M. A. Crowther argues that the workhouse commissioners who promoted the New Poor Law had no particular animus against the poor and never expected a total abolition of relief, yet their objectives were contradictory. "The framers of the law thus believed that they could encourage the growth of an industrial economy, while at the same time shore [sic] up the patriarchal society which that economy was eroding. The purposes were incompatible. The deterrent workhouse could not be used to revive the old society; rather, it added to the bitterness of the new."[21]

Because the workhouses were designed as deterrents, they necessarily had to be unappealing. Thus in appearance and in organization they took on powerfully negative associations, so that mechanisms designed to establish justice became punitive instead. Labor in the workhouses enforced discipline and did not anticipate profit; much of it was extremely noisome, as with oakum picking. Moreover, though a general image of the workhouse pictured able-bodied males engaged in the hard labor of rock breaking and so forth, in fact most workhouse labor was done by women, children, and the aged (Crowther 199).

Admission to these unappetizing workhouses was itself humiliating and assumed a punitive character. An applicant found him or herself in a situation resembling a trial, including the detail of standing in a dock for questioning and wearing a shapeless workhouse uniform once admitted. The "workhouse test" was a deterrent to unsuitable applicants for relief. The "applicant's real destitution would be judged by his willingness to abandon everything and accept relief inside the workhouse. The effectiveness of this test of destitution was ensured by requiring that the conditions inside the workhouse were 'less-eligible' than those of the lowest-paid worker outside."[22] This practice obviously required and created serious deprivation. It is no wonder that many Poor Law boards, especially in the north, disliked indoor and outdoor tests, considering both as nothing more than punishment.[23] Add to these hardships poor food, the dissolving of families, and substantial laboring duties, and the workhouse quickly becomes a symbol of oppression in which the poor who require charity and mercy are punished like criminals instead. Even the education and medical care provided through them become additional means of disciplining individuals to the requirements of the ruling order. In addition, the Poor Law administration was open to serious political abuse from the elective office of workhouse guardian, to the use of paid rate rolls to determine which citizens were eligible to vote.[24] Understandably, the prospect of the workhouse was an ominous threat hanging over those who lived on the margins of society. Dickens tapped their fear and disgust in *Oliver Twist* and *Our Mutual Friend,* but that loathing and sense of injustice was everywhere in the popular literature of the time, as this passage from a broadside ballad indicates:

> Her lifeless form lies in the grave,
> Her soul has gone to heaven,
> Where Workhouse Cru'lty is unknown
> And Poverty's forgiven. (Crowther 223)

In this instance, then, what might appear to be a benevolent institution for the care of the needy becomes an instrument for controlling aspects of the labor market, for suppressing patterns of social behavior, for enforcing values of the dominant classes, and, as a result, for punishing all those who will not or cannot live up to the necessary standards. It is not surprising that many Victorians, faced with these and other inversions and perversions of justice, might find appealing Jeremy Bentham's recommendations for reconceiving the system of English justice on a utilitarian rather than a moral basis, and treating offenders against the law as infirm and remediable fellow creatures instead of morally corrupt souls in need of salvation.

To say that the law may be reconceived according to a utilitarian rationale does not mean that it will abandon or exclude morality. John Stuart Mill, writing in the utilitarian tradition, explains that there need be no separation between utility and morality.

> While I dispute the pretensions of any theory which sets up an imaginary standard of justice not grounded on utility, I account the justice which is grounded on utility to be the chief part, and incomparably the most sacred and binding part, of all morality. Justice is a name for certain classes of moral rules, which concern the essentials of human well-being more nearly, and are therefore of more absolute obligation, than any other rules for the guidance of life; and the notion which we have found to be the essence of the idea of justice, that of a right residing in an individual, implies and testifies to this more binding obligation.[25]

Trying to reach below surface peculiarities of any individual community, Mill sought to ground his doctrine on the individual's right to be protected from harm by others and to be free to pursue his or her own good. Punishment is a natural response toward all those who violate these "primary moralities." But even Mill, in emphasizing the inviolability of the individual as the basis for a community's elementary system of justice, ignores the culturally grounded source of his thought. Leslie Stephen questioned Mill's privileging of the individual and substituted for it a social, contextual ethic. But no matter which scheme is promoted, it requires the indoctrination of the populace at large, and it is this that punishment, and to a much lesser degree, mercy, effect through different avenues during the century.

I have taken a hasty overview thus far of the English penal system of the nineteenth century and arrived at the conclusion that underlying its choices in constructing or applying a system of justice is the assumption that a single, though complex, general set of moral standards should prevail throughout the community. Even when proponents of this set of standards were secular, or even agnostic or atheist in their thinking, they tended to champion the same values of retribution, reform, and mercy. Of course there are many exceptions. James Fitzjames Stephen made no bones about calling for retribution and saving mercy for the merciful. When told that prisoners are our brothers, Thomas Carlyle responded with a diatribe against foolish philanthropy and declared prisoners his enemies not his brothers, fully deserving of an unmistakable retribution, which was, after all, God's own law.[26] But overall, from the beginnings of prison reform until well past mid-century, the general feeling was that the fundamental aim of punishment was to reform a recoverable human being.

To make their plans workable, reformers of various kinds agreed that state inspection or governance should replace the indiscretions of private prison contractors (Ignatieff 77).[27] The years after 1840 saw an acceleration in the replacement of small dynastic and paternalistic prisons by larger hierarchical ones.[28] Uniformity would serve reformatory purposes. William James Forsythe says that "All reformist approaches were essentially aspects of the pursuit of power through the mounting of reverberating discourse which demanded ever-increasing regulation" (7). Ironically, a pattern of reform based on the principle of love winning over the reluctant hearts of wayward brothers and sisters called for reduced freedom, through either the silent or separate system, increased hard, servile, sometimes pointless labor, and longer sentences. Forsythe explains that there were two general systems of thought guiding prison reform—Evangelical and Associationist. Both believed that criminal conduct was environmentally determined. Both accepted the need for suffering as a means of achieving reformation. Evangelicals believed criminals must experience suffering at the hands of earthly powers because human institutions should reflect the behavior of God and employ pain in punishment because pain can be regenerative. Associationists believed that personality was formed by experiences that give rise to sensations and that sensations must be changed in such a way as to obliterate the desire to renew criminal behavior—a form of what we now call behavior modification (10–11).

A preliminary aim of punishment was to arouse a sense of guilt in the prisoner and revive his or her conscience. Love was to replace anger. Both Benthamite and Evangelical could agree that punishment should involve a calculated pattern of discipline with social good and the offender's needs in mind. "It was the prison chaplain who would bind prisoners with the cords of love. He would persuade offenders to accept their sufferings as an impartial and benevolent condemnation. He would force them to accept their own guilt. It was he who would enclose them in the ideological prison" (Ignatieff 75). The prisoner was now a reluctant prodigal being welcomed into the fold. But to achieve this end the gospel had not only to be preached but practiced in the prison, so that the prisoner would internalize its values and set up a tribunal in his heart by which to judge his own conduct ever after. Not only was the chaplain to adhere to this method, but other officials were to demonstrate the same Christian attitude. Prison warders, for example, were to acquire moral influence over prisoners by performing their duties conscientiously but without harshness, never abusing or striking prisoners but always treating them with dignity (Forsythe 61).

In fact, however, it was extremely difficult to instill in operatives of the new prisons the kind of Christian bearing that reformers required. Moreover, practice at the local level often differed markedly from official purpose. "Local politics, interests, inertia and rates bills therefore played a great part in local prison policy, quite apart from the ideological appeal of the disciplinary systems" (Forsythe 105). Michael Ignatieff notes that the new prisons offered parish officers a broader opportunity to enforce family discipline, increasing, for example, the number of imprisonments of women for bastardy.

> Women with illegitimate children, agricultural laborers who stole turnips, weavers who embezzled their masters' yarn, apprentices who absconded—these were the chief objects of the new strategy of summary justice that Gloucestershire's new prisons made possible. Whatever reformative purposes Paul had in mind for them, these prisons in fact continued to carry out the old functions of the law, but with a new rigor—penalizing the passage from labor into crime, and enforcing the authority of landlords, masters, and parish officials. (109)

By the second half of the century a new attitude was beginning to emerge with the suggestion that criminals might be a separate class of beings with inherited, perhaps in irradicable tendencies to anti-social behavior. Cesare Lombroso in Italy was a prominent exponent of the idea of the criminal as a primitive, unevolved human type. Early reformist hopes were by the end of the century deeply tinged with pessimism.[29] Perhaps this was no more than a reflection of the larger movement of thought during the century, with claims for objective or scientific responses to human and natural events displacing to a large degree religiously grounded moral standards. Also, from the beginning of the reform movement another feature of the age was apparent. Michael Ignatieff points out that from around "the end of the Napoleonic wars, a language of discipline free from familial or animal-taming connotations began to make its appearance. The word 'cell' replaced the word 'apartment,' with its association to the household dwelling. Discipline displaced economy. Prison populations, not families, were referred to in official parlance. The metaphors of command also became increasingly military in derivation" (190). Partly this was because many of the new prison officals were former military men, but also at work was a growing interest in discipline of all sorts, not least the discipline of the workplace. Ignatieff again notes that the creators of the new factory discipline "drew inspiration from the same discourse on authority as the makers of the prison . . ." (215). We have already seen that one aim of workhouse education was to make children productive members of society. Certainly a chief aim of prisoner reform as well was to recover prodigals to useful labor, an aim easily identifiable with the welfare of the state.

In general, English law during the nineteenth century was decidely moving in a direction away from crude retribution and toward amelioration and mercy. A clear example of this tendency was the gradual improvement of laws involving debtors, which gradually allowed more protection for debtors than power to creditors until, with the passage of the Debtors Act and the Bankruptcy Act in 1869, all insolvents who had contracted nonfraudulent debts could discharge their liability through personal bankruptcy.[30] Even the New Poor Law may be seen as anomalous, as M. A. Crowther has suggested, since it was practically obsolete when it was devised, just before the rapid development of voluntary hospitals, charitable homes, and other types of asylum (271). Although law could not abandon the fundamental concept of punishment and could scarcely give serious consideration to outright forgiveness, it could increasingly temper the severity of its judgments and balance retribution with reformation. From the last man to stand in a pillory, which was at Newgate on June 22, 1830, to the last person publically hanged outside Newgate on May 26, 1868, the tide of English criminal law was toward a closer approximation of the popular conception of Christianity—justice tempered with mercy. English literature reflects this movement from concern with punishment to a regard for the individual citizen.[31]

NOTES

1. Michel Foucault's *Discipline and Punish: The Birth of the Prison,* trans. Alan Sheridan (New York: Vintage Books, 1979) (First published as *Surveiller et Punir; Naissance de la prison* [1975]) has been very influential among intellectuals, though it has from its first publication had serious critics. For example, Robert Brown, reviewing the Allen Lane edition of Alan Sheridan's translation in the *Times Liter-*

ary Supplement for June 16, 1978, made several critical points, in particular regarding Foucault's failure to account for the rise of corrective training as an alternative to severe penal servitude. Michael Ignatieff is perhaps the most prominent English revisionary scholar in this field. His *A Just Measure of Pain: The Penitentiary in the Industrial Revolution 1750-1850* (New York: Columbia University Press, 1978) caused a good deal of discussion. Subsequent references appear in the text. In his *Reconstructing the Criminal: Culture, Law, and Policy in England, 1830-1914* (Cambridge: Cambridge University Press, 1990), Martin J. Wiener suggests that revisionists go too far in depicting an onward march of surveillance and control in English penal policies (8), but he nonetheless agrees with the fundamental shift of interest represented by Foucault and Ignatieff (101).

2. See Michael Ignatieff's comparison, 67.

3. Joseph Adshead, *Prisons and Prisoners* (London: Longman, Brown, Green, and Longman, 1845), viiff.

4. Clive Emsley, *Crime and Society in England, 1750-1900.* (London: Longman, 1987), 69. Subsequent references in the text. See also P. B. Munsche, *Gentlemen and Poachers: The English Game Laws 1671-1831* (Cambridge: Cambridge University Press, 1981). F. M. L. Thompson notes that rabbits were a big business for the working class, and that new laws and more rigorous enforcement did not change such persons' minds that they were entitled to carry out their occupation. "Unsurprisingly," Thompson writes, "the number of poaching offences brought before the magistrates increased in sympathy with the number of gamekeepers and policemen, just as happened with drunkenness cases: there were about 4000 game law convictions a year in the 1840s and over 12,000 a year in the 1870s" (*The Rise of Respectable Society: A Social History of Victorian Britain 1830-1900* [Cambridge: Harvard University Press, 1988], 341).

5. Martin J. Wiener remarks that mid-Victorians felt reformation should be as painful as deterrence (111).

6. Clive Emsley writes: "The traditionalists were defending an aristocratic and paternalistic image of justice and focussed on the practice of the courts and the use of mercy; the reformers focussed on existing severity and proposed an image of impersonal justice in which the law was above the suspicion of dependence on any personal discretion. The problem for the opponents of reform was that moderate and often influential Tories, like Peel, were sympathetic to the reformers' image of justice" (222).

7. Edward W. Cox, *The Principles of Punishment, as Applied in the Administration of Criminal Law, by Judges and Magistrates* (New York: Garland Publishing, Inc., 1984 [originally published 1877]), 3. Subsequent references appear in the text.

8. Mr. Serjeant Ballantine, *Some Experiences of a Barrister's Life* (New York: Henry Holt and Co., 1882), 81.

9. John Bender, *Imagining the Penitentiary: Fiction and the Architecture of Mind in Eighteenth-Century England* (Chicago: The University of Chicago Press, 1987), 2. Subsequent references appear in the text.

10. Thomas Plint, *Crime in England, Its Relation, Character, and Extent as developed from 1801 to 1848* (London: Charles Gilpin, 1851), 147ff.

11. George Rudé, *Criminal and Victim: Crime and Society in Early Nineteenth-Century England* (Oxford: Clarendon Press, 1985), 123ff. Subsequent references appear in the text.

12. Douglas Hay and Francis Snyder, "Using the Criminal Law, 1750-1850: Policing, Private Prosecution and the State," *Policing and Prosecution in Britain 1750-1850,* ed. Douglas Hay and Francis Snyder (Oxford: Clarendon Press, 1989), 18. Clive Emsley comments, "The overwhelming majority of criminal prosecutions, more than eighty per cent, were conducted by the victims of crimes or, reflecting the dominance of the male in eighteenth and nineteenth-century society, most prosecutors were men" (138). In an essay entitled "The Criminal Law and the Detection of Crime," (*The Cornhill Magazine* 2 [December 1860], 697–708), James Fitzjames Stephen informed his readers that far fewer offenders were charged and prosecuted in England than on the Continent because England had no public official responsible for initiating prosecutions, a task that remained the responsibility of individual citizens. This lack, he explained, was the consequence of the English demand for individual freedom.

13. Lionel Rose, *The Massacre of the Innocents: Infanticide in Britain 1800-1939* (London: Routledge and Kegan Paul, 1986), 76.

14. F. M. L. Thompson asserts that limitations of family size were collateral decisions of the different classes. "In this fundamental matter of the family the classes worked out their own destinies and their own controls, from a common pool of techniques, and any appearance of a percolation downwards from the top of society to the bottom was a mirage of chronology rather than a fact of emulation" (84).

15. Olive Andersen, *Suicide in Victorian and Edwardian England* (Oxford: Clarendon Press, 1987), 192.

16. Andersen points out that the 1860s and 1870s were the heyday of enthusiasm for such counseling (297).

17. Martin J. Wiener notes that there was a tendency in the 1880s for prison doctors interested in deviance to classify offenders as medical rather than criminal cases (235).

18. In 1992, in the state of Michigan, the legislature struggled to find some means of controlling assisted suicide, for which no clear law existed. At the time of this writing, the question is still in dispute. Californians rejected a ballot proposal in California, November 1992, that would have made assisted suicide legal.

19. Derek Fraser, "Introduction," *The New Poor Law in the Nineteenth Century,* ed. Derek Fraser (New York: St. Martin's Press, 1976), 14.

20. Francis Duke, "Pauper Education," in Fraser (68).

21. M. A. Crowther, *The Workhouse System 1834-1929: The History of an En-*

glish Social Institution (Athens: The University of Georgia Press, 1981), 23. Subsequent references in the text.

22. M. W. Flinn, "Medical Services under the New Poor Law," in Fraser (67).

23. David Ashforth, "The Urban Poor Law," in Fraser (136).

24. Derek Fraser, "The Poor Law as a Political Institution," Chapter 5 in Fraser.

25. John Stuart Mill, *Essays on Ethics, Religion and Society,* ed. J. M. Robson, vol. 10 of *Utilitarianism, Essays on Ethics, Religion and Society,* ed. J. M. Robson, vol. 10 *Collected Works of John Stuart Mill,* 32 vols. (Toronto: University of Toronto Press, 1969), 255.

26. Thomas Carlyle, *The Works of Thomas Carlyle,* 30 vols. (New York: Charles Scribner's Sons, 1898), 20:66.

27. See also H. W. Arthur, *"Without the Law": Administrative Justice and Legal Pluralism in Nineteenth-Century England* (Toronto: University of Toronto Press, 1985), especially Chapter 4.

28. William James Forsythe, *The Reform of Prisoners 1830-1900* (London: Croom Helm Ltd., 1987), 113. Subsequent references appear in the text.

29. See Forsythe's Chapter 7. Forsythe writes of the period following 1860: "More generally the growing tendency to objectify the appearance and fixed traits of the criminal began to influence observers and explorers during this period towards a pessimistic attitude to the lowest class which might not be consciously theoretically supported by constitutional psychological or evolutionist theory but which plainly at least in part depended upon it, a potent mixture of ill-digested scientific concept and unmistakeable fear" (185). But Martin J. Wiener describes the tendency later in the century to distrust this primitivist view of criminals and to begin instead to blur the boundaries between deviance and normality (254ff.). Wiener also, however, records the increasingly determinist attitude of penal authorities.

30. Hugh Barty-King, *The Worst Poverty: A History of Debt and Debtors* (Wolfeboro Falls, NH: Alan Sutton Publishing Inc., 1991), 144.

31. Franco Moretti writes that "in the middle of the nineteenth century, the focus of attention shifts from execution to the trial. While the former underlines the individual's weakness by destroying his body, trials exalt individuality: they condemn it precisely because they have demonstrated its deadly greatness." (*Signs Taken For Wonders: Essays in the Sociology of Literary Forms,* trans. Susan Fischer, David Forgacs, and David Miller [London: Verso, 1988), 138.

PART TWO

Dickens

FOUR

Early Dickens

WHEN HE WAS thirty-two years old, at a time when, as Alexander Welsh has recently speculated, he might have just been through an identity crisis of some sort, Charles Dickens began writing *The Life of Our Lord* for his children. He felt that everybody ought to know the story of Christ because "No one ever lived who was so good, so kind, so gentle, and so sorry for all people who did wrong, or were in any way ill or miserable, as He was."[1] He cautioned his children not to be proud but to regard evildoers as deserving of pity because they might not have had opportunities to be better. Dickens makes very little reference to divine displeasure in this work, emphasizing instead mercy, compassion, and forgiveness. Though eliminating some and condensing much in his accounts of Christ's teaching, Dickens cites all the crucial passages about forgiveness. After telling the story of Mary Magdalene, he mentions Christ's lesson that the debtor with the greatest debt will appreciate forgiveness the most, and then summarizes the topic. "We learn from this that we must always forgive those who have done us any harm, when they come to us and say they are truly sorry for it. Even if they do not come and say so, we must still forgive them, and never hate them or be unkind to them, if we would hope that God will forgive us" (49). Later, he instructs his children that they must forgive if they hope to be forgiven, and tells the story of the bad servant, which he says illustrates the passage in the Lord's Prayer that reads, "forgive us our trespasses as we forgive those who trespass against us" (59–60). Dickens explains that the parable of the workers in the vineyard indicates that even those who truly repent late in life can be forgiven their sins, and he includes a substantial summary of the parable of the prodigal son. Set against these numerous instances of mercy and forgiveness is only one noteworthy account of punishment—the story of Judas. After Judas had betrayed Christ, Dickens relates, he was overcome with remorse and returned to tell the chief priests that he could not keep their money. "With those words, he threw the money down upon the floor, and rushing away, wild with despair, hanged himself. The rope, being weak, broke with the weight of his body, and it fell down on the ground, after death, all bruised and burst,—a dreadful sight to see!" (101–2).[2]

It strikes me as significant that the form of punishment Dickens chooses to explore in his narrative of the New Testament is self-punishment arising from a bad conscience. To a great degree this choice reflects the manner in which he constructed his moral world. Mercy and forgiveness are true signs of virtue. Against them is a wide array of behavior in different flavors of evil, but the overwhelming burden of punishment for that evil is brought on by the evildoers or their confederates themselves. I believe that Dickens' moral picture of existence deepened as he matured and that he became more and more willing to use his moral scheme as a means of structuring narratives. In the chapters to follow, I shall look briefly at the early works, then concentrate on the later novels to examine the way narrative strategies and character presentation are affected by the implementation of Dickens' moral scheme, based on the two counterweights of punishment and forgiveness.

Many of the *Sketches by Boz* are primarily descriptive, and therefore one would not expect a great deal of moral weight in them. They were designed to be light and amusing. Virgil Grillo remarks that Dickens' initial literary impulse was satiric and that the pervasive notion evident in the *Sketches* is that persons are actors and human action is comic drama.[3] Yet even in these early works, conspicuous instances occur where the young Dickens discloses the values underlying his narration or exposition. There are many examples, but an interesting, because recurrent, one is the fable of a deliquent son who is the occasion of his virtuous mother's suffering. In "Meditations in Monmouth Street," the narrator concocts the history of a man based on a set of clothing in a pawnshop. The narrator pictures this person as a boy carefully tended by his widowed mother, but subsequently falling among pernicious companions and treating his mother poorly. Later he becomes a drunken, violent parent himself, meanwhile letting his mother die alone in a workhouse. Continuing in his evil courses, he is eventually arrested and sentenced to banishment or the gallows. The narrator concludes his meditation: "What would the man have given then, to be once again the contented humble drudge of his boyish years; to have been restored to life, but for a week, a day, an hour, a minute, only for so long a time as would enable him to say one word of passionate regret to, and hear one sound of heartfelt forgiveness from, the cold and ghastly form that lay rotting in the pauper's grave!"[4] "Criminal Courts" focuses on an early stage at which this malignant progress might be halted and even reversed. The narrator sees an elderly woman of decent appearance leaving a law court with her fourteen- or fifteen-year-old son after his release from punishment for a first offense. At first the boy is stubborn and tough, resisting his mother's pleas to return home. Suddenly, moved by some unknown impression, perhaps by his mother's kindness, the boy bursts into tears, then, "covering his face with one hand, and hurriedly placing the other in his mother's, walk[s] away with her" (198). This stern vignette nonetheless suggests the potentially redemptive power of love, forgiveness, and remorse. "The Black Veil" is much grimmer, recounting the story of a mother who fetches a doctor to revive her prodigal son after he has been executed. When such a revival proves impossible, the mother promptly goes mad and is confined for the rest of her life.

This prodigal son pattern is replicated in similar accounts of prodigal husbands. "The Broker's Man" concludes with the pathetic tale of a woman whose hard work has sustained her lazy husband in his bad habits until an execution has been put on their property. Ill though she is, the wife manages to raise sufficient money over three days to save the property, but the subsequent improvement in the family's fortunes comes too late, for the mother has exhausted her strength. "Those children are motherless now, and their father would give up all he has since gained—house, home, goods, money: all that he has, or ever can have, to restore the wife he has lost" (33). "The Drunkard's Death" is very predictable. A man given to drink sees his wife die before him and trembles at her glance. But the loss of his wife does not alter his conduct. His neglected sons go bad and he himself must be tended by his long-suffering daughter. Through drunkenness and loose talk, he unwittingly assists the police in apprehending his fugitive son. As he is led away to prison, the young man curses his parent.

> "Listen to me, father," he said, in a tone that made the drunkard's flesh creep. "My brother's blood, and mine, is on your head: I never had kind look, or word, or care, from you, and alive or dead, I never will forgive you. Die when you will, or how, I will be with you. I speak as a dead man now, and I warn you, father, that as surely as you must one day stand before your Maker, so surely shall your children be there, hand in hand, to cry for judgment against you." (491)

This is a strangely powerful scene in many ways. In *The Life of Our Lord*, Dickens writes of Christ's promise that he would ascend to heaven and sit at the right hand of God, "beseeching God's pardon to sinners" (54). But those who do not repent and do not forgive will be judged and found wanting. How, then, it might be asked, will fallen sons be standing by in heaven to curse their parent? The sons are bad and they judge their bad parent and condemn him. Since the father has, by neglect, sped his sons to their degradation, he has earned their condemnation; in this sense his sins will be upon him when he comes to judgment whether his sons are actually present there or not. And if these sons are symbolically there in the form of a curse which is no more than the reification of his sins, will Christ beseech God's pardon for him?

I don't wish to make much of this brief melodramatic moment in a minor story, but it is worth indicating that some of the simplest narrative devices bear within them heavy charges of meaning that may too easily be overlooked. A son

cursing his father and threatening to bring charges against him at the foot of
God's throne presents a powerful reverberant statement about sin and punishment. When directed to an audience believing in judgment after death and
fierce, if not necessarily eternal punishment to follow, the scene becomes not
merely dreadful, but imposing by virtue of its affinity with conventional instruction. In some writing, an indictment of this sort might be a sufficient means of
identifying the nature of the offense and the judgment it deserves. But Dickens
does not depend upon having his readers accept the son's proleptic judgment as
certain; in addition, his story accomplishes similar ends within its own design by
incorporating a narrative punishment. The plot now begins to turn against the
sordid parent and quickly moves toward a "natural" retribution for his crimes.
The drunkard's daughter disappears. Left unattended, the father rapidly declines
and "the long-forgotten scenes of a misspent life crowded thick and fast upon
him" (492). Miserable and fearful of losing his mind, he determines to drown
himself. Only when he is in the water does he realize that he still wants to live,
but with his son's curse ringing in his ear, he is swept away and drowned. "A
week afterwards the body was washed ashore, some miles down the river, a
swollen and disfigured mass. Unrecognized and unpitied, it was borne to the
grave; and there it has long since mouldered away!" (494). The man's own way
of life has accomplished everything in this life that the curse signifies for the
next. He will go to judgment with his own reluctant suicide and all of his other
crimes still black upon him. As so often in Dickens, desecration of the body accompanies this disfigurement of soul. This tale is obviously guilty of melodramatic overkill. Heaped upon the repulsive father are the inevitable displeasure of
God, his son's curse, and finally his own self-violence. He is himself the author of
an increasingly intimate order of judgment, and is ultimately the specific agent
of his own punishment. The implied author has signaled the man's fate in regard
to the divine, made specific the son's forecast of his father's fate, and then openly
intervened to have the plot itself enact a preliminary punishment in this world.
Though similar situations will occur in later narratives, this bare-bones presentation is more extreme than later, more subtle versions; still, those later narratives
include the same basic elements, especially the prominent role of self-punishment.

The pattern of the prodigal son or husband is especially loathsome for Dickens
because it brings crime, sin, and vice into the home. Spurning filial obedience
and neglecting parental or spousal protection and care are very high on Dickens'
list of wrongdoing, and thus the prodigal narratives become clear fables of retribution or forgiveness. There is no need to point out how regularly Dickens
praised the home, even while overwhelmingly picturing unsuccessful homes and
families in his fiction. The prodigal narratives help to explain this practice, for
they regularly contrast the ideal relationship of family authority with trespasses
against it. The moral literature of the time, especially in Protestant England,
stressed the Fatherhood of God and the Sonship of Christ, the one just and wise,
the other caring, compassionate, and obedient. If real homes rarely had the kind
of authority and harmony that Victorians claimed to value, the ideal home mod-

eled on Christian values did. One could not more starkly contrast the one with the other than by the use of unwise, negligent, or reprobate fathers and delinquent, disobedient, and degenerate sons.

The Pickwick Papers is given over primarily to fun, but when the narrative means to convey a trenchant point, it frequently reverts back to one of these archetypal patterns. Thus the first serious story in the book is the bathetic account of the dying clown, his remorse for his dissolute ways, and his grotesque death accompanied by hallucinations before his wife and child. Like so many of these tales, the emphasis is upon self-punishment as the natural consequence of a vicious way of life. These are predictable cautionary tales, employing, in reverse, the tradition of the holy deathbed scene so very common throughout the century, as I noted in Chapter 1.5 But usually these tales incorporate a larger lesson. The second interpolated tale in *Pickwick* is called "The Convict's Return" and stresses the ingratitude of a delinquent son for his mother's care and sacrifices. This embedded narrative intensifies the convention by including both prodigal son and prodigal father. The son turns to crime and is eventually imprisoned. While in prison he learns of his mother's serious illness, prompting thoughts of better days which incline him to reconsider his conduct. The clergyman who is telling the story says, "I bore the mother's forgiveness and blessing to her son in prison; and I carried his solemn assurance of repentance, and his fervent supplication for pardon, to her sick bed" (77). The son's life is spared and he is transported instead, returning home many years later to find his mother dead and himself a stranger. His old surroundings remind him of his and his mother's sufferings at his dissolute father's hands and his rage against the man revives.

> 'And such was the return to which he had looked through the weary perspective of many years, and for which he had undergone so much suffering! No face of welcome, no look of forgiveness, no house to receive, no hand to help him—and this too in the old village. What was his loneliness in the wild thick woods, where man was never seen, to this!' (80)

By accident he encounters his father, and so powerful is his anger against the man that when the fearful parent strikes his son with a stick, the younger man seizes his throat, intending to strangle the hated creature. But, because the wretch, now a broken-down inmate of a workhouse, is his father, he cannot. As will generally be the case with Dickens' morally correct characters—and here the convict, who, we are assured by the clergyman who narrates the tale, "was truly contrite, penitent, and humbled," serves that role—the son is unable to carry out retribution himself. But thanks to the power of the implied author, who has organized the tale, justice is done anyway.

> 'The old man uttered a loud yell which rang through the lonely fields like the howl of an evil spirit. His face turned black: the gore

rushed from his mouth and nose, and dyed the grass a deep dark red, as
he staggered and fell. He had ruptured a blood-vessel: and he was a
dead man before his son could raise him.' (81)

As with the father in "The Drunkard's Death," this reprobate brings about his
own death. His bad conscience strikes him down when he recognizes his son in
what amounts to an embodied curse. Of course the physical circumstances of
death must be as repulsive as possible, recalling Dickens' gratuitous addition of
the details of Judas' death in *The Life of Our Lord*. Here Dickens works an interesting variation on this familiar story, for the son has truly repented of his offenses,
whereas the father has not. His sins come back to him and crush him, but the son
lives on to work humbly for the clergyman narrator.

If the returned convict is contrite, he still must lead a life humbled in more
ways than one. As we shall see, it often happens that even those who repent and
are forgiven must endure one or another form of punishment despite their return
to the company of the virtuous.[6] Dickens earnestly preaches and practices forgiveness in his narratives, but because he as earnestly believes that chastisement
of some form must follow transgression, he must frame strategies by which both
ends may be served. Sometimes the underlying rationale for these strategies is
directly exposed. Thus the narrator of "The Couple Who Coddle Themselves"
in *Sketches of Young Couples* (1840) breaks out unexpectedly, for such a light-
hearted series, with a moral indictment, warning that couples and individuals
"who fall into exclusive habits of self-indulgence, and forget their natural sympathy and close connexion with everybody and everything in the world around
them, not only neglect the first duty of life, but, by a happy retributive justice,
deprive themselves of its truest and best enjoyment" (596).

From the beginning, then, Dickens emphasizes the need for a compassionate
and forgiving nature, but also the inevitable self-punishment that follows transgression. Frequently in his writings, his narrators exhibit sympathy and understanding for human error and pity for its consequences. In "A Visit to Newgate,"
the narrator muses on how many people daily pass the building "utterly unmind-
ful of the throng of wretched creatures pent up within it" (597). He not only
thinks of those wretches but enters and examines their prison and conjures up at
one point the thoughts of a man on the night before his execution, tortured
thoughts and dreams that suggest how important and inaccessible repentance and
pardon seem in his circumstances. In the sketch "Hackney Coach Stands," the
narrator fancies how rich with tales a hackney coach's autobiography would be,
with its experience of different people and, even more, of the same people at
different stages of their histories, a notion that evokes an age-old pattern of decline. "The country-girl—the showy, over-dressed woman—the drunken prostitute! The raw apprentice—the dissipated spendthrift—the thief!" (84). The
narrator of the *Sketches* can find poignancy even in degraded scenes. A debauched
young woman, dying in a hospital from her boyfriend's brutality, says she won't

give evidence against him, then adds, "I hope God Almighty will forgive me all the wrong I have done, and the life I have led. God bless you, Jack. Some kind gentleman take my love to my poor old father. Five years ago, he said he wished I had died a child. Oh, I wish I had! I wish I had!" (243). This scene may be read as sensational sentimentalism, but it also demonstrates Dickens' firm belief in the need for granting and claiming forgiveness, no matter how vicious the conditions.

One more instance and I will have done with the *Sketches*. In the series entitled *Characters* there is a chapter on "Prison Vans" in which the narrator comes upon two teen-age prostitutes being brought to jail, the older with "two additional years of depravity [having] fixed their brand upon" her features, the younger weeping out of shame. Instead of making this coarse scene an occasion for denouncing the sinners, the narrator fastens the blame elsewhere. "These two girls had been thrown upon London streets, their vices and debauchery, by a sordid and rapacious mother." In a manner that was to echo throughout Dickens' fiction the narrator warns, "The progress of these girls in crime will be as rapid as the flight of a pestilence, resembling it too in its baneful influence and wide-spreading infection" (274).

From the outset of his career Dickens was deeply concerned with the need for withholding judgment, extending compassion, and, with evidence of repentance, assuring forgiveness. But he was equally convinced that transgressions required retributive punishment. These two contending impulses call for differing narrative methods, because, while charity and punishment must be kept apart, both must be exercised. The simplest resolution for this conflict of charity and punishment is having the sinner punish him or herself, a lesson repeated over and over in such routinely moralistic masterworks as Hogarth's *The Rake's Progress* or *Industry and Idleness*. It would be some time before Dickens would grapple with the dilemma in serious narrative terms.

I have already noted that the interpolated tales in *Pickwick Papers* are among Dickens' simplest instances of the punishment/forgiveness pattern. "The Madman's Manuscript" depicts the consequences of a life of debauchery: murder and haunted confinement in an insane asylum. The story is interesting because it shows the offender unrepentant despite the punishment that has followed from his crimes. He tries to blame heredity for his behavior, but an editorial note attached to the Madman's Manuscript calls in doubt a hereditary source for his madness. Disavowing his own responsibility leaves the madman in a hellish condition: haunted by terrors, uncompassionated by any fellow human, confined for the rest of his life with a phantasmal substitute for bad conscience, and doomed for a worse condition hereafter. Gabriel Grub, the morose, ill-natured sexton, is luckier. If he is neither a debauchee on the level of the madman, nor terminally alcoholic like the dying clown, he is a steady, self-pitying tippler and a generally unsympathetic fellow. Fortunately, in a prototype of Scrooge's experience, Grub learns from a Goblin King how to value life and to realize that properly nurtured and hard-working individuals find more happiness in life than drunken idlers, and are superior to adversity "because they [bear], in their own hearts, an inexhaustible well-spring of affection and devotion" (404). Gabriel accepts the lesson of his "punishment," which is nothing more than the natural consequence of self-indulgent drinking on Christmas Eve, whereas the madman does not and remains in a self-begotten hell.

There is one story more troubling than any other interpolated tales in *Pickwick* because it concentrates so ferociously on all that Dickens most disapproved—relentless vengeance at the expense of all softer feeling. This is the story of "The Queer Client." Heyling is cast into prison for debt, during which time he is helpless to tend his wife and child, who die. He vows revenge, then falls into a fever dominated by images of vengeance. Recovering from his illness, he discovers that his father, who refused to assist him while he was in need, has died, leaving Heyling heir to a fortune. Paternal guilt looms much larger in the tale than Heyling's father's intransigence, however, because Heyling's creditor and "enemy was his wife's own father," who had let his daughter and her child die in prison (290). It is interesting again how Dickens intensifies this situation, perhaps even to the point of improbability, by insisting on the extreme violation of domestic expectations. Two fathers, not just one, imperil their children's lives through conscious neglect. Heyling, as surviving victim of this cruelty, is predictably intent upon revenge. His first opportunity to indulge his appetite for vengeance comes when he lets his father-in-law's young son die before his eyes. Unsatisfied with that installment on the debt of revenge, Heyling strips the old man of all his belongings. But this too is not enough; Heyling traces the old man to his hiding place and consigns him "to the living death to which you devoted her [his daughter]— a hopeless prison" (295). The old man never goes to prison, though, for he dies as soon as Heyling has declared his final act of revenge.

Oddly enough for so melodramatic a tale, no overt moral accompanies it. Heyling is not a good man in his revenge, yet we never learn his fate. Instead, we have only a hint that by devoting himself to such a course of stern retribution he has forever separated himself from those he loved. The tale ends with the narrator's statement that Heyling's wife and child lie in the soft landscape of a secluded churchyard in Kent. Appropriately, given his treatment of his daughter, the old man's ashes do not mingle with theirs. But neither, apparently, do Heyling's, of whom not another word is heard after the accomplishment of his revenge. Ordinarily, Dickens would not permit the representation of so brutally unchristian a nature to pass without some qualification. But the only qualification here is in the bizarre nature of the leering old man who tells the story and the comic setting in which it is delivered. It is a rare instance of revenge being presented as purgative. It is also, of course, a story of retributive justice being done by one who takes upon himself all the moral responsibility for such an action.

Neither *Sketches by Boz* nor *Pickwick Papers* pictures religious organizations or individuals as compassionate and helpful, nor does either represent legal institutions or individuals as very just or effective in meting out reward or punishment.

This emphasis upon the ineffectiveness of the law will remain essentially unchanged throughout Dickens' fiction. Almost always the burden of enacting justice falls to individuals who have little or no official capacity to punish or assist
other people.[7] Pickwick is the first and in many ways the most stunning example.
After the burlesque early instances of his follies, Pickwick steadily progresses
toward a model of Christian humanity. He is not a paragon in intellect or sober
restraint, yet he clearly becomes the focus for all of the good feeling in the book.
However, he takes it upon himself to judge and punish his fellow men and spends
much of his time trying to hunt down and expose Mr. Jingle and Job Trotter. He
is motivated not only by the abuses he has suffered from Jingle and his sidekick,
but also by his indignation on behalf of the Wardle family and others. He determines to bring Jingle to justice, though his efforts rarely result in any true punishment. It is finally Jingle's own way of life that lands him in prison, where his
suffering, and thus his punishment, is extreme. When Pickwick discovers Jingle
and Job in the Fleet prison he is immediately generous with his coin. Soon, however, he extends that generosity to genuine concern. Jingle and Job typify the
suffering Pickwick sees all about him, and though he does not, like the Vicar of
Wakefield, set about helping his fellow prisoners to improve their conditions
materially and morally, he does do what he can to alleviate some suffering while
withdrawing into his private room. When Mrs. Bardell, who is responsible for
Pickwick being in prison, is herself arrested, she asks and receives Pickwick's
pardon. That pardon is on a larger scale extended to Jingle and Job as well, for
whom Pickwick provides the means of a new life. "He never had occasion to
regret his bounty to Mr. Jingle; for both that person and Job Trotter became, in
time, worthy members of society, although they have always steadily objected to
return to the scenes of their old haunts and temptations" (801).

Although Pickwick regards himself as a champion against evil, his enemies are
surely minor offenders and his character is ultimately unsuited to the genuine
punishing of any of them. He may mistakenly picture himself as a scourge of
wickedness, but the implied author knows better and sees to it that he ends by
forgiving Jingle and Job, who have inconvenienced him several times, and Mrs.
Bardell, who has seriously endangered his well-being. Perceiving his "enemies"
in a worse condition than his own, his best instincts surface and he offers them
aid. Dennis Walder observes that, in the end, *Pickwick* is "about discovering evil
rather than about acting upon that discovery," and to a degree this judgment
seems correct unless one regards forgiveness as a means of reacting to the discovery of evil (29). And Pickwick's identification with forgiveness increases as the
novel continues. Though there is no reason that Mr. Winkle and Arabella need
ask his pardon, they do, and he becomes a benevolent intercessor to Winkle's
father, a mission that ultimately succeeds. A series of forgivenesses follows as the
novel approaches its close. Winkle, Snodgrass, and Sam Weller are "forgiven"
their romances. The lovers' disclosures are benevolent rather than guilty, and
beneficences rather than punishments follow from them.

The parallel plot involving Tony Weller and Mr. Stiggins also turns on the

theme of retribution. Tony has every right to feel aggrieved about the dissenting
enthusiast who is troubling his home by wooing Mrs. Weller to the faith. Tony
actively seeks revenge and punishes Stiggins by arranging that he appear before
his congregation drunk to deliver a sermon on temperance. Later, when Mrs.
Weller is dead, Tony takes his punishment a step further and dunks Stiggins in a
trough. Dickens is willing to let Tony thus directly punish Stiggins in a retributive fashion because he wants the sense of direct punishment to be reinforced, as
it is so vividly in the interpolated tales, but he also wants it to be done in an
"acceptable" fashion. Tony is a rogue. He is willing to be dishonest and subvert
the law if necessary and he has no clear-cut moral values. He is, therefore, an
appropriate instrument for executing summary justice upon the wicked. Tony is
lovable but unrehabilitated. Over and over in Dickens' fiction some such figure
will emerge to expend the pent-up energy of poetic justice by performing an act
of retribution that good characters are not permitted.[8] In this way his narrative
methods satisfy the need both to see evil punished and to insure that the predom-
inating and superior power of forgiveness rules.

Dickens' earliest fictional narratives already contain all of the deep moral
structures that will characterize the architecture of his fiction. In these early
works the polarities of punishment and forgiveness are often crudely presented.
In later works, his narrative strategies will become far more subtle and sophisticated, but the ground for them will remain essentially unchanged.

NOTES

1. Charles Dickens, *The Life of Our Lord. Written for His Children During the
Years 1846 to 1849* (New York: Simon and Schuster, 1934), 11. In *Dickens and Religion* (London: George Allen & Unwin, 1981), Dennis Walder cites Dickens' letter
to the Reverend D. Macrae in which he says he wants his novels to convey the
lessons of the New Testament (1). Walder goes on to argue that Dickens was less
interested in doctrine and theology than in touching the religious consciousness
of his vast readership (4). Subsequent references appear in the text.

2. Dickens also tells how Peter cut off the soldier's ear when Christ was
taken in the garden of Gethsemane, but that is less an instance of punishment
than of simple defense.

3. *Charles Dickens' Sketches by Boz: End in the Beginning* (Boulder: The Colo-
rado Associated University Press, 1974), 9–10. Kathryn Chittick reminds us that
the magazine literature after which Dickens modeled the *Sketches* went for
amusement and variety, but that he was at the same time entirely capable of replacing fancy with accurate transmission of information as a parliamentary re-
porter ("Dickens and Parliamentary Reporting in the 1830s," *Victorian Periodicals
Review* 21, no. 4 [Winter 1988], 151–60). Chittick enlarges upon this theme mas-
terfully in *Dickens and the 1830s* (Cambridge: Cambridge University Press, 1990).

4. Charles Dickens, *Sketches by Boz, Illustrative of Every-Day Life and Every-Day People* (London: Oxford University Press, 1963). Subsequent references appear in the text.

5. One should consider as well the conventional tradition of charitable and punitive deathbed scenes in painting; for example, Jean-Baptiste Greuze's *Le Piété filiale* (1763) and *Le Fils puni* (1778).

6. This pattern applies even to protagonists who err, as with David Copperfield to a mild degree, and more severely with Pip.

7. It is worth remembering that Dickens grew up during a period when prosecuting criminals was, as Chapter 3 indicates, largely the responsibility of individual citizens. Only slowly did the police and the authorities assume that task as part of their regular duties.

8. John Kucich, in commenting on the functions of melodrama in Dickens' fiction, observes that, for his good characters, "melodrama allows a complete spending of the self into emotion freed from its ambiguous status—a general victory over repression" (*Excess and Restraint in the Novels of Charles Dickens* [Athens: The University of Georgia Press, 1981], 49). But he also points out that Dickens' heroes are kept free of the final violence associated with the victory of good over evil (50).

FIVE

Oliver Twist

THERE ARE at least three major categories of transgression presented in *Oliver Twist* (1837–38). At the most public level is the injustice represented in government institutions, including the abuses of the recently enacted New Poor Law of 1834 and those of the criminal justice system. The exemplar of workhouse injustice is Bumble, and of Old Bailey injustice, Magistrate Fang. Their names, of course, indicate their natures. Bumble represents muddled and perverse official thinking, Fang irrational and arbitrary use of authority.[1] As we saw in Chapter 3, the New Poor Law was systematically designed to make the poor suffer. The narrator of *Oliver Twist* says that those who formulated the new scheme "established the rule, that all poor people should have the alternative (for they would compel nobody, not they) of being starved by a gradual process in the house, or by a quick one out of it."[2] Separation of family members, hard work for all, and low rations were designed to make the workhouses proof against idlers fraudulently claiming economic help. Outdoor assistance, previously under parish discretion, was seriously altered when conveyed to a regional authority. Bumble explains the new thinking: "The great principle of out-of-door relief is to give the paupers exactly what they don't want, and then they get tired of coming" (168). Dickens reinforces the bitterness of this irony by having Bumble wear buttons on his uniform bearing the image of the parochial seal, "the Good Samaritan healing the sick and bruised man" (24). An institution designed to assist the needy had been consciously transformed into a mode of punishment, but, as Dickens saw it, a punishment of the innocent and therefore not a punishment at all but an imputable crime in its own right. Bumble is merely a functionary in an insensitive system, but Fang is an irresponsible individual in a presumably sound system. He is an example of what can happen when callous citizens, uninformed in the details of the law and motivated by personal vanity, are named to offices with powerful legal authority. Again, an institution designed to seek out justice dispassionately—and Dickens himself at one point in his career wanted to be appointed magistrate—has been converted instead to a punitive organ for venting individual passions, and those not the sweetest.

The second category of transgression is downright criminal activity, principally the operations associated with Fagin, Sikes, Nancy, and Monks, but shading off into the minor peculations of Bumble, Mrs. Mann, and others. These are *violations,* as opposed to *abuses,* of the legal system, though the two categories have a strange affiliation as we shall see in a moment. First, however, we must consider a third form of transgression—violation of the moral code. This is the most complicated of all because, as society in *Oliver Twist* is constituted, even the blameless feel the burden of guilt for these offenses.

I have presented these transgressions hierarchically from the most public to the most private. Thus, those who corrupt the true purposes of public institutions have the greatest potential for doing widespread harm, those who break the laws by individual crimes somewhat less potential, and those who, in their own hearts, trespass against moral law perhaps the least potential of doing direct harm to others. Of course these categories are not easily divisible. I would now like to rearrange this hierarchy according to the orders of infraction that are ultimately most serious. Those who knowingly break God's law are the most culpable, those who break man's law less so, those who distort or neglect some service or institution least so. As I have just noted, these are not easily separable actions; for example, someone who serves an institution that starves a child has already violated Christ's injunctions to charity. In *Oliver Twist* punishment is shaded roughly according to not only the nature of an offense, but to the degree of offense and the number of boundaries that the offense crosses. Poetic justice is active in the novel, with each category of sin evoking a roughly equivalent punishment.

There are numerous ways that mortals can be charged with moral obliquity, and *Oliver Twist* provides some interesting explorations of the appropriateness of these charges. There are, for example, three important morally "tainted" women in the novel whose offense is sexual in nature. Oliver's mother loved truly, but was unwise and agreed to intimacy without the benefit of marriage, though the man she loved meant no injury to her and died before he could remedy their error. Through most of the novel, except for a few modest hints, she is presented as "the same old story"—a woman who indulged her sexual appetite and paid the price. Nancy, by contrast, is a genuine hard case. She has worked the streets from childhood, is bound to Sikes by feeling and habit, and considers herself unredeemable, though the narrator presents several signs that she has not been utterly corrupted. Passing a prison, Nancy expresses compassion for associates now confined there. She is moved by Oliver's dilemma, and, because "there was something of the woman's original nature left in her still," she sets about helping the boy, a generous action that will cost her her own life (301). Rose Maylie is certain that Nancy is reclaimable. At first Nancy rejects the notion, but gradually she feels the influence of Rose's kindness. "Oh, dear Lady, why ar'n't those who claim to be God's own folks as gentle and as kind to us poor wretches as you . . . ? (350). When Mr. Brownlow offers to help Nancy to a new life, she refuses, but recognizes a change for the better in her own nature. By this minimal but significant alteration in Nancy's character the narrator suggests that, though she is a true fallen woman, if she could be freed from the corrupting influences around her she might yet be saved on the model of Mary Magdalene. What is clear in Nancy's case is that no one until Rose has even thought of helping her, let alone make an actual gesture to do so. This is, of course, an indictment of the church and its adherents who overlook sinners like Nancy. She hates the life she now leads, but since Fagin first put her into service as a child, she has known nothing else. Without external help she has little opportunity to improve. Just as the transgression of Oliver's mother is mitigated by her trusting love, so Nancy's is by the dominating influence upon her of environment. Both sinners may thus claim some pity and an accordant tempering of justice.

The third "tainted" woman is Rose Maylie. Because she is supposed to be illegitimate, she is not considered worthy of respectable society. She refuses marriage with Harry Maylie because she believes it all too likely that an ardent and ambitious young man married to "a wife on whose name is a stain, which, though it originate in no fault of hers, may be visited by cold and sordid people upon her, and upon his children also," might come to repent of his marriage (302). The narrative, by contrast, amply indicates that, far from being morally stained, Rose is a paragon of virtue. The association with moral transgression is false, and, the narrative implies, should be revoked.[3]

These three women represent very different versions of the consequences of sexual license. Nancy has never had a chance, yet still has not lost all of the original woman in her, which suggests that the original pattern is good in all of us. Agnes Fleming loved not wisely but too well, yet was certainly good-hearted and far from depraved. Rose has never sinned at all but must wear the badge of sexual indiscretion nonetheless. The injustice of Rose's case casts light backward on those of Nancy and Agnes, palliating the one's environmentally determined corruption and the other's loving weakness. Gradually Rose's compassionate, forgiving spirit comes to dominate the narrative. From her first introduction nearly halfway through the novel, Rose is literally "marked" for virtuous predominance. The narrator cannot say enough about her moral excellence, even to its manifestation in her physical appearance. "The very intelligence that shone in her deep blue eye, and was stamped upon her noble head, seemed scarcely of her age, or of the world; and yet the changing expression of sweetness and good humour, the thousand lights that played about the face, and left no shadow there; above all, the smile, the cheerful, happy smile, were made for Home, and fireside peace and happiness (212). This nonpareil woman's first significant act in the narrative is to protect the injured Oliver, preferring not to prejudge but to think the best of the boy. Her spirit of compassion repeats Mr. Brownlow's "forgiveness" of and trust in Oliver, a trust that, as Mr. Grimwig has suggested, seems misplaced when Oliver fails to return from an errand. Rose's sympathy also satisfies a sense of poetic justice. Although Brownlow does not know if Oliver has betrayed his trust, the reader knows that he has not. The narrator places Oliver in a strong moral position by thus having him unjustly charged with the ungrateful crime that he would most reject. This narrative sharing of confidence that Oliver is good and not evil releases one tension in the plot, for there will be no suspense about Oliver's moral character. At the same time, however, it generates another suspense concerning the disparity between Oliver's desert and the treatment he receives. Rose's intuitive trust in him is an installment on the "debt" owing to his unjust treatment.[4] It also signals an alliance between Rose and Oliver that will slowly extend itself to other good characters in the novel, and that will be certified by the revelation of their actual kinship.

The introduction of Rose and all she represents also constitutes the pivot upon which the narrative turns. Hereafter, though besieged, the forces of home, peace, happiness, and compassion begin to prevail. Oliver is never again in serious danger and Rose's spirit even manages to penetrate the criminal underworld. Her good influence on Nancy represents the first beam of light breaching that darkness, a light quickly extinguished by Bill Sikes. If the evil figures in the novel intrigue, conspire, and mystify, Rose's spirit of forgiveness and charity unravels those conspiracies as she joins forces with Mr. Brownlow. In consequence, she is herself rewarded with the solution to the mystery of her birth. Her reputation is entirely rehabilitated when Mr. Brownlow discloses that she is legitimate, though, significantly, the sister of the fallen Agnes. Meanwhile, Harry Maylie, abandoning his political and social ambitions, has become a clergyman with plans for a quiet, retired, and humble life of good works, married to Rose.

The plot of the novel indicates that sexual transgression is reparable, that sinners and those marked by sin need not despair, and that our proper course as human beings is not to judge but to forgive sinners if they repent and to help them to change their lives. The narrator reinforces this lesson by following it himself. He opens the novel with the scene of Oliver's illegitimate birth and the death of Oliver's mother. When it becomes clear that Agnes is acting out "the old story" of seduction and abandonment, a reader might easily suppose that he or she is witnessing an instance of narrative punishment. But subsequent events reveal that this is not the case. Agnes' sin is the most important transgression in the story because it brings into being young Oliver, who is its main subject, and whose career is that of "the principle of Good surviving through every adverse circumstance, and triumphing at last."[5] Thus, in narrative terms, Agnes' transgression is expunged by the victory of her son over evil, a victory which, in solving the mystery of Oliver's birth, extends its beneficial power by solving the mystery of Rose's as well. The orphans Rose and Oliver, tried by adversity, learn to be charitable to others and are thus happy. The narrator explains, "I have said that they were truly happy; and without strong affection and humanity of heart, and gratitude to that Being whose code is Mercy and whose great attribute is Benevolence to all things that breathe, happiness can never be attained." He goes on to picture Agnes' tomb in the old village church, where, he says, "I believe that the shade of Agnes sometimes hovers round that solemn nook. I believe it none the less because that nook is in a Church, and she was weak and erring" (415). The narrator forgives Agnes by assuming that God has already done so. And he who opened his story in a workhouse ends it in a church.

Rose suffers emotionally and symbolically, but the narrative does not punish her for her association with sexual indiscretion. Agnes and Nancy may be forgiven after the fact, their deaths serving the function of a perfunctory punishment. Agnes and Nancy sin, the one out of love, the other out of ill-training, and they must somehow be punished, but neither is malicious or exploitive or cruel to others. In short, they never sin against love. The same cannot be said regarding the conscious injustice of the workhouse and the predatory crimes of Fagin, Sikes, and their sort. Though Dickens provides no remedy for the abuses of the workhouse, he permits the plot of *Oliver Twist* to execute narrative justice on the law's representatives. Bumble marries Mrs. Corney for mercenary motives, but his marriage promptly tumbles him "from all the height and pomp of beadleship, to the lowest depth of the most snubbed henpeckery" (272). He utterly loses caste even with the paupers. No punishment could be more direct and fitting. This is both a natural punishment for a personal failing and a convenient narrative punishment by which poetic justice is done. In equally appropriate terms Mr. and Mrs. Bumble are punished as a pair, becoming "paupers in that very same workhouse in which they had once lorded it over others" (414). It is a long while yet before Dickens will threaten a public institution with spontaneous combustion, but the treatment of the Bumbles is a good beginning in that direction.

If the workhouse and baby farm pervert the very qualities of home that they might be expected to provide, by dissolving families and abusing the poor persons charged to their care, Fagin's criminal world parodies the virtues of both home and charitable institution, for it provides food, protection, society, education (of a sort), and amusement. What from one point of view might appear to be a happy family is, of course, utterly corrupt because behind the appearance of geniality is raw selfishness. Behind Fagin's apparent geniality, as behind the workhouse's apparent charitable concern, is an actual exploitation both cynical and cruel. All the number ones making up Fagin's "family" really serve old Number One himself, who is willing to sacrifice anyone for his own interests. Within this perverted household, virtuous behavior is punished; hence Nancy's good actions lead to her death, and Oliver is threatened and locked up like a bad boy for wanting to live a life free from crime, which Fagin calls the offense of ingratitude. Similarly twisted is Fagin's view of legal justice; he approves of capital punishment not because he believes in punishing those guilty of crimes, but because it is a tidy way to dispose of possible informants.

If Fagin is sly and insinuating, Bill Sikes is merely a cunning brute. Neither seems to have anything resembling a conscience, though Bill discovers something like one after he has killed Nancy. In his flight from the scene of the crime he is haunted by Nancy's phantom. Bill's feverish excursion bears a very strong resemblance to the earlier leisurely trip that he and his gang make with Oliver to commit the burglary at the Maylie house. It is as though our first view of his professional life prefigures its end. Soon after we meet Bill we see him reading the *Hue and Cry,* a publication with information about crimes, criminals, and the rewards offered for them. These are proleptic hints, for, at his end, a hue and cry has been raised for Bill himself. The circularity in his career is symbolized, whether intentionally or not, by the noose toward which he is aimed and with which he hangs himself accidentally when trying to escape from the rooftop of his hiding place on Jacob's Island. Cruikshank's illustration appropriately emphasizes the noose-like quality of Bill's escape rope. The inadvertently self-punishing nature of Bill's death is accentuated by his belief that Nancy's eyes appear before him, thus unnerving him and causing him to slip, fall, and be hanged. Since this is precisely the form of punishment he would have suffered had he been taken, the pronounced irony of his death is an obvious instance of narrative punishment calling marked attention to itself.[6]

Bill lacks a true conscience, but knows that he has committed an abominable crime, and thus superstitious fear serves the same function that conscience would. His own imagination turns against him, as do his fellow thieves when he returns to their company. Burglary is one thing, killing a lover out of fear for one's own hide is another. Sikes brings retribution upon himself with no apparent opportunity to be shriven of his crime. In Victorian literature this is a terrible prospect, for it means, in basic Christian terms, that the soul, black with its sins, will speed directly to judgment. It is not uncommon in the literature of the time for the narrative itself to overtly or implicitly permit a sinner about to die some brief respite to allow for repentance. Bill's unabsolved end is therefore the most extreme form of punishment that can come to him. In a highly melodramatic manner, the implied author refuses to forgive his representative of evil and consigns him to hell. By contrast with Sike's abrupt end, Fagin has more than enough time to regret his life of crime while he awaits execution, after having been informed upon by the confederates he was himself so willing to betray. Perhaps his state is even worse than that of Sikes, since he ignores the opportunity to repent, yielding instead to despair at the terrible prospect of death.

> He had sat there, awake, but dreaming. Now he started up, every minute, and with gasping mouth and burning skin, hurried to and fro, in such a paroxysm of fear and wrath that even they [his guards]—used to such sights—recoiled from him with horror. He grew so terrible, at

last, in all the tortures of his evil conscience, that one man could not
bear to sit there, eyeing him alone; and so the two kept watch together. (408)

This is conscience with a vengeance, but not repentance. It is the awareness of
guilt without contrition for offending, only a low animal fear at having to pay
the price. Much as Mr. Fairchild took his errant children to view the remains of a
hanged man on a gibbet, Mr. Brownlow takes the innocent Oliver to see Fagin in
his last hours because he wants to educate the boy. Oliver has seen Fagin confident in his successful crime, Mr. Brownlow says, and now he should see him
suffering the dreadful punishment for them. While Fagin fantastically tries to
gain Oliver's help in escaping, that marvellous Christian boy exclaims, " 'Oh!
God forgive this wretched man!' " (411). Vain as that prayer might be, it signifies
that Oliver, at least, forgives Fagin. Being genuinely good, Oliver wants nothing
to do with the actual punishing of Fagin, but the implied author has no scruple
about exhibiting the wretch's sufferings and thereby inflicting punishment upon
him. This is a clear instance of the difference Dickens established in his fiction
between "authorized" and "unauthorized" punishments. As author he may do
what his good characters may not. They must forgive or remain passive; the implied author will punish.

    One last major instance of transgression and punishment remains—that of
Monks, otherwise Edward Leeford. Leeford is not a criminal by profession but
aims his villainy at Oliver in order to retain the entire inheritance from their
mutual father. Leeford is careful to instruct Fagin against violence: "Anything
but his death, I told you from the first. I won't shed blood; it's always found out,
and haunts a man besides" (194). Leeford has a conscience of sorts and he scruples
at certain crimes, but he is vicious nonetheless. If Leeford is Oliver's nemesis, he
is just as much his own, for his iniquitous way of life marks his destiny. His fits
and his fear of being left alone are indicators, but Mr. Brownlow explicitly describes Leeford's condition, telling him he is one "in whom all evil passions, vice,
and profligacy, festered, till they found vent in a hideous disease which has made
your face an index even to your mind" (378). At the close of the novel we learn
that Leeford retreated to a distant part of the New World, where, having
quickly squandered his share of the money divided between him and Oliver, "he
once more fell into his old courses, and, after undergoing a long confinement for
some fresh act of fraud and knavery, at length sunk under an attack of his old
disorder, and died in prison" (412). The narrator does not stipulate what Leeford's disease is, but the fits and the disfigured face suggest syphilis, thus more
horribly indicating the physical as well as the moral retribution that Leeford
brings upon himself.

    The confrontation with the unmasked Leeford is one of the more curious epi-
sodes in the novel, when judged from the perspective of this study. Despite his
viciousness and his crimes, Leeford is not punished by any other characters, even
when in their power.[7] Mr. Brownlow presents Leeford with an unequivocal

choice, asking him to decide quickly if he wants him "to prefer my charges publicly, and consign you to a punishment the extent of which, although I can, with a shudder, foresee, I cannot control," or to appeal to his "forbearance and the mercy of those you have deeply injured" (373). Leeford wisely elects the second course and is asked no more than to make restitution to Oliver.[8] Clearly the good characters assembled together in this scene might justifiably feel some rage against this viper, might entertain some craving for revenge, at least some small impulse to punch him in the nose, if he still has one. Instead, they are all forbearing and merciful, and it is this response to Leeford's villainy that elevates them above ordinary humanity and makes them a composite model for our own behavior, a model we have seen taken to an extreme in Oliver, who prays for Fagin's forgiveness, and which is aptly imitated by the narrator himself in the narrative's conclusion when he forgives Agnes Fleming. If the implied author is willing to take on the task of executing justice and seeing to it that his narrative punishes scoundrels like Fagin, Sikes, and Leeford in their varying degrees, according to a melodramatic poetic justice, he just as importantly makes certain that his good characters just as melodramatically act virtuously, as represented in the Leeford episode by their restraint and mercy.

There is another context in which this mercy operates (for it is more mercy than forgiveness in Leeford's case). Monks says that when his despicable mother died, "she bequeathed these secrets to me, together with her unquenchable and deadly hatred of all whom they involved—though she need not have left me that, for I had inherited it long before" (397). Whether intended realistically or only symbolically, Leeford has inherited all of his mother's bad features and none of his father's good ones. He hates, is vengeful, and is selfish and self-indulgent. Leeford may thus be read as the embodiment of mankind's least appealing, most commonly sociopathic traits, the very traits which, if unrestrained, will most certainly bring their own grim consequences in the end. By contrast, Leeford's half-brother, Oliver, seems not only free from all such impulses but almost inoculated against external evil as well. Fagin tells Leeford that Oliver isn't like other boys in the same circumstances. Much earlier, the narrator explains that though Oliver looked frail as an infant, "nature or inheritance had implanted a good sturdy spirit in Oliver's breast" (5). This inheritance may refer only to his physical being, but it seems quite clear that we are meant to perceive his parents' best traits surviving in Oliver. When Oliver first comes to Fagin's establishment and is drowsing off into half-consciousness, the narrator comments, "At such times, a mortal knows just enough of what his mind is doing, to form some glimmering conception of its mighty powers, its bounding from earth and spurning time and space, when freed from the restraint of its corporeal associate" (58). Later, when Oliver is asleep after the attempted burglary at the Maylie house and Rose's tears drop on his forehead, he smiles in his unconscious state "as though these marks of pity and compassion had awakened some pleasant dream of a love and affection he had never known." In the same way a sound or an odor will "sometimes call up sudden dim remembrances of scenes that never were, in

this life; which vanish like a breath; which some brief memory of a happier existence, long gone by, would seem to have awakened; which no voluntary exer-
tion of the mind can ever recall" (216). In short, through steady association with
this context of eternity, Oliver becomes our touchstone for behavior in the temporal and finite world. It has often enough been pointed out that Oliver is a sort
of spirit or ideal making its pilgrimage through the material world, and the passages I have cited reinforce this notion. But if he is such an ideal, he also serves as
a practical model.

Though Oliver is regularly identified with references to the afterlife, the contrast such identifications create between this world and the next also becomes an
instructive tool. Witnessing the funeral of an infant brings home to Oliver some
truths about death that had not struck him when he worked for Sowerberry in
the undertaking trade. The narrator pauses to instruct us.

> We need be careful how we deal with those about us, when every
> death carries to some small circle of survivors, thoughts of so much
> omitted, and so little done—of so many things forgotten, and so many
> more which might have been repaired! There is no remorse so deep as
> that which is unavailing; if we would be spared its tortures, let us re-
> member this, in time. (247)

The true purpose of mercy, compassion, and forgiveness is to follow Christ's
teaching and to be good to others, but the negative version of this teaching is that
failure to follow Christ's precepts will engender a natural retribution. Lacking
mercy, compassion, and forgiveness, we prepare tortures of remorse for ourselves that could easily have been avoided. But if we respond positively to intimations of a timeless existence surrounding our own, and learn the lesson of the
deathbed, we will be less likely to make this mistake.[9]

Oliver Twist begins with Agnes Fleming's death and ends before her memorial
in an old village church. Part of this concluding paragraph I have already quoted,
but it bears repeating in this context. The narrator muses on the coffinless tomb.

> But, if the spirits of the Dead ever come back to earth, to visit spots
> hallowed by the love—the love beyond the grave—of those whom
> they knew in life, I believe that the shade of Agnes sometimes hovers
> round that solemn nook. I believe it none the less, because that nook is
> in a Church, and she was weak and erring. (415)

It is yet another deathbed that sets in motion the plot mechanisms that will link
these two significant references to death. In dying, Old Sally, who had attended
Agnes' death in the workhouse, provides the evidence that will solve the mystery
of Oliver's father and his relationship with Rose Maylie. Out of death comes
hope. Similarly, the grim scene of human mortality with which the novel opens is
also the beginning of Oliver's pilgrimage toward truth and virtue. The novel

emphasizes this circularity, connecting death and the hereafter with life's progress back to heaven by way of achieving redemption on earth. Just as Bill Sikes' journey into crime is replicated in his flight from justice, so Oliver's flight from injustice is mirrored in his victorious return to that very location where the mystery of his origins is disclosed. When Oliver receives his proper inheritance and has proven his goodness by being generous even to Leeford, he completes his career within the plot by praying for Fagin's forgiveness and projecting his own merciful sentiments into the next world. These two circularities complement one another and inhabit interlocking spaces in the novel.[10] If the first parts of the novel accumulate instances of perverted justice and outright crime and violence, the narrative progressively operates to exclude or diminish the polluting forces, increasingly bringing the powers of compassion, mercy, and forgiveness forward until there is no room left within the boundaries of the story for Fagin, Sikes, Leeford, and others like them. Only a foothold remains for evil in the likes of the Bumbles (now humbled, if not penitent) and Noah Claypool. The wicked have worked their own defeat, failing when there is no one for them to feed upon. The good have goodness always within them and are self-sustaining.

I have referred to *Oliver Twist* as melodramatic, but this description requires some clarification and qualification.[11] The novel does follow the structure of melodrama, which, according to Peter Brooks,

> moves from the presentation of virtue-as-innocence to the introduction of menace or obstacle, which places virtue in a situation of extreme peril. For the greater part of the play, evil appears to reign triumphant, controlling the structure of events, dictating the moral coördinates of reality. Virtue, expulsed, eclipsed, apparently fallen, cannot effectively articulate the cause of the right. Its tongue is in fact often tied by the structure of familial relationships: virtue cannot call into question the judgments and the actions of a father or an uncle or a guardian, for to do so would be to violate its nature as innocence.[12]

Thus far Dickens' fiction is roughly consistent with melodrama. The signs of good and evil must be clarified and isolated before the virtuous characters are reestablished. But Dickens goes beyond the merely melodramatic, even in *Oliver Twist,* by a concern for character and individuality. This concern for character will increase in depth and intensity in the novels to follow, but it is already evident in both good and evil characters in *Oliver Twist.* Here is Peter Brooks again.

> If in a novel by Dickens or a play by Ibsen we may be tempted to talk about "identity," the movement of the plot toward discovery of identity, and the moral anagnorisis that accompanies it, such terminology appears inappropriate in a theatre where persons are so very typological, and where structure is so highly conventional. Anagnorisis in melodrama thus has little to do with the achievement of psychological

identity and is much more a matter of the recognition, the liberation from misprision, of a pure signifier, the token for an assigned identity. (53)

But if Brooks draws this contrast between the simplifications of stage melo-drama and the more complicated contests of fictional narratives, he nonetheless concludes that melodrama fulfills a desire for justice that other approaches may not satisfy. "For in the absence of any more transcendent principles, melodrama must at last sacralize Law itself, a perfect justice of punishment and reward, ex-pulsion and recognition" (204).

Oliver Twist, and Dickens' fiction in general, seems to meet this description of melodrama, but the significant difference is that underlying the surface display of punishment and reward is a true belief in transcendent principles—the simple equations of the Christian creed. Ironically, though there is nothing like the sim-plifications of melodrama in Christ's teachings, they establish an ideal of what is right that may generate its opposite. Melodrama may thus be seen as a form of Christian Gnosticism where powers of good and evil contend, but where, in each individual manifestation of the contest, good triumphs. But if something like this moral conception underlies Dickens' writings, then the shapes his narratives take will include clear punishments, not at the hands of chivalric knights, but as con-sequences of evil itself, or through the intervention of a providential implied author. Poetic justice there must occasionally be, but virtuous characters must remain unpolluted sources of grace. Even in the later novels, when the good characters are themselves flawed, this principle will hold true. *Oliver Twist's* generally melodramatic structure rests, then, on the foundation of Christian be-lief that requires both forgiveness and punishment, and which must therefore exploit narrative strategies that will incorporate both satisfactorily.

Susan Horton has suggested that Dickens wanted to believe in a moral uni-verse in which good was rewarded and evil punished, and yet "he wrote novels in which Fate, as often as a just god, determines action and consequence."[13] She goes on to suggest that Dickens satisfied his own and his readers' conflicting de-mands by distributing his intentions into the variety of modes that he adopts in his novels. This ultimately leads to evident disharmonies between images and rhetoric and plot and rhetoric (35).[14] This is an acute perception of some difficul-ties in reading Dickens' fiction, but it is possible to locate a foundation level at which Dickens and his ordinary readers were able to reconcile not only the con-tradictions between God and fate, but those within language as well. Dickens' approach is essentially Carlylean. He believes that there are universal laws that guarantee an ultimate justice and that human beings cannot long counteract these laws, or the laws will undo them and their schemes. Folly is punished by the same kind of law that promises that an apple will fall when loosened from its bough.[15] Yet though Carlyle may sharply suggest in *Past and Present* (1843) that retaining the Corn Laws is stupid and even wicked, his remedy is not in specific legislation but in the change that individual men discover in their own souls before they seek to change the world. The two great transcendent moral polarities for Dickens and much of his audience were punishment and forgiveness. Punishment might come through human agency, divine justice, or natural law (read fate), but it must come in lieu of repentance. It is equally important to forgive those who offend, because forgiveness demonstrates the purity of our *own* soul even when it may have little to offer to a sinner.

Oliver Twist contains Dickens' first sustained mystery plot, a narrative device he would exploit for the rest of his career. Here again Susan Horton observes a disharmony. "We may not have, as we read Dickens, solved the 'puzzles' of poverty and disease and crime and of lumbering institutions such as the Court of Chancery, but as we solve the plot mysteries of Dickens's novels, we may *feel* that we have" (78). But the point of the mystery plots may be self-discovery through the disclosure of secrets, not the solution of social problems. Steven Marcus contends that "the protection of Dickens's satire is its innocence."[16] *Oliver Twist's* satire is general and operates in all directions, though the progress of the novel is toward not institutional reconstruction but the discovery of Oliver's identity and inheritance.

Peter Garrett is helpful in appreciating Dickens' mystery plots. He observes that the mystery plots have a narrative movement toward the discovery of secrets and the revelation of a hidden coherence. "The secrets toward which mystery plots are directed have a double location, in the minds of others and in the past."[17] They do not project well into the future in the way that prophecies of social justice might, except with one or two exceptions. *Oliver Twist*, Garrett says, uses the mystery plot to impose a resolution while confining the protagonist to a passive role, a feature of later Dickens novels as well. In *Oliver Twist* the mystery plot provides salvation, in *Nicholas Nickleby* retribution.

For Dickens, then, mystery and secrecy are central elements of narration not only because they generate suspense and keep the reader interested, but because the representation of one or another form of tracking or hunting down offers a special gratification to a certain moral sensibility, and because the disclosure of "the kill" is essential to the ground purpose of the narrative, which is the certification of virtue and the punishing of evil. The first comes through significations like forgiveness, charity, and self-sacrifice; the second from some means of repentance or retribution, all as means of modeling the procedures by which we all make our own souls. It has often been said that Dickens' novels call for a change of heart, but it might equally be said that by exposing the secrets of the human heart they call for the change and discovery of soul.[18]

NOTES

1. The figure of the inept magistrate or justice is familiar in the English novel, from Fielding's *Joseph Andrew* and Goldsmith's *Vicar of Wakefield* onward.

2. Charles Dickens, *The Adventures of Oliver Twist*. Oxford: Oxford University Press, 1987), 11. Subsequent references appear in the text.

3. Mrs. Corney represents a comic version of these "tainted" women. She follows a "respectable" route in attracting and winning Bumble, but because she is mercenary, she appears less virtuous than any of the conventionally deplorable female figures in the novel. She is, accordingly, punished in economic terms.

4. In "'The Parish Boy's Progress': The Evolving Form of *Oliver Twist*," *PMLA* 93, no. 1 (January 1978), 20–32, William T. Lankford discusses Rose's central role in the polarization of good and evil in the novel and also argues that the novel's two narrative perspectives—represented by realistic and melodramatic representations—embody the tension in its moral outlook.

5. Charles Dickens, *Oliver Twist,* ed. Kathleen Tillotson (Oxford: The Clarendon Press, 1966), lxii, from Dickens' Preface to the 3rd Edition.

6. Richard Maxwell carries this connection even further by suggesting that London is a maze, and "a maze is a kind of knot," and that the "gallows knots these associates together" (*The Mysteries of Paris and London* [Charlottesville: University Press of Virginia, 1992], 82–84).

7. There is an interesting parallel between the treatments of Leeford and Uriah Heep. Both are caught out by a band of lay persons (though Tommy Traddles is an attorney), who exact restitution but not retribution. Both nonetheless bring about their own formal punishment at the hands of officials of the law.

8. It is interesting that in this early novel Dickens separates the financial debt from the moral one. Leeford must cough up the money owed to Oliver, but he will not face the debt of his obliquities until he cashes in his chips and meets his maker. Later Dickens manages to draw the strands of financial and moral indebtedness together more intricately.

9. J. Hillis Miller has called attention to the "intimations of immortality" in *Oliver Twist,* and concludes from them that the only escape from this world is by death (*Charles Dickens: The World of His Novels* [Cambridge: Harvard University Press, 1965]). That, of course, was standard thinking for those who saw the world as a vale of tears. The point was to keep immortality in mind as a guide for one's conduct in this world.

10. D. A. Miller says that *Oliver Twist* requires a double plot—one with regulation secured in a minor way by the police and one with regulation secured in a major way by amateurs (*The Novel and the Police* [Berkeley: University of California Press, 1988]), 11. But Miller overlooks the fact that police are marginal in the novel because they were still marginal in society at the time of *Oliver Twist.* Only later would they become agents not only of detection and detention but of prosecution as well.

11. Edgar Johnson long ago called attention to the superficial conventions of melodrama in *Oliver Twist* and others have commented on them since (*Charles Dickens: His Tragedy and Triumph,* 2 vols. [Boston: Little, Brown and Co., 1952], 1:280ff.).

12. Peter Brooks, *The Melodramatic Imagination: Balzac, Henry James, Melodrama, and the Mode of Excess* (New York: Columbia University Press, 1985), 31. Subsequent references in the text.

13. Susan R. Horton, *The Reader in the Dickens World: Style and Response* (Pittsburgh: University of Pittsburgh Press, 1981), 7. Subsequent references in the text.

14. Other critics have, in one way or another, remarked on inconsistencies in Dickens' novels. John Carey begins by declaring that Dickens "reflects the popular mind in that he is able to espouse diametrically opposed opinions with almost equal vehemence," and then goes on to illustrate some of these opinions (*Here Comes Dickens: The Imagination of a Novelist* [New York: Schocken Books, 1974], 8). But these are precisely "opinions," not deep-seated moral convictions, where I argue Dickens knew his own mind very well.

15. Thomas Carlyle, *Past and Present,* ed. Richard D. Altick (Boston: Houghton Mifflin Company, 1965.), 18–19, and elsewhere.

16. Steven Marcus, *From Pickwick to Dombey* (New York: Basic Books, Inc., 1965), 59.

17. Peter Garrett, *The Victorian Multiplot Novel: Studies in Dialogical Form* (New Haven: Yale University Press, 1980), 52.

18. Barbara Hardy, *The Moral Art of Dickens* (New York: Oxford University Press, 1970). Hardy writes that the change of heart depends upon the convention of the moral double or opposite: "the hero is changed by seeing his situation or his moral defect enacted for him in external coincidence: by his twin, who forces a recognition of loathsome resemblance, or his opposite, who forces reluctant admiration and comparison. He sees his defect enlarged, isolated, unmistakably his own, but detached for inspection. And he acts on this recognition, and is irrevocably changed" (31).

SIX

Nicholas Nickleby

MUCH IN *Nicholas Nickleby* depends upon how money is used or abused; money is intimately interwoven with the moral values that the novel endorses.[1] At the false heart of this novel is avarice. Ralph Nickleby, the "man of business," represents heartless acquisitiveness. He recognizes himself as having only two principal interests, money and hatred. Though Ralph is the most powerful embodiment of cold, single-minded avarice, his antivalues are reflected in many other characters throughout the novel. Ralph says to Squeers, when conspiring with him to injure Nicholas, "You are, at least, as avaricious as you are revengeful. So am I."[2] Squeers is a nasty, cheating, greedy man, but he has a perverted sort of family affection that is beyond Ralph. Arthur Gride is as grasping as Ralph, but "Cringing and cowardly to the core," and susceptible to lust (710). Associated with these consummate figures of avarice are their prey, the wasters of wealth, Sir Mulberry Hawk (also a predator, as his name suggests), Lord Verisopht, Mr. Mantalini, and so on. Ralph is intelligent in making his money multiply, but to succeed by his dubious usury he has quashed all humanity within him. Upon receiving Nicholas' note denouncing Ralph for his behavior toward himself and his sister, Ralph recalls how, as a young man, he was unfavorably compared to Nicholas' father. "*He* was open, liberal, gallant, gay; *I* a crafty hunks of cold and stagnant blood, with no passion but love of saving, and no spirit beyond a thirst for gain." Then he resolves, "As a portion of the world affect to despise the power of money, I must try and show them what it is" (441).

Money and other forms of wealth play an important part in all of Dickens' novels to a lesser or greater degree, but in *Nicholas Nickleby* money is an ever-present key to the moral relations among people.[3] For Ralph money is power and he prides himself in being unhypocritical about his relish for it. On the other hand, unproductive wasters of money, like Hawk and Mr. Bray, are hypocrites to the degree that they do not wish to appear dependent upon the financial resources of others. They measure their worth by a financial valuation they know to be unsound. They must constantly derive funds from others to support their dubious self-respect. Other characters are dependent in more extenuated ways. Anticipating financial advantages for their children, the Kenwigses fawn upon their bachelor relative, Mr. Lillyvick. Learning of Lillyvick's surprise marriage to Henrietta Petowker, Mr. Kenwigs cries out: "'My children, my defrauded, swindled infants!'"(465). The Kenwigses have merely played at family feeling, whereas the true relationship with their relative has been economic. This theme of anticipated income and perverted family feeling is everywhere in the novel. Even Gride's lustful interest in Madeline Bray is greatly enhanced by the fact that she stands to inherit a modest income of which only he is aware.

As one might suppose, if the acquisition and expectation of easy money is rendered offensive in *Nicholas Nickleby,* innocence of finance and indifference to wealth are laudable. But unfamiliarity with finance can have disastrous effects upon the innocent who wander into its treacherous precincts. Nicholas and Kate's father had invested his money unwisely (at his wife's suggestion, in hopes of imitating Ralph's financial success), thereby leaving his family impoverished at his death. With genuine self-regard that reveals the hollowness of the Hawk genus, Nicholas and Kate do not wish to depend upon anyone but themselves for their well-being. They are willing to take up any work that is honest and insures self-respect. Kate, recollecting the better times she has known, tells Miss La Creevy that she "could not bear to live on anybody's bounty," including Ralph's (117). In an example of misguided education that casts ironic light on the money theme, Squeers asks Master Belling to repeat the first lesson his school instills into commercial pupils, which is "Never postpone business." But young Belling, with much prodding, produces instead: "Never—perform—business" (37). His version, though not a guiding maxim, nonetheless calls attention to what "business" generally represents in this novel.

But *Nicholas Nickleby* is not a novel dedicated to the abuse of business. It is instead a Carlylean objection to the cash nexus relationship that so often replaces a true consideration of human interdependencies. It is important, therefore, that Nicholas' benefactors should be businessmen who embody entirely different values from those represented by Ralph, the moneylender and speculator. The Cheeryble brothers carry on a legitimate trade, are kindly toward their employees, and charitable in general. They are the working model of how commercial wealth should be treated. Ralph's behavior is a perverted mockery of their conduct. When he finds Nicholas a job with Squeers it is to make certain that Nicholas will be humiliated, fail, and thus no longer have a claim upon him. Malice masquerades as charity; the apparent kindly gesture masks an evil intent. This reversal of the proper values of the novel in its most wicked character is repeated in other characters as well, most notably Squeers. He gives pious advice to the boys in his charge: "'Subdue your appetites, my dears, and you've conquered human natur,'" but the advantage to him is that he need not feed them so much (45). Later he tells his son, "'You always keep on in the same path, and do them things that you see your father do, and when you die you'll go right slap to Heaven and no questions asked'" (497). And of the captured Smike, the victim of so much evil intent on the part of Squeers and Ralph, this parody of a schoolmaster declares, "'Providence is against him, no doubt'" (499). Ralph and Squeers perform the same function in *Nicholas Nickleby* that the workhouse (and parodically Fagin's crew) does in *Oliver Twist*. An appearance of benevolence shrouds selfishness, thereby constituting a cardinal sin in Dickens' scheme of things—the betrayal and subversion of charity and love.

By contrast to the vicious acts of these mockers of the Christian code, the Cheerybles behave as the best sort of human should, hiring Nicholas for honest work based upon his evidently good character. When Ralph "generously" provides a dwelling place for Mrs. Nickleby and Kate, it is to utilize one of his own run-down properties, where they will be uncomfortable enough to want to go elsewhere. Meanwhile, he counts on Nicholas to misbehave sufficiently to justify his disowning of the family altogether. By contrast, the Cheerybles eagerly hand out charity to all those of whose need they are aware. They are grateful to Mr. Trimmers for calling their attention to charity cases. Even the antique weapons above their fireplace, a broken blunderbuss and edgeless swords, become "emblems of mercy and forbearance" in the Cheerybles' establishment (470). At the end of the novel, when Ralph dies intestate, Nicholas and Kate refuse to claim his wealth because they cannot endorse the manner in which it was accumulated. By this time, however, they have established themselves in a comfortable way of life and do not need an inheritance they have not earned.

If money, its acquisition, and its dispersal are important armatures for *Nicholas Nickleby*, the language of monetary exchange also finds its way into the values of the novel. Ralph Nickleby, for example, views human relationships in terms of money. When Nicholas refuses to give Smike up to Snawley, who Ralph represents as his true father, Ralph threatens to wear Nicholas down with legal proceedings. "'I'll prove you, and break your haughty spirit, strong as you deem it now. And when you make this house a hell, and visit these trials upon yonder wretched object (as you will, I know you), and those who think you now a young-fledged hero, we'll go into old accounts between us two, and see who stands the debtor, and comes out best at last, even before the world'" (594). Informed by the Cheeryble brothers of Smike's death, Ralph is delighted because he knows how deeply the loss touches Nicholas, and he exclaims, "'If you tell me that he is dead, I am in your debt and bound to you for life'" (785). By contrast, Miss Snevellicci, complimenting Nicholas on his attention to Smike, says it is very kind of him "'taking so much pains with him, and doing it all with as much delight and readiness as if you were coining gold by it!'" (386). Thus the language of commercial exchange is incorporated in the moral world of the novel to signify that the medium of exchange may be either viciously or benevolently applied. Money is power, money is value; but it may be the power to do good as well as evil, it may represent the values of charity and kindness as well as selfishness and pride. Money as such is neutral, but it facilitates malicious or benevolent action.

Throughout the novel greed masquerades as benevolence. The United Metropolitan Improved Hot Muffin and Crumpet Baking and Punctual Delivery Company is an early example. Ralph, as we have seen, is another—offering apparent charity to his brother's family, but intending harm. Squeers describes his enterprise as beneficial to society, though it is actually a convenience to unfeeling parents and an institution of suffering. Against the depradations of the greedy there is little help for those who suffer injustice, as the narrator pointedly observes when musing on the conditions in and near debtors' prisons. "There are many pleasant fictions of the law in constant operation, but there is not one so pleasant or practically humourous as that which supposes every man to be of equal value in its impartial eye, and the benefits of all laws to be equally attainable by all men, without the smallest reference to the furniture of their pockets" (603).

It seems quite clear, then, that the getting and giving of money is a central concern in *Nicholas Nickleby,* and that this getting and giving takes on a strong moral cast as it enters the language of moral values. Avarice is set against charity, vengefulness against benevolence. But beyond even this level of abstraction is another register in which money becomes the metaphor of eternal transactions. An early instance of a false comprehension of the idea that men may lay up treasures in heaven through their works on earth occurs, in a humorous form, in the tale of the Baron of Grogzwig. The narrator tries to explain the strange noises and effects in the Baron's old castle.

> I believe that one of the baron's ancestors, being short of money, had inserted a dagger in a gentleman who called one night to ask his way, and it was supposed that these miraculous occurrences took place in consequence. And yet I hardly know how that could have been, either, because the baron's ancestor, who was an amiable man, felt very sorry afterwards for having been so rash, and laying violent hands upon a quantity of stone and timber which belonged to a weaker baron, built a chapel as an apology, and so took a receipt from Heaven in full of all demands. (66)

This brief account condenses the usual pattern of a greedy rascal appropriating money by devious means for his own selfish ends, but adds to it the familiar ploy of trying, through a superficial moral virtue, to forestall the appropriate punishment. The joke here, of course, is that even the means for appeasing divine displeasure are misappropriated. The lesson of this tale applies to the novel as a whole, and its themes extend throughout the narrative. Though these themes are generally implicit in the actions of the narrative, occasionally they become explicit. At the beginning of Chapter 45, the narrator pauses to deliver a serious sermon that echoes the Grogzwig tale.

> There are some men who, living with the one object of enriching themselves, no matter by what means, and being perfectly conscious of the baseness and rascality of the means which they will use every day towards this end, affect nevertheless—even to themselves—a high tone of moral rectitude, and shake their heads and sigh over the depravity of the world. Some of the craftiest scoundrels that ever walked this earth, or rather—for walking implies, at least, an erect position and the bearing of a man—that ever crawled and crept through life by its dirtiest and narrowest ways, will gravely jot down in diaries the events of the day, and keep a regular debtor and creditor account with Heaven, which shall always show a floating balance in their own favour. Whether this is a gratuitous (the only gratuitous) part of the falsehood and trickery of such men's lives, or whether they really hope to cheat Heaven itself, and lay up treasure in the next world by the same process which has enabled them to lay up treasure in this—not to question how it is, so it is. And, doubtless, such book-keeping (like certain autobiographies which have enlightened the world) cannot fail to prove serviceable, in the one respect of sparing the recording Angel some time and labour. (567)

Ralph, at least, is not such a hypocrite. He adheres to one canonical maxim: Know thyself. He knows that he cares to gratify only the two passions of avarice and hatred, and assumes that all men are like himself and therefore in one way or another hateful.

Christ taught that human deeds are a kind of currency. He argued that we may lay up treasures in heaven through our good deeds on earth just as we lay up material wealth by our labors. Dickens' monetary metaphors allude to this message, insisting that our eternal reward depends upon how we treat our fellow humans. Essential to that treatment is a sense of charity. The Cheeryble brothers understand this. Ralph rejects the notion as nonsense. When his trials come upon him, he has no inner resources to support him. Only fleetingly does he have moments of doubt about the power of money. Touched by Kate's fine nature, Ralph meditates beside his cold fireplace amid his house's silent, dreary splendour on what she represents: "and in that one glimpse of a better nature, born as it was in selfish thoughts, the rich man felt himself friendless, childless, and alone. Gold, for the instant, lost its lustre in his eyes, for there were countless treasures of the heart which it could never purchase" (401). Kate is the principal embodiment of the best in human nature. In a sense she is also the principle upon which mankind can draw in moments of need. She has Carlyle's "light-fountain" within her that cannot be exhausted because it is a resource of the spirit. Because Kate represents a wealth that can be renewed by expending itself, she is the only person who can disturb Ralph with anything like a sense of compassion and affection. In fact, it could be said of Ralph, as it is of the central figure in Tennyson's "The Vision of Sin": "'He had not wholly quenched his power; / A little grain of conscience made him sour.'"[4] Kate stands for uncorrupted human virtue and is thus a proper object of affection. Ralph's great sin regarding her is in trying to make a profit by converting her into a commercial attraction for Lord Verisopht.

One of the vilest human activities in Dickens' code is to treat human beings as commodities. In one of his most powerful metaphors, the narrator of *Nicholas Nickleby* indicates early in the novel that human beings are the currency of eternal values, not to be debased through selfish transactions. The passage occurs in the tale of "The Five Sisters of York."

> "If we all had hearts like those which beat so lightly in the bosoms of the young and beautiful, what a heaven this earth would be! If, while our bodies grow old and withered, our hearts could but retain their early youth and freshness, of what avail would be our sorrows and sufferings! But, the faint image of Eden which is stamped upon them in childhood, chafes and rubs in our rough struggles with the world, and soon wears away: too often to leave nothing but a mournful blank remaining." (57)

This metaphor of human beings as the coinage of heaven was not an unusual one in Victorian times. Gerald Massey used a peculiarly developed version of it in his introduction to his poems.

> The child comes into the world like a new coin with the stamp of God upon it; and in like manner as the Jews sweat down sovereigns, by hustling them in a bag to get gold-dust out of them, so is the poor man's child hustled and sweated down in this bag of society to get wealth out of it; and even as the impress of the Queen is effaced by the Jewish process, so is the image of God worn from heart and brow, and day by day the child recedes devilward.[5]

Dickens' use of the figure in *Nicholas Nickleby* was not original, but it accorded very well with the network of references binding together the mercenary and moral themes of the narrative.

In this novel about money and heart, Ralph's pocketbook lies against his heart and smothers it; the same is true in varying degrees for other characters. But a pure and loving heart is the real gold of this book and it prevails. The conflict between money and heart ends with the dissolving of money into heart. The marriages that end the book are all triumphs of good hearts over financial impediments.

If the money theme is obvious and even obtrusive in *Nicholas Nickleby*, so is the narrative method. There are few of the skillful narrative devices in this early novel that are evident in *Dombey and Son* and onward. Given the thespian self-awareness of its theatrical episodes, the novel is itself appropriately theatrical.[6] It has often been remarked that Dickens was greatly influenced by the theatre of his day, notably by melodrama.[7] As in *Oliver Twist,* good and evil here are clearly distinguished from one another. Characters even assume stylized melodramatic postures and deliver stagey speeches, especially in confrontation scenes. This melodramatic equipment may be particularly appropriate to *Nicholas Nickleby,* which, more than most of Dickens' writings, is heavily overbalanced in the direction of hatred, revenge, and retribution. Countering these tendencies is much benevolence and charity, but surprisingly little forgiveness.

I use "melodrama" here, as with *Oliver Twist,* in its basic theatrical sense, not in the more penetrating manner in which Peter Brooks examines the subject. Dickens is not melodramatic in the manner of Balzac, but there are some resemblances. Dickens wants his created world to evoke the real world; he does not feel the "desire to express all [that] seems a fundamental charactistic of the melodramatic mode."[8] For Balzac, "The moral occult is not a metaphysical system; it is rather the repository of the fragmentary and desacralized remnants of sacred myth" (Brooks 5). But Dickens does operate on a fundamental metaphysic that retains the sacred teachings of the New Testament even as it simplifies the mysteries of the Old Testament into a system of secular metaphors.[9] In his early writings, and more subtly in his later writings, Dickens adheres to the melodramatic fashion of representing good and evil as recognizably opposed powers. Brooks describes the melodramatic mode as follows: "The polarization of good and evil works toward revealing their presence and operation as real forces in the world. Their conflict suggests the need to recognize and confront evil, to combat and expel it, to purge the social order" (13). And although Dickens maintained scriptural verity and assumed an attitude shared by most of his audience, his approach reflects Brooks' description of the function of melodrama in nineteenth-century writing, which is to become "the principal mode for uncovering, demonstrating, and making operative the essential moral universe in a post-sacred era" (15).

In melodrama, both villains and heroes or heroines voice their private feelings, either in monologues that we overhear or in direct address to other characters. The secrets disclosed by the unraveling plot are often plots themselves, schemes directed against other characters. In *Nickleby,* the narrative communicates Ralph's plots almost as quickly as he concocts them, sometimes by overhearing his inner reflections—as when he considers what will happen to Nicholas at Dotheboys Hall or when he imagines the consequences of using Kate as a lure to Lord Verisopht—sometimes by being present when he imparts his designs to others—as with Gride's scheme against Madeline Bray, or his own plan of revenge against Nicholas through Squeers. Sometimes details of his plots are conveyed to us by intermediaries such as Newman Noggs. The narrative need not withhold these plots from us in the interest of suspense, because the excitement for the reader in this novel is comparable to that of a playgoer at a melodrama or a horror movie—to know that something terrible threatens the good characters and yet be unable to prevent it. This constant threat of operational evil generates a corresponding energy directed against this evil that drives toward retribution at some point in the play or novel. The more "poetic" the justice the better. Hence the one important mystery that the narrative withholds from us throughout *Nickleby* is the secret of Smike's origins. Fittingly, Smike, the innocent medium for Ralph's acts of hatred against Nicholas, turns out to be Ralph's own son. His schemes all foiled, Ralph hangs himself in the very room where that son grew up in fear and dismay. The tool has turned in the villain's hand. The agency for his hatred fatally wounds him and, with a definite closure characteristic of melodrama, brings Ralph back to the source of his sin for consummate punishment at his own hand.[10] There is a satisfying circularity in Ralph's career resembling the circular pattern that brings Bill Sikes to his fate. If Bill Sikes dies by his own hand, he does so accidentally, though his bad conscience manifested in Nancy's phantasmal eyes helps him in that direction. By contrast, Ralph's is a conscious suicide, prompted as much by despair as by guilt. In both cases the scoundrel's punishment is the consequence of his own pattern of conduct. But a narrative punishment is at work with both as well: in the implied author's markers of the noose-like rope with Bill and in the location of Ralph's suicide.

Brooks notes that "One of the most immediately striking features of melodrama is the extent to which characters tend to say, directly and explicitly, their moral judgments of the world" (36). This trait is important because it eliminates irony and provides the spectator or reader with clearly stamped identifications. Ralph hates other members of the human race and imagines that all people are either open or secret graspers like himself, or plain fools. A Kate Nickleby disturbs him precisely because, if she is sincere, his world view is incomplete or false. To remain pristine in his evil Ralph must forget or repress any goodness in himself. He must force himself to regard human beings as commodities to be dealt with cold-heartedly, just as he deals with money. Habit makes this practice easy for Ralph, but he must struggle to reassert that habit after he has been in Kate's presence. Nicholas represents what Ralph might have become if he had not in his boyhood preferred money to heart. Ralph recognizes that in exact proportion as he becomes conscious of a lingering regard for Kate, his detestation of Nicholas augments. "It might be, that to atone for the weakness of inclining to any one person, he held it necessary to hate some other more intensely than before; but such had been the course of his feelings" (441). He keeps a ledger of emotions and must always balance the books. But Nicholas acts to scramble Ralph's entries, and thus intense emotional scenes are buttressed with financial references, either metaphorical or veritable. Exposing Ralph's repulsiveness to Kate, Nicholas drives the avaricious and vengeful man to an extreme pitch of malignity. This malignity will later be symbolized in Nicholas' powerful announcement to Ralph, at the moment Gride's scheme to marry Madeline collapses, that Ralph has lost ten thousand pounds. The financial loss signals Ralph's increasing failure to control other human beings. Power of all kinds is slipping

through his hands. At first this loss may seem gratuitous, but it is a direct analogue to Ralph's psychological metamorphosis. Hatred has clouded his vision.
The more he concentrates on taking revenge against Nicholas, the less dispas-
sionate he is about the purpose of his life. "The time has been when nothing
could have moved me like the loss of this great sum," Ralph reflects.

> "Nothing. For births, deaths, marriages, and all the events which are
> of interest to most men, have (unless they are connected with gain or
> loss of money) no interest for me. But now, I swear, I mix up with the
> loss, his triumph in telling it. If he had brought it about,—I almost feel
> as if he had—I couldn't hate him more. Let me but retaliate upon him,
> by degrees, however slow—let me but begin to get the better of him,
> let me but turn the scale—and I can bear it." (739–40)

Again Ralph must picture his loss and future victory in terms of his trade, of
measuring out portions until he once more turns the scale in his favor and the
gold of satisfied vengeance pours into his hands. But, of course, from this point
on Ralph will not win any victories, and what at first appear victories to him
actually become painful reversals—most notably the death of Smike. When
Ralph begins to fail his losses come thick and fast until he exercises his last form
of control, the power to choose his own death.

Punishment is not a surprise for transgressors in this novel. The warnings that
Nicholas issues to Ralph increase the tension building up to his final punishment,
and similar monitory signs occur in the careers of other wicked individuals.
When Nicholas arrives at Dotheboys Hall he instantly realizes that something is
very much amiss. The boys are as poorly treated as though they were "malefac-
tors in a jail." It takes little imagination to foresee trouble. "With every kindly
sympathy and affection blasted in its birth, with every young and healthy feeling
flogged and starved down, with every revengeful passion that can fester in
swollen hearts eating its evil way to their core in silence, what an incipient Hell
was breeding here!" (88). The signs that Hawk, and Verisopht, and Mantalini
will come to no good are abundant. Eventually, the reader will be able to say to
the characters what Mrs. Mantalini does when she puts her husband on an allowance: "'You have brought this on yourself'" (430). Mantalini has much further
to fall after he receives this rebuke, however, and his last appearance in the novel
is an apt one, as we shall see.

In *Nicholas Nickleby* Dickens allows his wicked and foolish characters to accumulate a burden of evil and folly that will crush them in the end. This is true of
much of the early writing and remains true, to some degree, throughout Dickens'
career. The relentless piling up of incident upon incident of malice, profligacy,
and imprudence, punctuated by warning signs of what the consequences must be,
creates the intense expectation that all of this evil and folly *must* be corrected.
And, true to the melodramatic form, Dickens does see to it that evil and folly

collapse before virtue. But unlike much melodrama, they collapse primarily by their own weight or by the treachery of other villains and fools, not as a result of the aggressive actions of the good characters. The increasing moral debt of such characters as Gride, Hawk, and Mantalini, in their different registers, is aptly figured in their bankruptcy, insolvency, or other monetary loss.

Elsewhere I have written that in many Dickens novels evil and objectionable characters dominate the fictional space for the greater part of the novel, but gradually their sources of power, generally external to themselves, begin to fail, whereas the upwelling of benevolence and good will in the virtuous characters gives them a force that not only sustains them as they are elbowed toward the margins, but which gradually permits them to retake narrative space until they exclude the worst types altogether.[11] In the previous chapter I quoted Peter Brooks' description of a similar pattern evident in melodrama. In both arrangements virtue passively endures until villainy is defeated by external powers, or defeats itself. In melodrama there is no strong prohibition to a hero's actively opposing the villain and helping to bring about the villain's downfall. In Dickens' novels there is such a prohibition, but Nicholas Nickleby offers us a partial exception to this rule. Nicholas does strike Sir Mulberry Hawk, for example, and he actively counterplots against Ralph and his associates. Moreover, Nicholas and Kate, the epitomes of virtue in *Nickleby,* are scarcely silent. Both denounce Ralph and both issue warnings. After the debacle at Dotheboys Hall, when Nicholas understands what fate Ralph had intended for him, he confronts his uncle, declaring that he will "keep strict account" of Ralph's doings: "'There will be a day of reckoning sooner or later, and it will be a heavy one for you if they [Mrs. Nickleby and Kate] are wronged'" (254). Ralph later recalls this warning and anticipates such a reckoning with the expectation that he will have a far superior stock of power. But at the climactic moment, when Nicholas and Kate save Madeline from Ralph and Gride, Nicholas once more speaks in apocalyptic terms: "'Look to yourself, and heed this warning that I give you!'" he says to Ralph. "'Day is past in your case, and night is coming on'" (720). He then delivers the stunning news about Ralph's lost ten thousand pounds. The reckoning is moral, though forcefully embodied in the loss of actual cash. The discourses of morality and money are closely intertwined throughout the novel, as we have seen, and thus even a final accounting must have its material manifestation.

Kate is not entirely passive. Plagued by Sir Mulberry Hawk's humiliating attentions, and provoked to an uncharacteristically excited state, she tells him, "'If no regard for my sex or helpless situation will induce you to desist from this coarse and unmanly persecution . . . I have a brother who will resent it dearly, one day'" (354–55). Kate's words are prophetic, for it will be Nicholas who later effectively ends that persecution and initiates the actions that lead to Hawk's decline. Kate denounces Ralph for his treatment of her; Nicholas' letter to the same purpose sounds almost like a curse. It concludes, "You are an old man, and I leave you to the grave. May every recollection of your life cling to your false heart, and cast their darkness on your death-bed" (425). This is strong stuff for a virtuous character in a Dickens novel.

In fact, Nicholas is one of the most physically aggressive of Dickens' good characters, though he is clearly a model of kind-heartedness as well. Chesterton explained this aggressiveness by describing *Nickleby* as a romance, thereby requiring three essential characters: St. George, the Dragon, and the Princess. Romance narrative also requires that the hero both love and fight.[12] Thus *Nickleby* goes as far as Dickens will allow in having a virtuous character actually administer some degree of punishment. Though driven to forceful action, Nicholas is fundamentally mild and loving. In his misery at Dotheboys Hall, he thinks primarily of his mother and sister. His charitable nature is evident in his protection of Smike. And yet he constantly employs force to correct a situation. Although he can control his impulse to punish Squeers for insulting him, Nicholas will not allow Squeers to punish Smike unjustly. Nicholas has begged Squeers to forgive Smike for his attempted escape from tyranny and pain (another ironic reversal of how the Christian virtues are supposed to work), but Squeers is determined to harm the boy. When Nicholas warns him, "' I have a long series of insults to avenge . . . and my indignation is aggravated by the dastardly cruelties practised on helpless infancy,'" Squeers responds by striking Nicholas with his cane, which the young man promptly seizes, beating the schoolmaster viciously in his turn (155). Squeers, so given to violence as a corrective measure, endures a similar violence himself. This is very satisfying to our sense of justice if we suspend the notion that good Christians are not supposed to employ violence. John Browdie, a positive character with whom we surely are to sympathize, goes so far as to congratulate Nicholas on his physical correction of the schoolmaster.

Nicholas has recourse to violence again when he corrects the actor Lenville's impudence and, most strikingly, when he responds to Hawk's blow with a whip, again using his attacker's instrument to beat him in turn and inadvertently causing Hawk's carriage to smash. Even in incidental matters Nicholas favors violent means of checking impudence, as when he feels inclined to smack Tom, the employment office clerk, for his crude admiration of Madeline Bray. The narrator's tone here is playful, but significant, since it prefigures two later scenes.

> Nicholas looked at the ugly clerk, as if he had a mind to reward his admiration of the young lady by beating the ledger about his ears, but he refrained, and strode haughtily out of the office; setting at defiance, in his indignation, those ancient laws of chivalry, which not only made it proper and lawful for all good knights to hear the praise of the ladies to whom they were devoted, but rendered it incumbent upon them to roam about the world, and knock on the head all such matter-of-fact and unpoetical characters, as declined to exalt, above all the earth, damsels whom they had never chanced to look upon or hear of—as if that were any excuse! (189–90)

This scene is comic because Nicholas himself as yet knows nothing about the handsome young woman he feels impelled to defend and therefore has no right to that office. That Nicholas' violent impulse is not endorsed by the narrative is made clear in the comic suggestion that he fails to adhere to the medieval law of chivalry that promotes violent behavior as a curative for most social differences. Dickens considered the medieval period a barbaric and benighted episode in human history. The narrator thus intimates that Nicholas does the right thing in this instance by suppressing his anger. The same is not true later when Nicholas confronts Sir Mulberry Hawk. This incident makes clear that when Nicholas' impulse to take action is endorsed by the narrative it is because he is taking action *for others* and not for himself. Nicholas wrangles with Hawk because the latter bandies Kate's name about in a disrespectful manner. Nicholas and John Browdie come to the physical aid of Frank Cheeryble, who is threatened by a crowd after he has struck Tom, the clerk who insulted Madeline, in order to defend Madeline's good name. If, in a comic scene, the narrator makes fun of medieval chivalry and commends Nicholas' restraint, when a serious incident occurs, the narrator seems to approve a modern version of the chivalric code.

Though capable of restraining himself, Nicholas gives way several times to violence in his attempts to establish justice. Physical punishment is part of his equipment for dealing with wickedness. When charged by Ralph with assault against Squeers, Nicholas replies, " 'I inflicted such punishment upon a wretch as he will not readily forget, though far less than he deserved from me' " (251). When Smike is concerned about Nicholas' downcast mood, Nicholas explains that he has an enemy who " 'is rich, and not so easily punished as *your* old enemy, Mr. Squeers. He is my uncle, but he is a villain, and has done me wrong' " (375). And when Smike has been liberated a second time from Squeers, Nicholas meditates "on a great variety of schemes for the punishment of the Yorkshire schoolmaster, all of which had their foundation in the strictest principles of retributive justice, and had but the one drawback of being wholly impracticable" (513).

Nicholas is a typical hero of romance in yearning to chastize the wicked. When Fielding's Joseph Andrews admits that, rather than forgive those who have robbed and beaten him, he would like to give them a taste of the same medicine, he is responding as most young men might. However, that is not the high Christian line, as Joseph is instructed by a pompous parson.[13] But if Nicholas is less Christian than he should be in dealing with his enemies, he is also very young. We are told several times that he has "a sufficient share of headlong rashness and precipitation (qualities not altogether unnatural at his time of life) . . ." (447). He has much to learn about the best ways of dealing with life, and the Cheeryble brothers will be good models to him. Dickens knew what he was doing with Nicholas and meant that he should be imperfect. He is not, like Oliver Twist, the principle of innocence surviving in a corrupt world; he is a more-or-less realistic young man. In his preface to the novel, Dickens writes, "If Nicholas be not always found to be blameless or agreeable, he is not always intended to appear so. He is a young man of an impetuous temper and of little or no experience; and I saw no reason why such a hero should be lifted out of nature" (xix). Dickens was to portray imperfect heroes again: Martin Chuzzlewit is more greatly flawed than Nicholas, as is Pip. One sign of Nicholas' immaturity is his readiness to use physical violence to achieve justice. Much as he may gratify our (and Dickens') sense of justice (and perhaps sadism) by pummeling wicked people, he is wrong to do so. The correct pattern is set forth by the Cheeryble brothers. When Charles Cheeryble calls upon Ralph to say that he has an important piece of information to impart, he tells Ralph that his visit is "in mercy to you" (767). He is less interested in making Ralph squirm than in sparing him pain. The Cheerybles tell Ralph that justice must take its course against the parties who plotted against Smike. "It is not in my power, or the power of my brother Ned, to save you from the consequences. The utmost we can do, is, to warn you in time, and to give you an opportunity of escaping them. We would not have an old man like you disgraced and punished by your near relation; nor would we have him forget, like you, all ties of blood and nature" (778). This is the orthodox line and Dickens feels compelled to include it. Ralph, of course, remains defiant and unrepentant. In the end, Nicholas will not be the instrument of Ralph's collapse; Ralph's own overreaching and the treachery of his confederates will bring him down, and he will accomplish the final "punishing" himself.

Revenge and punishment are closely linked in this novel. Nicholas says he has his own and the boys' injuries to "avenge" when he beats Squeers. He has been sorely provoked and believes that he is doing a just thing, but there is a tincture of vengeance in much of his thinking about punishment, as there is not in the Cheerybles. Nicholas is also sensitive about his proper pride and is a moderate version of the extreme forms of vanity all around him. A central instance of this extreme vanity, which highlights the essentially benign vanity of Nicholas, is Sir Mulberry Hawk. Hawk's interest in Kate is associated with his self-image. Presumably pursuing her for Lord Verisopht, he is intent upon "using his utmost arts to reduce her pride, and revenge himself for her contempt" (333). Appropriately it is Nicholas' family pride and concern for his sister that brings about the encounter that ends with Hawk's injury. When Ralph calls upon the invalid baronet he goads Hawk by saying how grieved he is that a relative of his "should have inflicted such punishment" on him. "'Punishment!'" Hawk immediately interrupts, touched to the quick. But Ralph continues to provoke Hawk, hoping to fire the nobleman to bloody revenge (491–92).

There is a good deal of spite and revenge in *Nicholas Nickleby*. Sometimes it is comic, as when the dishonored Mr. Lillyvick disinherits his faithless wife and revises his will in favor of the Kenwigs children. Though he says he does so "not out of revenge and spite against her, for she is below it," it is clear that he is motivated by precisely these feelings (690). But vengeance is a dangerous tool and can turn in the avenger's hand. Thus Hawk's scheme of revenge leads him to killing Lord Verisopht, exile in Europe, and eventual death in a debtor's prison.

Peg Sliderskew is another example. Out of spite and revenge against her employer, Gride, whom she rightly suspects of wanting to dismiss her when he marries, she steals documents he values but cannot pursue her for, because he wants to keep their contents secret. It is a fitting revenge upon Gride, but the theft brings justice upon Sliderskew too, not from Gride, but from Frank Cheeryble and Newman Noggs, who want the details about Madeline's fortune contained in the stolen documents. Sliderskew and Squeers, who is a confederate in Ralph's attempt to acquire the document out of revenge against Nicholas, are transported for their crimes. Meanwhile, back at Dotheboys Hall, the boys erupt in a vengeful rebellion and give the Squeers family a literal taste of their own medicine, until John Browdie intervenes to prevent anything serious from happening.

Nicholas Nickleby, though he is the protagonist of the novel, is not its moral center. In fact, he is much in need of moral instruction and that is the function of the Cheeryble brothers, as I have already indicated. Nicholas has a warm and kindly heart, but he is also proud and rash. He must learn to foster those kindly sentiments and to check the impulsive ones. This necessity makes Nicholas increasingly passive as the narrative continues.[14] While the narrative is increasingly giving itself over to the punishment of offenders and fools, Nicholas is learning not to enact revenge or retribution on his own account. If revenge is not directly tied to many of the punishments handed out in the closing chapters of *Nicholas Nickleby,* some form of retribution is stressed in almost all of them. Mr. Mantalini ends up living in a basement, the minion of a low washerwoman. Nicholas and Kate come upon him by chance, and the fallen monster of vanity, humiliated, tries to hide in a bed. "'Demmit,' he cried, in a suffocating voice, 'it's little Nickleby! Shut the door, put out the candle, turn me up in the bedstead! Oh, dem, dem, dem!'" (821). Nothing could be more fitting than to see the vain lady-killer in such a humiliating posture of submission, the slave of a coarse woman who has paid two pound fourteen for him, taking him out of prison to live with her "'like a gentleman'" (821). Mantalini has literally made his bed and must now lie in it. This is a trivial instance of retribution, but there are more awesome examples, most significantly Brooker's revelation that Ralph is Smike's father. "'I have been made,'" he says, "'the instrument of working out this dreadful retribution upon the head of a man who, in the hot pursuit of his bad ends, has persecuted and hunted down his own child to death'" (789). Ralph completes this retribution in a moment of "frenzy, hatred, and despair" (806).[15]

There is much revenge, spite, and punishment in this novel, and the generous sentiments of love, family affection, and charity abound, but there are few signs of forgiveness. Nicholas decidedly does not forgive Ralph; nor does Kate. The emphasis in this moral world is negative, stressing how a hating and vengeful nature will naturally bring upon itself a fitting retribution. At the book's end, evil has wrought its own demise, and charity prevails. The narrative is less concerned with encouraging forgiveness than with extirpating evil by "natural causes," using poetic justice and providential retribution as the main avenues of correction and foolish, weak, or evil individuals as the agents. The novel's narrative method is comparably straightforward. Adventures occur episodically and are not as tightly interrelated thematically and narratively as they will be in later novels. As in melodrama, the wicked seem to hold the upper hand and control the plotlines through much of the novel, but gradually the good characters assume control and resist the machinations that ultimately rebound upon their rivals. An interesting passage at the very end of the novel reveals to what degree the narrative is itself an agent of moral justice. We are past the major instances of punishment and reward and have come to the requisite accounting of minor characters, before concluding with the eventual fortunes of the good characters. The narrator explains that Arthur Gride managed to elude justice concerning unlawful possession of the will that named Madeline heir to a small fortune, but only "to undergo a worse punishment; for, some years afterwards, his house was broken open in the night by robbers, tempted by the rumours of his great wealth, and he was found murdered in his bed" (830). That this death is described as a punishment is extremely revealing, since such a fate for an old man rumored to be wealthy might have happened to virtuous or wicked alike. But so saturated are we—and the narrator—with how and why Gride and others like him acquired their wealth, that we immediately associate this consequence of that wealth as a form of retribution for an ill-spent life. In declaring this death a punishment, the narrator (perhaps unwittingly) indicates how narratives can be as slippery in designating consequences as can any other means of interpreting providence. Characters in nineteenth-century fiction often read providence as they like, making it suit their prejudices.[16] No one should claim to know the ends of providence. Yet it is human weakness to read just such purposes into events. If in life one might call the ruin of a rich but evil man providential, then in fictional narratives a character who deserves punishment and suffers may be seen as the object of providential retribution. The difference is that in fiction providence, in the form of an implied author, can reveal its intent. But just as we may attribute to providence the fall of a rich but evil man, so may our narratives give accounts of fictional characters who are obviously deserving of punishment but who are seen to be punished only because of that desert. The narrative itself becomes judge, jury, and executioner, and claims providential power to prove that "the good in this state of existence preponderates over the bad, let mis-called philosophers tell us what they will" (65).

NOTES

1. For John Lucas it is "the theme of lives sacrificed to financial interest which gives *Nicholas Nickleby* such coherence as it has" (*The Melancholy Man: A Study of Dickens's Novels* [London: Methuen and Co., Ltd., 1970]), 62.

2. Charles Dickens, *The Life and Adventures of Nicholas Nickleby* (London: Oxford University Press, 1960).

3. Grahame Smith's *Dickens, Money, and Society* (Berkeley: The University of California Press, 1968) treats this subject in a straightforward manner, but does not explore the metaphorically moral dimension that was always so present to Dickens' imagination.

4. Alfred Lord Tennyson, *The Poems of Tennyson*, 3 vols, ed. Christopher Ricks (London: Longman, 1987), 2:164.

5. Quoted in a biographical sketch of Massey by Samuel Smiles introducing *The Poetical Works of Gerald Massey* (London: Routledge, Warne, and Routledge, 1864), xi.

6. J. Hillis Miller concludes that theatricality so pervades the novel "that the central action of *Nicholas Nickleby* is the elaborate performance of a cheap melodrama, complete with sneering villains, insulted virginity, and a courageous young hero who appears in the nick of time" (*Charles Dickens: The World of His Novels* [Cambridge: Harvard University Press, 1965], 90).

7. See William F. Axton's *Circle of Fire: Dickens' Vision and Style and the Popular Victorian Theatre* (Lexington: University of Kentucky Press, 1956), Earle Davis'- *The Flint and the Flame: The Artistry of Charles Dickens* (Columbia: The University of Missouri Press, 1963), and Robert Garis' *The Dickens Theatre: A Reassessment of the Novels* (Oxford: Oxford University Press, 1965).

8. Peter Brooks, *The Melodramatic Imagination: Balzac, Henry James, Melodrama, and the Mode of Excess* (New York: Columbia University Press, 1985), 4. Subsequent references appear in the text. George Worth has devoted a book-length study to the subject in *Dickensian Melodrama: A Reading of the Novels* (Lawrence: The University of Kansas Press, 1978).

9. A number of studies have examined Dickens' use of the Bible in this way. Two that take rather different approaches are Bert G. Hornback's *Noah's Arkitecture: A Study of Dickens' Mythology* (Athens: Ohio University Press, 1972) and Janet Larson's *Dickens and the Broken Scripture* (Athens: The University of Georgia Press, 1985).

10. Ralph's suicide in the very room where his son spent his early years resembles Dorian Gray's death by his own hand in the room at the top of his house intimately associated with his childhood.

11. John R. Reed, "Confinement and Character in Dickens' Novels," *Dickens Studies Annual* 1 (Carbondale: Southern Illinois University Press, 1970, 41–54).

12. G. K. Chesterton, *Appreciations and Criticisms of the Works of Charles Dickens* (London: J. M. Dent and Sons, Ltd, 1911), 26ff. John Carey remarks that "Nicholas Nickleby is the first of the heroes to exercise his virtuous muscles on evildoers" (*Here Comes Dickens: The Imagination of a Novelist* [New York: Schocken Books, 1974], 28–29).

13. Henry Fielding, *Joseph Andrews with Shamela and Related Writings*, ed. Homer Goldberg (New York: W. W. Norton and Co., 1987), 47–48.

14. Steven Marcus comments that the Cheeryble brothers represent the traditional Christian view about the obligations of wealth but that like most philanthropists of the time they contributed relief without cure. Marcus finds these models of magnanimity unconvincing. However, they may be unconvincing because they *are* models. It is only through their unbelievable generosity, Marcus notes, that Nicholas can be passive. (*Dickens: From Pickwick to Dombey* [New York: Basic Books, Inc., 1965], 113, 123) Marcus does not allow that the nature of the Cheeryble actions is what is important, not their credibility, and that Nicholas' passivity in the pursuit of wickedness must gradually be converted into similar acts of charity.

15. Peter Garrett points out that the secrets in *Oliver Twist* and *Nicholas Nickleby* and the mystery plots involving them work out differently in the two novels. The mystery plot provides salvation in *Twist* and retribution in *Nickleby*. (*The Victorian Multiplot Novel: Studies in Dialogical Form* [New Haven: Yale University Press, 1980], 53)

16. See Thomas Vargish's *The Providential Aesthetic in Victorian Fiction* (Charlottesville: University Press of Virginia, 1985) and John R. Reed's *Victorian Will* (Athens: Ohio University Press, 1989).

SEVEN

The Old Curiosity Shop

THE OLD CURIOSITY SHOP is one of Dickens' least complex presentations of the punishment/forgiveness pattern, a pattern that is not always central to any given text, though it is implicit in all of Dickens' narratives. Evil must be punished and forgiveness remain the highest virtue, usually as represented in a character who is an orthodox Christian.[1] *The Old Curiosity Shop* is far more concerned with justice and injustice than with the working out of elaborate patterns of punishment and forgiveness. The rudimentary equation underlies this story but is not so prominent as in many other Dickens novels, perhaps because this story is so like a fable that it does not require elaboration of the punishment/forgiveness paradigm, already an entrenched characteristic of the fable tradition. Moreover, the clear emphasis in this novel on innocence, kindness, self-sacrifice, and endurance under suffering tends to dilute the clear opposition between punishment and forgiveness, just as the prominence of hatred and revenge in *Barnaby Rudge* intensifies that opposition.[2]

An important passage demonstrating the role of injustice in this novel occurs soon after Kit is arrested on the Brasses' charge that he has stolen money from them. Although certain of his innocence, Kit nonetheless suffers agonies of shame under the mere suspicion of guilt. The narrator fastens on this singular response. "Let moralists and philosophers say what they may," he comments, "it is very questionable whether a guilty man would have felt half as much misery that night, as Kit did, being innocent." Since the world is accustomed to injustices, it assumes that a clear conscience will be proof against unjust suffering. But, the narrator adds, "the world would do well to reflect, that injustice is in itself, to every generous and properly constituted mind, an injury, of all others the most insufferable, the most torturing and the most hard to bear; and that many clear consciences have gone to their account elsewhere, and many sound hearts have broken, because of this very reason; the knowledge of their own de-

serts only aggravating their sufferings, and rendering them the less endurable."[3]
Moreover, true innocence may be put at a disadvantage by injustice, as is Kit
when he makes an unprepossessing appearance before the court to plead his innocence, having been shaken by confinement, anxiety, and the novel setting of the
courtroom with all of its intimidating apparatus. In any case, consciences are peculiar entities. When Mrs. Quilp has been forced to extract information from
Nell for her husband, she is disquieted by her action. The narrator remarks that
in the majority of such cases, people are not troubled for long because "conscience is an elastic and very flexible article, which will bear a deal of stretching
and adapt itself to a great variety of circumstances. Some people by prudent
management and leaving it off piece by piece, like a flannel waistcoat in warm
weather, even contrive, in time, to dispense with it altogether; but there be others who can assume the garment and throw it off at pleasure; and this, being the
greatest and most convenient improvement, is the one most in vogue" (52). In
other early novels from *Pickwick* and *Oliver Twist* to *Barnaby Rudge* and *Martin
Chuzzlewit,* Dickens is at pains to disclose the vestiges of conscience, no matter
how misshapen, in the worst of his villains, but in *The Old Curiosity Shop* he seems
more inclined to demonstrate how the lack of conscience results in teratological
developments in the soul that are correspondingly manifested in the flesh. Quilp
is a monstrous grotesque illustrating this process.

The good people in this novel are frequently at a disadvantage precisely because they do have clean consciences and are therefore unable to penetrate the
wickedness so alien to them in the minds of others. Nell is the outstanding example. There is very little of forgiveness as a narrative or moral strategy in *The Old
Curiosity Shop* because the character most authorized to forgive does not survive
to dispense that grace. Before forgiveness may be exercised, a ground of virtue
must be established—a raw material of Christian potential. Against the confused
and corrupt world of adult misconduct in this novel, children stand out as the
locus of that raw virtue in a way impossible to imagine in *Oliver Twist,* where
vice permeates all ages alike. But *The Old Curiosity Shop* insists upon essential
trust in an untainted humanity locatable only in childhood and preservable only
through the memory of that childhood. This is the significance both of Kit's devotion to Nell's memory and of Dick Swiveller's transformation of the Marchioness. In this novel more than any other Dickens stresses the spiritual influence of
the powerless not through any act of charity or forgiveness, but by their very
existence. Hence the story of the schoolboy who dies young provides Nell with
the moral that those who survive should be grateful for being spared to do good;
the narrator adds that by dying young these creatures go early to heaven and are
spared the agony of losing those they love. This lesson is amplified later by the
schoolmaster when he says, "'There is nothing . . . no, nothing innocent or
good, that dies, and is forgotten.'" All have influenced others for good by their
example. "'Forgotten! oh, if the good deeds of human creatures could be traced
to their source, how beautiful would even death appear; for how much charity,

mercy, and purified affection, would be seen to have their growth in dusty graves!' " (406). And later, after Nell herself has died, the narrator assures us that for every innocent youth that dies, "a hundred virtues rise, in shapes of mercy, charity, and love, to walk the world, and bless it" (544).

When the brother of Nell's grandfather describes Nell as one in a line of women in the family serving as "the Good Angel of the race—abiding by them in all reverses—redeeming all their sins," he is talking about the Good Angel of a particular family, but the model is immediately applicable to the entire human race (524). And Nell is certainly the Good Angel and custodian of her wayward grandfather as well as the Good Angel and ideal for Kit Nubbles, who, influenced by her example, aspires to a life worthy of her approval. The novel ends with Kit passing on to his children, the next generation of youth who should in their turn be the repositories of virtue, the story of how Miss Nell died and went to heaven, as they will do if they are equally successful in remaining uncorrupted by the world. Implicit here is the romantic assumption that virtue is intrinsic to humanity, and is therefore most abundantly present in childhood and is lost gradually as the individual is exposed to the polluting and wasting influences of the world.

Since Nell is such a model and ideal, it does not signify if she dies at the end of the narrative, no matter how vigorously Dickens' readers protested against this conclusion. Dickens was determined to show that happy endings are not those in which characters marry and inherit fortunes, but those in which moral balance is restored. To make this point realistically, he had to include a few rudimentary truths. Nells die in this world.[4] The innocent might not be saved and rewarded in this world. The schoolmaster who has lost his favorite young scholar summarizes this crucial point at the end of the chapter describing Nell's death. " 'It is not,' said the schoolmaster, as he bent down to kiss her on the cheek, and gave his tears free vent, 'it is not on earth that Heaven's justice ends. Think what earth is, compared with the World to which her young spirit has winged its early flight; and say, if one deliberate wish expressed in solemn terms above this bed could call her back to life, which of us would utter it!' " (539).[5]

Dickens always requires some touchstone character who can be wholly trusted, whether an Oliver Twist, a Little Nell, a Tom Pinch, a Little Dorrit or a Joe Gargery. Each novel has one such character, but that character may function differently in each. Almost all of these characters are childlike in some way, but Oliver and Nell are genuinely children. The one survives evil to spread his goodness abroad in this world—though we are not interested in a detailed history of his adult life. The other endures evil, unscathed in spirit, but worn out in this world. She leaves her essence to be valued when she is gone. Dickens said of Oliver that he represented the principle of good persevering in evil surroundings. He saw Nell as the original narrator imagines her "in her future life, holding her solitary way among a crowd of wild grotesque companions; the only pure, fresh, youthful object in the throng" (13).[6]

Oliver is almost entirely passive in his goodness, being required more to resist evil than to precipitate good. Nell, on the other hand, must take on a positive, directive role. She bears the heavy burden of superintending her impaired and untrustworthy grandfather while realizing that she is the innocent occasion of his gambling mania, since he gambles not out of selfishness, but for the virtuous purpose of winning sufficient money to make her safe from care. When Nell shares her history with the kindly schoolmaster, he is astonished at how "'this child heroically persevered under all doubts and dangers, struggled with poverty and suffering, upheld and sustained by strong affection and the consciousness of rectitude alone!'" (344). Thanks to him, Nell finds security and makes the church her iconic setting—a tranquil place where nothing evil enters. Through her sufferings she has learned not to fear death. "With failing strength and heightening resolution, there had sprung up a purified and altered mind; there had grown in her bosom blessed thoughts and hopes, which are the portion of few but the weak and drooping" (388). Like a good Christian, she is resigned. Only once is this paragon asked to forgive, and that is by her grandfather at the outset of their troubles when she first learns that they are to be cast out of their home and become wanderers. In many ways it is good that Nell is never called upon for the obligatory late scenes of forgiveness that so characterize Victorian fiction, for much would have to change in this narrative if such scenes were to be made viable. The central narrative is a simple one of flight and pursuit. Nell is hounded into greater and greater purity until she comes to rest in the precinct of peace. Her reward will be a release from the soiling and spoiling world of matter. In her part of the narrative there are few of those partially good characters, who, after wicked or mistaken courses, repent and sue for forgiveness. In short, despite her harrowing experiences, Nell actually has little truck with the world. By contrast, Quilp, her extreme opposite, is precisely a man of the world, of matter, of materiality. He is a moral as well as a physical grotesque so maimed spiritually that he cannot help punishing himself on the way to harming others. He is a vehement exponent of hatred and revenge—sentiments diametrically opposed to Christ's message of love and forgiveness. Accordingly, the narrative leads him remorselessly toward self-punishment and self-induced destruction.

Nell is the model of all Christian virtue and Quilp the embodiment of impulsive, even irrational evil. Almost as soon as he is introduced he exhibits his cruelty in the most revered venue Dickens could think of—the home. As a punishment for gossiping with some women friends, Quilp makes his wife sit up all night long. When day breaks, she is still "sitting patiently on her chair, raising her eyes at intervals in mute appeal to the compassion and clemency of her lord, and gently reminding him by an occasional cough that she was still unpardoned and that her penance had been of long duration" (38). Quilp is sharply inscribed as an unforgiving beast, glorying instead in vengefulness. He pretends to be Dick Swiveller's friend, promising to help him win Nell as a wife, but behind Dick's back the dwarf exults "in the prospect of the rich field of enjoyment and reprisal

it opened to him" (173). Quilp develops animosities quickly. He takes an immediate dislike to Kit Nubbles and eventually engineers his arrest. Watching Kit
being led off charged as a thief, Quilp taunts him with a variation on Kit's earlier
insult to the dwarf. " 'Kit a thief! Kit a thief! Ha ha ha! Why, he's an uglier-
looking thief than can be seen anywhere for a penny' " (447). His glee in revenge
is so violent it terrifies the coachman who is transporting Kit. Quilp's treatment
of his hired boy, Tom Scott, is a mild variation on his punitive methods, though,
because there is an understanding between boy and master, these episodes are for
Quilp more in the nature of exercises than determined actions.

Quilp so delights in giving pain that he is willing to endure discomfort himself
to hurt others. He treats his confederates in this manner, making Sampson Brass
drink scalding liquor with him, for example, or making both of the Brasses sit
out with him in foul weather while they plot against Kit. Quilp is not a calculating "man of business" like Ralph Nickleby. Although one of his driving motives
is to make money, that aim always seems secondary to plain nastiness of spirit.
He thinks that he could get the single gentleman into his net too if it weren't for
Kit and his mother. The thought of their hindering him makes him rage: " 'I hate
your virtuous people . . . ah! I hate 'em every one!' " The narrator steps in to
confirm that this was not merely a vaunt but Quilp's real sentiment, "for Mr.
Quilp, who loved nobody, had by little and little come to hate everybody nearly
or remotely connected with his ruined client. . . . Above and beyond that
general feeling of opposition to them, which would have been inseparable from
his ravenous desire to enrich himself by these altered circumstances, Daniel
Quilp hated them every one" (360–61).

Dickens makes no attempt to analyze Quilp's character. There is no penetration of his mind and feelings as there is with, say, Jonas Chuzzlewit. But some of
his actions indicate that he is inherently self-destructive and that much of his
spite and animosity is generated by a clear view of his own despicable appearance and character. Thus he is intensely jealous of his wife, who was persuaded
to marry him for financial security. Also, he determines to pay back anyone who
makes derogatory comments about his dwarfish appearance. Many of Quilp's activities put him in physical peril, though he seems to care nothing at all for such
dangers as long as he can terrify and intimidate others. But all of this violent
feeling and acting hints at a nature that will dash itself to pieces. Quilp's own
idiosyncratic gestures of potential self-harm are reflected in his confederates,
who mirror many of his traits, a doubling that intensifies the heavily redundant
representation of Quilp's self-destructive leanings. Thus when the good characters set about unraveling Quilp's plot against Kit, they decide to influence Sally
Brass to incriminate Quilp. But, as Kit foresees, she is enough like Quilp in her
grotesqueness and impenetrability not to yield to their intimidations. One recalls
at such a moment that even when she and her brother were obliged to sit in the
rain to learn of Quilp's designs against Kit, Sally, uncomfortable herself, could
nonetheless take pleasure in Sampson's sufferings. After all, it is Sampson, Quilp's

weaker reflection, who gives way, and even then imitates his mentor by voluntarily betraying Quilp before the dwarf can do the same to him. Sampson gives
testimony against Quilp and then adds, "'Punish Quilp, gentlemen. Weigh heavily upon him. Grind him down. Tread him under foot. He has done as much by
me, for many and many a day'" (498–99). Brass' zeal shows that he wants not
justice but revenge, thus running true to Quilpish form. Like Quilp himself,
Brass is unconcerned with any institutional justice that may be served, being interested only in paying back those who have offended him. Unlike Quilp, he has
been too cowardly to do so until now, when he sees an advantage for himself as
well as potential satisfaction for an old injury. In *The Old Curiosity Shop,* as in
Oliver Twist, there is no honor among thieves. Those who live according to a
"code" of personal selfishness, hatred, and vindictiveness will dish their accomplices when it serves their turn to do so.

From this point of view Quilp has clearly generated his own fate. Can one
consistently treat one's tools contemptuously without anticipating some reaction? Even Tom Scott's little rebellions could have taught Quilp that other sub-
ordinates might eventually resent and resist his abuse. But it is precisely this
careless hazard of his own future that characterizes Quilp's brand of evil. He is
both shrewd and heedless, but the heedlessness tells and finally he, who has
hounded others mercilessly, finds himself the hounded one. Like so many of
Dickens' villains, he is hunted down. The narrator pauses to deliver a stagey announcement of the poetic justice provided by this reversal.

> And now, indeed, it seemed that Quilp's malignant career was
> drawing to a close, and that retribution, which often travels slowly—
> especially when heaviest—had tracked his footsteps with a sure and
> certain scent and was gaining on him fast. Unmindful of her stealthy
> tread, her victim holds his course in fancied triumph. Still at his heels
> she comes, and once afoot, is never turned aside! (501)

The language of punishment, subtler in later novels, is overt here, revealing the
moral foundation upon which the narrative rests. Punishment is essential, but in
the fashion already rapidly becoming characteristic of Dickens' fiction Quilp is
not incarcerated or otherwise officially punished for his crime. Instead, having
been warned by Sally that he is sought, he takes flight in the foggy night, falls
into the Thames, and is drowned. "The general supposition was that he had
committed suicide, and, this appearing to be favoured by all the circumstances of
his death, the verdict was to that effect. He was left to be buried with a stake
through his heart in the centre of four lonely roads" (549). The narrator reflects
that this sentence might not have been carried out, or, if it was, that Quilp's
remains were removed elsewhere. Nonetheless the judgment is narratively fitting because, although we as readers know that Quilp struggled to live and did

not voluntarily die, we also know that he was fundamentally self-destructive and that the course of his life so directly led to the kind of end he met that, morally, he was a species of suicide. Evil, the message goes, consumes itself.

Quilp is the most profound representative of evil in this story, but there are others who also require severe punishment, notably the Brasses and Fred Trent. The Brasses are presented as repulsive from the start, both physically and morally, and in their function as agents of Quilp they are clearly tainted by his evil. At first they appear relatively innocuous and comic, greedy but relatively harmless vermin. But Sally Brass' tyrannical conduct toward the Marchioness hints at greater registers of cruelty, culminating in the scheme to imprison and even transport Kit Nubbles. Conniving becomes plotting, which in turn leads to criminal action—planting evidence and perjury. Quilp, being an embodiment of evil, must be removed from the stage altogether. Pure evil cannot continue to inhabit the fictional world in which the principle of good has become triumphant. But agents through whom evil is enacted—figures like the Brasses—remain a potential threat in human existence. Human weakness is always in danger of yielding to temptation. Thus Sampson is punished with imprisonment, after which he and his sister are left to wander at the dim horizon of social existence among the "archways, dark vaults and cellars" of the city, creeping out into the streets only at night, "the embodied spirits of Disease, and Vice, and Famine" (549). Their narrative punishment consists of being transformed into the spoiled fruit of their own evil handiwork. Like fairy tale creatures they become what they have caused to be. The narrative that has embodied them and located them in the liminal moral world between the law as an institution and the lawlessness of their behavior now strips away all false supports, to let them plunge into the liminal underworld where they embody Sin. The punishment is both retributive and exemplary. As human actors they suffer the appropriate destiny they have made for themselves; as iconic types they warn those who follow the narrative to loathe their actions and not to repeat their transgressions.

The Brasses' punishment is logically related to all that has preceded. Gradually their increasing wickedness has become evident to the reader until retribution becomes necessary. This retribution is a degree beneath the extermination that Quilp suffers, but is nonetheless severe, and just as patently necessary. The dealing out of authorial justice at the end of the narrative also includes, however, an apparently insignificant detail, which nonetheless illuminates the moral armature for Dickens' story.

> The gamblers, Isaac List and Jowl, with their trusty confederate Mr. James Groves of unimpeachable memory, pursued their course with varying success, until the failure of a spirited enterprise in the way of their profession, dispersed them in various directions, and caused their career to receive a sudden check from the long and strong

arm of the law. This defeat had its origin in the untoward detection of
a new associate—young Frederick Trent—who thus became the unconscious instrument of their punishment and his own. (553)

A reader might first wonder what narrative purpose is served by recording the
fates of these minor characters in the summary chapter, and why they should be
coupled with young Trent. But in fact their guilt is closely linked to the central
progress of the story. Trent is an important reason that Nell's grandfather wants
to accumulate money for her security. He unwisely tries to do this by the short-
cut of gambling, an avocation to which he is entirely unsuited. At the lowest
point of Nell's adventure on the road, her grandfather steals from her to gamble
with List and his associates. More menacingly, they encourage the old man to
steal from Mrs. Jarley. Overhearing this advice to her grandfather, Nell loses no
time in resuming their flight. By driving the weary child into additional exposure and suffering, the gamblers thus have seriously contributed to her eventual
death. It is for this offense against Nell that they must be punished, not for the
violations of the law nominally reported. Similarly, it is appropriate that Fred
Trent, who was partly the occasion of Nell's trying pilgrimage, should be the
instrument of his own and the gamblers' undoing. "Punishment" is the word the
narrator uses, and these are, in fact, narrative punishments necessary for clarify-
ing the moral economy of the narrative as a whole, not simply for satisfying a
readerly curiosity about the eventual fates of minor characters. Trent is punished
not for breaking the law but for offending the innocent virtue represented in
Little Nell. These punishments are not circumstantial, but metaphysical. Not as
decidedly evil as Quilp and the Brasses, these characters nonetheless have chosen
the dark side of the Manichean struggle between good and evil. At the most elementary level of the narrative, they have accumulated a moral debt by gambling
with their heavenly reward. All of this punishment must be explicit in order to
make evident the justice that governs the universe, if not the affairs of men.

If there is no significant forgiveness at the end of this novel to balance the
checklist of punishments, there is something related—the dispensation of charity
or reward. Thus the brother of Nell's grandfather seeks out all who helped the
child in order to reward them for their kindness. Kit prospers, marries, and becomes the repository of Nell's memory. But perhaps the most intriguing instance
is that of Dick Swiveller.[7] Throughout the novel Dick appears as a careless
young man eager for money to support a desultory and dissipated life. He is amusing and lively and therefore attractive, but he lacks the character to earn money
through serious work. Being undisciplined and incautious, he is therefore dangerous in the hands of people like Quilp, Trent, and the Brasses. Midway through
the narrative, Dick, in debt and impoverished, finds himself established by Quilp
as a clerk to Sampson and Sally Brass. He regards this employment as a form of
punishment, a humiliating transformation. Disgusted to be the clerk to a "female
Dragon," Dick moodily ponders his case. "'Very good, very good! What shall I

be next? Shall I be a convict in a felt hat and a grey sit, trotting about a dockyard with my number neatly embroidered on my uniform, and the order of the garter on my leg, restrained from chafing my ankle by a twisted belcher handkerchief? Shall I be that? Will that do, or is it too genteel? Whatever you please, have it your own way, of course' " (253). Dick might almost be addressing himself to the narrator, since he is alone when he says this, but the narrator himself supposes that Dick is apostrophizing "his fate or destiny." In any case, Dick feels the shame of his altered condition, but does not admit responsibility for it; instead, he blames fortune. " 'Under an accumulation of staggerers, no man can be considered a free agent. No man knocks himself down; if his destiny knocks him down, his destiny must pick him up again. Then I'm very glad that mine has brought all this upon itself, and I shall be as careless as I can, and make myself quite at home to spite it' " (254). The narrator explains the utility of Dick's state of mind: by "throwing the responsibility of this and all other acts and deeds thereafter to be done by him, upon his unlucky destiny, [he] was quite resigned and comfortable: fully prepared for the worst, and philosophically indifferent to the best" (260).

Significantly, however, it is just when he is at the low point of his fortunes that Dick encounters someone far more miserable than himself—the diminutive serving girl working for the Brasses whom he later names the Marchioness. His growing attention to and kindness toward her creates a parallel mini-narrative that reflects Nell's career. As Nell comes to a quiet retreat under the care of the schoolmaster and others, the Marchioness gradually liberates herself from virtual slavery, thanks partly to Dick's interest. Eventually she escapes altogether from the Brasses to tend Dick on his sickbed. As Nell is sinking into the grave, the Marchioness is rising out of her dungeon. As Nell is transformed into an angel, the Marchioness is transformed into an educated young woman. And just as Nell's unselfish example makes others more conscious of the world's need of the virtues she represents, so Dick Swiveller achieves a purpose in life by securing a proper upbringing for the Marchioness even at the expense of his own comfort. His reward for this generosity is to win the charmingly altered young woman as his wife.

Dick has known the Marchioness only a short while when he is moved to meditation upon the poor creature's condition, ignorant of her own name and origin and unacquainted with any of the good things of life. He wonders, " 'can these things be her destiny, or has some unknown person started an opposition to the decrees of fate? It is a most inscrutable and unmitigated staggerer!' " (432). For someone who has been content to locate the responsibility for his own circumstances in destiny instead of his own conduct, the Marchioness' case opens the way to a new worldview incorporating a belief that, to some degree, individuals may shape their own fates and those of others. Gradually that is what Dick and the Marchioness do, and through sympathy and self-respect they establish an increasingly effective countercurrent to Quilp's selfish and malign directing of his own fate and his manipulation of the fates of others. As the narrative sweeps rapidly toward its close, Dick plays out a role often reserved for Dickens' central characters. Like Oliver Twist, Martin Chuzzlewit, Pip, and Arthur Clennam, to name a few prominent examples, Dick falls into an illness which functions as a moral passage.[8] He recovers to a life in which correct moral choices are easier to recognize. Having run Dick through this surrogate hero's pattern, the narrator offers him a narrative forgiveness. In this sense the illness might be considered a mild instance of therapeutic punishment. Dick has been unwise, profligate, and idle. But he is decent at the core and has suffered an appropriate humiliation and hardship for his misdeeds. He will not, very likely, be a very productive member of society on his annuity of £150 a year, but he has learned to care for others beyond himself and this is enough for him to be forgiven and rewarded.

The last instance of the narrator's charity to one of his characters requires that we address, if only briefly, the oddities of narration in this text. The history of this novel is familiar. It began as part of *Master Humphrey's Clock,* but soon absorbed the whole content of that venture. The narrating character who opens the tale with remarks about his night walks in the city to speculate on the nature and occupation of the people he sees does not last out the narrative. He claims to be removing himself from the narrative for dramatic purposes.

> And now, that I have carried this history so far in my own character and introduced these personages to the reader, I shall for the convenience of the narrative detach myself from its further course, and leave those who have prominent and necessary parts in it to speak and act for themselves. (28)

This is a remarkably awkward narrative move, given the care with which the narrating figure has been constructed and brought into immediate contact with some of the principal characters. The old narrator is clearly a moral man with great sympathy for his fellow creatures. He encounters young Nell on the street at night and escorts her home, noting that children come to us "fresh from God" (4). When he meets Nell's grandfather, he gently chides the old man for letting the young girl out alone in the dangerous city. He is present when young Trent badgers his grandfather and when Quilp arrives to lend him money. He becomes a familiar presence at the Old Curiosity Shop before suddenly declaring his withdrawal from the narrative. But that cannot be so blithely done, for he has made himself not merely the teller of the tale but an actor in it as well. What we have been led to consider our chief means of focalization in the text is suddenly withdrawn in favor of the supposedly unmediated performances of the characters. Of course, the characters do not speak and act for themselves but are made present to us through a new narrative voice more removed and privileged than the original first-person narrator, one who knows much more than do any of the characters whose experiences he relates. Moreover, this new narrator conveys their actions and speeches through the medium of his own interpretations. His metaphors and allusions, not the projected images of his characters, dramatize the scenes he presents. It was not to eliminate narrative mediation that the old gentlemanly narrator had to go, but to correct a flaw in the moral machinery of the tale. If the genial old narrator were to remain a character, he would be obliged, kindly fellow that he is, to interfere in some way to assist Nell and her grandfather. Since he is a man of keen intuition and judgment, he would be expected to act as a counterweight to Quilp. It is essential to the moral configuration of the narrative, however, that an accumulating weight of suffering be heaped upon Nell before she achieves peace and then death. Since she must flee from comfort into hardship, no kindly and trustworthy old man can be available from the outset to make available shelter and protection. The original narrator's potential role is filled near the end of the narrative by the brother of Nell's grandfather, also known as the single gentleman, but by then evil has played out its role and Nell is about to find her peace in heaven.

The narrator is extremely conscious of how necessary it is to present his story in balanced segments. We cannot relentlessly pursue Nell in her flight. To begin with, it would soon become wearing and perhaps even dull reading without some variation upon her adventures. Her pilgrimage is the thread and Quilp is the motivating nemesis, but there must be other agencies at work as well. Thus when Nell has reached a resting point with Mrs. Jarley, the narrator abandons her for a new and more menacing locale.

> As the course of this tale requires that we should become acquainted, somewhere hereabouts, with a few particulars connected with the domestic economy of Mr. Sampson Brass, and as a more convenient place than the present is not likely to occur for that purpose, the historian takes the friendly reader by the hand, and springing with him into the air, and cleaving the same at a greater rate than ever Don Cleophas Leandro Perez Zambullo and his familiar travelled through that pleasant region in company, alights with him upon the pavement of Bevis Marks. (244)

This is clearly not the voice of our original narrator, nor is it the voice of a sympathetic fellow character concerned about Nell's plight. It is the voice of a stage manager or magician who is concerned with the mechanism of his art, not the content. It is also implicitly the voice of a moral manager who must have a freedom not available to any of his characters to map out the trajectory of good and evil in his tale. Hence also the need to alternate scenes of Nell's physical trials and moral triumphs with those exhibiting greed, malice, and worse. Richard Maxwell keenly notes the change in the narrative. By the time the single gentleman is galvanizing the search for Nell, "It is no longer the energetic dwarf who seems to be pressing Nell toward her death; it is Humphrey and his style of allegorical narration."[9] It may be this change in narrative tone and strategy that has led many readers to identify the lively single gentleman with the narrator of the tale, even to the degree that he is supposed to be Master Humphrey, the original first-person narrator.[10]

The narrator must superintend the opposition of good and evil characters in the story, resulting in an alternation of episodes different in kind from those between Nell's journey and the wicked conspirators who have occasioned her flight. Nell represents an ideal perhaps impossible to preserve in this world. Thus her perfection, like that of the little scholar, does not survive long in it. But less perfect good people must not only survive but prevail, and hence the narrator must establish a subliminal contest between such good people and the consciously deviant. The Nubbles household opposes those of Quilp and the Brasses; so does the Garland household. At the climactic moment in the tale, when the single gentleman makes it known that he is searching for little Nell, the narrative swings away from Nell's story, as the controlling narrator openly exhibits his power to transfer our attention to Kit Nubbles' comfortable position in the happy household economy of the Garland family. The narrator can do this, he says, because "it happens at this juncture, not only that we have breathing time to follow his fortunes, but that the necessities of these adventures so adapt themselves to our ease and inclination as to call upon us imperatively to pursue the track we most desire to take." (281). The narrator has become a tease. He is clearly in control of the tale he is constructing for us and only plays at the fictions of "breathing time" and "necessities." He has already likened himself to a magical figure, and at the end of the novel he will repeat that motif. "The magic reel, which, rolling on before, has led the chronicler thus far, now slackens in its pace, and stops. It lies before the goal; the pursuit is at an end" (547). As he approaches the story's end, however, the narrator wishes to diminish his role as magical impresario of the fable we have witnessed, and he demotes himself to the mere chronicler of a magic reel already inscribed. Dickens probably had in mind the popular panoramic shows of his day where images rolled past viewers on a large sheet of fabric (or the miniature version with its small scroll in a closed portable box) to present the events of some historical or dramatic event.[11] In claiming to be such a chronicler the narrator makes himself redundant, since the spectator should be able to interpret the panorama without his help. At best he might be a commentator upon the scene as it passes. But the word "pursuit" gives away the narrator's true impulse. He is hunting down his objects of punishment. He will detail them to the very end of the text. Dickens has his narrrator play down his part in shaping the narrative because its moral arrangment must seem unforced. The superintending agency of the narrator must yield to providence and to the self-engendered consequences of human behavior. Quilp brings on his own demise. Nell earns heaven and leaves a seedbed of virtues on earth. But despite his attempt to disguise the narrator's role in assorting punishment and favor, Dickens cannot refrain from having his narrator run out a list of additional punishments and at least one forgiveness, as we have seen with Dick Swiveller, as though it is absolutely necessary that the ledger of good and evil be balanced at the end and a line be scored beneath the double entry.

This compulsion for moral closure may seem a narrative crudity, but given what Dickens is trying to achieve with the moral economy of his novel, such narrative strategies are fitting. The narrator cannot allow the kindly original narrator to continue his office because he could have intervened with help at the outset to forestall Nell's pilgrimage through the world of suffering to peaceful death. Nor would this narrator have been an appropriate voice to present the bizarre actions of Quilp and oddities of Swiveller and the Brasses. A less morally committed narrative voice was needed for that—the magical voice with its special effects of personification, metaphor, simile, allusion, and so forth. At the end of the narrative this second narrative voice must also give way to a somewhat different narrator who combines the virtues of the two preceding narrative voices, still employing a lively, conceit-loaded style, but bending that style to the purposes of punishment and forgiveness. When all the justice available has been doled out, the narrator himself erases the boundary between life and fiction with the concluding line of the novel. "Such are the changes which a few years bring about, and so do things pass away, like a tale that is told!" (555). With that line this tale is told and the narrator evaporates because the distribution of justice is complete. There is no other reason to end this tale here, just as in life there is no reason to draw a boundary between one moment and the next. We draw these boundaries when some deep expectation is met, when some need is gratified. It is not merely the death of Nell or her grandfather that makes this stage of the life journey an appropriate one at which to pause. After all, Kit, Dick, and the single gentleman live on, as their compressed proleptic histories indicate. The narrative ends here because the antagonistic forces of good and evil that it has generated have been brought back to a state of justice through the apportioning of punishment and charity. And so it is with this and every other novel that Dickens completed.

NOTES

1. Dennis Walder points out that in *The Old Curiosity Shop* Dickens does not explicitly provide support for a belief in Christ as mediator and redeemer, nor does he promote an explicit religious belief, nor is he sympathetic to the formal elements of Christianity (*Dickens and Religion* [London: George Allen and Unwin, 1981], 76). But all of Dickens' moral sentiments clearly coincided with basic Christian principles.

2. John Forster said of this novel, "I am not acquainted with any story in the language more adapted to strengthen in the heart what most needs help and encouragement, to sustain kindly and innocent impulses, to awaken everywhere

the sleeping germs of good" (*The Life of Charles Dickens* [London: Chapman and Hall, 1893], 93–94). Subsequent references in the text.

3. Charles Dickens, *The Old Curiosity Shop* (London: Oxford University Press, 1967), 453. Subsequent references in the text.

4. John Forster saw the artistic need for Nell's death and took credit for that feature of the narrative. "I was responsible for its tragic ending. He had not thought of killing her, when, about half-way through, I asked him to consider whether it did not necessarily belong even to his own conception, after taking so mere a child through such a tragedy of sorrow, to lift her also out of the common-place of ordinary happy endings, so that the gentle pure little figure and form should never change to the fancy. All that I meant he seized at once, and never turned aside from it again" (93).

5. Explicit as this assertion of death's positive qualities may be in the text, it is necessary to remember that the narrative is here treating a *blessed* death, not endorsing death outright. James R. Kincaid is right to note the complex character of death in this novel. "Death is seen both as a victory and as an escape from the pain which somehow comes from seeing others attain that victory. Dickens's ambivalence towards death neutralizes any meaning. The ambivalence is understandable, of course, but it does tend to weaken the novel by dissolving many of its ironies" (*Dickens and the Rhetoric of Laughter* [New York: Oxford University Press, 1971], 79). Subsequent references in the text.

6. Master Humphrey's vision of Nell is like her creator's. Dickens said, "I had it always in my fancy to surround the lonely figure of the child with grotesque and wild, but not impossible, companions, and to gather about her innocent face and pure intentions, associates as strange and uncongenial as the grim objects that are about her bed when her history is first foreshadowed" (xii).

7. Dick Swiveller has often been singled out as one of the most important characters in the novel. Gabriel Pearson ranked him with Quilp and Nell as one of the three instrumental forces in the novel (*"The Old Curiosity Shop," in Dickens and the Twentieth Century,* ed. John Gross and Gabriel Pearson [Toronto: University of Toronto Press, 1962], 77–90). James R. Kincaid treats him as the chief example of human regeneration influenced by Nell's behavior (99ff.). Garrett Stewart locates Dick at "the emotional hub of *The Old Curiosity Shop,*" a redemptive figure who is able to build a refuge in the imagination (*Dickens and the Trials of the Imagination* [Cambridge: Harvard University Press, 1974], 89), and Monica L. Feinberg carries this notion further in "Reading *Curiosity:* Does Dick's Shop Deliver?" *Dickens Quarterly* 7, no. 1 (March 1990), 200–11, by regarding Dick as a comic entertainer, who, like Dickens himself, becomes a good citizen through the agency of fiction.

8. See John R. Reed's *Victorian Conventions* (Athens: Ohio University Press, 1975), 14ff. for the conventional use of illness in Victorian literature. James R. Kincaid writes that "though Dick does become something of a classic hero, his illness is more than an archetypal purging; it is a symbolic rehearsal of death, a real brush with non-existence" (103).

9. Richard Maxwell, *The Mysteries of Paris and London* (Charlottesville: University Press of Virginia, 1992), 117.

10. The single gentleman reveals himself as the brother of Nell's grandfather but is also commonly identified with Master Humphrey. The text, however, suggests that he cannot be the latter because that narrator had become acquainted with the grandfather, whereas the single gentleman distinctly says that he is now seeing his older brother for the first time in many years when they meet over Nell's dead body. Moreover, Master Humphrey gives the impression of having lived a long while in London, whereas the single gentleman appears to be a new arrival. Whatever attempt Dickens might have made to equate the two men, neither the narrative manner nor the details of their careers permits that equation.

11. Richard Altick describes several different kinds of these devices in *The Shows of London* (Cambridge: The Belknap Press of Harvard University Press, 1978).

EIGHT

Barnaby Rudge

IF *NICHOLAS NICKLEBY* exhibits a preponderance of negative emotions and sentiments, *Barnaby Rudge* tilts even more to the violent and unseemly side of human behavior, while at the same time extending the mainly individual cruelty of *Nickleby* and *The Old Curiosity Shop* into the community as a whole. There is very little of forgiveness, mercy, or compassion in this novel, which rather seems designed as an encyclopedia of abuses against the human spirit, with special emphasis upon the passions of hatred and revenge.[1] Mostly the book examines acts of treachery, rebellion, and cruelty, and most of what passes for Christian spirit is false or a mockery. K. J. Fielding sees the novel as an expression of Dickens' own frustration. "Strongly as Dickens believed in authority and hated disorder," Fielding writes, "he was often exasperatedly rebellious. *Barnaby Rudge* spoke to his own times in urging that society itself was responsible for its ills."[2] He adds that "*Barnaby Rudge* is not unlike Dickens's other historical novel, *A Tale of Two Cities,* in using melodrama to image forces that he would have found it hard to analyse" (78).

The historical context of the novel concentrates on the Protestant Cause's detestation of Catholicism, but Dickens offers little ideological analysis of Lord George Gordon's position because difference in belief is less important to him than the paradigmatic prejudice the Protestant Cause represents. That it is not a good, just, or humane attitude is made manifest by its association with a weak-minded lord, the traitorous Gashford, and its many scummy supporters who have only general rage, private revenge, personal gratification, or all of the above at heart. The true Christian spirit is conspicuous here by its absence, having been supplanted by false Christianity. This approach is far different from Dickens' usual presentation of moral values, which is to reiterate, through numerous reflective examples, the central Christian doctrines of love, forgiveness, and charity as manifested in some principal model. By contrast, *Barnaby Rudge* is a dissertation

122

on the absence of Christian principles in the lives of almost all the characters of this book. Only Gabriel Varden, Mrs. Rudge, and perhaps Emma Haredale, signify the genuine pattern for human behavior. Very likely Dickens stressed the violent and cruel traits of human nature in *Barnaby Rudge* because it was set in an earlier period of English history which he viewed as markedly less satisfactory than his own imperfect time. As we have already seen in chapter 3, institutions and individuals in the eighteenth century were not squeamish about their means of achieving either justice or their political and personal ends. The Bloody Code that made so many felonies capital offenses was still warm in memory and hanging was still a common punishment in 1841 when Dickens wrote this novel.[3]

Barnaby Rudge is the titular figure of this novel not because he is its chief character, but because he embodies the contradiction of the society he inhabits. John Forster felt that in Barnaby Dickens intended "to show what sources of comfort there might be, for the patient and cheerful heart, in even the worst of all human afflictions," but Barnaby clearly reveals much more than that, for, in his simplicity, he is implicated in the vicious doings of the riot (108). The figurative language of the novel makes abundantly clear that the society of *Barnaby Rudge* is a society gone mad. A few examples from the beginning of the narrative should suffice to make the point. Rudge senior in disguise speeds toward London "with the fervour of a madman" (17). Encountering Rudge on the night road, Varden suspects him to be a madman (21). On a windy evening, a wig or a hat goes spinning past Varden on the street "like a mad thing" (40). This goes on until we get to the maniacal crowd, and to various inanimate objects imaged as insane. The current of this madness is indicated early and often by such little hints as the description of the sign above the door of the low tavern where the 'Prentice Knights meet, which pictures a rude effigy of a bottle swinging to and fro "like some gibbeted malefactor" (60). This crazed community will doctor itself by letting blood; brutish "insanity" will goad itself on to its own retributive end.

This feature of the novel has been recognized and needs no additional exposition, but it is important to stress the mixed nature of the society it depicts.[4] Tradition can be good or evil. It is evil in Mr. Chester, perniciously indolent in John Willet, and nurturing in Gabriel Varden. Innovation in the name of tradition is generally evil. Lord George Gordon's plea is to cleanse England of Catholicism, though, of course, Catholicism preceded Protestantism on the island. Sim Tappertit and his cronies call for a restitution of ancient rights, and want a revolution to gain them. Everywhere there is confusion about what is wisely established and what is merely entrenched, what is to be preserved and what is to be revived.[5] Perhaps the most notorious example of this confusion is Dennis the hangman, who wants to preserve his role of hangman with all of its traditional benefits by engaging in a revolution against the very system that sustains the need for hangmen.

Barnaby is the embodiment of these confusions. He is clearly a sweet soul who values the natural world and natural affections and who exhibits an exceptional fear of blood and violence. But Barnaby's good instincts are easily corrupted; thus Stagg can prompt him to desire the gold he would use for his mother's comfort at the very time that she is warning him about the dangers of gold. Despite his mildness, Barnaby plays a prominent role in the rebellion/riot that he does not truly comprehend. He is a compound of goodness, charity, and patriotism all corrupted and perverted to evil ends. In this manner he stands for the entire milieu of the novel.

All of this madness and error is like a maelstrom circulating around a central void—the unpunished murders that occurred years before at the Warren, Mr. Haredale's house. Although the reader does not immediately understand the narrative significance of the novel's opening chapters, in fact they are crammed with violence leading back to that central offense, thus early concentrating attention upon a private crime and raising the theme of fraternal conflict, since it is supposed that Reuben Haredale was murdered by his brother, Geoffrey, though there is no evidence to prove his guilt. The second chapter describes a potentially murderous encounter between Varden and the disguised Rudge, who is supposed dead, a gardener's dead body having been taken for his corpse. Chapter 3 presents the discovery of Ned Chester, wounded by Rudge. Chester is in love with Emma Haredale, whose father, we later learn, Rudge murdered. This concentration of violence and unpunished transgression in the opening pages of the novel creates an intense pressure toward retribution in the narrative to come, a pressure that is both supported and mocked by images of a bound energy that is ultimately released publically in the Gordon Riots.[6] Once the theme of murder and violence is clearly identified with Rudge, the action swings away for a while to investigate the subversion in Gabriel Varden's household, a microcosm of the disorder brewing in the larger community. But even while Varden is occupied with his personal difficulties, his awareness of the mysterious stranger (Rudge) and his connection with Barnaby and his mother keeps the central and enabling crime of the narrative present to the reader. Moreover, the subplot involving Ned Chester, his father, Mr. John Chester, Emma Haredale, and her father keeps the theme of the haunted Warren alive in the context not of crime, but of prohibition and generational conflict through the antagonism between Mr. Chester and Haredale, who oppose the union of their children.

At the center of the novel, then, and anchored in its past, is the abominable crime of a servant murdering his master out of greed and ambition. Having murdered his master and a fellow servant, Rudge tells his wife of his crime and thereby loses all of the values that wife and home represent. He is immediately an outcast for his sin and the effect upon his wife and son is perpetual suffering for the one and madness for the other. Rudge's crime goes unpunished by the law and remains a mystery. Indeed, injustice rather than justice seems to prevail, since the innocent Barnaby and his mother suffer for Rudge's act and the inno-

cent Geoffrey Haredale is never entirely free from suspicion, a condition that
blights his life. In reality, however, God's justice has been active all along. When
we first see Rudge he resembles a "hunted phantom" (17). Later, we learn that
since the moment of his crime he has been haunted by his deed, though he has
remained unrepentant. He is a kind of Flying Dutchman or Wandering Jew, tormented without the present hope of forgiveness and without the impulse to repent. He explains his condition to his wife.

> 'Hear me,' he replied, menacing her with his hand. 'I, that in the
> form of a man live the life of a hunted beast! that in the body am a
> spirit, a ghost upon the earth, a thing from which all creatures shrink,
> save those curst beings of another world, who will not leave me;—I
> am, in my desperation of this night, past all fear but that of the hell in
> which I exist from day to day.'

His wife, who should loathe him, is too fine a spirit—in the Dickensian scheme
of things—to give him up to justice. She cannot initiate punishment against him.
Instead she prays, "'Remove this man from me, good Heaven! . . . In thy
grace and mercy, give him one minute's penitence, and strike him dead!'" (129).
It would be a quick and merciful end—penitence and then death before any
backsliding can occur.

Rudge is a walking emblem of retributive justice executed upon oneself. Just
as his son represents the moral confusions of his society, Rudge senior represents
the incorporation of God's justice. He feels like a hunted beast, but though humans may be trying to hunt him down, the real hunting/haunting is done by his
own mind—or else by spirits, if we interpret the above passage literally. Rudge is
a variation on the Bill Sikes model. Present at the Maypole when the rioters are
attacking the Warren, he hears the warning bell ring, the same bell that rang the
night of his crime, and convulsively re-experiences his crime, tormented by the
sound of the bell. "He sank upon the ground, and grovelling down as if he would
dig himself a place to hide in, covered his face and ears; but no, no, no,—a
hundred walls and roofs of brass would not shut out that bell, for in it spoke the
wrathful voice of God, and from that voice, the whole wide universe could not
afford a refuge!" (420). In prison Rudge declares that he involuntarily revisited
the neighborhood of the Warren, being "chased and driven there, by him [Reuben
Haredale] and Fate. Because I was urged to go there, by something stronger than
my own will" (471–72).[7] Stagg, with whom he is speaking, says he supposes that
Rudge is now resigned and penitent, but Rudge replies that he has striven and
wrestled with the power that forced him to return. "'Has my whole life, for
eight-and-twenty years, been one perpetual struggle and resistance, and do you
think I want to lie down and die? Do all men shrink from death—I most of all!'"
(475). Rudge has responded particularly to the issue of being resigned, which he
is not. He has neglected the question of penitence, but he is not repentant either.

In fact, ~~it is precisely~~ his struggle against repentance that has made his life a hell. Repentance would presumably have brought him peace.

Rudge is obviously capable of feeling guilt. He has a conscience in spite of himself, but he has not made the proper use of it. Just as pain and suffering may be healthy reminders of our mortal condition, and stimuli to virtue, so a sensitive conscience should provoke repentance. But Rudge's false position is stressed by a secondary manifestation of his bad conscience, showing that part of his sin is his preoccupation with himself. When he hears the mob moving through Newgate, he is so engrossed with his own position as a hunted felon now trapped and unable to escape that he supposes the rioters are coming for him and suffers an agony of fearful expectation. "Thus fearful alike, of those within the prison and of those without; of noise and silence; light and darkness; of being released, and being left there to die; he was so tortured and tormented, that nothing man has ever done to man in the horrible caprice of power and cruelty, exceeds his self-inflicted punishment" (497).

Later, when Barnaby has learned who his father is, Mrs. Rudge acknowledges his vileness but instructs her son, " 'if we could win him back to penitence, we should be bound to love him yet' " (562). As we have seen in chapter 1, this is one traditional method of insisting upon the Christian principle of forgiveness. The truly repentant must be recuperated to the position they held before committing their offense. True repentance erases all. It would have been difficult, however, for Dickens to recuperate the dreadful Rudge narratively. Instead, the narrative pointedly introduces a scene immediately after Barnaby's meeting with his mother in which Mrs. Rudge has an opportunity to plead with her husband to repent, considering all the terrible accumulating consequences of his initial crime, which includes the condemnation of his son to death. But Rudge responds, " 'Begone! I curse the hour that I was born, the man I slew, and all the living world!' " (565). Rudge enlists himself among such sincere haters of mankind as Quilp, and thus releases us to despise him and glory in his punishment. He has done it to himself. At the same time, the implied author has acted like the God of the Old Testament who hardened the hearts of those he intended to punish, thereby confirming them in their faults and guaranteeing their punishment.

Part of the reason the world of *Barnaby Rudge* is so deficient in true Christian sentiment is that Dickens viewed the eighteenth century, the time in which its action is set, as a particularly inhumane period. The injustice, the recourse to violent and degrading forms of punishment, the arrogance of class and privilege are all prominent and have been sufficiently explained elsewhere not to require review here. But it may be argued, in a perversion of a post-structuralist trope, that the absence of true Christianity makes its presence all the more present. It is the otherness of eighteenth-century society that Dickens chooses to focus upon. Of course Christianity is not entirely absent; it shines through the miasma of terror and madness in the characters of Mrs. Rudge and Gabriel Varden. Yet such an unchristian age does not come about by accident. Dickens certainly believed that circumstances form human character, but entertained as well a corollary belief that human beings can alter circumstances. Unfortunately, the human capacity to transform the conditions of existence works both for good and for evil. And, in *Barnaby Rudge,* those with the greatest power and authority to effect change do not employ that power and authority fruitfully. In this book, the chief spokespersons for the ruling order of the eighteenth century are not pleasant figures. Lord George Gordon is the opposite of what a nobleman should be. He is a weak-minded fanatic, appealing out of vanity and confusion to the rabble, which he misreads. Haredale has distanced himself from social action, brooding on his private injuries and nursing ill will in his heart. Time and again he is characterized by his leaning toward passionate action. Mister Chester, later Sir John, is thoroughly cynical and self-absorbed, quite willing to exploit and injure others to secure his own gratifications. Gashford, a sort of gear moving between the fated wheels of Gordon, Haredale, and Chester, combines the worst traits of all these individuals. He is a cynical and selfish deceiver like Chester, an exploiter of the people like Gordon—as well as an exploiter of Gordon himself—and, like Haredale, he is unforgiving. Dennis admires Gashford and proposes a toast to this man of whom the hangman has heard it said "that he'd a surprising memory and wonderful firmness—that he never forgot, and never forgave" (338). In short, Gashford is the concentrated antithesis of Christian feeling.

Revenge is a prominent craving in many of these figures. Haredale wants to avenge his brother's death and has been stymied for many years. His life has been spoiled by his "gloomy thirst for retribution" (583). Chester, Hugh, and Gashford seek their various revenges against Haredale. And Gordon (benignly) and his followers (dishonestly) want revenge against the Catholics. Retribution dominates social and personal sentiment as a means of dealing with opposition. Even off-stage characters emphasize this theme. Hugh's mother purposely had him brought up in ignorance so that he would not imbibe any notions of gentleness and forgiveness, trusting that the god of her tribe would bring Hugh and his father together for her and her son's revenge.

Associated with this spirit of retribution and revenge is a more general disregard for human life. Hugh is a simple example, openly declaring his contempt for mankind. One of his formulations epitomizes his attitude: "'I'd sooner kill a man than a dog any day'" (160). Gashford also despises his fellow men, and Dennis values human life only to the degree that it should be preserved until he can take it away. Mr. Chester is the most subtle example of these haters of humankind. The narrator intrudes to instruct his readers on the nature of this grim misanthropy.

> The despisers of mankind—apart from the mere fools and mimics, of that creed—are of two sorts. They who believe their merit neglected and unappreciated, make up one class; they who receive adulation and flattery, knowing their own worthlessness, compose the other. Be sure that the coldest-hearted misanthropes are ever of this last order. (183)

The coldest-hearted in this book is Mr. Chester, as remote from the vehement, haunted Rudge with his bad conscience as he is from Haredale, who passionately believes in justice and wants it served. "The thoughts of worldly men," the narrator says, "are for ever regulated by a moral law of gravitation, which, like the physical one, holds them down to earth." They find no sign or pleasure in the wonders of the heavens. "They are like some wise men, who, learning to know each planet by its Latin name, have quite forgotten such small heavenly constellations as Charity, Forbearance, Universal Love, and Mercy" (217). But worldly and cynical as they are, they still may play the role of honesty to themselves.

> Men who are thoroughly false and hollow, seldom try to hide those vices from themselves; and yet in the very act of avowing them, they lay claim to the virtues they feign most to despise. 'For,' say they, 'this is honesty, this is truth. All mankind are like us, but they have not the candour to avow it.' The more they affect to deny the existence of any sincerity in the world, the more they would be thought to possess it in its boldest shape; and this is an unconscious compliment to Truth on the part of these philosophers, which will turn the laugh against them to the Day of Judgment. (174)

False as they are, such men cannot abandon the virtues that are important to all of mankind, though they may misunderstand those virtues. Laying claim to what they define as truth, they miss the Truth that makes their grotesque perversion evident. "So do the shadows of our own desires stand between us and our better angels, and thus their brightness is eclipsed" (217). Few persons in this novel can see past the shadows of their own desires; few can read the signs left everywhere about them to be interpreted. As in most of Dickens' texts, these signs are clear to the reader, at least in retrospect. But they are at the same time indications, even monitions to the reader, that he or she should not commit the errors of blindness into which the novel's characters fall. The narrative permits us to see into the hearts and minds of these characters so that we may register their folly and benefit from it. There would be no advantage in suppressing this information or revealing it only late in the narrative, for one great purpose of the narrative is to keep this foolish blindness constantly evident to the reader. There is little value in examining this practice in detail, but a few examples will serve the purpose.

Let me concentrate upon Mr. Chester and Haredale. When the two men are closeted together at the Maypole, the lounging habitués speculate that the meeting may end in a duel and "one of those stains upon the floor that never come out" (88). A stain of this sort that marks the scene of murder at the Warren symbolizes guilt. In fact, the meeting between Mr. Chester and Mr. Haredale, though not amicable, is cooperative because they both desire to prevent a marriage between Edward Chester and Emma Haredale. Although the meeting does not result in a duel between these hostile men, metaphors used to enhance the scene prefigure what will come to pass. Haredale remarks that he would not "enter the lists to combat with gentle compliments and masked faces" against one so accomplished in such arts as Chester, admitting that he is "not his match at such weapons" (91). After their conference, Mr. Chester repairs to "a great old spectral bedstead" whose ornaments have grown "hearse-like and funereal," while Mr. Haredale returns to his "ghost of a house" (96, 102). The analeptic and proleptic suggestions of haunting transgressions and foreseeable fatality permeate the episode and contribute to the accumulating force of guilt and moral debt. Just as there is a moral law that holds worldly men to the earth like gravity, so there is a moral law that will see justice done. Thus a ghostly power will eventually draw both men to the ruined Warren, where the suspended duel will take place and expiation be made. Such are the signs to the reader of a destiny preparing for these two men. The reader must interpret the signs and recognize their place in the moral economy of the novel. By way of instruction on how this may be done, the narrator provides an embedded sample case—Hugh's premonitory dream, in which he imagines himself about to be hanged. Hugh may not understand his dream, but readers certainly should, having been assisted throughout the text with numerous references to hanging as symbolically, if not actually, the ultimate punishment for trespass.

There is yet another suppressed text that we must interpret to fully comprehend the workings out of justice in this novel. In the significant interview between Chester and Haredale, Chester expresses his nihilistic view against Haredale's overcharged set of values.

> "The world is a lively place enough, in which we must accommodate ourselves to circumstances, sail with the stream as glibly as we can, be content to take froth for substance, the surface for the depth, the counterfeit for the real coin. I wonder no philosopher has ever established that our globe itself is hollow. It should be, if Nature is consistent in her works." (91)

From this point on Chester is consistently represented as false and hollow. He takes a seat in parliament to baulk his creditors, whereas men without such protection must go to jail for their debts. When he is knighted his honors are not for any contribution to society, but for his manners. Chester is false coin. Far from possessing any innate nobility, he is a hollow man who employs the basest tools for his purposes—the likes of Gashford and Hugh. Hugh is an interesting case because he is the bestial figure who will lead the mob that burns down the Warren, a gratifying event for Mr. Chester. Dickens was always interested in the covert relationships between gentility and crime—most obviously and extensively in *Great Expectations*—and that interest surfaces in *Barnaby Rudge* through the complex relationship between Mr. Chester, Hugh, and Hugh's mother. Near the end of the novel, Varden recounts the story of Hugh's mother to Mr. Chester: "'She had been tempted by want—as so many people are—into the easy crime of passing forged notes'" (578). She was caught in the first commission of her crime and she died for it. Having exploited her sexually, Chester seems to have done so criminally as well for his own pleasure and profit. The connection between actual counterfeiting and Chester's earlier use of the metaphor of counterfeiting illuminates an actual criminal texture underlying the moral texture that has long been evident in the narrative. Chester stands for the corrupted values of his time and his order in a manner later to be explored more subtly in *Great Expectations*. On the one hand, Pip's specious gentility is made possible through Magwitch's recovery from crime. On the other, Compeyson's appearance of gentility unjustly spares him the full burden of his crime. Compeyson receives a light sentence because he is a gentleman, Magwitch a heavy sentence because he is unconnected and poor. *Barnaby Rudge* suggests that Chester, now knighted and an MP representing the honor and order of the state, has been a pernicious subverter of the social order. Like Dennis, rioting in defiance of the government to preserve his function as hangman, Chester is circulating the false coin of his apparent worth which is all the while debasing the very institutions he is thought to sustain.

In condemning the "false coin" circulated by Lord Gordon and Gashford, the narrator pauses to explain that, in politics, an air of mystery appealing to the curiosity of the multitudes lends false priests, prophets, doctors, and patriots a temporary advantage over truth and common sense. That is because "Curiosity is, and has been from the creation of the world, a master-passion. To awaken it, to gratify it by slight degrees, and yet leave something always in suspense, is to establish the surest hold that can be had, in wrong, on the unthinking portion of mankind" (277). But if it can be effective to use mystery and curiosity in this way for evil purposes, it can be equally effective to employ the same devices for good—as in the spinning out of a narrative. It is precisely through the building up of several interlocking mysteries, some of which are evident (the secret of Dennis' "trade"), some of which are partially veiled (Hugh's background), some of which are long obscured (Rudge's identity), that the narrator keeps his narrative moving forward. At the same time, many discordant clues are distributed along the way so that, while some elements of the interlocking mysteries are revealed, others are made darker. There are no dramatic unveilings here—no Boffin shown to be his old good self, no Magwitch presenting himself to Pip. There are only the gradual unpeelings of the onion of mystery.

Appropriately, it is a mysterious power—providence, fate, or implied author, depending upon your affiliations—that draws Chester and Haredale back to the Warren, the focus of crime and retribution in the novel, where the imperfect Haredale will execute justice upon the vile and guilty Chester, thus satisfying the accumulated desire for his punishment that it has been the purpose of the narrative to create. Haredale becomes the instrument or agent of retribution even though he recognizes beforehand the error of his earlier preoccupation with retribution. With Rudge in the hands of justice, Haredale no longer seems to have an object for his revenge, yet the dynamics of the narrative itself have left the hunger for retribution unsatisfied. Rudge's punishment is ongoing throughout the novel; thus the unrepentant and arrogant Chester gradually supplants him as the true target for punishment. Haredale's swollen passion expends itself appropriately (for the narrative) upon this loathsome creature. But that is because Haredale himself is not a good man. He has lived in error and now, having served as the instrument of God, fate, and the implied author, he must suffer for his own violence. The means, predictably, is self-punishment. Immediately after killing Chester, Haredale retreats "straight to a religious establishment, known throughout Europe for the rigour and severity of its discipline, and for the merciless penitence it exacted from those who sought its shelter as a refuge from the world, he took the vows which thenceforth shut him out from nature and its kind, and after a few remorseful years was buried in its gloomy cloisters" (628).

It would be possible to examine in great detail the operations of guilt and retribution in *Barnaby Rudge,* but my basic point is that there is a consistent way that punishment and forgiveness dictate the nature of Dickens' narrative strategies. That most of the wicked characters bring their punishments upon themselves is predictable, and appropriate narrative avenues open up to entrap them, with the public riot being the most obvious. The wily and inured villain Chester receives his punishment at the hands of another person, but that other person must not, in Dickens' scheme, be a virtuous hero or heroine. Instead, the retributive agent is a flawed man who subsequently passes voluntary judgment upon himself and seeks sustained punishment on the hope of ultimate forgiveness, though that forgiveness is not so much as mentioned in the narrative.

At the end of the novel other forms of narrative punishment are quickly dispensed. Lord Gordon dies in Newgate, a convert to Judaism; Gashford descends into poverty and dies by his own hand; Sim Tappertit is reduced to shoeblacking and a contentious marriage; and so forth. Everywhere wickedness receives its due. But though punishment abounds, no compensating forgiveness fills the void left by the elimination of evil. Gabriel Varden pleads with Sim to repent his behavior just as Mrs. Rudge urges her husband to seek forgiveness from God for his offenses. But neither succeeds. Mrs. Varden realizes the error of her supporting the Protestant Cause, but Gabriel's forgiveness is silent. The only pronounced plea for forgiveness is Haredale's sincere and earnest suit for forgiveness from Edward Chester and Emma Haredale, a suit that is granted.

What is missing in this misanthropic eighteenth century, this materialist world of selfishness and narrow-minded arrogance, is the social manifestation of the Christian spirit. That spirit survives almost exclusively in Gabriel Varden, and there chiefly in a defensive manner, as though preserved in a strongbox. It does not significantly affect society at large, or even perceptibly influence the other good characters of the novel. *Barnaby Rudge* depicts a world overwhelmingly

moved by fear, hatred, envy, and other evil passions manifested in acts of revenge and rebellion. If goodness cannot correct such a fallen world, the very
laws of nature and morality will. Thus hatred and revenge bring down upon
themselves a self-engendered retribution, and the entire unmerciful society ends
morally as the rioters do physically, "the wretched victims of a senseless outcry,
became themselves the dust and ashes of the flames they had kindled, and strewed
the public streets of London" (526).

In *Barnaby Rudge* Dickens pictures a misguided society too preoccupied with
retribution and revenge to recognize the corrosive powers of these desires. An
entire social structure stands indicted for lack of mercy and forbearance and it
suffers wholesale punishment in the form of popular riot. If it is true that the
shadows of our own desires stand between us and our better angels, eclipsing
their brightness, then the obvious solution is to make those desires transparent or
to remove them altogether by turning our attention to the welfare of others.
Mercy, forbearance, and forgiveness are means to this end. By depicting a historical moment and social condition in which a flourishing obsession with punishment casts the love and forgiveness of true Christianity into obscurity, Dickens
means to force his readers to recognize in that malign Other the vicious desire
obscuring Christ's truth. Uncaring selfishness must be washed away not by
bloody suffering but by humility. This is a lesson that Martin Chuzzlewit learns
in Dickens' next novel.

NOTES

1. A. E. Dyson calls attention to the prominent place of hatred in *Barnaby
Rudge,* and at one point comments, "The problem confronting us seems more religious than social; there is a *mystery* of hatred, in the flagrant disproportions between cause and effect" (*The Inimitable Dickens: A Reading of the Novels* [New
York: St. Martin's Press, Inc., 1970], 52).

2. K. J. Fielding, *Charles Dickens: A Critical Introduction* (Boston: Houghton
Mifflin Co., 1964). Subsequent references appear in the text.

3. John Forster saw the punitive practices of that historical time as contributing to the riots. Of Dickens' novel he writes:

> Its scene is laid at the time when the incessant execution of men and women,
> comparatively innocent, disgraced every part of the country; demoralising
> thousands, whom it also prepared for the scaffold. In those days the theft of a
> few rags from a bleaching ground, or the abstraction of a roll of ribbons from a
> counter, was visited with the penalty of blood; and such laws brutalised both
> their ministers and victims. It was the time, too, when a false religious outcry
> brought with it appalling guilt and misery. Such vices leave more behind them
> than the first forms assumed, and involve a lesson sufficiently required to justify

a writer in dealing with them" (*The Life of Charles Dickens* [London: Chapman and Hall, Ltd., 1893], 108). Subsequent references appear in the text.

4. John Lucas discusses the old order of this novel as having fallen into its dotage (*The Melancholy Man: A Study of Dickens's Novels* [London: Methuen and Co., Ltd., 1970], 97ff. Steven Marcus calls attention to the old order's failure to recognize the character of uncivilizable energies around it. As these impulses are pulled apart "there begins the dreadful, familiar declension: power into will, will into appetite, and appetite, the universal wolf, seconded by will and power, becomes the universal prey that at last eats up itself" (*Dickens: From Pickwick to Dombey* [New York: Basic Books, Inc., 1965], 203). Marcus also observes that the conflicts between institutional authority and the populace are recreated in the novel's personal relations (184). Edgar Johnson shows how contemporary social abuses generated much of the indignation that Dickens expressed in *Barnaby Rudge* (*Charles Dickens: His Tragedy and Triumph. A Biography*, 2 vols. [Boston: Little Brown and Co., 1952], 1:311ff.).

5. The term "conservative" was itself problematic in this period. Disraeli focused on this fact in *Coningsby* (1844), with his question: What do the conservatives conserve?

6. Steven Marcus calls attention to images of boilers about to explode, persons portrayed as vessels under pressure, and so forth—images that Carlyle also used in *The French Revolution*—and then summarizes, "Even these few scattered examples suggest that the essential conception of the novel took shape in Dickens's mind in various ideas and images of compression and repression, of fermentation and intoxication, of swellings and explosions and of corrosive anxiety and tenseness stretched to the breaking point. These images, developed in the course of the novel's action, are brought to their consummate expression in the eruption of the riots: in the breaking down of restraints, in drunkenness, fire and general explosive violence" (206).

7. Rudge repeats these points in the conversation that follows (473–74).

NINE

Martin Chuzzlewit

A NUMBER OF themes prominent in *Nicholas Nickleby* reappear in *Martin Chuzzlewit*. The subversion of Christian principles through viewing life in terms of economic advantage, the perversion of natural affection through selfishness, and the inversion of Christian virtues through outright transgression are interconnected in this novel. Set against these entwined themes are positive depictions of trust, selfless affection, and the capacity to learn from adversity. Both positive and negative presentations conform to a regular narrative pattern disparaging vengeful and punitive sentiments and praising the genuine capacity for forgiveness, while managing to punish wrongdoers and forgive errant characters. As usual with Dickens, though forgiveness may be extended and received by the virtuous characters, they are debarred from directly punishing those who break moral, social, or legal rules.

The Chuzzlewit family, as its name suggests, is the victim of an age-old confusion of mind. Descending "in a direct line from Adam and Eve," its members are good illustrations of the consequences of the Fall.[1] They are easily given to various forms of crime, and display "an overweening amount of family pride," though that pride does not include fellow members of the family, for whom they display only distrust and dislike, as indicated by the gathering of predatory Chuzzlewits at Pecksniff's house when old Martin Chuzzlewit lies dangerously ill at the Blue Dragon. Mainly, the Chuzzlewit family, like much of humankind, is "remarkable for taking uncommon good care of themselves" (6). Far from being a peculiar social unit, the Chuzzlewit family is a pattern of almost universal human behavior.

Dickens clearly declares within *Martin Chuzzlewit* and elsewhere that the central theme of this novel is an exposure of selfishness, but at the moral heart of the book are two characters apparently incapable of selfishness—Tom Pinch and Mary Graham.[2] Significantly, Mary is the one woman for whom Tom feels genuine love—as distinguished from affection and regard—though his is a hopeless and therefore nobler emotion than that of young Martin Chuzzlewit, whose love is true, faithful, and requited. Martin gets the wife, Tom the ideal. Unlike young Martin, who requires much moral instruction before he is worthy of the affection of these models, Tom and Mary seem immune to error from the outset. Both have had difficulties to overcome and difficult situations to endure. They are both orphans dependent upon benefactors who are preoccupied with their own welfare and suspicious of others. Tom believes his mentor, Pecksniff, to be a model of virtue; by contrast, as the ward of old Martin Chuzzlewit, Mary cannot ignore his unpleasant nature. Tom and Mary, representing true Christian feeling, are appropriately distributed because their "benefactors" are, despite all appearances, the true antagonists in this narrative. Dickens indicated very early in his notes to himself about the novel that old Martin, an embodiment of selfishness, will be the nemesis of the consummate hypocrite, Pecksniff. For his notes to chapter 10 he writes, "Old Martin's plot to degrade and punish Pecksniff in the end."[3] Old Martin so presents his offer to seek refuge with Pecksniff after his disappointment with young Martin that, if Pecksniff could look past material advantage, he might read the old man's true retributive purpose. Old Chuzzlewit is blunt and even aggressive about his distrust of other people's motives, believing that his wealth has been a dangerous influence on those who know him. He tells Pecksniff, for example, to expect no gratitude for visiting his sickroom.

> "I have so corrupted and changed the nature of all those who have ever attended on me, by breeding avaricious plots and hopes within them; I have engendered such domestic strife and discord, by tarrying even with members of my own family; I have been such a lighted torch in peaceful homes, kindling up all the inflammable gases and vapours in their moral atmosphere, which, but for me, might have proved harmless to the end; that I have, I may say, fled from all who knew me, and taking refuge in secret places have lived, of late, the life of one who is hunted." (39–40)

Money gives old Martin no pleasure, only unhappiness. What's more, it appears to have been the chief cause of the breach between him and young Martin, a separation that the old man deeply regrets. So convinced is he of the corrupting power of money that he insulates his relationship with Mary by means of a solemn oath not to leave her any money when he dies, thus guaranteeing that she will have no expectations from him and thus no motive for wishing him harm.

Old Martin disguises neither his pessimism about human nature nor his conviction that greed underlies most human activities. He is galling, but candid. By contrast, Pecksniff is a hypocrite and a fraud, presenting himself as a moral man disinterestedly devoted to benefitting his fellow beings, but actually abasing him-

self whenever necessary and using whatever unscrupulous devices he must to
wrench profit or advantage from others. John Westlock, parting from Pecksniff
in anger, realizes how all of Tom Pinch's good qualities serve as inexpensive en-
dorsements of Pecksniff's moral character, Tom's true light illuminating the
carefully prepared false facade. Westlock recognizes that Pecksniff has committed one of the great sins in the Dickens decalogue—he has treated Pinch as a
commodity, a form of advertising. "'Pecksniff traded in your nature,'" Westlock tells the unconvinced Pinch (23). As we have already seen, the languages of
financial and moral debt interpenetrate one another in Dickens' novels and the
narrative energies associated with one may easily be transferred to the other.
Thus, if Pecksniff is an actual swindler, who uses his students' ideas for his own
enhancement, he is equally capable of presenting as his own moral collateral the
virtues of a Tom Pinch. John Forster saw Pecksniff as the chief object of Dickens'
moral judgment precisely because he represents the most elusive form of transgression. He mirrors the sin of selfishness all around him, indicating "more
plainly than ever that there is but one vice which is quite irremediable. The elder
Chuzzlewits are bad enough, but they bring their self-inflicted punishments; the
Jonases and Tigg Montagues are execrable, but the law has its halter and its penal
servitude; the Moulds and Gamps have plague-bearing breaths, from which sani-
tary wisdom may clear us; but from the sleek, smiling, crawling abomination of a
Pecksniff, there is no help but self-help."[4] Michael Steig comments that Pecksniff
is more profoundly disturbing than earlier villains "because he exists within 'respectable' society, and mirrors some of its pervasive ethical confusions."[5]

Pecksniff carries his financial and moral duplicity directly into the realm of
practical religion. He mouths the appropriate Christian sentiments while feeling
their opposites in his heart. Typical of this behavior is ostentatiously naming his
daughters Mercy and Charity after two of the central Christian virtues, and then
educating the girls to a hypocrisy resembling his own. Mercy and Charity are the
virtues most closely associated with benignity and forgiveness. Pecksniff knows
that forgiveness is the most highly valued Christian response next to direct love,
and he bends even this central requirement to his own selfish ends. Hovering like
a predatory raptor in anticipation of a comfortable bequest from old Martin
Chuzzlewit, Pecksniff keeps himself in readiness for a summons "to the bedside
of his penitent and remorseful relative, whom, in his ample benevolence, he had
made up his mind to forgive unconditionally, and to love on any terms" (43). Not
only does Pecksniff lack the saving grace of a forgiving nature, he unctuously
arrogates that condition to himself while eager to gratify his most vindictive
urges. While trying to obtain old Martin's aid in making Mary his wife, he
threatens harm to young Martin, though he exonerates himself to himself. "As to
any thought of revenging himself on young Martin for his insolent expressions
when they parted, and of shutting him out still more effectually from any hope of
reconciliation with his grandfather, Mr. Pecksniff was much too meek and forgiving to be suspected of harbouring it" (476). The narrator's use of free indirect

discourse, however, clearly reveals his own ironic view of Pecksniff's unworthy intentions. Even at the climactic moment of his exposure by old Martin, Pecksniff responds to the several denunciations of him by righteously simpering that although he has been wickedly deceived by most of the persons assembled to witness his discomfiture, he has "'forgiven those persons on the spot'" (811). To young Martin, who has just detailed a bill of lading of Pecksniff's sins, the oily rascal responds with a pious chestnut. He tells Martin that in contemplating the tomb, he should remember that Pecksniff, while reproaching him, forgave him too. "'That I forgave you when my injuries were fresh, and when my bosom was newly wrung. It may be bitterness to you to hear it now, sir, but you will live to seek a consolation in it'" (812). The impious scoundrel cannot leave his pious formulas alone. But by creating a character moved by small and large vindictiveness while trumpeting forgiveness and mercy abroad, Dickens has charged his narrative with a gravitational energy that must and will find release in the returning of this inversion of Christian order to its natural level and harmony. Though Pecksniff commits no crime as serious as murder or assault, his offense has the same energy because it defiles the highest Christian values of love and forgiveness. That is why the "reprisal, when it comes, has a brutality that exceeds the needs of comedy or even of poetic justice," in Alexander Welsh's words.[6]

Pecksniff's reference to the contemplation of last things fits into an overall pattern, amply noted by literary scholars, of biblical structuring in *Martin Chuzzlewit*.[7] The novel opens with a reference to the antiquity of the Chuzzlewit family reaching back to Adam and Eve, and ends with Tom Pinch at the organ "narrating" the story of his life that reaches from the present and the past into the future, which is evidently not merely an earthly future but an eternal one with an assured place for Tom in the heaven to which his music rises like a prayer. Many biblical references are straightforward, but throughout the narrative many reversals of the true biblical pattern also occur. Thus the Eden to which young Martin Chuzzlewit and Mark Tapley so hopefully travel turns out to be a wasteland resembling a landscape after the Deluge. The very next chapter following the description of this dreadful Eden opens with Pecksniff dressing himself in his gardening attire so that old Martin will discover him in this benign rustic occupation. "'You find me in my garden-dress,'" he says to Martin. "'You will excuse it, I know. It is an ancient pursuit, gardening. Primitive, my dear sir; or, if I am not mistaken, Adam was the first of our calling. *My Eve*, I grieve to say, is no more, sir; but:' here he pointed to his spade, and shook his head as if he were not cheerful without an effort: 'but I do a little bit of Adam still'" (384). The inhabitant of Eden that Pecksniff truly most resembles is the serpent, and when he encounters the irreproachable Eve of his garden he has a taste of heavenly humiliation. Encountering Mary "communing with Nature" in the sunny rural weather, Pecksniff takes the opportunity to voice his ambition of making her his wife, despite her declared aversion to him (480ff.). When the stalwart Mary expresses her resistance and leaves him, Pecksniff experiences a transformation that reverses Satan's metamorphosis from a toad to his proper form when touched by the angel Ithuriel's spear as he crouches down by Eve's ear. Pecksniff does not swell to full proportion, but withers. He suddenly appears "to be shrunk and reduced; to be trying to hide himself within himself; and to be wretched at not having the power to do it. His shoes looked too large; his sleeve looked too long; his hair looked too limp; his features looked too mean; his exposed throat looked as if a halter would have done it good. For a minute or two, in fact, he was hot, and pale, and mean, and shy, and slinking, and consequently not at all Pecksniffian" (485). Touched by the truth of Mary's noble character as Satan is touched by the celestial spear, neither can disguise his actual character, "for no falsehood can endure / Touch of celestial temper, but returns / Of force to its own likeness" (*Paradise Lost* IV, 811–13).

We first encounter Pecksniff when an angry and vengeful wind slams the door in his face, upsetting him at his own doorstep. This might serve as an emblem of Pecksniff's relationship to nature. He is neither the gardener Adam nor the benign spirit of the rural countryside; in fact, he lacks any true appreciation of nature either in mankind or in the material world. The narrator makes explicit this quality of Pecksniff's character when he remarks that Pecksniff's enemies "maintained that he always said of what was very bad, that it was very natural; and that he unconsciously betrayed his own nature in doing so" (34). Throughout the novel "nature" and "natural" are charged terms, often directing us back to that "natural" trait of the age-old Chuzzlewit clan, selfishness.

If Pecksniff notoriously perverts Christian virtues, he is equally outrageous in his pretense of moral righteousness. Believing that he can curry favor with old Martin by expelling young Martin from his home, Pecksniff quickly manufactures a supply of moral indignation "only to be equaled by the kindling anger of his daughters. What! Had they taken to their hearth and home a secretly contracted serpent; a crocodile, who had made a furtive offer of his hand; an imposition on society; a bankrupt bachelor with no effects, trading with the spinster world on false pretenses!" (160). The commercial metaphor used in Pecksniff's denunciation of young Martin is consistent with much of the false and true moral commentary in this novel, as it is with Dickens' fiction in general. It also reveals here the venal sources of Pecksniff's artificial fervor. In fact, Pecksniff's charges against Martin apply very well to himself. He has traded on Pinch's good reputation and old Martin will later accuse him of treating young Martin "as a speculation" to gain advantage from him (205). Driving Martin from his house, Pecksniff claims to pity the young man's voluntary withdrawal from "the flowery paths of purity and peace"; he theatrically strikes himself "upon his breast or moral garden," declaring that he cannot have "a leper and a serpent for an inmate" (210). So Martin becomes the serpent cast out from the garden by a virtuous, Adamic Pecksniff—a complete reversal of Genesis, as everything in Pecksniff is a reversal and parody of true Christian behavior.[8]

Pecksniff expresses his indignation a second time when he dismisses Tom Pinch for allegedly addressing Mary " 'with un-returned professions of attachment and proposals of love' " (499). His actual reason is that Tom has learned from Mary's accounts of Pecksniff's conduct what kind of man his benefactor really is. As with young Martin, Pecksniff's accusation, though not true of Tom, is true of Pecksniff, who has very recently forced his attentions upon Mary. He hopes, in sending Tom away, that his " 'deception may not alter my ideas of humanity' " (500). By punishing Martin and Tom for behavior more characteristic of himself Pecksniff unconsciously points to the nature of his own desert. He condemns himself in these deceitful judgments upon others. Each act of pretended moral outrage increases Pecksniff's moral debt.

The climax of the narrative is Pecksniff's downfall, and predictably the novel's chief moral forces of punishment and forgiveness are concentrated there. Although it follows the more melodramatic unmasking of Jonas, Pecksniff's undoing is more significant because, as old Martin recognizes, he is "the incarnation of all selfishness and treachery" (796). The vicious Jonas is *hunted down,* but the more insidiously corrupt and corrupting Pecksniff is *found out,* and once exposed to the light of truth is disempowered for evil. In a rare act of physical violence, which mirrors Tom Pinch's earlier and more astonishing blow to Jonas Chuzzlewit, old Martin begins his denunciation of the consummate fraud, Pecksniff, by thrusting him to the ground. In Hablot K. Browne's illustration, a copy of *Paradise Lost* is prominently displayed crashing to the floor along with Pecksniff. Clearly Browne had instructions from Dickens on this detail, or else noticed the implicit connections himself.[9] There is a passage in *Paradise Lost* that indicates how important the concept of free will is to the Christian scheme of responsibility, and thus to moral reward and punishment. This passage is echoed in old Martin's reminder to Pecksniff that "he had not trapped him to do evil, but that he had done it of his own free will and agency" (809). This assertion also echoes Pecksniff's denunciation of young Martin for voluntarily withdrawing himself from the paths of purity and peace. The scene of Pecksniff's coming to judgment also fittingly brings the real and metaphorical economic patterns of the narrative together. Much earlier the narrator had described Pecksniff's conscience with a trope from accounting.

The good man's enemies would have divided upon this question into two parties. One would have asserted without scruple that if Mr. Pecksniff's conscience were his bank, and he kept a running account there, he must have overdrawn it beyond all mortal means of computation. The other would have contended that it was a mere fictitious form; a perfectly blank book, or one in which entries were only made with a peculiar kind of invisible ink to become legible at some indefinite time; and that he never troubled it at all. (328)

Now, with Pecksniff brought to book, old Martin opens Pecksniff's moral ledgers for inspection and declares him "'Bankrupt in pocket no less than in good name!'" (807).

In unmasking Pecksniff, old Martin has to face some truths about himself and readily admits the faulty principle according to which he directed his life. He warns others like himself, to whom wealth cannot bring happiness but only the alienating of potential friends: "'take heed that, having cast off all whom you might have bound to you, and tenderly, you do not become in your decay the instrument of such a man as this, and waken in another world to the knowledge of such wrong as would embitter Heaven itself, if wrong or you could ever reach it!'" (807–8). Martin refers to the "penance" he has done living under Pecksniff's authority, but he sees it as a necessary tutelage to the falseness of a life he has based upon greed and selfishness. It is important to this scene that Pecksniff himself undergoes no such educative experience. Though people all around him are asking forgiveness, he never acknowledges his guilt. As we have already seen, he insists instead upon maintaining his moral superiority and dispenses forgiveness to others. This inability to learn, to repent, and to reform not only makes his decisive punishment appropriate, but justifies its continuance as well. Pecksniff will degenerate into a bad-spirited begging-letter writer, sponging upon Tom Pinch. But beyond that earthly destiny, we as readers can expect that, old Martin's warning not being heeded, Pecksniff will discover a more serious punishment in the hereafter. There is a kind of dustwagon in the afterlife where all the Weggses and Pecksniffs will be dumped—the unrepentant trash of the world. It is important to Dickens' fictional world that its boundary extend past material existence to a realm of true justice and love, for the very moral energies that power his narratives depend upon an eternal source. His characters are judged in the light of an authority that transcends that of narrator or implied author.

When Pecksniff extends his specious forgivenesses, he does so as a man sinned against, but his appearance has already changed and he lacks the sleekness that usually aids his deceptions. He stands "as if a host of penal sentences were being passed upon him," and, being touched by the truth once again, he is once more transformed into his shabby reality, as he had been before in the presence of Mary Graham's rectitude: "his discomfiture seemed to have extended itself even to his dress. His clothes seemed to have grown shabbier, his linen to have turned yellow, his hair to have become lank and frowsy; his very boots looked villanous and dim, as if their gloss had departed with his own" (810). The punishment that falls upon Pecksniff thus has an immediate material effect, to which the narrator calls attention. He already seems to have become a vagabond or convict, though his penal servitude will extend well beyond the confines of the material world. The implied author has considered it appropriate to render Pecksniff unrepentant, and thus excluded from the realm of goodness forever because he represents the most insidious and permanent evil tendencies in humankind, the very moral faults that wither sympathy and enlarge private appetites. These faults may be controlled and corrected but never extirpated. If we recognize them, if we find them out in ourselves, we are armed against them. But being permanently evil, they cannot themselves conceive of repentance and so they are eternally punished.

It is manifest everywhere in *Martin Chuzzlewit* that self-examination is a necessary exercise for fulfillment of character. We cannot find the seeds of Pecksniffism in us if we do not turn over the soil of our nature.[10] This narrative, more insistently than many other Dickens stories, stresses the important role adversity can play in irradiating fissures of weakness in character and therefore opening the way for reformation. Mark Tapley is the embodiment of this principle, searching out difficult circumstances so that he may test his character to demonstrate that he can be jolly in the worst conditions. He never fails in this determination. He is, of course, an excellent companion for young Martin, who discovers the extent of his own selfishness through painful experiences in the United States, most specifially at Eden. Before Martin leaves for America, he complains about the inconvenience he will suffer at being separated from Mary. Tom offers him some useful advice, suggesting that all will be well in time " 'and some trial and adversity just now will only serve to make you more attached to each other in better days.' " What never ran smooth can't be expected to change its character for us, he observes, " 'so we must take it as we find it, and fashion it into the very best shape we can, by patience and good-humour' " (98). This is precisely Mark Tapley's *modus operandi,* and the narrator makes sure that we see it working effectively both in him and in Tom Pinch.

Mary, the model of female excellence in this novel, "had had her nature strengthened by the hands of hard endurace and necessity; had come out from her young trials constant, self-denying, earnest, and devoted" (235). Mark's view that " 'we must all be seasoned one way or another' " by hard experience applies to all the characters in the novel. Many of these characters fail to benefit from the prophylactic quality of misfortune. Chevy Slyme, for example, gains nothing but increased spite from hardship because he feels so much is owed to him. A surprising and striking instance of the value of adversity is Mercy Pecksniff. As a flighty and thoughtless young woman, she teased Jonas mercilessly while he courted her, not realizing the consequences of marriage to such a man, though old Martin tried to enlighten her. After a short period of marriage, she has suffered enough to understand how painful life can be and has even learned to sympathize with others. She explains to Tom Pinch that she can value Chuffey: " 'You see how misery has changed me. I can feel for a dependant now, and set some value on his attachment' " (705). Later, after Martin's denunciation of her father, she forgives Martin for having judged her too quickly, admitting that before her marriage she was trivial: " 'I had no thought, no heart, no care to find one; at that time. It has grown out of my trouble. I have felt it in my trouble' " (828). Mercy thus serves as a clear example of how pain may benefit us if we know how to accept it in a Christian spirit. Her simple and paradigmatic case helps to illuminate what may be seen as more problematic cases. It is another instance of Dickens' use of redundancy to intensify his message.

Young Martin is, of course, the chief example of how adversity can improve one's character, though critics do not at all agree on his conversion.[11] After realizing, when Mark falls ill, how much he has depended upon his partner, young Martin comprehends the extent of his own selfishness and resolves on a course of "humility and steadfastness" for the future (525). Only after he has become aware of this flaw in his character can Martin frame an appropriate method for dealing with his problems. When Martin is preparing to leave for America, Mary tries to advise him to take a more judicious course than that of angry defiance of his grandfather.

> "Martin! If you would but sometimes, in some quiet hour; beside the winter fire; in the summer air; when you hear gentle music, or think of Death, or Home, or Childhood; if you would at such a season resolve to think, but once a month, or even once a year, of him, or any one who ever wronged you, you would forgive him in your heart, I know!" (242)

Mary's remarks condense Dickens' thinking on this point. They are the moral center of this novel. Martin's erroneous conduct is made all the more reprehensible through his inability to value the truth in Mary and in the message she conveys. Filled with his own sense of grievance, Martin rejects "mawkish forgiveness" as a ridiculous weakness (242). This is a dangerous attitude for any character in a Dickens novel and customarily signals either a punishment or some transformative experience ahead. For young Martin that experience is the ordeal of Eden. Humbled and changed for the better by his American adventures, Martin eagerly accepts Mark's advice that he should boldly and freely ask old Martin's forgiveness " 'as a gentleman should' " (663). When he first sees old Martin in his apparently subordinate relationship to Pecksniff, he is deeply moved. Even when blinded by selfishness, young Martin had valued the traces of the old man's ancient love. "But now, changed for the better in his worst respect; looking through an altered medium on his former friend, the guardian of his childhood, so broken and so bowed down; resentment, sullenness, self-confidence, and pride, were all swept away before the starting tears upon the withered cheeks" (665). He tells old Martin he now realizes that he should have been more considerate toward him and thought less of himself, and asks him for " 'forgiveness: not so much in hope for the future, as in regret for the past' " (668). In my reading of the novel, with Dickens' constant pattern of punishment and forgiveness in mind, this gesture signifies Martin's genuine moral conversion, whatever minor faults of character might remain.

This scene, a version of the prodigal son convention so familiar in Victorian literature, is conventional in another way as well.[12] The chastened youth returning to seek forgiveness from a parent or parent surrogate would normally be warmly welcomed back into the bosom of the family, his transgressions forgotten, affections renewed, and security assured. But against all such expectations, this scene in *Martin Chuzzlewit* frustrates one of the central dramatic expectations of the narrative, for the repentant Martin is sent away by his grandfather, who seems only partly to be following the lead of the slimy Pecksniff. This violation of the packed convention of forgiven prodigality adds a new zest to Dickens' narrative by suggesting that the easy ploy of admitting error is not sufficient, in itself, to constitute redemption. Earlier, when Martin is chafing at the injustice of Pecksniff winning a prize with an architectural design stolen from him, Mark Tapley soothes him with the assurance, " 'it'll all come right in the end, sir; it'll all come right!' " Now, his hopes of reconciliation dashed, Martin might repeat his early gloomy response: " 'And in the meantime—' " (555).

In the meantime, of course, one must endure and do what is right. What must come first is old Martin's own awareness, arising out of his own trials, that he too was partly responsible for young Martin's selfishness. Significantly, it is Mark Tapley who drives this truth home for the old man once he has learned it. Thus the two Martins exhibit versions of the same moral malady, presented at the beginning and the closing of manhood. If young Martin's adversity arises from his foolhardiness, old Martin's is a chosen role. The role is no less painful for that, though it has the consolation of remaining under the old man's control. The great emotion that should have been released in the prodigal scene must be postponed and reenacted because there are two prodigals involved, and one is the "father" whose role is to forgive. Some critics have been unhappy with old Martin's function in this narrative, but for the moral economy of Dickens' tale some such withholding of gratification, such as an instructive complication of the familiar convention, is necessary to convey the essential point that true forgiveness can be offered to the genuinely repentant only when the forgiver's heart itself is pure. Dickens' insight here, and his narrative strategy for conveying it, is superior to the simpler expectations of his critics, for he knows how intimately the shocks of storytelling are related to the purposes of educating. To affirm a simple lesson, a predictable convention is appropriate, but not so when a difficult lesson must be taught.

Old Martin, himself guilty of some of Pecksniff's sins, though not of his hypocrisy, uses Pecksniff's strategy of disguise and deception to allow himself a means of surveillance. As a daily domestic witness of Pecksniff's chicanery, the old man is able to accumulate the evidence he needs to unmask the villain. We might say that this constitutes Pecksniff's finally being *found out*—though others have sized him up correctly earlier. This is not a usual strategy for Dickens, though he will use it again later, especially with Mr. Boffin in *Our Mutual Friend*. More characteristic of Dickens' approach to clearly evil characters is the process I have broadly called *hunting down,* and the person who represents this object of justice in *Martin Chuzzlewit* is, of course, Jonas Chuzzlewit. It is significant that, whereas old Martin can expose Pecksniff and even deliver a retributive blow upon him, his plan to punish Jonas fails. On the face of it, there seems no good explanation for this swerve in the narrative. But it actually serves two important purposes, both related to the moral economy of the novel and rooted in the concepts of punishment and forgiveness.

Dickens withholds two principal secrets from us, though his omniscient narrator might at any time have let us in on them.[13] The first is completely masked until old Martin begins to take action against the two chief rascals of the narrative, and we discover that he was only feigning weakness and subservience. The other is gradually hinted at and disclosed by Jonas' uneasiness in the vicinity of his father's corpse, his dislike of the word "death," the appearance of Lewsome with his horrible secret, and Chuffey's mysterious outbursts about death and foul play when he witnesses Mercy's sufferings at the hands of Jonas.[14] Clearly we are meant to suspect Jonas of having somehow facilitated his father's death, particularly because he so often explicitly resents the old man's reluctance to die. It comes as no real surprise, then, when we witness Jonas' progress toward the murder of Montague Tigg. Thus, by the time Martin charges Jonas with poisoning his father, we are fully prepared to have the charge supported by evidence of various kinds. But at this juncture, when even Jonas believes himself guilty, Chuffey overcomes his customary stupor to reveal that Anthony knew about the poison, made up to look like his medicine, that Jonas acquired from Lewsome. He gave his son the impression that he was taking the poison, though he was not. In fact, on the night when Anthony died, says Chuffey, he was trying to tell Jonas that he forgave him, realizing that he himself had trained Jonas up "'to be too covetous of what I have to leave, and made the expectation of it his great business!'" (784). He planned to turn his fortune over to Jonas immediately and live humbly with faithful Chuffey, saying, "'I have sown, and I must reap'" (784). But Anthony dies of natural causes and, since Chuffey is sworn to silence about the poison, Jonas continues to believe that he has murdered his father. It is this belief that puts him in Tigg's power and drives him to an unnecessary homicide. But before taking up that part of Jonas' career, we should examine the leading traits of his character to explain why he is punished as he is.

Swinburne was one of the earliest critics to notice how much an advance in the depiction of villainy Jonas was over earlier wicked characters in Dickens' fiction.[15] And commentators since have appreciated Dickens' skill in exploring Jonas' character and his crimes.[16] There is no question that Jonas exhibits a wide array of the usual faults of Dickens' villains. To begin with, he views other people as commodities. From "his early habits of considering everything as a question of property, he had gradually come to look, with impatience, on his parent as a certain amount of personal estate, which had no right whatever to be going at large, but ought to be secured in that particular description of iron safe which is commonly called a coffin, and banked in the grave" (119). His interest in the Pecksniff girls is based upon the money that will come with them, and he chooses the prettier one, who is also the one Pecksniff supposedly values the least and will therefore pay the most to have married. This tendency to reduce humans to a form of currency is compounded in Jonas by a vindictiveness and perverseness of character that have little to do with greed. For example, Jonas cannot help being influenced by the expensive trappings with which Tigg has surrounded himself to make the Anglo-Bengalee Disinterested Loan and Life Assurance Company seem sound and legitimate; but "over and above the habitual distrust of his character, it was in his nature to seek to revenge himself on the fine clothes and the fine furniture, in exact proportion as he had been unable to withstand their influence" (441). Even inanimate objects generate a vengeful feeling in Jonas, though humans are the best objects for such emotions. Before and after their engagement, Mercy makes great sport of teasing and taunting Jonas. After one such episode, Jonas remarks to himself about the departing Mercy, "biting a piece of straw, almost to powder; 'you'll catch it for this when you *are* married! It's all very well now—it keeps one on, somehow, and you know it—but I'll pay you off scot and lot by-and-bye" (400).[17] And he soon lives up to his word, avenging himself viciously on the light-headed girl.

For Jonas life consists of acquisition and revenge—"taking in" and "paying off," as he has it in his commercial idiolect. Not surprisingly, when the truth begins to tell against him, he sees it swooping down upon him on "avenging wings" (782). But long before justice catches up with him, Jonas creates his own penitential circumstances, first in the anxiety occasioned by Tigg's knowledge of his supposed murder of Anthony, and then in the anxiety occasioned by his murder of Tigg. When Tigg prevents him from escaping to the Continent, Jonas has "the aspect of a man found out and held at bay; of being baffled, hunted, and beset" (634). He begins to plan Tigg's death, a sequence in the novel rightly praised for its satisfying grimness, since not only is the complicated psychology of intending murderer and suspicious victim well drawn, but the moral dynamics are nicely adjusted to both horrify and gratify the reader. Tigg is himself a scoundrel well deserving of punishment and so his suffering from fear of Jonas seems just. In a strange way that Dickens understood well, it is perversely refreshing to those who claim to be honest and virtuous to witness the dueling of rogues. Thus it almost seems suitable that Jonas should "accidentally" lead restless horses within inches of trampling out Tigg's brains. But, scoundrel that he is, Tigg's crimes do not justify a death sentence, and the burden of evil falls heavily on Jonas instead.[18]

Chapter 47, in which the murder takes place, opens by identifying Jonas with Cain, and with Jonas' dream of the Last Judgment, while for Tigg this time is filled with "the presentiment and vague foreknowledge of impending doom" (723). On the fateful night, it is almost as though the narrator offers Tigg a chance at safety. He can choose to return from Pecksniff's in the growing dusk by a lonely and retired footpath or by the public road. He chooses the fatal footpath, after which the narrator concludes with what amounts to an elegiac, moralizing valediction.

The glory of the departing sun was on his face. The music of the birds was in his ears. Sweet wild flowers bloomed about him. Thatched roofs of poor men's homes were in the distance; and an old grey spire, surmounted by a Cross, rose up between him and the coming night.

He had never read the lesson which these things conveyed; he had ever mocked and turned away from it; but, before going down into a hollow place, he looked round, once, upon the evening prospect, sorrowfully. Then he went down, down, down, into the dell. (724)

Once Jonas has committed the crime, it is important that he experience no penitence or remorse. The narrator stresses this fact. "There was no more penitence or remorse within him now," he says, referring to the period immediately following the crime, "than there had been when the deed was brewing" (777). And much later, though he is tormented by fear of discovery, Jonas remains unrepentant. "Still he was not sorry. It was no contrition or remorse for what he had done that moved him; it was nothing but alarm for his own security" (826). Like Pecksniff, Jonas must remain unrepentant and thereby deserve his punishment. If he were to repent, his character would be altered and his punishment would have to be changed as well. But just as Pecksniff's exposure is the appropriate punishment for his hypocritical, sneaking sins, Jonas' punishment must be appropriate for the vicious and violent sins of which he is the representative agent in this narrative. If Jonas feels no agony of remorse, he suffers torments of dread, waiting for the discovery of the murder and the consequences of that discovery. "For he knew it must come; and his present punishment, and torture, and distraction, were, to listen for its coming" (729).

It is typical of Dickens' novels that when the forces of good begin to expand their power and range of action, the villains' arenas of action begin to shrink, and this pattern holds vividly true for Jonas: "faster and faster the encircling ruin contracted and contracted towards himself, its wicked centre, until it should close in and crush him" (782). But, as we have seen, the final stifling gesture is forestalled. Jonas is not guilty of murdering his father. But this technical innocence provides only an ironic and temporary reprieve, since he is culpable in the murder of Tigg, which resulted from his belief that he was his father's murderer. Punishment will come, but at one remove. And exposure for this crime is certain because, just as old Martin has been secretly maintaining his surveillance over Pecksniff, Nadgett has been doing the same with Jonas. Jonas makes a last desperate attempt to avoid public punishment by using his most beloved resource, money. He offers a bribe for the privacy in which to commit suicide, but he lacks courage for the act and the bribe is returned. Finally he poisons himself in the carriage conveying him to prison.

Poetic justice has the son who sought to kill his father with poison take his own life in the same manner.[19] The needless crime against Tigg becomes the authentic offense for which Jonas is condemned. The narrator notes, "the fatality was of his own working; the pit was of his own digging; the gloom that gathered round him was the shadow of his own life" (713). Jonas has led a self-destructive career similar to those of old Martin and Anthony, only more concentrated and intensified and acted out literally to the end.[20] Anthony comes to regret his way of life and its influence on his son, and old Martin not only repents but reforms. Jonas goes to his fate unredeemed, and, as is so often the case with Dickens' violent villains, takes his own life. The self-punishment of this final act is simply the termination of a life of suppressed self-injury. Jonas' greed and resentment have tainted his life from the beginning. Like Tigg he has never valued religious faith, nature, or any of the other conventionally positive influences of life. He closes the books on his life with a heavy moral debt owing.

Enhancing the futility of Jonas' fate is the fact that a little reflection could have prevented his crime. The narrator remarks that if Jonas had listened to Tom Pinch's explanation of how he came to be the bearer of Tigg's note to him, he would have realized that Nadgett also knew his "secret," and he would thus not have been tempted to silence Tigg. Instead, he tells Tom, "'I'll pay you for the carriage of it one day, and settle an old score besides. I will!'" (712). Jonas' hostility to Tom is irrational and almost instinctive, for he is Tom's moral antithesis. One clear theme of this novel is that we reap what we sow, with the suggestion that our evil deeds come home to us. But Tom embodies the truth that we may sow good as well as bad seed and reap the reward for our virtuous acts. Jonas sows evil, Tom good. Tom's fidelity to Pecksniff may be foolish and mistaken, but it is nonetheless nobly motivated. Tom inclines to charity and trust. Even when he is forced to defend himself against Jonas' aggressive gestures, giving Jonas a good clout on the head with Jonas' own stick, he remains gentle and considerate, immediately going to his enemy's aid. "'Are you hurt?'" said Tom. 'I am very sorry. Lean on me for a moment. You can do that without forgiving me, if you still bear me malice. But I don't know why; for I never offended you before we met on this spot'" (393). The spot itself is significant, for it is the same footpath across the fields between Pecksniff's house and the village where Tigg will be struck down. Tom follows up his defensive blow with an apology and assistance and even instructs his victim on the moral niceties of the event, behavior very different from Jonas' heartless impenitence after the fatal blow he will deliver.

Surely this parallel is a conscious narrative gesture and a means for setting Tom's admirable qualities off against Jonas' loathsome traits. As Jonas' opposite, Tom functions as the lodestone of true, selfless values in this novel about selfishness. He is self-effacing in his dedication to Pecksniff, self-subduing in his undeclared love of Mary, and selfless always in offering help to others. A good sign in the arrogant young Martin is that he is willing to take money from Tom. There are certain people to whom being indebted is in no way compromising. When Pecksniff dismisses him, Tom does not deign to deny charges of misconduct alien to his nature. When he leaves, practically the whole village demonstrates its affection for him and its appreciation of his character, an appreciation symbolized in Mrs. Lupin's bountiful gifts. Nor is Tom "sage enough," as the ironic narrator remarks, to follow the "strictly rational and eminently wise proceeding" of revenging "himself upon mankind in general by mistrusting them one and all" because he has been disappointed in one man. Instead, he follows the "Christian system of conduct" and simply laments the loss of his ideal (556). Even Mercy Pecksniff says that she was always confident of his kindly and forgiving nature, though she never showed it.

J. Hillis Miller refers to Tom Pinch as an example of "the impasse to which total unselfishness leads," though noting that this would not have been Dickens' intention (121). And other scholars have criticized Tom as a creation. For example, Robert M. McCarron concludes that Tom may be successful as a "wise fool" but not as a "Holy Innocent."[21] But Dickens knew what he wanted to accomplish with Tom and made that aim explicit in his text. He may have failed with some readers, but his purpose went beyond wise fools, Holy Innocents, and impasses of unselfishness. More than once the narrator pauses to apostrophize Tom for his simple, unselfish goodness.[22] But it is his loving sister, Ruth, who summarizes his virtues best—"so faithful and so good . . . so true and self-denying . . . so gentle, and so kind, and even-tempered," and hopes that somehow the secret love of his heart might be satisfied (766). Tom has no such aspiration, trying only to lead a good life in the real world and not to be a hero out of books. If Jonas is punished by a poetic justice he has himself engendered, Tom receives the reward appropriate to his nature.

> "You think of me, Ruth," said Tom, "and it is very natural that you should, as if I were a character in a book; and you make it a sort of poetical justice that I should, by some impossible means or other, come, at last, to marry the person I love. But there is a much higher justice than poetical justice, my dear, and it does not order events upon the same principle. Accordingly, people who read about heroes in books, and choose to make heroes of themselves out of books, consider it a very fine thing to be discontented and gloomy, and misanthropical, and perhaps a little blasphemous, because they cannot have everything ordered for their individual accommodation. Would you like me to become one of that sort of people?" (767–68)

Tom does not regard his love as sorrowful but as a fine sentiment that makes him more sensible of affection and attachment, thus softening his nature in many ways and therefore not making him less happy. In Tom Pinch Dickens offers a hero quite unlike the active, passionate, Byronic creations of contemporaries like Bulwer and Ainsworth. If there is a justice that finds out the secret sins of the wicked, there is also a justice that finds out the secret virtues of the good. Tom Pinch reveals, by the end of Martin Chuzzlewit, the central importance of Christian charity. He is a marked example of a type that recurs in Dickens' fiction. Stephen Blackpool in *Hard Times* is another, less fortunate version.

But if Tom Pinch behaves charitably, the one character who might be expected by her name to exhibit such conduct represents instead the very opposite qualities. Charity Pecksniff demonstrates personal traits very much at odds with her name, being ungenerous and spiteful at the very least, and, as a Pecksniff, hypocritical. Appropriately, when she learns that Tom has beaten Jonas, she befriends him because she hates Jonas for preferring her sister to herself. How apt that Charity should respect Tom for the one act least like him, of which he is himself regretful.

Charity is a version of the stereotyped comic spinster. Her great ambition is to be married, not necessarily for love but for the appearance of things and the feminine triumph involved. She is furious and unforgiving when, after expecting that Jason will propose to her, he asks Mercy to marry him instead. Later, when she learns that her father hopes to make Mary his wife, Charity is mortally offended and insists on leaving home to live by herself. At Mrs. Todgers' rooming house she maneuvers the morose Moddle, who had fastened his heart on the now married Mercy, into a marriage proposal and then parades her engagement. Meanwhile, she takes spiteful pleasure in her sister's hymeneal misery. Of course she will be punished for this behavior, just as Mercy is punished for her flightiness. But there is a narrative difference in these punishments. Mercy tormented Jonas before marriage and he afterward returns the favor with brutal interest. It is serious punishment administered by one character upon another, and its effect is actually beneficial, for it teaches Mercy an important lesson. But Charity's punishment is far more the conscious act of the narrator, designed to achieve closure at the end of his tale. As other young characters in the novel are moving toward their predictable marriages—Martin and Mary, John Westlock and Ruth Pinch, Mark Tapley and Mrs. Lupin—Charity is "forgiving" her relations and inviting them to her wedding. This is clearly malicious and spiteful behavior disguised as cordiality. However, her anticipated triumph turns sour when she receives a note from Moddle after he has sailed for Van Dieman's Land. Charity's marital hopes are dashed and she faints away. The uncharitable Charity is doomed to lovelessness. And on this note the story ends. Or almost. For what remains is a coda describing Tom playing at his organ some time in the future—a last portrait of the heart of goodness at the center of the novel. Pecksniff and his shrewish daughter beg from him, but otherwise his life is rich and happy. His contrast to Charity, representing what she stands for in name only, is made clear in their apparently parallel circumstances. Tom has remained a bachelor as Charity has a spinster. But he has *chosen* a single life, his one love inacessible to him, whereas Charity has had the single life forced upon her. He finds his life rewarding; hers is a penance. The narrator, not Moddle, is the agent of justice here, securing in this conclusion evidence of the destinies of false and true charity. Like all the other wicked characters in this novel, Charity has brought her punishment upon herself, and, because she cannot recognize it as such, is doomed to endure its rigors forever. Meanwhile Tom, who anticipates no reward for his love and kindness through poetic justice, has the reward of a happiness that he has earned for himself through a life of forgiving kindness.

The organization of *Martin Chuzzlewit* has frequently come under fire, especially in post-Jamesian times. Kathleen Tillotson sees no accomplished design in the novel, which she considers loosely structured enough for "improvisation and modification. There was no narrative plan, no dynamic view of the interaction of the characters, such as we find in the long letter to Forster outlining the design of *Dombey*"[23] I think that this broad view is generally supported among critics because it allows for a general organizing principle on Dickens' part, yet leaves open the question of any closely followed structural pattern in the novel. Another related line of criticism has different consequences for the ultimate purpose of the novel. In *Comic Faith: The Great Tradition from Austen to Joyce,* Robert M. Polhemus examines Dickens' use of language and comes to the general conclusion that the comic vision of the novel tends to subvert its supposed moral design.[24] James R. Kincaid similarly argues that the "comic vision here is one of the most mature and moving in English literature, though perhaps it "does help upset [Dickens'] original design and damage somewhat the unity of the novel."[25] Kincaid goes on to prefer a grandly blemished work to the original design as presented by Forster. In a later essay, Kincaid continues this line of thought, suggesting, like Polhemus, that the parodic power of *Martin Chuzzlewit* works against its moral intent. Moreover, he suggests that the novel resists any final truth, remaining open to multiple readings.[26] In a related approach, Gerhard Joseph locates the tension between comic and moral vision within Dickens himself and concludes that, as a moralist, Dickens sought a certainty which, as an artist, he resisted. This opposition is figured in Tom's ordered world of the library and the labyrinthine impulse of the novel itself.[27]

These are skilled readings of Dickens' text, but they lack one ingredient that would help us appreciate just what Dickens was accomplishing in his narrative. Anthony Trollope explained that the characters in *Phineas Finn* simply developed as they were written, but nonetheless, he, as author, knew "the good and evil of my puppets, and how the evil would always lead to evil, and the good produce good."[28] Dickens composed according to a similar imperative, though with increasingly strict control. No matter how spontaneously his characters and plots might develop in his early compositions, the moral rigors remained firmly in place and were the instruments governing the larger narrative movements and strategies. While what we might call secular readings of his novels can and do produce exciting and illuminating insights, they run the risk of generating misinterpretations if they leave out the larger program according to which Dickens created his plots and characters. In the novels from *Dombey* on, Dickens brought an increasing degree of discipline to the planning and execution of his narratives, but what did not change was the armature of good and evil, extending eternally before and beyond human existence and founded on what Dickens believed to be a pattern of divine justice. What I have tried to suggest throughout this work, and wish to emphasize here because *Martin Chuzzlewit* is a flawed novel open to misreadings for many reasons, is that for Dickens the polarity of judgment and punishment against that of mercy and forgiveness constituted an unvarying frame upon which his narratives confidently wove themselves. I believe that if we keep this in mind we will remain as close as possible to what Dickens believed himself to be achieving.

NOTES

1. Charles Dickens, *Martin Chuzzlewit* (New York: Oxford University Press, 1951), 1. Subsequent references appear in the text.

2. Dickens' preface and his comments to John Forster and others indicate that his chief concern was to expose selfishness.

3. *Dickens' Working Notes for his Novels,* ed. Harry Stone (Chicago: The University of Chicago Press, 1987), 43.

4. John Forster, *The Life of Charles Dickens* (London: Chapman and Hall, 1893), 224.

5. Michael Steig, *Dickens and Phiz* (Bloomington: Indiana University Press, 1978), 60–61. Subsequent references appear in the text.

6. Alexander Welsh, *From Copyright to Copperfield: The Identity of Dickens* (Cambridge: Harvard University Press, 1987), 122. Subsequent references appear in the text.

7. See, for example, Bert Hornback's *Noah's Arkitecture: A Study of Dickens's Mythology* (Athens: Ohio University Press, 1972), 42ff. Chapter 5 of Welsh draws the relationship between *Martin Chuzzlewit* and *Paradise Lost.* And Sylvia Manning calls attention to the persistent inversion of the Eden theme in *Dickens as Satirist* (New Haven: Yale University Press, 1971), 71ff.

8. Jane Vogel's *Allegory in Dickens* (University, AL: The University of Alabama Press, 1977) and Janet L. Larson's *Dickens and the Broken Scripture* (Athens: The University of Georgia Press, 1985) are two works that deal with ironic uses of the Bible in *Martin Chuzzlewit* and other Dickens texts.

9. Michael Steig calls attention especially to the allusion to *Paradise Lost* in Phiz's illustration (77).

10. J. Hillis Miller examines the many ramifications of self-exploration and concern for identity in *Martin Chuzzlewit.* "Everywhere in *Martin Chuzzlewit,* then, we find in the characters a vacillation between the desire to be wholly autonomous and the even more intense desire to discover something outside themselves which will recognize their being" (*Charles Dickens: The World of His Novels* [Cambridge: Harvard University Press, 1965] 139).

11. See Sylvère Monod's *Martin Chuzzlewit* (London: George Allen and Unwin, 1985) for a survey of attitudes on Martin's failure as a character and doubts about the authenticity of his conversion (27ff.). Subsequent references appear in the text.

12. John R. Reed, *Victorian Conventions* (Athens: Ohio University Press, 1975), 239ff. See also Steig on the prodigal son motif (63).

13. Archibald C. Coolidge, Jr. calls attention to the importance of secrets in *Martin Chuzzlewit* in *Charles Dickens as a Serial Novelist* (Ames: Iowa University Press, 1967), 108.

14. Sylvère Monod details other clues to Jonas' guilt and foreshadowings of his fate (98).

15. Algernon Charles Swinburne, *Charles Dickens* (London: Chatto and Windus, 1913), 29.

16. Monod regards *Martin Chuzzlewit* as "one of the best illustrations of Dickens' curious and on the whole intelligent treatment of the theme" of criminality (92). George Gissing thought Jonas "mechanical," but "the earliest worth mentioning" of Dickens' "black-hearted" villains (*Charles Dickens: A Critical Study* [New York: Dodd, Mead and Co., 1924], 112). Philip Collins says that Jonas is pretty conventional until he experiences a troubling premonitory dream, after which Dickens' presentation of him is more original and effective (*Dickens and Crime* [Bloomington: Indiana University Press, 1968], 276).

17. See the later passage where he expresses a similar vindictiveness toward Tom Pinch (712).

18. Monod recognizes Dickens' pattern of punishment and the severity of Tigg's fate. The victim of crime is himself a criminal. "That, then, is Tigg's punishment, and it is final enough to satisfy any appetite for retribution" (105).

19. In his preface Dickens says poetic justice is not necessary as an explanation for the fates Anthony and Jonas Chuzzlewit, but the manners of their deaths still evoke a powerful sense of poetic justice.

20. Several scholars have noted Jonas' contribution to his own destruction. Sharon Whitehill is among the most explicit; she contrasts his self-destruction with Martin's moral regeneration ("Jonas Chuzzlewit: Archetype of the Self-Destroyer," *Dickens Studies Newsletter* 9 [1978], 70–73). J. Hillis Miller has an acute analysis of Jonas' process of self-division and self-destruction (126ff.).

21. Robert M. McCarron, "Folly and Wisdom: Three Dickensian Wise Fools," *Dickens Studies Annual* 6 (1977), 40–56.

22. See, for example, the narrator's extended praise of Tom's simplicity of soul that concludes Chapter 39 (616–17).

23. Kathleen Tillotson, *Novels of the Eighteen-Forties* (London: Oxford University Press, 1961), 160.

24. Robert Polhemus, *Comic Faith: The Great Tradition from Austen to Joyce* (Chicago: University of Chicago Press, 1980), 88ff.

25. James R. Kincaid, *Dickens and the Rhetoric of Laughter* (New York: Oxford University Press, 1971), 134–35.

26. James R. Kincaid, "All the Wickedness in the World is Print: Dickens and Subversive Interpretation," *Victorian Literature and Society,* ed. James R. Kincaid and Albert J. Kuhn (Columbus: Ohio State University Press, 1984), 273.

27. Gerhard Joseph, "The Labyrinth and the Library: A View from the Temple in *Martin Chuzzlewit,"* *Dickens Studies Annual* 15 (1986), 1–22.

28. Anthony Trollope, *An Autobiography,* intro. Bradford Allen Booth (Berkeley: University of California Press, 1947), 265.

TEN

Dickens' Christmas Narratives

CHARLES DICKENS viewed the Christmas season as a time to remind ourselves of the sweeter aspects of the Christian faith. Today we tend to focus on Scrooge's fearsome Christmas Eve ordeal, ending with the anticipation of his own death and the joyous relief of a second chance represented by a toothsome goose. But there is much more in these stories of peace and love than of terror and repentance.[1] All of the Christmas narratives emphasize the theme of redemption, but in the Christmas books, as distinguished from the stories, there is a greater suggestion of evil's effects and of the complexity of human relationships. Thus in the premiere Christmas Book, *A Christmas Carol* (1843), Scrooge comes on stage as a repulsive man, except perhaps for his sardonic wit. He delights in being recognized as privately and publically uncharitable. Like Mr. Langley in the story "Somebody's Luggage" (1862), he comes perilously close to casting his heart into a dungeon of its own making. Marley's ghost warns Scrooge that the chains he is currently forging for himself to wear after death will greatly outweigh those he sees encumbering his ex-partner. Not only has Scrooge refused to give charity, he refuses to accept any from his nephew, Fred. The consequence of this behavior, this rejection of the true spirit of Christ, is a form of punishment. In keeping with the motif of temporal liquidity in this story, the whole of Scrooge's adventure may be seen in mythic terms so that the day, night, and day of the narrative represent an entire life span. Christmas Eve sums up his life as it has been lived and his awakening to Christmas morning previews how it will be lived. Under these circumstances it is not surprising that immediately after we, as readers, have become acquainted with Scrooge's ungenerous nature, his punishment comes upon him in the form of a forced exploration of his own inner wilderness. The narrator, by collapsing time in his own narrative and blurring time in the accounts of Scrooge's visitants, puts his readers in the position of witnessing not

154

one episode in the life of a specific man, but an archetypal experience representative of mankind in general.

It may seem strange that Dickens began his tradition of Christmas narratives with a protagonist so deeply in need of penitence and forgiveness. It would have been so easy to emphasize the benevolent actions of a virtuous individual, but the Scrooge pattern is a recurrent one in Dickens' fiction—a somehow imperfect hero coming to a recognition of his limitations and amending them.[2] This pattern is not nearly so true of heroines. This hunting down and rooting out of some internal fault is the psychological equivalent of the discovery and pursuit of the villains that populate Dickens' novels. Scrooge's situation broadly resembles Mr. Dombey's. He has rejected love and valued property. His punishment is to discover through psychological travail the superior value of love and the poisonously ineffective nature of wealth. Mr. Dombey, too, has sealed himself in the prison of his own character and is spared a grisly confrontation with death through the renewal of love. Gradually Scrooge emerges from the dungeon of his self into the light of family affection, and into a recognition of his fellowship with all of humanity; like Dr. Manet he is reborn to life. The device that brings Scrooge to his knees is a proleptic vision of his own neglected grave. This life-size *memento mori* alerts Scrooge to the full, eternal impact of the lovelessness he has manifested. It sets him yearning for a second chance, which, of course, he gets, giving and receiving good will, and pleading for the forgiveness that he has needed all along. In retrospect, Scrooge does not seem so very mean because the whole narrative is bathed in the narrator's happy energy, as G. K. Chesterton observed, adding that "Scrooge is not really inhumane in the beginning any more than he is at the end. There is a heartiness in his inhospitable sentiments that is akin to humour and therefore to humanity; he is only a crusty old bachelor, and had (I strongly suspect) given away turkeys secretly all his life."[3] We may justly doubt that Scrooge was a secret benefactor during his mature years, but, for all his mistaken views of life, he is not evil.

Trotty Veck seems as remote from wickedness as can be, but *The Chimes* (1844) follows a design very much like that in *A Christmas Carol*, only far more benignly. Though Trotty Veck *is* a good man, he makes one serious error. In a moment of depression, after he has read an account of an impoverished mother's murder of her child, he wonders if the poor and common people like himself are not somehow inherently bad. This doubt violates the principle of hope and progress represented by the church bells, which therefore put Trotty through an ordeal much like Scrooge's. He is obliged to watch as the years pass and his daughter, Meg, and her husband, Richard, slide into poverty and disorder, until finally Richard is dying and poor haggard Meg is left alone with an infant daughter. Determined to prevent the child from growing up to a life of prostitution and vice, she aims to drown it. But Trotty interrupts this horrible vision to exclaim that he has learned his lesson and realizes that killing a child may be an expression of a mother's love, and not necessarily an unnatural act. Dickens himself had once been called to serve at an inquest to determine if a mother had purposely murdered her child, where he argued for the most lenient view.[4]

Trotty is actually guilty of two offenses. One is insulting the ideal of hope—a large, abstract notion represented by the bells of the church. The other is a rash judgment upon a fellow creature whose circumstances he does not understand. He must literally learn to put himself in her place. This caution about hasty judgment is all the more important among the poor because their lives are so greatly influenced by circumstances beyond their control. After his harrowing vision of the possible future, Trotty realizes "that we must trust and hope, and neither doubt ourselves, nor doubt the good in one another." He also has a sense of the providential scheme that makes hope possible because it will see to the "natural" assigning of punishment and reward. "'I know that our inheritance is held in store for us by Time to rise one day, before which all who wrong or oppress us will be swept away like leaves.'"[5] Trotty learns that we not only must forgive those who injure us personally, but we must be prepared to forgive those who do harm to our class or communal interests as well. A society in which forgiveness is confined to individual interactions will never rise to the vision of providential justice implicit in Dickens' writings and which he shared with his friend Thomas Carlyle.

The Chimes is essentially melodramatic, establishing Trotty at the center of a struggle between benevolence and selfish pride. On one side are Meg, Richard, Will Fern, and Lilian, all good-hearted but disadvantaged people. On the other are official types like Alderman Cute, who wants to put down suicide, Sir Joseph Bowley, a caricature of paternalism, and Filer, who values the good old times and thinks the poor have no right to be born. The prize in the contest between these two forces is the consciousness of Trotty Veck. That is why his self-doubt, which implies doubt of all of his kind, is such a grave betrayal and a potential victory for oppressors like Cute. But the characteristic feature of Dickens' plot is that none of the virtuous personages play any role in punishing the Bowleys, Cutes, and Filers. So the melodramatic conclusion never comes, though it hovers in the air perhaps more powerfully for remaining offstage. It *will* come and the wicked *will* suffer, but the good must not actively bring it about. It may be argued that this quietism is typical of Dickens' reforming spirit. He wants social improvements, but not through active rebellion or disorder by the poor and the disadvantaged. As I have tried to show, this avoidance of retributive or punitive gestures was a central tenet of his Christian beliefs, which underlay his social and political views.

Scrupulousness about human charity has another face in *The Chimes,* and the shape of the narrative, its locating of critical, even pivotal scenes, follows from the extension or withholding of forgiveness. In Trotty's vision Lilian, who has become a prostitute, brings money to the very needy Meg and Richard, but Meg cannot accept this money. She loves Lilian still, but as long as Lilian holds to her sinful ways she cannot accept anything from her. Nor can she forgive Lilian. As we saw in Chapter 1, humans cannot forgive sin; they can release others only from some injury to themselves. A modern reader less sensitive to the charged religious emotion of this scene might easily miss its enormous power and therefore equally overlook the significance of the scene where a repentant Lilian does ask forgiveness. Meg's refusal of the money galvanizes Lilian's conscience and she returns to Meg after abandoning the vicious life into which she had fallen. Dickens' narrators generally assure us that Youth and Beauty implement the ends of our Beneficent Creator, and so Meg is able to win Lilian back to virtue.

> 'Forgive me, Meg! so dear, so dear! Forgive me! I know you do, I
> see you do, but say so, Meg!'
> She said so, with her lips on Lilian's cheek. And with her arms
> twined round—she knew it now—a broken heart. (137)

The narrator confirms Lilian's repentance by having her die immediately. Meg's forgiveness now represents the usual acceptance back into the Christian fold of the truly repentant.

The Cricket on the Hearth (1846) is concerned with secrecy, misinterpretation, and forgiveness. This is a simple narrative about various kinds of matrimonial misunderstanding, conveyed by a curiously disembodied first-person narrator. Thanks to Tackleton, the effective villain of the piece, John Peerybingle comes to believe that his wife, Dot, loves a young stranger. John feels guilty of injuring his wife by having married a woman so much younger than himself. He tells Tackleton that he is willing to set Dot free to have the life she wants. "'Go, with my blessing for the many happy hours she has given me, and my forgiveness for any pang she has caused me'" (218). Another marriage problem is Tackleton's planned union with the much younger May, a mirror image of John's case but devoid of mutual love, for May is secretly in love with Edward Plummer, who eventually rescues and marries her. Meanwhile, blind Bertha Plummer envies May's projected marriage because her father, Caleb Plummer, has misrepresented Tackleton as a paragon of benevolence and grace. There is a typically Dickensian symmetry in the development of these two plotlines, for just as John is forgiving his apparently wayward wife, Caleb is asking his daughter's pardon. "'My dear blind daughter, hear me and forgive me! The world you live in, heart of mine, doesn't exist as I have represented it. The eyes you have trusted in, have been false to you'" (222). Bertha does forgive him and love him, realizing that all of his deceit was prompted by deep affection. By disclosing the secret of his deception, Caleb achieves forgiveness and solidifies his bond with his daughter. John's case is parallel, but different. If Caleb misrepresents the world to his trusting daughter, John misreads his faithful wife and is guilty of distrust. Even before Tackleton shows him Dot and the young stranger apparently in intimate conversation, John had been suspicious of his wife. But he kept this secret to himself, suffering in silence. Caleb's is an active secret, a lie about the world. John's is a passive secret, a fear about the truth. Though John is wrong about his wife, there are grounds for his suspicion because Dot has a secret of her own for which she blames herself. She has not told her husband that she has been actively assisting the romance of Edward and May, and her suspicious behavior is associated with this generous effort. John's suffering is self-punishment for an unworthy secret; Dot's self-judgment is for a secret charity. The virtues of humility and charity ironically lead to suffering because they are misinterpreted.

Implicit in *The Cricket on the Hearth* is a warning not to keep secrets, not to tell lies (even for an apparently good purpose), and not to rashly interpret the conduct of others. When the misreadings in this narrative are corrected, three couples are reconfirmed in love—Bertha and her father, Edward and May, John and Dot. But one misunderstanding remains. At the heart of this story is Tackleton, an unpleasant, uncharitable toymaker. There is a seeming paradox in the man's trade and nature, the one designed to provide innocent pleasure, the other to seek selfish comfort. The story leaves no doubt that Tackleton has a bad side, but at the end of the tale, when we expect the scoundrel to behave in some vindictive way toward the young lovers who have frustrated his purposes, and to be summarily punished for it, Tackleton instead sends the cake from his own aborted wedding to Edward and May's marriage celebration, followed by some toys for Dot's child, followed by himself, asking the others to "'Be gracious to me; let me join this happy party!'" (233). They are gracious to him, forgiving him as a changed man and admitting him to their charmed company. After all, this is a Christmas story.

But there is more to this surprising transformation. Just as the characters have had to deal with secrets, misrepresentations, misreadings, and rash judgments, so the narrator now reinforces his lesson by demonstrating to his readers that they too have misread Tackleton's character and judged it too quickly. No judgment is safe before the end of the story. As we have seen earlier, Dickens often represents life as a story in the midst of telling. All "final" assessments are therefore premature. A Scrooge may change overnight because good memories and a clear vision of a loveless life and death may redeem the best in him. So, too, a Tackleton. And there are preparatory clues. Nasty as the consequences may be, it is not necessarily unkind to warn an acquaintance that his wife may be unfaithful. And can a man whose occupation is toymaking be truly evil? If we, as readers, had read more charitably, perhaps this ending would have seemed less a surprise and more a fulfillment.

Forgiveness is important in the three stories I have mentioned so far, but everything hinges on it in *The Battle of Life* (1846). Like *The Cricket on the Hearth,* this story involves a good deal of misunderstanding. It opens on the scene of a great historical battle but immediately offers the hopeful reflection that, although the hideous traces of the fight lasted a long while, "Nature, far above the evil passions of men, soon recovered Her serenity, and smiled upon the guilty battleground as she had done before when it was innocent" (239). This fancy prefigures the action of the story, involving the apparent guilty flight of Marion Jeddler, which is actually the benevolent means of bringing Marion's sister, Grace, and Alfred Heathfield together. Marion is supposed to have run off with the "prodigal son," Michael Warden, who, at thirty, has almost ruined himself by wasting a large estate (262). "Prodigality" echoes throughout this tale intent upon fostering the values of home. After all, the message of the parable of the prodigal son is that he has sufficient humility and faith after his dissipations to return home and to seek forgiveness.

On the very evening that Marion decides to leave home secretly, she happens to read aloud a passage from a book that praises the virtues of home and comments on the sorrow of separation. She is much upset by the text, which continues, "O Home, so true to us, so often slighted in return, be lenient to them that turn away from thee, and do not haunt their erring footsteps too reproachfully." Don't remind such exiles of your blessings, the book advises, "but if thou canst look harshly and severely, do, in mercy to the Penitent" (269). This is an odd passage on the prodigal theme, in effect suggesting that Home should make itself appear unattractive so that those who desert the hearth will suffer less for their betrayal. In fact, it is precisely the aching memory of home that can generate the penitence that leads prodigals to return and to find salvation.

Marion's father, whose philosophy is "to look upon the world as a gigantic practical joke; as something too absurd to be considered seriously, by any rational man" chides her for being so emotionally moved by the book, which he calls " 'mere rags and ink' " (264, 269). Texts of this kind, however, are a significant theme in Dickens' Christmas writings, as Deborah Thomas has pointed out.[6] Marion is deeply moved because she, like Michael Warden, is about to play the prodigal; unlike Warden, her gesture is not an adventure in dissipation, but an act of generous love for her sister. The passage that Marion reads, recommending that Home make itself unattractive to the prodigal, seems to reinforce Marion's imminent "betrayal" of home and affection.

Soon after this scene Marion asks her father's forgiveness in advance for any pain or grief that she might cause him. The good doctor plays facetiously with the idea of forgiveness, but he soon has reason to consider it soberly. When Warden returns to the neighborhood, six years later Doctor Jeddler, after much suffering, had forgiven Marion at Grace's wedding. Warden allows everyone to believe that Marion has died, until she herself arrives to explain that, although Warden wished to possess her, he honorably assisted her in leaving home to stay secretly with a relative. Marion loved Alfred, but seeing that Grace loved him too, she sacrificed herself to make her sister happy. Meanwhile, Warden, having lived abroad on a tight budget, has recovered his fortunes and become a reformed prodigal.

Running like a countertheme in a fugue through this plot is the subordinate story of Clemency Newcome. As her name suggests, she represents uncomplicated virtue and she lives by two simple maxims, one on her thimble and one on her nutmeg grater. The one is "Forget and Forgive," the other, "Do as you would be done by" (255–56). Her kind ways help everyone, and even transform the sour servant Benjamin Britain into a cordial innkeeper and her husband. But through the narrative Clemency's maxims are not taken seriously enough. When Clemency shows her thimble with "For-get and For-give" engraved on it, the lawyers Snitchey and Craggs laugh at it. "'So new!' said Snitchey. So easy!' said Craggs. Such a knowledge of human nature in it!' said Snitchey. So applicable to the affairs of life!' said Craggs" (255). The lawyers have a view of life a degree bleaker than that of Doctor Jeddler, who considers life a joke. Snitchey's expression of life as a game introduces a more sinister note.

> 'I don't stand up for life in general,' he added, rubbing his hands and chuckling, 'it's full of folly; full of something worse. Professions of trust, and confidence, and unselfishness, and all that! Bah, bah, bah! We see what they're worth. But you mustn't laugh at life; you've got a game to play; a very serious game indeed! Everybody's playing against you, you know, and you're playing against them.' (251)

However, after Marion has returned and the secret of her purpose is revealed in all its sororal splendor, Doctor Jeddler revises his view, admitting that the world is a "'world full of hearts . . . and a serious world . . . and it is a world we need be careful how we libel, Heaven forgive us, for it is a world of sacred mysteries, and its Creator only knows what lies beneath the surface of His lightest image!'" (308).

The Battle of Life embodies the contest between a world of hearts that forgive and a world of distrust, selfishness, and antagonism. And, in the end, the narrator supports the forgiving side by concluding his tale with an account of Michael Warden's improved condition. Warden says that he has endured a term of self-reproach, learning his demerits, and makes his "'humble supplication for forgiveness'" to Marion "'when I knew her merit and my deep unworthiness. In a few days I shall quit this place for ever. I entreat your pardon. So as you would be done by! Forget and forgive!'" (311). The narrator coyly steps in at this point to remark that he has had the latter portion of this story from Time, with whom he is well acquainted, and been informed that Michael never went away but received his reward of Marion as a wife. "But," he adds, "as I have observed that Time confuses facts occasionally, I hardly know what weight to give to his authority" (312).

Deborah Thomas says that The Battle of Life is "mawkishly sentimental; the plot is implausible; the characters are poorly motivated and thinly drawn" (48), and she concludes that the book "is a clear failure" (51).[7] From a high literary point of view this is surely true, but the book may have a different and perhaps deeper level of modified success. The plot of this story is very contrived and highly improbable, but that is because it partakes more of the world of fable than of reality. It is Dickens' own version of a parable. And part of its lesson might be summarized by another maxim: "Judge not lest ye be judged." Warden's lawyers, knowing of his love for Marion and his intemperate ways, assume that he has run away with her. Everyone believes the worst of Marion. Yet this wickedness never generates hatred or vengefulness, only sorrow. Underlying this apparently spoiled world is a benign order (as represented by Clemency). Even the animosity between the two lawyers' wives turns out, after all, to be a fiction more illustrative of a common cause than of hostility. What for so long seems the deepest wickedness turns out to have been the most generous and benevolent behavior. The apparent conflict of life symbolized by the ancient battleground actually reveals itself as harmony, like curative Nature herself. And removing the mask of guilt discloses a radical innocence. The prodigals come home from their travels untainted, with no need for forgiveness, but only for welcome.

The Battle of Life is a misleading title, just as the plot itself is filled with misleading clues, for in the world of this story beneficence and forgiveness prevail. They only wait to be discovered. The great secret of the book, one perpetuated by the narrator's purposeful silence, is a good secret. The story may be viewed as a conscious reversal of Dickens' usual pattern, in which uncharitableness must be redeemed by witnessing some act of benevolence, as with Scrooge. But if this story is particularly devoted to a world dominated by the forgiving, even self-forgiving spirit, it is like almost all of the other Christmas books and stories in displaying so little of punishment. But given Dickens' view of what Christmas should be, it is entirely fitting that he excludes any serious degree of punishment from these narratives, illustrating instead the virtues he wishes to reinforce. When some punishment does occur, it is generally the self-punishment of a cramped heart. Even injury is turned to a good purpose. As Milly Swidger in *The Haunted Man* (1848) tells Mr. Redlaw, it is a good thing to remember the wrong that has been done to us so that we may forgive it. As John Butt has said, this last of the Christmas books stresses the importance of memory to man's moral condition (144ff.). Redlaw makes a compact with a ghost to forget a bad memory that haunts him. But the compact includes him transmitting his amnesia to others. Although the other characters have learned to live with human suffering through the recollection of an act of human sympathy, when they contract Redlaw's amnesia they become disagreeable egotists. Redlaw's effect is counteracted, however, by Milly, who revives their power of sympathy on the strength of her simple affections. Memory is especially important in *The Haunted Man,* in which Dickens intended to show that bad and good are inextricably linked in memory and we must recall both to derive the benefit of remembering. Dickens emphasizes the power of memory for good throughout the Christmas books and stories, in particular by turning the Christmas season itself into a talisman of memory, recalling the spirit of Christian forgiveness and charity.[8]

"A Christmas Tree" (1850) dwells heavily on the theme of redemptive memory through the narrator's recollection of the many children's tales he associates with Christmas. He is reluctant to leave the enchanted realm of these tales, but moves on to the story of Christ as presented in the Waits' Christmas songs, ending with the final scene: "again, dying upon a Cross, watched by armed soldiers, a thick darkness coming on, the earth beginning to shake, and only one voice heard, 'Forgive them, for they know not what they do.'"[9] This is the popular Scrooge paradigm in embryo. Memory leads to an encounter with death, and to the real meaning of Christmas as the birth of a savior who promises hope to mankind through a message of forgiveness and love. After this point the tale becomes more somber until it closes with Christ's injunction to remember: "'This, in commemoration of the law of love and kindness, mercy and compassion. This, in remembrance of Me!'" (18).

Most of the Christmas stories, even if they touch upon grisly subjects, are essentially upbeat. An interesting example, a kind of anti-Scrooge fable, is "The Schoolboy's Story" (1853). Here the boys at a private school turn on Old Cheeseman, who was once a student at the school but who has now accepted the post of second Latin Master, an action the boys regard as treachery. They put a ban on Cheeseman, which pains his kindly heart. One day Cheeseman is gone. The boys speculate that he has done away with himself out of shame. Learning instead that he has inherited a fortune, they anticipate his dire revenge upon them when he revisits the school. But when he returns, Cheeseman entertains everyone, saying that he couldn't enjoy his good fortune without exchanging congratulations with the students. "'If we have ever misunderstood one another at all, pray, my dear boys, let us forgive and forget'" (56). Of course it goes beyond that. After the predictable feasting Cheeseman, who, like Scrooge, had regularly suffered such a fate when he was young, asks who has to stay over the holidays at school. The narrator of the story is the only instance of such abandonment, so Cheeseman and his new bride take him away for a grand time at their home.

Sometimes the effort of forgiveness is not so simple. In "The Seven Travellers" (1854), Richard Doubledick witnesses the death in battle of his mentor, ideal, and friend, Captain Taunton, and vows to avenge it. When Richard conveys the news of her son's death to Mrs. Taunton, the young man and his friend's mother become attached to one another. Through a tangled set of circumstances, Mrs. Taunton becomes great friends with a family in the South of France. When Richard visits he discovers the French gentleman to be the officer responsible for his dear friend's death. He realizes that this is a fine man of excellent sentiments and is torn between his vengeful purpose and his respect for its object. Gradually his craving for retribution diminishes until he comes to feel the influence of his lost friend. "'Spirit of my departed friend . . . is it through thee these better thoughts are rising in my mind?'" The spirit of love and forgiveness triumphs, associated with the memory of a beloved friend. When Richard "touched that French officer's glass with his own, that day at dinner, he secretly forgave him in the name of the Divine Forgiver of injuries" (91).

This narrative is contrived to bring about the intense inner struggle between the desire to punish and the need to forgive. It is, in that sense, a narrative forgiveness comparable to the narrative punishments we have noticed elsewhere in Dickens' writings. This specially arranged forgiveness is important because it has an unusual trait—the chief act of forgiveness must be secret. Richard cannot identify the officer to Mrs. Taunton, for that would taint the friendship now so innocently uncomplicated. Nor can he confide the secret to his wife or to the officer himself. But the secrecy of this forgiveness is actually the highest confirmation of its sincerity. It is a triumph within the self that requires no approval or praise from elsewhere. Often forgiveness occurs in a dramatic, even melodramatic situation in Dickens' fiction so that, at least for modern readers, some of its force is lost in what appears to be a spectacular insincerity, if not on the part of the characters, then in the narrator himself. But unshared forgiveness, because unwitnessed, has the virtue of appearing more deep-seated and profound. Only we, as readers, view the happy spectacle and derive our own secret pleasure from it. Moreover, because of this sharing, we are more likely to internalize the experience and contribute to it in the manner described by Wolfgang Iser, especially since the role of forgiveness is so well established in the Christian interpretive community common to readers in nineteenth-century England, and is still widely felt today.[10]

But secret forgiveness may be a dangerous virtue, as the next year's Christmas story suggests. In "The Holly Tree" (1855), Charley narrates how he first encountered the Holly-Tree Inn on a detour through Yorkshire on his way to take ship to America because he believed that his beloved Angela Leath preferred his good friend Edwin to him. Charley intends "to write each of them an affecting letter conveying my blessing and forgiveness," which they will receive after he is at sea (98). He is stopped by a snowstorm at the Holly-Tree Inn and the bulk of his narrative is given over to stories about inns. Then, near the end of the tale, as Charley is about to resume his journey, Edwin arrives at the inn. They are surprised to see one another and Edwin exclaims, " 'Charley, forgive me!' " He, assuming that Edwin is conveying Angela to Gretna Green for a hasty marriage, replies, " 'Was this well? When I loved her so dearly! When I had garnered up my heart so long!' " (127). But no forgiveness is necessary, for the woman in Edwin's carriage is not Angela, but her cousin Emmeline, to whom Edwin will in due course be married. Charley returns to London and marries Angela. He admits to us, his audience, "I have never until this time, even to her, disclosed the secret of my character, and the mistrust and the mistaken journey into which it led me" (128). It is only at this point that we realize how much in need of forgiveness Charley is. He had imagined an injury which he intended to forgive in what now appears a pathetic, almost melodramatic, manner. But, after all, it is he who injured his dearest friends with untested suspicions and distrust. Unlike Richard Doubledick, whose secret forgiveness is a genuine act of self-overcoming which communicates its healing quality to the readers who alone know of it, Charley needs to confess the false basis for his forgiveness to some audience, if not to Edwin and Angela, because doing so represents a form of self-awareness essential for ultimate absolution. To forgive where there is no injury is to assume a position of moral superiority that is unjustified and that bears a strong resemblance to hypocrisy. Of course, Charley's is a light-hearted case told in retrospect and he knows that since he is writing down his memories for family members he will be found out at last. But, he says, he can bear it. "I began at the Holly-Tree, by idle accident, to associate the Christmas-time of year with human interest, and with some inquiry into, and some care for, the lives of those by whom I find myself surrounded. I hope that I am none the worse for it, and that no one near me or afar off is the worse for it" (129).

Sometimes all that is required to revive human sympathy is an example of Christian charity. In chapter 2 of "Somebody's Luggage" (1862), Mr. Langley, an apparently ill-tempered Englishman, is lodging in a French town. He has disowned his daughter, now left with a young daughter of her own. Langley is attracted by Corporal Théophile's jolly and kind treatment of a young girl, Bebelle. He makes their acquaintance and gradually comes to admire the friendship. After the corporal dies fighting a fire in the town, Langley finds Bebelle lying on his grave, and this evidence of deep human attachment melts his heart. He determines that he will "take away Bebelle to look for Théophile [his spirit, that is] in England and at his forgiven daughter's" (346). As he is leaving the French village, he has an early taste of his reward, as his landlady and her associate cry, " 'Homage to the friend of the friendless' " (348). But here, as with Charley in "The Holly-Tree," it is Langley who has benefited from his own generous act. His life was soured and headed in a bad direction until the model of man and child reminded him of what human relations are meant to be and how easily they may be coaxed in that direction by forgiveness. The refusal to forgive is a disease, an injury, an imprisonment of the unforgiving one, as Dickens makes quite clear: "so the dark shades and the hollow sounds and the unwholesomely locked currents of his soul were vanquished and set free. See to it, Vaubans of your own hearts, who gird them in with triple walls and ditches, and with bolt and chain and bar and lifted bridge,—raze those fortifications, and lay them level with the all-absorbing dust, before the night cometh when no hand can work!" (347).

A slightly milder version of this same pattern, which reflects Scrooge's prototypical example, occurs in "Mugby Junction" (1866). Mr. Jackson, who calls himself Barbox Brothers, after the firm he slaved for and came to own, has retired from business and is traveling to escape from his birthday. He had been disappointed in love when the girl he worshipped married his friend; and all his loveless life has been spent in bill-broking. In Mugby Junction he becomes acquainted with the cheerful invalid Phoebe and her thoughtful and kindly father, Lamps. He admires their good cheer in hard circumstances and resolves to contribute to it by buying Phoebe a musical instrument. On a visit to the city, after feeling the positive effects of his charity, Mr. Jackson encounters a young girl who first claims to be lost but later is revealed as Polly, the daughter of his old love, Beatrice. Heartened by the look of human sympathy in his face when she sees him buying his gift for Phoebe, Beatrice has the courage to reestablish contact with Jackson through Polly. Beatrice's terminally ill husband believes that a curse has killed their other children and will wither Polly too because of their treatment of Jackson. "'I now pray to you to forgive me, and to forgive my husband,'" Beatrice pleads (510). He does this implicitly by blessing Polly. In forgiving Beatrice and her husband, he has transformed the evil memory that spoiled his life into a positive experience. He returns to Mugby Junction with a far different attitude toward his fellow human beings. "For he was Barbox Brothers and Co. now, and had taken thousands of partners into the solitary firm" (514). The act of forgiveness here is nearly as contrived as that of Richard Doubledick's, but far from being a private and secret affair, it calls attention to the way an individual act of forgiveness can open the heart to a larger community.

The final example of the function of forgiveness in the Christmas stories is an involuted one. In "Mrs Lirriper's Legacy" (1864), Mrs. Lirriper and Major Jackman take young Jemmy Lirriper, Mrs. Lirriper's adopted child, to France because a dying man notifies Mrs. Lirriper that he has willed his property to her. "Mrs Lirriper's Lodging" (1863) told the story of how a young woman was abandoned in her pregnancy and delivered a child that remained in the care of Mrs. Lirriper and Major Jackman when she died. Now, at Sens, Mrs. Lirriper discovers that the dying man who sent for her is Jemmy's father. Mrs. Lirriper denounces him at first but sees that he is suffering and, with the memory of Jemmy's dying mother in mind, cries, "'O man, man, man . . . if your heart is rent asunder and you are truly penitent for what you did, Our Saviour will have mercy on you yet!'" (425). The dying man, though speechless, indicates that he would like to see Jemmy, knowing that the boy has been kept ignorant of his father. So Mrs. Lirriper and Major Jackman bring Jemmy to the death bed.

> "My darling boy, there is a reason in the secret history of this fellow-creetur lying as the best and worst of us must all lie one day, which I think would ease his spirit in his last hour if you would lay your cheek against his forehead and say, 'May God forgive you!'"
> "O Gran," says Jemmy with a full heart "I am not worthy!" But he leaned down and did it. Then the faltering fingers made out to catch hold of my sleeve at last, and I believe he was a-trying to kiss me when he died. (427)

In this instance Jemmy is able to forgive an injury done to him by his own father without knowing that it is a personal forgiveness he conveys. But because he has learned the general principle that forgiveness is a Christian's duty, he can forgive, as it were, in the abstract. The secret here is unlike that of Charley or Richard Doubledick. Jemmy will not know that he has forgiven a personal trespass, but only that all who err are open to God's forgiveness. The secret is kept exclusively from the person it most affects, but by preserving this secret, the narrator emphasizes the purity of the gesture. Jemmy realizes that he is not necessarily worthy to forgive others, but he knows that we can all, like Richard Doubledick, forgive in the name of the Divine Forgiver. At the same time that Jemmy's act remains pure of personal sentiment, it has the effect on his father of an individual act of forgiveness. This is, perhaps, the purest form of forgiveness available to human beings.

Dickens' Christmas narratives stress the need to recall the positive features of the Christian faith, and, though several of them deal with wickedness—such as "The Perils of Certain English Prisoners" (1857) and "No Thoroughfare" (1867)—or natural disaster, as in "The Wreck of the Golden Mary," the overwhelming mood of these works is redemptive, reminding readers that Christ's message of charity and forgiveness is most appropriately recalled, especially by memories of love and friendship, at the season most closely identified with him.

"No Thoroughfare," written in collaboration with Wilkie Collins, is, on the surface, closely related to melodrama, even describing its divisions as acts in a manner common with Collins. But the story also demonstrates fairly directly the kind of maneuvers Dickens felt necessary to achieve the moral justice he believed his fictions should convey. We need not review the entire plot here, but may simply concentrate on its central conflict. George Vendale's partner in a wine business, Walter Wilding, dies after failing to find the true Walter Wilding for whom he was mistaken when a child in the foundling hospital. Vendale is in love with the Swiss girl Marguerite Obenreizer and establishes an agreement with her guardian, Jules Obenreizer, that he can marry her when his income reaches a certain level. But Jules is secretly both George's rival in love and a thief. Serving as Vendale's guide in the Alps, Obenreizer drugs him, attacks him, and pushes him into a chasm. Marguerite, following behind, discovers his body and courageously descends on a rope to save him, but Act 3 ends with the revelation that Vendale's heart has stopped. The melodramatic confrontation comes when Obenreizer demands to have Marguerite returned to him. At this point the lawyer Bintrey reveals that Vendale is still alive and that all of Obenreizer's crimes are known. The narrative stresses the passivity of the good characters Marguerite and Vendale, and emphasizes the active role of the lawyer who says that to unmask Obenreizer " 'I not only had no scruple in digging the pitfall under your feet in the dark—I felt a certain professional pleasure in fighting you with your own weapons. By my advice the truth has been carefully concealed from you up to this day. By my advice the trap into which you have walked was set for you' " (Books, 651). Obenreizer is forced to give up Marguerite in exchange for a promise of no further prosecution, but he also spitefully reveals that Vendale is the missing foundling, Walter Wilding. Even this malicious gesture reacts against him, for it makes Vendale the heir to a fortune and reconciles the difference of station that had seemed to create a barrier between Vendale and Marguerite. On the very day that George and Marguerite are married, Obenreizer's broken corpse, crushed by an avalanche, is hauled away to burial.

The opposition of good and evil here could have been simpler. The disclosures about Vendale's birth and Obenreizer's crimes might have occurred spectacularly in the alpine setting. The struggle might have ended with Vendale pitching his evil antagonist to his death. But Dickens' pattern of justice will not permit Vendale to act in punishing the villain. The whole plot must be turned and twisted and certain coincidences employed to make Obenreizer the agent of his own destruction. Even then, Dickens does not permit even lawyer Bintrey to punish Obenreizer, but only to redeem his trespasses. Ultimately we witness author/providence executing condign punishment on Obenreizer, and expelling him from the narrative world at the very moment when the good characters are joined in happiness, usurping the narrative space by monopolizing its projected future. Whatever its aesthetic merits, "No Thoroughfare" is a stark model of the underlying moral scheme that regularly guides Dickens' narrative decisions.

NOTES

1. Long ago Louis Cazamian explained Dickens' Christmas philosophy as an attempt to extend the good sentiments of Christmas beyond the family into society at large. This doctrine includes the assumption that "Christianity inescapably ordained solidarity among men, which ought to find expression in the active solicitude of society's members for one another. Rich and poor alike had duties, though the latter already possessed unsuspected virtues: dedication and self-sacrifice were common among them and, contrary to expectation, they were morally superior to the rich" (*The Social Novel in England 1830-1850: Dickens, Disraeli, Mrs Gaskell, Kingsley*, trans. Martin Fido [London: Routledge and Kegan Paul, 1973], 135; original publication in French, 1903).

2. Harry Stone calls attention to a pattern of this kind in the Christmas stories in *Dickens and the Invisible World: Fairy Tales, Fantasy, and Novel-Making* (Bloomington: Indiana University Press, 1979), 19ff.

3. G. K. Chesterton, *Charles Dickens*, intro. by Steven Marcus (New York: Schocken Books, 1965), 170.

4. Charles Dickens, "Some Recollections of Mortality," in *The Uncommercial Traveller and Reprinted Pieces* (London: Oxford University Press, 1964), 195ff. It has been noted that Dickens also drew upon widely disseminated newspaper stories about such cases. See for example John Butt's *Pope, Dickens, and Others* (Edinburgh: Edinburgh University Press, 1969), 139. Subsequent references appear in the text.

5. Charles Dickens, *Christmas Books* (New York: Oxford University Press, 1987), 151. Subsequent references appear in the text.

6. Deborah Thomas, *Dickens and the Short Story* (Philadelphia: University of Pennsylvania Press, 1982), 50ff.

7. George H. Ford included *The Battle of Life* and *The Cricket on the Hearth* among the worst books ever written by Dickens in *Dickens and His Readers: Aspects of Novel-Criticism Since 1836* (New York: W. W. Norton and Company, 1965), 53.

8. Various scholars have called attention to the importance of memory in Dickens' writings, among them F. S. Schwarzbach, *Dickens and the City* (London: The Athlone Press, 1979), 61ff., and Audrey Jaffe, *Vanishing Points: Dickens, Narrative and the Subject of Omniscience* (Berkeley: University of California Press, 1991), 66ff.

9. Charles Dickens, *Christmas Stories* (New York: Oxford University Press, 1987), 11. Subsequent references appear in the text.

10. Wolfgang Iser, *The Act of Reading: A Theory of Aesthetic Response* (Baltimore: The Johns Hopkins University Press, 1978). Iser writes that "significance is the reader's absorption of the meaning into his own existence. Only the two together can guarantee the effectiveness of an experience which entails the reader constituting himself by constituting a reality hitherto unfamiliar to himself" (151). Later he adds that the "significance of the work . . . does not lie in the meaning sealed within the text, but in the fact that that meaning brings out what had previously been sealed within us" (157).

ELEVEN

Dombey and Son

DOMBEY AND SON (1846–48) is Dickens' first novel in which a "villain," after accumulating a heavy debt of injustice, is redeemed by his punishments.[1] A contemporary reviewer recognized how unusual and morally superior this approach was.

> When a fashionable novelist introduces misfortune as attaching to his hero, it is usually in a manner *retributive:* the *corrective* has seldom any place in his mind. Misfortune, as the just penalty of folly or vice, is in his opinion a very handsome stretch of morality. Mr. Dickens does more, for he applies to misfortune that which makes it truly valuable, its scriptural quality of correction: he makes it the dark cloud, and heavy storm, which precede the setting sun's beams of humility and resignation.[2]

The two chief offenses in this novel are pride and a mercenary attitude toward human relations. Not only is Mr. Dombey guilty of both, he views them as virtues. Unlike an obvious wretch such as Ralph Nickleby, who knows himself to be avaricious and a hater of his kind, Dombey misviews himself as a worthy benefactor. Writing from a psychoanalytic base, Lawrence Frank regards Dombey as blind to his own nature: "Dombey, who cannot see himself, is *'condemned to the repertoire of the images'* he mistakes for himself."[3] On the surface this is a plausible explanation of Dombey, who, Frank points out, must remain unconscious of himself if he is to ignore the effects of change and death that surround him. But Dombey's pose of virtue and self-assurance masks a fundamental condition of bad faith, for Dickens himself notes in his preface to the novel that Mr. Dombey undergoes no violent change in his nature. "A sense of injustice is within him, all along. The more he represses it, the more unjust he necessarily is. Internal shame and external circumstances may bring the contest to a close in a week, or a day; but, it has been a contest for years, and is only fought out after a long balance of victory."[4] Kathleen Tillotson and Arlene Jackson have both indicated how Dombey's awareness of his false position is signaled many times before his collapse.[5] Jackson stresses Dombey's complexity, "the mixture of a man who knew what he was doing, but who could not refrain from doing it" (113). What Dickens wants in Dombey is an ideal case for punishment—a willed bad deed, in this case protracted for years—that is nonetheless accessible to redemption, hence the suppressed bad conscience.

Dombey is proud of his family and of his business, and, as it turns out, he applies the same values to both. This confusion of priorities is most evident in Mr. Dombey's relationship with his son. Wanting a male heir who will grow up to take over Dombey and Son, thus continuing the family regime, he is impatient for little Paul to be done with childhood and enter the business world. Little Paul, however, does not have a businessman's way of looking at the world. He asks his father, "What's money?" and is not satisfied with his father's reply that money can get you what you want, because he knows that money could not save his mother (92). Dombey makes little Paul Sol Gills' creditor so that the boy will learn the power of money. But if money can make people come to you for favors, thereby putting them in your debt, it cannot keep you from the grave. Paul is taken out of circulation by the old-fashioned means of death. This obvious truth should serve as an instruction to Mr. Dombey, but his son's death does not change the businessman's commercial outlook.

Florence Dombey cannot take her brother's place in her father's heart, and instead becomes an irritating reminder of Paul's loss. Florence is not valuable to Dombey despite her being his daughter because a girl in "the capital of the House's name and dignity . . . was merely a piece of base coin that couldn't be invested" (3). Like so many other faulty characters in Dickens, Dombey regards human beings as commodities. When, upon his wife's death in childbirth, it is necessary to hire a wetnurse, Dombey impresses upon Polly Toodles that he desires "to make it a question of wages, altogether." He wants no emotional attachment to develop. "When you go away from here, you will have concluded what is a mere matter of bargain and sale, hiring and letting: and will stay away" (16).

The converting of human affections into marketable wares is a central theme of this novel, one that has been treated elsewhere and needs no great elaboration here.[6] But one feature of this theme bears examination. Daughters are particularly susceptible to commodification because they must be brought to the marriage market. This domestic version of the marketplace is one of the most familiar features of Victorian fiction. But there is an interestingly redundant treatment of this subject in *Dombey and Son*. There are many treatments of the marriage theme in this novel: daughters may be pampered or abused, successful or not in the marriage market, contented or not in their domestic arrangements. Three daughters, however, are of special importance—Florence Dombey, Edith

Skewton, and Alice Marwood. If Florence is a daughter Dombey cannot invest, Edith is a woman he can buy. Disgusted with herself and her mother, who has brought her up to consider the marriage market all-important, Edith nonetheless allows herself to be purchased first by Mr. Granger and then by Dombey. Edith and her mother are dramatically compared with Alice Marwood and her mother. Edith sells herself in good society through "convenient" marriages, whereas Alice sells herself as a kept woman and descends to the lowest level of society. Both rage against the situations into which they have voluntarily brought themselves. Both suffer humiliation for their free choices. Both blame their mothers for educating them to this means of acquiring money and comfort. Like Dombey, who is so cruel and heartless toward Florence, these mothers have estranged their daughters and been the initial cause of their suffering by not teaching them the superior value of honest feeling over mercenary scheming. Of course, it is a grotesque irony to have Mrs. Skewton, Edith's mother, constantly protest that she longs for nature and heart, the two things she has so rigorously excluded from her and her daughter's lives. Significantly, Mr. Dombey, who lacks natural affection for his daughter, also shows no interest in planning for her marriage. She has value to him neither in his commercial market nor in the marriage market. But ignored and unvalued as she is, Florence is thereby insulated against a mercenary point of view and becomes instead the custodian of heart and feeling. She carries on Paul's legacy of affection over calculation, and Paul's good-hearted but witless schoolfellow Toots is a walking emblem of that legacy in his loyal attachment to Florence. Lyn Pykett argues that Florence is not only constant to an ideal, "but she is also an idealized character who is presented in a non-realistic even anti-realistic manner." Arguing that *Dombey and Son* is not a *Bildungsroman* but a "sentimental romance" embodying the longing for an apparently lost or unattainable world, Pykett regards Florence as resembling the heroine of a folk or fairy tale; she "is tried and tested by experience and events, but she is not radically changed by them."[7] Audrey Jaffe adds that Florence's "love has power for the reader because it appears useless, and therefore pure; it finds its value not primarily, or not first, within the novel, but outside it, in the act of exchange that is reading."[8] Jaffe here assumes that Dickens' audience would value as pure what is useless. Although I do not disagree with Pykett or Jaffe, I would suggest that it is less the uselessness of Florence's love than the unselfish outpouring of feeling that would have appealed to Dickens' audience. Nonetheless, both are right in emphasizing the extratextual appeal of what Florence represents. Later I shall note that her forgiveness of others' offenses operates in the same way.

   This pattern of vitiated family relations is familiar enough in Dickens and in nineteenth-century fiction generally, but a small narrative detail gives it a unique application in this novel. As Alice Marwood lies dying, her mother raves about her daughter's former beauty and then makes the surprising disclosure that Alice is well born, since she is the illegitimate daughter of Edith Dombey's uncle

(825).[9] At first this announcement seems to be an unnecessary reinforcement of the already obvious parallel between the selling of daughters in high and low society; beauty is a valuable commodity in both. But more importantly, this information completes a circle of relationships in which Florence stands out as the incommensurate figure. This circle of relationships began when Mrs. Brown took young Florence into custody and deprived her of her good clothing, while sparing her rich curls through memory of her once-lovely daughter. Perverted as Mrs. Brown's values are, this scene emphasizes her genuine affection for her daughter while dramatizing Dombey's indifference to his daughter as a person, rather than merely as an extension of the family pride. Edith also feels genuine maternal affection for Florence, once more contrasting with Dombey's lack of feeling, an obvious failure on Mr. Dombey's part that hastens Edith's movement from indifference toward dislike and even hatred for him. If Mrs. Brown, Alice, and Edith represent women who have treated themselves as materials for sale, their shared connection with the unmarketable Florence, emphasizes her elevation above the commercial reduction of human beings to articles of purchase or exchange. To be valueless in the world's eye is to be superior in the moral realm. The curse of parental lovelessness carries for Florence the hidden advantage of sparing her from being put up for sale. It is not all bad to be base coin when good currency buys nothing but trouble.

I shall return to the role of punishment and forgiveness in this pattern of family relations, but first it is worthwhile to glance at some contrasts to it. The chief contrast is probably that of Harriet Carker, who has devoted her life to serving her disgraced but repentent brother John, thereby earning the dislike and contempt of her brother James. Giving up James and his riches, Harriet chooses to share John's meager life out of a sibling's love and a Christian's compassion. Her role as model of correct family behavior is certified through her befriending and even redeeming Alice Marwood. This kindness is more significant than she knows, since her brother James was the man originally responsible for Alice's fall, later spurning her and refusing to assist her when she was in need. Harriet's unselfish charity obliterates the family debt to the Brown household in the same way that John's long punishment in humiliation balances the family debt of honor in the House of Dombey.

It has often been noted that although Dickens praises natural affection, there are few traditional families in his fiction that demonstrate the ideal. As often as not it is one or more surrogate parents, or real or surrogate siblings, who behave as we all are advised to do. In this novel Sol Gills fulfills the role of father for Walter Gay, who matures into a worthy young man, sensitive and dutiful. Captain Cuttle is a backup parent for both Walter and Florence. These relationships, like that of Harriet Carter, contrast with Mr. Dombey's perverse lack of natural affection for his daughter. Mr. Dombey's pride is foolish, but not necessarily wicked. His almost absolute focus upon business is limiting, but not evil; he is an honest merchant, as his dealings during bankruptcy are meant to show. His real crime is his treatment of Florence. It is chiefly for this wrong that the narrative must punish him, and punished he will be precisely in those two areas where he is most likely to suffer: his pride and his wealth.

Much of the action of *Dombey and Son* is designed to position Dombey where he will feel the full weight of his offense. The main thrust of the narrative is to burden Dombey with a heavy debt of injustice to Florence. His condescending and even callous treatment of others enhances his radical mistreatment of his daughter. As we have seen, she is first overlooked because as a female Dombey she is valueless to the firm. After his wife's death, Dombey begins to feel something like aversion to Florence because he resents having been shut out from that tender moment when daughter and dying mother embraced. Now Dombey "almost felt as if [Florence] watched and distrusted him. As if she held the clue to some secret in his breast, of the nature of which he has hardly informed himself" (29). Florence is not conscious of such a clue, and instead desperately hopes to learn the secret of pleasing her father and generating in him the parental love she craves. But if she cannot understand her father, she represents perfectly what is amiss with him. Florence's secret is her surveillance of the happy family across the street and her vigil outside her father's door.[10] Dombey does not permit love for Florence to enter into his heart. The secret in his breast is the closed room of his affections—cold and stiff as the stately rooms that witness the christening ceremony of the infant Paul.

Dombey is a self-condemned man, though he does not realize this until after the collapse of his marriage and his business. But, as readers, we are provided with many clues to his condition. Dombey may feel shut out from the tender scene of his wife's deathbed, but it is much more typical for him to shut out others and shut himself up. Even to Polly, serving as young Paul's nurse, the solitary, brooding Dombey seems like "a lone prisoner in a cell, or a strange apparition that was not to be accosted or understood" (23). Dombey incarcerates himself again after his son's death, and this self-imprisonment corresponds to his shutting out Florence, though his redemption depends precisely on his letting Florence into the chilly room of his heart to release him. Instead, Dombey drives his loving child farther and farther from him. When Florence dares to penetrate to her father's private room to offer love and receive it in return, she is rebuffed with "not one touch of tenderness or pity," not "one gleam of interest, parental recognition, or relenting," but with downright dislike (255). The narrator is so offended by this unnatural behavior that he intrudes to call attention to this moment and proleptically mark its corresponding moment in the story not yet told, the shape of which is forecast by the very nature of his warning. "Let him remember it in that room, years to come. It has faded from the air, before he breaks the silence. It may pass as quickly from his brain, as he believes, but it is there. Let him remember it in that room, years to come!" (256). This scene is especially painful because, as witnesses to Dombey's genuine grief at the loss of his son, we are deeply inclined to compassionate him. Like Florence, we can understand and even feel the impulse to reach out a consoling hand to this proud and unwise man. But to have that compassionate gesture, embodied in Florence, so unceremoniously spurned only increases the resentment that has been building against Dombey; in fact, it intensifies this resentment exponentially, since it would have been more appropriate for him to be reaching out toward Florence instead of shutting her out.

The frustration of this scene is exacerbated by the narrator's inability to correct Dombey's imprudent behavior. Although the narrator's warning suggests a foreseen, foreplotted design to which he is privy, thus hinting at a providential and therefore just pattern for the narrative as a whole, the fact that the narrator does not arrogate to himself the power to open Dombey's eyes is consistent with his unwillingness to make a preordained pattern supervene upon the free will of the characters he describes. Their very freedom of will is what makes the characters responsible and thus guilty. Audrey Jaffe writes: "Omniscience can report what everyone sees and can show what 'no one' sees, but it cannot make characters see what it reveals. In *Dombey*, responsibility lies not in showing but in seeing, and it is up to characters to learn to see what they need to know. The narrator thus emphasizes his lack of management, an emphasis that is achieved in part through the novel's focus on habit" (103).

There are moments when a reprieve for Dombey seems possible. When the newly married Dombeys return from their continental honeymoon, Florence sits down to do her needlework in a room where her father lies apparently sleeping; actually he is watching her and beginning to experience a change of heart.

> But as he looked, he softened to her, more and more. As he looked, she became blended with the child he had loved and he could hardly separate the two. As he looked, he saw her for an instant by a clearer and a brighter light, not bending over that child's pillow as his rival—monstrous thought—but as the spirit of his home, and in the action tending himself no less, as he sat once more with his bowed-down head upon his hand at the foot of the little bed. He felt inclined to speak to her, and call her to him. The words 'Florence, come here!' were rising to his lips—but slowly and with difficulty, they were so very strange—when they were checked and stifled by a footstep on the stair. (503–4)

This positive tendency is abruptly terminated when Dombey witnesses Edith's mild and loving manner with Florence, a side of herself that she will not offer to him. His resentment is renewed and we, who know that he has wilfully turned away from the true vision of his daughter out of wounded self-love, can only feel a new increment in our dislike and a new urgency that this behavior be corrected.[11] In his working notes for the novel, Dickens wrote of this scene, "Mr. Dombey's discovery of what Edith *can* be. -Turns him against Florence. Tortures himself."[12] Clearly Dickens meant to redirect Dombey's cruel gestures against him. If he becomes less friendly to his daughter with an eye to punishing both Edith and Florence, he is at the same time tormenting himself.

In a later scene Florence approaches her truly sleeping father after his horse-riding accident and kisses him, thus reprising the episode I have just discussed and recalling the narrator's warning to Dombey. Again the narrator in his own person urges the sleeping man to awake, not merely from sleep but to a true recognition of his moral condition. He warns that "the hour is coming with an angry tread" (609). But the narrator knows that Dombey will not awake. He is like the Old Testament God who hardened the hearts of those he planned to punish. So while the narrator urges awareness, he knows that Dombey will get worse, not better, and that his doom is already established, but in so adjuring Dombey, he heightens the reader's awareness of Dombey's dereliction.

Dombey's unjust behavior, which had been mainly negligent, now becomes fiercely active. When Edith flees, Dombey takes out his anger on his daughter, actually striking her. This is too much even for Florence, who runs from her father's house and takes refuge at the Wooden Midshipman. Florence, who had been like Dombey's "better angel," "excusing him, and pleading for him," is cast out of what has scarcely been a heavenly home, in a parody of the fall of Lucifer. As is so often the case in Dickens' novels, it is the good angel who is cast out by the bad lord.[13] Dickens may not have intended such an equation, but he surely meant his readers to recognize that Dombey's behavior is the very opposite of what a Christian should do.

One trait of true Christianity is selflessness and concern for others, as embodied in Florence and Harriet in this novel. Self-sacrifice provides its own rewards in the pleasure of helping others. In Dickens' moral economy self-love, which would seem likely to provide pleasure through self-indulgence of vanity or the senses, in fact automatically brings its own forms of punishment. Dombey's "imperious asperity of temper," the cold, hard armor of pride in which he is encased, creates its own suffering, for it "is the curse of such a nature—it is a main part of the heavy retribution on itself it bears within itself—that while deference and concession swell its evil qualities, and are the food it grows upon, resistance and a questioning of its exacting claims, foster it too, no less. The evil that is in it finds equally its means of growth and propagation in opposites. It draws support and life from sweets and bitters; bowed down before, or unacknowledged, it still enslaves the breast in which it has its throne; and, worshipped or rejected, is as hard a master as the Devil in dark fables" (560). This armor bears another heavy retribution. "It is proof against conciliation, love, and confidence! against all gentle sympathy from without, all trust, all tenderness, all soft emotion; but to deep stabs in the self-love, it is as vulnerable as the bare breast to steel; and such tormenting festers rankle there, as follow on no other wounds, no, though dealt with the mailed hand of Pride itself, on weaker pride, disarmed and thrown down" (560–61). Thus even as he is increasing his guilt in preparation for some grand retributive move against him in the narrative, Dombey is already suffering the *automatic* punishment that his proud nature generates.

When Edith leaves him, apparently to give herself to Carker, Dombey does not recognize this rebellious and vengeful act as a punishment upon him, though, as Dickens points out in his working notes, she decamps on the anniversary of her wedding day, a fact that might have registered with another sort of husband (Stone 91). Though his personal pride is offended, he can still maintain his dignity despite being very much concerned about what the world thinks of him. But because he views himself as an avenger who will punish the false Carker, he is blind to his own position, the true blow falling upon him only when the business that sustains his family pride collapses. Chapter 59 is significantly titled "Retribution" in clear acknowledgment of the narrative's direction from the outset. This chapter delivers a real bill for Dombey's amassed guilt; Carker's crime is incidental.

Once more Dombey incarcerates himself. Though he wanders the emptied house at night, when day breaks he is back in his "cell," "shut up in his rooms again" (842). The narrative voice, with all the vehemence of a scriptural prophet, quotes his own warning that has come to pass as he knew it must and would. " 'Let him remember it in that room, years to come!' He did remember it. It was heavy on his mind now; heavier than all the rest" (838). Only when the material vanities of the world have been swept from him is Dombey broken down to the point that he recognizes the need for the love that Florence represents; now he can feel only "sorrow and remorse" for what he has lost (840). The secret in his breast that once led him to distrust his daughter now takes on an ominous character as he becomes a brooding wraith, pacing about with its hand in its breast, clenching a weapon. This picture of a spectral Dombey fulfills the expectation created by Polly's sense of Dombey as "a strange apparition" after the death of his wife (23). He was already infected with the malady that now becomes manifest. The secret in his breast was lovelessness, death-in-life, annihilation. Now, already a ghost in his own eyes, he is about to make his moral death material as well when Florence once more enters the room so long prohibited to her, bringing with her light and hope, and prevents his suicide. " 'Papa! Dearest papa! Pardon me, forgive me! I have come back to ask forgiveness on my knees. I never can be happy more, without it.' " The narrator cannot resist injecting his sentiment. Here is Florence, unchanged in her love, "Asking *his* forgiveness" (843). The narrator's indignation underscores the enormity of Dombey's transgression against natural affection. Like a stage manager, he focuses our attention on the brutal irony of innocence begging forgiveness of pride. Peter Garrett has argued that "there can be no doubt that Dickens repeatedly associates narrative elevation with danger and destructive violence." He says that "despite the claim made through [the narrator] that he only observes the action of impersonal physical and moral laws, the author is always implicated in the plot he has constructed"[14] Garrett is referring to a different scene in *Dombey* when he makes these remarks, but they certainly apply to the one that we are discussing here. The elevated, judging narrator decidedly makes us sense some impending violence. But the device is used here to enhance the moment of rescue, thereby intensifying both punishment and forgiveness. Although the narrator refuses to meddle with the implied author's grand design, he willingly highlights its significant phases. He has not constructed a narrative punishment but he happily glosses punishment when it comes.

Florence's seeking forgiveness includes a more profound irony since her gesture is precisely what will energize the still proud but already penitent Dombey.[15] As is characteristic of Dickens' good characters, Florence has had no part in her father's punishment. She has remained untainted, yet in seeking forgiveness she makes apparent both to Dombey and to readers that the retributions brought on by Carker, Edith, and Dombey himself have had their effect in opening Dombey's eyes to the moral truths so long obscured for him. At last he is able to say, "God forgive me, for I need it very much!" (844). Florence now leads him from "the room in which he had been so long shut up" into the freedom of true familial love, where he learns to cherish Florence's son, Paul, but especially her daughter, Florence (845).

Two converging plot lines occasion Dombey's overthrow—Edith's, aimed at his personal pride, and Carker's, aimed at his wealth. Both are nemeses to the House/house of Dombey. More interestingly, both are motivated by resentment and vindictiveness, the very sentiments that corrupt Dombey's relations with his daughter. Carker's animosity is masked and indirect. Dombey never suspects it. But this is another way for the narrator to disclose the true moral dimensions of his narrative. Dombey is blind to inimical as well as benign forces around him. But the narrator makes clear that the novel's readers are not. Carker's sinister nature is indicated from the outset by descriptions that emphasize his teeth and his feline manner. That Carker the Manager is a managing man is evident in his directing of Dombey at one extreme and his domination of Rob the Grinder at the other. But only gradually do his motives and aims become apparent. When little Paul dies, the narrator comments that "it would seem that there is something gone from Mr. Carker's path—some obstacle removed—which clears his way before him" (240). Carker arranges to have Walter, befriended by little Paul and Florence, sent off to Barbados, then establishes a subtle power over Florence.

Here and there the narrator offers clear signs about Carker's hostile sentiments. When Carker is praised for his skill at games and contrasted with Dombey, who plays no games, the Manager replies that Dombey has had no occasion to acquire such little arts, whereas to men like himself they are sometimes useful. The narrator indicates the menacing quality of this response: "It might be only the false mouth, so smooth and wide; and yet there seemed to lurk beneath the humility and subserviency of this short speech, a something like a snarl; and, for a moment, one might have thought that the white teeth were prone to bite the hand they fawned upon" (378). The narrator regularly demonstrates that Carker is the more accomplished of the two men but we do not know the range of Carker's resentment until his scene with his brother. James asks John if he has anything to complain of in Dombey and John says no. The Manager asks if John believes he has been kept on in his job "'as a cheap example, and a famous instance of the clemency of Dombey and Son, redownding to the credit of the illustrious house?'" (642). But John believes he has been retained for more kind and disinterested reasons. It is clear, however, that Carker harbors grievances against Dombey of many kinds, from his need to play the hypocrite and flatter his superior, to the humiliation of having his brother kept on in the company as a disgraced clerk, to the personal humiliation of being used as go-between for Dombey and his wife. Carker tells John that all the employees at Dombey and Son would delight to see their master humbled. "'There's not one among them, but if he had at once the power, and the wit and daring to use it; would scatter Dombey's pride and lay it low, as ruthlessly as I rake out these ashes'" (644).

Carker is Dombey's alter ego: unscrupulous shrewdness opposed to supercilious honesty, luxurious self-indulgence opposed to Dombey's chilly abstemiousness, indifference to family opposed to Dombey's obsessive regard for family dignity, concern for business reputation only insofar as it assures power and wealth opposed to Dombey's genuine dedication to business and the long-term accumulation of wealth. But the two are alike in their almost single-minded attention to money-getting, and it is in this arena that Carker is able to wound Dombey. He is determined not only to make his fortune at Dombey's expense, but to ruin the man and his business as well. Carker is thus the plot's embodiment of all those wealth-oriented forces in the book that are morally ruinous to Dombey's character, and are dramatized, as so often in Dickens, by financial ruin as well. One of Dombey's idols is Mammon, and Carker reveals how sorry a god that Mammon is.

Another of Dombey's idols is self, as represented in his own being and in his family's reputation. But Dombey's is a corrupted form of family and personal pride, for it depends not on a shared community of feeling and an appreciation of family and social relations, but almost exclusively on his arrogation of authority over all other family members and the chilly maintenance of the appearance of the family dignity in society. He is more concerned with ceremonies than with values, with presentation than with appreciation. When he purchases Edith Granger he expects to acquire an ornamental wife whose dignity matches his own, and who may provide him with another son to carry on the family tradition. Yet it is clear from early in their relationship that man and wife are very unlike in their likeness. Visiting Warwick Castle, they create a sort of composition standing together in one of the rooms while examining the works of art.

There was a difference even in the pride of the two that removed them farther from each other, than if one had been the proudest and the other the humblest specimen of humanity in all creation. He, self-important, unbending, formal, austere. She, lovely and graceful in an uncommon degree, but totally regardless of herself and him and everything around, and spurning her own attractions with her haughty brow and lip, as if they were a badge or livery she hated. So unmatched were they, and opposed, so forced and linked together by a chain which adverse hazard and mischance had forged: that fancy might have imagined the pictures on the walls around them, startled by the unnatural conjunction, and observant of it in their several expressions. (388)

When Edith, humiliated by Dombey in his efforts to make her subservient to his wishes, warns him more than once to forbear, he responds by intensifying his demands for submission. Ironically, it is Edith's love for Florence that brings the contest to its breaking point. Edith can bear much from Dombey, but will not be a party to a prolonged, unrelenting torture of Florence. She purposely runs off with Carker precisely to give the impression that she has committed adultery, because she wishes to wound Dombey as deeply as possible in his personal and family pride, knowing how much he values the world's opinion.

It is typical of Dickens' mature novels that even subplots reflect and refract the energies of the main plots; hence it is not surprising but entirely gratifying to realize that the entire sequence of events that leads to the marriage of Dombey and Edith is itself the consequence of a carefully planned strategy of revenge and vindictiveness. Major Joe Bagstock has come to think of Miss Tox as a romantic conquest of sorts. When she turns cool he investigates and discovers that she has associated herself with the Dombey household. He therefore befriends Dombey himself and assumes the factotem's role in Dombey's personal affairs that Carker supplies in his business dealings. He fawns by feigning blunt sincerity. By revealing Miss Tox's outrageous matrimonial hopes concerning Dombey, Bagstock achieves his revenge against the poor soul, punishing her for ignoring old Joey B. Bagstock is also the means by which Dombey visits Leamington and meets the lovely Edith Granger. The two phonies, Joey B and Cleopatra (a.k.a., Mrs. Skewton) plan the marriage and Dombey complies. It has been argued that Bagstock is a representation of libido, and that may be so, but he is also clearly a manifestation of the egoism so morally damaging to Dombey. Like Carker, he is an exaggeratedly sensual and expressive version of Dombey's stiffer traits.

To a great degree the Carker and Edith plotlines are redundant, since any narrative sequences designed to humble Dombey and prepare the way for his repentance and thus his salvation would have served. In another sense, however, the two plotlines reinforce the message of the main narrative. Carker, whose one shared interest with Dombey is acquiring wealth, loses that and his life because he gives in to his collector's impulse concerning handsome women. One woman

he has betrayed puts Dombey on his track, the other turns out to have betrayed
Carker in his turn, leaving him a confused fugitive hunted down less by Dombey
than by his own destiny.[16]

Carker may be the agent who punishes Dombey for his arrogance, but Edith
is the agent who punishes both.[17] However, in doing so she brings a similar punishment upon herself, for her agonizing pride and the knowledge of her debase-
ment are constant tortures to her, not to mention the additional torment that
Carker's awareness of her condition creates. In the great scene when she and
Carker begin to deal openly with one another, Dickens marks his characters with
indications of what is to come. Carker suggests that it is an injustice to hold him
responsible for what Dombey has made him do. But Edith responds, " 'If I had
done justice to the torment you have made me feel, and to my sense of the insult
you have put upon me, I should have slain you!' " (626). Carker, in his turn, tells
Edith that Dombey "intends that [he] shall be a punishment for [her] contu-
macy" (628). Edith clearly brings about her own punishment, which is actually
an extension of her earlier experience. She is guilty of having prostituted herself
in marriage, of having acquiesced in becoming a commodity. Her punishment is
extenuated, consisting largely of solitude and unpleasant memories. But though
she is sorry for the consequences of her actions, she retains much of her proud
defiance, admitting that she was guilty " 'of blind and passionate resentment, of
which I do not, cannot, will not, even now, repent' " (686). Arlene Jackson concludes that "Edith Dombey is a character whose complexity became too much
for her creator to handle" and that he ended by "punishing Edith for desertion of
a husband rather than rewarding her for faithfulness to a lonely and unprotected
child" (121). However, Edith's self-inflicted punishment is not artificially engineered by author or narrator, but is the natural consequence of her partial
repentance.

Together these three create a mirrored and mirroring cycle of retribution and
self-punishment, but set against this maelstrom of requital are counteracting
forces of forgiveness and mercy. The chief example, as we have already seen, is
in the John and Harriet Carker subplot. John Carker stole from Dombey and Son
but was retained in a lowly position. Never able to live down his disgrace, he
outlives his trespass, for he is truly repentant and free from vindictiveness. His
punishment lasts his entire life and even includes his sister, Harriet, for he
realizes that she has sacrificed much of her life to care for him. John has learned
from his early error and is a better man because of his punishment. This does not
mean, however, that the meting out of this stern punishment was correct, a point
made very clearly in Harriet's expostulation to Mr. Morfin: " 'Oh, Sir, after
what I have seen, let me conjure you, if you are in any place of power, and are
ever wronged, never, for any wrong, inflict a punishment that cannot be recalled; while there is a God above us to work changes in the hearts he made' "
(477). Mr. Morfin's response summarizes one of the chief moral lessons of the
novel. We go on in our clockwork routine from day to day, he says, and are "so

d____d business-like," that we become indifferent to everything around us. Midway through life Mr. Morfin has decided to become sensitive to the life around him, a conscious decision that prefigures Dombey's more violent transformation from businessman to man of feeling.[18] Habit, Morfin says, is all that the routine and businesslike individual will have to excuse himself to his conscience on his deathbed. "'Very business-like indeed, Mr. What's-your-name,' says Conscience, 'but it won't do here!'" (477).

Since Harriet Carker is obviously one custodian of the truth in this novel, her adjuration to Mr. Morfin may be taken as a gloss on the narrator's activity as well. As we have seen, the narrator does not disguise the fact that a retribution is building for Dombey, yet the punishment that descends threefold on Dombey— in the loss of pride, the loss of wealth, and the harrowing awareness of squandered filial affection—is a punishment that can be recalled. Though the narrator cannot spare those who remain unrepentant, he can revoke punishment for those who regret their sins. This is the central significance of Dombey's recuperation. Not only has Florence forgiven and saved him and offered him love; the narrator conspires to support her effort. Florence's emotional generosity is mirrored in the economic behavior of the Carkers. After James' crimes against Dombey personally and professionally, the angry businessman dismisses the innocent brother, John. John can understand this action, though Harriet wonders if it is lenient and considerate of Dombey to punish John "for the misdeed of another" (742). But these Carkers are as forgiving as their brother was unrelenting, and, when they inherit James' wealth, they enlist Mr. Morfin's help in seeing that the money will return to the bankrupt Dombey in the form of an anonymous annuity.

If Harriet and Florence are models of pure forgiveness, other characters also show their potential for decency through a capacity to forgive transgressions. Alice and Edith both forgive their mothers for educating them to the miserable lives they have known. Alice relents after helping to set Dombey on Carker's trail because she does not want his death charged to her moral account. The last meeting between Florence and Edith is awash with forgiveness. Florence tells her stepmother that she forgives her and will ask her father to do the same, suggesting as well that Edith pray to Heaven "'to forgive you all this sin and shame'" (867–68). Edith now announces that she is not guilty of adultery and concludes, "'I will try, then, to forgive him his share of blame. Let him try to forgive me mine'" (871).

Alice's deathbed scene, which immediately precedes the "Retribution" chapter, is also heavy with forgiveness; at its conclusion Alice dies with Christ's name on her lips. Harriet had just read to her from the history of Christ, who "had sweet compassion for, and interest in, [life's] every scene and stage, its every suffering and sorrow" (827). His teaching emphasized mercy and compassion, but even in the most Christian countries that teaching is all too often ignored and even subverted. Alice complains much earlier that the law that harangued her about her duty and was quick to punish her when she was an outcast and a deserted girl did nothing to save her when she was "'an innocent and helpless little wretch'" (488). Ultimately it is to this larger domain of social responsibility that the energies of punishment and forgiveness are meant to apply. For though the immediate application of punishment and forgiveness is highly personalized in the narrative, it is also clear that people do what they do largely as a result of their aculturation. A family that values pride and wealth above natural affection will eventually suffer the inevitable consequences of that unwise investment. Similarly, a system of law that overlooks the misfortunes of the poor while scrutinizing and punishing the predictable consequences of those misfortunes will sooner or later pay the price for such callous practices.

Chapter 47, entitled "The Thunderbolt," which concludes with Edith's flight, a flight that in turn begins the process of retribution for several characters in the tale, opens with a dissertation on "unnatural" behavior. It is not surprising that one trained from infancy, as Dombey was, to value money and family should have become such a monster of pride. Nor should we be surprised that so much vice, crime, and misery should rise from the slums that are obvious manifestations of society's neglect of the unfortunate. We may witness the physical consequence in disease. "But if the moral pestilence that rises with them, and in the eternal laws of outraged Nature, is inseparable from them, could be made discernible too, how terrible the revelation" (647). There follows an oft-quoted passage that I shall quote yet again.

> Oh for a good spirit who would take the house-tops off, with a more potent and benignant hand than the lame demon in the tale, and show a Christian people what dark shapes issue from amidst their homes, to swell the retinue of the Destroying Angel as he moves forth among them! For only one night's view of the pale phantoms rising from the scenes of our too-long neglect; and from the thick and sullen air where Vice and Fever propagate together, raining the tremendous social retributions which are ever pouring down, and ever coming thicker! Bright and blest the morning that should rise on such a night: for men, delayed no more by stumbling-blocks of their own making, which are but specks of dust upon the path between them and eternity, would then apply themselves, like creatures of one common origin, owing one duty to the Father of one family, and tending to one common end, to make the world a better place!
>
> Not the less bright and blest would that day be for rousing some who never have looked out upon the world of human life around them, to a knowledge of their own relation to it, and for making them acquainted with a perversion of nature in their own contracted sympathies and estimates; as great, and yet as natural in its development when once begun, as the lowest degradation known. (648)

"Social retributions" follow from our neglect of our fellow mortals, which itself follows from our "contracted sympathies." As Mr. Morfin says, habit will be no excuse for conscience on the deathbed. The law of nature declares that both trespass and indifference will bring retribution to loveless individuals and hard-hearted communities. Those who begin by shutting love out will end by being themselves imprisoned in the despoiled room of their own conscience, ready to pass mortal judgment upon themselves. Yet everywhere the lesson waits to be read. The secret that Florence hopes to discover, the secret that she bears in her own heart, the secret that rankles finally in the fallen Mr. Dombey's breast is as plain as nature: love begets love, sympathy sympathy, understanding compassion. Chiefly Florence represents the giving of love, even to the unworthy, out of the desire to be loved and to share in a community of love. Miss Tox, in her authentic affection for and interest in Dombey and his household, extends her sympathies and forms a bond with the Toodles family. And the world of the Wooden Midshipman is a model of a community based not upon the obligations of family relations, but on affections freely given and received, duties learned through love. To be capable of love, finally, is to be capable of forgiveness. Once again, as this novel ends, the good characters have remained untainted by selfish or cruel sentiments of revenge or retribution. The wicked have taken care of that for themselves, and when their business is done, Florence and Walter step forth to draw them back, penitent and forgiven, into the larger world of human sympathy. As Audrey Jaffe remarks, it is the *idea* of the family rather than any specific family that signifies in this novel, "and since 'family' exists within each individual, it hardly matters what form it takes externally" (108). But she adds a significant explanation for the way this novel of family affection plays out the narrative lines it does. Though a family is restored to natural feeling within the story, external to the narrative the novel has also created a family. "The novelist becomes the father of a newly forged community founded on feeling he has himself evoked." Dickens provides "an explicit use for the feeling the novel summons into existence: the novel and its author become mediators in the formation of an imaginary community" (108). Through its distribution of punishment and forgiveness, the narrative excludes those characters who have alienated themselves from the human family, but has opened itself to those (even those who have grievously sinned against that family) who, sooner or later, recognize their links with their brothers and sisters and plead again for admission to that forgiving circle of love.

NOTES

1. One possible exception is Jingle in *Pickwick Papers,* but it is difficult to think of that jolly scamp as a cold-hearted negative figure like Dombey.

2. Anonymous review, *Sharpe's London Magazine* VI (May 1848), 202. Quoted in *Charles Dickens: Dombey and Son and Little Dorrit: A Casebook,* ed. Alan Shelston (London: Macmillan Publishers, Ltd., 1985), 28. This reviewer admires Dickens' approach to fiction, saying "his high moral tone, and a certain internal evidence that he writes upon a conviction of the truths he is maintaining, place him in the first rank of the popular writers of the present day" (25). This valuation reveals how important sincere moral attitudes were to critics of fiction at this time.

3. Lawrence Frank, *Charles Dickens and the Romantic Self* (Lincoln: University of Nebraska Press, 1984), 42. Subsequent references appear in the text.

4. Charles Dickens, *Dombey and Son* (London: Oxford University Press, 1960), xv. Subsequent references appear in the text.

5. Kathleen Tillotson, *Novels of the Eighteen-Forties* (Oxford: Clarendon Press, 1961), 164ff. Arlene Jackson, "Reward, Punishment, and the Conclusion of *Dombey and Son,*" in *Dickens Studies Annual* 7, ed. Robert B. Partlow, Jr. (Carbondale: Southern Illinois University Press, 1978), 106ff. Subsequent references appear in the text.

6. There are numerous discussions of the theme of commercialism in *Dombey,* but Robert Clark's "Riddling the Family Firm: The Sexual Economy in *Dombey and Son,*" *ELH* 51 (1984), 69–84, deals more particularly with Florence's exchange value.

7. Lyn Pykett, "*Dombey and Son:* A Sentimental Family Romance," *Studies in the Novel* 19, no. 1 (Spring 1987), 19.

8. Audrey Jaffe, *Vanishing Points: Dickens, Narrative, and the Subject of Omniscience* (Berkeley: University of California Press, 1991), 78. Subsequent references appear in the text.

9. Susan Horton has an excellent discussion of Alice Marwood's role in *Dombey and Son* in *Interpreting Interpreting: Interpreting Dickens's Dombey* (Baltimore: The Johns Hopkins University Press, 1979), 130ff.

10. Jaffe makes this observation about Florence's secret, then goes on to explain the significance of Florence's observational role.

> While the narration attempts to separate itself from Carker's observations, however, it endorses Florence's. One of the primary ways in which *Dombey and Son* valorizes the private is by aligning itself, and consequently the reader, with Florence. Though she stands for the private and the domestic, she is (next to Carker) the novel's most penetrating observer. Seeing with Florence, narrator and readers—unlike 'the world' which pursues Dombey, and unlike the merely curious stranger—see for the sake of the private. It is Florence's vision, finally, that the novel naturalizes, and that naturalizes Dombey and Son—family, firm, and novel. (89)   •

11. Audrey Jaffe discusses the significance of watching in *Dombey and Son.* But in addition to characters viewing one another, Dickens' novel emphasizes

the reader's ability to oversee the activities hidden to the characters in the narrative, thereby intensifying a desire to see justice executed.

12. *Dickens' Working Notes for His Novels,* ed. Harry Stone (Chicago: Chicago University Press, 1987), 85. Subsequent references appear in the text.

13. In Hablot K. Browne's illustration "Florence and Edith on the Staircase," there are angelic and near-angelic figures that clearly allude to Florence's role. Michael Steig identifies originals for these and other art works in the illustration and provides a very helpful interpretation in *Dickens and Phiz* (Bloomington: Indiana University Press, 1978), 101ff.

14. Peter Garrett, *The Victorian Multiplot Novel: Studies in Dialogical Form* (New Haven: Yale University Press, 1980), 34–35.

15. There has been much unhappiness among critics with Florence's plea for forgiveness from her sinning father. But Arlene Jackson notes that "Florence has need of repentance, for she has rejected her father, and at a most critical time" (115). Nancy Klenk Hill justifies the psychological correctness of Florence's asking forgiveness of her father, not only because she is the person most wronged by him and thus most likely to move him to acknowledge his repentance, but also because this scene of mutual confession underlines the importance of suffering and the loss of pride in the Christian pattern of repentance, and the need to accept one's commonness before the Lord ("*Dombey and Son:* Parable for the Age," *Dickens Quarterly* 8, no. 4 [December 1991], 175–76). Dennis Walder goes so far as to regard Florence as a Christ parallel because she takes on her erring parent's sins. He also sees her as a projection of her father's conscience (*Dickens and Religion* [London: George Allen and Unwin, 1981], 136). Subsequent references appear in the text.

16. Carker's demise can easily be viewed as providential, a working out of divine justice. Dennis Walder so concludes that Providence sees to it that Carker destroys himself (125). But A. O. J. Cockshut is not comfortable with providential agency as a justification for Carker's end. "It would need a much stronger and more pervasive sense of Divine Providence than Dickens could rise to, to convince us of the artistic rightness of this semi-miraculous intervention" (*The Imagination of Charles Dickens* [New York: New York University Press, 1962], 103). For my purposes, we need not attribute the punishment to providence when we have the implied author nearer at hand to construct a narrative punishment for Carker.

17. Lawrence Frank suggests that Carker, in his infantile orality, "seems all teeth, but remains the toothless Son who cannot become a man, a husband, and a father" (54). Accordingly, when Edith unmans him he collapses and seeks out the train "as a mechanical instrument of retribution, an apt extension of a dehumanized Dombey and a manifestation of his own inner condition" (57).

18. From Dickens' own day to the present critics have objected to the abruptness of the change in Dombey. But John Forster explained that Dickens himself had regarded Dombey as a man suppressing his better impulses. When he

finally recognizes Florence's faithfulness, "the sense of his injustice, which has never quitted him, will have at last a gentler office than that of only making him more harshly unjust" (*The Life of Charles Dickens* [London: Chapman and Hall, 1893], 360). Dickens' own preface to the novel confirms his intention. Susan Horton has wisely cautioned readers of *Dombey* (and other texts as well) to be particularly cautious about assuming that intention and accomplishment are the same thing (105). In any case, the simple development suggested by Dickens and Forster is more complex and richer than it seems, as Edgar Johnson's comment on Dombey suggests.

> Even in Mr. Dombey's remorse, though, with a marvellous touch of psychological insight, Dickens shows him still his old self. If he had "heard her voice in the adjoining room," Dickens writes, "he would not have gone to her. If he could have seen her in the street, and she had done no more than look at him as she had been used to look, he would have passed on with his old cold unforgiving face, and not addressed her, or relaxed it, though his heart should have broken soon afterwards." In their superb penetration these few vivid words, for all their brevity, are equivalent to paragraphs of intricate psychological analysis (*Charles Dickens: His Tragedy and his Triumph*, vol. 2 [Boston: Little, Brown and Co., 1952], 640).

TWELVE

David Copperfield

DAVID COPPERFIELD (1849–50) is an anomaly among Dickens' novels for its gentleness. We tend to think of the Murdstones and Uriah Heep as distinctly unpleasant people, but Dickens' treatment of them is surprisingly temperate given his strong inclination to severe forms of retribution. This novel, deeply concerned about injustice, is also marked by a strong sense of innocent human folly. At the core of the novel is David's own sensibility, which changes over time. In his early years he is a sensitive, susceptible, and imaginative child, who must learn to survive in a world of harsh realities. He becomes an energetic, genial, but impetuous young man who must learn to chasten his "undisciplined heart."[1] Because of his experiences, and his knowledge of his own limitations and of the ease with which individuals can be shaped into unattractive forms, David's narrative is characterized by a greater compassion, even for serious offenders, than is common in Dickens' fiction. Moreover, David's narration incorporates a dual vision—while trying to convey the way his younger self viewed experience, the mature David must nonetheless incorporate the moral insights he has gained, though he need not disclose any narrative secrets as he proceeds. It is the ability to hold these two outlooks in solution and suspension that creates the peculiarly lenient tone of the novel.[2]

Hints about this "forgiving" trait in David appear humorously in several instances at different stages in young David's career.[3] The delightful scene of the waiter at the inn who cozens little David out of his food, unjustly charges him for stationery, and then requires a tip for his services is an outstanding example. There is no impetus to punish this rascal for exploiting a child. His very exuberance seems to excuse him. In fact, little David seems almost to blame for being such an easy, gullible target. Elsewhere young David is persuaded by a coach driver to yield his special place on the coach to a rough country gentleman. No doubt it is coincidence that both of these manipulators are named William, but it is no coincidence, I think, that neither these nor many other minor offenders are punished, not even the young scamp who steals David's money and his box when he is leaving London for Dover, or the old clothes man on the road to Dover who makes David wait so long for inadequate payment. These and many other impositions upon David are overlooked as moral offenses because they are represented partly as consequences of David's own youthful weaknesses, and partly because they provide so much entertainment in the narrative.

Perhaps the most notable example of Dickens' willingness to forgive here what he so often was inclined to punish is Mr. Micawber. Micawber is clearly improvident, self-indulgent, and self-aggrandizing. He borrows from his acquaintances to their misfortune and deals unscrupulously with creditors and the law. But aside from the constant discomfort of his life he is not punished for these behavioral traits. Acting in his favor to negate any need for retribution is his exuberance, his love of life, and his genuine capacity for friendship and family affection. Moreover, although he cannot manage to make a decent living, it is not because he has not tried.

Much of the misbehavior in the novel, then, is palliated by the narrator's self-awareness, by his consciousness of the role he may himself have played, and certainly by the role his imagination now makes him and all those in his history play. The tenor of this narration is gentler because it is the product of a character who has learned humility and sympathy, rather than the expression of an omniscient narrator who may be understood to control, not merely report on, the world of the narrative. There is, however, a flavor of omniscience to this narration rendering an account of a world we might say the implied author has created. But David knows that the stories he tells are inevitably made up largely of his imaginings, which themselves depend upon stories told by others. To sense one's own limited power to command the story of life is to feel sympathy for all in that condition, even one's earlier self.[4] After commenting on the painful experiences of his working days in London among strange people like the Micawbers, the narrator reflects:

> When my thoughts go back now, to that slow agony of my youth, I wonder how much of the histories I invented for such people hangs like a mist of fancy over well-remembered facts! When I tread the old ground, I do not wonder that I seem to see and pity, going on before me, an innocent romantic boy, making his imaginative world out of such strange experiences and sordid things. (169)

But it is this very capacity for creating imaginary histories that has provided young David with consolations against his own pain and given the power of narrating that gains him friendship and protection from Steerforth at Mr. Creakle's school. Ultimately this same power will secure him a place in society when he becomes a successful novelist. But the very power to create imaginary histories suggests a tendency to treat "real" histories in a similar fashion, and certainly the history that David is narrating has all of the same features that we find in Dickens' other narratives: its forms of characterization, its plays on language, its narrative prolepses, and so forth. And, as the passage above and others like it suggest, David is himself aware of how much his narrative skill influences the rendering of his own history. The implicit self-consciousness of David's narration, by resembling Dickens' own trademark qualities, automatically calls attention to the ways David's narration differs from Dickens', while nonetheless calling attention to an implied author who is neither David nor Dickens.

The Murdstones are the first genuine exemplars of unpleasantness in the novel. In an omniscient narration one would expect them to suffer some decisive retribution for their conduct, but David allows as much humor about them as he does moral judgment. Mr. Murdstone wants to marry David's mother, but sees the boy as an "incumbrance" (23). He is never kind to David once he becomes his stepfather. Personal distaste aside, "the gloomy theology of the Murdstones made all children out to be a swarm of little vipers" (55). As such they are in constant need of discipline. But what the Murdstones call "firmness" is "another name for tyranny," and both Murdstones are associated with imprisonment and confinement (49). Miss Murdstone's jewelry, handbag, and other appurtenances are likened to fetters, jails, and so forth; Mr. Murdstone actually shuts David up in his room after his rebellion, an experience that David refers to as "my imprisonment" (59).

The whole Murdstone sequence is characterized by injustice. Young David feels deprived of his mother's full affection and attention, natural enough even if his new father had been agreeable. But added to this deprivation is an accumulating sense of constraint and suffering. Mr. Murdstone's mode of education and discipline is even more strict and equated with pain than are the examples of Evangelical teaching discussed in chapter 2 of this study. Here is a famous example of Mr. Murdstone's method.

> 'David,' he said, making his lips thin, by pressing them together, 'if I have an obstinate horse or dog to deal with, what do you think I do?'
>
> 'I don't know.'
>
> 'I beat him.'
>
> I had answered in a kind of breathless whisper, but I felt, in my silence, that my breath was shorter now.
>
> 'I make him wince, and smart. I say to myself, "I'll conquer that fellow;" and if it were to cost him all the blood he had, I should do it. What is that upon your face?' (46)

A judgmental tone dominates the Murdstone sequence, a tone all the more offensive in its somberness, because it follows the comical descent of the capriciously judgmental Aunt Betsey upon Blunderstone Rookery on the advent of

David's birth. This daunting personality, so firm in her views and so narrow as well, is eccentric and amusing, no matter how much she terrifies Mr. Chillip the doctor. But the altogether more malign firmness and comminatory bearing of the Murdstones evoke no laughter. Aunt Betsey's manner is tyrannical, but even her first appearance reveals a heart that can warm to persons in whom she takes an interest. Under her brusqueness is good feeling, but the "gloomy taint that was in the Murdstone blood darkened the Murdstone religion, which was austere and wrathful" (52). They are congenitally cool, operating on theories and abstractions about right and wrong, not upon actual human responses.

And yet, bleak as this picture of the Murdstones is, the narrative implies that this is a recollection dependent upon the impressions formed by a young boy, impressions that the adult David may endorse but that he also has sense enough to distrust. After all, when he has lost his pretty young wife, even Mr. Murdstone feels genuine loss and sorrow. David recalls that "Mr. Murdstone took no heed of me when I went into the parlour, where he was, but sat by the fireside, weeping silently, and pondering in his elbow-chair" (129). There are other similar signs that Mr. Murdstone is not inhuman, but simply wrongheaded and crude in his human relations. Later in David's life, when he encounters Miss Murdstone again as the companion of Dora Spenlow, he is not as cowed by her, though she is still characterized by images of incarceration. Now, however, these images suggest self-imprisonment more than the desire to restrain others. Encountering Mr. Murdstone on the eve of that gentleman's marriage to another young woman, David can still resent the man and pity his future wife, but his fear and awe are gone. This change in his attitude suggests that David as narrator has had sufficient time to reflect on his experiences with the Murdstones and to conclude that these people require no dramatic punishment for their offenses, no turn of plot to make them suffer, perhaps in kind, for the pain they have occasioned others. David is content simply to remove them from the center of his own experience and consign them to its periphery. But the fact that they remain a part of the narrative also suggests that all such injustice and inconsiderateness, all such petty tyranny and cruelty, are part of life and cannot be shut out of our knowledge and our memory, as Redlaw in "The Haunted Man" discovers. Far better, in fact, to remember that cruelty so that we do not repeat it ourselves, as Aunt Betsey warns David when he finds himself inclined to reshape Dora according to what he would like her to be instead of accepting her for what she is. What punishment the Murdstones do suffer is noted near the very end of the novel when, as usual, the various punishments—such as they are—are doled out.

Significantly, at the end of the episode of David's disgrace, his mother embraces him and declares: "'I forgive you, my dear boy. God bless you!'" despite the displeasure of Miss Murdstone, who wants no softness for the young miscreant and says to him that "she hoped I would repent, before I came to a bad end" (62). In this contrast of attitudes as David is sent away from home, Dickens epitomizes two polar approaches to human error—loving-kindness, understanding, and forgiveness as opposed to anger, threat, and distrust.

It is interesting that the next stage of David's life begins with a punishment. He is sent to Creakle's school "in holiday-time as a punishment" for his misconduct (77). When the boys return from holidays, he bears the additional punishment of wearing a sign that reads: "Take care of him. He bites" (78). David did bite Mr. Murdstone and the sign is literally true, but it is nonetheless a cruel device for correcting a young boy in his first encounter with other young boys, a gesture almost certainly designed to start him off on the wrong foot. But Creakle's school is characterized by an injustice even greater than Murdstone's. Murdstone has the justification of religion to support his educational and disciplinary methods, but Creakle is simply a sadist. "He had a delight in cutting at the boys, which was like the satisfaction of a craving appetite" (89–90). Cruel as Mr. Creakle is, he does not have the solidity of a Murdstone, being more "like a giant in a story-book," an exaggeration, a monster (89). The pain he creates is real enough, but not invasive in the way that Murdstone's is. For example, though David cannot help reacting physically to his being punished by Mr. Murdstone, by biting, he later takes the blame for his behavior on himself, in the usual manner of early nineteenth-century child training. "My stripes were sore and stiff, and made me cry afresh, when I moved; but they were nothing to the guilt I felt. It lay heavier on my breast than if I had been a most atrocious criminal, I dare say" (58).

Creakle is not the villain of David's first school stage; he is too much like a cartoon, a fabular presence. It may at first sound strange to regard Steerforth as a school villain, but he is. The truly wicked and threatening presences in *David Copperfield* are those who are positioned to alter David's perception of himself by insinuating some aspects of their own nature into his. Murdstone threatens this infiltration through domestic coercion, Steerforth more dangerously through his charm.[5] Steerforth is already spoiled beyond redemption; he treats Mr. Mell with contempt, and thinks that monetary compensation will excuse his behavior, a clear sign in Dickens' fiction of serious moral obliquity. He is already a manipulator of other people, as his appropriation of David's allowance and other treasures suggests. And he is clearly a self-indulgent egotist, with a hint of something worse in his question to David: " 'You haven't got a sister, have you?' " (87)

Steerforth is dangerous because he is so engaging. When he returns to David's life, he returns as his "bad angel," against whom Alice, the paragon of the novel, must warn him. Upon this revival of friendship, Steerforth provides a clue to his character by giving David the ambivalent nickname Daisy and by taking charge of his naive friend, saying, " 'I feel as if you were my property,' " always a very suspect attitude in a Dickens character (290). But Steerforth is not evil in the manner of a Fagin, Quilp, or Ralph Nickleby; his is a thoughtless, self-indulgent transgression. He would rather not be as he is, as his random moments of depression indicate, but he makes no effort to discipline himself. " 'I wish with all my soul I had been better guided!' " Steerforth exclaims to David. " 'I wish with all my soul I could guide myself better!' " (322) But he cannot, and the result is an occasional bout of blue devils, or the nightmare that troubles his guilty mind like the nursery tales designed to frighten children from misbehavior. " 'I believe I have been confounding myself with the bad boy who 'didn't care,' and became food for lions—a grander kind of going to the dogs, I suppose' " (322). Given Dickens' own interest in moral tale-telling, this allusion to instructive children's literature is apt. Dickens did not approve of the more gruesome children's tales, but he commended fairy tales and other children's stories that established good Christian principles. Steerforth's true failing is that he lacks these principles, a lack that makes him a victim of his own ungoverned nature. Even his charm has no better motive than transient triumph. His social conquest of the Peggoty household, for example, "was a brilliant game, played for the excitement of the moment, for the employment of high spirits, in the thoughtless love of superiority, in a mere wasteful careless course of winning what was worthless to him, and next minute thrown away" (310–11).

Steerforth refers to himself as a "prodigal son," but has no intention of repenting (427). Even as he is planning to seduce Em'ly, he asks David to think the best of him if they should ever be separated. His treatment of Em'ly is commensurate with all of his relationships, for it repeats his tendency to use others as though they were currency for his own pleasure. He does not care about making a profit from others, as do Murdstone and Heep. These latter two characters confuse sexual and monetary attraction, the one in a rather bloodless fashion, the other with reptilian eagerness. Steerforth at least is interested *only* in pleasure, though all too often at others' moral, if not financial, cost.

Steerforth becomes a genuine representative of evil in the novel when Ham reads Em'ly's letter explaining her flight: " 'he's a damned villain,' " Ham exclaims (453). And he is, in the conventional melodramatic sense. But he is a victim as well, as the mature David, with this tragedy already in mind when he begins to tell his tale, realizes. His treatment of Steerforth is complex because it is already bathed in regret and in the knowledge of Steerforth's early death. When he recounts his last look at the sleeping Steerforth before that final vision of him aboard the foundering boat, David writes: "Never more, oh God forgive you, Steerforth! to touch that passive hand in love and friendship. Never, never more!" (437). Even after he discovers Steerforth's unworthiness, David cannot help but love him. This continued affection is a strange feature of *David Copperfield,* as is the benign treatment of its other wicked creatures. But it is possible for David to convey his own forgiving nature to the events of his experience because another form of justice sees to correcting the moral economy of his world. As Alexander Welsh has pointed out, David may forgive Steerforth early and often, but that does not prevent Dickens (or as I would prefer to say here, the implied author) from bringing retribution to bear in a scene that recapitulates a number of significant themes.[6] Ham sacrifices his life to save the man who has betrayed him; Steerforth goes down in a sailing vessel in the very neighborhood where he bought his boat and named it the "Little Em'ly," and he lies dead on the shore in the pose David has seen him in so often as he slept. Apparent innocence, moral shipwreck, Christian sacrifice are all brought together in a moment of retribution and transfiguration. Extremes of good and evil cancel one another in this powerful scene, though even in death Ham and Steerforth are kept apart, the citizens of Yarmouth thinking it would not be fitting for their bodies to lie in the same room together. So the principles of Christian sacrifice and pagan self-indulgence must always remain distinct and immiscible, no matter how much they are intertwined in our lives, no matter how much attraction they have for an innocent heart like David's, where they may lie down safely together, equally loved, equally regretted.

That Steerforth is not entirely to blame for his character is made quite clear throughout the novel. He laments the lack of a father to guide him, knowing that he has been spoiled by his infatuated mother. That infatuation is not identical with love, for it consists largely of pride, a pride that is not separable from personal pride. When Steerforth offends that sense of pride, Mrs. Steerforth is as inflexible and unforgiving as any Murdstone—at least on the surface. "'Let him put away his whim now, and he is welcome back,'" she says. But he is unwelcome "'unless, being rid of her for ever, he comes humbly to me and begs for my forgiveness'" (469–70). The child she has trained in pride will never return like the prodigal son, seeking forgiveness. Moreover, the forgiveness that Mrs. Steerforth proposes is a parody of the true Christian forgiveness that becomes a duty when the sinner repents and puts aside his sin. Her forgiveness is simply an acknowledgment that the sinner has been obedient to her authority. Similarly, Rosa Dartle's love is a parody of Christian love, or even of normal human affection. Her denunciation of Mrs. Steerforth shows where she locates the blame. "'Now,' she said, 'is your pride appeased, you madwoman? *Now* has he made atonement to you—with his life! Do you hear?—His life!'" (799) It is thus possible to see Steerforth as the product of an unwise parent, a wasted splendor that might have benefitted mankind instead of maiming in one way or another all those who cared for him, as he physically maimed Rosa for life.

In direct contrast to Mrs. Steerforth's unforgiving nature is Mr. Peggotty's genuine selfless love. In setting out to find Em'ly after her fall, he tells those he leaves behind to let her know, if they encounter her first, that his message to her is, "'My unchanged love is with my darling child, and I forgive her!'" (472). Unlike the forgiving Mr. Peggotty, Rosa Dartle can only desire condign punishment for the woman who has caused the breach between mother and son and removed Steerforth from her presence. "'I would have her branded on the face, drest in rags, and cast out in the streets to starve. If I had the power to sit in judgment on her, I would see it done. See it done? I would do it! . . . If I could hunt her to her grave, I would'" (471).[7] This willingness to undertake direct punishment and to hunt down the offender is precisely the form of behavior that Dickens will not permit to his genuinely good characters, though he frequently identifies such vindictive traits with his unsavory ones. But the vanity and pride of Mrs. Steerforth and of Rosa Dartle bring with them their own punishments in the unsatisfied cravings of their hearts. Mrs. Steerforth is condemned to relive over and over the moment in which she learns of the death of her beloved son. It is a suitable substitute for hell on this earth.

There is one major villain left to consider, but before I turn to Heep I will briefly discuss the female "transgressors" in this novel, chiefly of Martha, Em'ly, and Annie Strong, all of whom either break the rules of sexual morality, or appear to have done so. Of course, the most serious transgression of which young women are generally guilty in Dickens' novels is sexual imprudence. Three young women are considered guilty of this offense in *David Copperfield,* but each is considered to have sinned differently. Martha Endell has become a common prostitute, though she has "decency" enough to deplore her condition and wish to end it by suicide. Little Em'ly is seduced by the fascinating Steerforth with the additional enticement that he will make her a lady. Hers is a lapse of vanity and love; but if it degrades her, it does not corrupt her. Annie Strong is suspected of having married Doctor Strong while retaining an affection for her cousin Jack Maldon, and perhaps unwisely returning his passion. We later learn that she is innocent of any improper behavior. What becomes important for this range of female error is the the way others judge the condition of a "sinful" woman.

Dickens was a great believer in the value of suffering for purifying the soul, but he believed even more in the preservation of innocence. Thus, although Em'ly will become a saintly young woman when she is taken off to a new life in Australia, David can still say, looking back on all of her experience, that it might have been better for her to die as a child when she was still untainted.[8] When as a child Em'ly rushes along a pier toward the water, the young David fears that she will fall into the sea and drown. Then, as adult narrator, he reflects: "There has been a time since—I do not say it lasted long, but it has been—when I have asked myself the question, would it have been better for little Em'ly to have had the waters close above her head that morning in my sight; and when I have answered Yes, it would have been" (36). The passage does not suggest that it was an abiding sentiment with him, but that it was a genuine one, reinforced by a similar view of his own career. When young David returns from his first term at Salem House, he comes upon his mother nursing her new baby and he is included in the embrace. His recollection of this scene occasions a startling response. "I wish I had died. I wish I had died then, with that feeling in my heart! I should have been more fit for Heaven than I ever have been since" (109). To die is not such a bad thing; to die young may even be a good thing, for it insures purity and admission to Heaven. Although this may be a morbid line of thought, it does explain a thread of sentiment obvious throughout Dickens' novels and most prominent perhaps in *The Old Curiosity Shop* and *Dombey and Son.* But if the "Wordsworthian" view of children as closer to God makes their early departure something like a blessing for them, the obverse of that blessing is the curse of having to continue in life, heaping one species of guilt after the other upon a soul eager to remain pure enough for admission to Heaven. Life under such circumstances becomes a kind of double-entry bookkeeping, in which each individual starts with a certain amount of good credit but inevitably accrues debts through sin. One can only hope that enough of the true bullion will remain when one dies. No human action except forgiveness seems to approach the initial purity with which humans begin their earthly experience. Forgiveness is the clearest sign that the books are balanced. To some extent David is so lenient a narrator because in composing the book of his life he is trying to balance the book of his moral account. If the end of his story is to be salvation, he must prove himself a Christian and forgive all those who have trespassed againt him. The good Christian—and that is what David becomes—can no more tell a punitive tale than he can commit a retributive deed. Since it is his voice and his language that constructs the story, the story must be faithful to his character.

The two passages about earthly death that I have cited are not unique in Dickens. Elsewhere he expresses similar feelings, but in *David Copperfield* these passages have an additional narrative function. The first foreshadows Em'ly's subsequent ordeal; the narrator implies that she will behave in some way that will bring her pain and perhaps punishment for transgression. This proleptic casting forward of the line of the story not only gives Em'ly a greater interest for us, but it swathes her in the cloak of potential tragedy, thus sensitizing us to all of her actions. We are led to distrust her, a distrust that is only increased when we learn that she is considered by other persons in Yarmouth to put on airs and to speak of wanting to be above her class. This distrust subtly prepares us for Em'ly's fall and makes understandable the connection between Martha, Em'ly, and Steerforth. When Steerforth learns what kind of woman Martha is, his conscience troubles him because he has just been thinking of seducing Em'ly. Martha is like a warning spectre for Steerforth, which he recognizes—just as he does the nightmare of the greater kind of going to the dogs—though he overcomes both out of a selfish desire for pleasure and conquest. On the other hand, Martha is to Em'ly both a cautionary symbol of what becomes of women who err and an opportunity to show her compassion and sisterhood. In Phiz's illustration for the scene in which Martha pleads to Em'ly for help in leaving Yarmouth there are clues to the rightness of Emily's sympathy. Directly above Martha, mirroring her kneeling position, is a picture of Christ forgiving Mary Magdalene, and behind the door above Little Em'ly's head is a picture of Eve being tempted by the serpent.[9] The paradigm lesson seems to be that when woman falls she brings disaster upon herself and others, but that even in her most degraded state she is still capable of redemption and that the true Christian response is to understand such failings and be prepared to help the fallen when they repent. Mr. Peggotty, a touchstone of right feeling, has been able to improve upon an already admirable character. He learns that there remains value even in some of the most obviously outcast among us. When Martha offers her help in finding Em'ly, Mr. Peggotty revises his thinking. " 'The time was, Mas'r Davy,' he said, as we came down-stairs, 'when I thowt this girl, Martha, a'most like the dirt underneath my Em'ly's feet. God forgive me, theer's a difference now!'" (676). Mr. Peggotty is obliged to ask God's forgiveness for not having been forgiving himself.

Mr. Peggotty has learned what Rosa Dartle never can, for she wants only to punish. She tells Em'ly that she would like to see her whipped to death and suggests that the best solution is suicide. This unforgiving fury arises partly from envy, partly from frustrated passion. It is a secular version of the Murdstones' wrathful theology that emphasizes punishment over compassion. Counterbalancing Rosa's Mosaic harshness are Ham's more acceptable sentiments. "'Tan't that I forgive her,'" he tells David. "'Tan't that so much. 'Tis more as I beg of her to forgive me, for having pressed my affections upon her'" (737).[10] In a truly Christian mode, Ham understands that human malefaction cannot be so simply isolated. In some remote way he too may be guilty, and therefore must not judge Em'ly's weakness severely. That too is the meaning of the picture of Eve being tempted by the serpent. We are all children of fallen parents and condemned to repeat their error in our various degrees. In her farewell letter to Ham, Em'ly writes, "In another world, if I am forgiven, I may wake a child and come to you" (785). Everything at the end of the novel hinges on the crucial act of forgiveness. Indeed, there would be no such narrative as David Copperfield if David himself had not learned to be careful in his moral judgments and to forgive those who repent. Implicit in his lesson is an awareness germane to Ham's that he is himself not free from complicity in the misfortunes of others.

David's lesson, to trust love, comes to him from Annie Strong. And he seems determined to make us learn the dangers of his distrust along with him. In fact, his treatment of Annie Strong is an antidote to the very distrust he has created in the reader concerning Em'ly. David gradually provides clues to Em'ly's eventual dereliction, confirming our growing doubts about her character. Something similar happens with Annie Strong. Mr. Wickfield implies that the young woman's marriage to the much older Doctor Strong was motivated not by love but by a desire for economic security for Annie and her family. Again it is Mr. Wickfield who suspects that Doctor Strong wants young Maldon out of the way because of the danger to Annie's virtue. Mr. Wickfield is a dangerous guide in matters of this sort, since he is early portrayed as a man inherently suspicious of other persons' motives. Nonetheless, influenced by Mr. Wickfield's opinions and by his own reading of the Strong marriage, David comes to mistrust Annie too.

Since he is narrating these events long after the fact, David could tell us immediately all that he knows about Annie, but he purposely withholds information that would exonerate her. This withholding of information is a normal narrative device for creating suspense, and thus a desire on the reader's part to pursue the story. But there is a distinctly manipulative quality to David's approach. For example, on the eve of Jack Maldon's departure for India, something happens when he bids Annie goodbye—various clues suggest an embrace. Later, when David happens upon Annie seated on a stool by her husband's feet, he is struck by her look, but cannot interpret it. "Distinctly as I recollect her look, I cannot say of what it was expressive, I cannot even say of what it is expressive to me now, rising again before my older judgment. Penitence, humiliation, shame, pride, love, and trustfulness, I see them all: and in them all, I see that horror of I don't know what" (246). By opening his list with negative suggestions and concluding it with the word "horror," David compromises the positive elements of his list so that pride can be vanity, love can be unassigned, and trustfulness mere credulity. In calling attention to his inability to interpret Annie's expression even at the time of narrating, David underlines his position of privileged knowledge, his power to tell us what the upshot of this scene was. Yet he does not do so, preferring that we experience the same misgivings that he did, making us wait until after Em'ly's fall to discover that there is another kind of love that grows not out of physical attraction and social ambition, but out of tenderness, long affection, and respect.

We are led to suspect Annie just as David is largely because of the reactions of other people to her, Mr. Wickfield in particular, who dislikes any contact between Agnes and Annie.

> And now, I must confess, the recollection of what I had seen on that night when Mr. Maldon went away, first began to return upon me with a meaning it had never had, and to trouble me. The innocent beauty of her face was not as innocent to me as it had been; I mistrusted the natural grace and charm of her manner; and when I looked at Agnes by her side, and thought how good and true Agnes was, suspicions arose within me that it was an ill-assorted friendship. (281)

It is not until after Em'ly's fall that David returns to Annie's story with Uriah's plan to end the friendship between Annie and Agnes. David passes over the obvious recommendation in Annie's favor that Agnes, the touchstone of virtue and insight in the novel, has chosen to continue her friendship with the young wife. There could be no higher endorsement in this novel. That Uriah, an obvious rogue, should become Annie's chief enemy might be read as a mark in her favor. In any case, it is Uriah who informs Doctor Strong that his wife is too sweet on the now-returned Jack Maldon, and he solicits Mr. Wickfield's and David's own suspicions to support his charge. David is so furious at being implicated in this way that he declares Uriah a villain and, in an act very rare among Dickens' good characters, strikes him (619–20).[11]

Uriah's open charge ironically becomes the cause of a true reconciliation between Doctor Strong and his young wife, for the obvious constraint between them prompts Mr. Dick to bring them together again, allowing Annie to declare her faithful and enduring love for her husband. Annie's speech in this incident not only demonstrates her own unblemished virtue, but announces some of the key phrases that will apply to David's case. To explain her discovery that Maldon was not an appropriate partner for her, she declares that "there can be no disparity in marriage like unsuitability of mind and purpose"; she is thankful to her husband "for having saved me from the first mistaken impulse of my undisciplined heart" (660–61). The reconciliation is confirmed in words that will echo importantly later in the novel: "'Oh, take me to your heart, my husband, for my love was founded on a rock, and it endures!'" (663).[12]

In the end, not only has our distrust of Annie been unwarranted, but she is actually the guardian and exponent of all of the highest virtues associated with human love. She represents, moreover, the very course that David should have pursued—to have disciplined his heart and sought out a partner with suitable mind and purpose and there fixed his heart like a rock that endures. That our suspicion of Annie should prove false after our doubts about Em'ly have been confirmed I take to be a conscious strategy on Dickens' part, designed to emphasize again the Christian caution not to judge others too easily, since we cannot know their hearts. Moreover, if those who have fallen can still be pitied as Martha is pitied, and even be redeemed, as Martha is redeemed, then all such suspicion must at least be tempered by an underlying respect for common humanity.

It is this sense of common humanity that makes even the vilest creature in this novel somehow not worthless. The wicked characters retain an important trait missing in many of Dickens' villains—family affection. The Murdstones support one another and believe that they are doing what is right and just. Steerforth and his mother have a strong affection between them, though they share the same obstinate character. And the one redeeming quality in Uriah is his sincere affection for his mother and her reciprocated maternal love. Ralph Nickleby's greatest offense was cutting himself off from all "natural" family affection. Dombey's was to withhold that affection from his daughter. The list could go on. But no principal villain in this book makes that grave error.

The interesting feature of Uriah Heep is that he employs a superficially Christian mode to effect his villainy. His constant references to his own humble condition cannot help but create an increasingly cacaphonous reverberation of the beatitude: "The meek shall inherit the earth." As we have seen, this is a characteristic form of evil in Dickens' narratives; thus the workhouse betrays charity, Squeers betrays benevolent education, and the Protestant Cause betrays religion. The greatest sin against Christianity is to invert its formulas of good will. From David's opening description Uriah is unappealing both physically and behaviorally, yet from the start young David is equally struck by the natural affection demonstrated between the Heeps. If we dislike Uriah from the start, that is no reason for wanting to see him suffer.[13] Dickens is here playing out a narrative strategy not unlike the Annie/Em'ly equation. Despite reinforcing signs, suspicions against Annie's virtue were clearly unwarranted. Conversely, though the narration signals that Uriah is dangerous and not to be trusted, is, in fact, a clear manifestation of class *ressentiment*, mere aversion is not enough to justify moral judgment. This is a problem for David, but it is a problem for the reader as well. Our moral assessment of Uriah must be gradual and well documented. For example, when Uriah reveals his desire to possess Agnes, we may righteously yearn to thwart him not because Agnes is too good for him, but because his means and his motives are corrupt. He uses his power over Mr. Wickfield in trying to force Agnes to accept him, though her aversion to him is evident. This form of coercion does not sit well with his claim of "pure affection" for Agnes (381). The desire to forestall Heep's evil increases as we learn of the loss of Aunt Betsey's fortune, which we attribute to Heep, since by now we know that he controls Mr. Wickfield. Later, when David strikes him, Uriah refuses to quarrel, again grotesquely reflecting a distorted Christian resistance to violence; it is a wily turning of the other cheek. By this time, however, we have sufficient evidence to understand Uriah's behavior and we reject this mockery of Christian values. I have attributed these responses to us as readers because I assume that Dickens envisioned such a sympathetic and responsive audience. But he also understood his audience well enough by this time to forgo genuine melodrama for the most part and to play some interesting variations on the moral expectations invoked by his narrative.

Ultimately, of course, Uriah is unmasked, and it is not so unusual that the agent of this justice is the improvident Micawber. Nothing could be more remote from Heep's hypocritical scheming than Micawber's expansive failure. But here again family affection plays an important role. Micawber realizes the degree to which his nature has been altered by association with Heep when he feels himself alienated from his wife and children. Though as weak in his own way as Mr. Wickfield and others are in theirs, Micawber nonetheless has a core of real decency in him, indicated in various ways—for example, by never asking David for financial assistance, though knowing David very likely could not refuse him. And so, with proper theatrical flourish, Micawber exposes Heep's villainy.

But even now full punishment is withheld. Uriah must disgorge all that he has acquired illegally, but that is as much as Traddles, Copperfield, and Betsey Trotwood seem to want. Uriah charges that David has always been against him, leaving an opening for some straightforward moralizing on David's part. "'As I think I told you once before,' said I, 'it is you who have been, in your greed and cunning, against all the world. It may be profitable to you to reflect, in future, that there never were greed and cunning in the world yet, that did not do too much, and over-reach themselves. It is as certain as death'" (760). From David's point of view, then, Uriah has brought his downfall upon himself. David has wanted this, but he has not acted to bring it about because he has not known the extent of Uriah's villainy and hypocrisy. Uriah's false meekness discovers itself as a fierce drive for power and domination. David has become increasingly aware of Uriah's formidable abilities. But, according to Christian formula, the truly meek triumph after all because evil ultimately undoes itself, brings on its own natural punishment. Uriah is bested by a "fool" (Micawber), a questionable attorney (Traddles), and a naive young man (David). What could be more painful to a lifelong schemer? But he *is* bested and leaves the scene—apparently for good.

The later chapters of *David Copperfield* provide an interesting examination of the nature of forgiveness and punishment as Dickens understood them. As all of the main crises of the novel are being resolved, Dora is dying. Her death eliminates the need for any forgiveness between her and David. She will not become a burden to him as their lives grow more and more dissimilar. David will not have to seek her forgiveness for unwisely marrying her, and she will not have to seek his for proving so inadequate a spouse. To some degree her death is a punishment to David for his undisciplined heart, but it is also a providential release for both of them. In the light of David's willingness to have good people, himself included, die before they can be tainted by the world, Dora's death may even be seen as advantageous for her everlasting happiness. To make this point fully clear, the narrative has Betsey Trotwood's husband die soon after. David accompanies his aunt to the funeral service, after which she says, in summary of her miserable hymeneal experience, itself the consequence of her own undisciplined heart: " 'Six-and-thirty years ago, this day, my dear,' said my aunt, as we walked back to the chariot, 'I was married. God forgive us all!' " (782).[14]

In that "all" is the core of this novel's unusual tenderness, for it is an admission of universal human error and the need for compassion and forgiveness above all else. We must even learn to forgive ourselves. And this is David's next task. With the main actions of the novel over, he sets out on a continental tour that will run from months into years. By letter, Agnes teaches him to gain strength from sorrow. Finally he is reconciled to his condition, able to think gravely but not bitterly of the past, and to contemplate the future in a brave spirit. " 'It was right that I should pay the forfeit of my headlong passion. What I reaped, I had sown' " (830). But this genuine self-discipline and self-understanding are the very means by which he will earn another chance at creating a happy life. David is willing to acknowledge some degree of complicity, blame, or responsibility for some of the misfortunes that have occurred to himself and others. Though he is very far from a wicked person, he is sensitive to his own mistakes. Not all sins are active sins. In part David becomes involved in misdeeds because he invites abuse, or because he fails to comprehend it.[15] Even the prevailing mode of his narration largely withholds awareness of peccancy.

The voracious waiter we have already mentioned, but that instance of intimidation is only a beginning. When he is still young and inexperienced, David feels thoroughly daunted by the "respectable" Littimer, Steerforth's servant. Littimer's coolness makes David feel young and inept. Moreover, he fancies that Littimer is always capable of penetrating his defenses. "How was it," he asks himself, "having so little in reality to conceal, that I always *did* feel as if this man were finding me out?" (416). What David does not realize as a young man is that he feels "found out" because he has a strong moral sense and is aware of his own faults no matter how small they are. Littimer, on the other hand, is devoid of any genuine morality and thus is not troubled by his conscience. It is precisely this sensitivity to being found out, this vulnerability, characteristic of so much of Thackeray's attitude toward punishment and forgiveness as we shall see later in this book, that contributes to the genial mood of *David Copperfield*.

There is no better example of this geniality than the apparently unfortunate Tommy Traddles, so consistently punished by Creakles, so apparently luckless in his young manhood, but ultimately so successful in life, winning a fine wife and making a good career. If he first seems foolish and bungling, his is also one of the earliest voices raised for justice, since it is he who openly protests against Steerforth's treatment of Mr. Mell, and who later accuses him of shabby behavior. As grown men, he and David recall his schoolboy habit of drawing skeletons, which reminds them both of their days together at Creakles' school. "After we had both laughed heartily, Traddles wound up by looking with a smile at the fire, and saying, in his forgiving way, 'Old Creakle!' " (848). David is not as ready to forgive the old rascal, a familiar instance where a minor character is more benevolent than his or her central counterpart. Traddles is the Tom Pinch of this novel. And his forgiving nature does not extend merely to offenders in the past. Immediately after Heep's discomfiture, Betsey Trotwood denounces him as a "monster of meanness," but Traddles replies: " 'Really I don't know about that. . . . Many people can be very mean, when they give their minds to it' " (778). If this is not exactly forgiveness, it certainly is human understanding based upon a recognition of general human frailty, a recognition that lies beneath any person's sense of his or her own unworthiness. It is entirely appropriate that Traddles, so early a victim of injustice and a spokesman against it, should find his way in life as a lawyer. The novel is filled with suggestions that the law has very little to do with justice, and often inhabits the opposite camp. But though Mr. Waterbrook categorizes him as "one of those men who stand in their own light," Traddles does make his way by virtue of honesty, hard work, and good temper.

As the novel draws to a close, there is much settling of accounts. The punishments that were not handed out in any specific way earlier in the narrative are now stipulated. Mrs. Steerforth, we have already seen, will continue to suffer afresh the revelation that she has lost her beloved son, and Rosa Dartle will burn herself up with her own rage and frustrated passion. And in the later pages of the book the Murdstones are finally assigned their punishment. Mr. Chillip gives David an account of Mr. Murdstone's second marriage, including indications that Murdstone is proving as much a tyrant now as he did with David's mother, and that he is preaching ferocious religious doctrine. But the mild doctor protests: " 'And do you know I must say, sir, I *don't* find authority for Mr. and Miss Murdstone in the New Testament?' " He goes on to pronounce their fate. " 'However, as Mrs. Chillip says, sir, they undergo a continual punishment; for they are turned inward, to feed upon their own hearts, and their own hearts are very bad feeding' " (834).

A notable encounter turning on the issue of punishment and forgiveness awaits David and Traddles in their visit to the model prison run by Mr. Creakle, where Littimer and Heep are confined. Everything in this scene is topsy-turvey. Creakle, a model of tyranny and injustice, now represents the authority of institutionalized law. Whereas he once beat innocent young boys, he now pampers convicted felons. Meanwhile, the felons use Christian formulas as weapons against the truly virtuous. Littimer insincerely declares that he sees his past follies and hopes that his former companions may find forgiveness. He hopes too that David will "repent of all the wickedness and sin to which he has been a party," and asks David to tell Em'ly that he forgives her her bad conduct to himself and that he calls upon her to repent (853). Uriah's behavior is similar. He declares that it would be "better for everybody, if they got took up, and was brought here" to prison. But his greatest outrage in this scene is an embodiment of the technique of aggressive meekness that Nietzsche had in mind when he condemned Christianity as a subversion of the proper master mentality by a slave ethic. Uriah reminds David that he once struck him and implies that David has behaved poorly toward him in general.

> "But I forgive you, Mr. Copperfield," said Uriah, making his forgiving nature the subject of a most impious and awful parallel, which I shall not record. "I forgive everybody. It would ill become me to bear malice. I freely forgive you, and I hope you'll curb your passions in future. I hope Mr. W. will repent, and Miss W., and all of that sinful lot. You've been visited with affliction, and I hope it may do you good; but you'd better have come here." (854–55)

The impious parallel is of course with Christ, who forgave those who unjustly punished him. Uriah here assumes the role of the suffering yet forgiving Christ who extends his charity at the expense of his own comfort. That the archscoundrel of the book should thus usurp the role of the supreme model of morality not only indicates the centrality of the concept of forgiveness in Dickensian thought in particular, and Victorian thought in general, but also suggests a caution about too quickly assuming the role of judge and executioner. Though Uriah's charges against David are exaggerated and his forgiveness false, they contain a small grain of truth that is enough to make David and the reader wary of too quickly acting upon suspicion and appearances only.

Like Dickens' other novels, David Copperfield depends upon an ultimately melodramatic structure, though much attenuated. Versions of good and evil early stand opposed to one another in a contest that will increase and diversify through the narrative, with the agencies of evil dominating most of the story. Then the tide begins to turn, and, following a series of dramatic incidents, the powers of evil are eliminated or forced to the margins of the fictional world. It is as though the novel is constructed of huge blocks of energy that shift and sheer against one another depending upon sensitive points of leverage. There are many such points in the narrative, but I shall touch on just a few. One is Em'ly's flight with Steerforth. It represents not only the triumph of selfish wickedness, but the corruption of virtue as well, and it sets in motion the lines of action that will lead to Mr. Peggotty's recovery of Em'ly and to Mrs. Steerforth's loss of her son—versions of rewarded virtue and punished folly. Another such leverage point is the chapter entitled "Tempest," for here certain lines of narrative come to a close with a powerful implicit message. Ham dies trying to rescue the man who has callously betrayed him. He is the embodiment of selfless, compassionate action. But this selflessness is dangerously linked to his indifference about his own future. His Christlike self-sacrifice is colored by his abrogated future. Contrarily, though Steerforth's self-gratifying behavior is a model of wickedness, it is related to his charm and boldness as well.[16] So he dies in a dashing, heroic manner, defiant and brave to the end. The bodies of the two men will not be laid out together in the same room because the villagers consider such a move indelicate and insulting to Ham. This is the definitive separation of good and evil characteristic of melodrama. But David cannot comfortably live in a melodramatic milieu that calls for absolute distinctions and absolute judgments. David moves between his two friends, loving both and remembering them both for what is best in them, and thus reinforcing the caution of the entire novel that we risk committing an injustice ourselves if we judge too strictly, too sternly, too swiftly—as, for example, the Murdstones do. We must try to discipline our own hearts while recognizing that others have similar tasks, similar impulses to ward against. When we have faced and overcome our own weakness, we will be the more able to protect ourselves from the evil begotten by others, and to extend to them the understanding that their behavior too is complicated and difficult to judge.

Nonetheless, the narrative *does* judge, even if more mildly than in almost any other of Dickens' narratives.[17] Those who have misbehaved are all punished to some extent. Those who have learned restraint are, in some degree, rewarded and forgiven. Mercy, pardon, and forgiveness irradiate the closing chapters of the novel. While the characters learn to temper their animosities and modify their need to pass judgment, the implied author behind David's narrative voice sees to it that we, as readers, will be satisfied as the moral account books are totted up and ruled out. What the characters never do fully, the narrative does. It sees to the ordering of the world's moral economy.

NOTES

1. Charles Dickens, *David Copperfield* (London: Oxford University Press, 1966), 169. Gwendolyn B. Needham's "The Undisciplined Heart of David Copperfield," *Nineteenth-Century Fiction* 9 (1954), 81–107, is the significant essay on this specific theme.

2. Sylvia Manning provides an interesting explanation for this lenient tone in an essay on a different subject. In "*David Copperfield* and Scheherazada: The Necessity of Narrative," *Studies in the Novel* 14, no. 4 (Winter 1982), 327–36, she observes that in *David Copperfield* the powers of language operate as a defense against memory. Narrative, by establishing an order to events, "shores up the

gains of the present against the returns of the past" (334). "Heroism, as the establishment of a sure identity, depends upon the conquest of one's past" (335). Manning very acutely notes that the tone of the novel follows David's increasing maturity. "The turning of language's fluidity from malign to benign marks David's rise from helpless child to confident adult" (330). I would only add that the issue is all the more significant because this is a first-person narrative where the backward-looking narrator, whose subject is himself, has enormous latitude regarding the tone and manner of his telling. The subject arises again, with different consequences, in *Great Expectations*.

3. The relatively light tone of *David Copperfield* was not accidental, but playfully present to Dickens from the outset, as his early title trials indicate. One of these trials included the following; "The last living speech and confession of David Copperfield Junior of Blunderstone Lodge, who was never executed at the old Bailey" (*Dickens' Working Notes for His Novels,* ed. Harry Stone [Chicago: The University of Chicago Press, 1987], 131). Subsequent references appear in the text. This almost facetious parody of a gallows confession title suggests a very blithe attitude.

4. Lawrence Frank says that David must learn to tell the story of his life without repressing details and thus becoming fixated at some point in the past, as Mr. Dick so stunningly is in his attempt to narrate. He must also overcome the temptation of yielding to the attraction of the Other and therefore not achieving full maturity. Frank reads David's mastery of shorthand as emblematic of his ability to read the signs of his life (see chapter 2 of *Charles Dickens and the Romantic Self* [Lincoln: University of Nebraska Press, 1984]). Subsequent references appear in the text. J. Hillis Miller calls attention to the way language constitutes a mode of transcendence in *David Copperfield,* and surmises that "there is a secret identity between the linguistic enterprise of Micawber and that of Dickens himself, as it is transposed into the attempt by David Copperfield to tell all that he remembers about himself and his experience" (*Charles Dickens: the World of His Novels* [Cambridge: Harvard University Press, 1965], 151ff.). Subsequent references appear in the text.

5. Lawrence Frank argues that Steerforth is the greatest threat to David's welfare (67).

6. Alexander Welsh, *From Copyright to Copperfield: The Identity of Dickens* (Cambridge: Harvard University Press, 1987), 146. Harvey Peter Sucksmith discusses the sympathetic rendering of Steerforth as an example of Dickens' complex effect in narrating (as distinguished from his simple effect) to achieve a combination of "complexity and power" (*The Narrative Art of Charles Dickens: The Rhetoric of Sympathy and Irony in his Novels* [Oxford: The Clarendon Press, 1970], 201ff.). E. D. H. Johnson is one of several scholars who have called attention to the way Steerforth's death is a culminating point of several plot lines and is so located that "the narrator's memories have been ironically ordered to forecast this denouement" (*Charles Dickens: An Introduction to His Novels* [New York: Random House, 1969], 99).

7. Rosa Dartle, who has been branded on the face by Steerforth's youthful passion, appropriately wants to brand Em'ly in a like fashion. The one woman suppresses her admiration for Steerforth, the other unwisely yields to hers. Both are branded by Steerforth, who is the projection of their own desires, not the object of genuine love.

8. I believe that F. R. and Q. D. Leavis misread what Dickens is trying to achieve with Em'ly. They object that "Em'ly, who has not been a prostitute like Martha, is not allowed to forgive herself for her one false step, but must hang her head in guilt eternally" (*Dickens the Novelist* [Harmondsworth: Penguin Books, 1972], 116). They conclude that Dickens "was apparently endorsing the prejudices of his reading-public at this point, for though so humane a man could not at heart endorse such an attitude, and we know that in fact he did not, he is scarcely challenging it effectively. Here writing at two levels has muddled the message" (117). But the narrative is not here punishing Em'ly for her sexual delinquency, as Martha's case seems to verify. She is punished rather for her treachery to love, having betrayed both Ham and Mr. Peggotty and the innocence for which they stand.

9. Michael Steig explicates this illustration, indicating its clear implication "that Emily is being tempted to evil, while Martha is on the path to reform through her own remorse and others' forgiveness, although she does not yet recognize the path" (*Dickens and Phiz* [Bloomington: Indiana University Press, 1978], 126).

10. Ham resembles John Peerybingle in *The Cricket on the Hearth,* taking personal responsibility for having imposed his love on a perhaps unwilling partner. This sentiment occurs several times in Dickens with interesting variations and is related to the situation where a lover withdraws from competition because he or she feels that his or her beloved object would be better suited elsewhere, as with Marion Jeddler in *The Battle of Life.*

11. Audrey Jaffe notes that David's reaction in this scene feeds upon a more general anxiety in the narrative as a whole. To be watched or scripted by others is the principal situation David tries to avoid. In this scene Uriah is forcing David to play a part in the script he has concocted about Annie's guilt, and thus David is in danger of becoming a figure in a text to be read by others (*Vanishing Points: Dickens, Narrative, and the Subject of Omniscience* [Berkeley: University of California Press, 1991], 127).

12. In his working notes Dickens emphasized for himself the application of Annie's remarks in this scene. After quoting these remarks, he writes, "all brought to bear on David, and applied by him to himself" (Stone 171).

13. A. O. J. Cockshut considers Uriah a puzzling and unsatisfactory character because "physical repulsion, moral disapproval and class superiority are mingled, are boiled up together into a kind of broth where they become indistinguishable" (*The Imagination of Charles Dickens* [New York: New York University Press, 1962], 119). But Cockshut may here be exhibiting his own prejudices. I take this mingling of Uriah's character to be a purposeful ambiguity, ironically

aimed not only at Uriah but at those who expect conventional behavior from him so that they may judge him simply.

14. In his working notes for this scene, Dickens underlined the sentence "God forgive us all" (Stone 177).

15. Lawrence Frank argues that David, at least unconsciously, is implicated in Em'ly's seduction and Dora's death, and that his perplexity at critical moments in the narrative is a consequence of his failing to acknowledge this complicity (78, 88).

16. In the illustration entitled "I make the acquaintance of Mrs. Mowcher," Steerforth's wickedness is reinforced by the painting on the wall representing Faust's seduction of Margaret. The painting of a shipwreck beside it proleptically suggests Em'ly's ruin. The shipwreck image was frequently taken to signify moral collapse. Of course, Steerforth is to die in an authentic shipwreck.

17. J. Hillis Miller sees this judgment as part of the novel's "providential spirit." David's "destiny and identity and those of other people have been made by a metaphysical power, the power of divine Providence" (155–56). He quotes specific passages in evidence of this view.

THIRTEEN

Bleak House

BLEAK HOUSE describes a pattern of accumulated injustice and abuse that cul-
minates in a massive need for dealing out forgiveness and punishment. It satisfies
that need through the uncommon strategy of a double narration, into which the
two contending impulses are distributed. The novel is altogether a more sophisticated and complex accomplishment than what had preceded. As has often been
noted about this astonishing novel, the themes are reflected and repeated in what
appears at first to be a mere muddle but which, in the end, reveals itself as an
elaborate tapestry. G. K. Chesterton astutely noted that *Bleak House* presented a
change of artistic structure in Dickens' fiction. "The thing is no longer a string
of incidents; it is a cycle of incidents. It returns upon itself; it has a recurrent
melody and poetic justice; it has artistic constancy and artistic revenge."[1] Dickens'
usual redundancy of details makes the novel's message or messages inescapable.
The design of this novel depends upon belief in a universe operating according to
a rational plan and culminating in a Day of Judgment that assumes human responsibility and culpability.

Bleak House approaches the theme of retribution and mercy from a peculiar
angle, for it begins not at the Old Bailey, as one might expect, but at Chancery, a
court not concerned with punishment and forgiveness, but with ensuring fairness
in human dealings. This shift of venue in itself marks a transfer of emphasis from
the early works, where delinquencies are essentially personal and external (outright crimes of theft, aggression, betrayal) and are punished in a more-or-less
criminal arena, to the later works, where sins replace crimes insofar as a sense of
culpability is more widely distributed, and moral transgressions are seen to arise
out of subtler social and psychological sources. Most transgressions, in short, are
not simple criminal acts, but more involved collusions and complicities. Hunting
down offenders in this world is likely to bring us face to face with our own secret
failings.

If Chancery's purpose is to ensure equity in human dealings and to protect property and the unfortunate, then that function has long since been lost sight of and we can "look in vain for Truth" in the Court of Chancery now.[2] So much has this public institution perverted its purpose, that it *begets* injury and injustice instead of curing them. It is a far more elaborate perversion on the model evident as early as the workhouse of *Oliver Twist*. The indignant third-person narrator wishes that when the court is locked up at night, "all the injustice it has committed, and all the misery it has caused, could only be locked up with it, and the whole burnt away in a great funeral pyre" (7). At the very outset of this narrative, the machinery of justice is addled, more deserving of the execution of justice *upon* it than *through* it. But if to seek justice through Chancery is to court one's own ruin, how can justice be achieved? One answer is to depend upon the ultimate equity of providence, as Miss Flite and Mr. Gridley do. Miss Flite passively awaits a Day of Judgment when she will receive justice, and Mr. Gridley angrily and aggressively asserts, "'I will accuse the individual workers of that system against me, face to face, before the great eternal bar'" (215). But to recommend no action until God judges all people is not an entirely satisfactory method of dealing with injustice in this world. Though we must trust to providence, we must not leave all the work to providence.[3] Because human beings are, in Dickens' world, endowed with free will, they are obliged to seek out truth and justice. This was much simpler in the early novels when only deceit and mischief by wicked persons kept the virtuous from the truth. It is far less simple a task when the virtuous themselves are implicated in the ways of evil, which are as insidious as a disease or a wasting rot. One mode of implication is simply not confronting the evil that is evident. David Copperfield, in all his innocence, is nonetheless vaguely aware of his own involvement in some of the lamentable events he records, and ultimately he must acknowledge this involvement, if only symbolically or in his manner of recounting his life story. The good people of *Bleak House,* too, must not turn away from the reality of evil as though it were a foreign, excludable entity, but face it as a domestic familiar. Mr. Gridley wants to accuse his antagonists face to face in the hereafter. It is more important perhaps to recognize those antagonists as they press upon our own domestic preserves. John Jarndyce wishes to insulate himself from the effects of the legal case that bears his name, insufficiently alert to the insidiousness of the evil, "and even those who have contemplated its history from the outermost circle of such evil, have been insensibly tempted into a loose way of letting bad things alone to take their own bad course, of a loose belief that if the world go wrong, it was, in some off-hand manner, never meant to go right" (5).

The infection of indifference finds its way into Bleak House despite Jarndyce's efforts at quarantine, in the case itself, in the person of Richard Carstone, and through that embodiment of indifference to practical affairs, Skimpole. Both characters, it should be noted, are admitted by Jarndyce himself, and both are indulged to an excessive degree by his unwillingness to admit evil when it wears a comfortable domestic mask. Thus one of the best characters in the novel is deeply implicated in the tendency symbolized by Jarndyce and Jarndyce to let the evil we regard as external continue unabated under the illusion that it will never touch our protected asylum of virtue. The physical consequence of this tendency to let evil be is dramatically represented in the disease that migrates from Tom-All-Alone's—itself symbolizing neglect—by way of Jo, to Esther herself. The message seems to be that neglect will eventually strike, not through malice but through natural circumstances, to the very heart of innocence.

If the first note sounded in *Bleak House* is the incompatibility of human and divine justice, the second is the disparity between Christianity as Christ taught it and as too much of mankind interprets it. As we have seen, this is a consistent theme in Dickens' writing, from the hypocritical nonconformists of *Pickwick* to the all-too-serious Murdstones of *Copperfield,* and later to the grim Mrs. Clennam of *Little Dorrit.* If human beings have misread the lesson of love and mercy that Christ taught, how can they reap the benefits of his teaching? Characteristically, Dickens' misguided religious enthusiasts look back to a punitive Old Testament God, or they pervert Christ's message of love as Pecksniff and Chadband do. Miss Barbary, Esther's "godmother," tells her that "Submission, self-denial, diligent work, are the preparations for a life begun with such a shadow on it" (17–18). At first this declaration seems to be no more than one standard religious slogan of the age—that the true Christian must submit his or her will to God's will in order to earn salvation. Esther's "fallen" condition—her illegitimate birth—could in this light typify mankind's fallen condition from the sin of its first parents, a simple traditional message saying that, since we inherit guilt, we must be vigilant against it. But Miss Barbary's religion, though not Calvinistic, is nonetheless severe, emphasizing fear and the likelihood of retribution. Her attitude is directly contrasted with Christ's plea for a forgiving spirit when he lectures his audience about the penitent adulteress: "He that is without sin among you, let him first cast a stone at her!" (19). Miss Barbary's doctrine asserts that because we are all the heirs of sin we must take arms against it, whereas Christ says that because we are all sinners, we must be slow to judge the weaknesses of others.[4] Redemption may be through pain or through love, but it is best through love, something that the Barbarys of the world cannot allow themselves to acknowledge because their own religious zeal is so often the consequence of thwarted desire. John Jarndyce comments critically upon "the distorted religion which clouded [Miss Barbary's] mind with impressions of the need there was for the child to expiate an offence of which she was quite innocent" (237). Innocent though Esther is, she is the living proof of a serious moral failure that deprived Miss Barbary of the fulfillments of love and marriage.

Though educated by her sincerely faithful and even "charitable" aunt (she does take the responsibility for Esther's upbringing), Esther cannot follow her example. Ironically she admits that she could not "even love her as I wished" (15–16). Esther is the true representative of Christ's teaching, being kind, meek (in the best sense), and positively helpful without being foolish. J. Hillis Miller says that, in Esther, "Dickens shows the possibility of a truly moral life" (217). Her narration is thus necessary for us to perceive the fallen, unredeemed world of the novel from the proper forgiving point of view. Moreover, it amplifies another important issue in the moral construction of the story. Esther's first-person narration may be read as a form of confession, but a confession that requires no penance, for it reveals no sins by the narrator. Inevitably, Esther's narrative becomes a story about herself. As Lawrence Frank points out, she, like David Copperfield but less professionally, is engaged in an essay of self-creation. She too struggles to define a self-constructed identity as opposed to identities offered by others, with perhaps less success.[5] If Esther has no sins to confess, she knows which sins require repentance and is, through no effort of her own, connected with her mother's sin and with Hortense's crime, if only by physical resei•.blance.[6] But if she knows where the moral faults lie in the world around her, she is generally not free to designate them. This is true at both serious and trivial leveis, from her mother's sin to Mrs. Jellyby's domestic peccadillos. Esther's sometimes embarrassing willingness to engage in self-revelation in her narrative contrasts sharply with the general spirit of secrecy that pervades the novel. From childhood Esther has understood the efficacy of confession, telling all of her youthful secrets to her doll. But if she can tell her secrets after the events of the narrative are in the past, she cannot, while those events are under way, disclose the secrets of others, and in this way she too partakes of the mystification so much a part of *Bleak House*.[7]

Esther's personal candor and her reluctance to disclose the secrets of others is nicely balanced by Sergeant Bucket's professional object of finding out other people's secrets in order to make them useful for the general public, for preventing or punishing crimes. But like Esther he keeps as many secrets as he shares, for there is no point in publishing secrets that have no professional bearing. Tulkinghorn, another pursuer of secrets, has no intention of making them public unless such revelation becomes necessary for his own standing.[8] He seeks out the secrets of others to satisfy a personal hunger for power and respect, a form of addiction. Young Guppy is a secretmonger who wants to convert his discoveries into a form of legal tender. What distinguishes Esther from other custodians of secrecy is that secrets come to her unbidden as a consequence of who and what she is. They are of no *value* to her as they are to others. In many ways they may be seen instead as her burden.

Esther's willingness to tell her story represents genuine candor because she is never moved by self-interest. She does not immediately disclose everything she knows about others, or about herself, where personal modesty prevents it, even long after any embarrassment should be past. What she does tell she tells directly. By contrast, Skimpole, who pretends to innocent straightforwardness and is always ready to confess his unworldliness and his ineptitude with money and domestic efficiency, is anything but candid, disguising both his selfishly motivated deeds and the consequences of his genial attributes upon his suffering family.

If Esther's narrative presents the world from a truly Christian perspective, the third-person narrative concentrates on a more retributive outlook. Esther is slow to judge; the third-person narrator easily condemns, asks for judgment upon others, and utters warnings. He is often prophetic and apocalyptic and seems to enjoy scenes where evil and error are punished. The third-person narrator resembles an omniscient narrator who recounts the narrative punishments meted out by an implied author; he is a human instrument acknowledging the designs of providence, and thus constitutes a "historical" or "public" moral position for which, at the public level, retribution is the natural consequence of neglect and injustice. Tom-All-Alone's is one notable example that he singles out.

> There is not an atom of Tom's slime, not a cubic inch of any pestilential gas in which he lives, not one obscenity or degradation about him, not an ignorance, not a wickedness, not a brutality of his committing, but shall work its retribution, through every order of society, up to the proudest of the proud, and to the highest of the high. Verily, what with tainting, plundering, and spoiling, Tom has his revenge. (627–28)

Mildred Newcomb is correct, I believe, in seeing Tom-All-Alone's as a manifestation of the Carlylean notion of cosmic justice, which insists that the great soul of the world is just and not unjust. Tulkinghorn illustrates the same concept in another register. "Like all of the other notes of warning sounded by Dickens, Tulkinghorn's fate reflects an unquestioned assumption of some kind of retributive justice that not only rectifies inequality, but does so in a poetically appropriate way."[9] For the third-person narrator, Krook's death also prefigures the retributive fate that all authority employing false pretenses and injustice can expect. They, too, "inborn, inbred, engendered in the corrupted humours of the vicious body itself," will die of spontaneous combustion (456).

Dickens accepted Carlyle's picture of a universe driven by justice, of which retribution was an important part, but he also believed that individual sin brought its own particular punishment. Institutions that persist in their errors and crimes will eventually bring about their own destruction, from the Court of Chancery in England to the *ancien regime* in France. But those are long-range consequences, and Dickens liked to show justice working itself out at the private level as well. Lady Dedlock is the chief example of this pattern in *Bleak House,* and just as the public forms of negligence and trespass create a web or miasma of extended evil and misfortune, so Lady Dedlock's original sin gradually radiates into the lives of others, contaminating them in various ways. Her individual guilt thus involves consequences beyond the repair that simple repentance can bring. Though Esther may forgive her mother, she cannot erase the effects of her mother's sin. Esther says, "my duty was to bless her and receive her, though the whole world turned from her" (510). Esther's response is the correct Christian response, a fact emphasized by the circumstances under which Esther first encounters her mother. As Lawrence Frank explains, "The meeting occurs in the church near Chesney Wold and is introduced as the service begins, 'Enter not into judgment with thy servant, O Lord, for in thy sight [shall no man living be justified]'" (105). The Christian message of forbearance in judgment has here an extremely intimate and personal significance, preparing for a loving reconciliation of mother and daughter made poignant by the fact that this reconciliation can never be broadcast, because to do so would be to expose the very sin forgiven.[10] To this degree forgiveness seems to endorse transgression. At the same time, withholding judgment here calls attention to the malign delayed judgments of human institutions, represented by the Court of Chancery and characterized by self-interest. All those associated with the Court are shown to benefit from *postponing* judgment—something very different from *withholding* judgment. The Court of Chancery is thus a parody of Christian mercy, energized not by charity but by materialism. Its blue bags, its documents, its wigs and other paraphernalia disguise the self-interest of judges and lawyers, the most ignoble of which is Vholes. That is why Krook, with all of his garbage and greed, is so apt a metonym for the Court. Because it is not an individual, the Court has the license to judge. Indeed, this is its one central command—judge and judge promptly and fairly. It fails dramatically in this charge, whereas Esther fulfills her Christian duty instantly and without praise or reward.

If Lady Dedlock is forgiven by the person who counts most (and the discovery of Esther as a living child converts Honoria's betrayed love into surviving love), this forgiveness as Esther observes, does not free her from retributive punishment. Lady Dedlock has sinned not only in her fornication; she has sinned, perhaps more seriously, against love itself, abandoning Captain Hawdon for the position and wealth that Sir Leicester Dedlock can provide.[11] One register of her punishment is the vapidity of her daily life, but intensifying her suffering and hence her "punishment" is the increasing pressure to penetrate her secret, her crime. To be found out means much more in Lady Dedlock's case than it does in so many other instances of discovery and exposure in Dickens and Thackeray. Lady Dedlock's secret, once exploded, injures not only herself but those she loves and an entire way of life. The innocent are likely to suffer most. Accordingly, her maneuverings to avoid discovery transform her narrative from one of being found out to one of being hunted down.

Lady Dedlock is punished daily by the choices she has made, the bargain she has entered. Her prominence is always, to her, potentially dust. And echoes of her condition reverberate through the novel. Even innocent remarks carry heavy, unintended meanings for her. When Lady Dedlock meets John Jarndyce again after many years, he behaves in a very courtly way and she objects to his behaving like a courtier because of her reputation as a beauty. And he responds, "'You have achieved so much, Lady Dedlock . . . that you pay some little penalty, I dare say'" (255). Jarndyce knows nothing of what and how large that penalty is. Lady Dedlock's pride intensifies her suffering by its reflection in others. When Lady Dedlock upbraids her maid, Hortense, the young woman reacts by taking off her shoes and walking home through the wet grass. Esther says, "I supposed there is nothing Pride can so little bear with as Pride itself, and that she was punished for her imperious manner" (257). Punished first, that is, by Lady Dedlock's rebuke, but then again self-punished. Lady Dedlock's relationship with Tulkinghorn is similar, but here it is the proud lawyer who chafes the haughty woman; ultimately he will be the agent of her most severe self-inflicted retribution.

Only to Esther herself can Lady Dedlock acknowledge her condition. "'I must travel my dark road alone, and it will lead me where it will. From day to day, sometimes from hour to hour, I do not see the way before my guilty feet. This is the earthly punishment I have brought upon myself. I bear it, and I hide it'" (510). She admits that beneath the mask of pride she is conscience-stricken. "'Think that the reality is in her suffering, in her useless remorse, in her murdering within her breast the only love and truth of which it is capable! And then forgive her, if you can; and cry to Heaven to forgive her, which it never can!'" (512-13). This is desperate language, especially the last despairing cry, which is heresy, since the Christianity Dickens believed in excluded only the unrepentant and unremorseful from forgiveness. In fact, Lady Dedlock is making her nominal transgression out to be far worse than it is and, ironically, this is another consequence of her pride. If she could accept her offense for what it is and humbly face what follows she would be on the way to redemption. But she is unwilling to humble herself outwardly, and thus she intensifies her private pain. Lady Dedlock's metaphorical dark road will become a real one, down which she will flee in a desperate and futile attempt to preserve her secret. She has herself become the secret that must be hunted down and unveiled. When Bucket and Esther have tracked her to the grave of the man and the principle she betrayed, her last word to the world of the living remains: "Forgive" (808).

Lady Dedlock's chief antagonists roughly resemble her in the manner of their demise. Tulkinghorn's contemptuous treatment of Hortense leads to his death at her hands, out of a vanity and pride that beget her punishment for that crime. These proud individuals evoke through their own actions and attitudes the "natural" punishments for their offenses. We could go further to indicate how many more such self-punishers there are in this novel, including Captain Hawdon and Krook in their different ways, but the chief point is simply that much of the punishment enacted in *Bleak House* comes about without significant external agencies or narrative contrivance, but by the simple "law" of reaping what one sows.

That is the punishment side of the ledger, symbolized in the fable of The Ghost's Walk, an objectification and justification of human conscience at work. Conscience, in the Christian scheme is the inborn proof of a universal justice that we violate at our peril, but it is also our means of redemption, for it can lead us to change our ways and choose a better path, a pattern elaborated in Tennyson's "The Two Voices." Mr. Snagsby is a parody of this condition. Though he is entirely innocent of any crime or moral obliquity, he distributes half-crowns as conscience money to palliate any number of afflictions. He becomes so confused about his own moral position "that he entertains wandering ideas of delivering himself up to justice, and requiring to be cleared, if innocent, and punished with the utmost rigour of the law, if guilty" (461). Snagsby's case comically approximates the human condition. We can rarely be entirely certain of how our acts impinge upon others or how others interpret our actions and judge us. Only the very virtuous, the very wicked, or the very self-confident can avoid an occasional sense that they owe some debt or are subject to some penalty for their behavior. This outlook is deeply embedded in the Judeo-Christian faith founded on the concept of original sin. Snagsby's form of relief from bad conscience is not confession or self-committal, but surreptitious charity. In such a way the faithful in general may give money or promote causes as a means not so much of helping others but of guaranteeing their own moral standing and of warding off a bad conscience. In his impetuous charity, Snagsby is also a parody of Jarndyce's real charity, which is set against the unfeeling schemes of Mrs. Jellyby and that "moral Policeman," Mrs. Pardiggle, who administers "charity" as though it were castor oil (107). Because he has nothing to repent, Mr. Snagsby resorts to a cash transaction, thus indicating his moral impoverishment, an impoverishment enlarged and made ludicrous in Mrs. Jellyby and Mrs. Pardiggle, who replace charity with forms of coercion, and who emptily supply money where what is needed is sympathy and care. The very word "charity" is corrupted from its original meaning by their conversion of it into mercenary terms. Ultimately Mr. Snagsby's situation demonstrates that you cannot buy off a bad conscience. If Mr. Jarndyce did nothing but pay out cash to the unfortunate, he would be as dubious a moral figure as those others. But the money Mr. Jarndyce distributes is in addition to his other truly charitable deeds. Moreover, his cash payments follow not from his own sense of obligation but from his awareness of a national bad conscience.

Conscience, of course, is a powerful force for good. Perhaps the best example of its positive effect is Mr. George, the prodigal son of this novel. George regards himself as "a thundering bad son," a conviction that keeps him from returning to the mother he loves but whom he feels he has injured (296). He stays away so as not to embarrass his family, and, with his own case in mind, cautions young Woolwich Bagnet never to do anything to whiten the hairs of his good mother's head since a good conscience on that score will be valuable to him when he is a man. George becomes entangled in the Lady Dedlock mystery and feels a suppressed violence against Tulkinghorn, yet it is because of this mystery and this man that he reencounters his mother. The two first come together again in Tulkinghorn's chambers, though Mrs. Rouncewell does not recognize her son. Later, when George is in prison under suspicion of a murder he did not commit, Mrs. Bagnet brings his mother to him, and, in the abode of punishment, his displaced guilt is forgiven. Mr. George has committed no real offense to estrange him from his family. He is an innocent prodigal son who has imagined his delinquency, and when he returns home no fatted calf is required to mark his redemption, only the sincere affection of all his family, who are happy to incorporate him again in the old circle. Just as he is falsely regarded as guilty of murdering Tulkinghorn, so he falsely suspects himself of sins against his family. But like Snagsby, he is a man whose sense of guilt is groundless and thus impossible to absolve without the assistance of others. A groundless sense of responsibility for sin balances the concealment of sin in *Bleak House,* and the central figure for this sense is Esther Summerson.

If Mr. George's conscience was too tender and he felt the need for a forgiveness that was unnecessary except in his own scrupulous mind, others in the novel do require forgiveness, and the most important of these repent and receive it. We have already seen that Lady Dedlock could humble herself before her daughter and ask forgiveness for the injury done to her, which is less serious than it first appears, since Lady Dedlock did not consciously abandon Esther, whom she has, until this moment, believed dead. In granting forgiveness to her mother Esther takes to herself the burden of her mother's actions: "I felt as if the blame and the shame were all in me and the visitation had come down" (514).

Esther is not a source of blame and shame, but she feels responsible for them and wishes to spare others by helping to expunge both. To a great degree, Esther's role in the novel is as a surrogate for the Atonement. She is not simply a Christ figure and this is no simple typological gesture. But Esther suffers for the original sin of her mother that guides this plot, moving from the Fall to the Day of Judgment, and in her ordeal, symbolized in the scars left by her illness, she suffers for the crimes of society as well. Her ambition is to promote feelings of love, friendship, and mercy. She is the necessary touchstone by which we learn to justify Christian virtues in an otherwise apparently godless world. The Guppys of this world will be the better for having known an Esther, even if they grow up to be the ineffective Lord High Chancellors of the future. Perhaps only those lacking in almost all human feelings, such as the Smallweeds, will not benefit from her acquaintance. As is so often the case in Dickens' novels, the power of good begins to assert itself as the narrative approaches its conclusion. As *Bleak House* nears its end, Esther's spirit of forgiveness begins to expand and predominate. Lord Dedlock offers "full forgiveness" to his errant wife (763). And the repentant Richard Carstone says to John Jarndyce, whom Richard could not earlier forgive for holding what he nonetheless knew to be a correct view of him, "'And you, being a good man, can pass it [Richard's troubled dream of the Jarndyce and Jarndyce case] as such, and forgive and pity the dreamer, and be lenient and encouraging when he wakes?'" (870). Jarndyce can and does forgive, and the shriven Richard dies at peace.

This complex novel is about a good deal more than punishment and forgiveness, but I have tried to demonstrate the important role of these moral forces in the narrative's construction. Good characters do not undertake to punish the

wicked; other faulty characters or natural circumstances achieve what punishments there are. Some fallible characters, though discomfitted, are not really
punished at all; the Smallweed clan is one example. But their lives are shown to
be loveless and unappealing—like Scrooge's before his conversion. Forgiveness
works in the novel because it not only reinforces the virtues of those who are
already forgiving, but promotes the same feeling in others. Thus, after coming to
know Esther, Caddy Jellyby can say, " 'I hope I am better-tempered than I was,
and more forgiving to Ma' " (196). As the novel proceeds, both punishment and
forgiveness increase in intensity. In the central plot lines, the two are intertwined. Thus Lady Dedlock's dereliction brings on a stern punishment long before Tulkinghorn worms out her secret. Yet exposure of her sin ironically makes
full forgiveness possible—perhaps, the narrator hints, hereafter as well as on
earth. Richard Carstone's sufferings are the direct result of his wrong-headed
insistence on seeing the Jarndyce and Jarndyce case settled. When it ends, there is
no fortune left. The case has, in effect, consumed itself just as Richard has consumed himself. But only through this process can Richard recover his senses and
ask and receive forgiveness.

   In this novel one narrative voice judges all it surveys mercilessly; the other has
been regarded by some readers as charitable to a fault. But this dichotomy in the
telling of the tale is entirely appropriate for the elucidation of its moral content.
A world as perceived by the third-person narrator would be an uncomfortable
one for any kindly and sympathetic being, and yet the vitriolic temper of that
narrator serves to fasten blame and recommend punishment for transgressions at
the institutional and national level. His is a world of self-generated destinies or
fates in which evil deeds will come home to roost as they do in the Paris of *A Tale
of Two Cities*. But this angry moral attitude is inadequate as a total reading of
existence. We require as well the intimate, personal interpretation of the world
that only reluctantly passes judgment and that readily forgives. The two outlooks
are implicit everywhere in Dickens' fiction, but in this novel they assume independent identities to enact a Manichean drama not between good and evil, but
between judgment and mercy, punishment and forgiveness. This explicit separation also clarifies a point I have made throughout this study—that the implied
author is the agent of justice in Dickens' novels. It has been noted that Bucket,
who does a good deal of detecting and hunting down, but who does not himself
do any punishing, is a stand-in for the novelist himself.[12] Using the narratological
terminology of our day, perhaps we could say that he is the agent of the implied
author whose actions duplicate the process of the novel's narrative discourse.[13]
Bucket is "on the whole a benignant philosopher not disposed to be severe upon
the follies of mankind . . . but through the placid stream of his life, there glides
an under-current of forefinger" (712). So also the implied author, through his
two narrative voices, points by way of foreshadowing, metaphor, symbolic
scene, and downright indictment to the outcome of our acts, to the bad conscience we all carry about with us. Some of us are willing, one way or another,
to acknowledge our sins and shortcomings, real or imagined; others hide them

deep within themselves. But these shortcomings cannot be hidden from the self. Eventually the pointing forefinger will lead the guilty mind to reveal itself. The implied author's is the warning finger of destiny, which, like the pointing Roman on Tulkinghorn's ceiling, indicates the inevitable terminus for the train of actions we ourselves have set in motion. In Dickens' view that terminus will ultimately be the same for all of us when a symbolic Miss Flite frees her captive birds like liberated souls, and the Day of Judgment descends.

NOTES

1. G. K. Chesterton, *Appreciations and Criticisms of the Works of Charles Dickens* (New York: E. P. Dutton and Co., 1911), 151.

2. Charles Dickens, *Bleak House* (London: Oxford University Press, 1966), 2. J. Hillis Miller explores the significance of the Chancery case as a symbol of the human condition in *Charles Dickens: The World of His Novels* (Cambridge: Harvard University Press, 1965), 196. Subsequent references appear in the text.

3. J. Hillis Miller offers an extreme interpretation of the role of providence in the novel. "Providence is powerless to work in things for man and can only work through the heart of man himself. God has withdrawn himself from the world of *Bleak House*. He apparently does not exist immanently within things as an ubiquitous Providence ordering all events for good in mysterious ways. He does not exist in many events at all. He has left the human world and the objective world to human beings. It is their responsibility" (218).

4. Janet L. Larson discusses the opposition of wrath and love in the novel and Dickens' use of the Book of Job to show that the law of reward and punishment is superseded by the law of love (*Dickens and the Broken Scripture* [Athens: The University of Georgia Press, 1985], 172). The situation is not that simple for Harvey Peter Sucksmith, who sees the world of *Bleak House* as Manichean, with providence acting as both a loving and chastising force (*The Narrative Art of Charles Dickens: The Rhetoric of Sympathy and Irony in His Novels* [Oxford: The Clarendon Press, 1970], 354). Subsequent references appear in the text.

5. Lawrence Frank writes that Esther's challenge "is to create a viable identity within the act of writing an account of her life so that she may come into possession of her story, of her self" (*Charles Dickens and the Romantic Self* [Lincoln and London: University of Nebraska Press, 1984], 98). Subsequent references appear in the text. See also his concern about Esther's enigmatic nature at the end of the novel (123).

6. See Frank on the linkage between Jo's and Esther's confusion and sense of difference (109).

7. Audrey Jaffe says that Esther, like Tulkinghorn and Jarndyce, becomes the keeper of someone else's secret, a secret that she can keep because she has truly given it away (*Vanishing Points: Dickens, Narrative, and the Subject of Omni-*

science [Berkeley: University of California Press, 1991], 140). Jaffe sees Ether's scarred face as symbolic of her mother's sin (141).

8. J. Hillis Miller discusses the significance of secrets in *Bleak House* (170ff.). Graham Storey gives a summary assessment of the importance of secrets in the novel (*Charles Dickens: Bleak House* [Cambridge: Cambridge University Press, 1987], 28ff.).

9. Mildred Newcomb, *The Imagined World of Charles Dickens* (Columbus: Ohio State University Press, 1989), 118–19.

10. Timothy Peltason speculates on just why Lady Dedlock feels compelled to keep her painful secret and not simply flout the world, acknowledge her sin, and openly claim her daughter. He notes that calling attention to this aspect of the discovery scene between mother and daughter indicates its limitations, but admits that to pursue the issue would be to go "off into the regions of a novel we probably don't care to read and of the extra-literary space where Lady Macbeth's children are numbered," "Esther's Will," *ELH* 59 (1992), 681.

11. Harvey Peter Sucksmith misses this betrayal of the principle of love, I believe, when he complains that Lady Dedlock's punishment is out of proportion to her offense and that fate, in her case, is an entirely sinister force (352).

12. Karen Chase explores the way the detective figure crystalizes the task of detection in the novel (*Eros and Psyche: The Representation of Personality in Charlotte Bronte, Charles Dickens, and George Eliot* [New York: Methuen, 1984], 99). She observes that "Bucket belongs to the fictional universe and participates in its dramatic action. In this way, the detective becomes an incarnation of the divine narrative privilege that Dickens usuallly reserves for himself. He brings the plot's agency down to a human scale" (109–10). Bucket is the novel's principle of fate given human form.

13. Offering the reverse side of this equation, J. Hillis Miller proposes that "perhaps the real detective is the narrator himself, attempting through mere passive perception and the exercise of constructive intelligence to discover the laws of the world he sees" (176).

FOURTEEN

Hard Times

EVERYONE KNOWS that *Hard Times* contrasts the fruitfulness of the imagination with the barrenness of Utilitarian thinking. Everyone knows that the flexibility and generosity of Sissy Jupe and the circus world contrasts with the rigidity and selfishness produced by school and industry. Unquestionably this issue is paramount in the novel, but attitudes toward punishment and forgiveness are nonetheless significant and are characteristically presented here. Not only are values and sins rewarded and punished, with love and natural affection being promoted over selfishness and the exploitation of others, but in this novel the narrator assumes a judgmental role himself, thus creating a specific, parable-like narrative.

In *Hard Times* punishment and forgiveness are intimately related to narration itself because a central concern of the novel is to endorse its own enterprise and denounce enemies of that enterprise. The narrator takes sides at once. In the manner of Dotheboys Hall and other such deliberate denominations, the names in this narrative indicate from the outset how the dice are loaded. Gradgrind, M'Choakumchild, and Bounderby suggest by their names alone the negative character of one camp. Nor does the narrator hesitate to pass judgment openly on his characters. This partial description of Bounderby is designed to make him immediately repulsive to the reader: "A big, loud man, with a stare, and a metallic laugh. A man made out of a coarse material, which seemed to have been stretched to make so much of him. . . . A man who could never sufficiently vaunt himself a self-made man. A man who was always proclaiming, through that brassy speaking-trumpet of a voice of his, his old ignorance and his old poverty. A man who was the Bully of humility."[1] Gradgrind and M'Choakumchild are bullies of education, but at least they are not hypocrites. Gradgrind, we are told, is even an affectionate father after his manner. That they intend good does not signify, however, for the novel's imagery informs us that they are nonetheless dangerous persons. Gradgrind, for example, "seemed a kind of cannon

219

loaded to the muzzle with facts, and prepared to blow [the students] clean out of the regions of childhood at one discharge" (3). The narrator is too impatient with his bad types to allow them time to reveal their traits through actions and speech; he tells us directly what we are to think about them and their influence. Of Bounderby he says, "It was one of the most exasperating attributes of Bounderby that he not only sang his own praises but stimulated other men to sing them. There was a moral infection of clap-trap in him" (43).[2] And the narrator does not for a moment let us forget what his central theme is. At the beginning of chapter 8, entitled "Never Wonder," he says, "Let us strike the keynote again before pursuing the tune"; and that keynote is the Utilitarian principle "of educating the reason without stooping to the cultivation of the sentiments and affections" (49).

The narrator of *Hard Times* is particularly antagonistic toward Gradgrind and his associates because one target for their abuse is precisely the kind of story he appreciates and likes to tell. He is personally threatened by their inaesthetic views and quickly aligns himself with common people, who also enjoy his kinds of stories. "They sometimes, after fifteen hours' work, sat down to read mere fables about men and women, more or less like themselves, and about children, more or less like their own. They took Defoe to their bosoms instead of Euclid, and seemed to be on the whole more comforted by Goldsmith than by Cocker" (50). Narratives with believably human characters naturally appeal to all human beings, the narrator implies, because they offer surrogate experience of persons like ourselves and because they provide consolation and comfort. They are a means both of engaging life and of escaping life's pain. Thus Sissy could cheer her father by reading him tales from books like the *Arabian Nights,* which " 'kept him, many times, from what did him real harm. And often and often of a night he used to forget all his troubles in wondering whether the Sultan would let the lady go on with the story, or would have her head cut off before it was finished' " (59). Out of curiosity about the outcome of a fictitious history, we are able to postpone our miseries and avoid misconduct. In a life driven by necessity and apparently stagnated in a comfortless routine, narrative suspense provides a substitute for hope, a kind of useful anticipation not of what will become of one's own individual existence, but of the whole pattern of life in general. Fictional narratives are a double translation of sorts, converting ungovernable personal histories into orderly plots, which are then reconvertible to our own experience as imaginative means of ordering our lives, of turning our otherwise random experiences into life plots of our own. To violate this function of storytelling, which fosters the sympathies and affections in human nature, is thus a great transgression, as we shall see in a moment.[3]

In trying to spare his storytelling daughter greater suffering, Mr. Jupe creates a mirror image of Sheherezad's device by suddenly decamping, leaving Sissy to be educated at Gradgrind's school. He means to benefit his daughter by his absence just as Sheherezad means to save herself by her continued presence. His silence obliges Sissy to create her own fable about his departure and anticipated return, a kind of hopeful suspense, just as Sheherezad's narration, by coming each evening to a narrative suspension, reinforces the hope of her continued existence. This was, of course, Dickens' own mode of serial publication, by which he sustained his own purpose and encouraged a hopeful anticipation in his audience. It was for Dickens and his audience a mode of sympathetic association. Typically, Bounderby immediately assumes that Jupe has simply deserted his daughter and that's that; it is what that sort of person does. But the imaginative, that is to say, the sympathetic, mind seeks to go beyond the simple act and picture to itself some human reason for this behavior. Characteristically, those associated with the imagination tend to allow a benevolent motive for Jupe's conduct.

One of the grand ironies in *Hard Times* is that the great Utilitarian Bounderby is its most outrageous fabulist, having concocted an elaborate false autobiography very much dependent on the "rags to riches" convention of storytelling and enhanced by figurative language and illustrative detail.[4] His language is always colorful in a way that his and Gradgrind's principles theoretically forbid. The very emphasis upon synecdoche in referring to the working men as "hands" is an illustration of how thoroughly dependent human expression is upon communication that goes beyond the limits of fact.

Sleary's declaration that "People must be amuthed," and the narrator's outright announcement that he considers the English people hard-worked and that he "would give them a little more play" make it clear that human beings cannot do without storytelling of one kind or another (41, 63). Gradgrind and his kind deny the use of narration for amusement, permitting only those instructive narratives rapidly going out of fashion that we have glanced at in chapter 2 of this study. Organizations concerned for the welfare of the working class "wrote leaden little books for them, showing how the good grown-up baby invariably got to the Savings-bank, and the bad grown-up baby invariably got transported" (49). These are Mrs. Sherwood stories, only with an emphasis on commerce instead of last judgments.

Dickens' own narrative approximates the pattern of children's fables. As though counteracting the effect of the leaden books for grown-up babies, his narrator produces a bouyant children's tale for childlike adults, where "childlike" means unspoiled and imaginative, or, in a word, responsive. So from the early pages of his story, the narrator draws his imagery from just those works proscribed by the Gradgrind school to describe the school's deleterious effects. Thus M'Choakumchild sets to his preparatory work with his students "not unlike Morgiana in the Forty Thieves: looking into all the vessels ranged before him, one after another, to see what they contained. Say, good M'Choakumchild. When from thy boiling store, thou shalt fill each jar brimful by-and-by, dost thou think that thou wilt always kill outright the robber Fancy lurking within— or sometimes only maim him and distort him!" (8).[5]

The answer to this question is surely that the attempt to kill Fancy usually does result in some form of maiming and distortion. Three significant examples of this process are Tom and Louisa Gradgrind and Bitzer. The first and last learn to look out for Number One. Bitzer fulfills the promise he showed as prig in the classroom by becoming a spy in his adulthood. His attempt to arrest the fugitive Tom is phrased not in terms of justice, punishment, and moral values, but in terms of economics. Bitzer looks forward to personal advantage from the act. The narrator intrudes to lecture us that this is what the Gradgrind philosophy taught—"that everything was to be paid for. . . . Every inch of the existence of mankind, from birth to death, was to be a bargain across a counter" (288–89).

It is not surprising, then, to see that Tom and Louisa also have this trade-like view of human relationships. But their views differ in that Tom is prepared to barter Louisa to improve his own situation, whereas Louisa disposes of herself as a piece of property to benefit her beloved brother. Tom's sin is one of the most loathed in the Dickens register—the use of another human being for personal advantage. From the moment Tom lets his sister know that she could do him a great service by marrying Bounderby it is certain that he will have to be punished. Tom compounds this offense by stealing money from Bounderby's bank and then arranging for Stephen Blackpool to seem guilty of the crime.

The narrator thoroughly dislikes his character. After Tom has discussed Louisa's private circumstances with Harthouse, thus allowing that scheming gentleman an opening through which to appeal to her, the narrator offers his candid assessment of Tom. "The whelp went home and went to bed. If he had had any sense of what he had done that night, and had been less of a whelp and more of a brother, he might have turned short on the road, might have gone down to the ill-smelling river that was dyed black, might have gone to bed in it for good and all, and have curtained his head forever with its filthy waters" (137). In short, he recommends that Tom execute justice upon himself as so many of Dickens' self-punishers do in one way or another. But Tom is not fully aware of his transgression, despite his conscious intent not to behave himself once he leaves his father's house. He looks forward to the time when he will leave school and home and be rid of his education in facts. "'I wish I could collect all the Facts we hear so much about,'" he says to Louisa, "'and all the Figures, and all the people who found them out: and I wish I could put a thousand barrels of gunpowder under them, and blow them all up together! However, when I go to live with old Bounderby, I'll have my revenge.'" When Louisa focuses on the word "revenge," Tom explains, "'I mean, I'll enjoy myself a little, and go about and see something, and hear something. I'll recompense myself for the way in which I have been brought up'" (52). Better, the narrator implies, to have let him visit the circus, to have a look at life's amusements, than to have dried up all of his fancy so that when he breaks away it is to a life of common dissipations. But there is more to this revenge than simply having some fun, for the desire to escape his upbringing is inevitably also a means of punishing his father. He wants not only to enjoy himself but to live contrary to his father's teaching. Ironically, his mode of escaping from that life of facts and figures is to work in a bank where he deals with figures, and where his downfall comes through the misuse of money.

It is an interesting feature of this text, as David Lodge has noted, that the narrator accepts the language of one of his wicked characters. Harthouse first denominates Tom The Whelp, but thereafter the narrator uses the description freely as well. Lodge considers this appropriation a moral error on the narrator's part because "he has taken a moral cliché from a character who is morally unreliable and invested it with his own authority as narrator" (154ff.). But Harthouse, though he is morally unreliable, is an acute judge of character. Nowhere does the narrator suggest that he has misread other characters. Harthouse is wrong about how far Louisa will go to act upon her discontent, but he has not misunderstood her. More tellingly, he immediately senses Sissy Jupe's indomitable nature when she confronts him and wisely yields to it. The narrator simply acquiesces in Harthouse's "objective" assessment of the world into which he has moved as a discerning stranger. In a larger sense, however, it is Harthouse who, by using the expression "whelp," adapts himself to a moral pattern established by the narrator. The novel very early demonstrates that humans of the Gradgrind type cannot appreciate the "characters" of animals. A horse is simply an omnivorous quadruped, for example. But in the communal world of the circus, a horse is a partner, as is a dog like Merrylegs. These creatures exhibit the qualities of loyalty, affection, and obedience that humans all too often fail to demonstrate. Even an animal behaves better than a Tom Gradgrind or a Bitzer, who have been taught—supposedly against their inherent natures—to think first of Number One. It is worth noting that Tom's escape is effected through the obedience of Sleary's horse and dog, who prevent Bitzer from bringing Tom to justice. Thus the animal motif that Harthouse stumbles upon is already a prevailing rhetorical mode imposed by the narrator.

If the narrator shares nothing else with Harthouse's thinking, he shares his contempt for Tom. When Tom is finally undone, his life of error is pointed up by Sleary's account of a different kind of "whelp," the dog Merrylegs, who laboriously found his way back to the circus after Jupe's supposed death, as though looking for Sissy, and then died trying to perform his old tricks. Sleary marvels at the dog's instinctive ability to trace the circus people.

> " 'It theemth to prethent two thingth to a perthon, don't it, Thquire?' said Mr. Sleary, musing as he looked down into the depths of his brandy and water: 'one, that there ith a love in the world, not all Thelf-interetht after all, but thomething very different; t'other, that it hath a way of ith own of calculating or not calculating, whith thomehow or another ith at leatht ath hard to give a name to, ath the wayth of the dogth ith!' " (292–93)

Tom, the human whelp, proves less admirable than Merrylegs, the faithful and loving mutt, because the dog never violates the instinct to care that transcends human selfishness.

In his shame and humiliation, emphasized by the circus costume that he wears as a disguise, Tom is incapable of anything but fear and anger. Tom employs a version of statistics to depict his crime as normal and suggests that his father comfort himself with the fact that it is a law that so many people out of a given population will be dishonest. Mr. Gradgrind's apt punishment is to know that his beloved philosophy is responsible for the degradation of his son. This, combined with a similar causal relationship in his daughter's suffering, constitutes a form of poetic justice common in Dickens' fiction. It is one thing to be guilty of maiming many children through an educational method, but quite another to number one's own children among the worst instances of that system. In addition, one of Gradgrind's most successful products, young Bitzer, becomes the last nettle in his suffering as Bitzer attempts to prevent young Tom's escape. Bitzer has no compassion, thinking only of himself and of his potential reward. If Tom has enacted a version of the prodigal son parable, Bitzer has inverted the parable of the Good Samaritan.[6]

Gradgrind bids farewell to his son by asking him to atone by repenting for his crime, and concludes, " 'Give me your hand, my poor boy, and may God forgive you as I do!' " Tom is moved by his father's speech, but spurns Louisa, who calls after him "that she forgave him, and loved him still, and that he would one day be sorry to have left her so, and glad to think of these her last words, far away" (285). Later, as the narrator projects his narrative into the future beyond the time of the story, he asks if Louisa could see in the fire a letter in a strange hand saying that Tom " 'died in hospital, of fever, such a day, and died in penitence and love of you: his last word being your name' " (298). Gradgrind himself is equally repentant and will make "his facts and figures subservient to Faith, Hope, and Charity; and no longer [try] to grind that Heavenly trio in his dusty little mills" (297). Despite the aversion he demonstrates toward young Tom, the narrator does not arrange any narrative punishment for him; Tom's behavior is presented as the logical consequence of his training. Because Tom has been warped by this training and is therefore not entirely responsible for what he has become, his punishment is mitigated, equilibrated carefully to the degree of his freedom. The narrative even conspires with its characters, so to speak, to illegally assist Tom in his flight from official punishment. The narrator absolves himself from blame for this activity, however, by letting us know that Tom's exile has achieved what other forms of punishment might not have—repentance.

Louisa too is repentant, but her case is more complicated. She and Tom are implicated in more ways than one with Bounderby. Tom works in Bounderby's bank, but he also becomes a hypocrite and a liar like his employer, the chief fabricator of the novel. And Louisa creates a lying scenario of her life by marrying Bounderby without love, though there are signs that she recognizes the lie she lives, a life chosen to benefit her brother, whom she does love. When her false life becomes impossible and she is forced to flee from Harthouse's attentions, she returns to her father, telling him that she curses the hour she was bred through his philosophy to a life without sentiments of the heart and graces of the soul. She does not reproach her father, but she also does not forgive him.

Louisa's chief transgression, her marriage to Bounderby, is its own punishment for that transgression. Louisa is guilty of little except repressing all the good instincts in her heart; nonetheless, she feels a great need to seek forgiveness. For this she selects Sissy, who represents all of the natural impulses that she has ignored. Explaining her condition to Sissy, she cries, " 'Forgive me, pity me, help me! Have compassion on my great need, and let me lay this head of mine upon a loving heart!' " Sissy responds: "Oh, lay it here!" (226). With this scene of solicited forgiveness Louisa begins her redemptive recovery.

Louisa is tempted by Harthouse largely because he cares for nothing yet is interested in her. His role in her life is much simpler than she imagines, for, from the narrator's point of view, he is simply a "demon," "tempter," "Familiar," and "Devil" (133–34, 175, 179). That he is allied politically to the Gradgrind camp is simply another indication of its false values. If at first Harthouse seems out of place among Gradgrind and his political associates, it soon becomes clear that he shares with them a calculating mentality. In his working notes to *Hard Times* Dickens' intention is indicated, if not directly asserted. He asks himself, "To shew Louisa, how alike in their creeds, her father and Harthouse are?— Now the two heartless things come to the same end?" And he responds" "Yes. But almost imperceptibly."[7] Mildred Newcomb sees Louisa as an agent of retribution for the two men. Just as Edith Dombey brings down Dombey, her tyrannical Sultan, and Carker, his Grand Vizier, in one rebellious act, so Louisa brings down her father, the monster in the lecturing castle, and Harthouse, the drifting iceberg.[8] Harthouse is a larger example of looking out for Number One, even if it means selling his soul, which is of little use to him anyway. Interesting as he is as a figure in the melodrama of Coketown, he plays a surprisingly slight role in the novel's retributive scheme. When Sissy demands that he forget about Louisa and make reparation by going away, he is easily intimidated by her sincerity and departs. Just as his evil has been tepid and unsuccessful, the consequences of this episode are remarkably flat, but predictably perverse.

> The moral sort of fellows might suppose that Mr. James Harthouse derived some comfortable reflections afterwards, from this prompt retreat, as one of his few actions that made any amends for anything, and as a token to himself that he had escaped the climax of a very bad business. But it was not so, at all. A secret sense of having failed and been ridiculous—a dread of what other fellows who went in for similar sorts of things, would say at his expense if they knew it—so oppressed him, that what was about the very best passage in his life was the one of all others he would not have owned to on any account, and the only one that made him ashamed of himself. (235–36)

It is entirely fitting for a devil like Harthouse to suffer the modest punishment of being ever after nettled for having done a virtuous thing. His is an offered therapeutic punishment that goes unappreciated and thereby only compounds his guilt.

As a conventional seducer and unprincipled idler, Harthouse is necessarily bad, but the true villain of the novel is Bounderby with his cruelty toward workers, selfish exploitation of others, and pompous self-acclamation. He is both a tyrant and a buffoon. He is a nasty version of Gradgrind in his repressive Utilitarianism and a perversion of Sleary in his amusing fabrications. Bounderby might have been as delightful as that hypocritical rogue Pecksniff if he were not so sinister and influential. Perhaps Bounderby is most vile in his subversion of what is positive in the novel. In making himself the hero/victim of his autobiography he defames his family. In creating his fiction of heroic endeavor he betrays the moral potential of narration. Bounderby is a liar, not a storyteller. He has turned the constructive act of narration into a vehicle of self-applause and slander. He is a resilient form of evil, a negative model for Tom Gradgrind. Like Bounderby, young Tom is a devotee of Number One who ends up literally a clown, whereas Bounderby achieves that condition only metaphorically. The narrator calls off the hunting down of Tom because Tom's education has warped him and therefore mitigated his guilt. He is paroled into the new world. Bounderby, however, has committed the opposite sin of claiming to be entirely responsible for what he is, dismissing any suggestions to the contrary. His punishment is to be found out as a lying braggart and a heartless son. This betrayer of natural affection loses his household, too, when his wife runs away from home. Moreover, Mrs. Sparsit, as the person who brings Mrs. Pegler, Bounderby's mother, to light, has "audaciously anticipated him, and presumed to be wiser than he" (294). For this impertinence, and because she has made embarrassing false accusations against Louisa, Bounderby finds it necessary to dismiss her. Bounderby's self-constructed fable of grandeur collapses. Perhaps in the narrator's view the worst punishment a storyteller can suffer is to have his story discredited. And so Bounderby receives that degree of immediate punishment. But he is scarcely cowed by this reversal. Ever resourceful, Bounderby realizes that he can gain something even from what otherwise appears to be a failure. "At last he made the discovery that to discharge this highly connected female—to have it in his power to say, 'She was a woman of family, and wanted to stick to me, but I wouldn't have it, and got rid of her'—would be to get the utmost possible amount of crowning glory out of the connexion, and at the same time to punish Mrs. Sparsit according to her deserts" (294). He will squeeze as much profit out of Mrs. Sparsit as he does out of the "hands" in his factory.

Bounderby's hired ally in his fable of self-constructed grandeur, like her master, has a lively imagination in the service of wickedness. Like Bounderby she perverts the healthy purposes of storymaking. Bounderby concocts a fable about his own ascent from poverty to affluence, creates a role for Mrs. Sparsit as a lady, and attributes fantastic ambitions to the working class which actually mirror his own narrative of substituting wealth for want. Mrs. Sparsit is similarly inventive, though she applies her imaginative powers to Louisa, erecting "in her mind a mighty Staircase, with a dark pit of shame and ruin at the bottom; and down those stairs, from day to day and hour to hour, she saw Louisa coming" (201–2). She has no intention of interrupting Louisa's progress toward ruin, but waits "for the last fall, as for the ripeness and fulness of the harvest of her hopes" (205). In a direct reversal of Christian policy, Mrs. Sparsit does not strive to rescue her fallen sister but delights in a virtuous woman's progress toward sin.

Louisa does not follow Mrs. Sparsit's script, though Mrs. Sparsit assumes its accuracy and informs Bounderby that Louisa has eloped with Harthouse. The great tale-teller accepts this account as true and immediately goes to Gradgrind with the news, only to learn that Louisa has resisted temptation and returned to her father's home instead. In another kind of narrative, this situation might provide a conventional scene of forgiveness and reconciliation, not unlike that between Dr. Strong and Annie in *David Copperfield*. But Bounderby is no Dr. Strong. Hoping to resolve the problem between husband and wife and create a climate for remediation, Gradgrind suggests to Bounderby " 'that we may all be more or less in the wrong, not even excepting you; and that some yielding on your part, remembering the trust you have accepted, may not only be an act of true kindness, but perhaps a debt incurred towards Louisa' " (244). Bounderby is not interested in questions of mutual responsibility. For pardon he substitutes submission. He is peremptory by habit. Sustained authority has made him quick to judge and reluctant to change his mind. When his bank is robbed Bounderby promptly decides that Stephen Blackpool is the guilty party. He thinks only in punitive terms, as when he says of the organizers of the union, " 'We will make an example of half-a-dozen Slackbridges. We'll indict the blackguards for felony, and get 'em shipped off to penal settlements' " (150). Not a thought of negotiation, compassion, or charity. Why should he be different with Louisa? He demands that she return to his house within a day or never.

The breakup of Bounderby's household reveals the utter falseness of its values. It has been an anti-family. Bounderby is a bad son and a thoughtless husband. Louisa is an unloving wife, and Mrs. Sparsit is secretly Bounderby's enemy rather than his friend. Though she is dependent upon the brute and cannot openly rebel, she relieves her feelings by shaking her fist at his portrait. Once dismissed, however, she can speak her mind. " 'If that portrait could speak, Sir—but it has the advantage over the original of not possessing the power of committing itself and disgusting others,—it would testify, that a long period has elapsed since I first habitually addressed it as the picture of a Noodle. Nothing that a Noodle does, can awaken surprise or indignation; the proceedings of a Noodle can only inspire contempt' " (296).[9]

Bad as Bounderby and Mrs. Sparsit are, they are still ultimately comic figures and can be dismissed in basically comic terms. Revealed as having "built his windy reputation upon lies," Bounderby knows that witnesses to the event will spread the word in Coketown to his shame; "he could not have looked a Bully more shorn and forlorn if he had had his ears cropped. Even that unlucky female, Mrs. Sparsit, fallen from her pinnacle of exultation into the Slough of Despond, was not in so bad a plight as that remarkable man and self-made Humbug, Josiah Bounderby of Coketown" (263). The narrative punishment for these two is a projection into the future; Mrs. Sparsit will lead a cramped and uncomfortable life with Lady Scadgers, and Bounderby will die of a fit in the streets of Coketown five years hence. As an added stroke, the narrator indicates that after Bounderby's death his will, designed to commemorate him with a charitable Bounderby Hall, will begin "its long career of quibble, plunder, false pretences, vile example, little service and much law" (297). As he was determinedly uncharitable in life, the conversion of an intended benevolent institution into a nuisance after his death is poetic justice indeed, and also a statement of his true nature. If the good characters in *Hard Times* can do little to prevent Bounderby from getting his way, the narrator can arrange to frustrate all of his posthumous hopes. It is something like a retroactive Last Judgment on earth, and serves, as wills, debts, and other financial documents and terms do in Dickens, to foreshadow a similar frustration of Bounderby's hopes when he comes to his accounting at the real Last Judgment.

Last Judgment is a serious concern in this novel so much concerned with the material conditions of its characters. The focus of that concern is not with Louisa, Tom, and Sissy, who are crucial to the theme of opposing heart to fact, but with Stephen Blackpool and Rachael. When we first meet Stephen we are told that he has had his share of misery and we are assured that he is "a good power-loom weaver and a man of perfect integrity" (64). He is also, as his Christian name suggests, a martyr. All of the true injustice of the novel bears down upon Stephen. He is married to a drunken wretch from whom he cannot be freed because the laws require a great expenditure of time and money to secure a divorce. Only the wealthy can afford the £1000 or £1500 it would take to effect a divorce. In his frustration at this inequity in the law, Stephen objects that there are laws to punish him if he hurts his wife, flees from her, marries another woman, or lives with her in adultery. With so many laws to punish him, he cries out, "'Now a' God's name . . . show me the law to help me!'" (74). But there are no laws designed to help someone in Stephen's class and situation. As is customary in Dickens' fiction, official legal institutions are chiefly punitive or inept. Law is rarely supportive at the individual or the communal level. Stephen can only follow Rachael's advice when she tells him to let the law be.

Loving Rachael and seeing her wear her life away alone because she returns his love but cannot marry him, Stephen is tempted to let his wife die when the opportunity presents itself, but Rachael remains the true model of behavior. Despite the barrier that Stephen's wife is to her own happiness, Rachael tells Stephen that they must still treat her with compassion. Rachael's goodness makes her a visible emblem of Christian behavior for Stephen. "'Let me see thee setten by the bed. Let me see thee, a' so good, and so forgiving. Let me see thee as I see thee when I coom in. I can never see thee better than so. Never, never, never!'" (84). Because she is good and forgiving, Rachael represents all of the best in humanity and saves Stephen from his guilty dream of murdering his wife or letting her destroy herself. When Stephen is powerless to move, half in a trance, Rachael prevents his wife from accidentally drinking the poisonous medicine (presumably laudanum) at her bedside. This positive goodness, more than his dream of guilt and punishment, saves Stephen's soul alive, as he himself declares.

This domestic torment is only one form of injustice visited upon Stephen. He is ostracized by his fellow workers because he will not join the union. He must avoid Rachael lest he cause her inconvenience as well. But even these misfortunes are not all that is in store for Stephen. Bounderby fires him, saying, "'you are one of those chaps who have always got a grievance. And you go about, sowing it and raising crops. That's the business of *your* life, my friend'" (152). Bounderby is as adept at fabricating life stories for others as he is for himself. Without a job in Coketown, Stephen must look elsewhere for work. When he is gone he is accused of robbing Bounderby's bank, though the narrator makes it clear that the true thief is Tom Gradgrind and that the suspicions that fall upon Stephen are unjustified. Characters in the narrative doubt Stephen's innocence because he does not respond to Rachael's appeal to return and answer the charges against him. Slackbridge even boasts of how he punished Stephen by driving him away, claiming that the revelation of his theft now justifies that action. But Stephen has not purposely kept away. He is discovered to have fallen into an abandoned mine shaft. Badly injured, Stephen explains that when he learned he was suspected of robbing Bounderby's bank he believed that Louisa and Tom had plotted to make him appear guilty, and he was on his way back to Coketown to assert his innocence when his accident occurred. "'When I fell, I were in anger wi' her, an' hurryin' on t' be as onjust t' her as oothers was t' me. But in our judgements, like as in our doins, we mun bear and forbear. In my pain an' trouble, lookin' up yonder—wi' it [the star] shinin' on me—I ha' seen more clear, and ha' made it my dyin prayer that aw th' world may on'y coom toogether more, an' get a better unnerstan'in o' one another, than when I were in 't my own weak seln'" (273).

The injustice in his heart seems to precipitate Stephen into the pit as a kind of instant punishment, and the fall turns out to be a fortunate fall in that it teaches him the true lesson of Christianity and humanity—to bear and forbear. If, in this novel about materialism, there is no serious, clear-cut punishment for transgressors, there is at least a definite tilting of the scales in favor of forgiving. Stephen thought of the star shining above him while he lay in the pit as the star that led to Our Saviour's home. When he dies it becomes just that. "The star had shown him where to find the God of the poor; and through humility, and sorrow, and forgiveness, he had gone to his Redeemer's rest" (274).

The God of the poor. Is there another God for the well-to-do? Surely the poor need a God who will recommend them to heaven for their humility, sorrow, and forgiveness, but shouldn't all persons exhibit the same traits? The narrative suggests that they must. The comfortable classes have an additional requirement and

responsibility to improve the lot of their fellow beings, whereas the great responsibility of the poor is not to be impatient and violent. And it is here that two
branches of the central theme of this work come together and are joined through
the narrative's underlying scheme of punishment and, especially, forgiveness.

As we have seen, one great virtue of childhood is its capacity to become a
storehouse of good memory and hence of good behavior. Tom, and Louisa, and
Bitzer do not turn out well because they lack this reservoir of comely images of
virtue. Dickens makes this connection very clear when Louisa is returning to her
parents' cheerless home after her marriage.

> The dreams of childhood—its airy fables: its graceful, beautiful, hu-
> mane, impossible adornments of the world beyond: so good to be be-
> lieved in once, so good to be remembered when outgrown, for then the
> least among them rises to the stature of a great Charity in the heart,
> suffering little children to come into the midst of it, and to keep with
> their pure hands a garden in the stony ways of this world, wherein it
> were better for all the children of Adam that they should oftener sun
> themselves, simple and trustful, and not worldly-wise—what had she
> to do with these? (197)

Reason has dried up all these images and associations so that Louisa has no anchoring memories to preserve her in the face of temptation and unhappiness. Fortunately she can eventually turn to Sissy, who knows the value of such memories.
In the future that the narrator projects for Louisa she will be "grown learned in
childish lore; thinking no innocent and pretty fancy ever to be despised; trying
hard to know her humbler fellow-creatures, and to beautify their lives of machinery and reality with those imaginative graces and delights without which the
heart of infancy will wither up, the sturdiest physical manhood will be morally
stark death, and the plainest national prosperity figures can show, will be the
Writing on the Wall" (298–99). Louisa achieves the purpose that Dickens' novel
aims at, both in its message and in its very being. Its purpose is both to provide
generously for the graceful improvement of the lives of fellow citizens of all
classes by awakening their capacity for enjoyment and the appreciation of beauty
and charm, and thereby preventing the natural violent reaction against a life of
ugliness and deprivation, such as the narrator warns Utilitarian types against.
We must help not abuse the common people, he says. "Cultivate in them, while
there is yet time, the utmost graces of the fancies and affections to adorn their
lives so much in need of ornament; or, in the day of your triumph, when romance
is utterly driven out of their souls, and they and a bare existence stand face to
face, Reality will take a wolfish turn and make an end of you" (162–63). Just as
the excesses practiced by the French aristocracy of the *ancien regime* brought on
the "natural" consequence of the revolution, expressed in terms of the natural

forces of flood and fire, so in modern industrial England—a land of machines and mechanical thinking—it is necessary to remember the ultimate justice behind existence. The three books of *Hard Times* are named Sowing, Reaping, and Garnering, echoing Galatians 7:7, "whatsoever a man soweth, that shall he reap." This is a conventional piece of Christian wisdom common in Dickens' writing, but in this tale, concerned with a tendency among certain philosophical schools to divorce themselves from the natural, impulsive, and emotional side of humanity in favor of the logical, numerical and calculating side, the hoary axiom gains added force.

Many readers and critics have objected to Sleary's circus as a response to the Gradgrind school of thought. Amusement, this argument goes, does not constitute a sufficient counterweight to factual utility. But the circus represents only a few provinces in the realm of Fancy. Sissy is the spokesperson for imagination at the personal level. She represents the way imagination begets sympathy and understanding of others, and hence a capacity for charity and forgiveness. Sleary's circus may be affiliated with this sympathy and reluctance to judge, but what it more clearly illustrates is the communal advantage of persons brought together under the banner of imagination with a purpose of conveying pleasure. The circus represents the capacity to appreciate the efforts of others and to share in the necessary duties of the troupe. In fact, whereas Sissy represents the human advantages of imagination and love, the circus shows the practical utility of faith in the imagination and thus ironically cancels out the false Gradgrindian Utilitarianism that has not factored in imagination, love, and forgiveness.[10]

It is important in *Hard Times* that the oppressors, transgressors, and sinners are only modestly punished, for they also represent the educating, governing, and ordering classes. A severe punishment for these figures might imply the need for revolutionary change and the overthrow of unjust institutions. But Dickens did not advocate such measures. It is equally important that the model for forgiveness and humility should emerge from the ranks of the common people, from Stephen and Rachael to Sissy Jupe and Mr. Sleary. These are the voices of compassion learned through suffering and through the knowledge of amusement's curative powers. Just as the romances and fables of childhood are later transformed into happy memories that foster a charitable response to existence, so are amusement, ornament, and narrative comparable means of lodging in the memories of the common people a similar charity, an ability to bear and forbear. Dickens' readers must be prepared in their way to do what he is doing in his, to provide some such ornament to their lives. The novel ends with just such a plea, as the novelist steps before the curtain to address his audience.

> Dear reader! It rests with you and me, whether, in our two fields of action, similar things shall be or not. Let them be! We shall sit with lighter bosoms on the hearth, to see the ashes of our fires turn grey and cold. (299)

NOTES

1. Charles Dickens, *Hard Times* (London: Oxford University Press, 1970), 15.

2. Mark Lambert, in *Dickens and the Suspended Quotation* (New Haven: Yale University Press, 1981), characterizes the narrator's language regarding his subject as aggressive. "Attached to the thematic idea of the despotism of Fact we find: reader, I care more about my hatred for this thing than I care about your love; don't get in the way of my hatred" (121). This is a forceful, but perhaps somewhat extreme, statement of the case. But clearly the narrator is punitive. More modestly, Cynthia Northcutt Malone says, "Throughout the plot, the novel will watch closely and record in textual figures the deaths and disappearances of undisciplined bodies, so that the novel itself becomes a spectacle with a disciplinary function" ("The Fixed Eye and the Rolling Eye: Surveillance and Discipline in *Hard Times*," *Studies in the Novel* 21, no. 1 [Spring 1989], 16). The point is that this novel, unlike many others, is militantly committed to attack and retribution from the outset. G. K. Chesterton said that *Hard Times* represented Dickens at his sternest, an "expression of a righteous indignation which cannot condescend to humour and which cannot even condescend to pathos" (*Appreciations and Criticisms of the Works of Charles Dickens* [New York; E. P. Dutton & Co., 1911], 171).

3. Garrett Stewart has wisely noted that much of Dickens' enterprise as a novelist is to expose the falsification of the imaginative devices that reconcile human beings to their circumstances (*Dickens and the Trials of the Imagination* [Cambridge: Harvard University Press, 1974]). Without this constant struggle against fraudulent uses of the imagination, the proper uses are in danger of wholesale invalidation.

4. Critics have long been aware of Bounderby's and Mrs. Sparsit's roles as creative artists. John Butt and Kathleen Tillotson remarked on this anomaly in *Dickens at Work* (London: Methuen and Co., 1963), 208. In a recent monograph surveying critical attitudes toward *Hard Times,* Allen Samuels has again called attention to this subject (*Hard Times: An Introduction to the Variety of Criticism* (London: Macmillan, 1992), 78ff. Bounderby's version of Mrs. Sparsit's past seems highly exaggerated, too, as the narrator's tone concerning the Powler family suggests (50).

5. Robert Barnard emphasizes this use of fairy-tale themes in "Imagery and Theme in *Hard Times,*" reprinted in *Hard Times,* ed. George Ford and Sylvère Monod (New York: W. W. Norton and Co., 1990), 2nd ed., 373–74. David Lodge is also concerned with Dickens' use of fairy-tale rhetoric (*Language of Fiction: Essays in Criticism and Verbal Analysis of the English Novel* [New York: Columbia University Press, 1966], 159ff.).

6. Samuels, 88.

7. *Dickens' Working Notes for His Novels,* ed. Harry Stone, (Chicago: The University of Chicago Press, 1987), 259.

8. Mildred Newcomb, *The Imagined World of Charles Dickens* (Columbus: Ohio State University Press, 1989), 125.

9. Mrs. Sparsit overtly expresses her desire to see Bounderby humiliated (196).

10. Ruskin advances a similar argument in "The Veins of Wealth," in *Unto This Last* (1862).

FIFTEEN

Little Dorrit

LITTLE DORRIT, which was originally titled *Nobody's Fault,* might just as easily have been named *False Expectations.* In *Great Expectations,* which was to follow, Pip is led to expect gentility and the income to support it—a genuine but dangerous promise that goes amiss. In *Little Dorrit* several characters have unfounded expectations of special treatment and lapse into various forms of resentment when they are not satisfied. Exacerbating this pervasive mood of injured worth are those institutions—most noticeably the Circumlocution Office—which reward untalented persons for doing nothing at the public expense. It has often been pointed out that the prison in *Little Dorrit* is an emblem representing all of society, but it is worth adding that given the injustice of current circumstances most people deserve to be there.[1] Moreover, though the second chapter of the novel shows characters successfully passing through quarantine at Marseilles, the rest of the novel locates them in an atmosphere of disease and infection. The injustice that the narrative discloses must be corrected within the confines of the narration. Since many of the sins in this novel concern dereliction of duty and financial liability, offenses of idleness claiming reward and the usurpation of wealth must be punished in varying degrees. Sickness and disease play a significant part in this punishment, as do images of debt and payment. The economy of the narrative becomes associated with the economics of guilt and punishment.

As always with Dickens these themes and motifs are worked out in a spectrum of redundancies from minor to major examples. In this novel, as in other mature novels, most of the examples are interlinked. I shall examine several levels at which Dickens works out these themes, beginning with the personal, moving to the personal-become-public, then to the public, and finally to the religious, which is both personal and public.

From the novel's opening chapter, "a prison taint" is on everything.[2] Two lawbreakers are incarcerated in the Marseilles prison. Without palliating the

234

crimes of the prisoners the narrator describes the ugliness and discomfort of their imprisonment. The two prisoners are Rigaud, later called Blandois and Lagnier, and John Baptist Cavaletto. There is a wide range of culpability here, for Cavaletto is a humble fellow charged with mere smuggling, whereas Rigaud, who has most certainly murdered his wife, is a vain, blustering rascal. As Lionel Trilling pointed out, Dickens' novel does not recommend the elimination of prisons, and Blandois is one reason, for he is a genuinely evil man. "One of the effects of his presence in *Little Dorrit* is to complicate our response to the theme of the prison, to deprive us of the comfortable, philanthropic thought that prisons are nothing but instruments of injustice. Because Blandois exists, prisons are necessary" (ix). Rigaud is an intense example of those characters in the novel who consider themselves unjustly injured, thus owning the right or even obligation to repay their offenders. They feel that some *payment* is due to them. They are the creditors of society at large, or of some individual or institution.[3] This moral indemnification is often secret because it is involuntary. Rigaud, for example, does not broadcast his intention to seek the payment of revenge. After his release from prison for lack of evidence that he murdered his wife, Rigaud is scorned by the general public, who consider him guilty. "'I am a man . . . whom society has deeply wronged,'" he says, explaining to Cavaletto that he has been so abused by people in general that the police have had to protect him. He has even been kept away from his house and has had to survive on a tight budget. "'Such are the humiliations that society has inflicted upon me, possessing the qualities I have mentioned, and which you know me to possess. But society shall pay for it'" (132). Rigaud takes the reasonable indignation of the people as an affront to his character and uses it as an excuse to do whatever mischief he likes in order to get his way. Fittingly, this consummate hypocrite is the agent who eventually exposes Mrs. Clennam's hypocrisy—another example of Dickens' familiar practice of using one wicked agent to expose and punish another.

Appropriately, Rigaud becomes associated with Henry Gowan, another variation on the disgruntled individual who feels he has been defrauded of his due. Gowan wants for himself the security of place provided to the Barnacle clan; instead, he has to count on commissions for his paintings to survive. Having to work for his income embitters him.[4] But Gowan's character is nothing compared to the impassioned sense of injustice evident in Miss Wade. Miss Wade's pride, and what we would today perhaps call paranoia, spoil her prospects in life. She is a "nameless" person, but has the opportunity to marry well and lead a respectable life. Instead, thinking that her potential husband's family condescends to her, she becomes involved with Gowan, whose cynical view of life resembles her own. Gowan, who has never presented himself as very serious, throws her over, and this increases Miss Wade's bitterness. Miss Wade is the source of her own suffering, a fact made entirely clear in the chapter recounting her experiences, entitled "The History of a Self Tormentor." Her behavior is dangerous not only to herself, for she infects young Tattycoram with a similar discontent. Tattycoram is already inclined to disaffection, but Miss Wade fosters it and soon draws the young girl away from the Meagleses to live with her. When Mr. Meagles and Arthur Clennam go to visit her, they seek her dwelling down Park Lane, a wilderness where once-fashionable houses look like "the last result of the great mansions breeding in-and-in," as they seem "to be scrofulously resting upon crutches" (324). They find her dwelling down "one of the parasite streets" and are "summarily shut into the close black house" for their interview (325–26). The imagery here and elsewhere suggests Miss Wade's connection with disease and suffering. She might be dismissed to her own suffering if she did not affect others. Miss Wade forms one corner of an evil triangle, for she, like Gowan, employs Blandois, using him to spy on the Gowans. She wishes to get back at Gowan and to injure Pet Meagles, his wife. Mr. Pancks, who knows as much about her as anyone, says that "She writhes under her life. A woman more angry, passionate, reckless, and revengeful never lived" (540). She does not know her parentage, an ignorance she takes as a metaphysical affront, feeling that she deserves much more than the money that Mr. Casby doles out to her. Unlike many other orphans in Dickens—most notably Esther Summerson—she cannot face a life of apparent injustice with humility.

Each of these resentful and revengeful figures brings some degree of punishment upon him or herself. Gowan's is least significant, an idle disaffected life with a woman whose love he has misvalued. Miss Wade will be left to her self-punishment and will lose Tattycoram, who finally sees through her facade of concern to the vindictive heart hidden behind it. But Blandois' punishment is fully fitting. He represents the most debased form of modern pride and greed, and he is criminal and unfeeling in all things with no conscience whatsoever. After he has exacted his demands from Mrs. Clennam, he waits in the ancient Clennam house that he finds "Almost as dull as the infernal old jail" (786). Soon after, the house collapses, and when the debris is cleared away, searchers find "the dirty heap of rubbish that had been the foreigner" (794). If Blandois-Rigaud has had his revenge upon society, and in this case both metaphorically and literally brought down the House of Clennam, he has done it at his own expense. Dennis Walder calls attention to Dickens' conscious opposition of New and Old Testament values in *Little Dorrit,* with victory going to the former, but adds that "Dickens reveals in pursuing Rigaud a sympathy for that Old Testament ethic of revenge he otherwise rejects."[5] But Rigaud's end is not simply the result of a surrogate providence's wrath. Dickens carefully and methodically arranged for the precise character of Rigaud's end, emphasizing individual implication in our own fates rather than a god's ruling hand.[6] In this novel providence seems balanced by destiny. Breeding and inheritance play as large a part in human experience as any perceivable scheme of justice. James Kincaid says that "there is an undercurrent of black fatalism in the novel, even in its circular form, where characters swing back to meet each other and move from one prison to another"

(202). This kind of circularity was evident as early as *Oliver Twist,* figuring most prominently in Sikes' career, but now it is vastly more complicated, like a crowded ballroom of dancers as they work the revolving figures of a dance. Miss Wade's outlook is deeply deterministic; she assumes that what is destined to occur has been mapped out for us from the beginning. Earle Davis sees Henry Gowan as a person chained to environment and heredity, whereas Arthur Clennam, himself struggling against these influences, "is one of the central forces who illustrate Dickens' thesis about individual responsibility and freedom of the will."[7] Rigaud is not the harried victim of a vengeful god; his crimes themselves engender his destruction. He becomes materially what he has been morally through the entire narrative, a dirty heap of rubbish.

Although Dickens' projected title for the novel, *Nobody's Fault,* has often been taken as a sign that he meant to stress the imprisoning and determining nature of human existence, when read another way it suggests that "Nobody" *is* at fault or *has* a fault. The chapter headings "Nobody's Weakness" (I:16), "Nobody's Rival" (I:17), "Nobody's State of Mind" (I:26), and "Nobody's Disappearance" (I:28), indicate clearly the presence, not the absence, of faults. Arthur Clennam does have faults and he is to blame for certain errors. So are we all, with the possible exception of Amy Dorrit, which is why, perhaps, the novel ended up with the title it did.

Gowan, Wade, and Rigaud have little in the way of conscience, yet they bring about their own punishments. They are so *self*-conscious that they can never look beyond their own imagined deserts. They are the embittered alternatives to Arthur Clennam, whose self-consciousness is so preoccupied with the deserts of others that in his own affairs he is inclined to self-erasure. Gowan, Wade, Rigaud, and others like them stand in opposition to Little Dorrit. As J. Hillis Miller has remarked, "she derives all of her power to help her father and others around her from her preservation of the simplicity, loving-kindness, and faithful perseverance of childhood" (240). But she is almost unique in the tainted world of the novel.[8] Miller keenly observes that "*Little Dorrit* centers on the secrecy, the otherness, of Little Dorrit herself" (244). She alone is healthy in a world given up to moral deficiencies and maladies. To understand Little Dorrit is to comprehend life as it should be lived. But Little Dorrit remains a mysterious Other to those who are deeply self-involved. Again, Miller states that in *Little Dorrit* Dickens employs a "new way of showing many of his characters altogether aware of their spiritual states and even deliberately choosing them" (235). If in a novel like *Hard Times* the narrator freely judges and punishes his characters, in *Little Dorrit* he need scarcely interfere to bring misery to this set of self-tormentors.

If Gowan, Wade, and Rigaud all lack a conscience, they cannot help acting on something like conscience. For Dickens, the human mind, whether consciously or not, tends to operate on assessments of good and evil, no matter how perverted its perception. Lionel Trilling felt that Freud's view of the mind resembles Dickens' in that it is "at once the criminal, the victim, the police, the judge, and the executioner," and I think that he is right (viii). Athough I have examined some of these features already in Dickens' earlier work, I will now explore at greater length the way the broad concepts of debt and punishment engender dubious strategies for human conduct, and call forth intriguing maneuvers by the narrator who must record them. Rigaud, Gowan, and Wade all feel that a debt is owing to them from society and they use that feeling to justify their unjust and even criminal behavior toward others. They are utter egotists and utterly selfish. Their cases, though they affect others, are essentially private instances of moral and material debt and repayment. However, at the center of the novel is a more notable and more problematic instance of debt and payment, the case of William Dorrit.

Dorrit's circumstances are significant not only in themselves, as demonstrating the injustice of a civil law that, at the time, could keep an individual incarcerated indefinitely while preventing him the means to earn money to pay his debts, but also because they are intimately connected with the central character, Arthur Clennam, and his family. When Arthur Clennam first visits William Dorrit in prison he wonders if his mother is not somehow responsible for the misfortunes of the Dorrit brothers, and if her confinement is not a counterpart of Dorrit's. He is awakened from his sleep by his mother's spectral voice saying, "'He withers away in his prison; I wither away in mine; inexorable justice is done; what do I owe on this score!'" (89).[9] But the whole drift of this novel is more that inexorable *injustice* is done, and that we all owe a great deal on that score. This injustice ranges from the most personal level—say the Dorrit family's treatment of Little Dorrit—to that of the Circumlocution Office.[10] Institutional negligence and incompetence are stressed at the very opening of the Marshalsea chapters, in the description of how the prison functionaries maintain the fiction that smugglers and debtors are confined separately. Now and then an official comes to inspect. "On those truly British occasions, the smugglers, if any, made a feint of walking into the strong cells and the blind alley, while this somebody pretended to do his something; and made a reality of walking out again as soon as he hadn't done it—neatly epitomising the administration of most of the public affairs, in our right little, tight little, island" (57). We later learn that Mr. Tite Barnacle, high in the Circumlocution Office, is an important representative of the creditors who are responsible for keeping Dorrit in prison. Little is said about the injustice of a law that confined people indefinitely for a debt they had not the means to adjust, because Dickens is less concerned with the precise injustice of a given law than with the treatment of an entire population by those in authority. This pattern of incompetence and deceit is repeated in many ways, including resistance to Doyce's and Clennam's attempts to patent the former's invention, Mr. Merdle's swindle, and Christopher Casby's hypocritical exploitation of the inhabitants of Bleeding Heart Yard.

Arthur ironically asks Little Dorrit's forgiveness for following her back to the Marshalsea and making the visit to her father, with the explanation that his motive is to do the family a service if he can. He is troubled by what we might call an inherited bad conscience and he is determined to make reparation if he can.[11] Given his religious and secular background, he is as inclined as his mother to conceive of this reparation in financial terms. The "testimonial" he gives to William Dorrit is a ritual form established by the Father of the Marshalsea for preserving a certain tone in the prison, but it anticipates Arthur's struggles with the Barnacles and the Circumlocution Office to resolve the problem of Dorrit's debt. Though he does not fully understand his own position, Arthur's impulse is moral, though operating through commercial and political avenues. It is bitterly ironic, then, that when Dorrit receives his fortune and is released from prison, he views his debt to Clennam entirely in monetary terms. If Clennam, with the best of intentions, cannot clearly distinguish moral from money obligations, Amy Dorrit can. She understands the nature of being under obligation to others and urges Clennam not to offer testimonials to her father. She sees past the fiction warranting the practice to the debasing reality beneath. Only Little Dorrit grasps the heart of her father's case. " 'It seems to me hard,' " she says, " 'that he should have lost so many years and suffered so much, and at last pay all the debts as well. It seems to me hard that he should pay in life and money both' " (422). This, however, is the law, even if to innocent Little Dorrit it seems unjust. Clennam insensitively regards it as "the last speck . . . of the prison atmosphere upon her" (422). Clennam, accepting the law as it stands, is blinded to its inhumanity. Little Dorrit, though she does not consider what hardship might accrue to her father's creditors from his inability to pay, nonetheless sees the vicious truth that moral and financial indebtedness have become so unhealthily entangled that debt must be paid over and over in differing currencies.

And yet there is an additional irony here, for although there surely seems to be injustice in Dorrit's long confinement and in the difficulty of coming by any means to rectify his situation, there is a subtler moral code that justifies that imprisonment. Dorrit was not fit for the world of commercial transaction. At the time of his arrest he is "a very amiable and very helpless middle-aged gentleman," with "irresolute fingers" and a "trembling lip," who has no comprehension of his business affairs, which are perplexed "by a partnership, of which he knew no more than that he had invested money in it"; even the sharpest accountants can get nothing from him and give him up "as a hopeless job" (58–59). William Dorrit may be a gentleman, but he seems not to have understood the earning of money. Dickens says little about his history but enough to show that his gentility means more to him than his ability to earn a living. We may suppose that he was a member of the *rentier* class, living not from its own efforts but from interest on investments. This condition is replicated in prison, where Dorrit accepts the testimonials of fellow prisoners and the income from the labor of his relatives, on no better basis than that he somehow represents the gentlemanly class. In short, William Dorrit typifies an abuse in society at large, that so many "gentlemen" are given places—in the Circumlocution Office, for example—for which and at which they do not work. Like these people, he receives compensation for what he is, not for what he does. But like them, too, he finds himself uncomfortably circumscribed. Henry Gowan in this novel, and several characters in *Our Mutual Friend*, to name just a few examples in Dickens' fiction, are injured more than assisted by the possession of a small inheritance. It sustains them, but keeps them from any effort at larger application of their energies. Of course, the outstanding example of this training in unsuitability for a life of self-support is Pip in *Great Expectations*.

The low-grade punishment natural to place-men is dependency and subservience, a kind of imprisonment in the conditions set by their superiors. Dickens' fiction abounds with flunkies of one sort or another and almost always pictures them as prisoners of their condition. Sometimes they are embittered by that dependence. The Dorrit children are aggravated examples of their father's failing. Tip doesn't want to work for a living, but wants to be taken care of nonetheless. He makes unsuccessful forays into the world at large. "But whatever Tip went into, he came out of tired, announcing that he had cut it. Wherever he went, this foredoomed Tip appeared to take the prison walls with him, and to set them up in such trade or calling; and to prowl about within their narrow limits in the old slip-shod, purposeless, down-at-heel way; until the real immovable Marshalsea walls asserted their fascination over him, and brought him back" (76). Eventually they bring him back as a prisoner, not merely as a family member. Like his father, Tip petitions Arthur Clennam for assistance, and is resentful when not obliged, feeling that Clennam "hasn't used [him] like a gentleman" (375). If Tip inherits William's feckless and mooching tendencies without his style, Fanny inherits his sensitivity to family pride, but with added fierceness. She, too, however, is willing to swallow her pride for money. Mrs. Merdle buys her out of her initial relationship with Edmund Sparkler with supplements to her wardrobe.

From the very outset, the Marshalsea is another variation on How Not To Do It. When William Dorrit is still fresh in prison, his wife bears Amy. The doctor who attends her tries to ease Dorrit's mind by explaining to him that prison actually represents freedom; there is no anxiety, no rushing about, and no trouble to meet. In prison one finds peace, he says.

> Now, the debtor was a very different man from the doctor, but he had already begun to travel, by his opposite segment of the circle, to the same point. Crushed at first by his imprisonment, he had soon found a dull relief in it. He was under lock and key; but the lock and key that kept him in, kept numbers of his troubles out. If he had been a man with strength of purpose to face those troubles and fight them, he might have broken the net that held him, or broken his heart; but being what he was, he languidly slipped into this smooth descent, and never more took one step upward. (63)

If Dorrit is pitiable he is nonetheless responsible for his condition. He could have made an effort. But he succumbs to the malady of the Marshalsea, which brings with it a reversal of normal attitudes. Its inmates "come to regard insolvency as the normal state of mankind, and the payment of debts as a disease that occasionally broke out" (88).

Having been born in prison, Little Dorrit does not carry the errors of society with her into that preserve. She begins in humility and knows only service to others. Having lost nothing, having expected nothing, she resents nothing. Whether or not such a being is realistically credible, symbolically she fits very well into Dickens' scheme.

Difficult as Little Dorrit's circumstances are when her father is imprisoned, they become more painful to her when the family is at liberty. Before Little Dorrit had her occupations and ministering to her father to direct her attention, but after freedom from the Marshalsea her behavior is more restricted and confined, with the family and Mrs. General trying to alter her conduct. Though the Dorrits are out of prison, the experience haunts them, affecting each differently, but breaking out most dramatically when William Dorrit, in a sort of fit, publically lapses back to his former role as Father of the Marshalsea. This is the outward manifestation of a disease that has been breeding in him over the years, the disease of wanting something for nothing, of bad conscience for getting what one does not deserve. Pride and inflated self-regard often lead to a sense of injured worth for many figures in this book, and just as Mrs. Clennam's religious values are stated in accountants' terms, so are these social values presented in terms of wealth and poverty. William Dorrit's claim to preeminence in the Marshalsea presumably rests upon his gentility, but it rests as much on mere seniority. An abject scene with his daughter reveals how flimsy his position is, and how unwarranted his pretense of moral authority. When he receives his unexpected fortune and can live up to the station in society that he considers appropriate for his family, Dorrit remains haunted by the sense that he has no inherent worth to justify his position, only the money. He, Fanny, and Tip feel that much is owed to them, but Frederick and Amy endorse Arthur's and Doyce's view that we deserve nothing in this life except what we earn through our own honest effort. Dorrit insists on respect being shown to him as his due, an attitude that evokes torment over imagined and possible slights, most pitiably evident when, after his release from the Marshalsea, he scorns young John Chivery for venturing to offer a "testimonial" of former friendship. Dorrit has the decency to realize that he has overreacted, but the overreaction shows how little true gentility he has.[12]

Little Dorrit herself makes explicit the many metaphorical hints scattered through the novel when she reflects that English society in Italy "greatly resembled a superior sort of Marshalsea. Numbers of people seemed to come abroad, pretty much as people had come into prison: through debt, through idleness, relationship, curiosity, and general unfitness for getting on at home." She develops the analogy in great detail and concludes, "They had precisely the same incapacity for settling down to anything, as the prisoners used to have; they rather deteriorated one another, as the prisoners used to do; and they wore untidy dresses, and fell into a slovening way of life: still, always like the people in the Marshalsea" (511). Little Dorrit is not precise about the reasons for this penitential form of life, but the narrator's voice clearly suggests that idleness and misspent energies, like those of the Merdles and of Henry Gowan, exert their own punishing effects sooner or later.

The trouble, of course, is that the punishments that the idle and wicked bring upon themselves affect innocent persons as well, though in this novel many of the innocent victims, such as Little Dorrit and Pet Meagles, are strong enough to endure them. Long ago T. A. Jackson remarked that all of the good characters in *Little Dorrit* are victimized in one way or another. "Every character in *Little Dorrit* who counts on the side of Virtue and Heroism is, it will be seen, made to suffer, and that acutely" (168).[13] This suffering may be read to some degree as a form of punishment for their innocent connivance with the malign forces permeating their world. Elaine Showalter has argued that even Arthur and Amy have their negative shadow doubles—Rigaud and Maggy—to act out and release their primitive impulses.[14] It may be that the virtuous and heroic to some degree earn their suffering, but why should they endure pains disproportionately intense? It seems more reasonable to regard these characters as victims of injustice, unarmed sojourners in a hostile world. They cannot avoid the spreading contagion of the wicked and the idle.

But there is also an active and industrious wickedness that produces widespread suffering. Dickens' brilliant device of showing Mr. Merdle always holding one hand by the other, as though he were taking himself into custody, has often been remarked. It is a sign that the man knows himself to be guilty and what his punishment should be. He derives little pleasure from his financial prominence and spends his money "to satisfy Society (whatever that was), and take up all its drafts upon him for tribute" (247). As his wife points out, he is no ornament to that Society and would be better not to mix with it any more than necessary. He is an alien in his own mansion, dreading his own Chief Butler, who is "the Avenging Spirit of this great man's life" (557). Aside from the deference paid to his financial genius, Merdle lives in a purgatorial realm. Like Dorrit, he knows that he does not deserve the respect accorded him.

Mr. Merdle has a complaint that the Physician cannot diagnose. Eventually the complaint breaks out in a plague traceable to a definite moral infection, in this case financial speculation, which seizes the popular imagination and involves even such decent persons as Clennam and Pancks. The narrator is explicit.

> That it is at least as difficult to stay a moral infection as a physical
> one; that such a disease will spread with the malignity and rapidity of
> the Plague; that the contagion, when it has once made head, will spare

no pursuit or condition, but will lay hold on people in the soundest health, and become developed in the most unlikely constitutions; is a fact as firmly established by experience as that we human creatures breathe an atmosphere. A blessing beyond appreciation would be conferred upon mankind, if the tainted, in whose weakness or wickedness these virulent disorders are bred, could be instantly seized and placed in close confinement (not to say summarily smothered) before the poison is communicable. (571)

Dickens' use of the disease metaphor here suggests that treatment for this behavior should be more in the nature of cure or quarantine than punishment. Given the widespread agitation for penal reform in the early decades of the century, a movement that often pictured crime as the result of environmental forces, and thus to be regarded as a disease or handicap rather than brutally punished and suppressed, Dickens' metaphor is fully suitable for the time. The metaphor also implies how insidious many forms of wickedness are, and how difficult it is to separate the original agent of infection from those who transmit the disease to others. Like physical disease, moral weakness cannot easily be judged and therefore cannot easily be punished. But outright criminality and moral weakness suffer alike the consequences of their own folly. The widespread financial ruin that follows Merdle's suicide is the natural punishment, in the world of *Little Dorrit,* for the offense of speculation.

Merdle, like William Dorrit, who is equally terrified of Merdle's Chief Butler, has not earned his wealth. "He had sprung from nothing, by no natural growth or process that any one could account for; he had been, after all, a low ignorant fellow . . . he had never had any money of his own, his ventures had been utterly reckless, and his expenditure had been most enormous" (709–10). He even borrows the instrument he uses to do away with himself. Like Dorrit he unmasks himself, though his "disease" is directly mortal, whereas Dorrit lingers on awhile after the virulent outbreak of his sickness. Merdle punishes himself for his crimes, but even in doing so he cheats the law. Merdle has been an even greater fraud than Dorrit, who at least was born a gentleman. When the Chief Butler is informed of Merdle's suicide, he coolly gives notice and remarks, "'Mr. Merdle never was the gentleman, and no ungentlemanly act on Mr. Merdle's part would surprise me'" (708). Once Merdle is gone it becomes evident that "every servile worshipper of riches who had helped to set him on his pedestal, would have done better to worship the Devil point-blank" (710). When William Dorrit, who is more weak and ineffectual than wicked, dies, followed soon after by his gentle brother, Frederick, the reader is directed not to pass judgment too swiftly on the folly or weakness of either. They go not to be judged and punished. "The two brothers were before their Father; far beyond the twilight judgments of this world; high above its mists and obscurities" (652). It is a father they go to, not a judge. The same will not, one assumes, be true of Merdle.

Merdle's moral disease of selfishness, greed, and indifference to the welfare of others could be cured by the Physician, who possesses the necessary remedy and lives it out every day. He is not a proud or vain man. "Many wonderful things did he see and hear, and much irreconcilable moral contradiction did he pass his life among; yet his equality of compassion was no more disturbed than the Divine Master's of all healing was. He went, like the rain, among the just and unjust, doing all the good he could, and neither proclaiming it in the synagogues nor at the corners of streets." He is not a fraud like Dorrit and Merdle. "Where he was, something real was" (702). Whereas Bar knows all about the gullibility and knavery of people, Physician can give "a better insight into their tendernesses and affections" (703). In short, he is a Christian, and it doesn't hurt that he is "a great reader of all kinds of literature (and never at all apologetic for that weakness)" (704–5). It is fitting that he should be present at Merdle's extermination, his values immediately replacing those of the evil man. In a similar but far more lenient scene the good Frederick witnesses the passing of his weak and foolish brother. As the novel moves toward its close, a series of such displacements occurs, eliminating folly and wickedness, and replacing them with mercy and compassion.

The many diseases that break out in *Little Dorrit* are foreshadowed by the second chapter, which presents persons guilty of nothing more than possible exposure to disease deprived of their freedom through quarantine. This scene contrasts with and yet resembles the imprisonment scene of the first chapter, preparing the reader for the larger idea that there are many forms of confinement, voluntary as well as involuntary, some of which are salubrious to self or society, some of which are harmful. The two principal men in chapter 2 offer a contrast of another kind. Both Mr. Meagles and Arthur Clennam are shut up in quarantine, but whereas the one is energetic and hopeful, the other is largely cowed by life. He admits to having no will, purpose, or hope, and he blames his upbringing.

> 'Ah! Easily said. I am the son, Mr. Meagles, of a hard father and mother. I am the only child of parents who weighed, measured, and priced everything; for whom what could not be weighed, measured, and priced, had no existence. Strict people as the phrase is, professors of a stern religion, their very religion was a gloomy sacrifice of tastes and sympathies that were never their own, offered up as a part of a bargain for the security of their possessions. Austere faces, inexorable discipline, penance in this world and terror in the next—nothing graceful or gentle anywhere, and the void in my cowed heart everywhere— this was my childhood, if I may so misuse the word as to apply it to such a beginning in life.' (20–21)

To be confined may be punishment or protection. A prison keeps offenders in, but it keeps troubles out. Being held in quarantine is an inconvenience to the individual detained, but a benefit to the community at large. But if guilt and disease are as confused as blame and blamelessness, then confinement can be seen not as punishment of the guilty, but as an inescapable feature of human existence.

All of the detainees for quarantine soon have their liberty again, but some forms of confinement follow wherever one goes. Thus the gloomy Miss Wade sees all of existence as a kind of prison. " 'In our course through life we shall meet the people who are coming to meet *us*, from many strange places and by many strange roads,' " she says, " 'and what it is set to us to do to them, and what it is set to them to do to us, will all be done' " (25). Clennam himself refers to " 'this labyrinth of a world' " as though being at liberty is only a release into a larger species of confinement (19). Miss Wade's determinist outlook is only one manifestation of self-confinement.

The religion that has conditioned Arthur is what Dickens associated with the "gloomy enthusiast," characterized by a Calvinistic sternness arising from self-distrust and combined with a zeal aimed at redeeming the debt of real or imagined infractions.[15] In this novel, Clennam's mother is the outstanding example. Dickens is in keeping with the popular equation of money and moral obligation of his time, described in chapter 3 and asociated with Evangelical and Calvinistic religious opinions. The discourse of such religious sects draws metaphors for man's relationship with God from the vocabulary of commercial exchange, with an emphasis upon strict accounting, as though God were a higher sort of clerk more concerned with ledgers than with conduct. Such religion punished Arthur before he was guilty of any transgression. When he arrives in London on a Sunday, he notices the "penitential garb" of its melancholy streets (28). He remembers "the dreary Sunday of his childhood, when he sat with his hands before him scared out of his senses by a horrible tract which commenced business with a poor child by asking him in its title, why he was going to Perdition," and another when "he was marched to chapel by a picquet of teachers three times a day, morally handcuffed to another boy" (29).

Arthur finds his mother an invalid who has virtually willed her own confinement. Her religion is as grim as ever and she employs the moral bookkeeping I have just described to gratify her meaner impulses while insisting on her own rectitude. Mrs. Clennam, though a demanding woman, has not been able to make the family business—whatever it is—prosper. This situation, attributable to her conservative and grasping attitude regarding money, indicates something about her moral business transactions as well. She says that she can accept a hard but just bargain: " 'In my sinfulness I merit bitter disappointment, and I accept it' " (46). But the opposite side of that submissiveness is a totally unchristian fascination with the punishment of others.

Woe to the suppliant, if such a one there were or ever had been, who had any concession to look for in the inexorable face at the cabi-

net. Woe to the defaulter whose appeal lay to the tribunal where those
severe eyes presided. Great need had the rigid woman of her mystical
religion, veiled in gloom and darkness, with lightnings of cursing, vengeance, and destruction, flashing through the sable clouds. Forgive us
our debts as we forgive our debtors, was a prayer too poor in spirit for
her. Smite thou my debtors, Lord, wither them, crush them; do Thou
as I would do, and Thou shalt have my worship: this was the impious
tower of stone she built up to scale Heaven. (47)

When Arthur asks his mother if there is any reparation for which the family is
responsible, she replies with the opposing question: Have I not made reparation
in this room these fifteen years? At which point the narrator steps in to demonstrate the relationship between her secular and spiritual accounting.

Thus was she always balancing her bargain with the Majesty of heaven,
posting up the entries to her credit, strictly keeping her set-off, and
claiming her due. She was only remarkable in this, for the force and
emphasis with which she did it. Thousands upon thousands do it, according to their varying manner, every day. (50)

The narrator's censorious depiction of Mrs. Clennam is unrelenting, with the
one exception of her tenderness toward Little Dorrit. And the great disclosure
scene near the end of the novel discovers how deeply intertwined and confused
the secular and spiritual strains are in this fierce old woman. Rigaud knows her
secret and openly regards her as a thief. But she proudly recasts her story in
moral terms, insisting that she was motivated by religious principles, and citing
her upbringing as credentials. "'Mine was no light youth of sinful gaiety and
pleasure. Mine were days of wholesome repression, punishment, and fear'"
(774). She was married to Gilbert Clennam, supposing him to be the proper product of a similar education, but soon discovered that he had another love by whom
Arthur was born. Made aware of this vile abuse, she asks, could she doubt "'that
it was appointed to me to lay the hand of punishment upon that creature of perdition? Was I to dismiss in a moment—not my own wrongs—what was I! but all
the rejection of sin, and all the war against it, in which I had been bred?'" (775).
These sinners were "bound in the bonds of their sin" and delivered to her, and
she executed justice. She argues that the punishment she exacted was essentially
merciful, for she kept the sinners' secret and merely forced them to terminate
their guilty alliance; moreover, she considerately took the illegitimate Arthur
into her home to educate him according to her stringent improving religion.
Mrs. Clennam even claims that although sending Arthur's mother away with the
promise of modest support might occasion her some pain, that suffering would
work to her ultimate advantage. "'If in this, I punished her here, did I not open
to her a way hereafter?'" (777). Mrs. Clennam here claims the function of God,

who alone has the necessary knowledge to provide the opportunities for such therapeutic punishment.

The chief confusion in Mrs. Clennam's mind, requiring such sophistry, is between an injury to her own pride and a transgression against God's law. But as Frederick Robertson's sermon on "Joseph's Forgiveness of His Brethren" so clearly indicates, it is not the office of an individual to presume to enact God's justice.[16] Mrs. Clennam's language even echoes that of Joseph when he asks, Who am I to judge and punish? And there is always the familiar "Judge not lest ye be judged" to dissuade any person who is inclined to help God out with the administration of His justice. Such a role is particularly inappropriate for an injured party, since "justice" then so strongly resembles mere "vengeance." Mrs. Clennam has masked revenge with an argument based on strict religious principles, but the narrator intrudes to point out that in doing so she is reversing the order of creation, breathing her own breath into a clay image of her Creator. "Verily, verily, travellers have seen many monstrous idols in many countries; but no human eyes have ever seen more daring, gross, and shocking images of the Divine nature, than we creatures of the dust make in our own likenesses, of our own bad passions" (775). Merdle was worshipped like a Golden Calf or Mammon, whereas he was actually an unclean spirit spreading infection and unwholesomeness. That secular idolatry is bad enough, but Mrs. Clennam's religious version is worse, and also brings with it disease and unwholesomeness. The London Sunday, reflecting Mrs. Clennam's somber faith, is filled with the sound of bells "throbbing, jerking, tolling, as if the Plague were in the city and the deadcarts were going round" (28). The Clennam house leans on "some half-dozen gigantic crutches," almost as invalid as the woman cooped up within (31). This plague is like the plague that Merdle brings, but it is more pernicious because it is not only a moral disease like the other but an ontological contagion as well, creating a worldview and an otherworld-view that is wholly out of keeping with the healthy prescriptions of Christ. Mrs. Clennam says that in her imprisonment she forgets nothing. "'If I forgot that this scene, the Earth, is expressly meant to be a scene of gloom, and hardship, and dark trial, for the creatures who are made out of its dust, I might have some tenderness for its vanities. But I have no such tenderness.'" She ponders always a divine wrath that must be satisfied, and therefore looks upon her own confinement as a grace and favor. "'My affliction might otherwise have had no meaning to me. Hence I would forget, and I do forget, nothing'" (357). Mainly what she does not forget is the injury done to her. She misreads the letters inscribed in her husband's watch, taking the Do Not Forget to mean do not forget the evil done. But Flintwinch says to her, "'You know very well that the Do Not Forget, at the time when his father sent that watch to you, could only mean, the rest of the story being then all dead and over, Do Not Forget the suppression. Make restitution!'" (782). The last letters that Arthur's mother sent to Mrs. Clennam were "Prayers for forgiveness" (783). But the hard woman never forgave nor forgot, ignoring the prescriptions of a compassionate Christ. Hers is an Old Testament inclination, and the many references to plague, to Egypt, and to the East may suggest that her faith and the society characterized by Merdles and Dorrits and Barnacles reflect a latter day Egypt, where the chosen people are held in bondage for their sins, and where a plague will come to teach their tormentors that it is time for release.

It is a great irony that Mrs. Clennam's means of punishing wickedness takes the form of a dishonest financial maneuver. She withholds money provided by a codicil to her husband's will for Arthur's mother and for Frederick Dorrit's daughter, or, lacking that, his brother's youngest daughter, Amy Dorrit. Just as her conception of religion involves a commercialized accumulation and expenditure of merit and blame, so Mrs. Clennam's moral extortion takes the form of a pecuniary act, but she cannot deny that in acting according to a supposed moral code she breaks a secular law. Just as Dorrit's imprisonment for debt symbolically represents his unfitness for practical life and his presumptuous sense that he deserves what he has not earned, so Mrs. Clennam's misappropriation of money symbolizes her taking of God's law into her own hands and viewing a world that He made for love and forgiveness as though it were a world for sharp dealing and the calling in of accounts. More significantly, the repeatedly suggested notion that the money Mrs. Clennam has withheld would have spared Dorrit imprisonment is not necessarily true. There is no evidence, when the secret comes out, to verify the kind of balanced ledger of good and evil at which the text has more than once hinted.

All of Mrs. Clennam's machinations have brought only suffering; once she has been found out and her actions brought into the open, she herself can see them in a different light. She has all along realized that there is one truly innocent person in all of this affair—the one person whom she has truly injured, Little Dorrit. So she seeks out Amy at the Marshalsea, that moral prison so like her own, where she is tending Arthur, and learns the important lesson of the faith she has abused. "'I will restore to you what I have withheld from you,'" she says to Little Dorrit. "'Forgive me. Can you forgive me?'" And Little Dorrit responds as we know she will: "'I can, and Heaven knows I do!'" (789). When Mrs. Clennam tries to explain that she set herself against evil not against good, she receives a mild lecture from Little Dorrit against angry feelings and unforgiving deeds. It is precisely here that the balance in the narrative shifts decisively away from the Old and toward the New Testament—from retribution to love. "'Be guided only by the healer of the sick, the raiser of the dead, the friend of all who were afflicted and forlorn, the patient Master who shed tears of compassion for our infirmities. We cannot but be right if we put all the rest away, and do everything in remembrance of Him. There is no vengeance and no infliction of suffering in His life, I am sure. There can be no confusion in following Him, and seeking for no other footsteps, I am certain!'" Little Dorrit says this standing by her window in a softened light, unlike the black figure of Mrs. Clennam in the shade, no less an opposing visual power "than the life and doctrine on which she rested were to that figure's history" (792). Like the Physician who has followed Christ's healing ways, Little Dorrit has devoted herself to the care of others, and at this moment is ministering to an Arthur who is recovering from his own symbolic disorder. She is the touchstone of value in this book, apparently born to virtue. "Apparently," because, as Alistair M. Duckworth astutely points out, "If Little Dorrit is natural and benevolent (and she is), it is often by an act of the will, by a conscious fiction."[17]

If Little Dorrit's achievement seems effortless, Arthur's efforts to achieve the virtue and life he aspires to are constantly stressed. He is good, but lacking in confidence. Next to Little Dorrit he is the best we get. The need to counteract mean and hard business dealings during his working life has rescued him to honor and generosity; being bred in coldness and severity has rescued him to a warm and sympathetic heart; the cruel religion of his youth has "rescued him to judge not, and in humility to be merciful, and have hope and charity" (165). When Pet Meagles asks his forgiveness if she has unwittingly caused him pain, he gives her a chaste kiss and says that heaven knows he has nothing to forgive. No bitterness here and no recrimination, though much sadness and disappointment. He does not feel that he is entitled to Pet's love, nor that he is being defrauded of it by Gowan. Whatever her folly in marrying Gowan, Pet has not wilfully injured him and he knows it. He also knows that mere professions of faith and piety mean nothing. His mother's grim religion has not sunk into his heart, "so the first article in his code of morals was, that he must begin in practical humility, with looking well to his feet on Earth, and that he could never mount on wings of words to Heaven. Duty on Earth, restitution on earth, action on earth; these first, as the first steep steps upward" (319).

It is this very commitment to duty and restitution that lands him in prison. He has made the error of trying to profit without labor, of speculating to grow wealthy. No matter that his motives are good. His entire relationship with Doyce represents the value of earning one's own way and, as he well knows afterward, his speculating against Doyce's injunction is a betrayal of those values. At the same time, much more must be stripped from Arthur. He has had vain hopes about human affection. He loses Pet, and Flora Finching proves a grotesque caricature of his old love. He has wanted three things upon return from the East: to make reparation for some suspected injury his family has done, to find a worthy occupation to pursue, and to earn a good woman's love. In seeking to make reparation and in finding a worthy occupation he does win a good woman's love, but it takes him a long while to realize who that woman is. Only when he is in the Marshalsea himself, undergoing his own "punishment" for lacking wisdom and for being tainted with worldly expectations, does the truth come to him.[18] It is a form of conversion. Clennam realizes that Little Dorrit had always influenced his better resolutions. The narrator elaborates: "None of us clearly know to whom or to what we are indebted in this wise, until some marked stop in the whirling wheel of life brings the right perception with it. It comes with sickness, it comes with sorrow, it comes with the loss of the dearly loved, it is one of the most frequent uses of adversity. It came to Clennam in his adversity, strongly and tenderly" (720). Janet Larson has argued shrewdly that Arthur allows his Calvinist sense of deserved punishment to crush him.

> As Carlyle puts this religious legacy, Nature 'keeps silently a most exact Savings-bank. . . . Debtor and Creditor, in respect to one and all of us; silently marks down . . . Debtor, Debtor, Debtor, day after day, rigorously as Fate . . . and at the end of the account you will have it all to pay, my friend . . . neatly, completely, as sure as you are alive' (LDP [Latter-Day Pamphlets] 205). Dickens brings Clennam to debtors' prison partly to defeat this bookkeeping Theorem of the Universe, the Victorian formula by which Mrs. Clennam places acts of renunciation 'to her credit . . . in her Eternal Day-book.'"[19]

Dickens may, in Clennam's imprisonment for debt, be rejecting Mrs. Clennam's bookkeeping approach to her God and final judgment, but there is another kind of moral accounting that this episode endorses, one close to Carlyle's formula of a natural debt incurred by ill conduct and redeemable in this world. Arthur's imprisonment discloses to him his profound debt to Little Dorrit. His punishment is therapeutic; his sickness becomes a symbolic expulsion of error, calling Little Dorrit to heal him with the same traits of love, compassion, and mercy that she has demonstrated throughout the narrative. When Arthur refuses her offer of financial assistance to be released from prison, his refusal is more than the simple plot device, frequently employed in Victorian fiction, of male pride that will not be beholden to a woman. He is already deeply in Amy's moral and spiritual debt and he refuses to have that debt confirmed in material terms. He cannot accept money or love from her until he is worthy of both. And he does become worthy, and he does win her love, and the two of them go off "into a modest life of usefulness and happiness" (826).

All of the energies of the novel move from the pressure of punishment to the release of forgiveness. The opening chapters emphasize confinement and disease, subjects that are taken up and threaded together throughout the narrative. The closing chapters emphasize release from confinement and recovered health, and open into a new life beyond the narrative, as though the chosen people have journeyed out of the bondage of Egypt into the London wilderness to make their way toward their own Promised Land. Here, as in many of Dickens' novels, sustaining mysteries and withholding secrets is not simply a device to keep readers guessing and to maintain suspense. Mystery is one more means of emphasizing the claustrophobic nature of vengeful and unforgiving behavior. We learn many secrets during the narrative—especially the secrets in Arthur's and Amy's hearts, which they confide to themselves (though Maggie is an uncomprehending audience to Amy's fable). The secrets in the hearts of the wicked, however, are not disclosed until they actuate some significant transformation in private or public life. As we have seen, it is the thoroughly wicked Rigaud who hunts down Mrs. Clennam and finds out her secret.

Just as the narrator uses the language of dissent to expose the pernicious exchange practices of an immoral world, so he uses the complications occasioned by selfishness and deceit to evoke a strategy of survival that progresses from a largely punitive to a largely lenitive climate. He accomplishes this strategy by some intriguing reversals in the narrative. Some are reversals in the narrative's direction, others are reversals of expectation. Janet Larson discusses an example of the latter that is especially pertinent to this study. Larson assumes that Amy Dorrit is the central moral force of the novel, but adds that she is "at once more and less than 'the good Angel of the race'; her forgiveness must also be supplemented by formulas of debt and repayment, and guilt must be released through melodramatic events quite outside the circle of her powers" (272). In trying to protect her father, she is implicated in his evasions. Her angelic life-giving powers cannot contravene the consequences of certain deeds. In fact, Larson argues, forgiveness dissolves into mist in *Little Dorrit*.

> Amy's forgiving is unavailing in another sense: it does not release her from internal contradiction. In the system of forgiveness as a divine-human exchange, the payoff in forgiving *to be* forgiven is peace of mind. But the many acts of forgiveness that texture Amy's daily life do not dissolve her internal tension between her knowledge of good and evil, although they may keep some awareness of evil at bay. Amy's pain continues because there are still debts to be paid—paid again and again in her overwhelming sense of duty and her attempts to shoulder the burden of others' sins. (273)

Larson is correct, I think, in declaring that Amy Dorrit receives no peace of mind for the forgiveness she extends to others, but that is partly because she "forgives" in the sense of pardoning the deeds of others. True forgiveness comes only from God; human forgiveness attends the penitent individual. In many cases Amy Dorrit is "forgiving" individuals who have not repented. The perplexing irony here is that Amy's forgiveness does not excuse, exonerate, or cleanse the person forgiven, nor bring Christian gratification to her for having followed Christ's example. Dickens seems to be consciously calling attention to the proper function of forgiveness by demonstrating that Amy's generous and loving conduct cannot achieve much in isolation. Her forgiveness takes on much greater significance when it is evoked by a true penitential cry, as with Mrs. Clennam. Then her forgiveness signals the shift, mentioned above, from an Old to a New Testament atmosphere. Dickens purposely frustrates his readers' conventional expectation that Amy Dorrit's charity and forgiveness will achieve their aims in the customary clock-like manner of Victorian fiction, Dickens' earlier novels included. His own narrative resists the very message it seeks to deliver. It replicates the self-division of its hero and works out its purpose by testing alternate perspectives, as does this hero, coming to a clear statement of its purpose through the collision of these perspectives.

Alistair M. Duckworth proposes that *Little Dorrit* effectively deconstructs itself by questioning its god-terms, such as nature, reality, and Little Dorrit. All are seriously questioned in the text (129). As we have already noted, even Little Dorrit has to work at being perfect and employs some of the questionable strategies of other characters in the narrative. Janice M. Carlisle notes that Little Dorrit keeps the secret of Mrs. Clennam's debt to her from Arthur and thus begins her marriage with a deception. Similarly, Little Dorrit has recourse to fictionalizing, as do self-deceiving characters in the novel. Carlisle adds that Dickens himself withholds a good deal of information in his narrative, and she concludes that fiction is defined by what it cannot do in this novel.[20] To suggest this much is also to suggest an awareness by the narrator that novels cannot do all that one might hope. If *Hard Times,* in defending the imagination, was also defending the enterprise of novel writing, *Little Dorrit* seems to be a rueful acknowledgement of the limitations of that enterprise. Perhaps this is why the book is so often characterized as Dickens' most melancholy effort.

Randolph Splitter argues that the melodramatic catastrophe at the end of *Little Dorrit* represents a release of energy, an outward emblem of climactic revelations. But he asserts that the happy ending that follows "seems like a literary confidence-trick which fools us into thinking that the issue of guilt has been settled" (130). The narrative depends on compulsive, irrational character types or "humors" to distribute its energies.

> But the author of *Little Dorrit* is himself a kind of obsessive, compulsive humor who treasures up the secrets of his plot, revealing nothing more than teasing clues, until they explode in a final, melodramatic burst of revelations at the end. In this book, where every pleasure is suspect, tinged with guilt, Dickens himself, who seems to enjoy what he is doing, postpones full gratification and indulges instead in the mixed pleasure of waiting, holding onto his cards as long as possible. (131)

Splitter quotes Chesterton's saying that Dickens' "secrecy is sensation; the secret is tame" (132), and suggests that the machinery of melodrama discloses the hand of the novelist forcibly attempting to undo a guilt-ridden repression. But the ruse does not work, Splitter concludes. "It is true that the hero is not really freed from guilt, that the anxiety manifested in the novel is not dispelled; what Dickens gives us is an imitation of liberation, an elaborate sleight of hand. The point of the artifice—of which the artificer, the *auctor gloriosus,* is trying to convince himself—is that the nightmare of modern society is only a nightmare, a dream, a fiction, after all" (133).

Splitter's argument works up to a point. Just as Amy Dorrit's forgiveness cannot redeem a fallen world by itself, so Arthur Clennam cannot expunge guilt alone. Both attempt to rectify a world they find morally wanting in one way or another. Amy wishes to comfort, Arthur to redress. But it is precisely because neither is guilty of a specific offense to begin with that they cannot eliminate guilt. Arthur becomes capable of such erasure when he takes the infection of speculating. For this sin he is immediately punished, repents, and is forgiven and rehabilitated. Of all the other characters for whom this pattern is an option, only Tattycoram follows it out completely. By committing an error, Arthur also becomes responsive to Amy's love and forgiveness, so that her powers, too, can for once be fully implemented. Only in one another are Arthur and Amy able to fulfill their impulses to love, forgive, and make restitution. Other characters may be recovered, redeemed, forgiven, pardoned, and punished, but the only true reciprocity is between Arthur and Amy, who are finally united to face a largely uncongenial world. Elaine Showalter offers a helpful reading of the novel's ending. "The world of shadows has been encountered but not dispelled," she says; "the lovers pass along 'in sunshine and shade,' and around them the noisy and the eager, the arrogant and the vain, continue to fret. It is, however the 'usual uproar' (II, 34) of human conflict, rather than the poisoning unhealthy silence of the Marshalsea, which represents vitality, imagination, actuality. It is the clamor in which Dickens finds his own peace, in which he hears (to reverse George Eliot's famous line) the silence on the other side of roaring" (40).

Whether or not we regard the author as finding peace through the closure of his fiction, we can view the narrator as cancelling certain forces in his narrative and replacing them by others. The closing lines may be seen as the tidal success of a pattern of narrative reversals that move toward good. Reversals in narrative action serve a greater purpose than simply to revive interest in the story. Chief among these is Dorrit's release from prison, but as we have seen that release only confirms what the prison had signified—confinement for those who make unjustified claims upon society. Freedom becomes a path to sickness, disclosure, and death. Similarly, the reversal in Merdle's fortunes triggers widespread public retribution for folly, and the private unraveling of Arthur Clennam's affairs. Rigaud's stratagems bring him to Mrs. Clennam's, where the central mystery of the novel is finally aired—only to destroy the minatory agent himself and effect Mrs. Clennam's repentance. After all of the narrator's denunciations of Mrs. Clennam's commercial relationship with God, he simply proposes a revision of the pattern, letting his narrative reveal that in this prison of earth we must earn our salvation, working here to store up our treasures in heaven.

The pattern of the narrative produces gradual movement through stages of confinement to ultimate freedom. The prisoners and detainees of the first two chapters are confined for individual culpability or infection and are released to pursue their private ends; William Dorrit represents actual and psychological confinement. Both in prison and after his release he moves uneasily in a world partly private and partly public. Merdle is a wholly public figure until his death, a release that affects a wide spectrum of society. Finally, Mrs. Clennam's condition represents the last stage of release from a religion, worldview, and philosophy that makes all of existence a punishment. It is as though the reader moves through a series of boxes within boxes, the personal release leaving one still in private-public confinement, release from which leaves one still restrained by the world of social and institutional structures, which, once evaded, still leave one metaphysically enclosed until he or she is freed by the New Testament message of love, compassion, and forgiveness.

Speaking of what I have referred to as narrative punishment, Janet Larson describes Dickens' treatment of Mrs. Clennam. "In *his* role as disposer of all things in *Little Dorrit,* the novelist metes out the just deserts of silence and total stability to a woman who has so abused the potential of biblical and other language for unstable interpretation in her pursuit of fiction" (205). The implied author does construct narrative as well as natural punishments in this tale, but here the measure of mercy and recuperation is seriously diminished. He has structured his narrative to imitate the way each individual soul must work its way through the world and find true freedom at last. In the manner of its telling the narrative shows how arduous a task that is, how interwoven all of experience is and how necessary it might be to pick out the bad threads and begin again, as Carlyle suggests the need for an entire retailoring of the universe, including the tailor himself, in *Sartor Resartus.* In a similar fashion this novel shows the great undertaking that fiction is, and also what dangers and limitations it faces. In leading its characters to their minimal achievement, it reminds us of the complex effort that brought them there and, as the Third Volume of Amy Dorrit's life begins, the narrator's volume ends. As the narrative extends its qualified blessing on its protagonists, it solicits from us, its readers, a qualified blessing as well.

NOTES

1. The significance of the prison motif has been one of the major accepted features of the novel in modern criticism. Significant treatments of the theme appear in Lionel Trilling's Introduction to the Oxford University Press edition cited below, in Edgar Johnson's *Charles Dickens: His Tragedy and Triumph* (Boston: Little, Brown and Co., 1952), 2:883–903, and in J. Hillis Miller's *Charles Dickens: The World of His Novels* (Cambridge: Harvard University Press, 1965), 227–47.

2. Charles Dickens, *Little Dorrit* (New York: Oxford University Press, 1963), 3. Subsequent references appear in the text.

3. Randolph Splitter, in "Guilt and the Trappings of Melodrama in *Little Dorrit,*" (in vol. 6 of *Dickens Studies Annual,* ed. Robert B. Partlow, Jr. [Carbondale: Southern Illinois University Press, 1977]) stresses the connection between money and guilt in the novel, 120ff.

4. James Kincaid describes *Little Dorrit* as "more darkly moral than any novel before it," pointing out as well that it is filled with self-justifying characters. "The novel distrusts justifications and holds up the non-explaining Amy Dorrit as a reproof to all its other characters. Everyone else is a self-deceiver, more or less dangerous (Mrs. Clennam) or sad (John Chivery)" (*Dickens and the Rhetoric of Laughter* [Oxford: The Clarendon Press, 1971], 198). Another example of self-justification in a repellent proxy form is Mrs. Gowan objecting that her son must appeal to the Swinish Public for his income (*Little Dorrit*, 313).

5. Dennis Walder, *Dickens and Religion* (London: George Allen & Unwin, 1981), 171. Dickens' own working notes for chapter 31 of Book Two include the sentence, "Set the darkness and vengeance against the New Testament" (*Dickens' Working Notes for His Novels*, ed. Harry Stone [Chicago: The University of Chicago Press, 1987], 311). Subsequent references appear in the text.

6. In a rejoinder to James Fitzjames Stephen's negative review of *Little Dorrit*, entitled "Curious Misprint in the *Edinburgh Review*," (*Household Words* [August 1, 1857], 97–100). Dickens emphasized the care with which he had prepared for the catastrophic collapse of the Clennam house and the death of Rigaud, associating warning signs with the behavior of the characters.

7. Earle Davis, *The Flint and the Flame: The Artistry of Charles Dickens* (Columbia: The University of Missouri Press, 1963), 227.

8. Alison Booth, notes along with others before, that Amy Dorrit achieves happiness through sacrifice for others. She argues further that Amy, like George Eliot's Dorothea Brooke, is a prisoner of social fictions, but that both characters follow a pattern of confinement, exile, and a triumphant transformation of necessity into promise. "In both novels, the emphasis falls on the true 'progress' of the heroine, involved as she is in a complex of interdependent fates. Both novelists exempt their heroines from the defeating determinism of their worlds, albeit with a different bias" ("Little Dorrit and Dorothea Brooke: Interpreting the Heroines of History," *Nineteenth-Century Fiction* 41, no. 2 [September 1986], 196).

9. Dickens called attention to the parallelism of this imprisonment in his working notes (Stone 273).

10. It has long been evident that in *Little Dorrit* Dickens moved decisively in the direction of a sinister, pervasive, almost unspecifiable evil influencing society. T. A. Jackson, writing in 1937, commented that the real villain in *Little Dorrit* is no specific character. "Behind all these human phenomena, using them as its instruments, is a vaster and more impalpable Evil, of whose true being we get indications in the shadow of the Marshalsea walls, in the heart-breaking immobility of the Circumlocution Office, and in the terrifying gloom of Mrs. Clennam's theology" (*Charles Dickens: The Progress of a Radical* [New York: International Publishers, 1938], 165). More recently, James Kincaid describes the blighting effect of all that the Circumlocution Office represents (211ff.).

11. Randolph Splitter points out that "it is not money so much as guilt—a need to pay off debts, to make restitution—which is passed on from father to son" (123).

12. Peter Christmas discusses the opposition of gentility and reality in the novel in "*Little Dorrit:* The End of Good and Evil," *Dickens Studies Annual* 6, ed. Robert B. Partlow, Jr. (Carbondale: Southern Illinois University Press, 1977), 134–53.

13. A. E. Dyson also stresses that "in Little Dorrit the virtuous are certainly victims, who pay for their moral role with much of their lives" (*The Inimitable Dickens: A Reading of the Novels* [New York: St Martin's Press, 1970], 207).

14. Elaine Showalter, "Guilt, Authority, and the Shadows of *Little Dorrit,*" *Nineteenth-Century Fiction* 34, no. 1 (June 1979), 20–40. Subsequent references appear in the text.

15. Charles Dickens, "Sunday Under Three Heads," in *The Uncommercial Traveller and Reprinted Pieces* (New York: Oxford University Press, 1964), 638.

16. See chapter 1, pages 17–18.

17. Alistair M. Duckworth, "*Little Dorrit* and the Question of Closure," *Nineteenth-Century Fiction* 33, no. 1 (June 1978), 129. Subsequent references appear in the text.

18. Elaine Showalter, alluding to Julian Moynahan's assessment of Pip in *Great Expectation,* adds, "Clennam too is a dangerous young man, who is responsible for Mr. Dorrit's release from the Marshalsea into a world he can no longer inhabit, for Doyce's financial ruin, for Little Dorrit's love and Flora's disappointment, and for Mrs. Clennam's paralysis" (33). But surely this is a different order of responsibility from Pip's and perhaps more in line with the misfortunes generated by some of David Copperfield's actions.

19. Janet L. Larson, *Dickens and the Broken Scripture* (Athens: The University of Georgia Press, 1985), 235. Subsequent references appear in the text.

20. Janice M. Carlisle, "*Little Dorrit:* Necessary Fictions," *Studies in the Novel* 7, no. 2 (Summer 1975), 195–213.

SIXTEEN

A Tale of Two Cities

SOMETHING IS very wrong with justice in *A Tale of Two Cities* (1859). Both English and French legal systems seem more capable of persecuting the innocent than prosecuting the guilty. An outlaw like Jerry Cruncher may voice disgust at the inhuman legal punishment of quartering, but only from self-interest.[1] And when the mob overthrows corrupt authority in France, it imposes a mirror injustice, replacing one bloodthirstiness with another. The narrator specifically describes the self-appointed Tribunal as "unjust" (300). Many crimes in this book are punished, but not through official channels. As we have seen, this is true in much of Dickens' fiction, where public institutions rarely succeed in being just. Dickens wants a regime that combines a sense of justice with a sense of mercy, but under these requirements it is difficult to assign authority to punish. Christ recommended forgiving of offenders and advised turning the other cheek. Thus individual Christians must not exact justice. But if the unfeeling, mechanical, even corrupt state is unqualified to dispense justice, who has the moral right and the power and means to do so?

Like Carlyle and Ruskin, Dickens assumed that true justice is administered finally by providence. That does not mean that most offenses are not punished through human agency, but that the guiding power for such justice is divine. Human beings generate their deserts through their conduct and, in that sense, all punishments are self-begotten. Most of Dickens' novels focus on punishing offenses or patterns of offense in specific institutions or individuals. But *A Tale of Two Cities* emphasizes the fates of nations rather than of individuals. Because history does not forgive, there is very little discussion of forgiveness, or even pardon or mercy, in this novel, which is overwhelmingly occupied with illustrating the consequences of unwise, unjust, and inhuman behavior.[2]

Perhaps to convey a greater sense of the tragic dimensions of the French Revolution, the novel says little about providence, but a good deal about fate and destiny. At the outset of *A Tale of Two Cities* the narrator remarks that many years before the Revolution Fate had already marked the trees that would be used to construct the guillotine (2). Madame Defarge, knitting the names of those who are to be consigned to death when the Revolution begins, works "with the steadfastness of Fate" (106), suggesting an analogy with the Greek fates who spun, measured, and cut the threads of human life. Learning that Darnay/St. Evrémonde has married Lucie Manette in England, Defarge hopes that for Lucie's sake "Destiny will keep her husband out of France" (176).

This concern for the determining power of fate is reflected in the narrator's manner, for he regularly offers confident forecasts of what is to come. Partly this is because he is telling a story whose end—the French Revolution—is in the past and thus already known to his audience. There can be no suspense about the outcome of public events. But the narrator's many proleptic passages also confirm the rigidity of the events being related. Repetition of the motif clusters of wine/blood/stain and of hastening footsteps gathering into a crowd, along with direct forecasts by the narrator ("The time was to come, when that wine [blood] too would be spilled on the street stones, and when the stain of it would be red upon many there" [28]), enhance the foreknown events in an operatic manner, like the destiny motif running through Verdi's *La Forza del Destino,* or any of the value-laden motifs that accompany and foreshadow events in Wagner's operas.

But if these and other direct forecasts of what is to come suggest a known, predictable world, a second powerful tendency of the narrative is to insist upon the mystery that is within us. Despite the many indications that life is plotted by fate, in fact not all of these signs are accurate or trustworthy. Madame Defarge does not control the destinies of others, but is herself only part of a larger force. Madame Defarge points her finger "as if it were the finger of Fate" at Lucie's child, but the implied doom never comes to pass (253). The resurrection theme in the novel is intimately related to its "psychological" kernel, but it is also linked by its overt Christian association with the idea of forgiveness and redemption. Human sympathy is the amulet by which the charmed doors of the mind and heart can be reopened. When Lucie first succeeds in penetrating the muddle of her father's mind to touch his heart, he sobs tempestuously then yields "to the calm that must follow all storms—emblem to humanity, of the rest and silence into which the storm called Life must hush at last" (45). Dr. Manette is himself emblematic of the mystery that all humans are to one another. In his confused state following his release after more than seventeen years of imprisonment, "No human intelligence could read the mysteries of his mind in the scared blank wonder of his face" (46).

The narrator candidly announces this theme of the mysterious self at the opening of chapter 3.

> A wonderful fact to reflect upon, that every human creature is constituted to be that profound secret and mystery to every other. A sol-

emn consideration, when I enter a great city by night, that every one of those darkly clustered houses encloses its own secret; that every room in every one of them encloses its own secret; that every beating heart in the hundreds of thousands of breasts there, is, in some of its imaginings, a secret to the heart nearest it![3]

This is the inescapable condition of humanity; all efforts to fathom those nearest us are frustrated and ended by death. "In any of the burial-places of this city through which I pass, is there a sleeper more inscrutable than its busy inhabitants are, in their innermost personality to me, or that I am to them?" (10). Mystery and secrecy, as we have seen, are constant elements in Dickens' novels, but whereas in the earlier novels secrets generally have to do with concealed plots, unknown lineages, and so on, in the later novels secrets are just as often connected with internal states. The shift in this direction probably begins with *Dombey,* a pivotal novel in so many ways. In *A Tale of Two Cities,* personal and public secrets are intertwined and mysteries of the human heart are played out in public venues. In this novel as in others, secrecy is associated with suffering, death, and burial. But just as Dr. Manette, in being recalled to life from his "burial" in prison, becomes the embodied expression of a long-kept secret, so a major theme of the novel is that one way to counteract the power of death is through bringing to light the secrets within us, rooted as they are in suffering. This theme is related to Dickens' broader view that we must treasure memory—both good and bad—because out of memories come our resources for encountering the difficult experiences of life. In *A Tale of Two Cities,* secret memories are both private and communal. The communal "secrets" are already known to the reader because they are part of historical record, but the private secrets remain a mystery until the narrative exposes them to light. Thus, while the public narrative moves unswervingly toward its foreknown denoument, an accompanying narrative line presents a sequence of secrets gradually exposed to reveal the dark and bright elements harbored within human nature.

Mr. Lorry's suggestion to Dr. Manette that he might be able to defend himself against relapses in his mental health by sharing his secret with someone else is a straightforward version of Dickens' belief that the secrets of the heart may become useful when faced and shared. That which is repressed, that from which we unconsciously avert our gaze, only increases its power by being ignored. This is true in the history of nations as well as of individuals. The narrative, by temporally dislocating the order of its revelations, subtly indicates how complicated and insidious the perpetuation of evil can be, through the failure to face the secrets of the past. When Charles Darnay is arrested and "buried," "in secret," he both duplicates and anticipates Dr. Manette's history. Although Charles' confinement comes much later chronologically in the *fabula* of the novel, it is presented first in the *sjuzet.* Only after Charles' incarceration do we learn the details of Dr. Manette's unjust confinement by the St. Evrémonde brothers. Charles' imprisonment is a foreshadowing of the secret we will soon learn, and hence readable as a prolepsis or even a prophecy, but because it foreshadows a past event, it is also readable as an analepsis or recurrence, teaching us that history will rerun its scenarios until they are comprehended and consciously engaged. The two imprisonments are intimately linked. Dr, Manette recovers his full capacities in working to free his son-in-law. "For the first time the Doctor felt, now, that his suffering was strength and power" (257). His suffering having been made public, he is endowed with a productive strength that repression could never produce. Ironically, Dr. Manette is actually operating against his own scripting of history, but that revelation has yet to be made. At this point, what is important is the suggestion that torment can be transformed into triumph and that pain may be the agent of beneficial transformation.

The disclosure of our secrets is not always safe or constructive. The secret that the Doctor has himself deeply repressed comes to light and recondemns Charles to death. In the depths of his agony, Dr. Manette put in writing his curse on the whole St. Evrémonde family and now that curse has its effect. Like a pre-scripted fate, Dr. Manette's version of history now becomes the official text that the revolutionaries are determined to play out. Nested in this lesson on repression and revelation, suffering and salvation, is an even more basic moral ground. Hatred, rage, and vindictiveness are not the emotions that will improve human conditions. When hatred answers hatred, only more evil will be propagated in the world. Dr. Manette's cry for universal revenge against the entire family of his oppressors is as unjust as their behavior, and predictably begets additional suffering upon the victim who has become transgressor in his turn. In this way it reflects at the personal level what occurs at the public level with the violence of the revolutionaries. There are good and bad secrets in our hearts and we must learn to understand them ourselves and face them. Lucie's heart is "a mystery" to Dr. Manette, but it is clear to everyone that it is a benign mystery (128). So certain is Carton of the benignity of that heart that he wants "the last confidence of [his] life" to repose in Lucie's "pure and innocent breast" to be shared by no one else (145). This is the holy secret of another being's unselfish love.[4] Moreover, it is this love for Lucie that prompts Carton to look into "the mystery of [his] own wretched heart," and by facing its darknesses wrest from them a final shining victory (143).

Madame Defarge is the focus of error in *A Tale of Two Cities*, embodying the worst of human impulses and turning even apparent virtues into crimes. She is contrasted particularly with the Manettes, but with Darnay as well. If Madame Defarge's threads represent a terrible future, worked to its design out of the past and present, Lucie is herself "the golden thread" that unites her father's past and present over the gulf of his suppressed misery (74). And just as Lucie is the constructive force whose secret is a loving heart, so the secret in Madame Defarge's heart is an unforgiving hatred and a claim for revenge against all of the St. Evrémonde family. Dr. Manette has excluded Charles from his enmity—a form of forgiveness—but Madame Defarge has brooded on her injury until it has become a need for personal retribution. Her secret, saved until the last moment, is that the peasant family devastated by the St. Evrémonde brothers' cruelty was her family. As long as Madame Defarge labors for the oppressed she is triumphant and safe, but the moment she takes justice into her own hands she puts herself at risk, and in trying to injure Lucie and her daughter she destroys herself with her own weapon. Madame Defarge begins with a private family purpose and extends it to a public and "historical" dimension. By contrast, Lucie recovers her father, a figure publicly symbolizing historical oppression, and returns him to a rehabilitating domestic sanctuary. Lucie's love is opposed to Madame Defarge's hatred, and signifies the power of individual human effort to change events. Her golden thread is the bright line running through Madame Defarge's woven fate, and it can unravel at least a portion of that suggested destiny.

Describing the ambiguous behavior of the prisoners condemned by the revolutionary tribunal, the narrator offers a comment on human psychology that is closely related to this theme of secrecy and strength.

> Similarly, though with a subtle difference, a species of fervour or intoxication, known, without doubt, to have led some persons to brave the guillotine unnecessarily, and to die by it, was not mere boastfulness, but a wild infection of the wildly shaken public mind. In seasons of pestilence, some of us will have a secret attraction to the disease—a terrible passing inclination to die of it. And all of us have like wonders hidden in our breasts, only needing circumstances to evoke them. (267–68)

We all have mysterious, even dangerous and self-destructive impulses within us, but these must be brought to light and understood. The longer they remain repressed the more dangerous they become. Dr. Manette gradually comes to realize this and transforms suffering into active, positive power; Madame Defarge does not and enjoys letting her dark urges fester in her heart until, when freed, the tigerish impulses destroy her. But perhaps Carton is the most complex example of this process. He has resigned himself to a life of slow self-destruction, an undignified and fatal dissipation, until he meets Lucie. Her own goodness and the thoughts she inspires lead Carton to explore the mystery of his heart. Recognizing its treacherous features, Carton is nonetheless able to retrieve from all of its error one shining truth of love that matures into a stunning act of generous self-sacrifice. Carton's self-recovery is also an act of self-forgiveness; he has permitted himself to be the good man he previously could not believe in.

A Tale of Two Cities is, then, a history of individual secrets and their disclosures in the context of the permanent mystery of the human heart, but it is also a history of two nations in a specific period of chronological time. In this history, as I have already noted, there are no secrets because the major events are foreknown.

Yet this larger movement of the story is intimately related to the movement of individual careers.

The greatest historical guilt rests with the French aristocracy. The most obvious thing about them in this novel is that they are self-indulgent, arrogant, exploitive, and unjust. They cringe before their superiors and lord it over their inferiors. At the Monseigneur's reception in Paris there is an elegant turnout of court hangers-on. The narrator observes "that all the company at the grand hotel of Monseigneur were perfectly dressed. If the Day of Judgment had only been ascertained to be a dress day, everybody there would have been eternally correct" (101). But the whole point about Judgment Day is that all external ornament, all disguise, will be put aside and each individual will answer for his or her behavior. For most individuals some mercy will be required, since we are all fallible and likely to have some maculations to be forgiven and expunged. But the French aristocracy of *A Tale of Two Cities* has, as a class, institutionalized injustice and will have a heavy debt of guilt to pay. The narrator provides a sample of this behavior in the Marquis St. Evrémonde as he leaves the Monseigneur's party in a foul mood. The marquis urges his coachman to make speed, and, as a consequence, the coach runs down a child in the street. The marquis reprimands the poor people in the street for not being able to tend their children and is more worried about his horses than about the child. He throws the child's distraught parent a coin as a compensation for his loss. This callous behavior is emblematic because it manifests two central abominations in Dickens' moral economy— violation of family feeling, especially when focused upon a child, and the transformation of human values into monetary terms. When he arrives back at his estate the marquis is equally callous and arrogant toward his own tenants. He refuses to provide a simple marker for the grave of a woman's dead husband.

The marquis' actions offer representative and concrete examples of abuses by the French aristocracy. They are narrated in a manner calculated to excite common human sympathies, the narrator's method of weighting his plot toward retribution. But the accumulating burden of guilt is historical, not merely national. France may be a hell of injustice and cruelty, but England is not much better. "In England," the narrator remarks, "there was scarcely an amount of order and protection to justify much national boasting" (2). Even minor crimes were punished in a vicious and bloody manner and the kings of the time "carried their divine rights with a high hand" (3). Brutal and often fatal punishment took the place of any attempt to alleviate the conditions of the poor. The Old Bailey provided no better justice than the French system. The ogreish audience at Charles Darnay's trial finds him an object of interest because, if convicted, he will be drawn and quartered. The narrator comments that "putting to death was a recipe much in vogue with all trades and professions. . . . Not that it did the least good in the way of prevention—it might almost have been worth remarking that the fact was exactly the reverse—but, it cleared off (as to this world) the trouble of each particular case, and left nothing else connected with it to be looked after" (50).

And yet putting to death does not clear away the midden of accumulating social guilt. Putting to death is a public way of trying to forget. With the offender dead and buried, one may forget the occasion of the crime. One need not remember that a man stole a loaf of bread because he was hungry or pinched clothing from a line to sell for food because he had no means of employment. However, it is just as unhealthy for nations to suppress their memories, to turn their eyes away from suffering, as it is for individuals. Thus in the St. Antoine neighborhood in Paris where the Defarges have their wine shop, hunger is everywhere evident, indirectly attributable to neglect by the nation's ruling class. But this treatment has its consequences. "In the hunted air of the people there was yet some wild-beast thought of the possibility of turning at bay. Depressed and slinking though they were, eyes of fire were not wanting among them; nor compressed lips, white with what they suppressed; nor foreheads knitted into the likeness of the gallows-rope they mused about enduring, or inflicting" (29). A social evil may be repressed and forgotten, but as with the psychological operation of individuals, it will eventually find release and express itself all the more forcefully for having been so long held back.[5] The murder of the marquis is an individual event, but again symptomatic of what awaits his class when the hidden rage of the populace breaks into the open. Madame Defarge understands when she declares, "'Vengeance and retribution require a long time; it is the rule'" (170). A. O. J. Cockshut remarks that, perhaps influenced by Carlyle, Dickens treated the mobs in *A Tale of Two Cities* differently from those in *Barnaby Rudge*. The latter were "endowed with no serious meaning." By contrast the "Paris crowd is, from the start, an irresistible social force produced by inexorable causes."[6]

Madame Defarge alludes to the moral rule that evil brings its own consequences, a rule that was for Dickens a natural process as well. Thus the narrator uses images of such natural forces as storms and rising seas to describe the approach of the Revolution. As one sows so must one reap, the narrator suggests, elaborating the maxim when he explains that French aristocracy and British orthodoxy alike talk of "this terrible Revolution as if it were the one only harvest ever known under the skies that had not been sown—as if nothing had ever been done, or omitted to be done, that had led to it—as if observers of the wretched millions in France, and of the misused and perverted resources that should have made them prosperous had not seen it inevitably coming, years before, and had not in plain words recorded what they saw" (226).

And so the Revolution occurs. Secret hatred breaks into sight, becoming a kind of madness. The woman known as Vengeance typifies the unthinking violence of those who have broken from their repression with no constructive plan. They can only glory in the destruction of a power that once kept them "underground." Violent response to injustice, however, is not the answer, as Trotty Veck acknowledges in *The Chimes*. If it is not possible to pardon the outrages of the past, an individual or a people must not commit the equal error of perpetuating similar outrages in the present. The links or threads of act and consequence will in this case only fashion a continuing web of violence and retribution. Set against such a determinant sequence is the golden thread of love, forgiveness, and mercy embodied in Lucie Manette.

The connection between national and individual repression is focused in the St. Evrémondes' case. They rape a peasant girl and murder her brother. The St. Evrémonde brothers are humiliated not by the dastardly nature of these intimate crimes, but because the peasant boy dared to struggle against his oppressors on equal terms. It is to keep this embarrassing information secret that the aristocrats have Manette abducted and "buried alive." As witness to the truth, he becomes the memory they want suppressed, the secret they want hidden. But in Dickens' just universe the truth cannot be so easily concealed. The St. Evrémonde story comes to light in Charles Darnay's second trial and threatens to carry retribution to an extreme by destroying an innocent member of the family, just as the Revolution has gone to excess in slaughtering many innocent persons. Having renounced his aristocratic heritage, Darnay has immigrated to England where he lives by his own labor and is powerless to fulfill his mother's wishes, who, before her death, importuned him "to have mercy and to redress" the sins of his relatives (117). But Darnay does not know the secret crime that he is charged to redress. He inherits this secret responsibility as he inherits the name St. Evrémonde, but if he can divest himself of his name and his worldly inheritance, he cannot separate himself from his family history. When he later returns to France, he unknowingly plays two roles, though he is unaware of the private one. He hopes that he can do "something to stay bloodshed, and assert the claims of mercy and humanity," and imagines that he might have "some influence to guide this raging Revolution that was running so fearfully wild" (231–32). But his true name is a stigma dooming him to generic retribution no matter how much he has tried to renounce the abuses it represents. It appears that Darnay will unconsciously comply with his mother's appeal, redressing family derelictions with his life. National and personal patterns of trespass and retribution are made explicit with Madame Defarge's revelation of her personal stake in punishing the St. Evrémonde family.

Madame Defarge is the sister of the raped girl and murdered boy. Her whole involvement in the revolutionary cause has been fueled less by an abstract desire for justice and social progress than by a secret personal hatred, a craving toward private revenge. Madame Defarge is the reverse image of Darnay, just as she is of Lucie. Seeking to be just and to expunge the guilt of his class, Darnay is unaware of his own intimate involvement in a central, representative crime. By contrast, Madame Defarge's apparent concern for her class masks a private vendetta spurring her to public action. Ironically Madame Defarge, who has labored at bringing a specific destiny into being, dies "accidentally" by her own weapon when she struggles with Miss Pross in an effort to get at Lucie and her child. Dickens was fully conscious of the implicit moral balance he wished to achieve by this outcome, defending the use of accident in fiction generally, and specifically in the scene of Madame Defarge's death. "Where the accident is inseparable from the passion and action of the character; where it is strictly consistent with the entire design, and arises out of some culminating proceeding on the part of the individual which the whole story has led up to; it seems to me to become, as it were, an act of divine justice." Dickens adds that he purposely used the "half-comic intervention" of Miss Pross to emphasize the angry woman's failure and to contrast her mean death to a desperate but bold death in the streets. Madame Defarge's "mean death" is also opposed "to the dignity of Carton's."[7]

A Tale of Two Cities is a story of guilt and retribution, with retribution as its energizing core. While the narrative demonstrates that retribution operates at a historical as well as personal level, so that nations will eventually suffer for their crimes as individuals do, it must also denounce a retribution brought about by individuals motivated by hatred, vengeance, spite, and other unchristian emotions. The great grindstone used to sharpen the weapons of the revolutionaries provides one major symbol of the public nature of this bloody error. J. M. Rignall is wrong, I think, to assert that the grindstone scene demonstrates Dickens' impulse to solve violence with violence (579–80). The scene is very repulsive and surely Dickens intended it to evoke revulsion rather than gratification.

By incorporating fictional private histories, containing secrets to be disclosed through the narrative's progress within the larger historical, and thus known, story of the French Revolution—which contains no secrets about its development—the narrator can establish a tension between two ways of viewing justice in the universe in a manner that resembles the narrative strategy of *Bleak House,* where the more personal and private outlook is chiefly provided by Esther and the general and social by the third-person narrator. The great events that we describe as historical are governed by providence, or by fate, in the sense that implies inevitability. An unjust ruling class will inevitably suffer punishment for its conduct. At the personal level individuals are free to make crucial moral decisions that might bind them to or free them from "destiny," which is to say the evil consequences of bad acts. By choosing pardon, mercy, or forgiveness, individuals can break the chain of crime and revenge that leads to greater and greater suffering. If the grindstone is a symbol of the unthinking viciousness of rebellion, the guillotine is a symbol of its false justice. But even that symbol can be transformed. The positive power to transform symbols is at the heart of Sydney Carton's crowning act. Like all thoughtful human beings, Carton is something of a mystery to himself, and certainly he is a mystery to others, who cannot understand the waste he has made of his life. Carton is as he is partly because he can establish no clear identity for himself. He sinks his own identity into Stryver's work. He casually saves Darnay's life by calling attention to their apparent interchangeability. The one way he has of anchoring his nature is by the secret buried alive in his heart—his love for Lucie. But this, too, he shares with Darnay. Carton represents lack of initiative, whereas Darnay is all conscientious effort. But in the most dissipated among us, if only they have faith in some enduring belief or feeling, the power of transformation, or resurrection, as the language of the novel would have it, remains. He can *become* Charles Darnay. There is an oddly ceremonial quality to his rescue. The necessarily realistic change of clothes also resembles an investiture through which Carton assumes a phatic role among the condemned prisoners. By assuming Darnay's identity while retaining his own character, Carton divests himself of his worst self. His private secret of love for Lucie becomes the public secret of his disguise. The mystery of his nature becomes the sacrament of his act. As he mounts to the guillotine, this symbol of dreadful rage and revenge is transformed to a symbol of love. By Carton's act it comes to resemble Christ's cross; his death is an atonement reflecting the great Atonement that makes existence possible in a world complicated by evil destinies. Carton's act involves not only self-forgiveness but forgiveness for the violence that men do to one another. The great public crime of the Terror begets the great private sacrifice and redemption betokening love.[8]

If individuals can govern their own moral destinies, they are not therefore utterly free. National and personal histories not only resemble one another, they are inevitably intertwined, though not necessarily so melodramatically as in the case of Madame Defarge. The wood sawyer, as a figure associated both with the brutality of the French aristocracy and the violence of the revolutionaries, indicates that much human activity is thoughtless and habitual, easily guided by interested forces. To a degree, he represents the unalterable forces of destiny. But the very fact that such a destiny should be embodied in an individual human being suggests that deterministic forces are not inescapable after all. Roads are similarly important in this narrative. Like linear time, roads go from one locus to another. Lorry is carrying Lucie from Dover to Paris to accomplish a certain "destiny." But the very route that Lorry takes to enfranchise Dr. Manette later becomes the road that Charles Darnay takes toward freedom from revolutionary reprisal. The road of history may be reversed. The linear movement along a predetermined route may be altered and the new road may lead to freedom, not imprisonment.[9]

Another interesting feature of this novel emphasizes the role of analogous narratives embedded within the larger narrative. The narrator's task is to indicate the differences between historical and personal "fates," and to suggest how experience may be read to reveal the secrets of human destiny and to therefore change that destiny for the better. One way for the narrator to educate his characters and readers is to indicate by way of embedded narratives what might be expected in the main narrative, as Christ's parables illustrate his larger message. When Mr. Lorry meets Lucie at Dover to escort her to France, he tells her "the story of one of our customers" (20). This is an account of her unnamed father's circumstances, designed to prepare her for the revelation that he is alive. Dickens and other Victorian novelists frequently used this and similar devices, having characters break good or bad news gradually to their audiences, and so such an instance is not remarkable. Later an analogous tale prepares the reader for events to come in the same way that Lorry has prepared Lucie, though not so openly. Darnay recounts an anecdote about a prisoner in the Tower of London who had hidden a document in his cell that was later unearthed. Dr. Manette's response, and other clues, suggest that Dr. Manette knows of a similar case. Of course Darnay's anecdote, which does not mention the contents of the recovered documents, foreshadows Dr. Manette's hidden account, recovered by Defarge, describing the primal transgression that generates all of the events that follow. Dr. Manette's narrative is itself an analogue of the larger history of France—the suppression ('burying') of truth by the aristocracy to ensure the continuance of its own privileges.

This narrative device operates at a subordinate level as well. Thus in the embedded narrative about the historically real Foulon, the people are told that this rich speculator, supposed dead, has been found alive and brought back for execution. He had "caused himself to be represented as dead, and had a grand mock-funeral" to deceive the people whom he feared (212). This factual incident connects with the personal and fictional part of the narrative by preparing for the revelation about Roger Cly's false funeral. Revelation of Cly's ruse puts John Barsett in Carton's power, enabling him to carry out the rescue—the return to life—of the doomed Charles Darnay.

These narratives within the narrative and other anticipatory methods, such as the reiterated theme of approaching footsteps, create a predictive, proleptic effect very like that of statements in which the narrator openly anticipates the future. Such proleptic references seem to endorse a world of inevitable unfoldings where what will be is already existent, as though the future were foreknown and therefore already history. But these various forms of foreshadowing are transformed into a positive rather than pessimistically determinist version of anticipation when, at the conclusion of the novel, the narrator relates what Sydney Carton's words on his way to execution would have been ("and they were prophetic") if he had uttered them. Carton's conjectured story tells what the future will bring both for the individuals he loves and for England and France. The narrative that Carton projects into the future ends with Lucie's son telling Carton's story to his son. So the narrative we have just read becomes, at its conclusion, a story of a time gone by but made ever present by retelling, just as Carton's life, at the moment it ends, becomes an exemplary story worthy of being repeated.[10] Moreover, both Carton's story and Dickens' novel count on the instructive redundancy of frequent repetition to make memorable the errors of the past and the virtues of those who struggled against them. In letting Carton tell the story of the beneficent future, the narrator endorses his own task, for his novel is the calling to life of a communal memory, and its account of individuals who suffered intensely is designed to touch the heart and make it alive to injustice in its own day, much in the way the Christmas ghosts use the past and the future to revive Scrooge's heart. Only the wicked or foolish wish to forget. Even those like Clemency Newcome in *The Battle of Life,* who defend the maxim "Forgive and Forget," do not really mean to obliterate memory, but to forget the injury. Memory of good and bad, as *The Haunted Man* makes clear, is necessary to our very humanity. Unresolved suffering or injustice must be recalled, faced, and transformed into strength in nations as in individual human beings. Narratives can help us to do this; they can capture in a memorable form the moral energies that help us to understand the secrets of the human heart, and those great rules by which Dickens believed mankind was governed, rules ensuring that, in time, retribution comes to all who transgress and victory to all who suffer. This was Dickens' great hope and the moral foundation for the stories he told.

NOTES

1. Charles Dickens, *A Tale of Two Cities* (New York: Oxford University Press, 1967), 55.

2. W. H. Auden's "Spain" says "History to the defeated may say /Alas but cannot help or pardon" (*The Collected Poems of W. H. Auden* [New York: Random House, 1945], 185).

3. There has been a fair amount of discussion about the mystery of self in *A Tale of Two Cities,* but J. M. Rignall comments that, although the novel contains an unusual statement in the first person about the mystery of the self, in fact the characters in the novel prove to be quite knowable ("Dickens and the Catastrophic Continuum of History in *A Tale of Two Cities,*" ELH 51, no. 3 [Fall 1984], 575–87). Subsequent references appear in the text. Rignall makes a good point but forgets that the characters in the novel are knowable to us as readers, not necessarily to the other characters, and that only because we have the advantage of an omniscient narrator to reveal them to us.

4. K. J. Fielding says of *A Tale of Two Cities* that its Christian symbols are "partly parasitical . . . borrowed for a purpose not purely Christian," and that "what is holy in life is shown in terms of romantic love" (*Charles Dickens: A Critical Introduction* [Boston: Houghton Mifflin Co., 1965], 204). But it is Lucie's embodiment of Christian principles, not merely her physical attractiveness, that makes her the object of interest both to Darnay and to Carton.

5. Steven Marcus calls attention to this powerful awareness of repression in *Barnaby Rudge,* where individuals and objects resemble vessels that are likely to explode. These images, he suggests, are drawn from Carlyle's *French Revolution.* For Marcus, Dickens' conception of the novel took shape "in various ideas and images of compression and repression, of fermentation and intoxication, of swellings and explosions and of corrosive anxiety and tenseness stretched to the breaking point. These images, developed in the course of the novel's action, are brought to their consummate expression in the eruption of the riots: in the breaking down of restraints, in drunkenness, fire and general explosive violence" (*Dickens: From Pickwick to Dombey* [New York: Basic Books, Inc., 1965], 206).

6. A. O. J. Cockshut, *The Imagination of Charles Dickens* (New York: New York University Press, 1962), 71.

7. John Forster, *The Life of Charles Dickens* (London: Chapman and Hall, Ltd., 1893), 565. Harvey Peter Sucksmith discusses this passage and the general issue of retribution in Dickens, in *The Narrative Art of Charles Dickens: The Rhetoric of Sympathy and Irony in his Novels* (Oxford: The Clarendon Press, 1970), 238ff.

8. Edgar Johnson says that "Carton's renunciation is a deed of purification and redemption that is at once the consummation of a deeper justice amid the excesses of vengeance called revolutionary justice and a triumphant assertion of the saving and creating power of love" (*Charles Dickens: His Tragedy and Triumph* [Boston: Little, Brown and Co., 1952], 2:981).

9. Andrew Sanders calls attention to the use of roads in this symbolic and almost allegorical manner in *Tale* and in *The French Revolution* in *The Companion to A Tale of Two Cities* (London: Unwin Hyman, 1988), 109. J. M. Rignall regards these parallel carriage scenes as signifying an escape from history and from fiction (578–79).

10. Garrett Stewart offers an exciting and, I feel, convincing reading of Carton's death. He credits the death scene as an extremely significant feature of Dickens' enterprise in the novel. "No novel," he states, "could fasten more surely the always tacit bond between mortality and communicable narration. Carton's dramatized and consummating death scene is displaced into an articulate exemplum discovered at the very moment of his death to be recoverable in the telling, time out of mind. And so the tale recounted by Lucie's son becomes, in short—and of course in its shortened form—the title scene of *The Tale* that earns its closure by foreseeing it" (*Death Sentences: Styles of Dying in British Fiction* [Cambridge: Harvard University Press, 1984], 93).

SEVENTEEN

Great Expectations

DICKENS WROTE three first-person novels. In *David Copperfield* love and mercy overwhelm an impudent but largely personal evil. David himself makes mistakes and undergoes a therapeutic punishment which discloses his underlying innocence. *Bleak House* is thick with the atmosphere of social and personal guilt and employs memorable images and scenes to reinforce the notion that some form of punishment is inevitable for the violation of God's law, and that some form of forgiveness is always available for the repentant. But Esther Summerson, being a paragon, needs no punishment or forgiveness herself; her companion narrative voice is above punishment and forgiveness, like a prophet sure of his jeremiads. The atmosphere is the same in *Great Expectations* (1860–61), but the circumstances are very different. *Great Expectations* is an intriguing narrative because the first-person narrator is a flawed character who must be punished, but he is also a moral center of the text for the distribution of forgiveness. These circumstances call for a story far less comfortable about the separation of good and evil, the imputable and the innocent, and it also requires a peculiar mode of narration.[1]

Great Expectations is intensely moral, but the moral categories have purposely been dislocated. The narrative opens in a graveyard with a gibbet nearby, and soon incorporates a violent act by a grown convict against a young boy. The climate of infraction and punishment is thus established early and associated with the archetypal symbol of eternal judgment (the grave) and the practical symbol of human punishment (the gibbet), so that from the outset we are encouraged to equate, rather than conveniently separate, divine and human law. But the edicts of these two patterns of injunction are not always compatible, as in this instance. By employing threats and fear Magwitch gets Pip to bring him food, drink, and a file, though Pip, like Joe Gargery, is susceptible to softer appeals to charity. In this initial episode, what might otherwise have been an opportunity for Christian charity becomes a crime. In the very season commemorating the birth of the Savior, who instituted a creed based on charity and love, Pip is made to feel guilty for bringing food to a needy creature. Motivated more by anxiety and fear than by benevolence, Pip has to steal food from his own family to satisfy Magwitch's necessities. Since we know very well what sentiments Dickens considered appropriate at the Christmas season, we can easily assume that he fully intended the ironies of this situation, where mercy, compassion, and forgiveness are transformed into crimes. This self-conscious reversal of values is characteristic of the novel as a whole and focuses attention on the problematic nature of guilt and punishment.

Young Pip has a vague sense of Magwitch's guilty situation, as revealed in the images with which he describes the man. Magwitch walks carefully among the graves "as if he were eluding the hands of the dead people, stretching up cautiously out of their graves, to get a twist upon his ankle and pull him in."[2] Magwitch walks off toward the gibbet that once held a pirate and Pip thinks he looks "as if he were the pirate come to life, and come down, and going back to hook himself up again" (5). These images imply a complicated perception of guilt as something consciously aware of its blameable nature, which is both fearful and self-destructive. Later Magwitch risks his own freedom and safety to obtain revenge upon Compeyson, thus oddly and eccentrically placing himself on the side of the law and facilitating the recapture of both men, whereas Pip and Joe, both God-fearing and just persons, cannot help but oppose the law. Pip says, "I treasonably whispered to Joe. 'I hope, Joe, we shan't find them.' And Joe whispered to me, 'I'd give a shilling if they had cut and run, Pip'" (30). Once again conventional expectations about justice and punishment are strangely inflected.

When Magwitch is caught, he accepts responsibility for taking the food and file from the Gargery house, thereby showing a Christian spirit in protecting Pip. Joe in turn replies that they wouldn't have wanted Magwitch to starve and that he was welcome to the food. Thus trespass, charity, and guilt are all entangled and confused in this sequence, as are justice, mercy, law, and punishment. As if to point out how complicated the relationships between divine and human law are, Pip describes the black prison ship lying offshore as "a wicked Noah's ark" (36). This early unconscious knowledge pursues Pip secretly through his life, as the novel's chain motif demonstrates. Links of chains, whether iron or golden, bind Pip to his two false destinies associated with Magwitch and with Estella. Despite all the improvements in his condition, Pip can never escape a sense of affiliation with the guilt associated with crime, though his own fault lies in the realm not of human but of divine law. His guilt, though often reflected in the criminal associations around him, refers to sins against love.[3] There are other confused and mistaken codes in this novel, but surely an important one is the code regarding guilt-innocence/punishment-forgiveness, and it is to this code that I shall confine my remarks.

Pip has, in the opening scenes of the novel, an early opportunity to see how dangerous rash judgments of others can be; he experiences the tangled links of good and evil compressed into an otherwise melodramatic adventure. This awareness of the interpenetration of good and evil remains with him, largely unconsciously, through his youth and early manhood. Both Magwitch and Joe bind Pip with more metaphorical chains than he knows. All of these metaphors and themes, as they relate to the broader significance of the relationship between Pip and Magwitch, culminate in the scene of the old convict's appearance in court.

> The sun was striking in at the great windows of the court, through the glittering drops of rain upon the glass, and it made a broad shaft of light between the two-and-thirty and the Judge, linking both together, and perhaps reminding some among the audience, how both were passing on, with absolute equality, to the greater Judgment that knoweth all things and cannot err. Rising for a moment, a distinct speck of face in this way of light, the prisoner said, 'My Lord, I have received my sentence of Death from the Almighty, but I bow to yours,' and sat down again. (434)

As Magwitch is weakening toward death, Pip reads to him from the New Testament, and as the old man dies peacefully—itself a very good sign as deathbed literature had long confirmed—Pip says, "Mindful, then, of what we had read together, I thought of the two men who went up into the Temple to pray, and I knew there were no better words that I could say beside his bed, than 'O Lord, be merciful to him a sinner!'" (436). Magwitch, conscious of his crimes, may nonetheless at the end be as likely as the Publican to receive forgiveness, whereas the self-righteous Pharisee may not. Magwitch has a conscience of sorts, though the circumstances of his boyhood did not fit him for a Christian way of life. By contrast, Pip's boyhood would seem to have prepared him ideally to become a paragon like Esther Summerson, but there are complications. Mrs. Joe is not heavy on Christian meekness, though she is heavy with her hand and with Tickler, the wax-ended cane used for punishing Pip. She is an unloving, selfish woman, more brutal toward Pip in many ways than is Magwitch, who shows a greater appreciation for the boy. Pip cannot help but think ill of himself, a feeling that is grotesquely exaggerated by the "crime" he is contemplating on Christmas Eve. "Conscience is a dreadful thing when it accuses man or boy," the narrating Pip remarks; "but when in the case of a boy, that secret burden cooperates with another secret burden down the leg of his trousers [his buttered bread], it is (as I can testify) a great punishment" (10). In fact, Pip describes himself in terms appropriate to a criminal; he believes his sister "had some general idea that I was a young offender whom an Accoucheur Policeman had taken up (on my birthday) and delivered over to her, to be dealt with according to the outraged majesty of the law" (20). So the life that included religious instruction, a safe home, and food did not provide an adequate example of Christian practice, despite Joe's powerless generosity. Moreover, religion is used to subordinate Pip and make him grateful to his punitive sister. Uncle Pumblechook applies the parable of the prodigal son to Pip as a cautionary device (23). Ironically, it is through his pursuing the very ends and values fostered by Uncle Pumblechook and seconded by Mrs. Joe that Pip becomes a "prodigal." Though Magwitch is bred in crime and poverty, he redeems himself and performs an act of great charity that nonetheless operates harmfully and masks a selfish purpose. Correspondingly, Pip is bred to virtue and law but deviates from the mandates of sincere affection while aspiring to selfish aims of passion and possessions. In no other Dickens novel are benevolence and transgression so confused and interrelated, even to the degree that they mutate into one another. The anonymous reviewer in the *Atlantic Monthly* was surely correct when he claimed that, in *Great Expectations*, Dickens was seeking the "'soul of goodness in things evil'," but he might have added that he was also seeking the seeds of evil in things good.[4]

Great Expectations is chiefly about true and false affection. At the forge, Pip has examples of authentic feelings in Joe and Biddy and a model of insensitivity and lovelessness in Mrs. Joe. Throughout the novel, Dickens presents, in his customary fashion, many gradations and variations on this love and lovelessness. But for Pip the most striking example is at Satis House, where he becomes infatuated with Estella while at the same time witnessing the waste that misplaced love can make. Moreover, what was once a version of love in Miss Havisham has been transformed into vengefulness. Her aim is to avenge herself on men through Estella, to make them suffer as she suffered. This indiscriminate revenge is clearly unchristian. It ignores Christ's instruction not to return evil for evil and actually converts the highest of human feelings so championed by Christ, love, into a weapon of revenge. This is a total reversal of the teachings Dickens valued, and *Great Expectations* intensifies the outrageousness of Miss Havisham's sin by illustrating the wisdom of Christ's message by showing the consequences of ignoring it. Miss Havisham suffers the natural punishment of her conduct. She has so warped Estella's nature that the young woman can offer her sponsor none of the love she craves. Like the self-tormenting Miss Wade of *Little Dorrit*, Miss Havisham punishes herself in trying to injure others. By entombing herself in her dismal old house and living on spite, she has forfeited many healing influences and become diseased in mind. The punishment she has designed for others comes suffocatingly down upon her, as Pip sympathetically realizes after he has been disillusioned about his own circumstances.

And could I look upon her without compassion, seeing her punishment in the ruin she was, in her profound unfitness for this earth on which she was placed, in the vanity of sorrow which had become a master mania, like the vanity of penitence, the vanity of remorse, the vanity of unworthiness, and other monstrous vanities that have been curses in this world? (378)

By this time, Miss Havisham herself has fully realized the extent of her folly and how it has injured her and many others. She gives Pip a set of ivory tablets with her name written on the first leaf and says, "'If you can ever write under my name, 'I forgive her,' though ever so long after my broken heart is dust—pray do it!'" And Pip replies, "'O Miss Havisham . . . I can do it now. There have been sore mistakes; and my life has been a blind and thankless one; and I want forgiveness and direction far too much, to be bitter with you'" (377). Miss Havisham dies repeating this request for forgiveness and Pip can comply because he has become well acquainted with emotional suffering himself. He has learned to be cautious in his judgments upon others. Having much to forgive, he also has much for which he seeks forgiveness, though his errors and offenses are of a different order of magnitude from Miss Havisham's. Dickens' narrative choices in *Great Expectations* are determined in part by the need to create and satisfy the gestures of forgiveness that represent the underlying ideology of the text. Secrets and disclosures depend upon episodes of forgiveness. Love and charity, having been converted into their opposites, must, at critical junctures in the narrative structure, be redeemed to their proper roles.

If Miss Havisham's apparent generosity is revenge scarcely veiled, Magwitch's munificence is also a form of revenge, because he aims to get back at the society that made and then condemned him by creating a gentleman of his own. Thus Pip and Estella are both pawns in a game played out by injured parties trying, in misguided fashion, to even the score, thereby spoiling everyone's lives to some degree by giving free rein to a vindictive spirit. Of course Magwitch's case is very different from Miss Havisham's, but their careers parallel one another. And proof that Magwitch is not fully rehabilitated is his final execution of "justice" upon Compeyson. Of course, he too must "pay." But in the time before he is called away, he has an opportunity to draw closer to repentance (easier, of course, once Compeyson is dead), and he dies with Pip speaking Christ's words over him, asking mercy.

Estella is brought up without regard to expense, but she is confined, even in a sense imprisoned, for much of her youth in Satis House. Pip's case may seem different, but it is not. I have already mentioned that the chain metaphor keeps him linked to Magwitch, and he is as much a prisoner as Estella. His association with Jaggers' office and chambers, and his constant connection with crime and confinement culminate in Pip's visit to Newgate, when he himself "is consumed the whole time in thinking how strange it was that I should be encompassed by all this taint of prison and crime" from childhood on (249). And it is no accident that he should just have left Newgate to meet Estella, his fellow metaphorical prisoner, though at the moment he can only contrast the beautiful, proud, refined young woman with all that the prison represents. Soon enough he will learn that she is as deeply related to all that the prison signifies as he is—more so, for whereas he can shake the Newgate dust off, she has Newgate in her blood. The interjacence and transference of elegance and sordidness, of cold beauty and criminal passion, is another example in another thematic register of Dickens' consistent perplexing of good and evil in this novel.

The pattern of revenge displacing better emotions is played out again and again at different levels; one notable variation is the case of Mrs. Joe. The converting of virtues into abuses constitutes the central reason for punishment in the novel, self-inflicted or otherwise. Mrs. Joe is a simple example. The charity of assuming responsibility for the orphaned Pip becomes a workhouse experience for Pip, as though the "charity" were a bureaucratic means of displacing the security and comfort of the hearth and of life itself. We have already seen that Mrs. Joe is an unloving woman, but that trait is made worse by her transforming of charity into punishment. Her own punishment is to be brutally beaten into a mute and humbled condition. The weapon is a convict's leg-iron filed asunder. This detail signifies many things in the design of the novel, but one reading of it is cautionary. Our chief example of Mrs. Joe's mistreatment of Pip is associated with the memorable Christmas Eve on which he helps Magwitch. The leg-iron resembles the ghosts, spirits, and haunts Dickens liked to use, especially in the Christmas narratives, to alter the frozen hearts of unloving creatures. And this visitation, even if it is at the hands of the thoroughly repugnant Dolge Orlick, nonetheless has the effect of teaching Mrs. Joe about her own errors. At the approach of death, she asks Biddy to help her put her arms around Joe's neck, then rests her head upon his shoulder. "And so she presently said 'Joe' again, and once Pardon,' and once 'Pip'" (269).

Mrs. Joe's case shows how dramatically one may be punished for one's behavior, and though it is simply Orlick taking revenge on his master's shrewish wife, his act signifies much more. For Orlick is an unwitting agent of justice, and Mrs. Joe's asking forgiveness of Joe shows that she has learned something of the sort.[5] Swinburne was puzzled by Dickens' lenience toward Orlick, complaining that "he alone could have eluded condemnation for so gross an oversight as the escape from retribution of so important a criminal as the 'double murderer and monster' whose baffled or inadequate attempts are enough to make Bill Sikes seem comparatively the gentlest and Jonas Chuzzlewit the most amiable of men" (*Critical Essays*, 22–23). But Orlick's aggression has an oddly purifying effect; he operates as a species of evil conscience. The persons he assaults all deserve some form of correction; he simply carries the reprimands to extremes. Like Thackeray's Becky Sharp, he may be let off easily because he offers a caustic assessment of various forms of smugness. But he is not let off entirely, as Swinburne suggests. He is imprisoned for robbing Mr. Pumblechook's shop and for stuffing the merchant's mouth with seed, a neat retributive act in its own way.

In a peculiar way, Orlick may be seen as the means of Mrs. Joe's salvation. She has been punished not merely for her treatment of Orlick, but for her generally loveless nature. She can no longer actively atone, but she can demonstrate repentance and ask forgiveness, and this is a great deal, especially as it comes, in the Evangelical tradition, just before death. Orlick may be seen as an embodiment of the lower impulses in mankind, by which I mean the selfish and violent impulses. Thus he is associated with the selfishness and violence in Magwitch by way of the leg-iron, and he is related to Miss Havisham's aggressive selfishness by serving as her porter, his room there looking "like a cage for a human dormouse" (220). It is not much of a surprise, then, that Orlick should also play an important vengeful role in Pip's life, a role that almost ends that life. Appropriately, Orlick takes Pip captive on the marshes in sight of the hulks—the very scene where Pip's involvement with crime, confinement, and selfishness began. Orlick charges Pip with many offenses, but, interestingly, he claims that Pip is responsible for his sister's beating. " 'But it warn't Old Orlick as did it; it was you. You was favoured and he was bullied and beat. Old Orlick bullied and beat, eh? Now you pays for it. You done it; now you pays for it' " (404–5). This is a gross perversion of justice, but there is a queer logic in it. Our post-Freudian age has no difficulty assuming that there might be some truth in Orlick's claim, though not quite as Orlick sees it, for we have certainly seen that Pip had a grievance against his sister, that he charged her with freely beating him, and so it would not be surprising for him to harbor unconscious impulses of destruction toward her. In some remote and symbolic way, the authorial Pip's narrative assembling of these events—the linking of Tickler, convict, leg-iron, and Orlick—does permit him the abstract opportunity to punish Mrs. Joe, though Old Orlick is the vehicle of his wrath. Pip has a similar grievance against Miss Havisham. Is it so strange that, although he forgives her his many injuries, only moments later she is engulfed in flames and dies? Pip's own burnt hands almost signify a participation in the act—not merely that he tries to save her, but that he is intimately present at a retributive scene.[6] And is it so strange that another benevolent offender, Magwitch, should die under Pip's eyes, to go to his judgment with Pip's plea for mercy to the convict on his lips? Julian Moynahan has called attention to how dangerous an individual Pip seems to be, since so many persons closely associated with him come to harm (160). Whether we regard the phenomenon as a manifestation of an unconscious or conscious craving to punish on the part of Dickens or his narrator, the fact remains that those who injure Pip do suffer retribution, not at his hands, but often under his gaze. This pattern is in keeping with Dickens' need to see justice done in his narratives while not implicating his good characters in retributive acts.

But if the narrator who presents these retributive scenes may covertly gain satisfaction from them and establish them as important termini for the threads of his narrative, there is also building throughout the novel a pressure that will result in repentance, confession, and an appeal to forgiveness on the part of Pip. I have already mentioned the affiliations with crime and imprisonment that associate Pip with transgression and guilt. But there are subtler ways we gradually perceive the accumulating weight of his bad conscience. At one point Pip pauses, in spite of himself, to consider his position.

> As I had grown accustomed to my expectations, I had insensibly begun to notice their effect upon myself and those around me. Their influence on my own character I disguised from my recognition as much as possible, but I knew very well that it was not all good. I lived in a state of chronic uneasiness respecting my behaviour to Joe. My conscience was not by any means comfortable about Biddy. (258)

Earlier he had been driven by a sense of "repentance" to visit his hometown and stay with Joe (213). Coincidentally, on this trip he encounters the convict who had delivered the first gift from Magwitch. This association of Pip's moral uneasiness and the true source of his expectations, though unknown to him at the time (but known to the narrator in narrating time), feeds the growing tension in the narrative, intensifying the mystery and increasing the sense of some accumulating "debt." It is entirely fitting that one response to his sense of being corrupted by his expectations (and he cannot forget that Jaggers has predicted, "Of course you'll go wrong somehow . . ." [160]) is to try to put his and Herbert's finances in order and reorganize their lives. He even engages in some compensatory charity, becoming Herbert's secret benefactor, a genuine gesture of affection and generosity in contrast to the more problematic secret source of his own comfortable position. Secret benefaction has dubious merit throughout the novel. Jaggers has secretly conveyed Estella into Miss Havisham's keeping—a kindly act that has negative consequences. Magwitch secretly provides for Pip to the misfortune of both. Set against such hidden assistance is falsely claimed sponsorship. Uncle Pumblechook offensively boasts of his friendship to young Pip, and Miss Havisham lets him believe that she is his benefactor. In this atmosphere of redundant and tainted "charity," Pip's secret arrangement to find Herbert honest work stands out as an authentic gesture, even though it mimicks these other corrupted versions of benevolence. In his working notes Dickens stressed this, and he makes it explicit in the finished story. He instructed himself about Pip's charity to Herbert: "The one good thing he did in his prosperity, the only thing that endures and bears fruit."[7] In keeping with the moral economy of the novel, Pip's salvation is brought about through this untainted act of generosity, for he will humbly assume the position of clerk for the company in which Herbert has become a partner.

There are many large and small instances suggesting the relationship between economics and moral worth throughout this narrative so heavily charged with penitential language.[8] For example, Pip acquires an unnecessary servant more to indicate his status than to ease his life. And this show of vanity brings its immediate punishment. "I had got on so fast of late, that I had even started a boy in boots—top boots—in bondage and slavery to whom I might be said to pass my days." He has to find the boy a little to do and a great deal to eat, and so the boy becomes an "avenging phantom" that haunts him (206–7). Through Dickens' customary device of creating a real abstraction out of a metaphorical reality, the boy is soon denominated the Avenger. This is only one small instance of how numerous individual strands accumulate to establish Pip's moral indebtedness. What is interesting about his case is that he is morally sound enough to recognize that he is, in a vague manner, going wrong, for he is conscious *at the time* (not merely in later recounting) of his unwise conduct.

Pip is able to struggle against his failing in this direction just as he is able to recognize the folly of his love for Estella. But only the force of events gives him the real opportunity for repentance. After the several disclosures about Magwitch, Miss Havisham, and Estella, and just after Magwitch has died, leaving Pip without the material wealth he had anticipated but laden with moral debt, Pip falls ill. Sudden serious illness—brain fever or something similar—often functioned in Victorian literature as part of a narrative design indicating the humbling passage from error to truth.[9] When Pip revives in promising spring weather, faithful Joe is by his side. After his recovery Pip tells Joe and Biddy, who are now married, that he is going abroad never to rest "until I have worked for the money with which you have kept me out of prison and have sent it to you, don't think, dear Joe and Biddy, that if I could repay it a thousand times over, I suppose I could cancel a farthing of the debt I owe you, or that I would do so if I could" (519). At last Pip has a means of "repaying" both the material and the moral debt he has accumulated, the debt of inadequate affection and gratitude. The money debt is symbolic of his moral state and a concrete method for working out his penance and erasing his obligation. But another version of exculpation is also necessary.

> "And now, though I know you have already done it in your own kind hearts, pray tell me, both, that you forgive me! Pray let me hear you say the words, that I may carry the sound of them away with me, and then I shall be able to believe that you can trust me, and think better of me, in the time to come!"
>
> "Oh, dear old Pip, old chap," said Joe. "God knows as I forgive you, if I have anythink to forgive!" (455).

Significantly, when Pip and Estella meet again at the conclusion of the book there is no need to talk of forgiveness; both have suffered sufficiently to realize by now that neither has the authority to extend the forgiveness each would ask. And since there is genuine affection on both sides now, there is no call for forgiveness, the purpose of which is to restore that feeling to the hearts of men.

Having given a few examples of the many instances of penitential and punitive imagery and theme in *Great Expectations,* I now return to the way consciousness of the larger pattern of punishment and forgiveness present in this text affects narrative method. The story could, of course, be simply and directly told, but a great deal of its interest depends upon the suspense created by withheld information. As first-person narrator after the fact, Pip can reveal as much as he wishes, but it is in the author's interest to sustain mystery as long as possible and always to have some unresolved plot element in reserve until the very end. Thus, even when the major mystery of Pip's benefactor is revealed, there remain the resolutions of other mysteries recent or long-standing, such as the revelation of who attacked Mrs. Joe, what Estella's parentage is, and so forth. Because Dickens believed deeply in the moral responsibility of his calling, he also had to so arrange the narration that its tensions and disclosures would reinforce the principles the novel espouses. Since punishment and forgiveness play a large part in the moral structure of the work, one way to intensify their significance is gradually to let both tendencies accumulate force and then release those forces in close conjunction to one another. Hence Miss Havisham's punishment is clearly summarized and exhibited in the same scene in which she repents and asks for forgiveness, and Magwitch's symbolic trial and statement of punishment is speedily followed by his death and a plea for mercy toward him. Since the novel also emphasizes the inevitable consequences of human behavior, the coincidental release of these energies must, in retrospect, appear logical, something accomplished here by the involuted relationships of all parties concerned.

Great Expectations depends a great deal upon the concepts of justice and injustice.[10] Pip remarks that his sister's treatment of him made him highly sensitive to injustice. He refers to the injustice of undeserved suffering: "I had known, from the time when I could speak, that my sister, in her capricious and violent coercion, was unjust to me" (57). Estella's contemptuous treatment of him introduces a new dimension to this sense of unjust injury. This is injustice of the household, but it is linked to injustice of the state as well. Joe tells Pip that Mrs. Joe is "given to government," by which he means "the government of you and myself" (44). She is the authority in the house and the sole arbiter of punishment. She rules by mood and caprice, not by logic or compassion. In Magwitch's history we see that the same capriciousness can exist in the state's legal system. Compeyson is a gentleman who recruits Magwitch to his criminal purposes, but when they are both brought to trial their treatment is very different. "And when the verdict come, warn't it Compeyson as was recommended to mercy on account of good character and bad company, and giving up all the information he could agen me, and warn't it me as got never a word but Guilty?" (333). Later, what we see of Jaggers' profession indicates that the party who can pay the most for a talented lawyer is likely to have his or her way in court, not the party whose cause is just. Better to have Jaggers than justice on your side.

Dickens has arranged his narrative in such a way that what I shall, for convenience, designate public and domestic scenes alternate with one another to increasingly strange effect.[11] The opening chapters of the novel, though they offer some picture of the Gargery household, are chiefly focused upon the involvement of that household with the escaped convict. I call this block of six chapters a public segment of the narrative. The next few chapters provide a comfortable picture of the domestic activities, mostly pleasant, of Joe, Pip, and Biddy, contrasting immediately with the bizarre household of Satis House. There is no absolute separation of public and domestic, only a kind of tidal movement during which one dominates while traces of the other are present, so that, for example, in the long stretch from chapter 7 to chapter 17, notable reminders of the public world occur, such as the stranger with the file who delivers money to Pip, Pip's fight with Herbert Pocket, and the attack on Mrs. Joe with a leg-iron.

Chapter 18 brings word of Pip's Great Expectations and the flow of the narrative now reverses in the direction of the public world, situated largely in a London mainly characterized by Jaggers' profession and overshadowed by Newgate, though the domestic motif is preserved in the episodes of the Pocket household and of Pip's visit to Wemmick's home in Walworth. In the central portion of the novel, from chapter 27 to chapter 38, a tenuous balance is established between these two domains, the contrast being consciously typified by Pip's strong sense of unlikeness between the Newgate he has just left and the Estella he is going to meet. But with the return of Magwitch in chapter 39, the public world becomes increasingly dominant, with few glimpses of the domestic realm, the only positive such glimpse being Wemmick's marriage to Miss Skiffins, an important contrast to the constantly delayed marriage of Herbert and Clara and to the arranged marriage of Estella and Bentley Drummle, himself a real denizen of the public world, as Jaggers sees at once.

But if these two worlds at first appear to be separate, perhaps even polar opposites, a little examination proves them to be elaborately intertwined. Estella is not an embodiment of a happy household, but the daughter of a convict. The hearth is no haven for Pip, not only because of Mrs. Joe, but also because it housed (perhaps spawned) Dolge Orlick. Its tools appear time and again as reminders of its intimate connection with trespass. Satis House represents the violation of almost all domestic virtues and is itself intimately connected with the public world of crime, since Miss Havisham's condition is the result of Compeyson's desertion. Pip's description of Satis House emphasizes its iron bars and its prison-like character. It is a first cousin to Newgate. At the end of the novel these family resemblances will be revealed as genuine kinships, and Satis House is destroyed in a punitively symbolic way, representing the defeat of the public world and its perverted reflection in Miss Havisham's household. In the opposite direction, the imperfect world of the forge will be perfected by the marriage of Joe and Biddy after the narrative expulsion of Mrs. Joe, Dolge Orlick, and Pip. Julian Moynahan has argued that "Pip's career enacts his society's condition of being—its guilt, its sinfulness, and in the end, its helplessness to cleanse itself of a taint 'of prison and crime.'" Unable to redeem the world, Pip "can only lead himself into a sort of exile from his society's power centres" (167). But perhaps the point of this movement away from the public world of social power is that one cannot redeem a society if one is not morally superior to that society. Only Joe and Biddy are shown at peace in their own home. Whatever lies ahead for

Pip and Estella, we do not see them in domestic satisfaction. Although in his working notes Dickens refers to Herbert as "happily married to Clara Barley," he does not show us their happiness, nor does he disclose the domestic life of Wemmick and his bride (Stone 323). Wemmick tries to separate domestic and public worlds; Joe can operate comfortably only in the former. These two characters, in their different ways, display a self-understanding lacking to most other characters. Jaggers is perhaps the most intriguing character in relation to this opposition and interpenetration of domestic and public worlds, for he, in effect, has no domestic life. He has taken in a client as his housekeeper, and his business goes on about him in his dwelling. Only Wemmick, in a rare step out of character, suggests that Jaggers may have his eye on a home in the future, remote from Newgate and the Old Bailey. If these few characters seem to understand their relationships to the two spheres of domestic and public activity, most do not, Miss Havisham being the most glaring instance in her attempt to shut out the public world entirely. But there is no need to list other instances; our chief concern is with Pip.

A key misunderstanding of the direction his life will take occurs when Pip, having received word that he is to be brought up as a gentleman, makes a last visit to the marshes before leaving for London.

> If I had often thought before, with something allied to shame, of my companionship with the fugitive whom I had once seen limping among those graves, what were my thoughts on this Sunday, when the place recalled the wretch, ragged and shivering, with his felon iron and badge! My comfort was, that it happened a long time ago, and that he had doubtless been transported a long way off, and that he was dead to me, and might be veritably dead into the bargain. (139)

Far from being dead to Pip, Magwitch is the very agent of his transformation, and the symbols of his wretchedness will reappear to haunt Pip, as though trying to warn him of the fate toward which he has turned himself. And if there is a certain shame connected with Pip's relationship to the convict, we must remember that he also feels ashamed of the forge because he yearns for Estella's approbation. The mature narrating Pip pauses to reflect on how miserable it is to be ashamed of home, and associates that shame with moral fault. "There may be black ingratitude in the thing, and the punishment may be retributive and well deserved; but that it is a miserable thing I can testify" (100). We have long since become accustomed to viewing Pip as deserving of punishment for his guilt or shame.[12] But it is worth looking once more at what he has done. If we recall that Pip is telling his story long after he has learned the errors of his young life, and that his narrative therefore may fairly prefigure and foreshadow what is to come and draw connections that he might not have made as a boy, much of the imagery and many of the motifs he employs take on a greater meaning, as though carefully aiming toward a specific outcome. I have mentioned the prominent chain metaphor and several other details. Let me add a few more significant ones.

Pip accepts the invitation to Satis House to satisfy his mother and his uncle Pumblechook. This is a great thing for the family. He is spruced up and "put into clean linen of the stiffest character, like a young penitent into sackcloth, and was trussed up in my tightest and fearfullest suit. I was then delivered over to Mr. Pumblechook, who formally received me as if he were the Sheriff" (48). In this same episode, when Pip goes to Pumblechook's feed store, he wonders if the bulbs and flower seeds tied up in packets and kept in drawers "ever wanted of a fine day to break out of those jails, and bloom" (49). If we consider that Pip's name is also the name for seed, the resonance is clear enough. When he comes home from Satis House, Pip does not dare to tell the truth and invents outrageous lies which he later confesses to Joe, who cautions him that lying cannot lead to anything good. So in this brief account of his first visit to Satis House, Pip describes himself as a penitent, a prisoner, and a confessed offender.

Another scene associated with Satis House reinforces the picture of Pip as in some obscure way guilty for his behavior. He has fought Herbert Pocket and been spattered by his blood. "The pale young gentleman's nose had stained my trousers, and I tried to wash out that evidence of my guilt in the dead of night." Pip takes a practical, if immature, view of his crime. "I felt that the pale young gentleman's blood was on my head, and that the Law would avenge it" (87). Of course Pip is guilty of nothing. Herbert had forced Pip to the encounter, which was carried out in the manner of sporting rather than criminal behavior. So why should Pip feel such guilt? A closer look at his reaction to the fight provides some interesting information. Pip says that he felt but a gloomy satisfaction in his easy victory over Herbert. "I go so far as to hope that I regarded myself, while dressing, as a species of savage young wolf or other wild beast" (86). Pip feels that his behavior affiliates him with the public world of convicts and crime. Satis House is not an asylum from such conditions, but a memorial to them. The anger and vengeful energy displayed by Magwitch is characteristic of Miss Havisham as well. They are appropriate "parents" for Estella. To make this connection clearer, when Pip is given food at Satis House, Estella delivers it to him without looking at him, "as insolently as if I were a dog in disgrace" (57). Pip had particularly noted Magwitch's manner of eating like a dog. These and other signs and clues show us that the narrator is making a conscious and detailed connection between Pip and transgression, yet the only real offenses he commits are the understandable original sin of supplying Magwitch, and his betrayal of what Joe and Biddy represent: selfless love, charity, and forgiveness. Pip may be a decent boy, ill-served and keen to injustice, and he may grow into a young man with a good heart, but he is also insensitive to a certain degree, undisciplined in his emotions, and even selfishly proud. A clear sign of his culpability here is his treatment of Trabb's boy, whom he denounces vindictively to his master simply for his comic parody of Pip. A pure heart cannot be vindictive. Pip is not evil, but he is flawed, and his fault is closely allied to that of Magwitch. Jack P. Rawlins has written, "In terms of the novel's original vision, Magwitch is the epitome of a basic adult perversion: the desire to create, own, and exploit human beings as property and extensions of the ego" (175). We have seen that Dickens regularly condemns this attitude. But if Magwitch sins by wanting to own another human as though he were a commodity, Pip commits an almost equivalent sin in *disowning* human beings who exhibit the most human of virtues. To cast off authentic feeling is perhaps as wicked as trying to purchase it. Pip's chief sin is a failure of love. Significantly, Joe, who never fails in love, refuses to accept any cash compensation from Jaggers for the loss of Pip's services when Pip's Great Expectations take him away from the forge.

Pip must be punished not just once but several times. He is punished at the very moment his Great Expectations are fulfilled. His "reward" is to inherit Magwitch, an even more intense shame now that Pip is a gentleman than was his earlier boyish shame at being associated with the forge. This is a punishment from which he profits, learning to care for Magwitch as a real human being just as he once felt impulsive pity for this unfortunate being. Oddly enough, in this story of perverted and inverted moral actions, Pip forgives Magwitch for his "charity." His period of suffering has been a blessing after all. Pip is punished a second time in the encounter with Miss Havisham when he learns that she purposely misled him, that all of his hopes for Estella are unfounded, and that she will not be his. What reason to be kind, had I? Miss Havisham asks Pip. What reason has anyone to be kind but for kindness sake itself? Dickens might have responded, and did often enough, especially in the Christmas narratives. Pip's next punishment we have already looked at, but I wish to return to it briefly.

The weird scene in which Orlick has Pip in his power is emblematic of low revenge, but it is also a bursting forth of suppressed energy. As we have seen, Orlick blames Pip for Mrs. Joe's injury. Pip does not himself remind us at this point that he had experienced similar feelings at the time of the crime. Pip learned of the attack on his sister soon after he had attended Mr. Wopsle's reading of *The London Merchant* and somehow identified himself with the murderous protagonist. "With my head full of George Barnwell, I was at first disposed to believe that I must have had some hand in the attack upon my sister, or at all events that as her near relation, popularly known to be under obligations to her, I was a more legitimate object of suspicion than any one else" (113). This makes little sense considering Pip's age, the nature of the attack, and the fact that he has an alibi; Pip's response can only be read as an innocently paranoid fancy. And yet Pip cannot shed all responsibility. "It was horrible," he says, "to think that I had provided the weapon, however undesignedly, but I could hardly think otherwise" (114). Pip is obscurely implicated in his sister's misfortune.[13] Perhaps we might say there is a little of Orlick in all of us, but that most of us suppress him. Both Orlick and Pip charge Mrs. Joe with bullying and injustice. The connection between Pip and Orlick is made clearer when Orlick, in the confrontation scene, addresses Pip over and over by the name "wolf." This is the way Pip expressed his own self-loathing after his fight with Herbert. Pip has a violent side, and to some degree he bears resentment. There were three men at the forge. Two learned to pity themselves and resent others out of a sense of injustice. The third forgave, and offered kindness in return for harsh treatment. If Joe is the true model of manhood enduring injustice and responding with forgiveness rather than punishment, and Orlick is the false model of manhood avenging himself by force, Pip is in between, feeling the resentment, but not acting upon it, yet not forgiving it either. He is in a moral midworld, not in and not out of the public realm, not in and not out of the domestic realm. There is real resonance at the end of this scene with Orlick when among his rescuers Pip recognizes the one person he has truly injured vindictively—Trabb's boy.

In a psychological reading of the plot of *Great Expectations*, Peter Brooks locates "a quadripartite scheme of plots, organized into two pairs, each with an official plot, or interpretation of plot, standing over a repressed plot" (120). The numerous returns (thematic, of actual characters, and so on) revive the materials of the repressed plots, until the return of Magwitch makes explicit in Pip's own consciousness what the narrative has been accomplishing subliminally. "The return of the repressed—the repressed as knowledge of the self's other story, the true history of its misapprehended desire—forces a total revision of the subject's relation to the orders within which it constitutes meaning" (129). The narrative as a whole has been concerned with deciphering texts and shaping plots, but with the revelations instituted by Magwitch's return, all plots and the possibility of definitively reading them are called into question.

> In the absence or silence of divine masterplots, the organization and interpretation of human plots remains as necessary as it is problematic. Reading the signs of intention in life's actions is the central act of existence, which in turn legitimates the enterprise of reading for the reader of *Great Expectations*—or perhaps, vice versa, since the reading of plot within the text and as the text are perfectly analogous, mirrors of one another. (141–42).

Without challenging the value of this kind of reading, which illuminates the simple drives underlying a complex narrative, I would like to suggest that Brooks stops short precisely where I see a need for continued discussion. James Phelan also regards Brooks' reading of *Great Expectations* as limited, particularly in his turn to psychoanalysis. "Such a move presupposes that to explain the surface structure of texts, to explain the experience of reading, we need to move away from that surface and propose a model of its deep structure" (131). Phelan goes on to argue for greater attention to surface structure, especially as it relates to the mimetic effects of the text. But I would argue for a different kind of interest in deep structure; not the deep structure of a hypothetical model of human psychology or a theoretical model of history and economics based on Marxist principles, but a known underlying structure which formed a part of the visible and invisible ideology of the nineteenth century in England. I mean Christianity, especially in its popular and simplified form. Much recent criticism erects a barrier between the artistic text and its context. I am arguing for an ecology of the text whereby it is necessary to return the text to its historical, biographical, and especially moral setting to approach a sound, but by no means exclusive interpretation.[14] For Brooks *Great Expectations* ends with divine masterplots departed or silenced. But I suggest that Dickens is actually constituting such a masterplot in the moral design of his narrative. The rendering of punishment and forgiveness indicates the parameters of that plot. I would not go as far as A. O. J. Cockshut and argue that Dickens is rendering an account of his own guilt in the plot of *Great Expectations,* but I would argue that the reader of this novel is engaging in an experience somewhat different from that of reading texts within the narrative.[15] Brooks pays special attention to the opening scene of the novel as an example of the narrative's strenuous concern for deciphering texts, and he does a splendid job with the scene, but he does not explore the fact that young Pip's efforts at reading the world around him are presented with humorous irony by the adult Pip who already knows the entire fable; the reader, though caught up in young Pip's enterprise, nonetheless knows that he is receiving his information from an informed source and also knows that he or she is beyond the misreadings with which young Pip is struggling. Thus, if the sense of a masterplot may be obscured (especially by the use of first-person narration), the actual working out of a foreknown narrative suggests that there is a guiding consciousness more akin to Providence than to us as readers. And despite the surprises and reversals in the plot, the secret and the apparent forces guiding Pip's career, the overall structure of the moral universe of the world, is clear and readable.[16] Moreover, that decipherability is constantly enhanced by a redundancy of signals. Even the complicating of these signals by reversing the usual associations of crime, innocence, charity, and forgiveness serves to make their presence in the narrative more strikingly apparent, just as the interweaving of domestic and public narrative strains heightens the reader's awareness of how all-embracing the moral categories underlying the narrative are.

As we have seen, the text is rich with indicators of these moral categories, from obscure signs to outright statements, from the presentation of actual crime and its punishment to the very private shame of home with its retributive punishment. The folly of revenge, so clear in the careers of Magwitch and Miss Havisham, is echoed in numerous ways, from Mr. Wopsle's rendering of Revenge in Collins' *Ode on the Passions,* "throwing his blood-stained sword in thunder down, and taking the war-denouncing trumpet with a withering look" to young Pepper, nicknamed The Avenger because he keeps Pip's folly constantly present to his mind (40). And as usual in Dickens, the language of money and commercial exchange easily comes to signify the accumulation of moral debt and the need to have that debt repaid or forgiven.

At the end of *Great Expectations,* Pip has endured his several punishments and extended his several forgivenesses. He has learned to endure hardship and perhaps even further injustice. He has put his house in order. It is interesting that Dickens' first impulse was not to reward Pip with renewed love or great riches or any other palpable treasure. The new character he has won is his prize. In the second version, the union of Pip and Estella is conceivable only if we can believe that Estella, too, has endured the necessary punishment and learned the same lesson. In either case, the true purpose of the narrative has been served, demonstrating the self-punishing consequences of error, even when those errors are largely generated by others. As Pip looks back calmly now on the lesson of his life, over his shoulder the implied author rubs his hands, perhaps a little like Jaggers, washing off the crime and transgression it has been his duty to correct, and over his shoulder stands Charles Dickens, sure of the message he meant to deliver.

NOTES

1. I have found Robert B. Partlow's "The Moving I: A Study of Point of View in *Great Expectations*," in *Assessing Great Expectations*, ed. Richard Lettis and William E. Morris (San Francisco: Chandler Publishing Co., 1960), 194–201 helpful in approaching the first-person variations. Barry Westberg also notes that "who the narrator is makes all the difference," since Mr. Pirrip can amuse himself and us at Pip's expense as no other narrator could without seeming heartless or impertinent (*The Confessional Fictions of Charles Dickens* [Dekalb: Northern Illinois University Press, 1977], 119).

2. Charles Dickens. *Great Expectations* (London: Oxford University Press, 1975), 4. Subsequent references appear in the text.

3. There are many studies of guilt in *Great Expectations*, among the most prominent being Edgar Johnson's *Charles Dickens: His Tragedy and Triumph*, vol. 2 (Boston: Little, Brown and Co., 1952), 981ff., G. Robert Stange's "Expectations Well Lost: Dickens's Fable for His Time," *Critical Essays on Charles Dickens's Great Expectations*, ed. Michael Cotsell (Boston: G. K. Hall and Co., 1990), 63–72, and Julian Moynahan's "The Hero's Guilt: The Case of *Great Expectations*," *Critical Essays*, 73–86.

4. *Assessing Great Expectations*, 4. Barry Westburg comments on the connections between seeming opposites (125).

5. Orlick has been seen as Pip's alter ego or the expression of his aggression, but this approach, though intriguing, runs into difficulty when Orlick's anger focuses upon Pip himself. See especially Moynahan, 154ff., 159.

6. See Alexander Welsh on swift punishment after forgiveness in *From Copyright to Copperfield: The Identity of Dickens* (Cambridge: Harvard University Press, 1987), 146.

7. *Dickens' Working Notes for His Novels*, ed. Harry Stone (Chicago: University of Chicago Press, 1987), 323. Subsequent references appear in the text.

8. Philip Collins treats this theme in Dickens' works in general in *Dickens and Crime* (Bloomington: Indiana University Press, 1968), and Jeremy Tambling pursues the subject in a more fashionable recent mode in "Prison Bound: Dickens and Foucault," *Critical Essays* (182–97).

9. See John R. Reed's *Victorian Conventions* (Ohio University Press, 1975), 14ff., and Audrey C. Peterson's "Brain Fever in Nineteenth-Century Literature: Fact and Fiction," *Victorian Studies*, 19, no. 4 (June 1976), 445–64.

10. See, for example, John Lindberg, "Individual Conscience and Social Injustice in *Great Expectations*," *Assessing* (186–93), and John H. Hagan, Jr., "The Poor Labyrinth: The Theme of Social Injustice in Dickens's *Great Expectations*," *Critical Essays* (56–62). As their titles suggest, these essays explore the social aspects of justice and injustice rather than emphasizing more abstract concepts of moral justice.

11. Peter Brooks establishes a quadripartite plot arrangement in the novel (*Reading for the Plot: Design and Intention in Narrative* [New York: Vintage Books, 1985], 117ff. Subsequent references appear in the text.), which James Phelan restricts, for convenience, to the convict plot and the home plot (*Reading People, Reading Plots* [Chicago: University of Chicago Press, 1989], 122ff.). My distinctions differ in function from both of their designs but are necessarily related.

12. Different variations of this attribution of guilt to Pip occur in Stange and Moynahan, and also in Dorothy Van Ghent, *The English Novel: Form and Function* (New York: Holt, Rinehart and Winston, Inc., 1953) and in Jack P. Rawlins, "Great Expiations: Dickens and the Betrayal of the Child," *Critical Essays* (168–81). This last essay, as its title indicates, deals with a later and subtler form of guilt than that usually assigned to Pip.

13. Albert D. Hutter has an insightful essay ("Crime and Fantasy in *Great Expectations*," *Critical Essays*, 93–121) that is a corrective to some oversimplified readings of the novel and indicates how intimately connected characters are. Using a psychological approach, Hutter arrives at the following conclusion.

> In *Great Expectations* the pervasive guilt and criminality, the bizarre women and the frustrated love of the hero consistently resonate on several levels. Pip's fears and desires extend to all of the novel's relationships, its minor characters, its comedy and caricature, and even to the business context of Little Britain and the socially shared attitudes toward women. The social dimension of *Great Expectations* cannot be ignored, but does not in itself account for the novel's power. Dickens has created a richly suggestive story of individual growth that reveals the deepest wishes and conflicts of its hero, of its author, and of an age to which we still respond. (121)

14. It can be argued that one must know something about the author of a text before one can properly interpret the use of free indirect discourse and other narrative techniques.

15. A. O. J. Cockshut, *The Imagination of Charles Dickens* (New York: New York University Press, 1962), 160. Cockshut echoes Edgar Johnson, 988.

16. Max Byrd notes in " 'Reading' in *Great Expectations,*" PMLA, 91, no. 2 (March 1976), 259–65, that learning to "read" things aright is Pip's great task in a world where fantasy opposes a strict interpretation of reality. The person who reads truths correctly, i.e., morally, is the illiterate Joe.

EIGHTEEN

Our Mutual Friend

OUR MUTUAL FRIEND, like other late narratives of Dickens, is heavy with a
sense of accumulated guilt, and hence also with the pressure for justice to manifest itself. But the whole enterprise of executing justice has become profoundly
problematic. In *Great Expectations,* though Pip must suffer to achieve a true picture of himself, characters such as Joe and Biddy offer, in their candor, abiding
sources of good. But in *Our Mutual Friend* there are few who can afford candor
and even fewer who are qualified to act as judges. But if few are qualified to
judge, many are nonetheless eager to assume judgmental positions. There are, for
example, many characters in *Our Mutual Friend* who yearn to punish, but they are
a strange assembly and their views of what is wrong or wicked are tainted in one
degree or another by self-interest. Many characters innocently wish to see justice
done: for example, Boffin, who, virtuously wanting the murderer of John Harmon punished, offers a reward toward that end. But many other characters have
selfish motives for seeking to punish others. Silas Wegg wants to "punish" Boffin
for what he considers his impudence. Bradley Headstone's punishment of Eugene
Wrayburn is really an act of instinctive dislike and sexual jealousy. The Lammles
want to punish the Veneerings for encouraging their marriage, and all of society
for the financial condition they are in. Fledgeby wants to punish the Lammles out
of spite, and even Jenny Wren energetically punishes both her own father and
Fledgeby. But these personal acts of punishment scarcely have Dickens' endorsement, with the possible exception of Jenny's adding pepper to the wounds Lammle inflicts on Fledgeby.[1] One reason for devaluing the terms of desert and
punishment in *Our Mutual Friend* is to demonstrate that the supposed moral impulse to punish is often no more than a mask for achieving personal ends.
Another is to emphasize the limits of human understanding. Since we cannot
truly know what ideas and feelings move other humans to behave as they do, we
must not arrogate to ourselves the right to punish them. By forcing us, as wit-

289

nesses of unjust "punishment," to protest, Dickens reinforces our sense that only certainty will justify action against offenders, a certainty rarely if ever attainable in the real world.

The moral world of *Our Mutual Friend* is purposely depicted as desperately askew, and to the normal witness it at first seems a profound puzzle. Nothing reveals this confusion more than the way punishment and forgiveness are misunderstood or misapplied. From the first chapter we are introduced to an unclean world that needs the services of predators and scavengers. Gaffer Hexam is only the first example combining these traits. In one way or another many of the characters in the book are preying upon others. This means of subsistence may be as direct as the thieves who assault John Harmon, as crude as Bradley Headstone's manner of "lying in wait," which becomes his stalking of Eugene Wrayburn, or as utilitarian as Pleasant Riderhood's regarding seamen as her natural "prey."[2] It can be as muted as Weggs' drawing his wages from Boffin while planning to despoil him of his wealth, or as plain as the dependence of Twemlow, Wrayburn, and others upon allowances provided by wealthy relatives. This world, like many of its inhabitants—Charley Hexam is particularly singled out—is half civilized and half savage, a situation illustrated by Gaffer Hexam's moral distaste for Rogue Riderhood, charged with robbing a live man, compared with his own self-justification for taking money from the dead, who, he indignantly instructs Riderhood, *cannot* be robbed. "'Don't try to go confounding the rights and wrongs of things in that way'" (4–5).

But the rights and the wrongs of things are intentionally confounded in *Our Mutual Friend.* If Dickens purposely inverted Christian virtues in *Great Expectations,* in this novel he twists them until they are almost unrecognizable. Charley Hexam's offense, which makes him a parody of the prodigal son, is to seek an education so that he may better himself, a course that his father views as betrayal. "'Let him never come nigh me to ask me my forgiveness,'" Gaffer says (75). The whole parable is stood on its head, as the father refuses to forgive the son who does not want to waste his substance and swill with pigs. The newly married Lammles say of the "benefactors" who brought them together and facilitated their union, "'I never will forgive the Veneerings for this!'" (124). The Lammles have overreached themselves, of course, each thinking that the other had money. They are imposters who are especially outraged at having been imposed upon. Not only is there no love at the center of this marriage, but the self-interest itself is desperate. Like so many other figures in this novel, the Lammles decide to keep their secret and set themselves "against All England" (135).

Other imposters similarly see "virtue" in their own peculiar light. Rogue Riderhood's view of doing justice is to give false testimony against Gaffer Hexam for the reward money. Silas Wegg, proposing the Friendly Move, which is nothing more than a plan to appropriate Boffin's wealth, explains the justice of his motives to Mr. Venus: "Mr. Venus. It ain't that I object to being passed over for a stranger, though I regard the stranger as a more than doubtful customer. It ain't for the sake of making money, though money is ever welcome. It ain't for myself, though I am not so haughty as to be above doing myself a good turn. It's for the cause of right" (302). Later, when he believes he has Boffin in his power and is stating his demands, Wegg behaves as though he is bringing a tyrannical outlaw to justice.

Part of Dickens' effort in *Our Mutual Friend*, an effort that may have influenced his choice of a title, is to recuperate the original Christian scheme of punishment and forgiveness. As so often in his novels, he refracts his program through many different and redundant manifestations. I have just mentioned some of the perversions of Christian values that he uses to make this point. But there is an interesting and poignant case that makes clear the difficulty of putting into effect Christian principles in a world more than half given up to savagely selfish conduct. When the reader first encounters Jenny Wren she appears grotesque. She is both handsome and maimed; though a child, she behaves like an adult; though a pretty child, she utters vindictive sentiments. Don't talk to me about children, she says. They play and fight and mock creatures like me. " 'Oh! *I* know their tricks and their manners. And I'll tell you what I'd do to punish 'em. There's doors under the church in the Square—black doors, leading into black vaults. Well! I'd open one of those doors, and I'd cram 'em all in, and then I'd lock the door and through the keyhole I'd blow in pepper' " (224). Jenny's real name, Fanny Cleaver, has a menacing character, and she is much given to thoughts of how she will punish various figures, including her hypothetical husband and her very real wayward father, whom she abuses as a bad boy.

Jenny has assumed her punitive posture as a means of surviving in a world that is cruel to creatures like herself. Another scavenger, she lives upon scraps that she can pick up from Riah and shape into dolls' dresses. She cannot afford to be meek, and indulges her gentler feelings only when she is up on the roof of Riah's building, "dead" to the suffering world below. Then she can pity the suffering she sees, but when she is called to life again, she must put away such damagingly soft sentiments. Because she is imperfect in this way, unable to forgive those who have done her and her friends injury, she is liberated as few of Dickens' good characters are to indulge in physical punishment. When Lammle canes Fledgeby, Jenny adds pepper to his wounds to enhance their "curative" effect. By this Dickens makes ironically self-conscious allusion to his own characteristic tool of therapeutic punishment. It is characteristic of this narrative that an innocent child requires an aggressive manner to endure while one of the most Christian characters is a Jew.

The confusion of merit, demerit, punishment, and benevolence in *Our Mutual Friend* is related to a broader mystification. The world presented by the narrator is sinister, like a swamp where dangers hide in wait. In a world so dangerous to the innocent and so complicated for everyone, self-revelation is hazardous. So in this novel secrecy, suppression, withholding, and deception are commonplace, not merely among the wicked, but among the good characters as well. And the model for such deception is set by the narrator himself.[3] Many characters operate at the level of pretence and sham—the Lammles, for example, or the Veneerings. Others more designedly create mischievous fictions, such as Fledgeby's story that the kindly Riah is really the harsh creditor directing Pubsey and Co. Wegg and Venus concoct a secret plot against Boffin, and Riderhood is an outright liar. But there are other forms of dangerous suppression. Bradley Headstone tries to forget his origins, as does Charley Hexam after him. Headstone also tries to suppress his passions, but he does a poor job of it, because "even among school-buildings, school-teachers, and school-pupils, all according to pattern and all engendered in the light of the latest Gospel according to Monotony, the older pattern into which so many fortunes have been shaped for good and evil, comes out" (218). Riderhood, a regular denizen of the ancient swamp to which Headstone becomes a willing habitué, sees through Headstone's schemes easily. Good characters also find it necessary to keep secrets, play roles, or hide themselves. Most notable is John Harmon, who not only withholds his true identity, but assumes at least three other roles in the story before stepping forth in his "true" character. Boffin impersonates a miser, while Betty Higden and Lizzie Hexam run away and hide themselves out of self-protection and for the benefit of others.

If good and bad characters are given to playing roles, suppressing facts, keeping secrets, and so forth, the resolution to these many interlocking deceptions must be revelation, disclosure, confession, and prophecy. Lizzie is gifted with the last of these ways of penetrating a misleading world. She can read the futures of others in the fire but cannot see there her own destiny. Mrs. Lammle's disclosure to Twemlow of the plot against Georgina Podsnap brings her no serious redemption, but clears her conscience of a specific offense. Genuine confiding is a dependable sign of improved character; thus Lizzie and Bella signal a good turn in their careers when they share their private sentiments. Lizzie is able to speak her feelings, and Bella, admiring the genuineness of her new friend, reproaches herself for the false values to which she has so stubbornly adhered, giving herself a "penitential poke in the side" (528). The greatest disclosures come, of course, when Boffin reveals himself as unchanged and produces the appropriate evidence insuring that he and John will retain the Harmon wealth.

But if much of the energy of the novel is made up of secrets, disguises, and mysteries to be resolved by confessions and disclosures, this pattern is also deeply engrained in the manner of the story's narration. Although the narrator is clearly omniscient, he withholds a good deal of important information from the reader. We are not told, at first, that Harmon is alive.[4] The narrator lets him appear as a stranger accompanying Lightwood and others to the police station without enlightening us (23). Later Harmon comes on stage as the stranger who is renting a room at the Wilfer household, but we are not immediately made aware of his identity. For a considerable time the secret of Harmon's identity is withheld from us, and it is not disclosed until after he has employed yet another disguise as a seaman. Then, in his monologue, Harmon's whole story is brought out. By this time, however, the reader has had several clues to prepare him or her for this revelation. We had early been told that if Mr. Julius Handford, the stranger at the police station, had a twin brother on this earth it was John Rokesmith. So midway in the book a central mystery is resolved, but this resolution occurs just as another major mystery is developing—the apparent transformation of Boffin into a miser. Here again the narrator withholds information from us. We do not wish to see this good man go bad, but we are permitted no glimpses behind his disguise. To the contrary, we are offered some red herrings to make us accept his degeneration. Moreover, instead of alerting us to the true nature of Boffin's performance, the revelation of Harmon's secret seems to anesthetize suspicion, as though the trauma to the imagination of finally learning Rokesmith's story begets a temporary amnesia about all the indications showing Boffin to be an unalterably good man.

There is something more at work here than a narrator's reluctance to give up the suspenseful inertia of his narrative. Rather, mystery and disclosure are played off against one another in such a way that conventional expectations will be bruised and anticipations of resolution intensified. When Gaffer Hexam is being sought by the police, Riderhood assumes that Gaffer is in luck again when he sees the rope straining from Gaffer's boat; in fact, it is Gaffer himself who has died in the way of his trade—a sad sort of poetic justice. But this instance of predictable morality, though modest and dealing with a minor character, sets up an additional conventional expectation that poetic justice will be an operating force in the narrative. Thus when Riderhood is run over by a boat and brought to shore, the first supposition is that he has suffered Gaffer's fate and died practicing his vocation, punished, as it were, by the very river that he had dishonestly exploited. Riderhood not only does not die, but also violates all expectation for such a scene by being outraged with his rescuers instead of showing gratitude. This is because Dickens has prepared a yet more fitting demise for him. It will be death by water all right, but it will be a double death in which the alter egos Riderhood and Headstone—one patently savage, the other savage with a veneer of civilization—will drown together in the slime of the wier lock. Thus the apparent deviation from a pattern of poetic justice does not frustrate that expectation, but ultimately enhances it by delay and duplication. By apparently frustrating the reader's desire for a fitting punishment, Dickens actually whets that desire so that he may gratify it more spectacularly later. The case of Boffin's degeneration is similar. We have seen him fall into the hands of Wegg and been told quite authoritatively by the narrator that the guileful man has got the better of the simple one. We have seen how easily Rokesmith has gained Boffin's confidence. It is possible, therefore, to consider Boffin an easily led individual—as duped by the histories of misers as by dependents. And, since he praises misers for their prudence, it is also possible to see his interest as a perversion of a virtue. The worse Boffin becomes, the more narratively suitable Wegg's behavior toward

him is as a form of retribution gathering over Boffin's head. If the Golden Dust-
man has gone bad Wegg would make an entirely appropriate engine of punishment, as he himself declares. That Boffin turns out not only to be uncorrupted by
wealth, but actually to be teaching a lesson about money's corruptive power,
makes this mystery all the more instructive. Oddly enough, this mystery is not
resolved when its purpose is achieved. Though Bella learns from Boffin's deplorable treatment of Rokesmith that she is not mercenary after all, but is capable of
deep and genuine affection, she must wait a good while before she, and we, the
readers, are admitted to the secret of Boffin's behavior. Partly this is because
Boffin's pretence serves another narrative purpose—as bait to Wegg. But it
serves a larger narrative purpose as well that transcends the plot and extends to
the novel's readership. As Rosemary Mundhenk has argued, Dickens' careful
narration of Boffin's life as a miser aims at educating the reader, who "learns of
the error of easy judgments" (49). Dickens often taught this lesson in his fiction,
but he rarely used so elaborate a device as Boffin's performance to bring the
point home to his readers.

But if Dickens discourages facile judgments by his readers, he grants his narrator judicial powers. In the plan for his novel Dickens himself blatantly played
judge and executioner. The notes for Book Two, chapter 17 direct him to "Lead
up to Fledgeby's corporal punishment," and, more viciously, in the notes for
Book One, chapter 13, he writes bluntly, "Kill Gaffer retributively."⁵ But if he
schemed against his villains and saw to their punishment, he also directed his narrative in a more benign direction. When Bella wants to prove to Rokesmith that
she is repentant and reformed, she asks him to test her through some trial.
Dickens' narrator does the same with his readers. We have been put in a position
to judge the characters in the novel. Many are easily judged; they are outright
rogues or unquestionably decent. But lest we forget that judging our fellow mortals is an endeavor not to be undertaken lightly, we are also presented with several problematic types. Harmon/Rokesmith/Handford reveals himself slowly,
and we have little doubt along the way that he will turn out well, but just as he is
settling into a form with which we feel comfortable, Boffin requires our judgmental attention. Moreover, all along we have had to consider what sort of person Bella is and how she should be treated. It is entirely fitting that the great
climax of the novel comes at the convergence of the "testing" of these three
characters.

In the climactic scene in which Rokesmith is dismissed by the apparently degenerate Boffin, the denunciation he undergoes is supposedly a punishment for
his unseemly designs upon Bella. Ironically, of course, his dismissal is designed as
part of Bella's redemption, a bringing herself to herself. Rokesmith defines his
own punishment to Bella as loving her and being rejected and insulted for doing
so. Bella, ashamed to be the occasion of Rokesmith's dismissal, apologizes for her
earlier rude and imperious manner. "'As I am punished for it severely, try to
forgive it!'" (598). From this point on, scenes of forgiveness begin to abound.

Lizzie will forgive Eugene much later, but along the way, Pleasant Riderhood will forgive Mr. Venus, who, by confessing his part in the plot against Boffin receives the forgiveness of all concerned in that episode. And just as the pattern of forgiveness begins to accelerate, so does the pattern of punishment.

Rokesmith and the Boffins use the same set of deceptions to bring about the good end of rehabilitating Bella and to lay a trap for Wegg. They do not directly punish Wegg, but they let him punish himself. As the moment of his apparent triumph approaches, Wegg is worn down by greed and distrust because Sloppy has been persecuting him by his tireless attention to the dust heaps Wegg covets. John Harmon tells Wegg that he knew enough of him " 'to persuade Mr. Boffin to let us lead you on, deluded to the last possible moment, in order that your disappointment might be the heaviest possible disappointment.' " He then explains that Boffin has generously reinvested him with his father's property and adds that he has had all he could do to keep from physically punishing Wegg (789). But he *has* refrained, though Sloppy follows up this denunciation with his brand of justice by carrying Wegg out and plunging him into the dust cart in the street. The "mud-worm" is returned to his element.

Wegg returns to mud and filth because it is what he is composed of to begin with. He is a true dweller in the lower reaches of the Dismal Swamp. The good characters have merely let appearances guide him to his destiny, but they enjoy his torment and discomfiture nonetheless. Far more complicated is the condition that Bradley Headstone brings upon himself. Driven by jealously, and goaded by Wrayburn's insolence, Headstone, after much hunting down, finally strikes Wrayburn a murderous blow just as Wrayburn's conscience is picturing his pursuit of Lizzie in its true immoral light. Hunting down *his* prey, Wrayburn is himself being hunted. The motive power in both cases is sexual passion. Thus Headstone becomes the embodiment of Wrayburn's bad conscience and executes a form of justice on him immediately. He is the agent of retribution. But he is also a criminal and therefore his act, which brings about Wrayburn's redemption, becomes a torment to himself. Wrayburn decides that he does not want Headstone prosecuted because Lizzie's reputation would be ruined. " 'She would be punished, not he,' " Eugene declares (738). But if Wrayburn won't punish Headstone, Headstone will. He has no remorse for his violence against Wrayburn, "but the evil-doer who can hold that avenger at bay, cannot escape the slower torture of incessantly doing the evil deed again and doing it more efficiently" (708). What drives him to literal fits of anguish is the knowledge that his attempt to murder Wrayburn has actually confirmed Wrayburn's connection with Lizzie. "He thought of Fate, or Providence, or be the directing Power what it might, as having put a fraud upon him—overreached him—and in his impotent mad rage bit, and tore, and had his fit" (791–92). Headstone in his turn is hunted down by Riderhood, upon whom he had sought to place the blame for his act. Like Wegg, but on a grander scale, these two loathsome creatures tossed up from the Swamp return to their appropriate depths.

In the complex dramatic situation involving the Boffins, Bella, and Roke-smith, we may have a clue to Dickens' solution for the dilemma of punishment. The virtuous must not punish directly, but they may participate in a sequence of events that will lead the misguided to acknowledge their own fault and feel as punishment the discomfort that follows. As in the other novels I have discussed, self-punishment emerges as an acceptable mode. Wicked characters may punish other wicked characters, and that punishment stands as a just mode of retribution even though the punishers themselves become culpable for their deeds—witness the consequences for Lammle, Fledgeby, Wegg, Riderhood, and Headstone.

Fallible characters may themselves be the agents of punishment in Dickens' novels, but there are other modes as well. Chief among these is providential justice where, out of remorse or not, the offender's actions beget his or her punishment. We have noticed instances of this form of punishment elsewhere in Dickens' novels. The most consciously discussed example in *Our Mutual Friend* involves the attempted murder of John Harmon. In disguise, Harmon briefly sketches for Pleasant Riderhood the circumstances of how George Radfoot drugged and then robbed him.

> "Did you get the parties punished?" asked Pleasant.
> "A tremendous punishment followed," said the man, more seriously; "but it was not of my bringing about."
> "Of whose, then?" asked Pleasant.
> The man pointed upward with his forefinger and, slowly recovering that hand settled his chin in it again as he looked at the fire. (355)

Harmon's attacker suffered swift justice, but all justice cannot be so tidy; some must be worked out gradually. However, if we understand human experience in the light of providence, we realize that sooner or later justice *will* come. In this life, providential justice must always remain a mystery, for people cannot know for certain what crimes have been committed, who is guilty, and when guilt will be punished. This understanding lies behind the lesson Trotty Veck learns in *The Chimes:* "'I know that our inheritance is held in store for us by Time. I know there is a sea of Time to rise one day, before which all who wrong us or oppress us will be swept away like leaves. I see it as the flow! I know that we must trust and hope, and neither doubt ourselves, nor doubt the good in one another.'"[6] But good people like Trotty must not presume to chastise those oppressors themselves. The problem remains, then: How are the evil to be punished in a world that is unclear to those who live in it? Trotty's remarks refer to the condition of a specific social class, but the need to withhold judgment is universal because it is so difficult to know the sources of wickedness. Dickens presents a grim picture of this troublingly ambiguous yet tendentious moral climate in *Our Mutual Friend.* In describing Wegg's relationship with Boffin, he remarks, "The man of low cunning had, *of course,* acquired a mastery over the man of high simplicity" (185;

my italics). Mr. Inspector, the sympathetically drawn police officer, avers "that it was always more likely that a man had done a bad thing than that he hadn't" (159). But if we are justified in being skeptical about the goodness of our fellow mortals, we are not therefore permitted to act out our principles of justice upon them. Dickens assures us, in describing the triumph of the Boffins' simple virtue over old Mr. Harmon's selfish greed, that "this is the eternal law. For Evil often stops short at itself and dies with the doer of it; but Good, never" (101). Justice is in the nature of things, not in human hands.

Ultimately, then, evil will be punished and good rewarded. That is the eternal law. But we might never witness this scheme in daily life. As the schoolmaster in *The Old Curiosity Shop* says after the death of Little Nell, "it is not on earth that Heaven's justice ends."[7] The great power of fiction is to provide just such a record out of this world, which is nonetheless a model for justice in it. Story becomes destiny and the narrator providence. In short, the narrative itself becomes the final agent of justice, doling punishment appropriately. Dickens, through his narrative voices, openly takes sides among his characters; we generally have no difficulty distinguishing the good from the bad. In *Our Mutual Friend*, for example, he dismisses much of the waterside population as the "scum of humanity" and "moral sewage," and bluntly describes Fledgeby as the "meanest cur" (21, 268). But in this novel Dickens also introduces some degree of ambiguity. What are Rokesmith's motives? Is Bella really so crass? Has Boffin gone bad? Moreover, as we have seen, these good characters actually conspire and deceive in order to bring about good results. Although Rokesmith's secret history is hinted at early and revealed halfway through the novel, his participation in Boffin's transformation is withheld for some time, from the reader as well as from the other characters. Dickens behaves to his readers as Rokesmith does to Bella. A few characters in the novel know the whole story and can therefore intelligently predict its outcome; the reader must trust the narrator just as Bella must trust those characters.

Much of *Our Mutual Friend* is devoted to interpreting and composing stories, as the entire relationship between Boffin and Wegg suggests.[8] We are told that "What to believe in the course of his reading was Mr. Boffin's chief literary difficulty" (476). *The Decline and Fall of the Roman Empire* itself offers an interpretation of human life, but it is still only that, an interpretation, and we are meant to feel its limits and the limitations of its interpreters. The tales of misers' lives mean one thing to the virtuous, another to the miserly. Many characters in Dickens' novel project histories, but the wicked are self-serving in their lies and deceits and generally come to grief because selfishness clouds their vision. Jenny Wren offers a pathetic instance of innocent forecasting. She is prepared to punish her anticipated future husband because that projection of her life story contains all that she has known about family life with a man, her unreliable father. She can incorporate in her fiction only what she already knows. By contrast, the selfless Lizzie can correctly read the future in the coals for everyone but herself.

Dickens has given us a clue to the significance of fiction-making and storytelling in the continuing motif of the story that Mortimer Lightwood relates at the Veneering table. His story of John Harmon, the man from Somewhere, is interrupted by word that Harmon is dead, and so the story just begun seems to have come to an abrupt end. But it has not, though it changes its character radically as the novel continues, always introducing surprising new details while remaining intriguingly unpredictable regarding its conclusion, which coincides with that of the novel. Mortimer and Eugene are not creators or makers of this story; they simply transmit the story to an audience that cannot fathom its significance.[9] But ironically they are themselves mere incidents in the story of the man from Somewhere, which is, from the proper perspective, *Our Mutual Friend,* the story of John Harmon that Dickens' narrator is telling. And whereas Mortimer and Eugene, imbedded in a tale being told, cannot see their own future prospects, the narrator can forecast and bring to pass precisely what he anticipates, as Dickens' elaborate plans for the novel indicate. Eugene's case is the most dramatic. Mortimer asks him what the consequences will be of Eugene's interest in Lizzie. He says he has no idea. " 'Do you design to marry her?' " Mortimer asks. Eugene flippantly replies, " 'My dear fellow, I don't design anything. I have no design whatever. I am incapable of designs. If I conceived a design, I should speedily abandon it, exhausted by the operation' " (294). Later, more seriously, he admits that he does not know what he means and cannot look on to the end. But his nemesis, Bradley Headstone, does plan and form designs very carefully. And fittingly, it is at the very moment when parts of Eugene's thoughts start "unbidden, from the rest and [reveal] their wickedness" and he recognizes that he has reached the crisis of his story that the avenging Headstone strikes him down, obliging him to reenact in miniature the story of the man from Somewhere, almost drowning but recovering to a life of greater resolve (698). It is presumptuous, Dickens seems to suggest, to try to tell the story of someone else's life (i.e., judge him), when we do not even know the plot of our own.

The capacity to create a story for our lives that looks back to origins and forward to consequences, all shaped by patterns of justice and mercy, is an essential requirement in Dickens' way of dealing with the world. Obviously Dickens relished seeing his wicked characters punished and enjoyed the authorial power of making certain that they got what they deserved. The very ingenuity of some of these punishments testifies to the pleasure with which he meted them out. But punishment is also a purgative and corrective in an obviously fallen world. Dickens appears to be offering a fairly clear signal when he chooses for Boffin's reading *The Decline and Fall of the Roman Empire,* because much of his own narrative is a caution against the indifference of a governing class and the pride, greed, and general overreaching by the population at large.

Much of the wickedness and injustice in *Our Mutual Friend* is confined to the private worlds of its characters, but the broader application of Dickens' moral pattern is constantly reiterated. When told that some half-dozen people have lately died of starvation in the streets, Mr. Podsnap first objects to such a topic being raised at a dinner party, then declares of those starved, "Then it was their own fault" (140). Betty Higden makes it perfectly clear that, as far as she is concerned, the workhouse is designed less for mercy than for torment. The narrator himself steps in to chastise "My Lords and Gentlemen and Honourable Boards" who do nothing to change these conditions (199). The workhouse system, meant to deter idleness and false claims for assistance, is a gigantic error that punishes where it should succor. The poor, Dickens says, can see the injustice even if lords and gentlemen and honorable boards cannot. Moreover, if things do not change, a great reckoning will be forthcoming. Such consequences have been "the truth since the foundations of the universe were laid, and they will be the truth until the foundations of the universe are shaken by the Builder. This boastful handiwork of ours, which fails in its terrors for the professional pauper, the sturdy breaker of windows and the rampant tearer of clothes, strikes with a cruel and a wicked stab at the stricken sufferer, and is a horror to the deserving and unfortunate. We must mend it, lords and gentlemen and honourable boards, or in its own evil hour it will mar every one of us" (503). This unfortunate state of affairs results from inattention to Christ's message of love. "It is a remarkable Christian improvement, to have made a pursuing Fury of the Good Samaritan," but that is what modern English bureaucracy and official morality have done (506). Thus the great world of English government is as upside-down as the low world of Hexams and Weggs. Both have redefined justice and charity; both have corrupted justice and virtue.[10]

The moral model that Dickens preferred was that of a merciful, forgiving Christ. He also felt a strong need to see evil punished. Yet good people, and therefore good characters, must not punish directly. A few, like young Nicholas Nickleby when he beats Sir Mulberry Hawk or Jenny when she enhances Fledgeby's pain, may have the excuse of immaturity, impetuosity, or extreme provocation. After all, even Christ used violence to drive the money changers from the temple. But Dickens overwhelmingly does not permit his centrally virtuous characters to punish. Critics have often remarked the passiveness of Dickens' first-person narrators in *David Copperfield* and *Great Expectations*, but part of that passiveness is a consequence of the prohibition against their enacting punishment. They may, however, assemble the narratives that describe the punishments of all those who offend, and in that assembling point out the connection between offense and retributive agency. As Alexander Welsh observes, David may overtly forgive Steerforth for his sins, but the description of Steerforth's punishment comes on swiftly nonetheless.[11]

In *Our Mutual Friend*'s complicated story of deception and revelation, of creatures arising out of the depths to be transformed or returned to them, one of the most powerful agents in the development of the plot is the nature and manner of enacting punishment. As we have seen, most punishment comes about at the hands of imperfect or evil people. Thus Fledgeby punishes the Lammles by bankrupting them, and Lammle punishes Fledgeby by caning him. Headstone punishes

Wrayburn for his lust and is punished in turn by Riderhood, who, in turn, is punished by Headstone. Wegg is allowed to punish himself for his overreaching. One could go on, but the important point is that if good characters are permitted to pave the way for villains to do themselves in, they are not allowed to execute justice upon them directly because the truly virtuous must be slow to judge, quick to compassionate; they must be forbearing and merciful, and ready to forgive the penitent. On earth, assuming the role of judge and punisher is a risky maneuver because we know so little of one another and are not secure from doubts about our own virtue. Institutions designed to aid or punish rarely achieve their ends.[12] Only God has the real authority to punish. But Dickens realized that this *authority* can be imitated in fiction.[13] The narrator, in the role of Fate, Providence, or whatever directing power, can so arrange the distribution of justice that the moral pattern will not easily be mistaken. Like providence, the narrator may use vile agents to carry out punishments that no official scheme of justice would endorse. Also, he can so arrange the events of his plot and their ordering that a fundamental moral order will prevail, but for Dickens this involves the necessity of complicating the plot specifically to disengage paragon characters from the direct punishment of the guilty. And justice must be thorough; hence, even beyond the story as it is told, the narrator must reveal, at the opening of the last chapter, that "it is written in the Books of the Insolvent Fates that Veneering shall make a resounding smash next week" (815). This may seem like excessive and vindictive retribution on the narrator's part, but this little piece of proleptic information underscores the important message of the last chapter, which shows how temporary and insignificant "The Voice of Society" is, and how enduring are the charitable sentiments of Twemlow and Lightwood, who resist that voice. The narrator can dispense justice and the punishments prohibited to his good characters because, like God, he is the creator of their story and knows its real meaning and its end. By the elaborateness of his plotting he produces the coincidental circumstances, the ironies of fate, the sudden revelations that remove punishment from the hands of his virtuous characters and displace it to the wicked, who punish one another and themselves. His narrative tricks can engage us in the readerly partnership of mystery and disclosure, of accumulated indignation and gratifying release that teaches us to appreciate the moral pattern upon which the narrative itself is formed. The author is above the world of his begetting and can therefore offer to us, deep in the mystifying turnings of our own life stories, an experience of intricate moral certainty that none of us otherwise can know.

Dickens was not shy about asserting his moral opinions directly in the texts of his novels and elsewhere. But we do not require such overt assertions to arrive at a fairly secure notion of what Dickens felt about large moral issues, since the manner of his telling provides sufficient evidence for our conclusions. I have tried to demonstrate here that a definite moral base for Dickens' attitudes can be inferred from his literary method, especially as it relates to the subject of punishment. The narrator withholds information that tests the reader's assessments of characters, therefore implying a warning against rash judgment. The implied author does not permit good characters to execute punishment and emphasizes the tendency for the wicked to create their own punishments. By the very intricacy of his plotting, the implied author suggests a pattern of retribution that extends beyond the novel's text and encompasses it. This suggestion is magnified by the use of prolepsis, especially when what is foretold is the fulfillment of justice beyond the limits of the narrative's action. Similarly, on an opposite scale, repeated patterns of retribution reinforce the larger pattern in the novel as a whole, just as the many condensed stories within the narrative one way or another reflect and call attention to the direction of the novel as a whole. Taken together, these and other devices constitute a redundance of moral information that insures the successful transmission of the fundamental moral message of the literary work. In addition, these narrative devices lure the reader into making moral judgments more severe than those that the implied author will allow for his most sympathetic characters, promoting a self-correcting impulse in the reader that reinforces the novel's message of restraint. These are only some of the techniques by which moral signification can be perceived in a literary text, whether or not the author assists such a reading with open declarations. Thus, although any text may to some degree be deconstructed simply because language itself is so complex and so intricately involved with social structures and other signs, texts can nonetheless, through the redundance I have suggested, sustain a larger coherence that can be dissolved only through willful or capricious misreading, or through innocent ignorance of the language's contextual meaning. I believe that searching for these larger patterns of coherence is a worthwhile critical endeavor and one for which Dickens and his like would commend us.

NOTES

1. James R. Kincaid comments on "the fierce aggression" in the episode of Fledgeby's multiple punishment by Lammle and then Jenny. "The brutal nature of this comedy suggests not only its very basic nature but a negative impulse so strong that it reaches back to the physical, to the desperate satisfacton of a truly frightened man. Edmund Wilson remarked that Dickens was 'now afraid of Podsnap'; the humour indicates that he is, at any rate, afraid of the more elemental Podsnappery manifested in Fledgeby" (*Dickens and the Rhetoric of Laughter* [Oxford: The Clarendon Press, 1971], 236).

2. Charles Dickens, *Our Mutual Friend* (London: Oxford University Press, 1967), 217, 351. Subsequent references appear in the text.

3. I cannot agree with J. Hillis Miller's assertion that "There are no real secrets in *Our Mutual Friend* (*Charles Dickens: The World of His Novels* [Cambridge:

Harvard University Press, 1965], 289). He suggests that characters are immediately readable by one another through their speech patterns, gestures, and so
forth. But it seems to me that there is a good deal of misreading of character.
The novel abounds with real secrets, one of which is the secret that each person
is to her or himself—a major theme in *Little Dorrit,* for example.

4. Rosemary Mundhenk points out that the narrator does provide clues to
Harmon's identity, thus purposely inflating "the reader's confidence in his powers of detection and judgment" which will be shown inadequate in the case of
Boffin's masquerade as a miser ("The Education of the Reader in *Our Mutual
Friend,*" *Nineteenth-Century Fiction* 34, no. 1 [June 1979], 50). Audrey Jaffe observes
that surprise can be satisfying as a recognition of solutions in narrative, but if, as
in *Our Mutual Friend,* the reader does not know there is a mystery to be solved,
surprise operates in a much less reassuring manner, exposing the vulnerability
and lack of knowledge in the reader (*Vanishing Points: Dickens, Narrative, and the
Subject of Omniscience* [Berkeley: University of California Press, 1991], 154). James
R. Kincaid claims that Dickens offers a number of clues indicating that Boffin is
only playing a role as a miser, but I agree with Mundhenk that Dickens fully
intends to deceive his readers. Kincaid rightly argues, however, that Boffin "is
called upon to lend enormous positive support to the comic centre of the novel"
(246).

5. *Dickens' Working Notes for His Novels,* ed. Harry Stone (Chicago: University of Chicago, 1987), 363, 341.

6. Charles Dickens, *The Christmas Books* (Oxford: Oxford University Press,
1987), 151.

7. Charles Dickens, *The Old Curiosity Shop* (Oxford: Oxford Univerity
Press, 1967), 539.

8. See Stanley Friedman's "The Motif of Reading in *Our Mutual Friend,*"
Nineteenth-Century Fiction 28, no. 1 (June 1973), 38–61, for the implications of this
theme.

9. Lawrence Frank explores the ways in which Eugene Mortimer and his
antagonist, Headstone, must become novelists of themselves and create their sto-
ries rather than plagiarize conventional roles (*Charles Dickens and the Romantic Self*
[Lincoln: University of Nebraska Press, 1984], 190ff. More recently, Michal
Peled Ginsberg has affirmed this approach in "The Case against Plot in *Bleak
House* and *Our Mutual Friend,*" ELH 59 (1992), 175–95.

10. Various critics have shown how the apparent disarray of the world
depicted in *Our Mutual Friend* is actually made coherent as the novel progresses.
J. Hillis Miller demonstrates how "a large group of impenetrable milieus with
characters buried untouchably at their centers" reveals itself as "an immense
network of interrelations, none of which has an isolated existence" (285, 288).
U. C. Knoepflmacher argues that Dickens fragments the world of the novel to
reorder it (*Laughter and Despair: Readings in Ten Novels of the Victorian Era* [Berkeley:
University of California Press, 1971], 137–67). And Nancy Aycock Metz ex-

plores the representative role of Mr. Venus, whose occupation as "articulator" epitomizes the way in which the detritus of the world of *Our Mutual Friend* is turned to account ("The Artistic Reclamation of Waste in *Our Mutual Friend, Nineteenth-Century Fiction* 34, no. 1 [June 1979], 59–72). Aycock concludes about the novel's message, "Whatever is finally to be made of this world must be made out of such materials as are already at hand, however tainted and decayed, however partial and reversible the process of reclamation may be" (72). The glue for that reclamation is, in Miller's words, "the reciprocity of self-sacrificing love" (327).

11. Alexander Welsh, *From Copyright to Copperfield: The Identity of Dickens* (Cambridge: Harvard University Press, 1987), 146.

12. John M. Robson writes that "In *Our Mutual Friend* " 'crime' encompasses all wrong attitudes and actions: whatever is thought to require redress or punishment because it threatens or causes damage; whatever, to use a common nineteenth-century criterion, threatens 'security.' A constant question is, How can we be secure, in person and property? The obvious agencies for answers are the police and the law. But in his novel the former is (surprisingly for Dickens) no help, and the latter (not surprisingly for Dickens) proves woefully inadequate except for chicanery. Human beings and God (characters and author) must therefore do what they can supplying rough and/or 'poetic' justice" ("Crime in *Our Mutual Friend,*" in *Rough Justice: Essays on Crime in Literature,* ed. M. L. Friedland [Toronto: University of Toronto Press, 1991], 119).

13. Dickens was, of course, working in a well-established tradition. See Leopold Damrosch, Jr. *God's Plot and Man's Stories: Studies in the Fictional Imagination from Milton to Fielding* (Chicago: University of Chicago Press, 1985).

PART THREE

Thackeray

NINETEEN

Early Thackeray

THACKERAY IS temperamentally very different from Dickens. Whereas Dickens was a determined, highly-disciplined professional, proud of his craft and sure of his skill, Thackeray was comparatively slack and far more humble about the novelist's trade. Beneath this superficial difference the two men shared certain basic moral assumptions. However, where Dickens insisted on the Christian virtues, including mercy, love, and forgiveness, yet saw to it that his narratives guaranteed punishment of the wicked, Thackeray, though equally insistent on love and forgiveness, in a more tolerant manner often forbore any clearly defined pattern of punishment in his stories. For Dickens evil must be hunted down; for Thackeray it is sufficient that it be found out.

It is difficult to say how much temperament determines philosophy or vice versa. Certainly Dickens' worldview was consistent with his habitual behavior. He expected people to shape up and could be severe with those who did not. By contrast, Thackeray had a far more probationary attitude, assuming that others might know as well what was best for them as he did. Such rudimentary approaches to experience usually pervade an individual's opinions and beliefs. Thackeray's intellectual positions are clearly consistent with this fundamentally probationary view. Robert Kiely proposes that Thackeray had to be a humorist to achieve his aim of touching his readers' hearts rather than their minds, but also to assess the world around him in a humbly critical way. Kiely sees this approach in Thackeray's criticism as well as in his fiction. "Thackeray's criticism is nearly always tempered by sympathy, his sentimentality undercut by irony. But everywhere in his work the voice of the mimic can be heard. In the early sketches the fun seems to be for its own sake, but soon the adoption and exaggeration of accents and gestures becomes a way for the artist to draw near his subject without identifying himself with it altogether."[1] Thackeray's humorous approach, Kiely says, is an attempt at creating a natural and authentic voice that reflects and captures real experience. For Thackeray humor "is not a cover-up, a simplification of reality, but an evocation of complex, even contradictory, responses. The seriousness and sadness of the true humorist show through his best jokes, not in spite of them, but in subtle combination with them" (6).

Robert Paul Fletcher, examining the aesthetic grounds for Thackeray's art criticism, concludes that Thackeray preferred the rendering of "the historical and the accidental, the transitory moment and the surface detail, rather than the supposedly permanent and essential."[2] Because he is sceptical "Of human attempts to know (at least empirically) an objective reality," Thackeray resists a conclusive standard in art or in human conduct. "In both his art criticism and his practice as novelist, Thackeray exposes the role of perceptual hypothesis in sign systems" because he is fully alert to the subjective nature of perceiving, or of reading signs (44). This preference for the quick grasping of a temporary truth, evident in the best examples of caricature, translates into Thackeray's narrative method: "Both remain open to improvisation, willing to let the play of their perceptions determine the form and content of their work" (60).

Both Kiely and Fletcher stress Thackeray's openness to experience and his flexibility concerning standards and truths, and surely the whole tone of Thackeray's writing depends upon a mood of irony itself rooted in a broad scepticism. But the reluctance to take absolute stands in favor of passing "truths" dependent upon specific contexts also derives from a generosity of spirit at one with the essentially forgiving quality of Christianity. Thus Thackeray's narrative method, from my point of view, reflects his impulse to release his characters from punitive techniques and turns of plot, and to reach toward a more comprehensive acceptance of diffferences, even where these differences sometimes cause injustice and suffering. Only rarely does Thackeray's narrator insist upon or delight in an outright retributive punishment.

Although there is a pattern of growth and mellowing in Thackeray's writing, underlying his whole literary enterprise is a fairly well-established code of behavior. The difference between the exuberant early work and the wearier late work is perhaps as much a feature of social context as of individual physiology.

At the beginning of his career, Thackeray was a vigorous soldier in the literary wars of his time. But willing as he was to engage in the skirmishes carried out in the literary columns of the periodical press of the day, he disapproved of literary artists themselves using fiction as a form of propaganda. Reviewing Charles Lever's St. Patrick's Eve in the Morning Chronicle for April 3, 1845, he wished that novelists like Lever, Jerrold, and Dickens would eschew questions of politics and political economy, because otherwise they tended to make morality too obtrusive. Novelists, he felt, were increasingly using their fictions as mediums for social judgment. "You cannot have a question fairly debated in this way," he objected. "You cannot allow an author to invent incidents, motives, and characters, in order that he may attack them subsequently."[3] Novelists may be good at showing the condition of the poor, he admits, but they don't offer schemes for bettering social conditions. His own position is clear. "The novelist as it appears to us, ought to be a non-combatant" (74).

This position, taken early, remains basically consistent throughout Thackeray's career. In a review of Disraeli's *Sybil* in the *Morning Chronicle* of May 13, 1846, Thackeray declares that morals and manners are the novelist's best themes and hence he prefers romances that do not treat of politics and social problems, yet he is fair enough to acknowledge some of the truths expressed in Disraeli's novel. Thackeray did not lack political sympathies of his own; he simply considered fiction a poor, because unequal, forum for airing political issues. He is severe on *Coningsby* less for its exposures of and attacks upon Whigs and Conservatives than for its promotion of the vague project called Young England. The conclusion to his *Morning Chronicle* review of May 13, 1844, shows Thackeray's personal sentiments rather clearly (though influenced, no doubt, by the publication for which he was writing).

> We wish Sir Robert Peel joy of his Young England friends; and, admiring fully the vivid correctness of Mr. Disraeli's description of this great Conservative party, which conserves nothing, which proposes nothing, which resists nothing, which believes nothing: admire still more his conclusion, that out of this nothing a something is to be created, round which England is contentedly to rally, and that we are one day to re-organize faith and reverence round this wretched, tottering, mouldy, clumsy, old idol. (50)

Thackeray began his career as a writer at a time when authors dealt sharply with one another.[4] The reviewers for the quarterlies spoke their minds and were often cruel in their estimates of published work. Thackeray shows the influence of that climate, but is a good deal more temperate than many of his contemporaries, even when he means to scold. Writing in 1840 of fashionable French writers, he observes that Balzac, Hugo, and Sand assume godlike roles and warns that we should be wary of gods with lives like theirs. Sand's history, for example, is not very edifying. Thackeray discusses her *Indiana,* a novel sympathizing with an unfaithful wife, and remarks that Sand cannot be impartial, having been just such a wife herself. His conservative moral views become explicit when he judges writers, like Sand, who seek to change social conditions.

> And tell us who have been the social reformers?—the haters, that is, of the present system, according to which we live, love, marry, have children, educate them, and endow them—are they pure themselves? I do believe not one; and directly a man begins to quarrel with the world and its ways, and to lift up, as he calls it, the voice of his despair, and preach passionately to mankind about this tyranny of faith, customs, laws; if we examine what the personal character of the preacher is, we begin pretty clearly to understand the value of the doctrine.[5]

He admits Sand's artistic ability, but he deplores her morals.

Athough the young Thackeray disapproved of fiction serving as a pulpit, he was, from the outset, watchful of morals and sensitive about fiction's role in maintaining morality. He wrote an entire novel to counteract the popularity of Newgate fiction, saying that he wanted to show in *Catherine* (1839–40) what rogues were really like and not to glamorize them as Bulwer, Ainsworth, and others were doing with their Ernest Maltravers, Eugene Arams, and Jack Sheppards. Thackeray alludes to this misuse of fiction in The *Paris Sketch Book* (1840), where he playfully remarks that, Newgate and the highways (referring to highwaymen thieves) being fashionable at present in England, he will provide a corresponding Continental account of the notorious French thief, Louis Dominic Cartouche. There are some ironic turns in this brief biography. For example, the honey pots Cartouche steals as a boy at a Jesuit school turn out to contain hidden gold that the principal of the school is not supposed to have. "And now, see the punishment of avarice!" the narrator exclaims (84). He goes on to recount various of Cartouche's exploits, sardonically referring to one base act [the traitorous assassination of the leader of the gang of thieves of which Cartouche was a member] as a "great and celebrated stroke of genius," and to "an equally moral tale" of his murdering another partner in crime (89, 90). Thackeray obviously not particularly interested in Cartouche's punishment, concludes his essay without pursuing his subject's career to its close.

If Thackeray did not feature highwaymen and career thieves in his fiction, he certainly returned again and again to scoundrels of various sorts, especially so-called "men of the world" with a taste for gambling. Robert A. Colby describes *Barry Lyndon,* for example, as a move up from the outright criminality of *Catherine* to the world of the demirep.[6] Subsequent novels continue that move upward into the seamy margin of respectable society. No doubt Thackeray was influenced in this choice of rogue by his own weakness for gambling and his unfortunate experiences at the gaming table, experiences that must have made him especially sensitive to the likely consequences of a blackleg's life. The early story "Captain Rook and Mr. Pigeon" tells how Tom Rook, from a good family, gets among a bad set at college. While reading for the bar, he falls into debt and, going abroad to avoid the consequences, takes up the gambling and dueling life of a thorough rogue. He is a predator for whom nature supplies an abundance of pigeons. But the narrator has little sympathy for foolish Freddy Pigeon, who, he says, was designed for plucking. Is the blackleg's trade a good one? the narrator asks, and answers that it is not a good calling in the end, though some fellows have a natural genius for it. Captain Rook, he assures us, will end in prison; you can see several of him any time you go to Queen's Bench Prison. It is highly likely that Rook will end in a madhouse. In any case, it is a short career and Rook will die with disease, want, and bad memories as his deathbed companions.

The Memoirs of Barry Lyndon, Esq. (1844) is a more light-hearted and elaborate account of the same type, though Lyndon has social pretentions that the generic

Captain Rook does not. Robert A. Colby describes Barry as "An antiheroic hero, a comic figure with a tragic fate . . . the most deliberately paradoxical character in the Thackerayan cabinet of oddities" (216). Barry Lyndon is certainly a richer character study than Rook and other early Thackeray villains, but that is partly because he has an entire novel in which to develop, and partly because he tells his own story. At one point in his narrative he records the fate of his acquaintance the Chevalier de Magny, who gets into debt through gambling and compounds his difficulties by stealing to pay those debts. De Magny is arrested; his grandfather, appalled by these and other of the young man's dishonorable activities, brings poison to him in prison. Soon after, the Chevalier dies. Lyndon pauses to moralize, warning young men against gambling. Pious as this warning seems, it loses force when we realize that gambling is Lyndon's principal means of support and that his own memoirs are written from Fleet Prison, where he will eventually die from delirium tremens. This exemplum that Lyndon conveys to his readers has an important resonance that goes beyond the simple comic irony of a scoundrel preaching against scoundrelism. Lyndon assumes that the common respectable view is the correct one to communicate to his readers even if he does not abide by conventional moral standards himself. Moreover, Lyndon obviously believes that narratives should endorse moral values, whatever Thackeray might think. Lyndon's own fate is to be less honorable than that of de Magny, who at least has the decency to punish himself with suicide, sparing his family the discomforts of his disgrace. Thackeray thus shows concisely, in Lyndon's account of de Magny's case and later in Lyndon's own fate, the natural punishment that a life of folly begets. And he can achieve this amplified purpose without himself having to preach.

Thackeray never glamorizes his rogues, as he charged that the Newgate novelists did, but he rarely simplifies them into villains, either. Instead, he indicates that his scoundrels differ from the greater part of mankind in the *degree* of their immorality. If human beings are distributed on a continuum of reprehensible to admirable conduct and not divided, as Dickens was inclined to divide them, between the wicked and the good, with a mixed group in between, then it becomes infinitely more difficult to decide just where on the continuum the line between evil and good is crossed, especially since humans are much influenced by their own preconceptions and thus not adequately impartial in judging others. Describing the good-natured rascal Peter Brock in his first novel, *Catherine*, Thackeray makes a plea for realism. "Surely our novel-writers make a great mistake in divesting their rascals of all gentle human qualities: they have such—and the only sad point to think of is, in all private concerns of life, abstract feelings, and dealings with friends, and so on, how dreadfully like a rascal is to an honest man" (*Works*, 20:82).

Howard Walker in "Ravenswing" is a swinder, gambler, and general fraud, but he has breeding—enough to be accepted as a gentleman and to hobnob with aristocratic scamps. There is a certain panache to his selfishness and he is no fool;

that is to say, he is shrewd, though he ends up the victim of his own folly. Arrested for debt, he becomes angry when his wife fails to understand the maneuvers that would release him from the sponging house before additional claims upon him come in; nonetheless, when finally jailed, he lives comfortably in the Queen's Bench Prison. Walker's punishment is basically the legal consequence of his dishonest financial dealings. The judge who sentences him is particularly severe on his way of earning money. But the narrator claims that Walker "is not a bit worse than his neighbors" (*Works*, 20:290). Seeing Walker as a predictably fallible human being, Thackeray does not trouble to arrange a peculiar narrative punishment for this genial scamp, although eventually Walker dies from excessive drinking.

Since in his early writings Thackeray was largely a satirical and comic artist, it is not surprising that his narratives are filled with people of questionable character, fully deserving of chastisement or correction. Their frequent schemings, machinations, and follies cry out for some balancing setback. "The Amours of Mr. Deuceace" in *The Memoirs of Mr. Charles J. Yellowplush* (1837–38) is a typical example. For a time Yellowplush is a servant to the Honorable Algernon Percy Deuceace, fifth and youngest son of the Earl of Crabs. He is another of those characters so familiar in Thackeray's works who live on nothing a year. In fact, he is a gambler, a bad trade for a common man, Yellowplush says, but easy and profitable for "a real thoroughbread genlmn" (*Works*, 17:27). Of course Deuceace is a cheat, and of course he is looking for a wealthy woman to marry and thinks he has found one in Miss Matilda Griffin. Meanwhile, his father, Lord Crabs, comes uninvited to Paris to share in Deuceace's earlier booty. The old Lord is far cannier than his unsupportive son and easily outflanks the youngster. Lord Crabs suggests that Lady Griffin, whom Deuceace has rejected in favor of her stepdaughter, buy up Deuceace's English debts, which she does, and Deuceace is imprisoned for debt just before his planned marriage to Matilda. Lady Griffin firmly believes in revenge, and this is only a financial version of it. Before this, she provokes a duel between Deuceace and Monsieur de l'Orge, which results in the loss of Deuceace's left hand, a maiming punishment uncharacteristic of Thackeray even in his aggressive early writings. It is instructive that the individual so intent upon retribution is herself an entirely unappealing person. By contrast, Lord Crabs is not vindictive, as Yellowplush explains: "Now my Lord, roag as he was, was much too good-natured to do an unkind ackshn, mearly for the sake of doing it. He'd got to that pich that he didn't mind injaries—they were all fair play to him—he gave 'em, and reseav'd them, without a thought of mallis. If he wanted to injer his son, it was to benefick himself" (106). Nonetheless, when Deuceace is finally freed from prison and married to Matilda, who does *not* inherit a fortune, Lord Crabs does punish his son according to his fashion. He has outmaneuvered the young man and married Lady Griffin, who *does* inherit the fortune. Now he tells Deuceace that he should not have tried to outwit an old hand and says that he won't give a penny to help him in his trouble. Yellowplush last views Deuceace as a shabby man striking his wife out of impatience and anger.

Yellowplush is himself not innocent, as his prompt willingness to be bought by Lord Crabs suggests, though he asserts a belief in an ethical code, either directly or implicitly. For example, he openly declares it among servants' perquisites to appropriate goods and to nose into the business of their employers. Yet he is faithful to his master and even impersonates Deuceace so that he can escape his creditors and the law. Nonetheless, Yellowplush betrays his employer by assisting the rapid union of Deuceace and Matilda, and is rewarded with a position in Lady Griffin's establishment. About Deuceace's lamentable condition, Yellowplush feels only contempt for the deserved results of his erstwhile master's behavior. Yet generally aware of his own ambiguous standards of behavior, Yellowplush is inclined not to judge those around him too severely. This is true of several of Thackeray's narrators, from Ikey Solomon of *Catherine* to Pendennis of *Pendennis*. Awareness of one's own fallibility is as serviceable as Christian dogma in achieving moral tolerance. Only when Deuceace has clearly lost out in his cheating career does Yellowplush offer a negative assessment of him, but even then it is simply to express contempt rather than to judge the man. Yellowplush as narrator does not overtly condemn or punish Deuceace, but the implied author does. Thackeray wants us to witness the *natural* consequences of Deuceace's way of life. Not all the misbehaving characters in the story are punished. Lady Griffin and Lord Crabs suffer some discomfort and insult, but they end up with the material prizes they seek. Both Deuceace and his father have pursued selfish courses. One is punished and the other is not. This suggests that the young Thackeray was less interested in the authorial power of meting out justice and more inclined to let characters within his narratives dig their own pits to fall into. Of the two, Lord Crabs is the more amiable rogue, but also the more clever. That is why Deuceace fails. His "punishment" follows from his own overreaching ignorance, not from Thackeray's moral indignation. Deuceace is singled out for what little narrative punishment there is here, perhaps because, in addition to being a scoundrel, he is ill-natured, with little sense of humor and no self-criticism.

A different example of an uncritical fool is Bob Stubbs of *The Fatal Boots* (1839). At the outset of the first-person account of his adventures (one for each month of the year), Stubbs indicates that he considers himself a great and good but also an unfortunate man. At school he establishes a lucrative business lending money to other boys at interest. When Doctor Swishtail discovers his swindles he returns all of the money and flogs Stubbs. This is an early example of retribution following quickly upon Stubbs' transgression. In another episode Stubbs acquires a pair of boots from a shoemaker by pretending to be a lord, but he is found out; the boots are taken and his school fellows put Stubbs under a pump. Again, immediate retribution follows upon transgression. But there is more to this incident. Shoemaker Stiffelkind says to Stubbs, "'you have paid *something* for dese boots, but not all. By Jubider, *you shall never hear de end of dem.* 'And I didn't'' (*Works,* 19:350). This is Stubbs' first experience of delayed retribution. Years later, when Stubbs is engaged to Magdalen Crutty, a young woman with a comfortable fortune, her uncle turns out to be Stiffelkind, who denounces Stubbs and prevents the marriage.

By this time it is evident to the reader that Stubbs is his own worst enemy, and a mean and trivial one at that. He is no accomplished rogue like Howard Walker or Tom Rook, nor a hearty one like Barry Lyndon. He is a small-time cheat and liar. The lying gets him into trouble when he boasts to fellow militiamen of his liaisons with Miss Crutty and one Mary Waters, whom he had also hoped to marry. Mary's relative Captain Waters overhears this conversation and beats Stubbs, who then has to leave the militia and travel in Europe to avoid Waters' challenge to a duel. Later Stubbs meets a Jewish widow, Mrs. Leah Manasseh, who is supposedly very wealthy, but having wooed and won her, Stubbs is arrested for her debts. His lament is heartfelt. "What had I done to deserve it? Hadn't I always kept an eye to the main chance? Hadn't I lived economically, and not like other young men? Had I ever been known to squander or give away a single penny? No! I can lay my hand on my heart, and, thank Heaven, say, No! Why, why was I punished so?'' (383). To crown Stubbs' grief at this low moment in his career, Stiffelkind claims his debt for the forgotten boots. Meanwhile, Stubbs' supposed bride, actually a swindler who has married three men, runs off with what money Stubbs had.

Stiffelkind steps forward to assist the beggared Stubbs, first giving him work as a shoeblack, in which humiliating position he is seen by Magdalen Crutty, and then finding him a position as a general postman. Stiffelkind's compassion is one of the few instances of kindly sentiment in this story, except that of Stubbs' long-suffering mother, who now takes him to live with her until his drinking and carrying on ruins her business and he is left by himself to live on an allowance of £20 a year. He sells his story to a literary gentleman who says his adventures are moral, though Stubbs can't see that. The literary man is right, of course, since Stubbs' whole career is a record of selfish folly insistently tolling the message that offenses are punished both in the short and the long run and that, more often than not, we are the authors of our own misfortunes. But, like the dullards described in "Dennis Haggarty's Wife" in *Men's Wives,* Stubbs is entirely incapable of seeing his own error and stupidity. The Stubbses of the world lament the "punishments" inflicted upon them by fate or other individuals without understanding that these apparent punishments are really only the natural penalites for their selfish acts. Thackeray's narrator does not have to arrange poetic justice or narrative punishments when his characters so blatantly prepare their own misfortunes.

Mean-spirited and lacking self-criticism, Stubbs is inferior to most of Thackeray's rogues, but the graduated scale on which the unfortunate Stubbs is situated can also extend from terrible or trivial villainy to genuine innocence. Samuel

Titmarsh is an example. In *The History of Samuel Titmarsh and the Great Hoggarty Diamond* (1841), young Samuel hopes for a gift of money from his wealthy aunt, but she gives him a diamond instead. One way and another, the diamond brings Titmarsh to the attention of the nobility and also of his employer, Mr. Brough. Through all this Titmarsh does not lose his head. He adheres to his own standard of conduct and is faithful to Mary Smith, whom he marries. He seems to be prosperous and is advancing rapidly in Mr. Brough's insurance company, thanks to his superior's attentions. What he does not know is that he is being exploited for his connection with his wealthy aunt. Early hints indicate that Brough, who is eagerly selling shares, will soon suffer a financial collapse. Titmarsh does not see the crash coming and is arrested as representative of the company while Mr. Brough escapes to Calais.

In a pattern familiar in so many of Thackeray's tales, Titmarsh now hits bottom in the Fleet Prison, and when he is released from prison he finds himself and his wife impoverished. Their child is born and dies. Titmarsh pawns his diamond to pay for the infant's burial and immediately his fortunes take a turn for the better. Mary gets a job as a wetnurse to Lady Tiptof's baby. In his misfortune Samuel recommends the chapter in *The Pickwick Papers* that treats the folly of depriving honest men of their labor just when they most need it, by imprisoning them for debt. Titmarsh is an essentially good man who can recognize the injustice of a whole pattern of economic retribution and who seems to have suffered unjustly. Why, then, has he been so punished? Or is his fall simply an unfortunate turn of events in his life—fate, let us say? The answer is that the narrative is constructed not to punish Titmarsh himself, but to expose the folly of a whole mode of conduct, innocent enough in Titmarsh, but more blameable in other characters. This mode of conduct is founded in greed and arrogance. Titmarsh becomes a part of this pattern not because he himself aspires to wealth, but because his mother urges him to court their wealthy relative. Titmarsh's mother now appreciates her role in her son's misfortunes and apologizes for having obliged him to spend so much time with his odious aunt out of a desire to secure some financial advantage from her; Titmarsh adds that "she and I too were justly punished for worshipping the mammon of unrighteousness and forgetting our natural feelings for the sake of my aunt's paltry lucre" (*Works*, 12:134–35).

Although the story ends with Titmarsh's caution to his readers to be careful of their money and not to speculate with it, the narrative offers an interestingly lenient conclusion to the career of its chief financial offender, Mr. Brough. We learn of his alternately high and low fortunes on the Continent, but Titmarsh says we should at least admire him for his undaunted courage; besides, he figures there must be something good in a man whose family is faithful to him. In this passage the narrator's and the implied author's forgivenesses coincide. Brough has been an out and out scoundrel about money, but he has not been cruel, not been blind to his own failings, and not been cringing. If his family has been faithful to him, he too has been faithful to them. In short, Brough has sufficient redeeming features to excuse him from any punishment, beyond his business failure, that would condemn his conduct or satisfy some moral requirement of the narrative. It would be hard to imagine Dickens leaving a figure like Brough untouched by some retributive turn in the story's plot. In fact, punishment operates in a very confusing manner in this tale because it comes down hardest for a time on two of its least offensive characters. But that is because this punishment is not really retributive; it is therapeutic. And we shall see time and again that Thackeray was quite willing to invoke a narrative punishment of this kind to guide his good characters in a healthy direction.

This extended look at the kinds of "rogues" Thackeray singles out for punishment is not really the digression it appears to be. In fact, we have been looking at Thackeray's practice of depicting sin and retribution as distinguished from that of other authors of the time, where moral imperatives call for clear poetic justice or "providential" intervention, as with the death of George Locke from an infected garment made by workers he had exploited in Kingsley's *Alton Locke*. As we have seen, Thackeray did not consider melodrama and poetic justice realistic modes of representing human experience. In his early years he often mocked these conventional narrative approaches. In a review of Mrs. Gore's *The Snow Storm, a Tale of Christmas* in the *Morning Chronicle* for December 31, 1845, Thackeray makes fun of the utter conventionality of the tale.

> When a mysterious person comes back from India, or from 'the golden Americas,' just in the nick of time—after fifty years' absence—after oppressed virtue is at its last gasp, and is on the point of being sold up—after vice has had a career of prosperity, and has reached a disgusting climax of luck—you may be sure that somebody is going to be rewarded, and somebody else to meet with his just punishment. (MC, 105)

This oversimplified pattern of reward and punishment is not suitable fare for adults, though it is entirely acceptable where children are concerned, as Thackeray indicates in his review of John Edward Taylor's collection of traditional fairy tales, *The Fairy Ring,* in the *Morning Chronicle* for December 26, 1845. In these stories there are damsels shut up by ogres and princes in bright armor, "and vice is punished, and humble beauty and virtue rescued, as they always are in these kindly stories, which have made their way through all countries, and are told to happy children in every language in the world" (99).

Literary artists addressing an adult audience have to depict the world the way it really is, not in melodramatic or simplified forms. In drawing a picture of Lady Fanny Flummery, a caricature of the fashionable authoress in *Character Sketches,* Thackeray exposes the silliness of her writing and the social rather than artistic bases for her reputation. She succeeds chiefly on puffery by literary men. Thackeray thus concludes that Lady Flummery is not so blameable as those who cringe at her feet. After describing the sentimental and melancholy poetry of Ottilia Schlippenschlopp, Fitz-Boodle, the narrator, observes that real literary types are the least sentimental class of gentlemen. In fact, they must always be looking out for the main chance, literarily speaking, because they are in a world of severe competition. The abasements and puffery that attend Lady Flummery are part of a market economy that involves various returns on such investments of servility. A back must be scratched to have one's own back scratched. Some of the scratching, however, is frontal. Thackeray himself could be something of a harpy. Of Mrs. Gore's *Sketches of English Character* he wrote, "People's minds will not be refined or exalted by the perusal of this book" (MC 141). He judged Bulwer's poem, which Bulwer denied was his, rather severely: "'The New Timon' is not like Timon at all; the poetry, to our mind, is not like nature, though it is sometimes something like poetry" (133).

Thackeray was especially hard on Bulwer because he thought the man, though celebrated, not as good an artist as he believed himself to be; moreover, he considered Bulwer both intellectually and personally vain. Thackeray caricatured Bulwer's fiction, but also had Yellowplush censure his conduct. In "Mr. Yellowplush's Ajew," this lively literary servant meets Bulwig at his master's house. There is some moderate humor at Bulwer's expense and at the expense of literary people in general, but when Bulwig says he is going to be made a baronet for his eminence in literature, Yellowplush figures that under those circumstances he himself ought to aspire to a baronetcy as well. Yellowplush is more severe in "Epistles to the Literati," where he offers Bulwer some advice. He says he likes the baronet despite the sham sentiment and so forth in his writing, but recommends that, no matter how much Bulwer admires his own writing, he shouldn't protest when criticised because his complaints and whining just make people sneer the more. Nor should he jabber on about his baronetcy; such self-absorption only annoys folks further.

> With respeck, then, to the barnetcy pint, this is my advice: brazen it
> out. Us littery men I take to be like a pack of schoolboys—childish,
> greedy, envius, holding by our friends, and always ready to fight.
> What must be a man's conduck among such? He must either take no
> notis, and pass myjastick, or else turn round and pummle soundly—
> one, two, right and left, ding dong over the face and eyes; above all,
> never acknowledge that he is hurt. (*Works,* 17:154)

About *The Sea Captain,* Bulwer's play that saw some heavy criticism, Yellowplush says, don't give excuses in the preface to the play. "Fie, man! take courage; and, bearing the terrors of your blood-red hand, as the poet says, punish us, if we've offended you: punish us like a man, or bear your own punishment like a man" (17:156). Thackeray as Yellowplush could give this intelligent advice, but though he was eager to hand out critical punishment in the form of reviews or fictions (especially in the parodies in *Novels By Eminent Hands*), he was as little inclined as most of his contemporaries to bear his punishment like a man, and occasionally cried out himself when hit in a tender spot.

As I have noted, Thackeray did not like to see fiction employed for extraneous purposes. Yellowplush chides Bulwer for his exalted vision of his calling, a chiding that will seem a little wrongheaded to Thackeray himself within a few years. "Away with this canting about great motifs! Let us not be too prowd, my dear Barnet, and fansy ourselves marters of the truth, marters or apostles. We are but tradesmen, working for bread, and not for righteousness' sake. Let's try and work honestly; but don't let us be praying pompisly about our 'sacred calling'" (17:157). Here and elsewhere Thackeray suggests that he has no great respect for his own calling, a sentiment that was to appear again in *Pendennis* and occasion a serious dispute. By emphasizing the humble nature of his craft, Thackeray was not trying to belittle its office. He was simply consistent in suggesting that all human activities are best enacted with humility rather than as an expression of personal or group vanity. And though he disliked overt preaching in fiction, he never doubted that it should have some form of moral underpinning, if only the dubious morality of normal daily intercourse. Even in his early writings Thackeray could invoke his own moral purpose and wish to hold himself and other writers to a worthy code of conduct—witness the extended criticism of his fellow artists that *Catherine* represents. He welcomed negative responses to *Catherine* because such criticisms indicated that the taste for Newgate fiction was passing. Moreover, he frequently championed the importance of his craft, declaring that sham stories are more agreeable than real ones and just as instructive. "What is more, one could, perhaps, meet the stoutest historian on his own ground, and argue with him; showing that sham histories were much truer than real histories; which are, in fact, mere contemptible catalogues of names and places, that can have no moral effect upon the reader" (16:96). In part, the severe criticism that literary artists offered one another followed from their support of certain moral (and political) values. They simply differed on what those values were. But another part of this severity was simply a matter of self-interest and taking sides. In an essay on pictorial artists in *Character Sketches,* Thackeray comments that literary artists can take criticism better than painters because they *assume* personal hostility (17:374). In "An Essay on Thunder and Small Beer," that served as a Preface to the second edition of his Christmas Book for 1850, *The Kickleburys on the Rhine,* Thackeray records the negative assessment, by a London *Times* literary critic, of his book in judicial metaphors. The critic is depicted as a punitive judge who has found out the secret motive in Thackeray's heart—he writes for money. And don't we all, he asks, including the critic who berates me?

Robert A. Colby has suggested that Thackeray did not become serious about conveying a realistic and accurate picture of society until after his success with *Vanity Fair,* but from the beginning Thackeray was interested in being truthful, though profoundly aware of how relative the truth can be (36). Because he is following an actual Newgate account, the narrator of *Catherine* explains that he can't indulge in the devices used by romance writers, but must stick to the truth (20:83).[7] He consistently reminds the reader of the difference between his rendering of criminal conduct and the romancers' methods. Approaching the murder toward which the narrative moves, he calls it the "interestingly horrific" part of the book for people whose taste approves "foul Newgate garbage" (20:178). A brief imitation of Ainsworth's style heightens the contrast between Ikey Solomons' blunt style and that of the Newgate romances. Solomons boasts of the appropriately unnatural style he has employed in the climactic scene when Catherine and her lover, Count Galgenstein, discover the head of Catherine's murdered husband above them on a post. At the end of the tale he repeats that his whole purpose in relating the story has been to show immorality for what it really is. Of course there is always some degree of irony in Thackeray's narration, and certainly we must consider that this moral narrative has been offered for our improvement by Ikey Solomons, the notorious "prince of fences," who is himself writing from prison.[8] Moreover, as Colby points out, Thackeray also satirizes genteel society, as it is reflected in the distorting mirror of the criminal underclass. "The object of the author of *Catherine* . . . was to *lower* the respectable of society by exposing what they had in common with criminals. This was a strange way to 'pardon humanity,' but Thackeray's concern then and thereafter was not so much with unjust laws and penal institutions, as with 'what is false within'" (164).

We have seen that the typical rogue of Thackeray's early fiction is the gambling man-of-the-world, but the most common targets of his satire are pride and hypocrisy, especially the former in its many manifestations. *The Book of Snobs* (1846–47) is a good example. Much of this work depicts the toadying to and aping of the upper classes. A snob is at one point defined as a person "who meanly admires mean things," such as rank for rank's sake (14:11). The *nouveaux riches* marrying into the ranks of the nobility and clerics who seek wealth and station are some examples, though Thackeray also calls attention to the admirable example of poor, dedicated clergymen untempted by snobbery. There are numerous examples of folly, some of which result in suffering, but there is little attempt to punish vanity. *The Book of Snobs* is chiefly a work of exposure, not of chastisement. To a great extent it is designed to help the reader discover snobbery in his or her self, a means thereby of finding out one's own weaknesses and correcting them instead of judging the actions of others, and also a means of placing judgment, when it must be made, on a suitable foundation. A snob does not do this. You are a snob, the narrator comments, "if you lightly despise a man for doing his duty, and refuse to shake an honest man's hand because it wears a Berlin glove" (72).

There are a few narratives that serve as admonitory fables, such as the account of Sackville Maine, who, having made money in coal, is spoiled by club life and luxuries and brings his family to ruin, after which he is reestablished by his inlaws on a more modest scale. This therapeutic "punishment" simply indicates the inevitable consequences of economic irresponsibility. In other cases persons are shown to resist snobbery. Thus Raymond Gray and Emily Harley Baker marry for love against the objections of their ambitious families, but the plain unpretentiousness of their wholesome existence wins over the influential Goldmore, who promotes Gray's legal career. The point of the book is summed up in two statements made near the end. On the negative side, the narrator declares, "it seems to me that all English society is cursed by this mammoniacal superstition; and that we are sneaking and bowing and cringing on the one hand, or bullying and scorning on the other, from the lowest to the highest" (14:222–23). The ending words of this series of portraits are more positive. The narrator says, never forget, "if Fun is good, Truth is better, and Love is best of all" (225). Rather than fastening on means to punish the proud and hypocritical, Thackeray prefers to exhibit their faults and make us almost pity them for their foolishness. Love is best, and for love we often need forgiveness first.

Any unwarranted assumption of superiority spurs Thackeray's sarcasm, whether national, provincial, or personal. He frequently makes fun of the national vanity of foreigners, especially of the French, as Thackeray's parody of his own Yellowplush, entitled *Crinoline,* demonstrates. But he was equally severe and more often so with his countrymen. The English national sense of superiority is deplored in *The Book of Snobs,* especially in its evocation of dislike by people of other countries. Thackeray repeats this charge many times in his writings. A typical example occurs in *Little Travels and Roadside Sketches* by Michelangelo Titmarsh, who notes that the Belgians and the French dislike the British for their insolence.

> This is why we are hated—for pride. In our free country a tradesman, a lacquey, or a waiter will submit to almost any given insult from a gentleman: in these benighted lands one man is as good as another; and pray God it may soon be so with us! Of all European people, which is the nation that has the most haughtiness, the strongest prejudices, the greatest reserve, the greatest dulness? I say an Englishman of the genteel classes. (16:356–57)

One of Thackeray's more extended send-ups of the English as a nation is "Miss Tickletoby's Lectures on English History" (1842) in which national shibboleths are unceremoniously toppled. The piece implicitly criticizes traditional history by alluding to its fictional qualities and its obviously prejudicial character. Miss Tickletoby explains that she is not going to report Boadicea's speech because accounts of it differ widely, and hence she assumes the actual words are unknown and she refuses to quote words that were never uttered. She is disrespectful toward England's rulers, declaring that England has had kings for one thousand years, but only one great one, Alfred. We won't come to another one in history until George Washington, the American Alfred, she announces, prompting one parent to declare her a radical and to threaten removing his son from her school. She describes Edward the Confessor as a spooney and William Rufus as a liar to his people, though she adds that all politicians behave so. Other institutions besides royalty come in for their digs. When King Canute feels remorse for his many crimes against his people, his bishops say that his sins are forgiven by the church because the king is its generous benefactor. This is a particularly strong thrust at the arrogance of authority, because it was widely believed by various denominations that true forgiveness comes only through God, and only after genuine repentance.

Miss Tickletoby is unrelenting in her exposition of the crimes, follies, and rascalities of England's rulers, but she is just as sharp with her own charges. From the opening explanatory lecture, we learn that Miss Tickletoby is a stern educator, as her name suggests. The narrator tells us that Miss Tickletoby believes in the effectiveness of corporal punishment, not in modern leniency. We see her in action punishing Master Spry. John Carey absurdly claims that her implementation of caning approaches a form of Victorian pornography.[9] If that were so, we would have to X-rate a good deal of Thackeray's writing, where caning is frequently dwelt upon as a punishment at school, sometimes as an improving exercise, as Carey notes, and sometimes as brutal folly (Carey, 27).

Recounting the affair of King Henry II with Rosamund Clifford, Miss Tickletoby says that when Queen Eleanor found out about this dalliance, she offered Rosamund the choice of suicide by sword or by poison, and asserts that Queen Eleanor served the woman right (26:46). But if Miss Tickletoby endorses punishment, she does not approve of institutionalized murder. Despite her approval of Rosamund's fate, Miss Tickletoby is obviously against capital punishment. Having described how King Edward I eventually had the great Scottish warrior William Wallace hanged, she adds that murder and hanging were common then; "nay, they were thought to be just and laudable, and I make no doubt that people at that period who objected to such murders at all were accused of 'sickly sentimentality,' just as they are now, who presume to be hurt when the law orders a fellow-creature to be killed before the Old Bailey" (26:67).

If Thackeray regularly returns to the national sins of vanity and pride, he is predominantly concerned with the personal, more foolish forms they take in individuals. In "Little Poinsinet," Thackeray gives an account of the various tricks played on a vain, gullible, dwarfish fellow who lived in Paris in the 1760s to dramatize the moral that foolish pride deserves the mockery it invites. *Cox's Diary* (1840) is a farce about a barber and his family's elevation to the gentry, followed by their economic failure. Mrs. Cox, who has been chiefly responsible for the family excesses, admits her error, says she has punished her family, and declares that she repents her behavior. Orlando Crump, once Cox's assistant, is spurned by the family in its glory, yet he is faithful to them, providing Cox's salvation by taking him back as a partner. *A Little Dinner at Timmins'* (1848) follows a similar pattern on a smaller scale, when Mr. and Mrs. Timmins' decision to give a party gets entirely out of hand. The conclusion of the narrative emphasizes the folly of giving a party beyond one's means. Timmins is in debt, the people he has entertained are alienated, he has gained a reputation for extravagance, and he is in danger of losing clients as well as an inheritance from an uncle.

What there is of punishment in these tales is not the kind of narrative punishment that will interest us later, but straightforward description of the consequences of foolish behavior. Correspondingly there is not much occasion for forgiveness either, though, as we have seen, there is sufficient moralizing. But the early works do give numerous instances of how best to behave, either through direct instruction or through suitable models.

Throughout his career Thackeray located the truest virtues in women. He is often harsh on women's vanity and cruelty (especially to their own sex), but his best models of virtue are also women. Beatrice Merger in *The Paris Sketch Book* is a young French servant of all work who, despite poverty and hardship, remains grateful to God for what work and food she has. Coming to Paris, she is able to live more comfortably while preserving her virtue. Thackeray suggests that a lady or a bishop could learn from her faith, humility, and charity. Another good example from the *Paris Sketch Book* is Mary Ancel, who is prepared to marry a man she dislikes to save her father's life, but who boldly speaks the truth against her oppressor when that danger is past. Mary Ancel combines the self-renunciation of a Beatrice Merger with the more active courage of a Laura Pendennis. But women need not endure hardship or actively combat evil to be good influences. Mr. Brown in "Mr. Brown's Letters to His Nephew" advises his nephew to make himself welcome at homes where he'll converse with women because women have a good influence and are improving for young men.

But virtue is by no means the exclusive domain of women, as Dennis Haggerty of "Dennis Haggerty's Wife" demonstrates. Entirely misguided in his affection for an unattractive young woman, he is willingly ensnared into marrying her after she has been disfigured and blinded by smallpox. His fidelity and love are genuine, but wasted on a worthless object, for his wife and mother eventually send him away to pine and die from heartbreak and poverty.

Much of what Thackeray wrote for *Punch* in his early years was meant to be comic and satirical. To this degree it is also "punitive," as any satire might be regarded. In fact, however, most of the writing is little more than a repetitive pattern of exposing humbug. The Fat Contributor goes so far as to declare Athens, the source of much suffering for schoolboys who had to study the Greek classics, a humbug. His description of the city is very unflattering. He makes fun of Brighton and even reveals himself to be guilty of vanities he deplores in others, thus preparing for the Snob Papers by one of themselves. Only occasionally do the *Punch* papers take up subjects that call for moral judgment, and then the conditions are frequently both comic and ambivalent. "The Froddylent Butler" is a brief narrative, based on a real instance, about a butler who tampers with his master's wines until they are unmistakably bad, thus making his fraud evident. He is arrested and punished. But the point of the story is not the moral offense and its punishment, but the monumental stupidity of the butler. Morally reprehensible behavior occurs as well in "Hobson's Choice, Or, The Tribulations of a Gentleman in Search of a Man-Servant." Nagged by his wife to hire a male servant, Marmaduke Hobson begins by employing his greengrocer's son as a page. But the young man, who had been quite decent, changes in Hobson's service. He begins to consume a great deal of food and grows mischievous and lazy. When he is discovered comically imitating Mrs. Hobson's mother, retribution is immediate and he is fired. Though Hobson's house has been robbed under peculiar circumstances while a Mr. Abershaw has been his servant, no evidence can be found about the perpetrator, though Abershaw leaves unpunished when the investigating police officer recognizes him as a known thief. These servant/master farces are commonplace materials of the times in which the masters come off looking no better than the servants and the point is to make fun of folly, not to punish misbehavior.

Only rarely does Thackeray's persona become morally involved in the subject of his paper, but in one instance it does so vigorously. "On The Snob Civilian" (August 1846) touches on the civilian criticism of the military, occasioned by the death of a hussar following a severe flogging. The military's response to such criticism is that civilians don't understand the army. *Punch's* sarcastic remark is that, army men being known for their learning and intelligence, nothing could be more snobbish than to oppose them.

> When men such as these, and the very highest authorities in the army, are of opinion that flogging is requisite for the British soldier, it is manifestly absurd of the civilian to interfere. Do you know as much about the army and the wants of the soldier as Field-Marshal the Duke of Wellington? If the Great Captain of the Age considers flogging is one of the wants of the army, what business have you to object? You're not flogged. You are a Pekin. To lash fellow-creatures like hounds may be contrary to your ideas of decency, morals, and justice; to submit Christian men to punishments brutal, savage, degrading, ineffectual, may be revolting to you; but to suppose that such an eminent philanthropist as the Great Captain of the Age would allow such penalties to be inflicted on the troops if they could be done away with, is absurd. A word from the Chiefs of the army, and the Cat might have taken its place as an historical weapon in the Tower, along with the boots and the thumbscrews of the Spanish Armada. But, say you, very likely the Great Captain of his Age, the Duke of Alva, might have considered thumbscrews and boots just as necessary for discipline as the Cat is supposed to be now (26:369–70).

There is more to this simple incident of excessive punishment, however, because the case exists in a larger framework of justice that has to do with unequal treatment based on class, so Thackeray makes the injustice explicit.

When the tipsy young Lieutenant of the 4th Dragoons cut at his Adjutant with a sabre, he was reprimanded and returned back to his duty, and does it, no doubt, very well; when the tipsy private struck his corporal, he was flogged, and died after the flogging. There must be a line drawn, look you, otherwise the poor private might have been forgiven too, by the Great Captain of the Age, who pardoned the gentleman-offender. There must be distinctions and differences, and mysteries which are beyond the comprehension of the civilian, and this paper is written as a warning to all such not to meddle with affairs that are quite out of their sphere. (371–72)

With the exception of a few direct passages of this kind specifically attacking harsh forms of punishment and urging greater humaneness in judging human beings (including a famous one that I shall mention later on), Thackeray's early writings concern themselves very little with punishment and forgiveness in any serious way. As we have seen, he is punitive in the spirit of the time insofar as satire and comic exaggeration are punitive, and he is forgiving insofar as he allows some good and wicked characters to redeem their circumstances or go unpunished for transgressions. The exposure of pride, wickedness, hypocrisy, and worse offenses is Thackeray's chief mode of "punishing" his subjects through aggressive humor. But from about the time of *Vanity Fair* (1848), he becomes less punitive in his efforts to foster humane behavior and increasingly willing to offer positive models to imitate. If his rogues were generally not all bad, his examples of virtue were also compounds of strength and weakness. But by the time he had achieved success with *Vanity Fair* and *Pendennis,* he was prepared to offer direct advice on good living through his spokesman Mr. Brown in "Mr. Brown's Letters to His Nephew." Much of Mr. Brown's wisdom has to do with proper dress and social intercourse, but it is all founded on the concept of proper respect and sympathy for oneself and others. "Begin your day with a clean conscience in every way," Mr. Brown says. "Cleanliness is honesty. A man who shows but a clean face and hands is a rogue and hypocrite in society, and takes credit for a virtue which he does not possess" (16:238). Although Thackeray consistently reminds his readers to be slow to judge others because some secret motive may prompt their actions, just as secret motives make our own conduct rational to ourselves, he nonetheless advocates as great an openness or honesty as is possible, and directs most of his satire toward those who consciously pretend to be something they are not. In describing what kind of wife his nephew should seek out, Mr. Brown especially commends a woman who has humor and who is cheerful. His definition of the latter term summarizes Thackeray's ideal character.

What, indeed, does not that word 'cheerfulness' imply? It means a contented spirit; it means a pure heart; it means a kind and loving disposition; it means humility and charity; it means a generous appreciation of

others, and a modest opinion of self. Stupid people, people who do not
know how to laugh, are always pompous and self-conceited: that is,
bigoted; that is, cruel; that is, ungentle, uncharitable, unchristian.
(12:318)

Mr. Brown tells his nephew that we must be gentle with our neighbors' failings as we hope to be forgiven, a central tenet of Thackeray's moral philosophy.
Robert A. Colby has rightly observed that "The prophet's admonition 'Judge
not, lest ye be judged' could well be affixed to Thackeray's books," while arguing that, perhaps in the spirit of the great French critic of his time, Victor Cousin, Thackeray advocated a spirit of universal sympathy condensed in the classical
motto: *Homo sum; humani nihil a me alienum puto* (26, 34). Still, Thackeray realized
how difficult it was always to live by this principle and gave a notable example
in Dr. Solomon Pacifico's confession in "The Proser." The Doctor sees a Mrs.
Trotter-Walker at the opera and remembers that years ago she did not wish to
make his acquaintance, probably because he did not seem entirely genteel. The
slight still rankles. "We forgive injuries," he observes. "We survive even our
remorse for great wrongs that we ourselves commit; but I doubt if we ever forgive slights of this nature put upon us, or forget circumstances in which our self-
love had been made to suffer" (16:333).

By the time he wrote the gently moralizing essays of *Sketches and Travels in
London,* Thackeray had become more serious about the responsibilities of authorship. Earlier he had objected to fiction that was oppressively didactic, and eagerly satirized novels for their artistic liabilities.[10] Now, when Mr. Brown
notices *Pendennis* and *David Copperfield* being read by members of his club, he
comments on the moral responsibility that a novelist as popular as Dickens has to
his audience. But if Thackeray became increasingly concerned with providing a
strong moral base for his writings, he did so in a manner quite different from
Dickens. Dickens was deeply interested in seeing cruelty and vice punished, and
arranged his narratives so that this retribution was almost always accomplished.
By contrast, Thackeray emphasized the role of forbearance and forgiveness. Unlike Dickens, Thackeray was never much interested in the operations of legal
systems and seldom called for their application or their reform. In *Notes of a Journey from Cornhill to Grand Cairo* (1846), he casually observes the casual nature of
the prison at Rhodes. He remarks upon the beheading of an Arnaoot soldier in
Egypt. Informed that another beheading might take place the next day, he says
that it would make a good chapter, but he won't go. "Seeing one man hanged is
quite enough in the course of a life" (12:352).

Thackeray here refers to his attendance at the execution of Courvoisier, recorded in his essay "On Going to See a Man Hanged" (1840). The essay is less
about the criminal justice system than about justice in a larger sense, justice related to the whole arrangement of a society in which the privileged receive favored treatment that they do not deserve while the powerless suffer. The hanging

of one individual comes to signify, in its total context, the conflict of forces within English society and the arbitrary violence used to sustain an unequal justice. Thackeray says of the common folk in the crowd gathered to witness the execution that they are allowed no say in government and thus have no reason to value their "leaders" in Parliament. Though there is some disorderly behavior, Thackeray approves the good sense, morals, and knowledge of the crowd in general, and contrasts this prudence with the bad behavior of the aristocrats present. When Courvoisier appears, he bears his punishment like a man, Thackeray says, admitting, however, that he closed his own eyes at the crucial moment. Thackeray's judgment here on public execution is unequivocal. He feels that he has abetted a crime of wickedness by one set of persons against their fellow. The government, he sneers, commits the victim to God's mercy, but offers him none on earth. He does not believe that the crime of murder necessarily requires extermination, nor does he accept the death spectacle as a deterrent, and he wants the practice abolished. He comes away from Snow Hill with disgust for murder, *"but it was for the murder I saw done"* (14:452).

Thackeray took up this subject earlier in "The Case of Peytel," in *The Paris Sketch Book,* where he declared that, although he couldn't say if Peytel was innocent or not, he believed the evidence so poor that it did not warrant taking the man's life. Again, Thackeray emphasizes the injustice involved in the prosecution. He gives an account of Peytel's death and the nature of the crowd at the execution, and then directs an apostrophe at a generic representative of the law.

> Say, Mr. Briefless, do you think that any single person, meditating murder, would be deterred therefrom by beholding this—nay, a thousand more executions? It is not for moral improvement, as I take it, nor for opportunity to make appropriate remarks upon the punishment of crime, that people make a holiday of a killing-day, and leave their homes and occupations, to flock and witness the cutting off of a head. (16:279)

For Thackeray, then, there is little fascination in violent crime and the legal activities of pursuit and retribution. Unlike Dickens, who identified closely with the policeman's impulse to hunt down and punish, Thackeray had scant interest in these concerns. His prisons are almost entirely debtors' prisons, his representatives of the legal system as often questionable lawyers as honest ones, and more likely bailiffs' men than police officers. When Thackeray visited prisons—such as the women's prison in Paris—he was content to describe what he saw, not offering opinions on comparative theories of punishment as Dickens was likely to do. From early in his career, and increasingly thereafter, Thackeray's narratives are concerned less with the linear movement of chase, capture, and chastisement than with the expanding circle of disclosure and discovery. In a comic variation of the Faust legend entitled "The Painter's Bargain," Simon Gambouge makes a deal with the devil and soon after is caught trying to pawn a plate from a restaurant. The result is remorse, but Thackeray presents this remorse in sceptical terms. "The effects of conscience are dreadful indeed. Oh! how fearful is retribution, how deep is despair, how bitter is remorse for crime—when crime is found out!—otherwise, conscience takes matters much more easily. Gambouge cursed his fate, and swore henceforth to be virtuous" (12:73). The true grief is being found out in our wickedness or folly. To behave in such a way that you cannot afford to have your conduct known is not only likely to involve vice or indiscretion; it is to place yourself in the unappealing position of having to keep secrets. Barry Lyndon, who has been but a poor private, gains power over Princess Olivia and the Chevalier de Magny because he knows their secret. "And this," he says admiringly of himself, "is a proof of what genius and perseverance can do, and should act as a warning to great people never to have secrets—if they can help it" (19:159). In the major fiction, Thackeray's narrative method plays heavily on the role of secrets, the significance of disclosure, the punishments that hypocrisy, lying, and deceiving bring upon their perpetrators, and the need always to incline toward leniency, if only because there is likely to come a day when your own story will be made public and your conduct assessed.

NOTES

1. Robert Kiely, "Victorian Harlequin: The Function of Humor in Thackeray's Critical and Miscellaneous Prose," *William Makepeace Thackeray,* ed. Harold Bloom (New York: Chelsea House Publishers, 1987), 19. Subsequent references appear in the text.

2. Robert Paul Fletcher, "'Mere Outer Works' and 'Fleeting Effects': Thackeray's Novelistic Art and the Art of the Novel," *Journal of English and Germanic Philology* 91, no. 1 (January 1992), 46.

3. William Makepeace Thackeray, *Contributions to the Morning Chronicle,* ed. Gordon N. Ray (Urbana: University of Illinois Press, 1955), 72. Subsequent references appear in the text.

4. There are various studies that describe the lively scene among the periodicals and their contributors during this period. Political sentiments were still strong and complicated the periodical scene early in the century, as Iain McCalman has indicated in *Radical Underworld: Prophets, Revolutionaries and Pornographers in London, 1795-1840* (Cambridge: Cambridge University Press, 1988). M. H. Spielmann's *The History of Punch* (New York: Cassell, 1895) and Arthur Prager's *The Mahogany Tree: An Informal History of PUNCH* (New York: Hawthorn Books, Inc., 1979) detail the high spirits associated with the contributors of that landmark publication, while Spencer L. Eddy, Jr., *The Founding of The Cornhill Magazine* (Muncie, Indiana: Ball State Monograph Number Nineteen, 1970), discusses

the change of character in periodicals of the middle years of the century. Nigel Cross provides a comprehensive study of writers for the periodical press in the nineteenth century in *The Common Writer: Life in Nineteenth-Century Grub Street* (Cambridge: Cambridge University Press, 1985).

5. *The Works of William Makepeace Thackeray,* 26 vols. (Philadelphia: J. B. Lippincott Company, 1901), 16:232.

6. Robert A. Colby, *Thackeray's Canvass of Humanity: An Author and His Public* (Columbus: Ohio State University Press, 1979), 222. Subsequent references appear in the text.

7. Colby indicates how much Thackeray embellished the rudimentary Newgate account of this criminal episode. He also examines the function of the narrator, Ikey Solomons, himself a real criminal of the period (150ff.). Thackeray named his narrator Ikey Solomons, Jr., but he clearly meant to identify him with the real criminal.

8. Richard Altick notes that Ikey Solomons was under governmental detention at Hobart Town, Tasmania, where he was to die in 1851, but would still have been remembered by Thackeray's audience. Altick also remarks that Solomons was associated with Fagin in *Oliver Twist* (*The Presence of the Present: Topics of the Day in the Victorian Novel* [Columbus: Ohio State University Press, 1991], 601). See also J. J. Tobias' *Prince of Fences: The Life and Crimes of Ikey Solomons* (London: Vallentine, Mitchell, 1974).

9. John Carey, *Thackeray: Prodigal Genius* (London: Faber & Faber, 1977), 29.

10. See Thackeray's "Plan for a Prize Novel," where he specificially comments on the faults of didacticism (*Works* 15, 104).

TWENTY

Vanity Fair

YOU KNOW that you are in for an uncommon read when, early in your novel, a young woman declares, "Revenge may be wicked, but it's natural," as Rebecca Sharp does in the second chapter of *Vanity Fair* (1847–48). She goes on to admit, "I'm no angel," a view the narrator promptly confirms: "And to say the truth she certainly was not."[1] He also acknowledges the moral unusualness of his tale when he announces that "we may be pretty certain that persons whom all the world treats ill, deserve entirely the treatment they get" (1:12). And he adds, "The world is a looking-glass, and gives back to every man the reflection of his own face" (1:12). In short, we invite a treatment that we imagine is our due. But this outlook makes for a very slippery code of conduct. If we project a smiling face unto the world, should we be satisfied with its returning blandishments? Becky Sharp certainly learns to smile into the looking glass, and surely part of the world smiles back, but smiles do not seem to be enough—and I am not talking here about the money the Rawdon Crawleys perpetually lack. Thackeray's metaphor of the mirror also suggests what Tennyson offered as his contribution to world wisdom: "Every man imputes himself."[2] Looking into the mirror of the world, we discover there our own traits. The innocent will see innocence, the wicked will discern mischief. Implicit in this view is the inevitable distrust the wicked will feel about "the world," because they know the bad secrets in their own hearts and suspect the bad secrets in others as well. The great suffering for the innocent of this world is to discover evil; for the wicked, it is to be found out. But if what we see in the world around us is our own reflection, that does not mean that we wish that reflection to be recognized as our own, and so we establish an elaborate game of disguise. Ina Ferris comments on this feature of *Vanity Fair*. "Reality is hidden or ignored as the creation of false appearance becomes the norm and the central 'fact' of existence. So Becky's 'happier days' are

not days of innocence but days 'when she was not innocent, but not found out'
(Ch. 64)."³

Underlying the moral structure of Thackeray's fiction is the pervasive insecurity of human existence. This insecurity takes many forms, of course, and largely
accounts for the title of *Vanity Fair*. To a great extent we are all pawns or puppets
in a game or play arranged by powers beyond us. We will be disposed of as those
powers direct. That being so, we must not be too quick to arrogate virtue to
ourselves and folly, error, or crime to others. When financial disaster forces the
Sedley family down to the very hem of respectable society, the narrator warns
against the automatic contempt that poverty generates in the fortunate, as it does
in Mr. Osborne. How many of us think to compassionate the poor, he asks:
" 'There must be classes—there must be rich and poor,' Dives says, smacking his
claret—(it is well if he even sends the broken meat out to Lazarus sitting under
the window). Very true; but think how mysterious and often unaccountable it
is—that lottery of life which gives to this man the purple and fine linen, and
sends to the other rags for garments and dogs for comforters" (2:275). This warning concerns chances of good or bad financial fortune, but before long the narrator extends his caution to the realm of morals when he tries to palliate Amelia's
offense of accepting money from Mr. Osborne, her father's enemy. "Be gentle
with those who are less lucky, if not more deserving. Think, what right have you
to be scornful, whose virtue is a deficiency of temptation, whose success may be
a chance, whose rank may be an ancestor's accident, whose prosperity is very
likely a satire" (2:276). Thackeray knew very well how chance could alter an
individual's career. Not only was he a dangerously compulsive gambler who
learned to control his passion, but he lost a small fortune through business speculation. His metaphor of fortune, chance, and gambling was no random choice,
but rested on painful experience of the world's way. Early commentators on the
novel quickly recognized Thackeray's strategy of offering characters not susceptible of simplistic judgments. John Forster singled out Becky Sharp.

> She commits every conceivable wickedness; dishonours her husband,
> betrays her friend, degrades and embrutes herself, and finally commits
> a murder; without in the least losing those smart, good-tempered, sensi-
> ble manners and ways, which ingratiate her with the reader in spite of
> all their atrocities. In this we may think the art questionably employed,
> but it is not to be denied that it is very extraordinary art; and it is due
> to Mr Thackeray to add that he has been careful to explain the blended
> good and evil in this woman by very curious and impressive early de-
> tails of the circumstances of her birth and bringing up.⁴

Elizabeth Rigby applied this principle to all of the characters of the novel.

> With few exceptions the personages are too like our every-day selves
> and neighbours to draw any distinct moral from. We cannot see our

way clearly. Palliations of the bad and disappointments in the good are perpetually obstructing our judgment, by bringing what should decide it too close to that common standard of experience in which our only rule of opinion is charity.[5]

If some are born smiling into the looking glass of the world and others awake to it wearing a frown, that does not mean the one values the smiling, or that the other cannot unlearn her scowl. As we have seen, Becky learns to smile, and, despite some failures, maintains the smile sufficiently to get a portion of the looking glass to smile back, if only cloudily. But Becky is not content merely with succeeding in the lottery of life; she wants the risk and thrill that make the gambling worthwhile. There is more than one reason why Becky and Rawdon are so profoundly associated with gambling. It is not only the way they make a perilous living; it characterizes their very mode of existence. As we have seen in the previous chapter, from the outset of his career Thackeray was inclined to depict gamblers as almost certain losers in the long run. One very likely consequence of gambling was debt. In many Victorian narratives, including *Vanity Fair,* actual debt and the bankruptcy that often followed were frequently equated with moral impoverishment.[6] For many writers, including Dickens, as we have already seen, the very language of investment, income, debt, and forgiveness of debt was a means of representing moral judgment and mercy in this world and in the next. With Thackeray, however, poverty of pocket or of spirit is as likely to be fortuitous as it is to be earned, and the "punishment" for either capricious.

The narrator, who urges his readers not to judge others hastily, is generally willing to abide by his own advice, but upon occasion he feels the need to offer evaluations. He insists that he is not preaching, but simply telling the truth. At one point he pauses in his storytelling to discuss his objective. He has just quoted Becky's wickedly amusing letter from Sir Pitt Crawley's household and has remarked that she might have been more high minded in her correspondence.

> But my kind reader will please to remember, that this history has "Vanity Fair" for a title, and that Vanity Fair is a very vain, wicked, foolish place, full of all sorts of humbugs and falsenesses and pretensions. And while the moralist, who is holding forth on the cover (an accurate portrait of your humble servant), professes to wear neither gown nor bands, but only the very same long-eared livery in which his congregation is arrayed: yet, look you, one is bound to speak the truth as far as one knows it, whether one mounts a cap and bells or a shovel-hat; and a deal of disagreeable matter must come out in the course of such an undertaking. (1:94)

In telling the truth, however, he may still serve as a moralist by determining the fates of his characters. He describes the emotionally stimulating strategies of an Italian storyteller and of the French stage, the aims of which are to excite and involve their audiences in sentiments against the villains of their tales, and he then distinguishes his own role. He has set his two examples together "so that you may see that it is not from mere mercenary motives that the present performer is desirous to show up and trounce his villains; but because he has a sincere hatred of them, which he cannot keep down, and which must find a vent in suitable abuse and bad language" (1:95). A quiet style will do for the present chapter, he says, but promises "fine language" when he comes to the "harrowing villainy." This inflated language, with its alliteration and stiff passive voice that Thackeray frequently used to parody Ainsworth, Bulwer, and others, evokes the spirit of melodrama, but anyone having read this far in the narrative would be perfectly aware that he or she was involved in a comedy, and that the narrator's pronouncements are ironic. The narrator expatiates on his intention of passing judgment upon his characters as he goes along.

> And, as we bring our characters forward, I will ask leave, as a man and a brother, not only to introduce them, but occasionally to step down from the platform, and talk about them: if they are good and kindly, to love them and shake them by the hand; if they are silly, to laugh at them confidentially in the reader's sleeve: if they are wicked and heartless, to abuse them in the strongest terms which politeness admits of.
>
> Otherwise you might fancy it was I who was sneering at the practice of devotion, which Miss Sharp finds so ridiculous; that it was I who laughed good-humouredly at the reeling old Silenus of a baronet— whereas the laughter comes from one who has no reverence except for prosperity, and no eye for anything beyond success. Such people there are living and flourishing in the world—Faithless, Hopeless, Charity-less; let us have at them, dear friends, with might and main. Some there are, and very successful too, mere quacks and fools: and it was to combat and expose such as those, no doubt, that Laughter was made. (1:95–96)

I have dwelt on this familiar passage from *Vanity Fair* because I want to emphasize how consciously Thackeray was playing with the moral conventions of Victorian narratives. He called his book a "Novel Without a Hero," suggesting that his readers were not to look for a Nicholas Nickleby or a Crichton in it. His characters would be mundane types, like his readers. But that does not mean he could not depict the mundane virtues and villainies of such people and comment on them if he chose, even if, while judging others, he admitted his own ass's ears. Sometimes those judgments are purposely ambivalent. Of the French maid who has witnessed the breakup of Rebecca's establishment after Rawdon finds her alone with Lord Steyne, and who carries off many valuables and later enjoys Lord Steyne's patronage at her milliner's shop in Paris, he says, "May she flourish *as she deserves*" (2:242, emphasis added). Finally, as Juliet McMaster points out, the authorial presence is not Thackeray but a fallible narrator, a commentator who on his own is no ultimate authority.[7] A world in which all admit to being fools is a comic world where salvation and correction come in the form of laughter. In such a world, hunting down scoundrels to execute justice upon them is less important than finding out their frailties. The degrees of punishment are significantly reduced because the fundamental sentiment pervading this comic world is pardon. Robert Siegle, in exploring the reflexive nature of *Vanity Fair's* narrative, remarks that, "In effect, asking us to compare the conventions of sentimental romance and moralistic censorship undermines the stature of each code's implicit assumptions."[8] The narrative method is thus itself a means of enforcing a moral response without stipulating the specific nature of that response.

Still, the world of *Vanity Fair* is an unjust world and that injustice must be noted. Fittingly, Thackeray begins by indicating injustice toward the young through the tyranny of schoolkeepers, first Miss Pinkerton and then Dr. Swishtail. Youthful experience of tyranny and injustice is significant because "with some persons those awes and terrors of youth last for ever and ever" (1:10). The young are perhaps most sensitive to such abuse. "Who amongst us is there that does not recollect similar hours of bitter, bitter childish grief? Who feels injustice; who shrinks before a slight; who has a sense of wrong so acute, and so glowing a gratitude for kindness as a generous boy? and how many of those generous souls do you degrade, estrange, torture, for the sake of a little loose arithmetic, and miserable dog-latin?" (1:47). Much of what appears to be tyranny on the part of schoolmasters and parents is well-intended assistance gone wrong. The narrator suggests that little harm would result "if parents would not insist upon directing their [children's] thoughts, and dominating their feelings—those feelings and thoughts which are a mystery to all" (1:50). Being keenly sensitive to new experience, children are likely to regard such meddling as a form of abuse, an attitude fostering discontent, resentment, and restlessness.

School is not the world in miniature, but it is a miniature world.[9] Although that world is *governed* by adults, it is often *ruled* by children themselves. Usually the bullies dominate. This is the case in Swishtail's school and, according to the narrator, is normal. "Torture in a public school is as much licensed as the knout in Russia," the narrator explains, touching upon an incident where Cuff, the school bully, brutalizes young George Osborne. Dobbin, perhaps revolted by this tyranny, or moved by a desire to test Cuff, interferes and ultimately whips the fellow. Here is a simple, concise instance of cruelty punished in the most direct fashion. You use your fists to stop a bully from misusing his. Virtue triumphs in the simplest, most measurable terms. This rudimentary schoolboy scene recurs so consistently in Thackeray's writing that one is tempted to conclude that it represented for him nostalgia for a simple world in which injustices were blatant and open to direct means of retaliation and correction. But uncomplicated transgressions and immediate remedies are not Thackeray's usual way. Even in this primitive instance of immediate retribution for evil done, the issues are complicated. Though he has been rescued from Cuff, young Osborne is "rather ashamed of his champion," partly because Dobbin's father is a grocer and thus of a lower caste than himself (1:52). Nor is the enemy unworthy. To prevent Dobbin from being punished, Cuff admits to Dr. Swishtail that Dobbin justly stopped him from bullying a little boy, "By which magnanimous speech he not only saved his conqueror a whipping, but got back all his ascendancy over the boys which his defeat had nearly cost him" (1:53).

This episode presents Thackeray's method in microcosm. At first glance it is easy to sum up the moral situation. A bigger boy is treating a younger boy cruelly and is punished by a third boy. Complicating the issue, however, is the public school ethos condoning physical intimidation. Thus, although Cuff has overstepped the line, he has not initiated any new and shocking line of conduct. It is unclear, too, whether Dobbin's motive in defending Osborne is so very pure. Though he may dislike this form of bullying, he may also be taking this opportunity of using physical means to avenge himself for the jibes and insults directed at him because of his family background. So the villain here is not unmistakably evil, nor the hero pure. To emphasize this point, Thackeray has Cuff assume a "heroic" role by "saving" Dobbin, a reversal of the preceding scene, with Cuff now playing the rescuer and Dobbin the rescued. Moreover, Cuff achieves his heroism by utilizing the Christian version of triumph, meekness. He is penitent and forgiving—when it proves practical to be so. Villainy, punishment, and charity all are very complicated when examined; therefore, without close examination, no severe judgment should be passed. This is not a version of "to know all is to forgive all," but perhaps a more Thackerayan "to know oneself is to forgive all," for time and again Thackeray reminds us of how easily we might find ourselves the subject of unjustly severe judgment.

Injustice between classes, already hinted at in the Dobbin school episode, also constitutes a form of disguised punishment. Much has been written about the subtle ways nineteenth-century society managed to conceive of the poor as responsible for their own condition and therefore deserving of the suffering occasioned by it. This attitude was occasionally institutionalized by laws such as the Anatomy Act of 1832 or the New Poor Law of 1834.[10] But while the comfortable classes exploited and punished those beneath them, they could be seen as accumulating their own enormous debts of transgression in the eyes of heaven. Dickens warned those in power quite vividly that they would suffer for their mistreatment of the lower classes, either by revolution here or by judgment hereafter. Thackeray is less inclined to harangue in this manner, but he too consistently exposes the injustice implicit in the relations of the classes. Relentlessly he nudges his readers to admit their own ambiguous moral position. When Becky reckons that she could be an honest woman on £5000 a year, Thackeray comments:

> "And who knows but Rebecca was right in her speculations—and that it was only a question of money and fortune which made the difference

between her and an honest woman? If you take temptation into account, who is to say that he is better than his neighbor? A comfortable career of prosperity, if it does not make people honest, at least keeps them so. An alderman coming from a turtle feast will not step out of his carriage to steal a leg of mutton; but put him to starve, and see if he will not purloin a loaf. Becky consoled herself by so balancing the chances and equalising the distribution of good and evil in the world." (2:80–81)

That last sentence suggests that we have just been treated to a sample of free indirect discourse reflecting Becky's views, though not necessarily those of the narrator. But here and elsewhere there is no reason to suppose that the narrator does not feel some affinity for Becky's jaundiced view of society. Just because Becky is wicked does not mean that she is not acute. And just because the narrator slyly attributes these sentiments to Becky does not mean that his own text does not endorse them, despite his earlier disclaimer that he is not responsible for his characters' opinions and expressions.

John Carey is clearly wrong when he argues that Becky's whole sin is that she does whatever she can to escape from poverty.[11] This simplification overlooks one of the central infractions in Thackeray's moral canon—using others heartlessly for one's own ends. Thackeray constantly reveals the selfishness prompting actions in even the best of his characters, but calculated exploitation is another matter. Nonetheless, it is this very ability to calculate dispassionately what must be done, and to whom, that makes Becky such a capable critic of society and its pretentions. She aspires to the privileged class, but she has the outsider's eye for its weaknesses and faults, including its treatment of those beneath it.

There are whiffs of class injustice throughout the novel. For example, when Becky writes to Amelia to describe Sir Pitt Crawley's household, she mentions his interest in rural matters. "Sam Miles had been caught poaching, and Peter Bailey had gone to the workhouse at last" (1:88). The game laws were, of course, designed by the landed aristocracy and their allies to preserve their game even if that left pests to destroy farmers' properties. Country squires saw these as just and necessary laws, but it is unlikely that many tenants recognized them as anything but unjust coercion by their superiors.[12] Peter Bailey as likely went to the workhouse because he could not pay his rent as that he was improvident. That Bailey's family has been on the Crawley land for one hundred and fifty years and is treated no better than this intensifies Sir Pitt's offense.

There are other instances of this sort in the novel, but the chief example of economic injustice by the aristocracy against the lower classes is Rawdon Crawley's crude betrayal of Raggles. This honest fellow had once been at the head of Miss Crawley's establishment, saved money, and left her service when he married. He prospered as a grocer, bought a fine house for rental purposes, and prospered again. Out of affection and respect for the Crawley family, he rents his house to Rawdon and Becky. When their fortunes collapse, Raggles suffers most because the Crawleys have paid him nothing for house, services, and even food-stuffs. The narrator allows himself a digression on this interesting theme.

> I wonder how many families are driven to roguery and to ruin by great practitioners in the Crawley's way?—how many great noblemen rob their petty tradesmen, condescend to swindle their poor retainers out of wretched little sums, and cheat for a few shillings? When we read that a noble nobleman has left for the Continent, or that another noble nobleman has an execution in his house—and that one or other owe six or seven millions, the defeat seems glorious even, and we respect the victim in the vastness of his ruin. But who pities a poor barber who can't get his money for powdering the footmen's heads; or a poor carpenter who has ruined himself by fixing up ornaments and pavilions for my lady's *déjeuner* or the poor devil of a tailor whom the steward patronises, and who has pledged all he is worth, and more, to get the liveries ready, which my lord has done him the honour to bespeak?— When the great house tumbles down, these miserable wretches fall under it unnoticed: as they say in the old legends, before a man goes to the devil himself, he sends plenty of other souls thither. (2:15)

This passage is an obvious response to the customary attribution to servants of petty theft and cheating their masters, an attribution that Thackeray's narrators often make themselves.[13] The pilfering of household supplies by servants was both a stereotyped comic piece and a serious social complaint. But Thackeray wants to be sure that both sides of that story are told, suggesting that predation is not one-sided. Thus Betsey Horrocks, the servant girl, is very attentive to and affectionate with Sir Pitt in his dotage, hoping to be made "her ladyship" for real as she is called by Sir Pitt in jest. "But Fate intervened enviously, and prevented her from receiving the reward due to such immaculate love and virtue" (2:53). She is even prevented from retrieving a few mementoes and sent packing by Mrs. Bute Crawley. Given their relative opportunities, all classes demonstrate a tendency to take advantage of other classes.

In Victorian fiction up to this time the overwhelming tendency was to make certain that injustice and outright criminality were punished, both through explicit injury and embarrassment coming to pernicious individuals and through the mechanics of the plot. The rooted convention of this literature was to describe derelictions and then have them exposed and corrected in the story. But in *Vanity Fair* and Thackeray's fiction in general, though we are meant to feel that exploiting and injuring others deserve some form of punishment, his narratives frequently refuse to assign specific punishments for such transgressions. Betsey Horrocks will not really be hanged, as Mrs. Bute threatens, though she will be expelled from Queen's Crawley and she will have wasted her efforts. Similarly, the aristocrats who end up in the Fleet Prison or in exile abroad may be considered to have received a degree of punishment following naturally from their injudicious way of life, but in Thackeray's own stories, wicked noblemen like Lord Steyne do not suffer such retribution for their sins.

If the narrator of *Vanity Fair* exposes iniquity without maneuvering to punish it, he takes pains to examine in some detail the petty retributions that his characters exact. Within as well as across the different ranks of society there is a tendency to exploit others, and a corresponding desire to see supposed offenders punished. Miss Crawley represents the upper class in her treatment of her relatives. She is wealthy; they are not. They wish to remain in her favor because they hope for a comfortable inheritance when she dies. Knowing this, she plays one relative off against another. Thus, although she knows that Bute Crawley's son, James, is a questionable young man, she receives him kindly when he is sent to her on a visit, and "by way of punishing her elder nephew [Pitt Crawley], Miss Crawley persisted in being gracious to the young Oxonian" (1:426). Petty spite and retribution of this kind are pervasive in *Vanity Fair* and they cross the ranks. Thus Miss Crawley's maid Firkin, who has been displaced in the old lady's favor by Becky Sharp, "found a gloomy consolation on returning to London, in seeing Miss Briggs suffer the same pangs of jealousy and undergo the same faithless treatment to which she herself had been subject" (1:160). Becky, of course, is alert to all of these mundane faults and exploits them. Though guilty of the same maneuverings for favor, she has sense enough to accept defeat without malice and to rearrange alliances. That is to say, she is a superb hypocrite. Thus, when Miss Crawley dies and leaves her money to the Pitt Crawleys, Becky, on a peacemaking visit to that family, expresses her satisfaction with circumstances, blaming Mrs. Bute Crawley's avarice for the estrangement between her household and Lady Jane's.

> "She succeeded in making us poor," Rebecca said, with an air of angelical patience; "but how can I be angry with a woman who has given me one of the best husbands in the world? And has not her own avarice been sufficiently punished by the ruin of her own hopes, and the loss of the property by which she set so much store? Poor!" she cried. "Dear Lady Jane, what care we for poverty? I am used to it from childhood, and I am often thankful that Miss Crawley's money has gone to restore the splendour of the noble old family of which I am so proud to be a member. I am sure Sir Pitt will make a much better use of it than Rawdon would." (2:76–77)

Becky here mimicks Christian charity and forgiveness while still managing to condemn Mrs. Bute and to praise Lady Jane. But what is in shortest supply in the world of Vanity Fair is genuine charity, love, and forgiveness. These scenes might be viewed as reenactments of the rudimentary conflict between the schoolboys Dobbin and Cuff. Miss Crawley may be a bully, but her oppressions are invited and even promoted by a social system that values money and place above all else except appearances. That her family should kowtow to her is not unusual and she expects it. But she is also a victim because she can never expect true affection and regard. And through her consciousness of material power she loses her spiritual heritage. Those who contend against her have very mixed motives as well, and though they triumph over her in one way or another, ultimately they suffer their own defeats. Good actions thus have questionable motives, and cruelty can be explained as social and not merely individual in its development.

George Levine describes Thackeray's reluctance to submit to the simpler moral structures of most Victorian fiction: "Against the rigor of Victorian moralism and, perhaps, his own desires, Thackeray created worlds not ordered by the standards of Christian virtue but, rather, mixed, compromised, contingent, unfair—though on the whole, not too unfair. His sentimentality and his moralism merge in commentary on the fact; but they do not alter the fact."[14] But acquaintances could say that "If Thackeray did not wish all the world to be good, he certainly was only too happy, when he did meet what he thought good, to recognise and admire it."[15] Similarly, if Thackeray did not alter the fact of injustice in his fictional world, he nonetheless incorporated in his fictional strategies the means of making his audience lament a world so heavily weighted toward the immoral, so little appreciative of the rudimentary Christian values he endorsed even when he did not render them triumphant. Jack P. Rawlins says that Thackeray wanted to make his readers aware of the difference between the way they read and the way they lived. "We read romantic novels with an easy moral absolutism and live according to a more pragmatic creed. By casting us as the characters of his novel, Thackeray asks us to account for the discrepancy" (13). Wolfgang Iser, however, claims that Thackeray's narrator goes out of his way "to prevent the reader from putting himself in [the character's] place," forcing the reader to become skeptical and critical like the narrator himself (Iser 107). But he adds, in agreement with Rawlins' perception, that the reader's heightened sense of judgment permits the narrator to "compel the reader—at times quite openly—to reflect on his own situation, for without doing so he will be incapable of judging the actions of the characters in the novel" (48). Thus, if Thackeray does not solicit his readers' sympathy for his characters, he nonetheless subversively cautions them to be wary of passing judgment on beings no less worthy than themselves. If this is not exactly forgiveness, it is at least a fair degree of charity. Gordon N. Ray points out that Thackeray, when young, was an aggressive artist: "Telling the truth to Thackeray meant describing life as he had seen it during the bitter years since he came of age. 'He was created,' he told Dr. John Brown, 'with a sense of the ugly, of the odd, of the meanly false, of the desperately wicked; he laid them bare: them under all disguises he hunted to death.'"[16] But this early hunting to death gradually became a more restrained laying bare. To look into one's own sinful heart, the lesson goes, should be sufficient restraint when we feel the impulse to judge and punish.[17]

Janice Carlisle has argued that the rhetorical art of Victorian fiction was born out of moral necessity, even though the application of that rhetoric can extend from George Eliot's "clerical" role to Thackeray's Punch-like clown figure, who implies no high moral seriousness in narrator or characters.[18] Carlisle says that Thackeray's narrator in *Vanity Fair* is acquainted with characters like Becky, Rawdon, and Amelia, and hence initiates an analogical process that comes to include the reader as well (56). Through this process Thackeray exploits the difference between the authorial and actual audiences. As Peter J. Rabinowitz explains, the narrative audience is truly a fiction; "the author not only knows that the narrative audience is different from the actual and authorial audiences, but rejoices in this fact and expects his or her actual audience to rejoice as well."[19] But Thackeray pushes this, as he does a number of Rabinowitz's other "rules" or conventions, to some extreme limits, and he is fond of violating as well as gratifying expectations in impudent ways. In *Vanity Fair* and the novels that follow, Thackeray purposely blurs the difference between narrative and actual audience, a blurring that was facilitated by the serial appearance of his stories, in publications that carried advertisements for products used by fictional characters and actual readers alike, and which carried essays on subjects alluded to within the fictional texts, even including references to other fictional texts—Thackeray's or someone else's. So as Carlisle indicates, Thackeray's attempts to enforce self-knowledge and self-judgment on his readers need not be strident, but may proceed slyly. Juliet McMaster adds that Thackeray's method—a convention-bound but convention-warping realism that rejected the simplified moral world of melodrama and romance—obliged his readers to think for themselves (35–36).

Thackeray coerced his readers into thinking for themselves in various ways, of which narrowing the gap between narrative and actual audiences was just one. Another was to meddle seriously with what Rabinowitz calls the rules of configuration, which have to do with the form the work of fiction takes. The very nature of the narrative choices he made were determined by the moral structures upon which he depended and which he felt he shared with the greater part of his audience. But these moral structures need not be explicit, at least not from the outset. Much of the moral flavor of a narrative depends upon what is withheld or revealed, and when. Narratives—both fictional and purportedly true—may be viewed as secrets in the process of disclosure.[20] One of the pleasures of reading is to anticipate correctly the revelation to come; another is to do so incorrectly. To have your readerly expectations disappointed may be a far greater pleasure than to have them fulfilled, and the former is likely to be a more powerful learning experience than the latter. But Thackeray was able to exploit even this situation by pretending to renounce secrecy, yet still without providing disclosure.

This and other narrative strategies were possible for Thackeray because he avoided the more dramatic and sensational episodes in life and concentrated on the familiar and even the banal. Petty graspings and strugglings after place, power, and pence—the kind of episodes that Thackeray chiefly deals with—require no external power to exact justice. They all too often bring their own punishment. Rose Dawson could have been the contented wife of Peter Butt the farmer instead of the miserable Lady Crawley, married to crude and violent Sir Pitt, "but a title and a coach and four are toys more precious than happiness in Vanity Fair: and if Harry the Eighth or Bluebeard were alive now and wanted a tenth wife, do you suppose he could not get the prettiest girl that shall be presented this season?" (1:98–99; see also 1:173). Sir Pitt is no better off in his sphere, where he is a grasping landlord and avid speculator. But the meanness of his approach defeats his aims. "He had a taste for law, which cost him many thousands yearly; and being a great deal too clever to be robbed, as he said, by any single agent, allowed his affairs to be mismanaged by a dozen, whom he all equally mistrusted. He was such a sharp landlord, that he could hardly find any but bankrupt tenants; and such a close farmer, as to grudge almost the seed to the ground, whereupon revengeful Nature grudged him the crops which she granted to more liberal husbandmen" (1:102).

Not only do these sorts of people bring their own forms of suffering—interpretable as punishment—upon themselves, as the narrator himself here observes, but they also become cautionary objects to others. After Sir Pitt's stroke, he becomes a pitiable figure moaning for Lady Jane, and crying and sobbing when she leaves the room, after which his nurse screams out at him, " 'Hold your tongue, you stoopid old fool,' and twirl[s] away his chair from the fire he loved to look at—at which he would cry more. For this was all that was left after more than seventy years of cunning and struggling, and drinking, and scheming, and sin and selfishness—a whimpering old idiot put in and out of bed and cleaned and fed like a baby" (2:60). Nobody is concerned about him when he finally dies. Aside from Betsey Horrocks and a favorite old pointer, "the old man had not a single friend to mourn him, having indeed, during the whole course of his life, never taken the least pains to secure one." The narrator adds, however, that even the best and kindest among us would be surprised to learn how soon our survivors would be consoled. "And so Sir Pitt was forgotten—like the kindest and best of us—only a few weeks sooner" (2:78).

The passages about Sir Pitt indicate both that his last days are not pleasant and that no honored memory of him will survive. They also imply that these conditions directly follow from his unappetizing way of life. But lest the reader feel smug in witnessing Sir Pitt's sordid end, the narrator also makes evident the likelihood that, with or without Sir Pitt's moral obliquity, his fate might nonetheless be ours as well. Any person who has a stroke might suffer the same indignities that Sir Pitt does, whether a cunning boozer and rogue, or the best and most virtuous of persons. And the narrator explicitly says that even the kindest and best among us will be quickly forgotten after death. So, though Sir Pitt is a cautionary figure, the caution is much muted by the simple facts of human existence. The tone is somewhat different where Miss Crawley is concerned. This selfish woman, so spirited in company, so cruel to acquaintances and dependents, loses her confidence when she becomes ill. Becky Sharp tends her and knows "how peevish a patient was the jovial old lady; how angry; how sleepless; in what horrors of death; during what long nights she lay moaning, and in almost delirious agonies respecting that future world which she quite ignored when she was in good health." The narrator converts this picture of suffering into an emblem of human folly. "Picture to yourself, oh fair young reader, a worldly, selfish, graceless, thankless, religionless old woman, writhing in pain and fear, and without her wig. Picture her to yourself, and ere you be old, learn to love and pray!" (1:160). Despite its ironic context, the adjuration to learn the value of love and prayer is serious, though it is reinforced by an appeal to vanity. Miss Crawley is perhaps less repellant in her ludicrous worldliness than in her being deprived of all virtues *and her wig.* All the moral qualities she lacks are condensed into the striking image of the wigless old woman.

There are many object lessons of this kind to demonstrate that humans do not require a specific agent of justice to punish them for their folly, since folly begets its own evil consequences. The relationship between Mr. Osborne and Mr. Sedley is another small instance of this truth. Once friends and neighbors, Osborne and Sedley become enemies, even though Sedley helped set Osborne up in life. Osborne was under "a hundred obligations" to Sedley, but that, the narrator indicates, only makes him the more implacable. "When one man has been under very remarkable obligations to another, with whom he subsequently quarrels, a common sense of decency, as it were, makes of the former a much severer enemy than a mere stranger would be. To account for your own hard-heartedness and ingratitude in such a case, you are bound to prove the other party's crime" (1:211). Osborne here seems the vile fellow who deserves to be punished. But Sedley is himself capable of behaving unwisely out of revenge. Though he at first opposes Amelia's marriage to George Osborne (rightly, as the reader might think), the gratification of delivering a solid blow to his enemy Osborne, who also opposes this union, reconciles him to the marriage.

The struggle between these two men continues in some measure throughout the novel. And though no other characters in the story punish them for their offenses, the author provides limited forms of narrative punishment to imply a form of superhuman justice in operation. Sedley, who is so vain about his income and social position, loses his fortune and is bankrupted, leaving him not only poor, but humiliated in one of the most wearing of Victorian forms of shame. Osborne, who is so proud of the gentleman son he has produced, loses that son twice—first through his disobedience in marrying Amelia, and second in death. Yet both men remain essentially blind to the connection between their vanity and their suffering. Despite their intelligence, they are among those types Thackeray referred to as the dull in "Dennis Haggerty's Wife," people so self-involved and impercipient that they fail to make the most obvious associations that might compromise their own self-love. When Mr. Sedley is dying, the narrator imagines him reviewing his life and discovering that there is "no chance of revenge against Fortune" (2:323). And this ultimate condition, in which we are powerless to punish the forces that have made us what we are, and the prospect of which should make us reflect on what energies most suit that condition—those of revenge and retribution, or those of love and forgiveness—leads the narrator to a brief speculation about facing death. Is it better, he wonders, to face death when one is rich and successful, or when one has lost the game of life. He concludes that one is more easily reconciled to death in the latter case because resignation and hope are more likely then than when, in the full splendor of worldly success, one is forced to yield all material goods and all earthly expectations.

The "punishments" Osborne and Sedley suffer result from their own conduct and attitudes, though they neither see the connection nor recognize their pain as a form of punishment. These sufferings are, however, readable to Thackeray's audience as storytelling devices for demonstrating the moral difference between foolish and wise modes of living. In this sense they are what I call "narrative punishments," in the same way that Dickens' narrative punishments often involve a providential action worked into the plotting of his stories. In the instance of Osborne and Sedley, Thackeray satisfies his Victorian audience's expectation that the folly of these two men will evoke some form of poetic justice. Thackeray's authorial audience greatly resembles his contemporary actual audience. It may be that that is still the case for a majority of modern readers. A significant difference is that more modern readers are likely to identify the narrative punishment for what it is—a storyteller's strategy to manipulate his readership toward a given end.

Earlier I referred to storytelling as the gradual disclosure of a secret known to the teller but not to his or her audience. This feature is common to all fiction, but in Thackeray's narratives there is an added fascination with disclosure itself, at both the grand and trivial level. Disclosure, especially slow and subtle disclosure, is a major narrative instrument in Thackeray's hands. Being found out, not undergoing some physical form of correction, is Thackeray's preferred version of punishment. One of the most striking passages in the novel involves a combination of physical punishment and exposure—the climactic scene when Rawdon returns home unexpectedly to find Becky and Lord Steyne alone together. Rawdon strikes his lordship, scorns Becky, and leaves for good. The discovery here is primarily Rawdon's. He and Becky have schemed enough together to realize for a certainty that they are neither of them angels. But Rawdon does not expect Becky to betray *him*. Finding Becky alone with Lord Steyne after she has claimed that she could not ransom him from a sponging house forces Rawdon to conclude that he is as much her dupe as others are. Once aware of this, he cannot forgive her or resume life with her. He is not really a bad man and there is enough sincerity in him to make him fundamentally good. After rejecting Becky and turning to Lady Pitt Crawley for sympathy, Rawdon does change his ways. John Carey is right in describing him as one of the few convincing repentant sinners in Victorian fiction (184).

If most of the shock of discovery is Rawdon's when he finds his wife alone at night with a notorious rake, and he seems to execute obvious justice on his betrayers, the episode is far more complicated than this basic interpretation suggests. Rawdon has been a morally questionable figure to this point, with only a narrow range of behavior within which he can claim a right to justice. But he has been a faithful and loving husband. From this one clear moral vantage point he justly punishes Lord Steyne, who deserves such punishment—except that he supposes he is merely gathering the fruits of an expensive contract to which all parties have agreed. He complains to Becky in front of Rawdon: "'I have given you thousands of pounds which this fellow has spent, and for which he has sold you'" (2:227). Steyne is almost as surprised by the turn events have taken as Rawdon, and even suspects that he is the victim of a concerted plot. The secret now revealed, however, is that Becky has been deceiving both men and stashing away a good bundle of loot for her own emergencies. Even if she has not betrayed her husband sexually, she has been far from candid with him and has encouraged Lord Steyne to believe that Rawdon is pimping for his own wife.

Another complication in this scene is Becky's claim to be innocent, meaning, presumably, sexually innocent. The narrator offers no certainty about the matter. "What *had* happened? Was she guilty or not? She said not; but who could tell what was truth which came from those lips; or if that corrupt heart was in this case pure?" (2:229).[21] This is the same narrator who, much earlier, allowed himself the "omniscience of the novelist" to reveal Amelia's and Rebecca's secrets (1:183). Yet now he finds himself incapable of discovering what really happened. That is to say, the "omniscient" author has decided, provocatively, to become his appealing little sinner's confederate by choosing not to disclose her secret. But whether or not she is literally guilty may be beside the point. The narrator allows Rawdon to express what is perhaps the morally appropriate judgment: "'If she's not guilty, Pitt, she's as bad as guilty; and I'll never see her again,—never'" (2:257). Near the end of the novel, this decision is reinforced when Becky's son refuses to see her. If these responses can be taken as punishment for Becky's behavior, then she is punished, but there is no significant narrative punishment, for after this setback she begins a new career of mischief that finally leaves her a comfortable matron who "busies herself in works of piety" (2:430). And this despite the narrator's hints that Becky may have assisted Jos Sedley to his grave.

Though Becky is unquestionably an immoral person and her immorality is disclosed to us unequivocally, Thackeray feels no need to punish Becky with a retributive turn of plot. But if Becky is wicked, she is not clearly evil; moreover, she can be friendly, charming, and, upon occasion, truly kind. Her conduct may be pardonable as well because of her upbringing. In fact, Thackeray relents toward Becky because he himself is largely responsible for her situation, as he earlier admits after the crucial moment in her life when she and Rawdon, newly married, still have the opportunity to win the favor of old Miss Crawley by going down on their knees before the old spinster and avowing all; they would, he says confidently, have been forgiven in a twinkling. "But that good chance was denied to the young couple, doubtless in order that this story might be written, in which numbers of their wonderful adventures are narrated—adventures which could never have occurred to them if they had been housed and sheltered under the comfortable uninteresting forgiveness of Miss Crawley" (1:190–91).

Thackeray here suggests that if what happens to his characters is initially the novelist's responsibility, he cannot condemn them without implicating himself. Unlike Dickens, who, except for occasional hortatory episodes, wishes to maintain the illusion of separation between his creative effort and the world he creates, Thackeray constantly calls attention to the fictive nature of the story and of the narrator's involvement in it. But the narrator simultaneously continues the pretence that the story he narrates is independent of him. Near the end of the novel he describes how Dobbin learns Rebecca's history from the great society gossip Tapeworm and adds, "it was at that very table years ago that the present writer had the pleasure of hearing the tale" (2:404). All the time, however, he is simply teasing an audience that wants to get on with the narrative, which it accepts at face value. Instead, the narrator obliges his readers to pause frequently and reassess the nature of their own activity. Thus while describing the pleasant Continental interlude, when Dobbin accompanies Amelia and young George abroad, the narrator observes, "It was on this very tour that I, the present writer of a history of which every word is true, had the pleasure to see them first, and to make their acquaintance" (2:344). The reader, who has frequently been told that he or she is reading a novel, and who began reading with the full expectation that the subject was fictitious, must now be reminded that the "true story" the narrator is presenting is nonetheless a fabricated history. Yet this is the same narrator who earlier declares, when giving information about Rebecca's authorship of Rawdon's letters, "The novelist, who knows everything, knows this also" (1:408). As we have seen, however, the novelist who knows everything occasionally admits his own and his story's incomplete foreknowledge, as when he declares at the beginning of chapter 18, "Our surprised story now finds itself for a moment among very famous events and personages, and hanging on to the skirts of history" (1:207). Also, despite his frequent moralizing within the narrative, the narrator occasionally disclaims any high objectives. "This, dear friends and companions, is my amiable object—to walk with you through the Fair, to examine the shops and the shows there; and that we should all come home after the flare, and the noise, and the gaiety, and be perfectly miserable in private" (1:225).

In short, because Thackeray wants to keep in suspension both the forward drive of his narrative as an invented story and his audience's consciousness of his creative effort, both the illusion of real events and the outright announcement of their fictiveness, he is not inclined to present either internal or narrative punishments for his characters, since such punishments would enhance the effect of partial closure in the way that a caesura affects the rhythm of a poetic line. Internal punishment is allowable and even necessary for varying the energy of the narrative. There must be some crises, no matter how modest. But narrative punishment involves a more serious focusing of moral energy and hence most narratively contrived punishments relate to minor figures. Moreover, Thackeray's tendency to see both sides of a problem or ethical situation makes him reluctant to judge one side or the other too quickly. It is usually sufficient simply to exhibit the evidence. Hence, to return to Becky's case, he does not find it necessary to visit any serious punishment upon her. She has her ups and her downs and reaches the end of the novel in a satisfactory position. Past the end of the novel, she fares even better, being described as Lady Crawley in *The Newcomes*.[22] No other character brings justice to bear upon her, no institution punishes her, and providence does not correct her. The one form of "punishment" that Thackeray employs is to displace Becky to the margins of the narrative as the novel proceeds, a technique that Dickens also used to show favor to his good characters over his wicked ones. But without any other condemnation, this is a modest, though thoroughly narrative, form of moral judgment.

Another reason for Thackeray's clemency toward Becky is that, even while she aspires to all the good things of Vanity Fair, she is never taken in by them or self-deceiving about her own motives. She cheats others, but never herself. Not only does this make her more appealing to the self-scrutinizing Thackeray, but it makes her an excellent agent for exposing all of Vanity Fair itself. Juliet McMaster describes Becky as a punishment to Vanity Fair (105). She serves this function as a general scourge throughout the book, but she is also a healthy nemesis to individuals within the text, and, because she is not good herself, she has Thackeray's license to indulge her whims for making the proud, self-righteous, pretentious, and so forth, wince. She reveals George Osborne's own paltry heart to him, exploits Lord Steyne's lust, and, in a delightful instance of poetic justice, refuses to sell her horses to Lady Bareacres, who has snubbed her, when that lady seeks to flee Brussels in terror. These are only a few instances, but the point is that Becky is one of Thackeray's most effective means of energizing his narrative. He can therefore easily allow her to plea-bargain her way out of any serious comeuppance.

This does not mean Thackeray is unwilling to use his authorial powers to judge and punish his characters. Often, however, such narrative punishments are muted. For example, Lord Steyne is a minor figure in this novel clearly deserving of punishment, but the punishment he receives is chiefly of the self-inflicted kind. He is a vain, proud, and selfish man, whose vanity, pride, and selfishness sometimes occasion him pain. At the simplest level, Rawdon avenges himself on the lord by physically striking him. Captain Macmurdo, Rawdon's intermediary, says to the lord, "'The affair ain't a very pretty one, any way you take it; and the less said about it the better. It's you are thrashed, and not us; and if you are satisfied, why, I think, we should be'" (2:256). And so the punishment ends and there is no need for the "honorable" course of fighting a duel. Secretly Steyne is further humiliated and infuriated by being the source of Rawdon's fortune, for it has been his influence that secures Rawdon a colonial appointment (albeit a potentially lethal one). Steyne is eager to punish those who offend him, beginning with his own family; he "never forgives," and so, when Becky angers him, he sees to it that no ministers on the Continent will receive her; there is even a suggestion that her life might be in danger if she stays in Rome while Lord Steyne is there (2:382). But this unforgiving nature exacts a price upon itself as well, and after the Becky episode Steyne looks out on a world "of which almost all the pleasure and all the best beauty had palled upon the worn-out wicked old man" (2:381).

With Steyne, Thackeray has both arranged for a vile person to suffer from his sinning and added to that suffering an edge of authorial retribution in his description of the libertine outlasting his libertinage and left to gnaw on his rotten heart. But Thackeray was capable of offering summary sentences on his characters as well. It is abundantly clear that he does not care much for the adult George Osborne. He wants his readers to regret that this vain and selfish young man marries Amelia. His behavior is deplorable. Not only is he a gambler, but he is soon inclined to be indifferent and even unfaithful to his wife. On the night before his unit is called to the battle of Waterloo, George invites Becky to adultery and is so exulted by his anticipated success that he gambles wildly and wins. Soon after, realizing that he is going to a mortally dangerous adventure, he reconsiders his behavior. "Oh, how he wished that night's work undone! and that with a clear conscience at least he might say farewell to the tender and guileless being by whose love he had set such little store!" (1:357). Looking at his wife in bed just before he leaves, he thinks, "Good God! how pure she was; how gentle, how tender, and how friendless! and he, how selfish, brutal, and black with crime! Heart-stained, and shame-stricken, he stood at the bed's foot, and looked at the sleeping girl" (1:358). George's conscience can be stimulated only in the most serious moments, but that is not enough to spare him, and he dies on the field of battle on the first day. Although he makes no further moral judgment upon George Osborne within his text, Thackeray's opinion was stated clearly in a letter written at the time he composed this section of the novel. He tells his mother that Dobbin and Briggs are the only characters with real humility as yet, though Amelia's is to come "when her scoundrel of a husband is well dead with a ball in his odious bowels" (Letters, 2:309).

If there is not much in the way of outright punishment in Vanity Fair, there is also very little forgiveness. The narrator remarks, with evident bite, "But those who know a really good woman are aware that she is not in a hurry to forgive, and that the humiliation of an enemy is a triumph to her soul" (2:55). Juliet McMaster acutely observes that, in Thackeray, "To be unforgiving is the proper vice of the virtuous" (92). Of course a really good woman would forgive: the narrator is ironically alluding to those who pride themselves on their piety while lacking true charity. Unfortunately, there are far more of this sort in the world than there are true Christians. And, since forgiveness is technically the reward a sinner receives for repentance, there is small occasion for forgiveness in Vanity Fair. The narrator believes "that remorse is the least active of all a man's moral senses—the very easiest to be deadened when wakened: and in some never wakened at all. We grieve at being found out, and at the idea of shame or punishment; but the mere sense of wrong makes very few people unhappy in Vanity Fair" (2:82).

But what of the genuinely good characters in *Vanity Fair*, those who have demonstrated love, charity, and so forth? If we are to talk of such people, we must talk of William Dobbin. Earlier I chose young Dobbin's fight with Cuff as a model of how Thackeray treats his characters in their moral crises. There is a good deal of ambiguity about motives and action in that scene, and such ambiguity continues throughout the novel. For brevity's sake I shall concentrate here only on Dobbin, but these observations apply to other characters as well.

After the school episode, Dobbin becomes significant in *Vanity Fair* again only when he urges George to be faithful in his commitment to marry Amelia, despite the change in the Sedley family's fortunes. Complicating his participation in this romance is his own love for Amelia. Having convinced George that marrying Amelia is the right thing to do, Dobbin must inform George's father of his son's decision. He calls on Mr. Osborne "with a half-guilty secret to confess," and feels "doubly guilty" because of his instrumental role in bringing about a situation that will enrage the older man, who unsuspectingly greets him with his usual warmth (1:274–75). Dobbin is a dependable moral barometer in the novel and his sense of guilt is justified, for he not only is offending Mr. Osborne, but he is aware that his own motives are not entirely pure. Why had the marriage to be pressed on so precipitately? George would have recovered quickly and Amelia eventually from the separation. Dobbin examines his role.

> It was his counsel had brought about this marriage, and all that was to ensue from it. And why was it? Because he loved her so much that he could not bear to see her unhappy: or because his own sufferings of suspense were so unendurable that he was glad to crush them at once— as we hasten a funeral after a death, or, when a separation from those we love is imminent, cannot rest until the parting be over. (1:276)

Again and again Dobbin's conduct is presented in terms of transgression and crime, though always, despite his own romantic involvement, he is trying to do what he supposes best for Amelia. A sample of how this discourse of transgression operates is the scene where the troops have been called up for the battle of Waterloo and Dobbin hopes to get a last view of Amelia before the regiment leaves. The narrator's tone is ironically judgmental when he remarks that Dobbin's "selfishness was punished just as such odious egotism deserved to be." He got a view of Amelia, but it was a sight of suffering and dismay, the remembrance of which "haunted him afterwards like a crime, and the sight [of which] smote him with inexpressible pangs of longing and pity" (1:368). Dobbin is punished for the "selfishness" of wanting no more than a glimpse of the woman he has selflessly assigned to another man. His punishment is to feel longing and pity for that woman's suffering. It is a strange world in which compassion and love should require punishment, and of course it is not the moral world that Thackeray endorses. His inverted use of the language of crime and punishment is designed to call into judgment the kind of world where such values are so topsy-turvy.

Of course the whole history of Dobbin's love describes a pattern of error. He has made Amelia into an idol impossible of real existence. He spends his life worshipping her, accepting her indifferent friendship, and only very late in their relationship, when she has learned to value Dobbin's love, does he admit that he "loved her no more, he thought, as he had loved her. He never could again." He admits to himself, " 'It was myself I deluded' " (2:419). Dobbin recognizes his own delusion only after Amelia finds out, thanks to Becky's revelations, how false her own idol, George, has been. These disclosures are sufficient punishment not to require additional suffering for error. Amelia and Dobbin will have an agreeable union, but nothing like what either of them might once have anticipated from marriage. Dobbin is "punished" for his affectionate folly, and Amelia for her ignorance. And yet both are admirable in their ways. We have seen how sincerely generous Dobbin's behavior is, despite its admixture of selfishness called love. And Amelia, the narrator remarks ironically, "was a woman of such a soft and foolish disposition, that when she heard of anybody unhappy, her heart straightway melted towards the sufferer; and as she had never thought or done anything mortally guilty herself, she had not that abhorrence for wickedness which distinguishes moralists much more knowing." Amelia intuitively responds like a Christian, whereas the moralist prefers to judge. There is little doubt that this passage recommends Amelia's response above that of more punitive types. An additional comment by the narrator reinforces this interpretation. "This lady, I believe," he says, "would have abolished all gaols, punishments, handcuffs, whipping, poverty, sickness, hunger, in the world; and was such a mean-spirited creature, that—we are obliged to confess it—she could even forget a mortal injury" (2:390). How bitterly ironic that in Vanity Fair one must "confess," or reveal, or find out the deplorable Christian charity of this woman. But in Vanity Fair forgiveness and compassion are poor tools for success. Amelia struggles against her virtues, trying to accommodate herself to the moral climate of Vanity Fair. Pondering the husband she has lost and the child who has been taken from her by the Osbornes, "her selfish, guilty love, in both instances, had been rebuked and bitterly chastised. She strove to think it was right that she should be so punished. She was such a miserable wicked sinner. She was quite alone in the world" (2:277).

A loving, compassionate, forgiving heart has no better chance of reward and happiness in Vanity Fair than a cold and scheming one. Thackeray may see to it that his narrative punishes some characters outright—a George Osborne, for example. But other punishments, like Lord Steyne's, are subdued. Generally there is little to choose between the fates of virtuous and wicked characters. Who is better off at the end—Amelia and Dobbin, or Becky? And if Thackeray is reluctant to punish his characters, is he inclined to forgive them? Is Amelia, who has a husband she loves, but whose full love is no longer returned, forgiven for her earlier blindness? Is Becky, in being materially comfortable, forgiven for her wickedness?

Perhaps the only clear indication of Thackeray's own sentiments emerges in relationship to childhood and children. The childhood training of George Osborne and Becky Sharp has made them different kinds of rogues. The one has been spoiled into utter egoism and selfishness, the other has been honed by necessity and hard times to look out for Number One. The one great criterion for respect in Vanity Fair is affection for children and childhood. This division is most apparent in the ways Amelia and Becky respond to their sons. They represent a diagram: loving mother with a genial son, who is saved from being spoiled by the interposition of a loving surrogate father, as opposed to unloving mother with a genial son, who is saved from neglect by a loving, repentent father. Young Rawdon's refusal to see his mother becomes a far more significant act coloring the closing pages of the novel when seen from this perspective.

Like Dickens, Thackeray believed that there was something remedial, even redemptive, in the memory of happy childhood.[23] A sign that Rawdon Crawley is recoverable occurs when he and Becky return to Queen's Crawley as a married couple. Becky enters triumphantly, but "Rawdon was rather abashed, and cast down on the other hand. What recollections of boyhood and innocence might have been flitting across his brain? What pangs of dim remorse and doubt and shame?" (2:70). Memories of childhood can keep the conscience alive. Moreover, it is witnessing his sister Jane's fine motherly behavior and acknowledging his responsibility for young Rawdon that makes him aware of the need for moral improvement, if not for himself, then for his son. In his inarticulate way, he says to Jane, "'I'd like to change somehow. You see I want—I want—to be—'" (2:226). But he can't verbalize his desire. Nonetheless, we learn indirectly that Rawdon does change, for he dies of yellow fever at Coventry Island, "most deeply beloved and deplored" (2:430).

This report comes to us in the same paragraph that describes the Dobbin family's encounter with Becky. Amelia scurries off and Dobbin seizes his little Janey, "of whom he is fonder than of anything in the world," and whisks her away from the polluting influence. His gesture of protection makes Amelia realize that Dobbin's deepest love is not for her but for their daughter, and it is on this tenuous note of compromised fulfillment that the novel ends. But Amelia's melancholy discovery at the end of the tale is only one in a series of disclosures and exposures that make up the rhythm of the novel as it "finds out" one secret after another. The plot of this novel is not so much complicated as it is attenuated, depending less upon suspense than upon recognition. When the revelations come, they may greatly or mildly surprise the characters within the narrative, but they should not surprise the reader. Both narrative and actual audiences have been well prepared for the scene where Rawdon discovers that his wife has, one way or another, betrayed him; they have been slowly accustomed to accept Dobbin's disillusioning realization that he has defrauded himself in love; they have been absolutely primed for Becky's revelation to Amelia of George's baseness.

Thus, the disclosure or discovery of transgression, folly, or crime requires no further punishment. For this reason there are few punishments carried out by one character against another, or by the narrator against his characters. I have said that the narrator of *Vanity Fair* rarely indulges in narrative punishment. However, like Dickens' narrators, he may use subtler patterns of imagery and allusion to create a sense of fatedness that anticipates some form of moral retribution. Maria DiBattista's excellent examination of the charades in *Vanity Fair* shows how such indirect means can be employed to reinforce an underlying moral pattern that is not necessarily made explicit in the story itself. DiBattista writes, "The charades' suppressed Ovidian theme of metamorphosis and their Aeschylean vision of sexual fate and familial doom combine to revive the repressed but never forgotten memory of unexpiated and unexpiable sins that will be violently avenged."[24] The hidden retribution in the charades extends from familial to national dimensions. But the narrative does not openly explore the details of these implications. Instead, it emphasizes the open secret all humans share—that our hopes, noble or vile, are more likely to be disappointed than not, and that the failure to achieve them will be pain enough in this world. If we do not find ourselves forgiving others for their treatment of us, at least we must learn to forgive ourselves. The point of the narrative is to show that punishment is a sorry objective in a world so ambiguous and uncertain. It is perhaps best after all to conceive of life itself as no more than a fiction, with ourselves the powerless characters within it, and so the novel concludes:

> Ah! *Vanitas Vanitatum!* which of us is happy in this world? Which of us has his desire? or, having it, is satisfied? —Come children, let us shut up the box and the puppets, for our play is played out. (2:431)

And yet in that very *Vanitas Vanitatum* there is, echoing Scripture, a suggestion that a greater text for our lives does exist, but is unknowable in its details and appreciable only when our own desires do not obscure the lesson of compassion so earnestly presented eighteen hundred years before this particular Vanity Fair came into being.

NOTES

1. *The Works of William Makepeace Thackeray,* 26 vols. (Philadelphia: J. B. Lippincott Company, 1901), 1:11.

2. Hallam Tennyson, *Alfred Lord Tennyson: A Memoir,* 2 vols. (New York: The Macmillan Co., 1905), 2:76.

3. Ina Ferris, *William Makepeace Thackeray* (Boston: Twayne Publishers, 1983), 35.

4. John Forster, quoted in *Thackeray: The Critical Heritage,* ed. Geoffrey Tillotson and Donald Hawes (New York: Barnes & Noble Inc., 1968), 56.

5. Elizabeth Rigby, quoted in *Heritage,* 80.

6. See chapter 8 of John R. Reed's *Victorian Conventions* (Athens: Ohio University Press, 1975) and "A Friend to Mammon: Speculation in Victorian Literature," *Victorian Studies* 27, no. 2 (Winter 1984), 179–202, Barbara Weiss's *The Hell of the English: Bankruptcy and the Victorian Novel* (Lewisburg: Bucknell University Press, 1986), and chapter 17 of Richard Altick's *The Presence of the Present: Topics of the Day in the Victorian Novel* (Columbus: Ohio State University Press, 1991).

7. Juliet McMaster, *Thackeray: The Major Novels* (Toronto: University of Toronto Press, 1971), 5, 9.

8. Robert Siegle, *The Politics of Reflexivity: Narrative and the Constitutive Poetics of Culture* (Baltimore: The Johns Hopkins University Press, 1986), 56. U. C. Knoepflmacher, *Laughter and Despair: Readings in Ten Novels of the Victorian Era* (Berkeley: University of California Press, 1971), Wolfgang Iser, *The Implied Reader: Patterns of Communication in Prose Fiction from Bunyan to Beckett* (Baltimore: The Johns Hopkins University Press, 1974) and Jack P. Rawlins, *Thackeray's Novels: A Fiction That Is True* (Berkeley: University of California Press, 1974), are critics who have stressed the part the reader plays in the moral construction of the novel.

9. This concept became traditional in the English novel, as John R. Reed indicates in *Old School Ties: The Public Schools in British Literature* (Syracuse: Syracuse University Press, 1964). A notable extended treatment of the idea occurs in E. M. Forster's novel *The Longest Journey* (1907).

10. Ruth Richardson's *Death, Dissection and the Destitute* (London: Penguin Books, 1989) offers a fascinating picture of the establishment's attempt to change earlier fostered views of the poor as deserving of their condition, when attempting to legalize the use of paupers' bodies for anatomical experimentation.

11. John Carey, *Thackeray: Prodigal Genius* (London: Faber & Faber, 1977), 178.

12. See chapter 3, especially note 4.

13. This convention is exploited many times in *The Yellowplush Papers.*

14. George Levine, *The Realist Imagination: English Fiction from Frankenstein to Lady Chatterley* (Chicago: The University of Chicago Press, 1981), 157.

15. *Thackeray: Interviews and Recollections,* ed. by Philip Collins, 2 vols., (New York: St. Martin's Press, 1983), Vol. 1, 70.

16. Gordon N. Ray, "*Vanity Fair:* One Version of the Novelist's Responsibility," in *Thackeray: Vanity Fair: A Casebook,* ed. Arthur Pollard (London: The Macmillan Press Ltd., 1978), 97.

17. A. E. Dyson, "An Irony Against Heroes," *Casebook*, 181.

18. Janice Carlisle, *The Sense of an Audience: Dickens, Thackeray, and George Eliot at Mid-Century* (Athens: University of Georgia Press, 1981), 61, 33–37.

19. Peter J. Rabinowitz, *Before Reading: Narrative Conventions and the Politics of Interpretation* (Ithaca: Cornell University Press, 1987), 98.

20. The underlying point of Frank Kermode's *The Genesis of Secrecy: On the Interpretation of Narrative* (Cambridge: Harvard University Press, 1979) is that human beings are inveterate interpreters of the world around them, as though it were a text to be decoded and brought to some sense of fulfillment, but the complexity of the world inevitably increases rather than diminishes mysteries found there, the more intensely we try to penetrate them.

21. Richard D. Altick has no doubt about Becky's guilt. He asserts, "of course Becky and the lecherous lord were lovers" (*The Presence of the Present: Topics of the Day in the Victorian Novel* [Columbus: Ohio State University Press, 1991], 599). In a letter of May 1, 1848 to the Duke of Devonshire, Thackeray declared, "There is no sort of truth in the stories regarding Mrs. Crawley and the late Lord Steyne" (*The Letters and Private Papers of William Makepeace Thackeray*, ed. Gordon N. Ray, 4 vols., [Cambridge: Harvard University Press, 1945], 2:375. Subsequent references appear in the text.

22. In *The Newcomes,* Dobbin from *Vanity Fair* and Clive Newcome mention that Rebecca has become Lady Crawley (5:176). In his letter to the Duke of Devonshire of May 1, 1848, Thackeray gives a little more detail of Becky's career.

"She took the style and title of Lady Crawley for some time after Sir Pitt's death in 1832; but it turned out that Colonel Crawley, Governor of Coventry Island, had died of fever three months before his brother, whereupon Mrs. Rawdon was obliged to lay down the title which she had prematurely assumed.

The late Jos. Sedley, Esq., of the Bengal Civil Service, left her two lakhs of rupees, on the interest of which the widow lives in the practices of piety and benevolence before mentioned. She has lost what little good looks she once possessed, and wears false hair and teeth (the latter give her rather a ghastly look when she smiles), and—for a pious woman—is the best-crinolined lady in Knightsbridge district" (*Letters* 2:376).

23. See Ruth F. Glancy's "Dickens and Christmas: His Framed-Tale Themes," *Nineteenth-Century Fiction* 35, no. 1 (June 1980), 53–72, for a treatment of this subject in Dickens' Christmas stories.

24. Maria DiBattista, "The Triumph of Clytemnestra: The Charades in *Vanity Fair,*" in *William Makepeace Thackeray*, ed. Harold Bloom (New York: Chelsea House Publishers, 1987), 128.

TWENTY-ONE

Pendennis

PENDENNIS is a story of growth. That is a simple way of describing the narrative. A more sophisticated description might call it a story of moral growth. But both of these descriptions are far too simplistic and misleading to be of any real help, though most attempts to categorize the novel as part of the Victorian *Bildungsroman* tradition depend to a great degree upon such simplifications. For Thackeray moral growth was complex because all issues of morality were complex. And if discovering vanity in others could be the modest equivalent of punishment in his novels, discovering vanity in oneself could be the means of self-forgiveness and "salvation." Morality is not simple in Thackeray's fiction because good and evil, virtue and vice are not as distinct and separable as melodrama and much of the literature of early and mid-Victorian literature would have it seem. The complexity of Thackeray's approach is indicated early in the novel, when the narrator announces that if hardships of various sorts produce their corresponding virtues, "so the very virtues, on the other hand, will generate some vices."[1] The narrator has in mind Mrs. Pendennis' vice of family pride rooted in her otherwise virtuous nature. Such a weakness does not stop with its owner; it spreads its insidiousness abroad. Thus virtuous women may, by one fault, occasion disorder for many other persons, even those they most love. Mrs. Pendennis, for example, loves and pampers her only child, Arthur. "This unfortunate superstition and idol-worship of this good woman was the cause of a great deal of the misfortune which befell the young gentleman who is the hero of this history, and deserves therefore to be mentioned at the outset of his story" (3:18).

This brief passage already hints that whatever errors he may commit, Arthur Pendennis is not entirely responsible for them. Nonetheless, he must learn to accept responsiblity for all that he does, a process that involves his discovering what he is. Having been taught to think of himself as special and gifted, he is poorly equipped to uncover his own faults. And it does not help to have his vanity reinforced by his mother. Ultimately, he must find himself out in his own self-deception, as the narrator suggests we all must, if we wish to live authentically. "How lonely we are in the world! how selfish and secret, everybody! You and your wife have pressed the same pillow for forty years and fancy yourselves united. —Psha, does she cry out when you have the gout, or do you lie awake when she has the toothache? . . . and, as for your wife—O philosophic reader, answer and say, —Do you tell *her* all? Ah, sir—a distinct universe walks about under your hat and under mine—all things in nature are different to each . . . you and I are but a pair of infinite isolations, with some fellow-islands a little more or less near to us" (3:189).

In the last chapter I suggested that fictional narratives may be viewed as secrets in the process of disclosure, with Thackeray's own strategy being a combination of candor and evasion. He claims to forgo suspense and surprise, but he cannot abandon the technique of revelation. Thackeray frequently draws analogies between fictional narratives and real life. Each life is a story in the process of telling that looks different depending on who does the telling. But in every case that story is a secret slowly being opened to examination, and even when the teller and the subject are the same there is no guarantee that he or she will comprehend all that the secret reveals, or that he or she will be capable of articulating the secret in an entirely open manner. Not only does our vanity and our conditioning prevent us from recognizing and evaluating disturbing features of the narratives of our lives, but their motive forces may remain a mystery as well. Frequently we require the interpretation of a disinterested or warmly interested party to help us discover the secret of our own life story. Pendennis is fortunate in having friendly interpreters—some wise and some unwise—who help him to establish a sound communication between his infinite isolation and the fellow islands around him.

The notion of life as a narrative has become a commonplace of modern critical writing in various disciplines. What makes Thackeray's narrators so interesting is their reluctance to claim that they represent full literal truth, while nonetheless aiming to convey a larger moral truth. Laura Fasick has examined this quandary in "Thackeray's Treatment of Writing and Painting," arguing that "the narrative presence in Thackeray's fiction deliberately thwarts any readerly hunger for a simple, let alone a sentimental, idea of truth."[2] The narrator's awkward situation is self-defeating, for he must try to convey a truth that he does not believe will change his reader, and yet only by telling the truth can he achieve any authenticity as a writer of merit.

For Thackeray's implied author, however, writing is based on a keener than usual perception of life's horror, an ability to confront the sordid reality of the self that is inevitably also a confrontation with universally faulty human nature. But such knowledge is not redemp-

tion: it is guilt. No wonder he celebrates painting: it may be intellectually inferior to writing, but for that very reason it is innocent as
writing never can be. (90)[3]

Pendennis is a particularly interesting novel in this regard because it is about writers and the writer's obligations, written by a man who had only recently come to
a full admission of the writer's moral responsibility.[4] Again, however, it is worth
remembering that if a life is like a story being told, it is not truly a story under
the control of a narrating voice, a point Jack P. Rawlins and others have suggested.[5] Moreover, as Rawlins reminds us of Thackeray's narrators in general,
their authorial self-awareness "in its most overt form trains a similar objective
critical scrutiny in the reader" (151). Thus the narrator's exposures of his own
fallible opinions and references to his own minor vices make him a compassionate judge when he comes to evaluate Pendennis' faults, and we, as readers, are
taught to face our own secrets, admit them, and extend pardon to others as weak
as ourselves. Needless to say, despite such notable examples as Pip, this is not the
same as Dickens' method, which, by and large, offers a narrator firmly located
on trustworthy moral ground.

   If Pendennis is weak, he is nonetheless one of the more agreeable characters in
the novel. Still, an anonymous reviewer in the *Athenaeum* listed only four amiable
characters in the novel, and Pen was not among them.[6] The likeable but undisciplined young Pendennis is characterized by enthusiasm and self-concern; he
quickly becomes accustomed to having his own way. Disliking the constraints of
school, Pen does not return after his father dies, but is tutored by a local curate.
This is unfortunate not because he thereby misses the experiences of public school,
but because the curate, admiring Arthur's mother, conspires in spoiling the boy.
By the time he has reached an age to make romantic mistakes, Pen has little experience of self-control and no sense of proportion. There is an ironic shading to
Pen's first romantic infatuation, which seizes him at a performance of the play
The Stranger, Benjamin Thompson's English version of August von Kotzebue's
Menschenhass und Reue (Misanthropy and Repentance), a very popular play in the
nineteenth century. The theme of this play might, in a much modified form, serve
as the armature for Thackeray's own narrative, which moves from youthful disillusionment and worldliness to a renewed valuation of people and things.

   Pen's first infatuation is with the handsome young actress, Emily Costigan,
known as the Fotheringay. He is so smitten by the actress that he scarcely attends
to the play, though, despite many weaknesses, it offers an important set of messages. The narrator remarks that "in the midst of the balderdash, there runs that
reality of love, children, and forgiveness of wrong, which will be listened to
wherever it is preached, and sets all the world sympathising" (3:48).[7]

   Pen is introduced to the world of dissipation and passion through his friend
Harry Foker and his acquaintance Colonel Costigan, the Fotheringay's father.

Pen does not take to dissipation, but he plumps heavily for passion. Foker is vulgar and free-spending in a manner that suggests he is on the high road to hell. The narrator does not tell us this outright, but the usual clues are there. On the other hand, we are candidly informed that Costigan's ruined appearance is the direct result of hard living. The narrator claims that he knew Costigan himself and offers a succinct picture of the man. Since this apparently indifferent reference to Costigan appears just as Pen is discovering the pleasures of the dubious world of theatrical people, it takes on a monitory character. "Poor Cos! he was at once brave and maudlin, humorous and an idiot; always good-natured, and sometimes almost trustworthy. Up to the last day of his life he would drink with any man, and back any man's bill; and his end was in a spunging-house, where the sheriff's officer, who took him, was fond of him" (3:58–59). We may all be fine fellows with our admirable traits, but it is not these alone that will determine our fates, since we are equally driven by our follies and weaknesses, and if we cannot control these, they will lead to a natural sort of retribution—severe or bland, as the case may be. So at the outset of Pen's career in the world of romance and of literature, the narrator cautions against the dangers of both. Throughout the novel love and literature will summon various forms of retribution and forgiveness. But we begin with love.

The narrator informs us early in his story that "love makes fools of us all," referring specifically to Smirk's love of Helen Pendennis and Pen's infatuation with the Fotheringay (3:52). But though love can be the source of error, as with Helen's love of her son, it is essential to decent human makeup. The narrator indicates as much when he excuses Pen's rash obsession. "Let the poor boy fling out his simple heart at the woman's feet, and deal gently with him," he says. "It is best to love wisely, no doubt: but to love foolishly is better than not to be able to love at all. Some of us can't: and are proud of our impotence too" (3:81). Foolish love may be a weakness, but lovelessness is the true sin against humanity in Thackeray's code just as it is in Dickens'. If some persons wound themselves through loving, others injure themselves or others by their failure to love. Pen must learn the proper form of love; and his model is always before him in Laura Bell. But he must suffer through mistaken affections before he achieves the wisdom of loving her.

Thoughtless and impulsive early passion must clearly be restrained. Worldly-wise Major Pendennis asserts to Pen the folly of a man marrying his "superior in age or his inferior in station." He allows that it might be difficult to give up the loved object, but asks, "what would have been the trifling pang of a separation in the first instance to the enduring infliction of a constant misalliance and intercourse with low people?" (3:93). An instance of such enduring affliction in marriage is Francis Bell, Laura's father. Having rashly contracted an unequal alliance, he then fell in love with Helen Thistlewood. Forced to marry the woman to whom he had so passionately declared his love, he thus lost the woman he truly loved. The "punishment" for these lovers is severe, but is meant not as a narrative punishment of guilty characters, but as an exemplary warning to the reader. There are numerous warnings about unwise marriages in this and other novels by Thackeray, though early misalliance through passion seems the most forgivable. By contrast, when a man or a woman sells him or herself for wealth or station, the act is conscious and calculated and the subsequent pain at least foreseeable, if not measurable. But youthful passion cannot foresee in that way, as the cases of Pen and later of George Warrington illustrate.

Pen's first great error is romantic, but thanks to Major Pendennis he is spared serious harm. Failing to convince Pen of the terrible consequences of the marriage he contemplates—social ostracism, career impediments, and so forth—the Major simply pays off Costigan, who instructs his daughter to write a letter dismissing Pen. Pen suffers intensely, but this form of suffering may be called punishment for folly in the same way that a hangover may be called punishment for excessive indulgence. This is not moral or narrative punishment, though it is one of Thackeray's chief means of seeing that his characters harvest the bitter crop of their unwise actions. It is a lesson in cause and effect, distinguishable from retribution.

Unlike Dickens, Thackeray was often willing to let his fallible heroes execute justice on those they considered offenders. Pen, suffering still from his loss of the Fotheringay, is made the subject of much crude humor in his village. When a young fellow by the name of Hobnell mocks him, Pen strikes him with his whip and then beats him. Sobbing afterward, he explains to Doctor Portman, the local minister, that the coward had insulted him, "and the Doctor passed over the oath, and respected the emotion of the honest suffering young heart" (3:180); and there is every reason to suppose that Thackeray and his narrator concur with the kindly sentiment. Though others consider Pen's aggressive conduct to be as foolish as his romance, Pen argues that, as a gentleman, he is required to defend his honor. It might be argued that Pen's anguish stems as much from his wounded vanity as from disappointed passion. As always in Thackeray, an apparently simple situation proves subtly complicated and therefore difficult to assess with any degree of certainty. As Pen matures, vanity intrudes more consciously into his amours, to the degree that he is in danger of failing to respond authentically.

Pen is not unique in this respect. The narrator admits that Pen is very weak and very impetuous, very vain and very frank, very generous and very selfish, "and also rather fickle, as all eager pursuers of self-gratification are" (3:215). Pen is simply normal in this regard. The narrator says of most men, "As long as what we call our honour is clear, I suppose your mind is pretty easy. Women are pure, but not men. Women are unselfish, but not men. And I would not wish to say of poor Arthur Pendennis that he was worse than his neighbours, only that his neighbours are bad for the most part. Let us have the candour to own as much at least" (3:218). Much of the early praise for Thackeray's fiction referred to his ability and willingness to show both good and bad in his characters.[8] And certainly this willingness to forgive his own characters' venial sins on the grounds of common humanity is an open enunciation of what the narrative itself seeks to accomplish.

We have seen that Thackeray was deeply concerned with telling the truth about human behavior, even if that truth might be relative and dependent upon the perceiver. Unlike Dickens, who rarely allowed serious flaws in his heroes and heroines, Thackeray insisted that his heroes and heroines manifest normal human failings. With *Pendennis*, however, he seems to be experimenting with narrating the history of a fallible protagonist without alienating an audience accustomed to the convention of unequivocal virtue in its heroes. Part of Thackeray's method is to mask his unorthodox liberality through the use of familiar literary conventions, such as allusions to the Bible and other devices. Pen's early career offers a bland approximation of the prodigal son, for example. Yet the whole account of Pen's deviating from the straight and narrow is detoxified by the narrator's positioning relative to his subject.

Pen passes through his first trial scarred, educated, but certainly not perfected. His second trial comes when he enters college, where he achieves an excellent reputation among his peers, but privately avoids study, preferring smart clothing and interesting company. As a spur to his memory of college life, the narrator has Pen's verses before him. Though the poems were unsuccessful in competition, Pen had them privately printed. These and other documents from Pen's university days the narrator has found "lately in a dusty corner of Mr. Pen's bookcase" (3:226). The introduction of these palpable documents helps to distance Pen's university days of youthful ambition and vanity. At the same time, in a familiar Thackerayan device, they support the narrator's regular references to Pendennis' present circumstances, and, in a familiar Thackerayan ploy, underscore the narrator's intimate relation with the mature Pendennis who is the present-day friend of the man who is composing his biography. A basic convention of fiction is to trust third-person narrators, and thus we are encouraged to assume that Pendennis is a decent fellow worthy of the narrator's regard. In short, we are inveigled to believe that, whatever his conduct in the past, he has survived it and become an acceptable acquaintance in his maturity. Any judgments we might be inclined to make of young Pen's behavior are thus undercut, and the narrator's own negative assessments take on a tone of indulgent irony. Chapter 19 is entitled "Rake's Progress," but is far more innocent than that designation suggests, though it does describe Pen's involvement with a gaming set and his carelessness about debts. The narrator assures us that "this narrative is taken from Pen's own confessions, so that the reader may be assured of the truth of every word of it," though he provides few details about Pen's excesses (3:240). The narrator summarizes his approach. "We are not presenting Pen to you as a hero or a model, only as a lad, who, in the midst of a thousand vanities and weaknesses, has as yet some generous impulses, and is not altogether dishonest" (3:241).

This disclaimer that Pen is not a hero recalls *Vanity Fair,* which was also, by its author's assertion, heroless. The cautious expressions "has yet some generous impulses" and "not altogether dishonest" might suggest that these impulses will pass away and the dishonesty become complete, but as I have just suggested, the narrator subtly takes pains to reassure us that Pen has instead outlived his vanities and weaknesses and become worthy of the acquaintance of our urbane and sympathetic narrator. Whether it is Pen or the narrator who interprets his confidences as "confessions," the word emphasizes the movement of character development from early errors in the period of his academic disgrace to a state where Pendennis will repent of his folly and reform his conduct. If the "hero" is presented to us as guilty and deserving of the sentence passed upon him, he is also obviously deserving of our sympathy and mercy. We know beforehand that our investment will be rewarded.

Pen fails at Oxbridge and leaves in disgrace. He is aware of the pain he has given to others—most notably his mother—but his chief suffering comes from wounded self-love. This, the narrator suggests, is the immediate and natural punishment for the transgressions of which Pen is guilty. Chapter 21 is entitled "Prodigal's Return," emphasizing Pen's abasement, but again exaggerating the extent of the parallel. Pen is no more a serious prodigal son than he was a true rake. But the pattern of waste, loss, and repentance is there. And the inevitability of this conventional pattern, whether from the Bible or from Hogarth, suggests that punishment in some form is certain and only forgiveness remains in doubt. For Pen, however, there is no doubt because his mother practically embodies this virtue. When she sees her shamed son again, Helen's face beams "with love and forgiveness—for forgiving is what some women love best of all" (3:262).

As Thackeray often suggests, mere forgiveness is not always—and perhaps not nearly—enough. To pardon the offender is a beginning; to reverse his conduct is another matter. It falls therefore to the sturdier Laura to recommend a painful course of corrective action. She takes the practical measure of lending Pen money to pay his debts and expunge his academic dishonor. Pen is determined never to return to the scene of his disgrace, but Laura urges that, "as some sort of reparation, of punishment on himself for his—for his idleness, he ought to go back and get his degree, if he could fetch it by doing so; and so back Mr. Pen went" (3:263-64).

The language of punishment and forgiveness is everywhere in this second painful trial, a trial that gives Pendennis an opportunity to examine his own character and to discover its weak seams and faults. Despite this opportunity for self-discovery through serious self-examination, Pen decides instead to sequester himself with his books, his idleness, his loneliness, and his despair. Laura intends to make Pen the instrument of his own correction; punishment is what she says, but discipline and self-knowledge is what she means. Pen is simply not yet receptive to this course of repentance. He sees his sufferings not as punishments for his folly, but as misfortunes. He yearns less for forgiveness than for vindication. To revert to our earlier language, we could say that he still sees his life as a story in the writing, and his lapses as intrusions external to the narrative he is constructing. In short, he is still immature. The fact is that Pen has been spoiled and is finding it difficult to improve himself. Nor is his worldly uncle an entirely satisfactory guide. At this point Pen encounters a third trial. If his passion for the Fotheringay was foolish, it was nonetheless spontaneous and sincere. His behavior at school was imprudent but followed from high spirits and conviviality, not viciousness. Now, however, Pen demonstrates an insincerity in his flirtation with Blanche Amory, signaled by his adapting poems originally written for Miss Emily Costigan to his "romance" with Blanche.

Jealous of Blanche, Laura yields to an unaccustomed attack of evil spirits, which results in a quarrel between the two young women, an estrangement that does not persist because "Laura was always too eager to forgive and be forgiven," and Blanche has not understood the grounds for the brief antagonism (3:312). Pen does not appear in quite so good a light in this affair. At a ball, he is pleased to have the two prettiest women in the room quarreling over him. "He flattered himself that he had punished Miss Laura" by preferring Blanche as his dancing partner (3:332). Moments later he and Blanche have an accident on the dancing floor which puts them both in a ludicrous light. Though Pen is quick to satirize and make fun of others, he cannot bear to be laughed at himself. As if this were not humiliation enough for Pen's sensitive nature, he promptly becomes embroiled in an argument with Mirobolant, the French chef at the Clavering household.

The abruptness of Pen's own embarrassment after he has gloated over his punishment of Laura evokes a small case of narrative punishment, as though the narrator cannot resist pricking the young man's inflated ego. But if Pen's humiliation at the ball serves as a form of poetic justice concocted by the narrator, it may also be seen as issuing from Pen's own vain and thoughtless behavior. He is petty in wanting to punish Laura and oversensitive about his own *amour propre*. He is a snob and insensitive concerning Mirobolant. Still, unwise as he has been, he is far from a desperate case. At Laura's suggestion, Pen asks Mirobolant's pardon, making her feel that "there was goodness and forgiveness still" in Helen's son (3:346). That goodness is also revealed in Pen's eagerness to redeem his poor performance at college and thereafter. When given the chance to go to London and prove himself, he exclaims, " 'If I can get a chance to redeem the past, and to do my duty to myself and the best mother in the world, indeed, indeed, I will. I'll be worthy of you yet' " (3:325).

Laura provides the money for this opportunity. Accordingly, Pen feels obliged to offer himself sacrificially in marriage, a marriage his mother desires. He tells Laura that, though he scarcely feels he has a heart to give, he would like to consider himself bound to her, and concludes, "Let me go away and think that I am pledged to return to you. Let me go and work, and hope that you will share my success if I gain it. You have given me so much, dear Laura, will you take from me nothing?" Rhetorically the offer has a noble ring to it but is still an expression of Pen's self-love, since it presumes that he is a desirable partner and that he is doing Laura a favor in offering himself. Laura senses this, of course, having witnessed a good deal of Pen's selfish behavior. Her response to the young man has depths of meaning: "'What have you got to give, Arthur?'" (3:355). She knows that Pen is proposing not out of true love, but out of gratitude for her financial support and from a desire to please his mother. On these terms she cannot accept, though it is plain that she loves Pen. So Pen's supposed sacrifice is immediately transposed into Laura's real sacrifice, since nothing would please her more than to be Pen's wife—as soon as Pen is worthy.

Lennard J. Davis states clearly a common view of the novel when he says that its plot normally involves the movement of its protagonist from insecurity to security, imprudence to prudence.[9] Davis' main argument in *Resisting Novels* is that readers should be conscious of fiction's insidious ability to inculcate middle-class ideology. In his mature fiction, Thackeray openly endorsed conventional middle-class morality and arranged his plots to seem to reinforce that morality. But at the same time he was subverting that very morality, by time and again demonstrating both its potential for harm and the dangers of its limiting view of life. Pendennis' career fulfills the basic movement that Davis describes, but it does so with some interesting variations. It is instructive to contrast Pen with David Copperfield, who was before the public at the same time. Where Pen clearly misbehaves and acts foolishly at the prompting of his own impulses, David is almost entirely the victim of others' actions. David's one true folly—his marriage to Dora—nonetheless arises from an honorable, if misguided, affection. He occasionally acts unwisely, never ignobly—if we excuse his one night of dissipation in the amused hands of Steerforth and his friends. Moreover, though he says at the outset that he might not be the hero of his own story, it very quickly becomes clear that he will be, in all senses. It would be a while yet before Dickens could bring himself to create a genuinely fallible hero. Arthur Clennam is crippled in character, but he is evidently a victim like David, though damaged in a way David never is. Arthur is nonetheless a good and generous man. Pip is the first Dickens protagonist who develops serious weaknesses of character and who behaves in relatively unappealing ways to those around him. But Thackeray has chosen to make Pen almost unattractive and to set his readers against him, something he will do again later with Philip Firmin. Pen's early blunders in love and at school are predictable episodes in a young man's life, but once he moves to the great world a new set of standards applies.

To some degree Pen's "punishment" for his youthful folly is exhaustion of sentiment. He feels that he no longer has a heart to give, that his emotions are shriveled, that his youthful passions are over. And so, for the time being, romance departs from his life as another stage in his maturation opens. But the pattern he has thrice experienced, of foolish enthusiasm and false pride followed by a humbling lesson, will have to be repeated in a new setting—the London world of law and literature.

This life begins with Major Pendennis forgiving his nephew and visiting him in his rooms in the Temple. He is willing to offer the young man advice about urban life. His are worldly values and he aims to find Pen a rich wife—to his mind a better prospect than a lawyer's career. The narrator quickly assures the reader that Pen, though he may be a degree more cynical than previously, has remained chaste and has not become mean-natured in money matters. If a great deal remains for him to learn, he nonetheless has a basically sound foundation from which to begin. Moreover, by comparison with Mr. Paley, the industrious young drudge who restricts his capacious intellect to the narrow study of the law, Pen's carefree manner and high spirits appear attractive. The contrast of lively and curious Pen with cramped Mr. Paley offers an ironic reversal of the idle and industrious apprentice parable. "The one could afford time to think, and the other never could. The one could have sympathies and do kindnesses; and the other must needs be always selfish. He could not cultivate a friendship or do a charity, or admire a work of genius, or kindle at the sight of beauty or the sound of a sweet song—he had no time, and no eyes for anything but his law-books" (3:377). Typically, Thackeray rebels against the simplistic association of effort with virtue and idleness with vice. Now and again it is good for the serious Sandfords of the world to take a holiday.[10]

But Pen errs in the other direction, making most of his days holidays. He is enjoying his London life more than he is improving as a law student. When an embarrassment about money prompts a confession to his new friend George Warrington that he needs some source of income, George introduces him to the world of journalism. The dangers of Pen's happy-go-lucky style of living are represented in the careers of Grub Street denizens. A notable early example is Captain Shandon, whom Pen visits in Fleet Prison. Though Shandon is not dispirited by the inconvenience of confinement for debt and carries on his business more or less comfortably from this location, the very likelihood of such imprisonment serves as an "Abandon Hope" for all those who stand at the entrance to Grub Street with dreams of prosperity. Shandon shrugs off imprisonment and diverts himself with drink, card playing, and the conversation of friends, but his wife lacks such diversions and suffers more deeply than her coarse husband. The narrator exclaims, "Oh, what varieties of pain do we not make our women suffer!" (3:422).

Shandon is a talented and accomplished man, but not a wholesome character. In fact, what Pen sees of the literary world makes him dubious of any great claims for literary artists. Forgetting that his connections have been chiefly with hack writers, he begins to pontificate about his new calling. After a discussion of literary genius in which Warrington claims that there's less of it than people suppose, Pen remarks, " 'It does not seem to me, Warrington, that we are much better than our neighbors.' " This comment, innocuous in itself, is nonetheless the first sign of a new and valuable trait in Pen, a growing awareness that he is not a privileged being deserving special treatment. It is a preliminary indication of genuine maturation and is soon reinforced by his response to his new occupation. Prepared to earn his own living by writing and thus cease to impoverish his mother, Pen admits that he would relish honor and fame, but at the same time he sets himself a personal code of conduct. " 'If Fortune favours me, I laud her; if she frowns, I resign her. I pray Heaven I may be honest if I fail, or if I succeed. I pray Heaven I may tell the truth as far as I know it: that I mayn't swerve from it through flattery, or interest, or personal enmity, or party prejudice.' " And the narrator observes of him, "He went on with these musings, more happy and hopeful, and in a humbler frame of mind, than he had felt to be for many a day" (3:428).

Early critics, as I have already indicated, took umbrage at Pen's realistic assessment of the writing profession and assumed that he was voicing Thackeray's own views. That does not seem to have been the case, since Thackeray had already declared his sense of the seriousness of his craft. Jack P. Rawlins has shown how Pen's attitude and approach to writing are different from those of Thackeray (138ff.). But, for Thackeray, Pen's opinions about the *trade* of writing are healthy insofar as they represent an advance in self-judgment. His discoveries about himself now are assisted by his mentor, Warrington, who will not pamper him or shield him from the truth. Pen's commonsense approach to authorship is therefore a positive step in his career. An early reviewer commented that *Pendennis* had no real story to tell but derived its continuity "from the fact that it narrates certain adventures which befall Mr. Arthur Pendennis" (*Heritage*, 99). But this view overlooks the nature of these adventures, for Pen's progress comes, as I have already suggested, through a sequence of tests or trials of his character, progressively offering him greater and greater opportunities for self-assessment. He is unwittingly being urged to uncover the secret of his life story. He cannot do so until he recognizes and controls his vanity.

The birth of Pen's genuine humility coincides with the beginning of his new profession. To be a successful artist requires a high degree of self-examination. To be candid with oneself is the best way to tell the truth. When David Copperfield becomes a successful author, we learn little of his internal examinations; he still seems a rather naive young man. But Thackeray demonstrates, in the gradual transformation of his callow and less-than-sensitive young man into a more introspective and serious individual, the workings of character necessary to form a serious literary artist. That Pen's personality develops coincidentally with his art is perhaps Thackeray's way of indicating to his readers that the essential relationship between author and reader is sympathy. On his part, the author should arrogate little power over his characters, who remain free to sin and repent, and on their part his readers must learn to acknowledge the repentance and to forgive those sins.

Pen has one more arena in which to make mistakes before he begins his serious movement toward integration and integrity, symbolized by his growing power as a writer. He must undergo the apprenticeship of Grub Street. The literary world of this time, as I have already indicated, had a rough-and-tumble quality to it.[11] Rivalries, both political and aesthetic, were strongly felt and strongly expressed. A good deal of literary bruising took place. As a novice literary critic, Pen exhibits an aggressive, judgmental manner, much as Thackeray did when he began his career as a reviewer and parodist. "The courage of young critics is prodigious," says the narrator; "they clamber up to the judgment seat, and, with scarce a hesitation, give their opinion upon works the most intricate and profound" (3:455). Pen finds the judgment seat comfortable and hands out his punishments and rewards freely. But when he learns that he is expected to puff books published by Bungay and attack those published by Bacon, he has qualms. Pen is willing to treat his own side kindly and hit the enemy hard, "but with fair play. . . . One can't tell all the truth, I suppose; but one can tell nothing but the truth" (3:457). His editor, Captain Shandon, cannot appreciate Pen's fastidiousness, since the "veteran Condottiere" had "fought and killed on so many a side for many a year past, that remorse had long left him" (3:457). Pen insists on honesty, though he is willing to continue his role as a hanging judge.

But even judges are not above the law, and "A punishment, or, at least, a trial, was in store for Mr. Pen" (3:458). Thackeray wittily plays with the word "trial" here, suggesting both an ordeal and an appearance before a judge for sentencing. The occasion is his pseudonymous publication of some verses in the *Spring Annual*. Pen refuses to review this volume and it is given instead to Mr. Bludyer, who enjoys a "reputation for savage humor," and employs it on the *Spring Annual*, and, above all, on Arthur Pendennis' poetry.

This chastening experience apparently teaches Pen a lesson, though we are given no details about it. If the sting of punitive criticism teaches Pen a measure of charity in his own judgments, a much greater step toward genuine maturity is signaled by his ability to discipline his feelings and his talents, and transform painful personal experience into an artistically satisfying novel entitled *Walter Lorraine*. Just as George Warrington is able to influence Pen's thinking for the better, he both actually and symbolically helps Pen convert a passionate and sentimental effusion into a successful novel. Ironically, while Pen was attempting to be the author of his own life story, he continued to blunder, ignorant as he was of oncoming events, and ignorant as he was of the true nature of the influences that guided him. Now, obliged to turn "real life" into a romance, he learns what it means to shape a story, and, succeeding at that, realizes how different such stories are from the mysterious sequences of events that constitute actual living.

Pen's narrative success marks a fundamental turning point in his career, as the narrator explains.

> There are some natures, and perhaps, as we have said, Pendennis's was one, which are improved and softened by prosperity and kindness, as there are men of other dispositions, who become arrogant and graceless under good fortune. Happy he who can endure one or the other with modesty and good humour! Lucky he who has been educated to

bear his fate, whatsoever it may be, by an early example of upright-
ness, and a childish training in honour! (4:43)

The narrator's surprising moral exclamation is not so inappropriate as it may
seem, for he is marking the point at which Pen genuinely begins to benefit from
the positive features of his upbringing and to control the less appealing consequences of his having been spoiled. Pen does not leap immediately to great
virtue, but his improvement hereafter is fairly steady. He has decided that it is
important to do one's work in the world, not to stand aside as an observer or to
flee from it. He explains to Warrington that man's condition is "to be born and
to take his part in the suffering and struggling, the tears and laughter, the crime,
remorse, love, folly, sorrow, rest" (4:36). Warrington understands this position
all too well. He has been the good angel helping Pen to organize both his life and
his fiction through just such an awareness of the responsibilities inherent in both.
Self-denial is one of those responsibilities, one that Warrington learned the hard
way through an unwise marriage in his youth, a contrasting example of the real
danger that Pen escaped in his adventure with the Fotheringay. Warrington has
not yet shared this story with Pen, however.

Pen's first serious moral test—serious because now he is the person in a position to control events, not merely to react to the attractions and manipulations of
others—is the episode with Fanny Bolton. But before taking up this important
adventure, I must call attention to another aspect of Thackeray's developing narrative. Up to this point, the various incidents and entanglements have been
straightforward. The infatuation with the Fotheringay, the imprudence at the
university, and the flirtation with Blanche were all open and evident. Neither
Pen nor his associates have been secretive about their actions and their aims.
Both Foker and the Major typify this kind of openness, though in radically different ways. Pen himself has been ignorant of the motives of others, assuming
that other people are as candid as he is; but to this point no one actually resorts to
concealment. With the appearance of Altamont, the element of genuine secrecy
enters the novel. Just as Pen begins to unlock the secrets of his own talents and his
own best nature, the world around him becomes complicated by deceptions, disguises, and mystifications. Pen's new awareness is itself endangered by some of
these secrets.

Altamont's secret gives him power over Sir Francis Clavering. But this is only
one of several patterns of secrecy in the novel from this point forward. Major
Pendennis says, apropos the persistent rumors about Sir Francis, "Don't look too
curiously into any man's affairs, Pen, my boy; every fellow has some cupboard in
his house, begad, which he would not like you and me to peep into" (4:72). Even
the admirable Warrington has a secret. He does not explain why he devotes his
obvious talents to hack journalism, but mentions briefly, in a cautionary way to
Pen, "'I had a fatal hit in early life. I will tell you about it some day. You may,
too, meet with your master. Don't be too eager, or too confident, or too worldly,

my boy'" (4:85). The narrator could easily choose to disclose these secrets, just as he confided to his readers the secret of Laura's jealousy over Blanche Amory. By withholding information he authorizes the blatant secrets of his narrative, thereby inspiring curiosity and suspense, devices that he had abjured in roughly half of his narrative.

It might seem that Thackeray is following the Major's advice by keeping his nose out of other people's closets, but the constant references to the accumulating secrets clearly signal to the reader that revelation is inevitable, no matter how long delayed. Pendennis is himself not a secretive person. His sins have been open and obvious, even flaunted. Significantly, his successful novel exhibits his private experiences for public view. The craft of writing thrives not on removing from view but on disclosure. Truth pulls back the curtain. The disclosure of hidden truths through fiction is the most discreet means of finding out the skeletons in other people's closets. Pen, as the representative of authorship, thus increasingly embodies the truthfulness and openness that should mark his craft. Moreover, the aim of fiction's finding out is to teach us what we have in common, and therefore make us more humble about ourselves and more forgiving toward others.

As the narrative moves from candor to obvious concealment, characters that earlier gloried in their powers now begin to feel misgivings and even remorse. Sir Francis' misgivings are embodied in Altamont. Clavering has been habitually careless about his debts; now Altamont's claims upon him make him conscious of his financial position. Foker, so jolly and carefree as a young rogue, has become enslaved by the lovely Blanche, while realizing that he lacks the virtues to attract her. "'I misspent my youth,'" he complains, "'and used to get the chaps to do my exercises. And what's the consequences now? Oh, Harry Foker, what a confounded little fool you have been!'" (4:15). Mrs. Clavering, meanwhile, is not happy with her husband or her daughter, and her son is growing up terribly spoiled.

Midway through the narrative, then, Pen is emerging slowly as a man of moral substance who is turning his talents to use and improving his character, while those who once attracted him with their position or advantages are now seeing the emptiness of their existence. It is perhaps no accident that both Foker and Pen are interested in Blanche. But now it is Foker who is the infatuated youth and Pen who can see Blanche for the flirt that she is. In a parody of his uncle's worldliness, Pen declares that he intends to marry for money, a rational marriage. However, he is not as blasé as he pretends to be; he is a healthy, sociable young gentleman who even boasts of his "sympathy with all conditions of men" (4:104). It is this geniality that brings him into contact with Fanny Bolton, yet another form of temptation.

Pen generously assists Costigan in admitting Mrs. Bolton and Fanny to Vauxhall Gardens. But though Fanny is pretty, fetching, and apparently impressed by Pen, he cautions her, "'you mustn't call me anything but sir, or Mr Pendennis, if you like; for we live in very different stations, Fanny.'" And the narrator, with a slight dig at his male readers, remarks, "Well, the truth is, that however you may suspect him, and whatever you would have done under the circumstances, or Mr Pen would have liked to do, he behaved honestly, and like a man" (4:115–16).

Being honest is not enough to shield Pen from suspicion and slander. Mr. Bows, who was devoted to and exploited by the Fotheringay, now fears that Pen intends to ruin Fanny, and tells him so. At first indignant at the charge, Pen softens towards Bows and promises that he will not take advantage of the susceptible young woman. He cannot so easily deal with discussions of his "secret sin" at the village of Clavering. It is typical of Thackeray's irony in this tale that the open and candid Pen should be assigned a guilty secret without his knowing it. Young Huxter, offended by Pen's haughty behavior, retails his slanderous version of Pen's behavior. The chapel-going crowd "did not wait to hear whether he was guilty or not. They took his wickedness for granted: and with these admirable moralists, it was who should fling the stone at poor Pen" (4:153). Someone does in the form of an anonymous letter to Pen's mother, detailing his crimes. Of course she is very upset, but Laura, after reading the letter, angrily denounces the cowardly letter-writer and dismisses its charges as false. But Helen responds, "'It *is* true, and you've done it, Laura. . . . I will never forgive you, never!'" (4:154).

Helen distrusts Pen and credits the announcement of his corruption because she has seen him behave in a selfish and self-gratifying way all of his life, a way that she herself has sponsored by her indulgence of him. By contrast, Laura has helped Pen to resist self-indulgence and to strengthen his own character by facing down humiliation and failure. She has witnessed his moral recuperation more than once. Helen recalls Pen's lapses, Laura his redemptions. Helen forgets that Pen has been punished and learned from the punishment, Laura remembers that Pen has been able to humble himself after being humiliated by others. Both are correct. It is all a matter of faith.

At this point the narrator intervenes to expose an implicit secret that has remained untouched since the title page. The full title of the novel reads: *The History of Pendennis, His Fortunes and Misfortunes, His Friends and His Greatest Enemy.* Now the narrator reveals that greatest enemy to be Pen's own self, "and as he had been pampering, and coaxing, and indulging that individual all his life, the rogue grew insolent, as all spoiled servants will be" (4:157–58). Pen grows moody because he is unaccustomed to self-denial, but he nonetheless persists in avoiding Fanny, and thereby temptation. Unsurprisingly for a Victorian novel, the effort makes Pen ill. His sickness is a thoroughly conventional trope of Victorian plots, a physical manifestation of a moral crisis.[12] With predictable irony, Thackeray adds his own special twist to this convention by making the embodiment of temptation the specific cause that brings on the symptoms of moral fever; the "infection" that brings his malady to a head treats his sickness as well. And this irony generates a greater one, for when Helen and Laura, the one disbe-

lieving and the other trusting in Pen's virtue, come to his sickbed, they find
Fanny there. Fanny's act of Christian charity perversely confirms Helen in her
false assumption and converts Laura from truth to falsehood. Both women now
believe both Pen and Fanny guilty. Neither woman shows "any the faintest
gleam of mercy or sympathy for Fanny," and they can only deplore Pen's obvious
physical and supposed moral condition (4:171).

The irony here is peculiarly Thackerayan. Fanny is essentially a good girl.
Her response to Pen's illness is genuine and she behaves precisely as a good Christian should. Moreover, she is fulfilling the female's traditional role as nurse. But
it is precisely her carrying out these good actions *where she does not belong* that
outrages the good women who want to perform those offices themselves. They
cannot recognize Fanny's charity, and all too easily presume her guilt. What is
more, they tar the innocent Pen with the "shame" of Fanny's kindness. In his
first individual effort at self-denial and consideration for the welfare of others,
his first truly Christian act, Pen receives his most deeply wounding accusation
and is betrayed by those who love him most. This form of injustice clearly calls
for more ordinary retribution, and the narrator will pay off the offenders with
different degrees of narrative punishment.

As the illness convention requires, when Pen recovers from his physical illness, he discovers himself cured of his "mental malady" as well (4:184). Realizing
that he does not love Fanny, he is suddenly freed from the dis-ease that had preceded his disease. Nonetheless, the affection had been authentic and the temptation real, as Pen later confides to Warrington. This confession, in itself, is a sign
of his increasing strength. He is willing to address his own weakness and to acknowledge it as weakness. Warrington applauds this manifestation of Pen's increasing self-awareness, an applause stimulated by his own unfortunate early
love passage, which is adverted to once more at this stage of the narrative. Warrington says that he had a shattering experience early in life which he will relate
to Pen later. This attenuation of Warrington's secret accords with the general
use of secrecy in the second half of the novel, for it too is a version of disclosure,
or "finding out," that must take place before individuals or societies can know
what internal weaknesses they have to confront.

As if to emphasize the folly of early infatuation, Fanny's attachment to Pen
mirrors his passion for the Fotheringay. Pen's punishment had been the anguish of
losing the woman he thought he loved. Fanny's is far more particular: "What
could Fanny expect when suddenly brought up for sentence before" Helen and
Laura, asks the narrator, who quickly provides his own answer. "Nothing but
swift condemnation, awful punishment, merciless dismissal!" He adds that women
are particularly severe with their own erring sisters. Drawing upon a favorite
Thackerayan pool of metaphors for sensuality, the narrator explains, "When our
Mahmouds or Selims of Baker Street or Belgrave Square visit their Fatimas with
condign punishment, their mothers sew up Fatima's sack for her, and her sisters
and sisters-in-law see her well under water." Admitting that he, too, is a Turk

and approves of the sack practice, the narrator nonetheless recommends prudence. "But O you spotless, who have the right of capital punishment vested in you, at least be very cautious that you make away with the proper (if so she may be called) person" (4:189).

Here again is the Christian message not to be hasty in judging one's fellow beings. Christ taught compassion and forgiveness. If punishment is to be an acceptable and even principal mode of guiding human conduct, it becomes all the more important that the right person be punished. And the more severe the punishment, the more certain a judge must be of an offender's guilt. A judge's own spotlessness is not an adequate credential for judgments of this kind. As the narrative develops, we discover that such rash judgments can engender reactive judgments that punish the punishers. Hence when Pen finally learns that Fanny was forcefully driven from his sickroom, he instantly passes judgment. Fanny herself forgives everyone involved, but Pen exclaims, "'I'll never forgive the person who did it'" (4:239). Since that person is his own mother, Pen's angry judgment leads to an estrangement between two persons who otherwise love and respect one another deeply.

Pen's intemperate judgment upon his mother has the beneficial effect of prompting Warrington to tell the story of his own early error. He had married very young and very unwisely and his boorish and faithless wife and her relatives have remained a nemesis to him because, having separated from his wife and her family, Warrington continues to supply them with an annuity. He could never make a fortune or achieve fame without their claiming his money and his name. Warrington admits that he has found it very difficult to forgive these people who have cheated him, especially, as he intimates, because he would have liked to bestow his affections elsewhere, such as on Laura. The moral, which Warrington had offered to Pen before, is not to yield to rash emotions and not to marry out of one's station.

Warrington's revelation of his secret has an immediate remedial effect. He has shared his story with Pen, Pen's mother, and Laura. Helen now realizes her error and throws herself into her son's arms. All along Pen had been the one needing forgiveness for his various transgressions, and when it came his turn to judge, he was too stern. Now he learns the need to temper judgment with mercy. If it took wounded vanity to teach him the merits of merciful judgment in the world of literary criticism, it is love that teaches him the lesson of lenience toward those who have injured us by abusing those we consider to be under our protection. "'Yes, dearest Mother,' he said as he held her to him, and with a noble tenderness and emotion, embraced and forgave her. 'I am innocent, and my dear, dear mother has done me a wrong'" (4:250). Helen admits her need of forgiveness and hopes that God, too, will forgive her for her errors, which have been mainly those of excessive affection, a weakness that Thackeray time and again singles out for criticism; it is a central theme in *Vanity Fair*.[13] But if Pen can pardon his mother by recognizing the love and concern that motivated her, the author does not exercise similar moderation but executes a grave narrative punishment upon her.

Promptly after her forgiveness is assured, Helen dies and instantly becomes a talismanic source of moral strength for Pen. The narrator explains that after Pen ends his public mourning for his mother, he will carry her memory in his heart and will have recourse to it when tempted or successful, and find comfort in it when suffering, until he passes into the next life beyond sin. "Is this mere dreaming, or, on the part of an idle story-teller, useless moralising? May not the man of the world take his moment, too, to be grave and thoughtful? Ask of your own hearts and memories, brother and sister, if we do not live in the dead; and (to speak reverently) prove God by love?" (4:306). But this can be so only if we have parted from our loved ones in love and forgiveness.[14] Thus Pen's reconciliation with Helen is a crucial turning point in the narrative, proving the individual merit of both and insuring for Pen a source of comfort and strength in his subsequent life. If Helen has become the author's exemplary victim, her punishment at least makes her a martyr as well. Pen's memory of a sainted mother is for him what innocent and cheerful virtue is for Laura. The virtuous are favored by fortune, but they also have a treasure like a diamond in their breasts, for virtue "is a talisman against evil, and lightens up the darkness of life" (4:372). Just as Dickens saw his virtuous characters as fountainheads of creative energy managing to outlast the voracious but barren outlaws, so Thackeray saw his virtuous characters as possessed of a secret jewel upon which they may survive as moral capital that can never be spent, always renewing itself and thus protecting its owner.

The "secret" of Pen's sin is exposed as false. Forgiveness erases the injury that this misunderstanding created. Harmony revives among the virtuous characters. By contrast, those lacking virtue are not so fortunate. Precisely at this stage of the narrative, when the finding out of Warrington's and Pen's secrets has led to such splendid consequences, Sir Francis Clavering's secret becomes known. He was married to a woman whose husband was reported dead, but who reappeared. This is Amory, introduced to us as the mysterious Altamont, who has been blackmailing Clavering. Major Pendennis, who has found out Amory and Clavering's secret, offers Sir Francis a more discreet form of blackmail not to expose him. In an attempt to secure the best financial arrangements for Pen, the Major insists that Lady Clavering's fortune will be secured to herself and to her legitimate daughter, and that young Frank Clavering will be disqualified, while Sir Francis will live abroad on an allowance. Clavering has been found out, but the suffering he endures is designed less to punish him for his offenses than to protect others. But if he is not to be punished, he is not to be forgiven either. Mrs. Bonner, Lady Clavering's "aide-de-camp," says Clavering is worse than her mistress' first husband: "what's the use of my Lady paying his bills, and selling her diamonds, and forgiving him?" (4:284–85). The main thing is simply to get rid of him. Those who struggle to keep their secrets, especially when those secrets operate to their own advantage and against the legitimate interest of oth-

ers, are likely to feel the pain when they are found out. The exposure of Clavering's crime reveals his moral impoverishment and leads to a comparable financial
loss as well. Clavering has no inner resources.

Sir Francis and Colonel Altamont are representative bad men. But most of
Thackeray's fiction is concerned with the middling orders of men, both morally
and socially. A significant conversation between Pendennis and Warrington emphasizes their differing approaches to dealing with injustice in the world, and
hints at the lesson Thackeray hopes to convey in his novel as well as the methods
he uses to convey it. The two friends are talking about political reform. Pen admits that he is no better than his neighbor, but wants it understood that the reverse is also true. Sceptical of political solutions for social inequality, he affirms a
gradual approach to reform. He would prefer that the monarchy die a natural
death, not be violently displaced. Warrington accuses him of having a conservative nature and says Pen would have sacrificed to Jove had he lived in the time of
the persecuted Christians. Pen replies that the main drift of his argument is
against such persecution. "What I argue here is, that I will not persecute. Make a
faith or a dogma absolute, and persecution becomes a logical consequence"
(4:313). But George claims that Pen is a Laodacian and indifferent about all belief, including his own. Pen insists that he simply urges a considerateness toward
the beliefs of others. What that amounts to, says George, is that the saint's hymn,
poet's ode, and Newgate thief's chant are all equal. Pen reminds George that
Christ on the cross listened to the exclamations of a thief, and to him "the wisest
and the best of all teachers we know of, the untiring Comforter and Consoler,
promised a pitiful hearing and a certain hope. Hymns of saints! Odes of poets!
who are we to measure the chances and opportunities, the means of doing, or
even judging, right and wrong, awarded to men; and to establish the rule for
meting out their punishments and rewards?" He concludes that men are too presumptuous in arrogating judgment to themselves. "Our measure of rewards and
punishments is most partial and incomplete, absurdly inadequate, utterly worldly,
and we wish to continue it into the next world" (4:314). Measured by the alti-
tude of heaven, Pen says, "the tallest and the smallest among us are so alike diminutive and pitifully base, that I say we should take no count of the calculation, and
it is a meanness to reckon the difference" (4:315).

Plausible as this view seems, and as much in keeping with the underlying
moral structure of Thackeray's novel as is any other single statement in the book,
it is not definitive. The narrator carefully distances himself from Arthur Pendennis' Olympian view, and in fact describes the young man as a sleek Sadducee who
would ride away from John the Baptist and his followers to go home and muse on
the preacher and audience, then turn to his Plato and other diversions. Although
Pen's sentiment may be a satisfactory one, it is not an answer. In Arthur's
scheme, there would be no purpose in punishing, little purpose in taking any
moral action. But in a fallible world made up of widely differing codes of conduct, some degree of judgment is necessary. If Pen's overall view is correct, his

employment of it is not necessarily appropriate. But it is a good deal more appropriate, and a good deal more Christian than his uncle's moral position, which asserts that the indignities that attend those who transgress "ought to be a lesson to a man to keep himself straight in life, and not to give any man a chance over him" (4:351). This is a strictly selfish and worldly defensive position that does not even include an impulse to virtue or a commendation of generosity.

Pen may have achieved a degree of wisdom and a suitable moral outlook by the time he has weathered the Fanny Bolton episode, but both his wisdom and his morals are still compromised by his worldly ambitions, for he plans to marry Blanche for money and position, not from love and respect. And he is fully conscious of his fault. Before his mother's grave "the sight of the sacred stone had brought no consolation to him. A guilty man doing a guilty deed: a mere spectator, content to lay down his faith and honour for a fortune and a worldly career," he knows himself to be unworthy of his mother's memory (4:379). This incorrect behavior brings its own embarrassment. The Major has encouraged Pen to court Blanche because he knows she is destined for her mother's fortune, but circumstances change and the fortune and the seat in Parliament that Pen had counted on now seem to be reverting back to young Francis Clavering. Pen declares that he and the Major have been playing a guilty game and have overreached themselves. He considers himself "rightly punished" by the loss of fortune and Parliamentary seat, but since he has promised marriage to Blanche he feels honor-bound to go through with it, even though he does not love her and she will have only a modest fortune (4:426). Laura, admiring his honorable and generous heart, applauds his decision, though it may give her pain for other reasons. Pen has less respect for his own conduct and tells Laura that she wouldn't think as she does if she really knew him. "Love you know; but the knowledge of evil is kept from you" (4:435).

Pen's assertion is more significant than he can suppose, for the narrator has established a context in which even the paragon, Laura, has had her lapse and her secret. But this secret is not the kind that exposes Clavering, nor is it a false secret like Pen's; it is a generous and loving secret. Not many pages before, Pen had asked Laura if she would have accepted a proposal of marriage from Warrington if he had been free to offer one and she had answered with thorough honesty: yes. "The gentle girl had had her secret, and told it" (4:382). Unlike others with real or supposed secrets, Laura does not have to be found out. She offers up her secret herself, just as Warrington had done to help his friends. In her realization that she can entertain two loves in her heart, she discovers a certain brand of guilt and decides that she had been wicked and proud about Arthur's real and imagined failings. She sees herself as too confident and unforgiving. " 'I never forgave from my heart this poor girl, who was fond of him, or him for encouraging her love; and I have been more guilty than she, poor little artless creature! I, professing to love one man, could listen to another only too eagerly; and would not pardon the change of feelings in Arthur, whilst I myself was changing and unfaithful' " (4:383). Like Warrington, Laura is a model of what it means to look into one's own secret heart fearlessly.

The real secret that Laura has kept, though it has been clear to readers, is that throughout the narrative she has continued to love Arthur. When Arthur is honorably released from his obligation to Blanche, he hurries to Laura at Lady Rockminster's, offers himself, and is accepted. " 'What a sly demure little wretch you have been,' the old lady whispers to Laura, 'and how you have kept your secret!' " (4:464). But a secret of fidelity is nothing to be ashamed of. By contrast, Blanche, who has been playing a multiple game with her various suitors and who has been deeply implicated in the Clavering secrets, has kept one secret from everybody, especially from Harry Foker, her new fiance—that the rogue Altamont is her father. Harry charges her with cheating him and cancels the relationship, and is for a long time after unable to pardon her treachery.

Blanche's secret, because it is selfish and designed to exploit another person, deserves punishment. But although Foker withholds his forgiveness, no character steps forward to provide such punishment. The narrator himself must see to Blanche's fate, and in so doing, suggest the manner in which real punishments occur. The narrator now reveals that Amory had been married before he took Lady Clavering as a wife, making her marriage invalid and Blanche an illegitimate child. No character within the narrative delights in Blanche's discomfiture, but the reader is permitted the gratifying feeling that devious, heartless, and vain Blanche has received the punishment she deserves. Thackeray's readers have known all along that Blanche is a superficial and unappealing person whose conduct merits some reproof, and so the implied author satisfies their supposed desire to see her actual condition reflect her moral state. What could be worse in the moral world of the time than illegitimacy? Nothing in the plot requires this additional fillip to Blanche's case; it is a clear instance of the implied author deciding to punish his creation. He does here as he did not do with Becky Sharp, because whereas Becky was his partner in exposing the vanities of the world he depicted, Blanche is the object of his satire. She is the ultimate figure of hypocrisy that must be unveiled. Blanche is indeed a snob, and, as David Masson pointed out in his review of *Pendennis,* Thackeray was the chief literary expounder of "Anti-snobbism"; it was the one moral evil he could not resist punishing (*Heritage,* 125).

When he thinks he is within a day of winding up the sad story of his youth, Pen prostrates his spirit humbly before the throne of his final judge. Aware of his own failings, Pen acknowledges that we can never know what influences have operated on our fellow beings, and therefore can never comprehend what little events might have made them different for better or worse. "Who can weigh circumstances, passions, temptations, that go to our good and evil account, save One, before whose awful wisdom we kneel, and at whose mercy we ask absolution?" (4:454). He prays that he may begin the next phase of his life as a better man.

The prayer works, of course, because he has every intention of making it work. He deserves forgiveness not only from the characters in the novel but from the narrator as well. A fine fellow like George Warrington has not won any laurels (or Lauras) in the struggle of life, but we must be reconciled to such apparent inequity. "If the best men do not draw the great prizes in life, we know it has been so settled by the Ordainer of the lottery," says the narrator as he draws his tale to a close. But if the Ordainer has ordained a lottery where chance and hazard are the governing powers, what is to be said of the scheme by which we live? Perhaps it is a lottery only in the sense that *we* cannot know the outcome, though the *Ordainer* can. We see the strong fail, the virtuous go unrewarded, and many other apparent injustices, but this does not mean we should complain. Quite the contrary; the fellow feeling that such a perception of the world breeds is the true solution to human suffering, and "knowing how mean the best of us is, let us give a hand of charity to Arthur Pendennis, with all his faults and shortcomings, who does not claim to be a hero, but only a man and a brother" (4:495).

The narrator has unremittingly shown us his main character's many faults and measured them against his virtues. No one is virtuous enough to go blameless, but we are all encouraged to reflect before we judge. And this is perhaps harder for the very virtuous than for those who know they have sinned. Yet it was, in the Victorian Christian ethos, the most spotless of all, Christ himself, who enjoined forgiveness upon us. So the narrator arranges the various secrets that drive the second half of his novel to illustrate not that some of us are wicked and some are not, but that we will all very likely be found out, and that what has been hidden will be exposed. If what is hidden is vile, we will suffer for our vileness. If the reverse, we will not be shamed. Secrets shared in the interests of others are actually beneficial to those who share them. Significantly, the narrator has, by his many interjections, made it perfectly clear that the actions of his story are in the past, so that as we approach the end of the novel all of the secrets now appear innocuous. "At his present mature age all these pleasures are over; and the times have passed away too," the narrator says of Pendennis (4:464). Thus, in a sense, we are seeing a world predestined. We know that Arthur has not come to grief. The narrator has kept few secrets from us, except those incidental to the progress of his story. The events of Pendennis' life are laid out like a story that is told—but only after the fact, and only by someone sympathetic and forgiving. *Pendennis* furnishes perhaps the most pronounced appeal by a narrator for his audience to forgive his creation, and the progress of the narrative amply illustrates the manner and means by which such forgiveness should be extended.

NOTES

1. William Makepeace Thackeray, *The Works of William Makepeace Thackeray*, 26 vols. (Philadelphia: J. B. Lippincott Company, 1901), 3:18. Subsequent references appear in the text.

2. Laura Fasick, "Thackeray's Treatment of Writing and Painting," *Nineteenth-Century Literature* 47, no. 1 (June 1992), 79. Subsequent references appear in the text.

3. See Helene E. Roberts' " 'The Sentiment of Reality': Thackeray's Art Criticism," *Studies in the Novel* 13, nos. 1–2 (Spring-Summer 1981), 21–39, for a discussion of Thackeray's preference for realistic detail in art. His views resemble the early Ruskin, but without Ruskin's insistence that an accurate representation of nature is a moral act recognizing the value of God's creation.

4. In a letter of February 24, 1847, Thackeray writes to Mark Lemon: "A few years ago I should have sneered at the idea of setting up as a teacher at all, and perhaps at this pompous and pious way of talking about a few papers of jokes in Punch—but I have got to believe in the business, and in many other things since then. And our profession seems to me to be as serious as the Parson's own. Please God we'll be honest & kind was what I meant and all I meant. I swear nothing more" (*The Letters and Private Papers of William Makepeace Thackeray*, 4 vols., ed. Gordon N. Ray (Cambridge: Harvard University Press, 1945), 2:282.

5. Jack P. Rawlins, *Thackeray's Novels: A Fiction That Is True* (Berkeley: University of California Press, 1974), 135. Subsequent references appear in the text.

6. *Thackeray: The Critical Heritage,* ed. Geoffrey Tillotson and Donald Hawes (New York: Barnes & Noble, Inc., 1968), 91. The reviewer listed as the amiable characters Helen, Laura, Foker, and Warrington.

7. See Peter K. Garrett's *The Victorian Multiplot Novel: Studies in Dialogical Form* (New Haven: Yale University Press, 1980) for a discussion of the significance of this scene (97ff.).

8. David Masson applauded *Pendennis* for this quality: "So also, in almost all his other characters [besides Pen himself] his study seems to be to give the good and the bad together, in very nearly the same proportions that the cunning apothecary, Nature herself, uses" (*Heritage* 116).

9. Lennard Davis, *Resisting Novels: Ideology and Fiction* (New York: Methuen, 1987). See especially, chapter 4.

10. Thackeray would have disapproved of Sandford's officious piety as much as Dickens did. In a letter to Mary Holmes, a young friend, the paternal Thackeray indicated both his liberal approach to religious faith and his awareness of its use in children's literature. He disapproved of missionary enthusiasm and favored tolerance. "You must shut up your dear convictions of faith in your own heart. If you proselytize it's all over with you. With my young ones for instance—no guardian angels, no Saint Cecilias;—we are of the Clapham Theology. We rather consider Little Henry & his bearer the right kind of thing. You needn't throw a grain of incense on our Altars; but you must, you know, be tolerant to our Idols" (*Letters and Private Papers* 3:20). To his daughter Anne he wrote, about the same time, that Christ provided a new and superior law contradictory to the old and that Scripture, though merely a book, contained divine truths. "And so bless my darlings and teach us the Truth. Every one of us in

every fact, book, circumstance of life sees a different meaning & moral and so it must be with religion. But we can all love each other and say Our Father" (*Letters and Private Papers* 3:96)

11. Gordon N. Ray calls attention to some of the rough character of literary exchanges (*Thackeray: The Uses of Adversity 1811–1846* (London: Oxford University Press, 1955), 90, 222.

12. See John R. Reed's *Victorian Conventions* (Athens: Ohio University Press, 1975), 14ff.

13. See, for example, Ina Ferris' *William Makepeace Thackeray* (Boston: Twayne Publishers, 1983), 40ff.

14. In an amazing letter of April 30, 1846, Thackeray advised Edward Marlborough Fitzgerald to let his wife and children separate themselves from him and not publicize the fact that he brought his mistress into his home and even introduced her to his daughter. He suggests that Fitzgerald repent and improve himself, becoming worthy again of his wife. "Depend upon it that tender & affectionate creature who has pardoned you so much without repentance on your part, will not be hard-hearted when you amend. But prove it. You are bound to do this as clearly as any other criminal" (*Letters* 2:343).

TWENTY-TWO

Henry Esmond

HENRY ESMOND shows how considerably Thackeray had mellowed over the years, especially when compared with *Barry Lyndon,* his first real novel. Lyndon gives an account of his military and romantic adventures in such a way that the reader can easily discern the folly and evil of which he is himself unaware. Exalting himself in all things, he nonetheless produces the self-portrait of a vain, selfish, and heartless man. I suggested earlier that all novelistic storytelling resembles the gradual disclosure of a secret. In *Barry Lyndon* two varieties of secret are being disclosed: the materials of the narrative that remain unknown to us because they are fictional, and the "truth" about Lyndon himself, hidden in the events he narrates and disclosed to us through his language, which masks this truth from himself. This process of disclosure is complicated by the impossibility of knowing just when Lyndon is lying, exaggerating, or telling some version of the "truth." Yet despite this ambiguity, Lyndon is certainly assisting us in finding him out in all his baseness.

Unlike Lyndon, Esmond is presumably conscious of what his language communicates to his special audience (the narrative is composed for his family) and includes, in the interest of truth, passages that redound to his own credit and might otherwise be mistaken as boastful. Esmond's modest inclusion of self-praising passages enhances the truthfulness of his narrative just as Lyndon's crude boasts diminish our trust in his telling. Although it is a keen analysis of a vicious nature, *Barry Lyndon* concentrates on a rapid sequence of incidents and adventures. *Esmond* also contains many significant actions, from private duels to conspiracies against the Crown, but these incidents occur as necessary parts of a narrative that is far more concerned with subtleties of individual psychology and personal relations. The novel follows the general pattern of the historical romance, but its substance is transformed in the direction of personal and domestic concerns rather than issues of grand conflict and dynastic politics.[1]

If Lyndon is a self-revealing liar and braggart, Esmond appears to be a scrupulously honest witness to truth.[2] He bares his mind and his heart. In what seems a serious parodic manner, Thackeray shifts the balance of the historical romance from war-with-love-added to love-with-war-added. Esmond conspicuously plays down his experiences in battle, concentrating instead on his experiences with the complex behaviors of human beings, including himself. Furthermore, though it contains the usual instances of punishment and forgiveness, this novel emphasizes the preliminary sentiments of loving and caring, so that it almost becomes a treatise on how to avoid the necessity for punishing and forgiving.[3] Almost, because Thackeray is depicting the real world, in which no degree of sympathy or understanding can forestall conduct by others requiring pardon or correction.

Esmond may be a truth-teller, but that does not mean he need abjure the techniques of interesting storytelling. Thus, although he could have informed us at the outset of his tale that he is an aristocrat mistaken for a bastard, he saves that information for later disclosure, letting his readers know the facts at the point when, in the sequence of his own experiences, he learned them. In doing this he is faithful both to the history of his own perceptions and to the traditional narrative principles of suspense and surprise. On the other hand, by his use of occasional proleptic glances, we know a fair amount about how things will turn out, not only within Esmond's recounted youth, but beyond it into the time of the telling and thereafter. An example of this anticipation occurs within Esmond's narrative when, as a young boy, Esmond witnesses firsthand the rancor of a crowd against the Catholic Castlewood family. Colonel Esmond of Walcote extricates Harry from the struggle, and Esmond as narrator comments, "The boy did not know how nearly in after-life he should be allied to Colonel Esmond, and how much kindness he should have to owe him."[4] This remark anticipates the central experiences of Harry's life, for it is through Colonel Esmond's inheritance of the Castlewood estate that Harry becomes a member of the family and begins his lifelong devotion to Rachel, Lady Castlewood.

A forward glance of another sort shows us the narrator in his narrating time, looking back upon the experiences he is recording. Concerning his youthful vow that nothing will separate him from his mistress, he remarks, "Now, at the close of his life, as he sits and recalls in tranquillity the happy and busy scenes of it, he can think, not ungratefully, that he has been faithful to that early vow. Such a life is so simple that years may be chronicled in a few lines. But few men's life-voyages are destined to be all prosperous; and this calm of which we are speaking was soon to come to an end" (7:73). In explaining his principles, Esmond says that he has brought up his own children with little of the servile spirit in them, and adds that he wants his grandsons to represent him as nature made him; "so, with regard to his past acquaintances, he would speak without anger, but with truth, as far as he knows it, neither extenuating nor setting down aught in malice" (7:76).

Telling the truth in Esmond's narrative requires both candor and tact. He can confess his own thoughts and speculate about the actions of others; he can report

approximate conversations and even cite documents; but when it comes to the
private thoughts and feelings of others, he must move gingerly. This is especially
true with his most problematic character, Rachel. Since he is presumably writing
his narrative for his own descendants, he can leave certain important facts un-
mentioned until their place—most significantly, that he will end up married to
Rachel. There are numerous clues to this effect, including the fact that his daughter is named Rachel and that he frequently halts his narration to say that a given
moment in his past would remain with him forever, that Rachel has told him of
how she came to the knowledge of his inheritance, and that his present affections
remain firm (7:109, 363, 255). In retrospect, the reader can appreciate how much
has logically been left unsaid, given the supposed audience for Esmond's memoirs. But beyond Esmond the narrator is Thackeray the author, who is determined to tell a good story and to make it rich and rewarding as well. Esmond
may recount his experiences, but it is Thackeray, or that handy intermediate
concept, the implied author, who makes these experiences resonate with one
another. The dueling episodes, for example, take on moral overtones that Esmond himself does not explore, but which are implicit in the movement of the
narrative as a whole. The first Mohun duel ends with the death of the better
man, Francis, Viscount Castlewood, and creates a temporary estrangement between Henry and Rachel, supposedly because she considers him responsible for
her husband's death.[5] In the second Mohun duel, Henry defeats Mohun, not out
of revenge, but to protect the young Francis, Viscount Castlewood, for which he
earns the gratitude of the family. The third Mohun duel ends with Mohun's death
but also with that of the Duke of Hamilton, another good man and Beatrix's
intended husband. In the first instance, Rachel's loss of her husband was actually
a liberation from what had become a loveless marriage, a guilty liberation that
makes her fully conscious of her "sin" of loving Esmond. In the second duel,
Esmond, who now knows that he has the real claim to being Viscount Castlewood, nonetheless keeps his secret and protects the young man who enjoys the
title. By contrast to these two self-repressors, Beatrix feels only selfish vexation
that her material ambitions are frustrated by Lord Hamilton's death. The first
duel exposes one woman's true, rich feelings to herself, the second records Esmond's secret nobility in two senses, and the third exposes another woman's
crassness to all.

Another example of authorial arrangement is the relationship of Esmond to
Richard Steele. In temperament they are unlike—the one melancholy, the other
exuberant. But in taste and sentiment they are close. Both are sensitive to the
feelings of others and both appreciate good writing—Joseph Addison being a *to-
pos* of their agreement on this matter. Early in his narrative Henry describes his
unpleasant upbringing, which, he says, accounts for his melancholy tendencies;
"as those tender twigs are bent the trees grow afterward; and he, at least, who
has suffered as a child, and is not quite perverted in that early school of unhappiness, learns to be gentle and long-suffering with little children" (7:21).[6] A little

later Steele explains that the loss of his father at five years of age and the grief that accompanied it " 'has made me pity all children ever since; and caused me to love thee, my poor fatherless, motherless lad' " (7:68–69). Hidden in the rough and ready trooper is a gentle spirit; conversely, and more obliquely, we learn that hidden in the gentle and scholarly Esmond is a potential warrior. When occasion demands, he proves worthy of personal and public combat, and for a time enjoys the departure from his customary temperament. Though Steele will eventually write a treatise on *The Christian Hero*, he cannot live by the code of conduct his book describes, although Esmond, out of affection and gratitude rather than religious principle, can.

The full title of Steele's book is *The Christian Hero: an Argument Proving that no Principles but those of Religion are Sufficient to make a Great Man,* and it concludes with praise for King William as an illustrious prince whose character and actions serve as a bridle and a check upon tyranny. The principal argument of the book is for the control and direction rather than elimination of the passions. Steele sets forth his basic assumptions about the nature of justice in this world early in his text.

> Thus are Men hurry'd away in the Prosecution of mean and sensual Desires, and instead of Employing their Passions in the service of Life, they spend their Life in the service of their passions; yet tho' 'tis a Truth very little receiv'd, that virtue is its own Reward, 'tis surely an undeniable one, that Vice is its own Punishment; for when we have giv'n our Appetites a loose Rein, we are immediately precipitated by 'em into unbounded and endless Wishes, while we repine at our fortune, if its Narrowness curbs 'em, tho' the Gratification of 'em were a Kindness, like the Indulgence of a Man's Thirst in a Dropsy; but this Distemper of Mind is never to be remedied, till Men will more unreservedly attempt the Work and will resolve to value themselves rather upon a strong Reason to allay their Passions, than a fine Imagination to raise 'em.[7]

He asserts that "nothing is more daring than Truth" and "nothing more Chearful than Innocence" (11). Believing in a providential design for human history, Steele emphasizes Christ's humble appearance as a way of persuading mankind to obey God's injunctions, but his argument for the importance of placing reason in control of passion and soul in dominion over sense achieves its climax with a plea for sympathetic human behavior. We are framed, he says, for mutual kindness, good will, and service, and the Saviour has commanded us to love one another.

> But this extensive Magnanimity, according to the Rules of our Faith, is not to be bestow'd on those only who are our Friends, but must reach also to our very Enemies; though good Sense as well as Religion is so

utterly banish'd the World, that Men glory in their very Passions, and pursue Trifles with the utmost Vengeance: So little do they know that to Forgive is the most arduous Pitch human Nature can arrive at; a Coward has often Fought, a Coward has often Conquer'd, but a *Coward never Forgave*. (80)

In a world torn between Virtue and Vice, Innocence and Guilt, the best principles for success and useful service remain Christ's simple recommendations for humility, forgiveness, and love. Esmond, though he is a far from perfect being, nonetheless professes a desire for the truth as he can comprehend it, and does generally behave with humility (which nonetheless may mask a kind of pride) and forgiveness.[8] Like most Thackeray characters, he has faults, but Esmond, like Dobbin, approaches a true gentlemanly character.

By exploiting the similarities and differences between Esmond and Steele, the narrator makes clear his purpose of establishing the former's credentials as a model of the Christian hero *in the context of his times*. Like the two Viscounts Castlewood who protect him, Esmond exhibits a generous spirit and physical courage, but he also subdues his private impulses and emotions through self-discipline and introspection as they do not. Though his ideal is so to conduct himself that he will never require punishment or sue for forgiveness, invariably his affectionate behavior is misinterpreted and misunderstood, and eventually it is he who must forgive injuries. I shall return to this important subject later, for it offers an interesting way of viewing Thackeray's tactical approach.

Esmond stands in contrast to a gradation of other "heroes," from the genial Captain Westbury and noble General Webb to the treacherous Lord Mohun, but his nature is best read as representing a humble and achievable variation on the supposedly Great Characters represented in this novel chiefly by King William, the Duke of Marlborough, and James Stuart III, pretender to the English throne. The last of these, first introduced as a remote figure of greatness, proves morally repugnant on near acquaintance. What is true of James is, in Esmond's mature view, true of the Stuarts in general.

'Tis a wonder to anyone who looks back at the history of the Stuart family to think how they kicked their crowns away from them; how they flung away chances after chances; what treasures of loyalty they dissipated, and how fatally they were bent on consummating their own ruin. If ever men had fidelity, 'twas they; if ever men squandered opportunity, 'twas they; and, of all the enemies they had, they themselves were the most fatal. (7:206)

Again, discussing the Stuart intrigues against King William, Esmond rejects their unscrupulous recourse to employing base agents and planning for ambush and assassination. " 'Tis humiliating to think that a great Prince, possessed of a great and sacred right, and upholder of a great cause, should have stooped to such baseness of assassination and treasons as are proved by the unfortunate King James's own warrant and sign manual given to his supporters in this country" (7:210).

Esmond offers these sentiments in old age, long after his disillusionment with James III, who loses his opportunity for kingship by lustfully pursuing Beatrix Esmond, itself an insult to his firmest supporters. But Esmond's progress from high Toryism, Catholicism, and the Stuart cause is gradual, not a sudden revulsion. His respect for the Castlewoods, for example, is based upon personal gratitude and loyalty, not deference to their rank. When he meets with honorable behavior—as in a Steele or an Addison—he values the behavior itself, not the rank of the individual. Indeed, exalted as the individual may be, and as worthy of commendation for his achievements, Esmond cannot approve what he finds ignoble. Hence, despite his appreciation of Marlborough's military genius, Esmond deplores the man.

> Perhaps he could not have been the great man he was, had he had a heart either for love or hatred, or pity or fear, or regret or remorse. He achieved the highest deed of daring, or deepest calculation of thought, as he performed the very meanest action of which a man is capable; told a lie, or cheated a fond woman, or robbed a poor beggar of a halfpenny, with a like awful serenity and equal capacity of the highest and lowest acts of our nature. (7:260–61)

Esmond reiterates his disapproval in many places, but Thackeray seeks both to mitigate this personal animus and to humanize Esmond through the narrative ploy of a fictive footnote. Esmond's daughter, Rachel, who has edited the text, reports that Esmond told many more stories against Marlborough than appear in his memoirs, but that this hostility resulted from a personal slight the great Duke offered Esmond, which he never forgave. Information of this sort has helped to fuel a tendency among critics of *Henry Esmond* to be extremely suspicious of Esmond's narrative, reading in it numerous signs that throw into question his ability to render fairly and accurately the people and events that have affected him. Yet while Thackeray always allowed for the fallibility of his narrators, that fallibility did not necessarily discredit their accounts.[9] Whether Marlborough's slight to Esmond was real or not, no such personal affront is necessary for Esmond to revile a prominent figure whose position assured him respect and influence, but whose private behavior was selfish and immoral, and whose public conduct was disloyal. Esmond, though like all humans entirely capable of error, nonetheless maintains a high standard of moral behavior. Thackeray thus adds to the picture of his Christian hero the irony that even his adoring daughter has not fully appreciated the values that prompted his actions, but reduces them instead to her simpler and more personal standards. Later, in *The Virginians,* Thackeray would amusingly explore the rigid and unreflective morality according to which Esmond's daughter, Rachel, sought to govern her own, her sons', and her dependents' lives.

The clear model of elevated excellence in *Henry Esmond* is King William. Though the leader of the Whigs and Protestants, William nonetheless earns Esmond's admiration because he is a tactful politician and a good military strategist. Above all, he is a compassionate man, living up to the commendation accorded him by Steele. After describing the underhanded devices of the Stuarts, Esmond declares, "The noble Prince of Orange burst magnanimously through those feeble meshes of conspiracy in which his enemies tried to envelop him: it seemed as if their cowardly daggers broke upon the breast of his undaunted resolution" (7:210). This is high praise for an opponent, though naturally it is uttered long after Esmond has abandoned the Stuart cause. Elsewhere Esmond has offered evidence that William's behavior compared very favorably, in Christian terms, with that of the Stuarts. Esmond recounts how, during the 1695 conspiracy, William was provided with the names of gentlemen involved in the plot against him; "with a noble wisdom and clemency, the Prince burned the list of conspirators furnished to him, and said he would know no more" (7:127).

Esmond admires William's magnanimity, his ability to overlook even the most serious offense in the interests of a higher good. The wisdom of his practice is evident in the determination of the first Francis, Viscount Castlewood, after learning of this leniency, never to engage in a conspiracy against what he now considered "one of the wisest, the bravest and the greatest of men" (7:127). Later the Jesuit Father Holt is released from prison and put on shipboard "by the incorrigible forgiveness of King William" (7:212). It is clear from these and other instances—such as that of King William's absence of malice toward his noble enemy Lord Arran, whom he released twice from prison without trial despite that Lord's inability to give his word that he would not again conspire against the king—that what Esmond admires most about William is his ability to rise above any sense of personal injury, his willingness to appreciate the ideas and feelings motivating others, and his Christian tendency to prefer forgiveness over punishment.

Many critics have offered revisionary estimates of Esmond's character because of implicit revelations of character hidden in his first-person narration or hinted at in Rachel's preface and notes. But it is important to keep in mind the kind of rules of reading that Peter Rabinowitz calls to our attention. One kind of metonymic enchainment he describes in his rules of signification is the assumption that the presence of one moral quality is linked to that of another that lies more or less contiguous to it.[10] Thus charity or self-effacement might imply genuine humility, love, and so on. Reinforcing this kind of reading is another kind of chaining; many narratives ask us, "in the absence of evidence to the contrary, to assume a kind of innocence by association: we trust the friends of our friends and the enemies of our enemies" (90). Esmond's admiration for King William and affection for Steele are indicators of this kind. Esmond can love the generous but errant Steele for his genuineness and his good heart and he can admire, even as he opposes him, a ruler who exhibits the Christian values that Esmond himself is striving to live by. I believe that recent critics have labored too hard to undermine the nobleness of Esmond's character. Thackeray may have concluded in his self-deprecatory way that Esmond was, after all, a prig, but later, in *The Virginians,* he had Beatrix, now a worn-out old woman with no illusions, describe him as a truly fine man.

Esmond's narrative depicts King William as courageous, forbearing, long-suffering, and generous, a Whig interpretation that Thackeray shared. These are the best features of Esmond and Rachel as well. Other great men in the novel are deeply flawed in one way or another. The Duke of Marlborough is calculating, vain, and not a little treacherous. He appears vindictive and ungenerous in his behavior—most notably in his treatment of General Webb. Ultimately, his lack of scruple leads to retribution—a fall from power and position. This retribution, however, following Steele's beliefs in *The Christian Hero,* is rendered as a natural consequence of his actions, a return upon his hubris, not as a punishment concocted by a storyteller to satisfy the moral expectations of his readers. The case of James Stuart III is different. Here the entire account of the young Stuart's visit to England, to be on hand for kingship as Queen Anne lies dying, is fabricated precisely to illustrate the folly of a weak, passion-driven, self-indulgent character. Esmond records the event as history, but the implied author employs it to point out a moral.

These three characters are real historical figures, and thus the trajectories of their lives and the large outlines of their characters are pre-inscribed in the narrative, but there is, thoughout the novel, a fictional pre-inscription that works toward a comparable sense of inevitability. Because Esmond's narrative is a backward-looking account of his life, his rendering of it is determined by the events that actually happened. However, just as Ikey Solomon claimed to be constrained by the Newgate account of Catherine Hayes yet managed to incorporate enormous amounts of created material, so Esmond is not as limited in the construction of his story as it may first appear. He admits that his organization of experience is an artifact composed of slowly acquired information and changed outlooks.

> 'Tis not to be imagined that Harry Esmond had all this experience at this early stage of his life, whereof he is now writing the history— many things here noted were but known to him in later days. Almost everything Beatrix did or undid seemed good, or at least pardonable, to him then, and years afterwards. (7:142)

Also, the manner of interpreting past events is inevitably determined by their outcome. Thus Esmond reports that in the midst of his scheme to return James

Stuart to the throne he wished the deed undone. "He was not the first that has regretted his own act, or brought about his undoing. Undoing? Should he write that word in his late years? No, on his knees before Heaven, rather be thankful for what then he deemed his misfortune, and which hath caused the whole subsequent happiness of his life" (7:461). Esmond has to catch himself up in a cliché about the failure of his project and realize that it was actually a happy failure. If the "novel" of Esmond's life had ended with the collapse of James' attempt to claim the English throne and Esmond's loss of love for Beatrix, the tale would have ended sadly, if not tragically. The story does not end with sentimental and melancholy deprivation—the romance's obverse of the domestic novel's happy marriage ending—but continues on to another volume in Esmond's career, which involves marriage and domestic joy, though not what we have been led to expect.

Determined, then, the events of the story must be, but that does not apply to the judgment of those events, nor to their narration.[11] Esmond eschews direct chronology, for example, beginning his first chapter with the new Viscount Castlewood and his wife discovering the melancholy and lonely orphan Henry Esmond, whom they immediately befriend. He then turns not to his own previous history but to an account of Thomas and Isabella Esmond, Viscount and Lady Castlewood, but without the explanation of why he becomes a part of their family. Most of the narrative presents a consistent chronological development, but this slight reorganization dramatizes some experiences and withholds crucial information. Within the pattern of what actually happened, Esmond is nonetheless free to interpret, shape, and even sensationalize some features of the story.[12] Similarly, he takes the liberty of rendering characters through description and through reconstituted or imagined dialogue. Sometimes these procedures are elaborate.[13] For example, Esmond re-creates a dialogue with Rachel in which she re-creates her dialogue with Isabella in which she reveals the secret of Henry's legitimacy (7:362). Though complex, this account of conversation nested in conversation is comparatively straightforward. There is much more implied in Esmond's rendering of Richard Steele's account of his conversation with Rachel. Though Rachel has separated herself from Esmond in anger for his part in the duel that took her husband's life, the words that Steele repeats from their conversation contain a meaning unknown to Steele at the time, and undisclosed by Esmond in the time of his telling. Steele reports Rachel as saying, " 'It may be, in years hence, when—when our knees and our tears and our contrition have changed our sinful hearts, sir, and wrought our pardon, we may meet again—but not now' " (7:194). What is left unsaid is that Rachel is herself suffering the guilt of loving Esmond at a moment when the death of her unloved husband leaves her free to acknowledge that love. Her real reason for alienating Esmond is not hatred, but love, as the talismanic button she preserves from this episode reveals at the very end of the narrative. Moreover, a slip of the tongue reveals her sustained interest in Esmond's welfare. She says, of the Dowager Lady Castlewood, " 'The mistress of this house has relented very much towards the late lord's son

. . . and has promised me, that is, has promised that she will care for his fortune'" (7:194). It is unlikely that Steele would have taken the trouble to repeat these words with their exact hesitations and corrections, and Esmond could do so at the time of his narration only with the intent of revealing their significance. In fact, the meticulousness of this report of Rachel's remarks is the implied author's way of planting clues for the later explanation of Rachel's behavior.[14] Indeed, much of the effort to reverse the traditional reading of Esmond as an ordinarily flawed human being, nobly seeking to record the truth as he understands it, could be challenged by examining the function of the implied author in this narrative, an examination that is beyond the purpose of this study. But J. Hillis Miller's brilliant effort to present *Henry Esmond* as an indirect story or parable of the "erasure of Henry's picture of himself and its replacement by another truer picture" depends too much upon reading the text as a consistent pattern of discourse, whereas I would suggest, as does Miller himself, that a good part of the narrative's meaning reaches us over Esmond's head through the nuances of the implied author (103). As Scarry and Miller have indicated, there are many contradictions and double meanings embedded in the text of *Esmond,* so many, in fact, that they suggest a conscious design. But truth itself is called so much into question in the text that it is highly problematic to suggest that a "truer" picture of Esmond erases his own estimate of himself. Perhaps it would be safer to say that at least one other estimate of his character is laid beside his own for comparison, just as other readings of the sequence of events he narrates are possible.

One way to locate some interpretive stability in the face of this mystification is to establish a ground that is redundantly reinforced throughout the text, and further reinforced by the interpretive "success" that ground affords. I suggest that the moral ground underlying the whole operation and purpose of the narrative is roughly equatable with basic Christian principles, a ground that Thackeray could take for granted in his reading public, even if he often chose to tease them about their commitment to it. Much of our final opinion of Esmond depends upon how well he manages to approximate to his own declared models—for example, Rachel in one arena and King William in another. One source of confusion about Esmond is that he is speaking from a point beyond his narrative while at the same time trying to recapture the feel of experiences in their historical time (narrative, as distinguished from narrating, time). This means that at the same time Esmond is seeking to evoke long-past emotions, he is judging affairs with the intellectual advantage of hindsight. To declare, as Garson does, that Esmond the memoirist still has not forgiven the boy he fought with in childhood to defend Rachel's character is to ignore a basic feature of the narrative (390). Esmond *recalls* the emotions that moved him, but does not necessarily *repeat* them. In fact, the virtue of referring to some deep ground for the narrative is to realize that the moral position from which Esmond writes is precisely that of forgiveness and pardon. His false idols and enemies are gone, chiefly self-punished, and he retains his true idol—though not necessarily the one he most passionately desired and about whom he was disillusioned. Esmond was wrong to support the Stuarts and now, at the time of telling, values all King William stood for instead; Esmond was wrong to pursue Beatrix, who, in retrospect, can be seen to have been selfish and cruel from infancy onward, and Esmond now values what Rachel stands for instead. Part of what Esmond has to forgive is his own early errors.

If Esmond's narrative is determined by his belief that he is truthfully record-ing a personal history that is essentially concluded, the implied author's narrative is similarly determined by its taking place in a historical period long past, whose sequence of events is thus unalterable. But just as Esmond has a great deal of latitude in relating his personal memoir, so the implied author has great liberty in rendering the events of an earlier time. Just as Esmond must reconstruct conver-sations and imagine scenes that he did not witness directly, so the implied author can make history live by creating fictional characters like Esmond himself. At their different levels, both agents are doing the same thing, though one is profer-ring fiction and the other "truth." However, since Thackeray more than once argued that serious fiction is as trustworthy a manner of telling about the past as declared history, there is little to choose between these two approaches, and the novel gains in resonance by being a commentary on its own mode. Thackeray recognized early what has so concisely been pointed out by Hayden White: once past events are rendered in a narrative, they embody an ideology and move to-ward a moral conclusion.[15]

At the outset of this novel, Esmond himself objects that histories are too preoccupied with kings and great doings, providing too little sense of ordinary life. "In a word, I would have History familiar rather than heroic: and think that Mr. Hogarth and Mr. Fielding will give our children a much better idea of the manners of the present age in England, than the *Court Gazette* and the newspapers which we get thence" (7:2). Of course it is not just manners with which Thack-eray is concerned, but morals as well. But neither history nor fiction should smugly pass judgment on the events and people of the past or present. Thackeray had warned against such an attitude in his reviews of contemporary novels. Like Thackeray, Esmond asserts that we should not be too quick to judge other people's lapses. He can look as calmly upon the Lord Mayor's procession as upon that of a prisoner going to Tyburn for hanging. "I look into my heart," Esmond confesses, "and think I am as good as my Lord Mayor, and know I am as bad as Tyburn Jack" (7:4). This brief introduction touches most of the novel's important purposes—to offer an honest account of ordinary existence and to view the great and the common as equal before the eyes of human judgment and sympathy, though al-ways with the proviso that we first survey with an equally critical and compas-sionate eye that nearest province for moral evaluation, our own heart.

The two central characters in this novel are good and pious people; they are models of Christian character. Yet each behaves unwisely, each acts generously to ill consequences, and each feels the need of some "punishment." The two—Rachel and Esmond—are alike in other ways. Each has a secret that at first appears shameful, but which ultimately proves ennobling. Each performs a generous act of self-renunciation. Each, though acutely attentive to the secret promptings of the heart, to some degree misreads those promptings.

I have already suggested that all novels depend upon disclosing mysteries, and that Dickens and Thackeray carry out this activity in different ways. Dickens "solves" mysteries; Thackeray exposes secrets, though often ironically. In his review of *Esmond*, John Forster complained that "Mr. Thackeray hangs over the fictitious people on his paper too much as their creator and their judge," and seeks out not the benevolent secrets of his characters, but only their hidden baseness.[16] And J. Hillis Miller explains that "The activity of Henry's narration, in relation to other people, is a process of unveiling, as he shows the tawdriness and vanity, the lack of intrinsic worth in one person after another" (96). Yet Forster is wrong to say that Thackeray judges his characters in *Esmond*. Though Esmond himself may do this, Thackeray tends to remain aloof, though he does occasionally bring narrative punishment to bear. And the charge that Esmond's narrative only exposes the hypocrisy and nastiness of characters is to miss the exquisite irony that the two most significant secrets in the text, though apparently tainted, prove to be those most admirable and liberating when unveiled.

It is interesting that the first two books of *Henry Esmond* end with scenes of penitence and forgiveness, and the last book with episodes of punishment and reward. On the surface, all of these scenes have to do with matters of honor and gallantry; more profoundly, all deal with questions of individual human responsibility. Book One ends with the breach between Rachel and Esmond over the death of Francis, Viscount Castlewood. Book Two ends with another duel, and the recollection of the circumstances of the earlier duel. Book Three ends with punishment and, most significantly, self-punishment. All of these critical episodes are deeply related to the two central secrets of the narrative, secrets that are gradually made evident to the reader while being withheld much longer from the characters. The relative pace of these disclosures will be discussed later, but first we should examine the significant points where the three books end, remembering that this is the one novel Thackeray planned and composed in its entirety before it was published, thus suggesting stricter control of the larger aspects of structural design.

The last chapter of Book One is complicated by antagonistic emotions. Lord Mohun has insulted Castlewood by trying to seduce his wife—hence the duel. Realizing that he has lost his wife's love by his own philandering, Castlewood says of the duel, " 'If I live, that villain will be punished; if I fall, my family will be only the better' " (7:165). A desire to punish and a low sense of self-worth are not good conditions for the human spirit facing a crisis. But part of Castlewood's self-judgment results from Rachel's emotional estrangement. Earlier Castlewood had confided to Esmond that, though Rachel had forgiven him for leaving her to escape the danger of smallpox, she would not forgive his taking up with another woman. Now, when Castlewood admits to Esmond that he is going to fight over his wife, Esmond says it is unthinkable that Rachel has sinned. Castlewood replies, "'Do you fancy I think that *she* would go astray? No, she hasn't passion enough for that. She neither sins nor forgives'" (7:164). Rachel, however, believes that she has sinned precisely because she has had the passion to love not Mohun but Esmond. Similarly, she believes that she requires forgiveness from God, whereas it is apparent to the reader that she must learn to forgive herself.

The conclusion to Book One is thus a strange amalgam of error, misunderstanding, and unwise action. Nonetheless, an appropriately conventional ending to Book One makes it appear simpler than it is, largely because its many reverberations are not yet evident. (If the Viscount knew where Rachel's love was fixed, he might not be dueling Mohun, etc.) Mr. Atterbury, the clergyman who attends the dying Lord Castlewood, tells Esmond, "'He has made a clean breast to me. He forgives and believes, and makes restitution'" (7:174). For the first time Esmond learns, in Castlewood's written confession, that he is Thomas, Viscount Castlewood's legitimate son, and thus heir to the Castlewood title and properties. Esmond magnanimously burns the confession and Castlewood dies with a blessing on his lips.

Book Two ends with fewer submerged implications and serves as a counterbalance to the movements of Book One's conclusion. Young Frank, Viscount Castlewood, is determined to force Lord Mohun into a duel out of revenge for his father's death, but this time Esmond is successful in provoking Mohun first, so that it is he, not Frank, who meets Mohun on the field of honor. Esmond explicitly addresses and clarifies his motives in this encounter. "If Captain Esmond had put Mohun out of the world, as he might, a villain would have been punished and spared further villainies—but who is one man to punish another?" Thus renouncing not only his own intention to punish Mohun but the whole concept of individual retribution itself, Esmond explains his simple purpose. "I declare upon my honour that my only thought was to prevent Lord Mohun from mischief with Frank," and to this end Esmond only disables his opponent (7:327). The Castlewood ladies are proud of Esmond for this act, which recalls to Rachel her husband's death, of whom she now has a revised estimate. She says she has often felt that since his death Francis' love has come back to her. "'Perhaps he is here now, Harry—I think he is. Forgiven I am sure he is: even Mr. Atterbury absolved him, and he died forgiving. Oh, what a noble heart he had! How generous he was!'" (7:334). If the first duel severed Rachel from Esmond, this duel symbolically repairs that rent, though it has been made up in other ways during the interval. To some degree Esmond's act of traditional male valor recuperates Castlewood's character by locating it in the arena not of folly, but of family honor. Esmond's noble action reflects back on that of his mentor and, conversely, Rachel's praise of her redeemed husband acts as a veiled encomium for Esmond. A selfless, nonpunitive action thus generates analeptic and proleptic grace, bringing honor not only to the actor but to others as well. Ironically, Esmond's one true violent act, which superficially appears to be revenge, fosters love and forgiveness instead.

The end of Book Three is different, with Prince James Stuart and Beatrix bringing their own misfortune upon themselves. After the fact the prince realizes how vast the consequences of his pursuit of Beatrix will be. He has lost a crown, Beatrix, and the loyalty of followers like Henry and Viscount Castlewood. But he has sufficient understanding to recognize his own fault in this loss. He asks Esmond's pardon, offers him symbolic satisfaction through crossed swords, and then embraces him. He is both punished and forgiven, and stands at the end of the novel as a crowning example of the importance and true nature of both. No external punishment is required and forgiveness is readily extended after repentance. The individual case of the prince, because so monumentally significant, is a powerful endorsement of the overall moral structure of the novel.

Because Esmond regularly renounces retribution as an acceptable motive for conduct, it is entirely within his moral code that he follows James Stuart to Castlewood not to punish him, but to prevent dishonor to the Castlewood family. The implied author, however, need not be so scrupulous. Thus, although the Prince's punishment is self-engendered in Esmond's narrative, it is narratively engendered in the implied author's fable, invented precisely to establish the moral point that unwise acts bring their own retribution. Moreover, although Esmond may be supposed to recount his story in a roughly chronological manner, with a minimum of art, the pattern of forgiveness and punishment emphasized by the endings of the three books of the novel clearly reveals the implied author's purpose. If Thackeray will not allow his Christian hero to punish—for what man has the right to punish another?—he has no such reservations about his implied author, who, by existing extradiegetically outside and "above" the realm of his characters, can see to it that a broader justice prevails. He can act as the force— call it Fate or Providence—that creates a design and therefore an explanation in human experience.

That Esmond will not punish does not mean he will not fight; beginning with his early scrap with Bryan Hawkshaw, who speaks slightingly of Lady Castlewood, Esmond proves himself quite effective in combat. But he is fastidiously not punitive. His nature is given over much more to caring, protecting, and reverencing—and yet, simple as these impulses should be to understand, Esmond is regularly misunderstood, especially by those for whom he cares the most. And it is by them that he is most injured. The whole burden of Esmond's character perforce inclines toward forgiveness and pardon. The smallpox incident is a significant early example. Esmond is attracted to the blacksmith's daughter, Nancy Sievewright, with whom he spends an hour tending her ailing brother. Sexual attraction and compassion are both involved. When Esmond tells the Castlewoods that he has been exposed to infection and gives the circumstances, Lady Castlewood becomes angry, immediately suspecting him of baser intentions than he felt. Added to Esmond's grief at having brought the disease into the household is Rachel's anger at his conduct. As yet we do not, as readers, fully understand

Rachel's anger, but with hindsight it is apparent that she already entertains a warm feeling for Henry and is as jealous of his affections as of her husband's. Jealousy of beautiful women, we are told, was her single fault (7:77). Rachel is conscious of her mixed motives, and soon after her outbreak returns to take Esmond's hand and apologize. " 'I beg your pardon, Henry,' she said; 'I spoke very unkindly. I have no right to interfere with you—with your—' " (7:87). The sexual implications of the whole event nonetheless remain significant to her. Immediately afterward Rachel suggests it is probably time that Henry go to the university.

Esmond suffers a more serious misunderstanding, as we have seen, after Francis, Viscount Castlewood's death. Wounded himself and in prison, Esmond must endure Rachel's upbraiding instead of her gratitude, her blame for her husband's death instead of appreciation for his effort to prevent it. "It seemed," Esmond says, "as if his very sacrifices and love for this lady and her family were to turn to evil and reproaches" (7:180). At a moment when he has the power to respond vindictively toward this family, he overlooks Rachel's injustice to him as well as Lord Castlewood's. That nobleman had done Esmond a great injury by withholding the truth about his standing in the family. But Esmond takes no revenge; instead he forgives all and magnanimously leaves the Castlewood estates in the hands of Rachel and her family, a decision with which he is later satisfied and which he reaffirms explicitly. Esmond has to bear up after Rachel's cruel blow, "at once the sense of his right and the feeling of his wrongs, his honor and his misfortune" (7:184). But he does bear up. "If there be some thoughts and actions of his life from the memory of which a man shrinks with shame, sure there are some which he may be proud to own and remember: forgiven injuries, conquered temptations (now and then), and difficulties vanquished by endurance" (7:185). He has long since forgiven and blessed the soft hand that wounded him then, he adds, but "no time, tears, caresses, or repentance can obliterate the scar" (7:185). Esmond is the constant reinforcer of the idea that forgiveness is the proper mode of conduct, but it is also he who reminds us that if forgiveness can heal, it cannot undo.

There are other misunderstandings of Esmond's behavior, but these are the most significant and involve his central relationship—the mutual affection with Rachel. Ironically, when Esmond does see Rachel again, hastening to Walcote at the rumor of Thomas Tusher's conjugal hopes, he is warmly accepted and "it seemed as if forgiveness and love were awaiting the returning prodigal" (7:237). Of course, Esmond is more Samaritan than prodigal.

If Esmond's acts are regularly misread negatively only to be forgiven later, Rachel's transgressions remain hidden to all but herself, though awareness of them would make any compassionate observer judge leniently. Esmond does not endorse punishment, but punishment is an important part of Rachel's way of thinking because she believes herself guilty and therefore deserving of correction. When she visits Esmond in prison and chastizes him for his involvement in her husband's death, she assumes that she is the focus of this suffering. The problem, she says, began when she asked her husband to keep Esmond with them.

> "I saw that they boded harm to us—and it came, I knew it would. Why did you not die when you had the small-pox—and I came myself and watched you, and you didn't know me in your delirium—and you called out for me, though I was there at your side? All that has happened since was a just judgment on my wicked heart—my wicked jealous heart. Oh, I am punished—awfully punished! My husband lies in his blood—murdered for defending me, my kind, kind, generous lord—and you were by, and you let him die, Henry!" (7:179)

What is missing in this diatribe is Rachel's admission of her own love for Esmond, a fact made abundantly clear by her appropriating at this time the button from his coat that is a memento of her secret love. Later, when they are reconciled at Walcote, Rachel says: "'I knew you would come, Harry, if—if it was but to forgive me for having spoken unjustly to you after that horrid—horrid misfortune.'" She now knows that Esmond did all that he could to prevent the duel between Mohun and Castlewood; "'but it was God's will that I should be punished, and that my dear Lord should fall'" (7:232). Now Rachel reveals her pure devotion for Esmond and, reflecting on this moment, Esmond concludes that only true love lives after you, not vanity, ambition, wealth, or fame. He offers to stay with Rachel, but she pictures her life as essentially over, whereas his is just beginning. If there were now cloisters for women in England she would retire to one and pass her life in penance, she says. "'But I would love you still—yes, there is no sin in such a love as mine now; and my dear lord in heaven may see my heart; and knows the tears that have washed my sin away—and now—now my duty is here, by my children whilst they need me, and by my poor old father, and—'" (7:235). Esmond wants to add himself to the list, but she says no; she had wished to die when she sat by him in his dangerous encounter with smallpox, but she would have died in sin, she says. "'It is over now and past, and it has been forgiven me'" (7:235). To a very great degree Rachel is her own judge. It was she who found herself guilty and worthy of punishment; it is she who, feeling that punishment and suffering have cleansed her, can declare herself forgiven. But the language of moral judgment simply masks Rachel's different ways of dealing with a strong affection that she cannot and does not wish to dismiss. The life story that she considers over has merely reached the end of its first volume.

As the rest of the novel shows, Rachel's love is not over, merely suppressed. And if her sin is forgiven her—and it is unclear who did the forgiving—it seems to be on condition that she not allow that love to be gratified. The true punishment for this denial of love is to see Esmond fall in love with and suffer at the hands of her daughter, the beautiful, selfish, and heartless Beatrix. When Rachel's "sin" is truly found out it is revealed as the highest of virtues—true and enduring love. Rachel has understood the secret of her heart from its inception and sought to keep it. Though she confesses her love for Esmond, she does so only in the context of renunciation. Much later, after the disaster of James Stuart's failed attempt at the throne, Rachel admits the true nature of her love and accepts Esmond as her husband rather than her son. By contrast, Esmond has always openly expressed his admiration for and devotion to Rachel, but has never viewed it in erotic terms. This misunderstanding of his own love is increased by his passionate attraction to Beatrix. Finally, the two lovers, whom Beatrix quickly recognizes as suited to one another, are rewarded for their fidelity. About the same time that Beatrix remarks the compatibility of her lover and her mother, she also notes that Rachel "has had a great sorrow in her life, and a great secret; and repented it" (7:391–92). Beatrix assumes that this sorrow was not over her father's death. Rachel's secret can be found out only when Esmond, cured of his infatuation with Beatrix, discovers in his own heart the depth and nature of his love for Rachel and asks her to be his wife. "And then the tender matron, as beautiful in her autumn, and as pure as virgins in their spring, with blushes of love and 'eyes of meek surrender,' yielded to my respectful importunity, and consented to share my home" (7:514).

There is no reason to keep either secret from the narrative audience, since Esmond's family would already know the basic details—that Rachel loved Henry and that Henry was legitimate. And yet these secrets are parceled out in installments throughout the narrative. Esmond's first secret is that he is illegitimate, his second that he is not. The first is not his alone to keep; the second is. To keep the first is only natural and an act of self-regard; to keep the second is a selfless act of generosity. When he finally reveals that secret, Esmond is in a position to control its consequences. He can claim the honor of his condition and renounce its privileges. Thus the gradual disclosure of Esmond's secret corresponds to the psychological and political movement of the novel from dependence upon and support of inherited authority to the assertion of individual freedom and authority by merit. Privately and publicly Esmond moves from the divine right of kings to republicanism (even democracy). By comparison, Rachel's shameful love for a younger man not her husband is gradually revealed as an admiration for those traits she has always valued (and sought first in Francis Castlewood)—those of the Christian gentleman. In admitting her "worship" of Esmond, she reveals as well the real virtue of her character. As Esmond liberates himself from emotional and political illusions, the disclosure of his own secret within the narrative becomes increasingly important, though its revelation to the reader has long since worked to authorize Esmond's actions. By contrast, though Rachel's secret is also made evident to readers to enable us to understand her behavior, within the narrative it need never be disclosed to anyone but Esmond himself. Though Esmond recounts the events by which these secrets are found out, the relationship of these secrets to the larger narrative is actually controlled by the implied author, who shapes the design of the novel in conformity with the rudimentary Christian values of love and forgiveness.

Henry Esmond ends exalting love and the union of true hearts, with no need for forgiveness between the lovers. Rachel and Esmond provide a counterlesson to much of the behavior in the novel, signaled by the last escapade in which an unprincipled prince tries to debauch a manipulative sexual tease. We have already seen what punishment the prince suffers for his lack of wisdom. But Beatrix's punishment is also severe, and openly stressed both by the narrative and by the characters within the narrative. The narrative slowly establishes an interesting pattern in Beatrix's career. From the first, she has a mischievous and jealous nature. Moreover, she respects rank and wishes to be recognized for her inherited and thus "unearned" station. She also wishes to enhance that station, but her various romantic alliances regularly misfire. Young Lord Blandford is her first significant conquest, but he sickens and dies. Esmond is never really in the running because his position seems so inferior to Beatrix, whose sights are set very high. Rachel warns Esmond about Beatrix' callous nature, but of course it does no good. Beatrix accepts Lord Ashburnham, but that arrangement comes to nothing. Meanwhile, Esmond says that, according to court scandal, she has been a dozen times on the point of making great matches. Finally she is engaged to marry the great Duke of Hamilton, but again her matrimonial ambitions are dashed when Lord Hamilton is killed in a duel. When Esmond delivers this news, Beatrix can think only of her own injury, and Esmond exclaims, "'O woman, O sister! . . . can you bring no mourners but your revenge and your vanity? God help and pardon thee, Beatrix, as He brings this awful punishment to your hard and rebellious heart'" (7:426). Esmond views this event as the kind of therapeutic retribution that operates elsewhere in Thackeray's fiction to direct good characters into proper courses. But Beatrix is not an essentially good character who will accept redirection in her moral life. If Esmond sees her loss as therapeutic punishment within the narrative, we recognize it as *narrative* punishment long prepared for and anticipated in earlier episodes. It is the implied author's way of acting as Providence, to show that eventually bad conduct is likely to bring its own form of retribution.

But if the Old Testament God can harden the hearts of those he intends to punish, thus justifying the punishment, so the implied author can harden Beatrix' heart so that she does not learn from her chastisement. After the Lord Hamilton tragedy, Esmond says, "We knew that her pride was awfully humbled and punished by this sudden and terrible blow; she wanted no teaching of ours to point out the sad moral of her story" (7:429). That she may read the moral does not mean she will profit from it, but Esmond is unwilling to judge this willful creature too severely.

> I know one that prays God will give you love rather than pride, and
> that the Eye all-seeing shall find you in the humble place. Not that we

should judge proud spirits otherwise than charitably. 'Tis nature hath fashioned some for ambition and dominion, as it hath formed others for obedience and gentle submission. The leopard follows his nature as the lamb does, and acts after leopard law; she can neither help her beauty, nor her courage, nor her cruelty; nor a single spot on her shining coat; nor the conquering spirit which impels her; nor the shot which brings her down. (7:430)

Esmond seems prepared to excuse Beatrix' actions as the inevitable consequences of a nature she cannot control. But such a view of existence is inconsistent with a belief in individual free will and moral responsibility, which underlies Thackeray's fiction. Esmond wishes to excuse, but the implied author is less willing to spare his exemplary figure.

Beatrix confesses to Henry that she has a cold, ambitious heart, and that she is not good, but this self-knowledge does her little good since she persists in her unwisdom. Instead of repenting and reforming, she intensifies her efforts, raising her sights to the prince himself. When her family recommends that she leave London to avoid the attentions of the lecherous prince, Beatrix takes umbrage at their "distrust" (7:480). Leaving London with plans to lure the prince to Castlewood, Beatrix hypocritically declaims, "'Farewell, mother; I think I never can forgive you; something hath broke between us that no tears nor years can repair'" (7:481–82). "Forgive" is not a familiar word in Beatrix' vocabulary and it is no surprise that it should apply here negatively. But Rachel, who is undeceived by Beatrix' expressions of injury, has some simple advice. "'Go, child,' says her mother, still very stern; 'go and bend your proud knees and ask forgiveness; go, pray in solitude for humility and repentance'" (7:482). Rachel, who has followed just such a course, has learned humility and patience and been rewarded for those virtues, but her headstrong daughter charges forward and destroys not only her own plans but those of James Stuart as well. In her vanity and ambition she betrays herself, her acknowledged king, and the great cause of restoration. Surely she is punished, but just as significantly she is also an agent of retribution. Fulfilling the pattern of her selfish life, at the apogee of her efforts, with the future king besieging her, victory is snatched away and she is obliged to retrieve her fortunes on the Continent. We shall hear more of her subsequent career in *The Virginians,* but *Henry Esmond* ends with Beatrix in exile, adventuring on the Continent, and with Esmond and Rachel in loving retreat in the New World. J. Hillis Miller observes that Beatrix "must be cast out of the novel like a scapegoat, with all the sins of society upon her. Henry in the end repudiates her as without value, as immoral, as not worth loving" (114).[17] But Esmond does not punish Beatrix, though the narrative he is made to tell does. As a forgiving and loving man, Esmond must not punish Beatrix, but the implied author can institute his own version of natural law and natural justice. Miller argues that Beatrix is Esmond's "unrecognized alter ego, his mirror image in a changed sex," and that like Esmond she is deeply melancholic. "She has the melancholy of her nihilism. She knows that we are alone, alone, alone, and that no prize is worth winning. This is Thackeray's knowledge too. It lies behind that irony he wears like a cloak he cannot remove" (113). But if Beatrix has this part of Thackeray's and Esmond's knowledge—if she has beforehand a knowledge that Thackeray and Esmond acquire through the disillusionment of early enthusiasms—she lacks what Thackeray and his most genial characters possess: a knowledge of human weakness that recognizes the need for charity and forgiveness in a world of violated illusions, not least the forgiveness of our own vanity, foolishness, and error. Beatrix has no real secrets to be discovered. Esmond has cloaked her in illusion and found that illusion to be his own contrivance. Beatrix has always been transparently a selfish and baneful beauty. By contrast, the secrets of Rachel and Esmond, so carefully unveiled in the progress of the narrative, reveal virtues desperately needed in their world. Finding out and forgiveness become one, and disclosed secrets become agencies of grace.

This history honoring love, humility, and patience is told by a man who embodies all of the Christian virtues along with good manners and courage.[18] His daughter adds a footnote about Esmond's nature. "He was the humblest man, with all this; the least exacting, the most easily contented; and Mr. Benson, our minister at Castlewood, who attended him at the last, ever said: 'I know not what Colonel Esmond's doctrine was, but his life and death were those of a devout Christian'" (7:478). And so is his narrative devoutly Christian, because always forgiving. Esmond's motto might be that it is better to suffer than to injure, and to some degree this is Rachel's motto too. So there is no delight in Esmond's narrative at the discomfiture of the wicked, with the possible exception of the Duke of Marlborough. By contrast, the implied author of *Henry Esmond* may indulge in instructive punishments though his central character does not, and so the novel's repeated patterns lead to the multiple punishment that climaxes the narrative, in which the most beautiful of Englishwomen is punished for her misuse of that beauty and the most exalted Englishman is punished for the weakness of his character. It is no small achievement to so exalt the virtue of forgiveness and nonetheless manage, despite the forgiving nature of your narrator, to see retribution done.

NOTES

1. Robert A. Colby writes that "Even where critics felt that Thackeray carried introspection too far, or thought his hero overly melancholic, there was general agreement that he had advanced the historical romance intellectually beyond his greatest predecessor" (*Thackeray's Canvass of Humanity: An Author and His Public* [Columbus: Ohio State University Press, 1979], 325). Subsequent references appear in the text.

2. Many recent critics have been skeptical about Esmond's honesty as well as his basic goodness. Juliet McMaster is particularly aggressive in *Thackeray: The Major Novels* (Toronto: University of Toronto Press, 1971).

3. In his review of *Esmond* in November of 1852, George Brimley said that the ideal aspects of human conduct were no longer merely implicit as in Thackeray's previous fiction. "The medal is reversed, and what appeared as scorn of baseness is revealed as love of goodness and nobleness—what appeared as cynicism is presented as a heart-worship of what is pure, affectionate, and unselfish" (*Thackeray: The Critical Heritage,* ed. Geoffrey Tillotson and Donald Hawes [New York: Barnes and Noble Inc., 1968], 141). Thackeray seldom endorsed any virtuous figure entirely, and it is just like him to have responded to Trollope's praise of the novel as his best with the remark that nobody reads it. " 'If they like anything, one ought to be satisfied. After all, Esmond was a prig' " (*Heritage* 166).

4. *The Works of William Makepeace Thackeray,* 26 vols., (Philadelphia: J. B. Lippincott Company, 1901), 7:39.

5. J. Hillis Miller explores the significance of the repeated duels and the structural importance of what he calls the secret identity between Henry and Lord Mohun in *Fiction and Repetition: Seven English Novels* (Cambridge: Harvard University Press, 1982), 103. Subsequent references appear in the text.

6. Marjorie Garson aptly indicates how childhood experiences affect Esmond, but is unconvincing in suggesting that the mature Esmond resents children ("Henry Esmond's Love of Children," *Nineteenth-Century Fiction* 36, no. 4 (March 1982), 387–406. Thackeray frequently expressed his own love for children. See, for example, references in volume 1 of *Thackeray: Interviews and Recollections,* 2 vols., ed. Philip Collins (New York: St. Martin's Press, 1983), 58, 78, 85, 88, and others.

7. Richard Steele, *The Christian Hero,* ed. Rae Blanchard (New York: Octagon Books, 1977), 8–9. Subsequent references appear in the text.

8. Elaine Scarry, "*Henry Esmond:* The Rookery at Castlewood," *Literary Monographs* 7: *Thackeray, Hawthorne and Melville, and Dreiser* (Madison: The University of Wisconsin Press, 1975), 3–43. Scarry distinguishes Esmond's concern for subjective rather than objective truth, though she concludes that contradictions within his narrative indicate how elusive subjective truth, like all other forms of truth, can be. Subsequent references appear in the text.

9. See *The Adventures of Philip,* where the narrator admits that his version of the story might be very different from some other narrator's interpretation (11:349)

10. Peter J. Rabinowitz, *Before Reading: Narrative Conventions and the Politics of Interpretation* (Ithaca, NY: Cornell University Press, 1987), 89. Subsequent references appear in the text.

11. J. Hillis Miller skillfully explores the role of memory and the nature of the many proleptic hints about Esmond's destiny (91ff.).

12. Robert A. Colby records Robert Louis Stevenson's opinion that the end-

ing of *Esmond* is pure Dumas (335). Thackeray would probably have been pleased, since he often remarked that he would have liked to have had Dumas' talent for recounting action.

13. The use of a dramatic technique to evoke the past was part of the armory of historians such as Macaulay, Carlyle, and Froude, popular in the earlier part of the century. This method was challenged by the "scientific" historians who followed. See Rosemary Jann's *The Art and Science of Victorian History* (Columbus: Ohio State University Press, 1985) for a thorough examination of this shift in approach among English historians of the nineteenth century.

14. Elaine Scarry declares that Esmond's belief in truth is not shared by Thackeray. "Esmond's narrative, then, offers subjective truth as an alternative to objective truth, subjective history as an alternative to objective history. But Esmond's narrative is not Thackeray's novel" (5). Because Thackeray, as author, does not intrude his voice to help us see beyond Esmond's level of perception, this novel offers an excellent example for applying the notion of the implied author—an agency that makes possible an assembling of the text's meaning that transcends the awareness of its narrator.

15. Hayden White, "The Value of Narrativity in the Representation of Reality," *Critical Inquiry* 7, no. 1 (Autumn 1980), 5–28.

16. John Forster, *Heritage*, 146ff.

17. J. Hillis Miller argues that Beatrix is one of Henry's alter egos. Henry's narrative is based on the claim of total memory, but Beatrix "is the personification of reading or narrating as forgetting. . . . If Henry, Thackeray, and the reader are drawers of lines, weavers of webs, Beatrix is the unweaver" (114). There is much merit to this argument, but it slights Thackeray's amused assault upon his own narrative enterprise. As with Becky Sharp, he can use Beatrix to unveil many of the hypocrisies of the world she inhabits, but she is excluded from Esmond's world because she offers no positive solution. Like Becky she has no real love, and the worlds of Esmond and Dobbin end with a measure of love, if not the distracting passion of youth.

18. Many critics, among them Juliet McMaster, J. Hillis Miller, and Marjorie Garson, have made an effort to picture Esmond as an untrustworthy narrator and not the loving figure so long supposed. However, I believe that it is sounder to consider Esmond "unreliable" in the old-fashioned sense, but otherwise trustworthy. That is, he makes errors of perception and judgment, but he is nonetheless presented by Thackeray as an admirable figure. I share Elaine Scarry's view that, though Henry's account is inaccurate, even at the subjective level, it is not untrue to certain values, and that Henry is absolved from any dishonesty in his narrative. When he was preparing to begin the novel, Thackeray wrote to Jane Brookfield, "A story is biling up in my interior, in wh there shall appear some very good lofty and generous people. Perhaps a story without any villain in it would be good, wouldn't it?" (Gordon N. Ray, *Thackeray: The Age of Wisdom 1847-1863* [London: Oxford University Press, 1958], 176). Though he could not

do without a villain, I believe he meant Esmond to represent the good, lofty, and generous qualities. That love was a pervasive virtue of the text is evident from Carlyle's reaction against the book, finding love too dominant, "represented as spreading itself over our whole existence, and constituting one of the grand interests of it; whereas love—*the thing people call love*—is confined to a very few years of man's life; to, in fact, a quite insignificant fraction of it, and even then is but one thing to be attended to among many infinitely more important things" (Ray 191). But it was precisely Christian love, not just *the thing people call love,* that Thackeray meant to depict.

TWENTY-THREE

The Newcomes

THE NEWCOMES opens with what the narrator calls "a farrago of old fables"—a wolf in sheep's clothing, an ass in a lion's skin, a fox, an owl, a crow, and a frog all commenting on one another. The narrator interrupts this fabling to describe the indignation of a supposed literary critic who complains about the narrator's plagiarism and also his contemptuous way of depicting human nature. "There is scarce one of these characters he represents but is a villain," the critic complains.[1] Accusations of cynicism were commonplace in critical responses to Thackeray's writing, and this self-conscious opening to *The Newcomes* indicates his attention to such criticism. In fact, this novel marked a conscious change. Robert A. Colby says that "As the most accessible and least ironical of Thackeray's novels, *The Newcomes* brought Thackeray his greatest prestige along with the widest public esteem that he ever had, establishing his claim to be taken seriously as a writer among respectable readers."[2] The narrator humbly acknowledges that "If authors sneer, it is the critic's business to sneer at him for sneering" (5:5). *The Newcomes* thus begins with a complex judgment scene, with the narrator relating how the characters in his animal fable are all punished one way or another, while himself being "found out" in his theft of old tales by the critic who proceeds to denounce him; the narrator slyly returns the favor, remarking that the critic's "livelihood is to find fault. Besides, he is right sometimes" (5:5). The narrator then asserts that no stories are new and that his own story that we are about to read consists of familiar character types and themes. But he promises to withhold the moral until the end.

A complex pattern of moral assessment is laid out in this interesting opening. At first glance it appears that the narrator arranges the poetic justice of his fable, apportioning the proper punishment for each transgression. Indeed, the understood purpose of such animal fables is to point out a moral, frequently by using narrative punishments that fit the crime. In this way they parallel the form of children's stories of the time. Introducing the literary critic complicates matters considerably. The critic is himself a judge, revealing the narrator's crime of theft. The narrator's stories are not his own. This means that the narrator has not, in fact, arranged the punishments of the various animals. Their fates were predetermined and the narrator merely recounts the preexisting stories. But if the narrator is right in saying that all stories are old stories already known, then the critic's judgment upon him is meaningless, since any story that is told already exists and thus each new narration is, in the critic's terms, a theft. We as readers have been rash to assume that the narrator himself was acting as a retributive agent; the critic is similarly rash in assuming that the narrator has misappropriated his narrative. The narrator himself is not candid when he says that he will keep his moral a secret until the end, for the "moral" of his storytelling is already evident in the cautionary opening: Do not be overhasty to pass judgment on the tale, the teller, or the one who interprets the teller. A tale may convey a moral, but since there are no new stories the significance of the story must not be in its message but in its telling.

To complicate matters further, this story is being told by a character from an earlier Thackeray novel, whose own story—an old one—would have been known, or available, to Thackeray's audience. Thackeray explained about *The Newcomes* to Sarah Baxter, "I am not to be the author of it. Mr. Pendennis is to be the writer of his friend's memoirs and by the help of this little mask (wh I borrowed from Pisistratus Bulwer I suppose) I shall be able to talk more at ease than in my own person. I only thought of the plan last night and am immensely relieved by adopting it."[3] It is not clear why this device would provide Thackeray such relief from speaking in his own voice, unless he wished to avoid earlier charges by literary critics and others that his outlook was too cynical. If Pendennis rather than Thackeray were speaking, that complaint could be forestalled. Ironically, however, this novel was seen as Thackeray's least cynical. Perhaps Pendennis speaks in a manner more optimistic than what Thackeray would have permitted himself.

The emphasis upon human weakness and a pervasive willingness to pass judgment on others suggests, in the opening pages of *The Newcomes,* that we are about to engage a tale in which such judgments will be both plentiful and fallible. As if to confirm this point, the first episode of the story proper offers just such a situation. Encountering his old school fellow Clive Newcome, the narrator is introduced to his father, Colonel Thomas Newcome. At an inn they join some convivial singers, and even Colonel Newcome offers a song, explaining that he learned it in his schooldays by slipping out of Grey Friars to hear the great Incledon sing. He adds, " 'I used to be flogged afterwards, and served me right too' " (5:13), an apparently inconsequential reminiscence that takes on greater significance moments later when, angered by Captain Costigan's singing a bawdy song in front of boys, Colonel Newcome berates Costigan and marches out with his son in tow.

Clive seemed rather shamefaced; but I fear the rest of the company looked still more foolish.

"Aussi que diable venait-il faire dans cette galère?" says King of Corpus to Jones of Trinity; and Jones gave a shrug of his shoulders, which were smarting, perhaps; for that uplifted cane of the Colonel's had somehow fallen on the back of every man in the room. (5:15)

This early scene anticipates and encapsulates much of what is to follow, and the Colonel incorporates a central concern of the novel—how to protect the innocent without using force against the wicked. The Colonel comes on stage as an agreeable man with fixed moral principles, prompt to express his sentiments when confronted by what he considers reprehensible behavior. He seems prepared to check evil influences with punitive measures if necessary, but has the self-control to stay his own hand. The Colonel's attitude, though it might be associated with his military training, actually is intimately connected with the larger themes of the novel that deal with family relations, charity, and revenge. The Colonel's attitudes toward punishment and compassion have been shaped by his upbringing. His stepmother was a zealous Methodist with a firm belief in the value of punishment. "Tommy was taught hymns, very soon after he could speak, appropriate to his tender age, pointing out to him the inevitable fate of wicked children, and giving him the earliest possible warning and description of the punishment of little sinners" (5:22). His parents do not agree about punishing Tommy, his father disliking the ease with which the stepmother resorts so quickly to physical correction. When Tommy runs away from home, however, it is his father who finds the "prodigal" and whips him.

Very likely the father suffered more than the child; for, when the punishment was over, the little man, yet trembling and quivering with the pain, held out his little bleeding hand and said, "I can—I can take it from you, sir;" saying which his face flushed, and his eyes filled, for the first time; whereupon the father burst into a passion of tears, and embraced the boy and kissed him, besought and prayed him to be rebellious no more—flung the whip away from him and swore, come what would, he would never strike him again. (5:27–28)

If punishment was a familiar part of his training, young Tom learned compassion and love as well. And later we see that, if he can be easily roused to righteous anger, he knows the appropriate response to that anger as well. At a dinner party Clive is so offended by his cousin Barnes Newcome's behavior, especially his mocking of Colonel Newcome, that he throws a wine glass at him. Next day the Colonel is certain of what must be done—to go and ask pardon. He tells of how he himself once forgave a young soldier an insult given over wine, and how some of his friends sneered at him afterward, doubting his courage. But he proved himself in war and the man he forgave became his fast friend, dying at his side in battle. The Colonel says, "'We must go and ask Barnes Newcome's pardon, sir, and forgive other people's trespasses, my boy, if we hope forgiveness of our own.'" The narrator confirms the importance of this scene by adding, "His voice sank down as he spoke, and he bowed his head reverently. I have heard his son tell the simple story years afterwards, with tears in his eyes" (5:185).

An interesting feature of this episode is the way embedding one story within another reinforces the message of the narrative, for it is really just one story retold. The Colonel tells of forgiving Jack Cutler in order to persuade Clive that he should forgive Barnes, and the narrator tells Clive's story presumably to encourage each reader to value the act and follow its example. The narrator's storytelling, then, is just a more complicated version of the Colonel's, in a long tradition of moral exempla. He has signaled this from the outset by declaring that all stories are old stories. Among the best-known old stories are the parables told by Christ, and the narrator here associates his characters with those parables by alluding more than once to the story of the prodigal son. We have already seen that Tom Newcome could play the prodigal in his youth, but, grown old, he becomes the forgiving parent to Clive, who assumes the prodigal's role. But just as Pendennis himself was described as a prodigal son, while exhibiting only the slightest portion of that offspring's profligacy, so Clive is anything but a model of misconduct. Indeed, if he is a prodigal he is one less in need of being forgiven than of offering forgiveness.

Clive is a good young man, though not always as considerate as he might be. The Colonel abandons his comfortable pursuits among military friends to look after Clive's welfare, but Clive "gave his parent no more credit for this long self-denial than many other children award to theirs. We take such life offerings as our due commonly" (5:247). The attentive reader will note how smoothly the narrator has moved from Clive as offender to *we*, who behave in the same way.[4] Implicating the reader is a consistent tactic in this novel, one that appears in many forms. For example, the narrator anticipates his reader's rejection of his cynical view of human nature and imagines him exclaiming, I wouldn't behave in this way, to which he responds, "Be it so. *You* would not. But own that your next-door neighbour would. Nor is this, dear madam, addressed to you; no, no, we are not so rude as to talk about you to your face; but, if we may not speak of the lady who has just left the room what is to become of conversation and society?" (5:69).

The narrator asserts again the notion first broached in the opening fable that human beings are strongly inclined to judge their fellows, through the most innocent gossip or the most condign condemnation. The narrator reminds his readers that they are not innocent of this practice, and, in telling his story as a higher kind of gossip, becomes a judge in his own right. But woven into his pattern of judging is also a palliating tendency to understand the weaknesses of human nature. Thus even his heroes are fallible. The narrator says of Clive Newcome,

"He is, in a word, just such a youth as has a right to be the hero of a novel" (5:78). But since he is the hero of a Thackeray novel, he will have his faults, which brings us back to the narrator's admission that Clive is selfish enough not to realize all that his father is doing for him. "Did we not say, at our tale's commencement, that all stories were old? Careless prodigals and anxious elders have been from the beginning:—and so may love and repentance, and forgiveness endure even to the end" (5:248).

There is an abundance of weakness, error, and outright mischief in humankind, and thus all the more need for love and forgiveness, says the narrator, and this is a familiar Christian assertion. But in order to disturb the self-righteous, who might otherwise accept his conventional bromide and ignore its application to themselves, the narrator takes the assertion further. After describing how Mrs. Brian Newcome's interference is alienating Colonel Newcome and his brother, the narrator comments, "The wicked are wicked no doubt, and they go astray and they fall, and they come by their deserts; but who can tell the mischief which the very virtuous do?" (5:251). If all were known, Thackeray's narrator reminds us time and again, we would all—including those who suppose themselves virtuous—have many errors and worse to answer for. As a form of instruction in the kindly art of discretion, the narrator goes out of his way to treat the subject of his history generously. Early in the novel he recounts a tour of the estate of the Marquis of Carabas during which one guest asks of the guide, "'And now, madam, will you show us the closet where the skeleton is?'" The narrator dilates on this suspicion that amidst all the beauties and treasures of the palace there is a secret closet that no one but its owner visits, then asks, "Have we not all such closets, my jolly friend, as well as the noble Marquis of Carabas?" (5:153). But if Pendennis, as narrator, can call attention to our closets, our guilty secrets, he can also be discreet by choosing not to open them for inspection. Telling of Clive's disenchanting passion for an actress, he wonders if Clive's friend Moss took him "behind the scenes," but decides not to explore the subject; "over this stage of Clive Newcome's life we may surely drop the curtain" (5:253).

Relentlessly the narrator drives home his broad assumption that we are all guilty of something and should therefore be considerate when we judge others. The tendency to be virtuously judgmental is perhaps most dangerous when it ceases to be individual and becomes a national trait. Describing the marriage market among the English community at Baden, the narrator touches on the subject of English virtue. "Do not, however, let us be too prematurely proud of our virtue," he warns.

> Shame! What is shame? Virtue is very often shameful according to the English social constitution, and shame honourable. Truth, if yours happens to differ from your neighbour's, provokes your friend's coldness, your mother's tears, the world's persecution. Love is not to be

dealt in, save under restrictions which kill its sweet healthy free commerce. Sin in man is so light that scarce the fine of a penny is imposed; while for woman it is so heavy that no repentance can wash it out. Ah! yes; all stories are old. (5:364)

The specific point here is that "virtuous" English mothers put their virtuous daughters up for sale. Condemn others for their sins as they may, they are, in the narrator's eyes, guilty of a sin comparable to or greater than those of many they denounce for "losing" their "virtue." Like Dickens, Thackeray makes broad allusions to Christ's willingness to forgive and sympathize with those who err, including the woman taken in adultery.

But the spirit of Christian charity should not end with those we like or those we do not know. More demanding is the need to be charitable to those we dislike. Even with those offensive characters whom he labors to make us loathe—such as Barnes Newcome—the narrator requires fair play. Clive is outraged when Clara Pulleyn agrees to marry Barnes, but Clive's kindly friend Lord Kew admonishes him for this swift condemnation, reminding him that he can see no good in Barnes because he considers Barnes an enemy and Barnes returns the favor. "'It depends on the colors in which a fellow is painted. Our friends and our enemies draw us,—and I often think both pictures are like,'" Kew comments, recommending a little Christian sentiment. "'Give Mr. Barnes the benefit of common charity at any rate; and let others like him, if you do not'" (5:397).

Now and then the narrator is explicit about his function as a moralist. In giving an account of the errors that land Jack Belsize in prison for debt, he refuses to criticize either Jack or Lord Kew, who sends his brougham to Queen's Bench prison and gives a public party on the day Jack is liberated. "I am not here to scourge sinners," he says; "I am true to my party; it is the other side this humble pen attacks; let us keep to the virtuous and respectable, for as for poor sinners they get the whipping post every day" (5:373).

This passage reveals many things about punishment and forgiveness in *The Newcomes* and, to a great extent, in all of Thackeray. Though a major feature of Thackeray's approach is to recommend mercy, compassion, and forgiveness, prompted largely by the recognition that no one is without fault, another impulse in his fiction is to provide support for traditional morality by reinforcing the idea that transgressions require correction. In the passage just quoted, however, the narrator clearly announces that he is not going to waste his time guiding blatant rogues and scoundrels to their just deserts, but will occupy himself more fruitfully in applying his whip to offenders who do not admit to their sins—those, in short, who have an unhealthy tendency to consider themselves in line for reward rather than punishment. The people he attacks are snobs. This means that Thackeray chooses not to exploit narrative patterns calling for rapid sequences of adventure and deeds of heroic or demonic action, where poetic justice or cause-and-effect consequences can be demonstrated with melodramatic force and simplicity. It is precisely the heightening and simplifying of emotions characteristic of melodrama that Thackeray avoids. His narratives instead develop slowly and expansively, for they must incorporate not only the narrow channel of individual character but also the broad reaches of the social context in which character is developed. To a great degree Thackeray's program is directly opposed to the *hunting down* pattern so much a part of the melodramatic approach, and for which Dickens had such a fondness. Melodrama isolates guilt and evil, but in Thackeray's scheme of things we are all infected by the virus of evil and all bear guilt of one form or another. If we will keep in mind our own closet with its skeleton or skeletons, we can imagine being *found out* and appreciate the sympathy, understanding, and pardon that we would then desire for ourselves.[5] Thackeray's narratives must have a diegesis that is complex enough to allow both for the partial exoneration of those who are outright sinners and for the partial inculpation of those who are apparently virtuous but unwittingly or hypocritically tainted.

As we have already seen, Thackeray's narrators have a great deal to say about their manner of narrating. Here, for example, is how the narrator opens chapter 24.

> This narrative, as the judicious reader no doubt is aware, is written maturely and at ease, long after the voyage is over whereof it recounts the adventures and perils; the winds adverse and favourable; the storms, shoals, shipwrecks, islands, and so forth, which Clive Newcome met in his early journey in life. In such a history events follow each other without necessarily having a connection with one another. One ship crosses another ship, and, after a visit from one captain to his comrade, they sail away each on his course. (5:301)

The seafaring metaphor continues, making the point that the story we are following is not rigorously structured; in an account of this kind the narrator claims he "dresses up the narrative in his own way," making up conversations that he couldn't have heard, and so forth (5:302). This is an amusing justification, familiar in the English novel, for why a fictional history has so much "fiction" in it. But another purpose in this byplay is to indicate the casualness of the narrative, its lack of a perceivable teleology aiming it toward a specific conclusion. As Mrs. Mackenzie remarks, the novel of life doesn't end with the third volume of marriage, a sentiment that Thackeray had expressed through M. A. Titmarsh in *Rebecca and Rowena.*

To reinforce the casual nature of his narrative, the narrator often proleptically releases the tension of suspense that might entice his readers on and intensify the demand for precise closure. At the end of chapter 16, for example, the narrator describes Clive as he is in the writing time of the history—apparently in

happy and comfortable circumstances, exhibiting a painting of his father to his
children (5:217). We thus know that he has weathered the journey and is safe in
harbor. In a much more explicit instance, the narrator shows how old Lady Kew
intends to form her grandson, Lord Kew, marry him to her liking, and leave him
her money. For the narrator, this is a moral danger for the young man.

> Have you taken your children to the National Gallery in London,
> and shown them the "Marriage à la Mode"? Was the artist exceeding
> the privilege of his calling in painting the catastrophe in which those
> guilty people all suffer? If this fable were not true, if many and many
> of your young men of pleasure had not acted it, and rued the moral, I
> would tear the page. You know that in our Nursery Tales there is
> commonly a good fairy to counsel, and a bad one to mislead the young
> prince. You perhaps feel that in your own life there is a Good Principle
> imploring you to come into its kind bosom and a Bad Passion which
> tempts you into its arms. Be of easy minds, good-natured people! Let
> us disdain surprises and *coups-de-théatre* for once; and tell those good
> souls who are interested about him, that there is a Good spirit coming
> to the rescue of our young Lord Kew. (5:417)

The narrator first establishes the moral dimensions of Lord Kew's situation and
reviews the kind of moral simplicities and artistic devices often used to exploit
such dilemmas for an audience's sake, but he then specifically renounces all such
devices. In the process, however, he establishes his own moral position.

When Lord Kew is ill from the fever following his injury in a duel, his
mother, Lady Walham, comes to him. She is a kindly and religious person. The
narrator segues from her to himself and his trade. "Our history has had little to
do with characters resembling this lady. It is of the world, and things pertaining
to it. Things beyond it, as the writer imagines, scarcely belong to the novelist's
province. Who is he that he should assume the divine's office, or turn his desk
into a preacher's pulpit?" (5:489). But if the narrator is unwilling to venture into
speculations about the next world, as Dickens is never reluctant to do, this does
not mean that he eschews all sermonizing. He may not be a minister in a pulpit,
but like us all can read a moral in the secular world around him.

> I have said this book is all about the world, and a respectable family
> dwelling in it. It is not a sermon, except where it cannot help itself,
> and the speaker pursuing the destiny of his narrative finds such a hom-
> ily before him. O friend, in your life and mine, don't we light upon
> such sermons daily—don't we see at home as well as amongst our
> neighbours that battle betwixt Evil and Good? Here on one side is Self
> and Ambition and Advancement; and Right and Love on the other.
> Which shall we let to triumph for ourselves?—which for our children?
> (5:506)

This passage illustrates Janice Carlisle's assertion that by the time Thackeray wrote *The Newcomes* he had abandoned the use of the alienating narrator and used this persona as a mediating device instead. She adds that *The Newcomes* requires active audience participation and, accordingly, trusts that audience's sophistication (120, 140). Thackeray could also trust that audience's appreciation of the moral paradigm from which he was operating.

Plots, and narratives more generally, contain either explicitly or implicitly some moral or ideological scheme. Once a story begins its movement through time it is on its way toward a destination, even if that destination is no more than a terminus. In all of his major fictions, Thackeray is preoccupied with time, and, while fully aware of the inescapability of its effects in life, he strives to control its effects in his narratives. John Carey claims that "The circlings of time in Thackeray's later novels, then, though they look like advanced literary structures, mark a retreat from his awareness of time's irresistible linear progression."[6] But Thackeray's narrators constantly call attention to the inescapably linear nature of time in life, even as they struggle against the linearity of narrative, not to deny the effects of time, but to counteract and disorder conventional responses to reading. Thackeray does this more in *The Newcomes* than in any of his novels we have discussed so far. Moreover, though in the preceding novels there were always secrets to be found out, *The Newcomes* eschews that mode of inducing readers to continue. No story can be told without unknown events being related and thereby, in simple temporal order, revealed. But that inherent kind of secrecy in narrative is not the same as secrets in the diegesis that are revealed or withheld by the narrator or the implied author. Becky Sharp, Blanche Amory, Henry Esmond, and Rachel Castlewood have their secrets—all of which are revealed both to the reader and to characters within the narrative, though not necessarily at the same time. But *The Newcomes* has no significant secrets of this kind. What it substitutes is "plots," or what we might even call "anti-plots"—sequences of events that trace experiences toward an explicable end, with the strange addition that one or more sequences swerve severely away from predictable directions. These are more than simple variations on conventions and seem instead specifically designed to call plotting itself into question as a vehicle of moral judgment. By concentrating on what I like to think of as a permanent ground in Thackeray's worldview—his attitudes toward punishment and forgiveness as actions reflecting a code of values—it is possible to watch this narrative juggling in action.

One important plotline of the first volume of the novel deals with the relationship among Ethel Newcome, Lady Kew, and Lord Kew. As a young woman, Ethel is sprightly; by seventeen she is a truthful girl but also a "severe Diana" (5:312). Clive considers her proud and says she would serve well as a model for Judith, Salome, or Diana (5:318). Lady Kew wants to arrange a marriage between Ethel and her grandson, Lord Kew, who has been a somewhat profligate young man. These two handsome and proud individuals develop along similar, though not parallel lines, as illustrated by an incident at a ball. Ethel, elegantly dressed, dances and flirts to annoy Lord Kew, among others. Kew is grieved by this behavior, forgetting "that if young men have their frolics, sow their wild oats, and enjoy their pleasure, young women may be permitted sometimes their more harmless vagaries of gaiety, and sportive outbreaks of wilful humor" (5:441). The next day, as Lord Kew is delivering a sermon to Ethel on her inappropriate behavior, she receives a letter detailing the young man's youthful indiscretions and shows it to him. Lord Kew had felt justified in remonstrating with Ethel for her own good. Moreover, although he had passed a reckless youth, "he was sad and ashamed of that past life, longed like the poor prodigal to return to better courses" (5:447). Now he takes his share of the pain "as a boy at school takes his flogging, stoutly and in silence" (5:448).

At this point at least two significant things are happening. A young woman who has misbehaved in the presence of her fiance is justly reprimanded by him— a scene that we might expect in much of the domestic fiction of the day. The plot, however, shifts the emphasis away from the chastising of Ethel to the sins of the sermonizer. A standard situation thus changes character, as it appears that the real narrative purpose for this dramatic scene is to impose an ironic poetic justice by finding out Kew's misconduct. But the true narrative punishment for Kew is yet to come, and this intense little moment between the engaged couple reveals instead the peril in which we always stand when we presume to instruct others in morals, ethics, or mere etiquette. The narrator indicates Kew's mistake before the young man goes preaching; the revelation of his immorality is no secret to us as readers and its disclosure in the text does not really constitute a punishment. It is rather a warning not to judge quickly, and also not to take the course of narrative and the shape of plot for granted. It is, perhaps, a *mis en abime* of the procedure of this novel as a whole.

Lord Kew is basically a good person, but a corrective is necessary to define his course in life. That corrective comes on speedily. Through Madame d'Ivry's maneuverings, he becomes involved in an argument with Monsieur Cabasse that leads to a challenge. Kew is sorry for the whole scene. "He thought of the past, and its levities, and punishment coming after him *pede claudo*. It was with all his heart the contrite young man said 'God forgive me.' He would take what was to follow as the penalty of what had gone before" (5:462). Madame d'Ivry was part of what had gone before and it is she who brings this particular punishment upon Lord Kew. But he is sorry for *all* the errors that have gone before. Especially to someone essentially kind, generous, and thoughtful, errors of this sort are particularly wounding. And wounded Lord Kew is literally in the duel that follows, which seems a yet more intense installment of the punishment that follows from his prodigal youth. On his sickbed, which might easily become his deathbed, Lord Kew resolves that if he lives he will make amends for the days gone by. He is reconciled now to his pious mother, who tends him:

> as the mother and son read together the beloved assurance of the divine
> forgiveness, and of that joy which angels feel in heaven for a sinner

repentant, we may fancy in the happy mother's breast a feeling somewhat akin to that angelic felicity, a gratitude and joy of all others the
loftiest, the purest, the keenest. Lady Walham might shrink with terror at the Frenchman's name, but her son could forgive him, with all
his heart, and kiss his mother's hand, and thank him as the best friend
of his life. (5:497)

This "punishment," then, though following naturally from Lord Kew's
youthful dissipations, now becomes an opportunity for changing his life, beginning with an act of forgiveness. Lord Kew's mildness and new demeanor are set
off by his grandmother's fury when he tells her that he has broken genially with
Ethel. Ethel, for her part, is humiliated by Lady Kew's meddling. And on this
note the first volume ends. Kew's punishment is both the natural consequence of
his youthful self-indulgence and a plot-oriented, therapeutic narrative punishment designed by the implied author to emphasize the centrality of forgiveness in
the moral scheme of the story. And despite many objections about Thackeray's
cynicism and his depiction of a world basically wicked, at the time he wrote *The
Newcomes* he was profoundly concerned with moral life, though somewhat bored
with storytelling.[7] But bored or not, he still wanted his stories to provoke responses, and thus the "completion" of the Ethel/Lord Kew anti-plot reverses
expectations. The predictable course of events might involve Lord Kew's death
in the duel and Ethel's repentance for her frivolous behavior. Instead, the young
rake repents and reforms while Ethel feels not repentance but humiliation for the
way Lady Kew has attempted to direct her life.

Volume One of *The Newcomes* deals chiefly with the developing relationship
between Colonel Newcome and his son, with Clive's associations with various
friends while he progresses as an art student, with Ethel's relationship with Lady
and Lord Kew, and with the affairs of the Brian Newcome family. Ethel is the
central figure from this side of the family in Volume One, but Barnes Newcome,
presented as a very unappetizing young man, becomes important in Volume
Two. Volume One ends dramatically with the conversion of the prodigal son,
Lord Kew. The career of Barnes Newcome is a counterpoint to that of Kew. The
young lord has been good-natured but unwise; Barnes is cynical and malign from
the start. If Ethel is a major part of the anti-plot in Volume One, Barnes serves
that function in Volume Two.

Clive's friend Jack Belsize falls in love with Clara Pulleyn and she returns the
feeling, but Jack has no prospects and so their marriage is forbidden. Barnes becomes interested in Clara, and, despite Clive's disgust at Clara's union with a
man who maintains a former mistress and two children, the marriage takes place.
Barnes' mistress shows up at the wedding ceremony and makes a scene. This little episode, though not made public in the press, thereby avoiding damage to
Barnes and his new wife, is nonetheless the implied author's way of hinting to
the reader that even if the results of our sins do not return in the substantive form

of a woman and two children, they nonetheless are always waiting like crouched lions to spring upon us.

Barnes is successful in business and becomes an MP, but he is not a gentle and loving husband, and soon his domestic life becomes a torment for him. Lady Kew upbraids Barnes for his treatment of Clara, objecting that the young woman who had been properly tamed is now becoming rebellious under his authority. His mistreatment of Clara has made Barnes' life miserable; not only does she torment him herself, but Jack Belsize, now wealthy as Lord Highgate, threatens to deal with him if he uses violence against her. But Barnes' behavior toward his wife is only one mark against him. Colonel Newcome offers to turn over the bulk of his fortune to Clive if Barnes will negotiate a match with Ethel. Barnes pretends that he wishes to help but says that Ethel is guided by Lady Kew. When the Colonel realizes that Barnes is not acting honestly by him and even lies to him about Lady Kew's being in town, his attitude toward Barnes changes abruptly.

> Now this gentleman could no more pardon a lie than he could utter one. He would believe all and everything a man told him until deceived once, after which he never forgave. And wrath being once roused in his simple mind and distrust firmly fixed there, his anger and prejudices gathered daily. He could see no single good quality in his opponent; and hated him with a daily increasing bitterness. (5:188)

And a little later, when he discovers that Barnes never delivered his letter to Ethel, the Colonel denounces his relative in public and the enmity is entrenched.

The Colonel admits that he has always distrusted Barnes in his heart and relied upon him against his "better instinct," having struggled against the feeling for ten years, "thinking it was a wicked prejudice and ought to be overcome" (6:213). George Warrington asks him why we should overcome such instincts. " 'Why shouldn't we hate what is hateful in people, and scorn what is mean?' " Warrington says of Barnes' infamous behavior. He concludes, " 'Sir, unless somebody's heel shall crush him on the way, there is no height to which this aspiring vermin mayn't crawl' " (6:213). In the conventional version of the wicked husband plot, the wife is miserable and may either die of grief and neglect or rebel and run off with a lover. The narrator holds this plot in abeyance as he develops Barnes as a dishonest relative as well. In both plot lines Barnes deserves punishment and reverses are forthcoming accordingly.

Chapter 17 of Volume Two is entitled "Barnes' Skeleton Closet," recalling the illustrative example of the Marquis of Carabas castle in Volume One. Pendennis says he is now going to discuss truths about mistakes in marriage and "if you will not hear of this, ladies, close the book, and send for some other" (6:226). He pities poor Clara and paints her situation with sharp irony:

> suppose a young creature taken out of her home, and given over to a hard master whose caresses are as insulting as his neglect; consigned to

cruel usage; to weary loneliness; to bitter bitter recollections of the
past; suppose her schooled into hypocrisy by tyranny—and then, quick,
let us hire an advocate to roar out to a British jury the wrongs of her
injured husband, to paint the agonies of his bleeding heart (if Mr. Advocate gets plaintiff's brief in time, and before defendant's attorney
has retained him), and to show Society injured through him. Let us
console that martyr, I say, with thumping damages; and as for the
woman—the guilty wretch!—let us lead her out and stone her. (6:230)

Later Pendennis again denounces the motives that led to Barnes' marriage, and in
the process reiterates one of the main themes of the novel as a whole—the great
abuse of the English practice of marrying for economic reasons, a socially accepted sin that frequently brings its own punishment.[8] Meanwhile, Clara and
Belsize, meeting secretly, have renewed their love. When Barnes learns of this
he behaves so outrageously that some of his servants promptly resign, and Clara
leaves with Highgate and some servants who sympathize with her. Barnes gets
an award of damages in the Court of Queen's Bench and brings a bill of divorce
to the House of Lords. Clara, meanwhile, is miserable and lonely because she is
outcast, even though she is now under Lord Highgate's protection. And, Pendennis asks, is Barnes' conscience bothered by the suffering he has caused her?

Why should Sir Barnes Newcome's conscience be more squeamish
than his country's, which has put money in his pocket for having tram-
pled on the poor weak young thing, and scorned her, and driven her
to ruin? When the whole of the accounts of that wretched bankruptcy
are brought up for final Audit, which of the unhappy partners shall be
shown to be most guilty? (6:270)

Pendennis dismally concludes the chapter with no hope of change: "and St.
George of England may behold virgin after virgin offered up to the devouring
monster, Mammon (with many most respectable female dragons looking on)—
may see virgin after virgin given away, just as in the soldan of Babylon's time,
but with never a champion to come to the rescue!" (6:271).

Pendennis openly displays what the appropriate simple version of the plot
should be here. The suffering woman is rescued by her hero and her tormentor is
punished. But because English society's values are askew, this romantic plot plays
out differently. Clara is rescued but finds little joy in her situation. Meanwhile,
Barnes is rewarded for his conduct. We might say that Barnes has been punished
insofar as his beastly treatment of his wife has been found out and his skeletons
are on public view. But if he endures some embarrassment and humiliation, he
nonetheless is the successful suitor at law, and it is Highgate who suffers a financial penalty, and Clara an emotional one. Highgate is no St. George, nor even a
Caponsacchi, for he loves the lady and is self-interested. At least he gets to knock

Barnes down and to spare Clara his further abuse. Hypocrite and liar that he is, Barnes naturally dislikes having his private behavior made known, but the disclosures scarcely alter his *modus operandi*. It is true that he is furious to think that the scandals in his family have precipitated the end of his plan for Ethel to marry Lord Farintosh, but he nonetheless goes on with his personal mean-spirited machinations. I shall return to Ethel's termination of her engagement to Farintosh later, but now I want to follow the course of Barnes' career, especially in his relations with Clive and the Colonel.

The Colonel is eager for some opportunity to take Warrington's advice and crush the verminish Barnes; Clive is similarly incensed. Of Barnes he says:

> "if ever I can punish him I will. I shouldn't have the soul of a dog, if ever I forgot the wrongs that have been done me by that vagabond. Forgiveness? Pshaw! Are you dangling to sermons, Pen, at your wife's leading-strings? Are you preaching that cant? There are some injuries that no honest man should forgive, and I shall be a rogue on the day I shake hands with that villain." (6:316)

Warrington sees the conflict in military terms and remarks that he wouldn't want Clive and the Colonel ranged against himself, but Pendennis says that as enemies he would prefer them to Barnes, for you would never know how the latter would strike. And strike he does, using his banking connections to adversely affect the Bundelcund stock upon which the Colonel's fortune depends. Barnes' treason and Clive's spiritlessness about his life anger the Colonel, transforming his character; "hate and suspicion had mastered him, and if it cannot be said that his new life had changed him, at least it had brought out faults for which there had hitherto been no occasion, and qualities latent before." Pendennis turns to his reader at this moment when it might be easy to condemn the Colonel for his loss of charity. "Do we know ourselves, or what good or evil circumstance may bring from us?" The answer, of course, is that we do not and should therefore not be hasty to pass sentence on others. "Thrice fortunate he, to whom circumstance is made easy; whom fate visits with gentle trial, and kindly Heaven keeps out of temptation" (6:332).

Barnes' wickedness has contaminated both Clive and the Colonel, but particularly the latter, and now Thackeray makes obvious the correct pattern of behavior regarding human malice. George Warrington supports Clive and the Colonel, declaring that war and justice are good things; "I have not the least objection in life to a rogue being hung. When a scoundrel is whipped I am pleased, and say, serve him right." But Laura Pendennis, a model of good behavior and a touchstone of good sense, disagrees.[9] Revenge is wrong, she declares.

> "Let alone that the wisest and best of all Judges has condemned it. It blackens the hearts of men. It distorts their views of right. It sets them

to devise evil. It causes them to think unjustly of others. It is not the noblest return for injury, not even the bravest way of meeting it. The greatest courage is to bear persecution, not to answer when you are reviled, and when a wrong has been done you to forgive." (6:332–33)

The Colonel's uncharacteristic enmity is so great that he is even drawn into opposing Barnes for a seat in Parliament, against Clive's advice. To indicate how wrong a course the Colonel is now pursuing, Pendennis comments that by trying to shape his son's life according to values he considers appropriate, he has effectively deprived Clive of art and given him ledgers and Rosey Mackenzie instead (6:349). Indeed, in his own unhappiness, Clive has come a long way from his earlier censorious and pugnacious attitude. Now he recommends that his father leave further punishment of Barnes " 'to time, to remorse, to the Judge of right and wrong; who better understands than we can do our causes and temptations towards evil actions, who reserves the sentence for His tribunal' " (6:355). Later Clive repeats his advice. We are the victims of fate, he says, appealing to his father's own fatalist creed, and must all endure as best we can, praise be to Allah. But the Colonel can't ignore Barnes' villainy. Clive says, " 'Let us leave him to Allah too,' " and, reverting to the war imagery used before for the relationship between these two and Barnes, he suggests breaking up camp and not doing battle. " 'Let us have peace—and forgive him if we can' " (6:377). But the old soldier won't consider retreat, and goes on to campaign against his enemy, allowing the public exposure of Barnes' early sins to humiliate and discredit him—a just punishment, the Colonel seems to think, for the man's many offenses. The tactic works and the Colonel soundly defeats his opponent.

With Colonel Newcome's victory over Barnes the traditional plot seems to assert itself. The heroic Colonel has defeated his rascally enemy in what serves as a punishment for his many trespasses. Justice seems to be served. But, as the battle imagery might suggest, there is something unsettling in this plot. Has the battle been fairly fought, or do we discover that the victor has employed the tactics of his enemy and won by tricks instead of valor? The novel's underlying moral scheme discredits the Colonel's victory and requires a therapeutic punishment, such as the one that enabled Lord Kew's redemption. What has happened to Barnes will soon be beside the point as the focus turns to the judgment that falls upon the Colonel. In fact, Barnes will go on to other worldly successes and will seem not to have been punished at all, since he survives his defeats and remains wicked. But the narrator has already indicated that he is less concerned with bullyragging rogues than with cajoling the ordinary citizenry. Barnes' anti-plot lets him avoid the expected retribution that his behavior would demand in a conventional Victorian novel.

We must remember that The Newcomes is a novel in which the narrator has openly pledged to scourge the so-called virtuous community; it is now time for the good Colonel to endure the consequences of his errors. The narrator earlier cautioned that intended good acts might cause as much mischief as intentionally wicked ones. Surely the Colonel has been unwise, though well-intentioned, in his management of Clive's life. But the keenest evidence of his misjudgment comes with the collapse of the Bundelcund Bank and the loss of his fortune. In the midst of his victory over Barnes comes a stunning defeat. Whereas Barnes' punishments have come at the hands of his fellow characters, this bankruptcy takes on a different character. Bankruptcy was a serious reality in the nineteenth century, but in fiction of the time it served, beyond financial distress, the emblematic purpose of signaling a collapse of moral values.[10] The implied author's power over the narrative is foregrounded in his exercising his privilege of punishing the Colonel for his many mistakes.

The implied author's presence is particularly evident at this critical juncture in Pendennis' explanations.[11] Readers have been right, he says, in their doubts about the Bundelcund Bank. He himself has dropped several hints that the concern is not safe, such as Warrington's worry that the Colonel controls all of the family money and the indication that the Colonel has lately changed his entertainments and associates. Pendennis explains: "I disdain, for the most part, the tricks and surprises of the novelist's art. Knowing, from the very beginning of our story, what was the issue of this Bundelcund Banking concern, I have scarce had patience to keep my counsel about it" (6:397). But he *has* kept his counsel and he *has* used the novelist's trick of secrecy. Or so it would seem, except, as he himself acknowledges, it has been a secret less and less maintained. The readers *have* felt an increasing misgiving about the Colonel's fortune. This is not a secret that must be found out but rather an undisclosed eventuality. In fact, the Bundelcund Bank is the equivalent of Nemesis. And now it comes crashing home, just when the Colonel's least appealing qualities have been demonstrated and gratified, because it is time for the Colonel to be humbled and redeemed. Pendennis claims to be telling the foreknown story of his friends, but this is simply to say that he is the scribe who records providence, fate, or destiny. In no way can Pendennis alter the story he has to tell. At this stage we see the Godlike hand of the implied author behind or above his spokesman. Characters within the story have tried to caution the Colonel and he has not heeded them, but sudden disaster brought about by the implied author himself cannot be ignored. It is the lesson of Lord Kew all over again, and the last chapters of Volume Two echo those of Volume One; repentance and reformation follow punishment; having been ruined in the world, the Colonel resumes his earlier gentle and humble manner.

After the collapse of their fortunes, the Newcomes are obliged to scale back their household severely. Clive's mother-in-law becomes aggressively contemptuous, and, as Clive explains, some of her taunts and gibes wound the Colonel deeply, "but he deems this is his punishment and that he must bear it as long as it pleases God" (6:425–26). Household life becomes a torment, increasingly extenuated but nonetheless painful. Clive tries to make a living from art, Rosey is unhappy and pregnant, and there is always the resident demon, Mrs. Mackenzie, who provides operating expenses for the family. Meanwhile, the Colonel refuses an offer of support from a wealthy old schoolfellow and humbly becomes a pensioner at Grey Friars school. This is the total fall of vanity from power to abasement, the half-turn of the wheel of fortune, in medieval art an emblem to remind humankind of its tenuous position, and to urge humility. But if the Newcomes have been punished for their animosity and their extravagance, they have been punished therapeutically. Significantly the chapter dealing with the Colonel's ruin is entitled "Belisarius," suggesting the noble misfortune of a great general's fall into beggary. This sly hint is supported directly in a later chapter, when Pendennis comes upon the Colonel in his pensioner's role at Grey Friars.

> The steps of this good man had been ordered hither by Heaven's decree: to this almshouse! Here it was ordained that a life all love, and kindness, and honour, should end! I heard no more of prayers, and psalms, and sermon, after that. How dared I to be in a place of mark, and he, he yonder among the poor? Oh, pardon, you noble soul! I ask forgiveness of you for being of a world that has so treated you—you my better, you the honest, and gentle, and good! I thought the service would never end, or the organist's voluntaries, or the preacher's homily. (6:450)

The Colonel has been totally recuperated. He is again the simple, honest, noble soul to whom we were first introduced. Though he wandered from his proper path, he never failed in his best attributes, as the psalm read at Founder's Day at Grey Friars suggests.

> 23. The steps of a good man are ordered by the Lord, and he delighteth in his way.
> 24. Though he fall, he shall not be utterly cast down, for the Lord upholdeth him with his hand.
> 25. I have been young, and now am old, yet have I not seen the righteous forsaken, nor his seed begging their bread. (6:450)

From this point on the Colonel again represents the proper acceptance of what Fate, or the Lord, has ordained. That he has resumed his role of Good Man is made clear by his good death. As the last peal of the chapel bell sounds, the Colonel says "Adsum" and dies, and Pen comments, "It was the word we used at school, when names were called; and lo, he, whose heart was as that of a child, had answered to his name, and stood in the presence of The Master" (6:504).

Another important trajectory from pride to humility occurs in Volume Two—that of Ethel Newcome. In the first several chapters of the volume it is clear that Clive, who loves Ethel, has little chance of winning her because her family and Lady Kew plan a high marriage for her; indeed, Lady Kew is already working on Lord Farintosh as a likely suitor. Clive is hurt and angry at Ethel's treatment of him and at her behavior in general. Pendennis goes so far as to consider Ethel "a flirt" (6:39). As narrator, Pendennis remarks that a young woman of spirit who allows herself to be pulled about in pursuit of a husband is in an awkward position as a heroine, and he says he would depose her in that very sentence if he could. "But a novelist must go on with his heroine, as a man must go on with his wife, for better or worse, and to the end" (6:91). Yet despite this fanciful attitude toward Ethel, Pendennis presents the extenuating circumstances of her situation, beginning with the by-now-familiar question of whether we who judge her are any better than our neighbors. After all, she is simply a young girl in the hands of others, reflecting the traditions in which she has been raised.

> Oh, to think of a generous nature, and the world, and nothing but the world to occupy it!—of a brave intellect, and the milliner's bandboxes, and the scandal of the coteries, and the fiddle-faddle etiquette of the Court for its sole exercise! of the rush and hurry from entertainment to entertainment; of the constant smiles and cares of representation; of the prayerless rest at night, and the awaking to a godless morrow! This was the course of life to which Fate, and not her own fault altogether, had for a while handed over Ethel Newcome. Let those pity her who can feel their own weakness and misgoing; let those punish her who are without fault themselves. (6:96)

Early in Volume Two, then, the theme that closed Volume One is restated. Before we assess others, we should consider their circumstances and look into our own hearts. We cannot help but be dismayed or heartened by the behavior of others, but we must temper our judgments with sympathy. Pendennis particularly urges young women to be gentle in their assessments of the motives of other females, since they are likely to exhibit similar weaknesses themselves (6:111). This caution to women is repeated, then goes underground while the narrative turns its attention to the male errors of the Colonel and Clive as they pursue an elegant and luxuriant lifestyle—to which they are not really suited—and marshall their forces to defeat Barnes Newcome instead of more wisely leaving him to his own undoing.

The scandal that leads up to Barnes' divorce teaches Ethel how false her own ambitions have been. She tells Lord Farintosh, whom she has agreed to marry, that she accepted him for the wrong reasons, apologizes to him, and frees herself. The Colonel has not forgiven Ethel for rejecting Clive's affection and considers her acceptance of an inferior creature like Farintosh shameful. "Her engagement to this man was a blot upon her—the rupture only a just punishment and humiliation" (6:303). We have just been treated to Mrs. Hobson Newcome's pious consideration that Ethel is suffering the "punishment of worldliness and vanity, the evil of marrying out of one's station," and to her warning her own daughters

away from "Ethel's *conduct* and *punishment.*" Since Mrs. Hobson Newcome is a
thoroughly unappealing character, we should realize that the Colonel is wrong
to second her opinions. In fact, Pendennis does not stop with this suggestion of
guilt by association; he leaves us no doubt that, though the Colonel is a righteous
and tender-hearted man, his sentence on Ethel is wrong. Pendennis and Laura
know Ethel better and their attitude is much different.

> Noble, unhappy young creature! are you the first of your sisterhood
> who has been bidden to traffic your beauty, to crush and slay your
> honest natural affections, to sell your truth and your life for rank and
> title? But the Judge who sees not the outward acts merely, but their
> causes, and views not the wrong alone, but the temptations, struggles,
> ignorance of erring creatures, we know has a different code to ours—
> ours, who fall upon the fallen, who fawn upon the prosperous so, who
> administer our praises and punishments so prematurely, who now strike
> so hard, and, anon, spare so shamelessly. (6:303)

Now, when Ethel becomes more closely identified with Laura Pendennis, and,
in her sorrow, begins to reveal her admirable moral traits, she and the Pendennises learn that Clive is going to marry Rosey Mackenzie. So Ethel's mistakes in
the marriage market come to an end just as Clive's are beginning. Thus, in
another instance of anti-plotting, the narrative rescue of Ethel from an unwise
marriage does not result in a happy conclusion. The usual Victorian fare would
have united her with Clive in a proper union of true hearts. But Thackeray is
determined to violate these simple expectations, and, having spared Ethel from
matrimonial woe and set her on a path of moral recuperation, plunges Clive into
the very error that he and his father had earlier inveighed against. Clive and
Ethel are not like David Copperfield and Agnes Wickfield, who are justly
matched after David's mistaken love for Dora Spenlow; they are not quite so
innocent. Ethel is perhaps the greater sinner of the two, with her acceptance of
the marriage market values, but she also proves the stronger in her "redemption." Like Lord Kew, she gains strength and maturity from her humbling.
Again, this can be seen as a narrative punishment that is therapeutic rather than
retributive. What Pendennis says of Colonel Newcome's admirable humility as a
pensioner could apply to the cases of Ethel and Kew as well: "who would not
have humbled his own heart, and breathed his inward prayer, confessing and
adoring the Divine Will, which ordains these trials, these triumphs, these humiliations, these blessed griefs, this crowning Love?" (6:453).

An interesting feature of *The Newcomes* is how, as the novel moves toward its
conclusion, feminine virtues—highlighted by contrasting feminine failings—
begin to dominate and force male violence, aggression, and self-involvement to
the margins. Laura Pendennis' recommendation of forgiveness over revenge is,
perhaps, the point at which the tide reverses. Her advice is rejected, but in the
remaining narrative revenge is painted as folly and the wisdom of resignation

and pardon is more frequently applauded. Ethel's case is the most closely attended of those illustrating the higher value of charity, humility, and self-suppression. To emphasize that these values have been superior, though largely overlooked, from the beginning of the narrative, Thackeray stresses the resemblance of Ethel and Clive's unhappy relationship to that of the Colonel and Madame de Florac. The latter two had been deeply in love, but Léonore de Blois was forced to marry Count de Florac, to whom she was faithful without loving him. The Colonel never lost his love for Léonore, whose name is on his lips as he is dying. For Pendennis, Madame de Florac is the highest model for human behavior. "I see in such women—the good and pure, the patient and faithful, the tried and the meek—the followers of Him whose earthly life was divinely sad and tender" (6:459).

Just as Madame de Florac's story is the submerged foundation for the entire novel—her enduring love for Thomas Newcome, her fidelity as a wife, her excellence as a mother—so the values she represents remain the ground for true judgment in the narrative.[12] What is true remains largely hidden until some crisis or tragedy tests us and then we find, past vanity, pride, and arrogance, what values will truly serve. Therefore, as the novel draws to its close, the mildness and mercy of Laura, Ethel, and Madame de Florac come to the fore. The latter two are at the Colonel's bedside when he dies. And the splendid virtues of these women are only the finer for the contrast with Mrs. Mackenzie's ill-bred harangues and Rosey's jealous passion. In a variation of a familiar Victorian convention, the wealthy young lady is able to "rescue" the young man she loves through a timely cash contribution. Ethel sees to it that money Lady Kew had wanted Clive to inherit becomes his, despite Barnes' resistance. Moreover, she advises Clive, temporarily estranged from his suspicious and pregnant wife, to return to her. "'She will be sure to ask for her husband, and forgiveness is best, dear Clive'" (6:498).

That last clause perhaps constitutes in itself the short version of *The Newcomes*. But *The Newcomes,* extended version, is much more than a recommendation of forgiveness; it is a detailed examination of how human beings, through the experience of some personal loss or error, some disadvantage or mistake, come to appreciate the greater power of forgiveness over punishment. By finding out or being found out in our own failings we may learn how chary we should be of condemning others and of longing to injure them. They will be judged, the novel says, but by a Judge with far more evidence about the case than we have. Juliet McMaster concludes that a major theme of *The Newcomes* is that poetic justice does not operate in life.[13] Moreover, it is precisely because poetic justice does not work out in life that it must sometimes be made to do so in fiction, although that poetic justice may not appear in the guise we expect. The implied author constructs anti-plots to frustrate our easy digestion of the tale we are consuming, and fabricates narrative punishments, which, like the Lord's visitations, prove to be our best means for salvation.

Yes, the longer version of *The Newcomes* was necessary, but it is, after all, only a fable. And the new narrative voice, taking over from Pendennis, who himself fades into Fable-land, explains that anything can happen in Fable-land; wicked people die appropriately and the weak are rescued: "And the poet of Fable-land rewards and punishes absolutely" (6:506). But his rewards buy nothing and his blows cannot be felt. With Pendennis now clearly relieved of his role as narrator and assigned to Fable-land, the implied author must decide where his tale is headed, for Pendennis did not say if Ethel married and, if so, who she married after Clive was freed by Rosey's death in childbirth. But it is precisely here that the long telling of the story becomes so important. On various occasions Pendennis had commented on his role as narrator, explaining that as narrator he was now and then obliged to embellish his tale and to imagine events and conversations that he has not witnessed. At the conclusion of the story the new narrative voice points out that Pendennis had to get his information about Ethel's private experiences from somewhere, and he speculates that her husband—very likely Pen's good friend Clive, confided them. And how did Pendennis get all those private letters, and so forth? The narrator concludes that the very detailed information available in the narrative is proof of its happy ending, and that it is his belief "that in Fable-land somewhere Ethel and Clive are living most comfortably together," but he allows the reader to settle Fable-land as she or he likes, because anything you like happens there (6:506).[14]

This returns us to the disturbing and complicating fact that all things do not happen as one would like in *The Newcomes*. There is much error, sin, and suffering in the novel and it is shared by the virtuous and the vicious alike. Not all the toads burst in their wicked rage. It may be that in Fable-land anything can happen, but it is an unwise author who seeks to make his Fable-land approximate real life, then set about creating impossible heroes and heroines with impossible lives. The true privilege of Fable-land is not to punish the unsavories and reward the delectables, but to be able to render in detail the generally invisible motives and influences that move people to act as they do, and by demonstrating that—a few true monsters aside—most people please or offend our moral sensibilities for reasons not far removed from our own. The implied author himself often refuses to judge, though he will often allow his surrogate narrator to do so. More often, however, this narrator will caution his readers not to judge. The implied author is inclined to forgive or to punish therapeutically. He is not very interested in narrative punishment of Sir Barnes Newcome and his breed, and when he "punishes" his good or middling characters it is to give them an opportunity to reconstruct their lives. In *The Newcomes,* Thackeray rearranges the priorities of a familiar saying: Be judged lest ye judge.

NOTES

1. *The Works of William Makepeace Thackeray,* 26 vols. (Philadelphia: J. B. Lippincott Company, 1901) 5:5.

2. Robert A. Colby, *Thackeray's Canvass of Humanity: An Author and His Public* (Columbus: Ohio State University Press, 1979), 387.

3. *The Letters and Private Papers of William Makepeace Thackeray*, ed. Gordon N. Ray, 4 vols. (Cambridge: Harvard University Press, 1945–46), 1:297–98.

4. Various critics have called attention to the reader's complicity in Thackeray's narrative method. Jack P. Rawlins' *Thackeray's Novels: A Fiction That Is True* (Berkeley: University of California Press, 1974) and Janice Carlisle's *The Sense of an Audience: Dickens, Thackeray, and George Eliot at Mid-Century* (Athens: University of Georgia Press, 1981) are two works that note how Thackeray makes his readers aware of conventional thinking and of the conventions of narration. Subsequent references appear in the text.

5. Whitwell Elwin recognized Thackeray's aims when he wrote in his 1855 review of *The Newcomes*, "Those who are not too dull or too hardened to learn will rise up from these volumes with an increased scorn of everything ungenerous, sordid, and deceptive, and there is no one so perfect that he will not stumble in his progress upon infirmities which are his own" (*Thackeray: The Critical Heritage*, ed. Geoffrey Tillotson and Donald Hawes [New York: Barnes & Noble, Inc., 1968], 233–34).

6. John Carey, *Thackeray: Prodigal Genius* (London: Faber & Faber, 1977), 147. Jean Sudrann's "The Philosopher's Property: Thackeray and the Use of Time," *Victorian Studies* 10, no. 4 (June 1967), 359–88, offers a far more satisfying exploration of Thackeray's "Janus-faced time who destroys man, yet through the power of memory, redeems the days and nights of his existence into a pattern of significance and joy" (378).

7. Gordon N. Ray, *Thackeray: The Age of Wisdom 1847-1863* (London: Oxford University Press, 1958), 238.

8. See the narrator's explicit statements about the inevitability of natural retribution (6:256, 271).

9. As early as Whitwell Elwin there was uneasiness about Laura's role as a paragon (*Heritage* 241). More recently Ina Ferris has indicated that Laura is objectionable for being too moral ("The Demystification of Laura Pendennis," *Studies in the Novel* 13, nos. 1–2 [Spring-Summer 1981], 122–32). But Thackeray was always willing to let even his best characters exhibit faults. And, after all, Laura was nurtured by that very loving and kind, though distinctly flawed, woman, Mrs. Helen Pendennis.

10. See chapter 8 of John R. Reed's *Victorian Conventions* (Athens: Ohio University Press, 1975) and his "A Friend to Mammon: Speculation in Victorian Literature," *Victorian Studies* 27, no. 2 (Winter 1984), 179–202. See also Barbara Weiss's *The Hell of the English: Bankruptcy and the Victorian Novel* (Lewisburg: Bucknell University Press, 1986), and chapter 17 of Richard Altick's *The Presence of the Present: Topics of the Day in the Victorian Novel* (Columbus: Ohio State University Press, 1991).

11. It might appear convenient here simply to refer to Thackeray, or even "Thackeray," since all readers understand that a real being in his own person, or

as rendered through a persona, wrote the story. But because Thackeray was particularly chary of passing judgment on his characters and applying his personal values to his fictional plots, the notion of an abstract agency such as the implied author operating between author and narrator is especially convenient.

12. Ina Ferris argues that "Through its ominous repetitions and parallels (particularly between generations) *The Newcomes* conveys a sense of human life as inevitably flawed. There is something inimical in life itself, the novel implies, something beyond the reach of social reform or goodwill or love itself" (*William Makepeace Thackeray* [Boston: Twayne Publishers, 1983], 97).

13. Juliet McMaster, *Thackeray: The Major Novels* (Toronto: University of Toronto Press, 1971), 172.

14. Thackeray did not want to end his novel with the highly conventional union of his heroine and hero, considering it artistically wrong, but he yielded to the pressure of the readers who had followed the serial for many months and who had desires of their own about its outcome (Ray 244).

TWENTY-FOUR

The Virginians

MUCH OF what we think about *The Virginians* comes down to the issue of its narrators.[1] The first narrator (hereafter referred to simply as the narrator, in contrast to George), who draws upon the historical documents that provide the substance of the narrative, is a mid-nineteenth-century man, perhaps Arthur Pendennis, standing in for Thackeray. This narrator thinks in "modern" terms and often digresses to compare Victorian and Georgian manners. The second narrator is George Warrington, one of the characters in the narrative, an eighteenth-century aristocrat telling his own story long after the main incidents are over. This division of narrators may be one reason why *The Virginians* has met with much less favor than Thackeray's earlier novels. If, in *Henry Esmond,* Thackeray had experimented with telling an entire story from the first-person point of view of one of its central actors, in *The Virginians* he gave this experiment a turn of the screw, telling his story in the sterescopic vision of essentially third and first persons, one extradiegetic and one diegetic. In this the novel resembles Dickens' *Bleak House,* except that where Dickens alternates his two narrators, Thackeray permits one narrative voice to cede authority entirely to the second. There are interesting consequences from this decision since, contrary to conventional expectations, authority moves from the narrator with the broadest view to the narrator within his own story.[2]

Janice Carlisle observes of *The Virginians* that before they rejected him, Thackeray had already alienated his readers.[3] She argues that Thackeray had lost faith in the moral value of his art, and thus his novel lacked both the tension between ideal and actual and the moral complexity and ingenuity that had characterized *Esmond* (143–44). Susanta Kuman Sinha, in an article defending Thackeray's use of authorial comment, states, "*Vanity Fair* with its authorial comments fully shows Thackeray's acceptance of the novelist's moral obligations towards his readers. In this novel as well as *Pendennis, Henry Esmond* and *The Newcomes*

Thackeray is fully able to establish the artistic validity of his moral comments. But in his later works like *The Virginians,* the comments do not have the same appeal."[4] I agree that *The Virginians* lacks the force of *Esmond,* but that lack is partly the result of Thackeray's curious narrative experiment, demonstrating that moral purpose and narrative method are almost always inescapably intertwined in serious artistic efforts of the Victorian period.

One problem with the two narrators is that they live in two different moral climates. Although the narrator constantly makes sarcastic comments designed to show that Victorians share many of the weaknesses for which they condemn their less fastidious forebears, he nonetheless clearly asserts that there has been substantial improvement over the last hundred years in moral and social conditions.[5] The first narrator thus is able to perceive, judge, and convey the historical events of his story from a morally superior and historically privileged position. George, on the other hand, writes out of the "inferior" moral and social atmosphere of his time and judges it subjectively according to his own temperament. To make matters more difficult, Thackeray gives both narrators ironic and worldly voices which must nonetheless convey substantially different world views. The similarities and contrasts between these narrators create many intriguing narrative dilemmas.

Not the least of the metanarrative complications is the first narrator's claim that he is telling a true story based upon family letters. But the open secret for his readers is that this "history" is the continuation of an earlier "novel" whose authorship was claimed by one William Makepeace Thackeray, whose name appears at the head of this narrative as well, a seemingly trivial point if the narrator did not keep the schizophrenic character of his work ever-present to us. A glance at some examples of this practice from the early part of the novel may help to illuminate its effects. The narrator claims that he is developing his narrative from the Virginians' letters, but because those letters are far from complete accounts, he has tried to imagine the conditions under which those letters were written. "I have drawn the figures as I fancied they were; set down conversations as I think I might have heard them; and so, to the best of my ability, endeavoured to revivify the bygone times and people."[6] But if there are no letters, the whole effort rests on nothing but the narrator's fancy. A few pages later the narrator alludes slyly to the open secret of the narrative when he comments that "[as] nothing is unknown to writers of biographies of the present kind," he is able to give conversations that took place outside the hearing of anyone who left records for him to inspect (8:18). "Biographies of the present kind" could refer to the imaginative license claimed earlier, but equally to the fact that Thackeray's readership knew they were reading a novel. And yet Thackeray continues to tease. Reflecting on George's letters to Harry from the military campaign against the French, the narrator becomes pensive. "As we look at the slim characters on the yellow page, fondly kept and put aside, we can almost fancy him alive who wrote and who read it—and yet, lo! they are as if they never had been;

their portraits faint images in frames of tarnished gold. Were they real once, or are they mere phantasms? Did they live and die once? Did they love each other as true brothers and loyal gentlemen? Can we hear their voices in the past?" (8:122). This last question is followed by a long letter from George describing his experiences, in which Thackeray tries to capture the appropriate and believable tone of an eighteenth-century gentleman.

Much is happening here. The narrator, in referring to the apparent insubstantiality of his characters, reminds his readership that they *are* phantasms since they exist only as characters in a novel concocted by a nineteenth-century novelist. Yet these long-dead fictional characters "live" through the simulated voices the novelist creates for them and will, in that way, outlive the living phantasms who read about the imaginary ones. At the same time, by his detailed references to the script on yellowed paper and the tarnished frames of the portraits, the narrator becomes a first-person narrator with a participating role in the narrative, a move which forces the reader to recognize the presence of an implied author behind him. By "overhearing" the epistolary discourse of one brother addressed to another, we are obliged to imagine an audience for George's letter and to accept George as an embedded narrator. But when the narrator dramatizes himself as part of a scene with the already-mentioned props before him, he obliges us to recognize the acute difference between Harry as narrative audience and ourselves as actual audience. But, if we consider that this is a fictional history and that the aforementioned props are not real, we suddenly discover that we are being pulled in the direction of narrative audience ourselves, and can recover only by admitting that there is an agency, an implied author, beyond this narrative voice and that we are the actual audience of that author.

This toying with the reader may seem merely an exhausted author's mode of prodding his jaded Pegasus, but I would like to indicate some important issues it raises. The narrator wants us to see him as a contemporary individual meditating upon the past. This permits him to draw comparisons and moralize from time to time. But this moralizing occurs in the sustained context of a phantasmal world in which all things pass away, including ourselves. As the narrator sighs at the end of *The Newcomes,* anything can happen in Fable-land, but the rewards and judgments have no significance. If we must make allowances for manners of the past that seem ignoble and coarse by our higher standards, perhaps we can make the next step of viewing our own contemporary behavior with the same degree of compassion and understanding. If we *are* better, let us *be* better. If we can forgive offenses in the past, can we not do the same in the present? Perhaps we can transfer compassion from Fable-land, where it doesn't count, to our daily lives, where it does.

When the narrator moralizes, he takes a fairly consistent line. Generally he is trying to spare someone's feelings. Sometimes it is the fine-minded reader. I won't shock the present audience, he says, with the "lively jokes" the Castlewood ladies laughed at, but which would be considered improper today (8:56). In doing this the narrator calls attention to the similarity or disparity between the authorial audience and the actual audience, though this comparison is deeply compromised by the likelihood that he does not take it seriously himself, but speaks ironically. Again not wanting us to suffer in suspense, the narrator promptly informs us, when Harry and his horse have a spill, that Harry is not dead. "How can we afford to kill off our heroes, when they are scarcely out of their teens, and we have not reached the age of manhood of the story? (8:213). This concern has not prevented the narrator from apparently killing off George—one of his two heroes. But the passage I have quoted also alludes to the open secret of the novel—that it *is* a novel, with its story in the hands of an author who has fabricated all the "evidence" upon which it stands. It also should recall to an attentive reader's mind the second paragraph of the narrative, which explains that "the subjects of this story, natives of America, and children of the Old Dominion, found themselves engaged on different sides in the quarrel, coming together peaceably at its conclusion, as brethren should, their love never having materially diminished, however angrily the contest divided them" (8:2). Here is the outline of the larger plot, an outline that should have informed any reader from the outset that George is not dead. The narrator is all the more slippery but candid, then, in saying that he cannot kill off his heroes so early. It is not the expediency of decorum regarding heroes and stories that prevents him from committing authorial murder, but the simple fact that he has already, in the preceding narrative, granted both heroes lives long enough to outlast the Revolutionary War. This constraint upon the narrator actually originates with the implied author. The narrator, remember, presents himself as telling a story about people who are real to him. He is therefore of the fictive world himself and incapable of creating that world. He tells a story that has originated elsewhere. This detail will take on significance later when it becomes necessary to discuss his disappearance. When the narrator wants us to respond sympathetically to a character, he coaches us; thus he expresses pity for Lady Maria Esmond, understanding how she suffers at the hands of her cruel aunt, the Baroness Bernstein (née Beatrix Esmond) (8:239). And later he shows sympathy for her position as a middle-aged woman in love with a very young man. Elsewhere he advises women with only common looks not to envy their beautiful rivals, since the attractions of youth fade rapidly, whereas ordinary individuals will remain comely into old age (8:283). Assuming that his readers object to the hypocrisy in Harry's letters to his mother, where Harry neglects to tell her all the truth of his activities in England, the narrator lectures them on the inevitability of such a case. "There must be a certain distance between me and my son Jacky. There must be a respectful, an amiable, a virtuous hypocrisy between us. I do not in the least wish that he should treat me as an equal, that he should contradict me, take my arm-chair, read the newspaper first at breakfast, ask unlimited friends to dine when I have a party of my own, and so forth. No; where there is not equality, there must be hypocrisy" (8:311–12). In another place, despite the prevailing

Victorian prejudice in favor of work, the narrator offers a paean to "blessed Idleness. . . . Dear slatternly smiling Enchantress! They may assail thee with bad names—swear thy character away, and call thee the Mother of Evil; but, for all that, thou art the best company in the world" (8:299).

What characterizes these intrusions, lectures, and asides to the reader is a general appeal to understanding and sympathy, an urging toward a more sympathetic, even forgiving, cast of mind. When comparing the morality of 1858 with that of 1758, the narrator says we are certainly more moral now and wouldn't tolerate a Fielding or a Richardson. Young men led a deplorable life of drinking and gambling then, he continues, but we're not better; we simply have fewer temptations. The narrator is grateful for the change and won't condemn Harry Warrington's dissipations: "I, knowing the weakness of human nature, am not going to be surprised; and, quite aware of my own shortcomings, don't intend to be very savage to my neighbor's" (8:428). Keeping to his word, he is even gentle concerning religious hypocrisy, claiming that he hasn't met any real religious hypocrites. "Folks have their religion in some mental lock-up, as it were,—a valuable medicine, to be taken in ill-health" (8:467). And when an opportunity arises to judge Harry after his financial collapse, the narrator can be sarcastic toward his audience. Yes, sting him with remorse when he's down, he says. "No pity on him, I say, my honest young gentlemen, for *you,* of course, have never indulged in extravagance or folly, or paid the reckoning of remorse" (8:473).

The narrator promises not to be savage with his neighbors, among whom we should include his characters. But at one point he offers some peculiarly savage advice, telling men that the best way to retain the love of women is through rough treatment with only a slight admixture of love and kindness, since too much kindness makes them indifferent. Assuming that female readers will be enraged with this recipe for male behavior, he hastens to explain that he is only joking and that he does not advocate thrashing their sex. This uncharacteristically brutal advice should have passed as ironic, comic, or exaggerated comment, but, by supposing that he must confess that he is being facetious, he also implies that his readers are not alert enough to pick up his humor. In a very modest version of his macho advice, then, he actually does treat his female readers roughly, by his low estimate of their ability to appreciate his tone. But the ironic advice has the additional function of focusing on the perversity of human conduct. All too often in Thackeray's fiction, mild and loving persons are treated condescendingly by the objects of their affection. We need mention only Amelia Sedley and Clive Newcome to make the point. And the point is, after all, that affection and sympathy do not always have their desired effect. In short, human beings are imperfect and must be accepted as such. And yet it is difficult for us not to judge.

In discussing Lady Maria's incriminating private letters, which would be embarrassing if made public because they candidly assess her acquaintances, the narrator declares, "I for one, and for the future, am determined never to speak or write my mind out regarding anything or anybody. . . . When this book is concluded, I shall change the jaundiced livery which my books have worn since I began to lisp in numbers, have rose-coloured coats for them with cherubs on the cover, and all the characters within shall be perfect angels" (8:367). This passage demonstrates several things. First, that the narrator can surprise us by voicing an unpopular sentiment, advocating ill treatment of women; second, that he can fool us because we do not recognize his ironic tone; third, that we have been duped into defending *his* usual position of sympathy, pity, and even kindness against coercion and condign judgment. And this last point is perhaps the most important, for it calls attention to the narrator's underlying message before and after this episode—that we should be reluctant to interlope upon the secrets and motives of others, and be slow to judge and condemn, inclining instead to compassion. The narrator thus establishes himself as a gentleman wise in the ways of the world, but inclined to forgive most offenses as instances of human weakness. In this character he is very different from George Warrington, who takes over narration midway through the second volume. But to explore this difference it will be necessary to turn our attention from the narrators to the story that is being told.

An incident early in the novel sets the stage for the moral economy to follow. In an account of Harry and George Warrington as boys, we learn that the twins are affectionate toward one another but different in temperament. George is studious and mild, whereas Harry is inclined to an active life. However, though George is quiet, he quickly becomes indignant when his mother presumes to punish his servant boy. "A fierce quarrel between mother and son ensued out of this event. Her son would not be pacified. He said the punishment was a shame—a shame; that he was the master of the boy, and no one—no, not his mother—had a right to touch him; that she might *order* him to be corrected, and that he would suffer the punishment, as he and Harry often had, but no one should lay a hand on his boy" (8:32–33). A corresponding incident occurs later. Determined to retain dominion in her own house, Madam Esmond directs the unpopular tutor, Mr. Ward, to punish George for disobedience, explaining, "When I was headstrong, as I sometimes was as a child before my spirit was changed and humbled, my mamma punished me and I submitted. So must George" (8:53). Of course, her nature has not been humbled, and she remains a headstrong person who should recognize the same imperious qualities incipient in her son. George has asked pardon already but his mother dismisses the gesture. What bothers George is not punishment itself but the chastising of an aristocrat at the hands of a hireling. He tries to explain, but his mother is inflexible. To dramatize the importance of this matter, George picks up a tea-cup prized by his mother because it belonged to her father. As an object lesson, he points out that once such a cup is broken it can never be mended. Once again he admits his error, stoutly declaring, " 'I have been wrong. Mr. Ward, I ask pardon. I will try and amend' " (8:54). This is his offer of peace toward his mother, but she misunderstands, regarding his gesture as a sign of fear, and she refuses to relent. George lets the cup drop and it shatters on the marble hearth, a symbol of his determination never to feel the same toward his mother again. She would not pardon him and he will never forgive her. That the symbol of this breach is a cup representing a bond between a child and a parent only reinforces the intensity of George's purpose and the enormity of the offense. Thus begins early George's career of contesting the authority of moral hierarchies.

But the scene does not end here. Mr. Ward takes George off to carry out Madam Esmond's instructions but immediately reappears bleeding from the head, followed by Harry. " 'I don't care. I did it,' says Harry. 'I couldn't see this fellow strike my brother; and, as he lifted his hand, I flung the great ruler at him. I couldn't help it. I won't bear it; and if one lifts a hand to me or my brother, I'll have his life,' shouts Harry, brandishing the hanger (8:55). When Ward later asks who is to compensate him for this insult, George suggests that, although they are only fifteen, the Warrington boys can offer the gentlemanly opportunity of a duel for redress. Ward rages, " 'This to a minister of the Word!' " Harry's response emphasizes the simple and direct nature of his moral code. " 'Well, well, if you won't fight, why don't you forgive?' says Harry. 'If you don't forgive, why don't you fight? That's what I call the horns of a dilemma.' And he laughed his frank, jolly laugh (8:56). It is clear from this early episode that Harry is easily inclined to fight but equally quick to forgive, whereas George is slower to use violence, but likely to nurse a grudge for a long time. The two boys' conflict with George Washington clarifies this difference between them.

Mrs. Mountain shares with George her fears that Washington plans to marry Madam Esmond, and shows him an improperly acquired letter of Washington's that seems to provide evidence. George is furious and pursuades Harry that the marriage is likely and must be prevented. Harry is reluctant to become involved because he greatly admires Washington; nonetheless, he agrees to go along with George, who so provokes Washington that a duel seems inevitable until Mrs. Mountain announces her error and explains that Washington is engaged to a different widow. Harry immediately embraces Washington, delighted at the way things have turned out, but George, though he apologizes to Washington, remains cool to the man. Later he says, " 'I feel somehow as if I can't forgive him for having wronged him' " (8:124). Harry is open, sociable, and somewhat naive; George is ruminative, intelligent, but cool and inclined to distrust others. After the duel has been averted, Washington says to George, " 'take a true friend's advice, and try and be less ready to think evil of your friends' " (8:119). In dramatizing, here and elsewhere, the difference in temperament between the two brothers, the narrator has at the same time presented them both as admirable but imperfect young men. Harry's faults are those of an active, naive, and self-indulgent individual, whereas George's are those of a skeptical brooder. It is worth remembering later, when George takes over the narrative, that all that he recounts is filtered through this intellectually sophisticated, but doubting, distrustful, and proud nature. But just as Esmond's obvious limitations should not be used to discredit his testimony and provide grounds for impugning him as a character, so should George be considered a biased and perhaps inaccurate but otherwise truthful and reliable historian. After all, Thackeray makes abundantly clear throughout his writings his conviction that all narratives are inescapably biased by the agent of narration. The divided narration in *The Virginians* is a means of exploring this truth.

The Virginians does not present punishment and forgiveness as prominent, overt themes, as do *Vanity Fair* and *Pendennis*. Through much of Volume One there are few explicit scenes or commentaries involving these two responses. But the opening scenes alert us to the quickness with which punishment becomes a mode of controlling behavior within the community of the novel, as well as the ambivalence toward forgiveness demonstrated by some of the central characters. It is important for everything to follow that Thackeray has his novel open with its focus upon Madam Esmond. In stereotypical Victorian thinking, women are the authentic agents of forgiveness. But Madam Esmond is instead a proud, unrelenting woman, who, while violating the basic tenets of Christianity, professes to be its stoutest adherent. This is blindness, not hypocrisy. In beginning with a major character of this sort, Thackeray clearly indicates that a central undercurrent of his narrative will set a tendency to severity and judgment against a tendency to leniency and trust. The twin Warringtons embody the virtues and drawbacks of these two different tendencies, and the narrative itself embodies the dynamic interplay of these tendencies. The first part of the novel is narrated by a sophisticated but nonetheless appeasing narrator, recording the adventures and misadventures of the generous and naive Harry, who is gradually overwhelmed by his own faults and the ambitions of others. He has used too little judgment, been too trusting. Later, George's history describes how his more calculating, wary, and unbending character reduces itself to a low point very like Harry's precisely because it lacks Harry's gentler, more outgoing, more sympathetic traits. The need for some balance among these qualities is signified in the love between the brothers, which survives conflicting allegiances in the war between their countries.

That George records his own downward trajectory and does not hesitate to pass judgment on himself is an important clue to Thackeray's purpose in bringing a sharper sense of human frailty to the entire issue of moral judgment. In *Henry Esmond*, Esmond could aspire to be the Christian Hero described by Richard Steele. But in *The Virginians* Harry is too unreflective and too much like the lively Steele himself ever to consider such a role and George too skeptical about himself and mankind to pretend to it.[7] If two such admirable men, the novel suggests, cannot hope to fulfill that active Christian role, who can? And if none can, perhaps we should admit that the ideal, though unattainable, is not unworthy of our efforts, much in the way that Tennyson's Arthur requires his followers to swear to vows that no man can keep but which every man should take.[8] And if we recognize that even the best of us are blameable, perhaps we will cease the redundant blaming and begin to pardon and forgive instead, even as we hope for those mercies in our own peccant state. I believe that Thackeray used the divided narrative to instantiate some such message in the very form of his work. The reader need not depend upon an implied author to read through George's narrative, as was helpful in Esmond's case, because the implied author has provided a narrator to make explicit many nuances only implicit in Esmond's narration.

With the first volume of *The Virginians* well under way, and deeply involved with Harry Warrington's adventures in England, especially his romantic entanglement with Lady Maria Castlewood, the subject of forgiveness comes under the narrator's scrutiny. The occasion is a reconciliation between Madame Bernstein and Lady Maria after they have exchanged sharp differences of opinion.

> What can there be finer than forgiveness? What more rational than, after calling a man by every bad name under the sun, to apologise, regret hasty expressions, and so forth, withdraw the decanter (say) which you have flung at your enemy's head, and be friends as before? Some folks possess this admirable, this angel-like gift of forgiveness. It was beautiful, for instance, to see our two ladies at Tunbridge Wells forgiving one another, smiling, joking, fondling almost, in spite of the hard words of yesterday—yes, and forgetting bygones, though they couldn't help remembering them perfectly well. I wonder, can you and I do as much? Let us strive, my friend, to acquire this placable, Christian spirit. My belief is that you may learn to forgive bad language employed to you; but, then you must have a deal of practice, and be accustomed to hear and use it. You embrace after a quarrel and mutual bad language. Heaven bless us! Bad words are nothing when one is accustomed to them, and scarce need ruffle the temper on either side. (8:394-95)

The narrator clearly discounts the specious forgiveness displayed by these two women, but the passage prepares for a more suitable exhibition of the genuine virtue. Lady Maria and the Reverend Sampson are both arrested for debt while Harry is away from Tunbridge. When he receives word of the arrests, he speeds back and provides money enough to release both, feeling pleasure in his power to convert their sorrow into joy. Sampson is so grateful that he confesses his part in assisting Lord Castlewood's machinations against Harry, and admits that he has in his possession Harry's supposedly lost pocketbook containing Lady Maria's compromising letters. Harry tells him to get the letters "'and let me try and forgive you having seized upon them.'" Sampson responds, "'My benefactor, let me try and forgive myself'"(8:408). The clergyman retrieves the pocketbook but the letters are missing. Nonetheless, Harry "accepted Sampson's vows of contrition, and solemn promises of future fidelity, and reached his gracious hand to the chaplain and condoned his offence" (8:409).

Harry's is a warm, enthusiastic nature, as his foolish love for Lady Maria and his zestful entry into the world of gambling and drinking suggest. This warmth, so much a threat to his own well-being, is a benefit to others, for he easily compassionates and readily forgives. Thus, even as Harry is playing the forgiving benefactor to Sampson, he himself stands in need of forgiveness for his performance as the prodigal son. When Harry returns to the fast life of London, the narrator thinks of Madam Esmond remembering her son in her prayers. "When the Prodigal Son was away carousing, were not love and forgiveness still on the watch for him?" (8:421). And, as with the Prodigal, Harry's sins bring their own punishment. He loses his entire patrimony through gambling. "He was the Prodigal amongst the swine—his foul remorses; they had tripped him up, and were wallowing over him. Gambling, extravagance, debauchery, dissolute life, reckless companions, dangerous women—they were all upon him in a herd, and were trampling upon the prostrate young sinner" (8:460). Ironically, Harry is himself confined for debt soon after he has played the valiant role of rescuing his friends from a similar imprisonment. What better evidence that we all might require the same forgiveness that we are adjured to extend to others?

At this sorry turn of events George Warrington returns from the dead, arriving in England just in time to aid his unlucky and unwise brother. Harry now proves his good nature in his genuine delight at seeing the brother who displaces him as heir to the Virginia estate. Before Harry's imprisonment, the good and generous Colonel Lambert had returned expensive gifts that Harry had sent to his daughters, an act that offended Harry and led to his estrangement from the Lamberts. Colonel Lambert proves his Christian nature by forgiving Harry and coming to his assistance. Later he is happy to meet George and Harry again in society. "Generous hearts sometimes feel it, when wrong is forgiven, when Peace is restored, when love returns that had been thought lost" (9:24). The Lambert family, with the exception of son Jack, is a model of good feeling and virtue. The Colonel is brave and wise, his wife a trifle weak but kind and loving. Theo is modest and good, her sister, Hetty, lively and aggressive. But all are generous and thoughtful toward others—even Hetty, who goads Harry for his failure to occupy himself with a worthy career. Set against the Lamberts is the supposedly religious and moral family of Sir Miles Warrington. But these are mean, ambitious, and hypocritical people. George is cool to their enthusiastic welcome because he knows that, despite their protestations, they abandoned Harry in his need. When George blunders by refusing the Prince of Wales' offer to accompany him on a military campaign, the Warringtons look upon him with ghastly pity.

> Who does not know that face of pity? Whose dear relations have not so deplored him, not dead, but living? Not yours? Then, sir, if you have never been in scrapes; if you have never sowed a handful of wild oats or two; if you have always been fortunate, and good, and careful, and butter has never melted in your mouth, and an imprudent word has

never come out of it; if you have never sinned and repented, and been a fool and been sorry—then, sir, you are a wiseacre who won't waste your time over an idle novel, and it is not *de te* that the fable is narrated. (9:131)

The narrator here explicitly signals one major drift of his story—that it is addressed to fallible human beings who have sinned and who hope for forgiveness.

Though hypocrisy is often regarded as the principal target of Thackeray's satire, he could also defend it as a social benefit. What, in fact, are manners but a form of hypocrisy? In this novel Thackeray incorporated no major secrets, no sins hiding a criminal past or disreputable relationship. We have already seen that the "secret" of George's survival was nothing of the kind, and we shall return to that point again later. But it is worth considering briefly how hypocrisy—often truly repellent and depicted as such in Thackeray's writings—can be justified.

Commenting on various slanders about George circulating in society, the narrator laments the sordid details that others fabricate about our lives. But counteracting this form of fictionalizing is another mode of pretense—the fortunate disguise of our true feelings. When women put on good faces to meet unwelcome guests, the narrator offers a rhapsody on this behavior. "Oh, let us be thankful, not only for faces, but for masks! not only for honest welcomes, but for hypocrisy, which hides unwelcome things from us. . . . I say the humbug which I am performing is beautiful self-denial—that hypocrisy is true virtue. Oh, if every man spoke his mind, what an intolerable society ours would be to live in" (9:74–75).

Unlike Dickens, so eager to unmask the guilty, the foolish, and the hypocritical, Thackeray is absolutely terrified that the masks might be pulled away and that we will be obliged to gaze upon what is disclosed not only in others but in ourselves. The great pain is to be found out in our folly, hence masks and hypocrisy are blessings helping us to tolerate our neighbors and ourselves. Knowing that we are all weak sinners, we should also be prepared to pity our neighbor when he or she *is* found out in crime or folly. Hypocrisy and forgiveness are two facets of the same "virtue."

It is interesting that, as the novel focuses more and more on the cool, intellectual George, it begins to change its character, and eventually its very voice. The narrator's intrusions speak less and less about moral issues and more and more about the craft of writing. The real business of life is of small consequence to the novelist, he explains. Experiences of the battlefield, for example, are better left to historians like Carlyle (9:101; 9:136). Novelists are more interested in those left behind than in those who must fight (9:179). The narrator calls attention to his own text by quizzing his readers on the original from which he has borrowed the design for the initial letter that opens his chapter (9:156). Corresponding to this increased reference to the writer's craft is the development of George's vocation as a writer. George begins to associate with theater people, and composes a play of his own. It is a tragedy describing how the hero, Carpezan, joins invading Turkish forces to fight against his ruler, the King of Bohemia and Hungary, because the king seduced Carpezan's wife, whom the warrior then executed. Carpezan slays the king on the field of battle but is himself killed by Solyman the Turk. As he lies dying, Carpezan crawls toward an expiring opponent once his friend, kisses his hands, and gasps—"'Forgive me, Ulric'" (9:165). Within this novel of divided loyalties, contending kingdoms, and domestic antagonisms, George's tragedy offers an intensified version of similar issues, a version that ends with a plea for forgiveness, as Thackeray's own novel might be taken as a belated and muted plea for England to forgive the colonies that broke violently from their parent to establish their own separate existence.

The events of George's play are highly dramatic and crimes are committed all round, but Samuel Johnson, approving the play, comments on its moral quality.

> "I would have no play contrary to morals or religion: nor, as I conceive, is Mr. Warrington's piece otherwise than friendly to them. Vice is chastised, as it should be, even in kings, though perhaps we judge of their temptations too lightly. Revenge is punished—as not to be lightly exercised by our limited notion of justice. It may have been Carpezan's wife who perverted the King, and not the King who led the woman astray. At any rate, Louis is rightly humiliated for his crime, and the Renegade most justly executed for his." (9:167)

It would be possible to dismiss Johnson's remarks as the outmoded views of an earlier age, except that they fully endorse the program of Victorian expectations concerning what literature should accomplish. It may seem surprising that the unrelenting George should write a play stressing the importance of forgiveness, but during this part of the narrative a softening force is operating upon George, for he has fallen in love with Theo, who returns his affection. At this point George himself assumes the role of narrator.

George is writing in middle age, with a sarcastic manner muted by his affectionate relationship with his wife. He comments freely on his family, especially poking fun at his son Miles, who is interested chiefly in the sporting life and not in literary pursuits. For the most part, the tone of the novel changes very little with the new narrator, though the perspective does. George recounts the vicissitudes of his courtship of Theo. Madam Esmond interferes in a way that leads to a temporary separation of the lovers. George writes a stern letter of rebuke to his mother, who responds by placing the case before the tribunal of God, saying that she will abide by the consequences and hopes that George will do the same. The memory of his mother's response leads George to reflect how when "our pride, our avarice, our interest, our desire to domineer, are worked upon [we are] for ever pestering Heaven to decide in their favour." If the Americans won, were they right, and does that mean that a defeated Poland was wrong? George does not endorse such appeals and cannot believe that God meddles in human disputes.

> We appeal, we imprecate, we go down on our knees, we demand blessings, we shriek out for sentence according to law; the great course of the great world moves on; we pant and strive, and struggle; we hate; we rage; we weep passionate tears; we reconcile; we race and win; we race and lose; we pass away, and other little strugglers succeed; our days are spent; our night comes, and another morning rises, which shines on us no more. (9:322–23)

George and Theo take their destiny in their own hands and marry in secret, fearing that the Lambert family will leave for General Lambert's governorship of Jamaica before they can accomplish the deed any other way. They know that they and their abettors are guilty of offending the best of men. "The deed done, all we guilty ones grovelled in the earth, before the man we had injured. I pass over the scenes of forgiveness, of reconciliation, of common worship together, of final separation when the good man departed to his government, and the ship sailed away before us, leaving me and Theo on the shore" (9:334). With this direct admission of guilt and the model of forgiveness again presented to him by a noble and magnanimous gentleman, George's narrative begins to show more and more strands of punishment and forgiveness through its weave, though George's attitude is different from that of the previous narrator. That genial spirit had emphasized our need to forgive others, to withhold rash judgment, to consider what is common to all of us and to appreciate human weakness. George is no such softy. In an editorial note, the narrator declares himself not answerable for inconsistencies in George's narrative. George, the narrator observes, says that "he speaks 'without bitterness' of past times, and presently falls into a fury with them. The same manner of forgiving our enemies is not uncommon in the present century" (9:363). Here the implied author bluntly specifies George's unforgiving nature, a trait that has not left him since he let his mother's favorite teacup serve as a memorial of malevolence. George does not claim to be a forgiving sort. Thinking of the hardships of his early married life, he exclaims, "There are some acts of injustice committed against me which I don't know how to forgive; and which, whenever I think of them, awaken in me the same feelings of revolt and indignation. The gloom and darkness gather over me—till they are relieved by a reminiscence of that love and tenderness which through all gloom and darkness have been my light and consolation" (9:364). Without the kind of love and virtue represented in the mild Theo, what would have become of the saturnine George? He is an ordinary man of an age when men were more disposed to quarrel than to appease, more concerned with their honor than with their benignity. George is frank and assertive; the narrator cajoles. The one expects nothing of his readers, scarcely even that they should read; the other has designs on a clearly defined readership. In this difference, Thackeray exhibits two different character types as they address the same subject matter, but also two different social climates. A man of George's time could not afford to be as forgiving as the narrator might like, unless he was exceptionally sure of his own strength. George is not that exception. He freely admits to his pride. If he has committed a wrong, he says, he will ask pardon, but as something due to his own pride. He cannot imagine how men can live hypocritical lives and wonders if they wear masks for themselves in private as well. Unlike the narrator, who wryly praises hypocrisy, George despises anything devious and indirect.

> If I choose to pass over an injury, I fear 'tis not from a Christian and forgiving spirit: 'tis because I can afford to remit the debt, and disdain to ask a settlement of it. One or two sweet souls I have known in my life (and perhaps tried) to whom forgiveness is no trouble,—a plant that grows naturally, as it were, in the soil. I know how to remit, I say, not forgive. I wonder are we proud men proud of being proud? (9:399)

If George cannot easily forgive, he also dismisses the idea of a directly retributive providence in favor of a belief in punishment naturally following by cause and effect. When little Miles Warrington dies accidentally, Lady Warrington believes his death is a punishment for her worldly ambitions. And when Harry marries Fanny Mountain against his mother's wishes, Madam Esmond says, " 'I'm punished for my crime' " (9:396). But this arrogating of direct punishment to oneself is a grotesque form of vanity, supposing that the Almighty has singled out an individual for special regard—no matter that it is of a punitive nature. George regularly indicates his discomfort with such tracings out of God's purpose, making this discomfort precise when he discusses the consequences of the British practices during the war with the colonies. "But that I *dare* not (so to speak) be setting myself up as interpreter of Providence, and pointing out the special finger of Heaven (as many people are wont to do), I would say our employment of these Indians, and of the German mercenaries, brought their own retribution with them in this war" (9:453).

If George has his mother's pride and obstinacy, at least he has a self-knowledge that she lacks. When Mrs. Mountain, who has mortally offended Madam Esmond by assisting her daughter's marriage to Harry, asks for a deathbed interview, the stern Madam Esmond supposes that her former housekeeper wants "to pray my forgiveness for her treachery towards me." She explains, " 'I sent her word that I could forgive her *as a Christian,* and heartily hope (though I confess I doubt it) that she had a due sense of her crime towards me. But our meeting, I considered, was of no use, and could only occasion unpleasantness between us. If she repented, *though at the eleventh hour,* it was not too late, and I sincerely trusted that she was now doing so' " (9:408–9). Not surprisingly, Mrs. Mountain refuses further communication with her former friend, since the behavior of this supposedly religious woman is actually a deplorable example of how not to behave. Claiming to forgive as a Christian, Madam Esmond dwells on the continuing sinfulness of the sinner and stresses the injury to herself. This is no forgiveness at all, only verbal battering with "forgiveness" as the weapon. Through Theo's mediation, Madam Esmond also "forgives" Fanny by accepting her curtseying attentions. But George declares, "rather than be forgiven in that way, I own, for my part, that I would prefer perdition or utter persecution" (9:419). George shares his mother's pride but not her vanity. She cannot see through her own behavior to interpret it for what it is. In George's terms, she wears her mask in private, too. Though proud, George is at the same time humble in his refusal to see himself as a figure of special interest to the Divine. Though incapable of thorough forgiveness, and thus, in Thackeray's terms, something short of a Christian Hero, he has the sense to value this and other Christian virtues in Theo, and he has the understanding to beg forgiveness when he knows himself to be a transgressor. It is highly significant that his tragedy of Carpezan ends with the implied recognition that forgiveness is a higher act than revenge. The one nourishes the soul, the other consumes it. Johnson, as a literary critic, endorses the orderly morality of George's play, and George as narrator does not contradict him.

But there is a difference between life and the theater. If George can compose a tragedy with "correct" morality, achieving the same ends in an autobiography is not so easy. He is obliged to describe injustices and injuries that go unpunished and devotions that go unrewarded. And yet the presence of the first narrator reminds us that George's narrative is limited to his own angle of perception. The narrower the perspective of the narration, the less capable it seems of avoiding the coloring of its source. George's character is not overly sanguine and so his view of the world is jaundiced. By contrast, the more broadly informed and historically privileged first narrator can afford a more benign view of human existence. But then, he is not obliged to close the narrative he has begun. *The Virginians* is thus an experiment in the relationship of moral judgment to narration. Esmond was required to tell his story and give it shape at the same time, knowing that his version of the story must ever be open to question precisely because it is his story and takes its shades from his nature, which is so much kinder than that of his grandson George and therefore allows for so many more considerate exchanges among the characters who make up his cast. By writing in a posthumous mood, and using the third person to describe himself, Esmond conveys some sense of historical distance and detachment. *The Virginians* shows that such detachment must always be largely illusory no matter how meritorious the teller. The first narrator assumes the office of detached and privileged agent and allows George's voice freedom only after his own worldview is established. The two narrators perhaps come closest when the narrative touches upon the conflict between the new world and the old.

Pride, inconsiderateness, and injustice at the domestic and personal level are evident throughout the narrative of *The Virginians* and are especially prominent in

George's narrative. But these issues are magnified when they rise to the level of two nations in contention.[9] The impulsive and more innocent Harry sides with the Americans and George, prouder and colder and more intellectual, allies himself with England. But, writing long after the wars, George prefers not to assign blame. He allows that there was good and bad on both sides and that what stand one took was largely determined by established allegiances and interests. At this elevated level George is willing to forgive and forget, even if he was on the losing side. He is also able to mark out the figure of a truly great man who manifested the Christian attributes so sorely needed among mankind. Against his own prejudices George recognizes the splendor of Washington—"Washington inspiring order and spirit into troops hungry and in rags; stung by ingratitude, but betraying no anger and ever ready to forgive; in defeat invincible, magnanimous in conquest, and never so sublime as on that day when he laid down his victorious sword and sought his noble retirement:—here indeed is a character to admire and revere; a life without a stain, a fame without a flaw" (9:430–31).

The narrative describes the wartime adventures of Harry and George and praises Washington several more times, then ends rather tamely with Sampson assisting George to secure the American estates against any claim by Lord Castlewood. But the moral climax of the novel is George's praise of Washington, interesting as a fictional device because a fallible fictional character ends up praising a real, supposedly infallible man.[10] In a novel excusing the inferior morality of the past, a real man arises out of that "immoral" time as a model of human behavior. Devoted to a high cause, he places forgiveness over punishment and depends more upon affection than upon anger. That this model of virtue should also be an American carries an additional message to the British reader. If your enemy is forgiving and magnanimous in victory, cannot you be generous in defeat?

The narrator who begins the tale for us may seem to disappear from the narrative, but in a way he remains present, if only in footnote form. More broadly, his narrative *contains* George's narrative, just as it contains the other written documents that form the basis of his account. And it contains George's narrative in another way, for the long-gone, proud, and unforgiving George nonetheless leaves a testament of what the ideal man's behavior should be. Prominent in that behavior is the capacity to forgive. And in the narrator's encompassing narration it is this tendency toward compassion, forgiveness, and patient effort to understand and excuse that determines the casual flow of the narrative discourse. Also, in a novel that praises hypocrisy—or a judicious reticence—it is the narrator who describes secret behavior and hidden motives, whereas the first-person George, writing in a confessional journal, confesses nothing even as he asks, Does any man confess all? Indeed, at a point where George declares that he will make a clean breast of it, the editor/narrator informs us that three pages are torn out of the manuscript, reinforcing the notion that reticence, and even hypocrisy, as George himself half admits, may be the wiser mode (9:403–4).

There is no question but that *The Virginians* is a weaker novel than most, perhaps all, of Thackeray's mature works. But I suspect it is so because Thackeray was attempting a difficult narrative experiment. The divided narratives I have already discussed, but the issue of reticence can bear some attention. As we have seen in earlier chapters, Thackeray's narrator, while largely abandoning suspense as a literary strategy, does not give up curiosity. If he keeps secrets to a minimum, he continues to employ a narrative reticence, not offering information available to him until he feels it appropriate. The missing pages of George's manuscript may be akin to the narrator's closing the curtain on Clive's infatuation with an actress in *The Newcomes,* but there is what appears to me a significant and tantalizing difference. To begin with, it seems that George did inscribe his sins, though they were deleted later. Confession and honesty and truth seemed best. But who decided that they were not? If George himself, then he knows all the facts and chooses to withhold some. If Theo or some other, the motive might be to spare oneself, George, or the potential audience. This mutilated manuscript stands for the nature of reticence in the novel as a whole. The narrator has argued for the benefits of hypocrisy, but perhaps a significant weakness of the novel is that there is too little penetration of the masks, too much reticence. Other novels had scamps like Becky Sharp to puncture other people's pretences. *Esmond* had what I believe Thackeray meant to be an honest self-appraiser. But George does not fully fathom his own nature, nor does either narrator plumb the characters put before us. Lacking here is the narrative teasing that withheld information provides, as well as the delight of gradual disclosure. Like Hetty's undeclared love for Harry, much of the withheld information is guessable, but like Hetty's love, it ends in silence and stagnation. Disclosure and discovery are Thackeray's strengths, and *The Virginians* offers less of both than any of Thackeray's novels. We, as readers, have been so wholly taken into the secret that the only discoveries of significance are the ones we make about ourselves.[11] And, judging from responses to this novel over the years, they have not been memorable.

As I have already said, punishment and forgiveness are not central themes or dialectical or dialogic forces in *The Virginians* as they are in other Thackeray works, but the need to mute the former and promote the latter nonetheless leads to an intriguing narrative arrangement, a narrative experiment perhaps ineffective for Thackeray's contemporaries and for posterity, but nonetheless instructive of how much the need to make certain moral assertions clear could determine the manner in which Thackeray was willing to tell his stories.

NOTES

1. Robert A. Colby comments on the way critics complain about the dissipation of interest in *The Virginians* with the shift of narrative center from Harry to George in the midst of events, and with the change from omniscient to autobio-

graphical point of view (*Thackeray's Canvass of Humanity: An Author and His Public* [Columbus: Ohio State University Press, 1979], 406). Gordon N. Ray also considers the injudiciousness of starting with the more attractive Harry (*Thackeray: The Age of Wisdom 1847-1863* [London: Oxford University Press, 1958], 383). Subsequent references appear in the text.

2. Shlomith Rimmon-Kenan offers a summary statement of the relationship between these narrative stances. "Knowledge, conjecture, belief, memory—these are some of the terms of cognition. Conceived of in these terms, the opposition between external and internal focalization becomes that between unrestricted and restricted knowledge. In principle, the external focalizer (or narrator-focalizer) knows everything about the represented world, and when he restricts his knowledge, he does so out of rhetorical considerations (like the attempt to create an effect of surprise and shock in 'A Rose for Emily'). The knowledge of an internal focalizer, on the other hand, is restricted by definition: being a part of the represented world, he cannot know everything about it" (*Narrative Fiction: Contemporary Poetics* [London: Methuen, 1986], 79). But Mieke Bal indicates that there are complications in this simple narrative power relationship. Focalization is not as transparent as it seems. "Firstly, it appears that various focalization *levels* can be distinguished; secondly, where the *focalization level* is concerned, there is no fundamental difference between a 'first-person narrative' and a 'third-person narrative.' When EF seems to 'yield' focalization to a CF, what is really happening is that the vision of the CF is being given within the all-encompassing vision of the EF. In fact, the latter always keeps the focalization in which the focalization of a CF may be embedded as object" (*Narratology: Introduction to the Theory of Narrative*, trans. Christine van Boheemen [Toronto: University of Toronto Press, 1985], 111–12).

3. Janice Carlisle, *The Sense of an Audience: Dickens, Thackeray, and George Eliot at Mid-Century* (Athens: University of Georgia Press, 1981), 143.

4. Susanta Kuman Sinha, "Authorial Voice in Thackeray: A Reconsideration," *English Studies* 3 (June 1983), 233.

5. In his 1859 review of *The Virginians*, Goldwin Smith missed the significance of this point, objecting to Thackeray's exhuming the epoch of the early Georges because morally it is "the epoch which of all others might be advantageously left to its repose" (*Thackeray: The Critical Heritage*, ed. Geoffrey Tillotson and Donald Hawes [New York: Barnes & Noble, 1968], 289).

6. *The Works of William Makepeace Thackeray*, 26 vols. (Philadelphia: J. B. Lippincott Company, 1901), 8, 3. The narrator of *The Newcomes* makes similar admissions.

7. Ina Ferris sees *The Virginians* in dialogue with *Henry Esmond*: "*The Virginians* reinterprets Esmond's narrative with its affirmation of a self fulfilled through time and completed by the love of Rachel. Thackeray not only rewrites but rereads *Henry Esmond* in a sophisticated narrative strategy that sets the two texts in

play against each other" (*William Makepeace Thackeray* [Boston: Twayne Publishers, 1983], 106).

8. *The Poems of Tennyson,* ed. Christopher Ricks, 3 vols. (London: Longman, 1987), 3:289.

9. Gerald C. Sorenson notes that both American and British characters have counterbalancing faults and virtues ("Beginning and Ending: *The Virginians* as a Sequel," *Studies in the Novel* 13, nos. 1–2 [Spring-Summer 1981], 114–16). Since both sides are involved in what amounts to a family quarrel—both in the Esmond-Castlewood clan and in the England-colony relationship—forgiveness and understanding are especially important. Subsequent references appear in the text.

10. Robert A. Colby observes, however, that even the tribute paid to Washington in this novel emphasizes human failing (412). George's respect for Washington mirrors Esmond's for King William.

11. Sorensen concludes of the novel, "The re-creation of the past is, then, a means of understanding ourselves in relation to the time we have experienced, and also implicitly a means of evaluating, of placing in a 'right' order, or emphasis, those events that have touched us" (118).

TWENTY-FIVE

The Adventures of Philip

AS ITS FULL title suggests, *The Adventures of Philip on his way through the world shewing who robbed him, who helped him, and who passed him by* concentrates on a specific feature of the moral world. Because the novel is concerned primarily with charitable sentiments and acts in a world mainly insensitive and self-serving, there is far less in it about punishment and forgiveness than in any of the other substantial novels. In fact, it is almost as though Thackeray is consciously working against his usual concern for these central moral concepts. Perhaps he felt it was time to turn his attention to other issues, though in *Denis Duval* he was to return to his customary treatment of punishment and forgiveness in a livelier format than usual.

Thackeray seems, in *Philip*, to be attenuating his moral world as much as he can. Dr. Firmin is among the most wicked figures in the novel, but he is never utterly condemned by the narrative, no matter how much individual characters damn him. The admirable Dr. Goodenough loathes Firmin, a clear signal that we may be permitted to do so as well. Yet Pendennis, as narrator, remembers the Doctor's generosity to him when he was a boy, his genuinely gentlemanly manners, and—an important sign with Thackeray—his good dinners. Furthermore, though Philip begins young manhood at odds with his father for the Doctor's sins against Caroline Brandon, he forgives his father for economic and financial crimes against himself. The Doctor is clearly reprehensible, yet he is such a smooth rogue that he emerges, as the story develops, more as an amusing scoundrel than a convincing demon. In some ways, he even parodies the figure of the self-punishing scamp.[1]

But Dr. Firmin, and many other characters in *Philip*, are too complicated or contradictory to be so facilely categorized. Juliet McMaster argues that *Philip's* interest is weighted toward psychology rather than social progress.[2] Another way to say the same thing is to suggest that Thackeray is less interested in plot than in character. Going a step further, we might consider that by concentrating upon the elaboration of character Thackeray is experimenting with a means of diminishing the force of linear plot, of testing fiction's power to be effective without dependence upon story making. In *The Genesis of Secrecy,* Frank Kermode argues that "The more elaborate the story grows—the more remote from its schematic base—the more these agents [of fable] will deviate from type and come to look like 'characters.' "[3] If the elaboration of narrative, or *sjuzet,* of the paradigm, or *fabula,* converts agents of narrative into characters, how much more do elaborated characters obliterate the schemata of plots as, in their representations of human psychology, they more and more blur the simple moral outlines originating in fable or parable. Thackeray specifically called attention to how far his characters and plots in *The Newcomes* departed from the simple old moral fables, and yet at the same time reminded us that, if we wish to support morality, we are obliged to retell the same old stories. If in the title for his novel Thackeray wishes to identify his rudimentary fable, in the working out of his narrative he self-consciously delays the operations of plot and favors the exposition of character.

The early part of *Philip* suggests a very rough parallel with *Little Dorrit,* introducing a son who feels that some evil moral debt burdens his parent. It takes the entire narrative of *Little Dorrit* before Arthur Clennam fully understands the crime his mother has committed. Philip, on the other hand, knows the skeleton in his father's closet from very early on. Though he claims often enough to eschew the novelist's tricks, Pendennis is very slow in answering his own question: What skeleton was there in Dr. Firmin's closet? He nonetheless supplies enough clues for an astute reader to guess that Firmin's chief skeleton is his false marriage to Caroline Gann, now a nurse known as the Little Sister, who goes by the name Caroline Brandon. The unfinished novel entitled *A Shabby Genteel Story* was an account of this love relationship. Pendennis eventually shares the necessary information about this family sin, which Philip tries to alleviate by befriending Caroline Brandon, just as Arthur Clennam unconsciously palliates his mother's crime by his kindly treatment of the Dorrits. But whereas Dickens sees to it that Mrs. Clennam is punished in her way and Mr. Dorrit in his for their different moral lapses, Thackeray allows Dr. Firmin to survive his fall morally unredeemed, and Caroline Brandon, though no saint, to be elevated above the normal level of approval among Thackeray's characters. Pendennis actually calls attention to his own restraint in passing judgment. In chapter 5, when he is still teasing us with the question of why Philip was in revolt against his father, Pen reflects that if we knew all the facts in a case, we would probably judge others differently, and worries that he might be painting Dr. Firmin too black.[4] Pendennis is here trying to follow Thackeray's injunction about the proper behavior of novelists toward the beings they create. Of Charlotte Brontë, Thackeray wrote to Mary Holmes: "I think Miss Bronte is unhappy and that makes her unjust. Novel writers should not be in a passion with their characters as I imagine, but describe them good or bad, with a like calm."[5] As though to highlight Pendennis' tolerant position, Thackeray makes the central character of his novel weak in precisely this regard. One of Philip's chief faults is that he is judgmental. Trustful until betrayed, he then becomes completely mistrustful. Hating hypocrisy, he goes to the opposite extreme of being too blunt. Pendennis pauses after this account of his friend's failings to adddress the reader directly. "My dear young friend, the profitable way is the middle way. Don't quite believe anybody, for he may mislead you; neither disbelieve him, for that is uncomplimentary to your friend. Black is not so very black; and as for white, *bon Dieu!* in our climate what paint will remain white long?" (10:199).

I believe that Thackeray was consciously writing against convention in *Philip,* but, as Peter Rabinowitz observes, "No matter how much a writer wishes to play with conventions . . . he or she can do so only if the readers share those conventions to begin with. Indeed, the more a writer wishes to undermine tradition, the more imperative it is that the tradition be understood to begin with."[6] In a novel explicitly calling attention to Christ's parable of the good samaritan, traditions concerning charitable behavior are likely to be prominent. And, though the world represented by the implied author is peopled chiefly by rogues, Pendennis may still behave like a Christian and treat them charitably. Thinking particularly of Dr. Firmin, Robert A. Colby says that "in his continuous probing of the 'refinement' of crime, Thackeray progressed from verdicts of outright guilt to those of 'not proven.'"[7]

One convention that Thackeray shared with other novelists of his time is what I have called therapeutic punishment, in which a character suffers some form of retributive pain or disadvantage for his or her behavior, leading to a reformation of character or a later access of good fortune. Such punishments, usually a form of benevolent narrative correction arranged for by the implied author's moral scheme, serve to strengthen good characters and to reform less virtuous ones. In *Philip,* Philip's loss of fortune might be viewed as a version of this device except that it is difficult to attribute the loss to any action of his own. Moreover, the full title of the novel suggests a different moral reading of the plot and encourages us to view Philip, with all his admitted faults, as a victim of the actions of others—he is the traveler fallen among thieves.

The great opportunity for Thackeray to utilize therapeutic punishment in this novel is with Dr. Firmin, but he resolutely refuses to have the old leopard change his spots, and instead increases his burden of guilt by having him outrageously claim to be a victim himself, most atrociously when he suggests that he has been ruined by the excesses of the son he has so blatantly robbed and defrauded. Thackeray seems thus to be consciously writing against convention, not only by not having Dr. Firmin reform his character after his fall, but by having him become insidiously worse by his assuming an air of plausible gentility in New York while continuing to draw upon his son's slender resources, ultimately through outright forgery. But Philip himself feels that his father has paid his debt by being outcast from home and respectability, and says he is no longer angry with him because he has suffered enough (10:392). Pendennis, too, forbears to abuse the Doctor, saying that even in his financial collapse the wily fellow managed to rescue as much as possible from his creditors, thus conceding that we cannot really change our character. "All is vanity, look you," he says; "and so the preacher is vanity, too" (10:331).

If Dr. Firmin's ruin is not a form of therapeutic punishment, neither is it the implied author's opportunity for a narrative punishment by which sin is chastened through plotting. The narrative instead emphasizes that what happens to Dr. Firmin is a natural retribution for an incautious way of life. No matter how little it serves to alter his behavior, it is readable as a punishment for his sins and a payment of his moral as well as pecuniary debts. If his breastbeating here rings false, and his shifting of blame for his circumstances off his own shoulders and onto the operations of an evil fate remains unconvincing, there is one area where Dr. Firmin feels an authentic pang of guilt, if for the most selfish reasons, and this guilt, has to do with his treatment of Caroline Brandon and its consequences for his later life.

We have already seen that it is knowledge of Dr. Firmin's false marriage to Caroline that estranges Philip from his father, and Dr. Firmin genuinely suffers from this deep division between himself and his son. Moreover, his guilty secret makes him vulnerable to blackmail by the Reverend Tufton Hunt. Pendennis tells us that Dr. Firmin feels shame and remorse at the alienation from his son and humiliation at having to lie to Caroline. Knowing himself guilty of a crime against her, he reasonably fears that she might claim legal marriage to him as a means of punishment. To forestall such an act, Dr. Firmin exploits Caroline's affection for Philip. If she claimed marriage, she would make Philip a bastard. Dr. Firmin confesses to Caroline that his money has been lost in financial speculations and he avers that this bad luck is a punishment for his treatment of her. Whether he believes this or not, he facilely uses the language of moral debt and payment to avoid further claims.

Pendennis says it would truly be a punishment for Dr. Firmin if he were now forced to acknowledge Caroline as his real wife, but the suffering the Doctor feels is chiefly the pain of exposure. "'You think about your wrong now it may be found out, I dare say!'" Caroline exclaims in disgust (10:269). But, as we have seen time and again, the fear of being found out in our guilt and our shame is, for Thackeray, itself a punishment for that guilt and shame, second only to actual public exposure. No further punishment is necessary in his code, especially since Thackeray doubted that sinners were capable of much improvement on their own. Dr. Firmin mouths the usual appeals for heaven to forgive him in his repentant mood, but he is motivated by fear and selfishness. By forgiving Dr. Firmin for abandoning her and by deceiving those who wish to prove Philip a bastard through her claim that she knew her marriage was a sham, Caroline earns the right to heap coals on her erstwhile lover and reveal his turpitude to him.

Dr. Firmin is, therefore, punished for his original crime against Caroline, and for his reckless waste of his own and Philip's fortunes. But these punishments are the natural consequences of folly, not corrective measures employed by an implied author to warn his readers off similar courses. Indeed, so futile does such an effort seem to Pendennis, that he openly asserts his sympathy for Dr. Firmin, declaring that justice should not have brought such a heavy judgment upon him; there is, of course, more than a touch of irony in this "softness" (10:272). He goes on to wish that we could all take the punishment for our crimes on our own shoulders and not make others suffer. And perhaps this is the key notion about punishment in this novel—that the crimes we commit may bring punishment in their wake, a punishment that all too often reaches beyond the perpetrator of the crime to those who are entirely innocent and sometimes even unrelated to the original offense. Even if it is well that the wicked man be punished for his dereliction, what of the man's wife and her poor babes!

The retribution that Dr. Firmin suffers is the chief instance of punishment in Volume One of *Philip,* and it is deeply involved with secrecy. Secrecy, here as elsewhere, does not necessarily include suspense. Pendennis explicitly eschews the use of suspense. As early as the second chapter he explains that Philip is now a prosperous, mature fellow with boys of his own. He will not, we are reassured, die of consumption or blow his brains out from despair at the end of this memoir. "No, no; we will have no dismal endings" (10:132). This is only the first of several such reassurances serving to direct our curiosity not to Philip's ultimate fate, but only to the circumstances of his difficult years. The implied author does not want us to be lured through the promise of an attractive mystery solved at the narrative's conclusion; instead he wants us to loiter through the narrative, enjoying its various incidentals along the way.

Just as the narrative makes little use of the larger devices of mystery and suspense to hold attention, it also abjures ambivalence about its central characters. In the second chapter of the novel, Pendennis reports that even as a boy visiting the Firmin household he was aware of Dr. Firmin's and Mrs. Firmin's faults, but he nonetheless acknowledges that they were kind to him. Pendennis wants his account of the past to be as balanced as possible, knowing that in recording the life of his friend Philip, he is likely to be biased in his favor. Thus Pendennis informs us that, as a boy, he came vaguely to discern that the Doctor was "an old humbug," whereas, given the Doctor's later behavior, he could easily be called something far worse (10:140). The point, however, is that we see from the start that the Doctor is a morally flawed, untrustworthy figure.

This directness in the presentation of character is not of the same order as that of other novels of the time where, with the first presentation, characters are fixed permanently in a moral or social structure and their future behavior made almost entirely predictable. Take Disraeli's description of Coningsby as a young man. A lovely woodland scene, we are told, "had fallen on a heart still pure and innocent, the heart of one who, notwithstanding all his high resolves and daring thoughts, was blessed with that tenderness of soul which is sometimes linked with an ardent imagination and a strong will."[8] There is certainly no mystery here. The narrator has opened Coningsby's nature to us and certified him as an admirable type. Each trait so presented will not change. Disraeli's characters *fulfill* their natures in the actions of the plot. But in *Philip* we are warned by the narrator himself that his moral judgments may be incorrect. He does not disguise his opinions of the characters he describes, but the only inevitability in their destinies stems from the fact that the story is being told from a chronological standpoint after all of its events have taken place. Because this is so, Pendennis has access to the secrets of his characters' motives.

Since Dr. Firmin is presented as flawed from the outset, it is reasonable to assume that he has erred at some point in his past career. Thus chapter 3 begins, "Should I peer into Firmin's privacy, and find the key to that secret? What skeleton was there in the closet?" (10:142). The skeleton, as we have already noted, is Caroline Brandon. The implied author here makes the narrative decision not to withhold this secret but to lay it out immediately, because it is not the pursuit of a mystery by which Thackeray means to enchant us, but the workings-out of the consequences of human actions. So we are told the events of *A Shabby Genteel Story* and the subsequent history of Caroline Brandon, who encounters her betrayer again, coincidentally, at the sickbed of his son. We later learn that Philip's alienation from his father dates from the episode of this illness, and it is not long before Pendennis reveals that Philip prevented his father from marrying again after the death of Philip's mother by telling him that he knew of the obligation to Caroline Brandon.

The great secret of Volume One is out of the closet very quickly. To make the revelations more credible, Pendennis calls attention to his own manner of narrating. To his readers Thackeray was the author of a novel entitled *Philip*, narrated by the created character, Arthur Pendennis, but Pendennis' story is supposedly a veracious memoir of his real-life friend Philp Firmin. Thus Pendennis is at pains to explain the sources for his text.

> I could not, of course, be present at many of the scenes which I shall have to relate as though I had witnessed them; and the posture, language, and inward thoughts of Philip and his friends, as here related, no doubt are fancies of the narrator in many cases; but the story is as authentic as many histories, and the reader need only give such an amount of credence to it as he may judge that its verisimilitude warrants. (10:146)

Later, admitting that most people's stories are compounds of truth and lies, though we all insist that our own are not subject to contradiction, Pendennis archly assumes "the character of infallible historian" (10:164). This is simply a complicated and playful way for Thackeray to remind us that what we call histories are themselves constructs, composed by historians out of fact ("truth") and speculation ("lies"). Again and again Thackeray claimed that novels could be as *truthful* as histories—truthful to human experience, that is. Miss Tickletoby refuses to report Queen Boadicea's speech to her troops before they go into action, "because, although several reports of that oration have been handed down to us, not one of them, as I take it, is correct, and what is the use, my darlings, of reporting words (hers were very abusive against the Romans)—of reporting words that were never uttered?" (26:18).

The upshot of this characteristic Thackerayan approach is that readers are both to disbelieve the persons and events in the text and to accept them as authentic representations of life. The openness with which secrets are disclosed, the refusal to employ suspense, the acknowledgement of decent qualities in offensive people and offensive qualities in decent people (notably Philip himself), are meant to evoke a sense of real-world experience. Insofar as punishment is concerned, that means repudiating melodrama and other unlikely manifestations of retribution in this world. Characters bring their own sufferings upon themselves to a very great degree; the rest may be assigned to providence or fate, just as good fortune might, but Thackeray is reluctant to play the role of providence and use his narrative as a punitive tool. Pendennis offers the Twysden family as an example of how most people invite retribution. Talbot Twysden is proud of the dinners he gives but which others consider notoriously bad; the whole family looks down on all those beneath them and truckles to their superiors. They are particularly cringing to their relative Lord Ringwood, from whom they hope for some advantage. Pendennis cannot resist some lively metaphors to distinguish the nature of this relationship.

> When old Ringwood, at the close of his lifetime, used to come to visit his dear niece and her husband and children, he always brought a cat-o'-nine-tails in his pocket, and administered it to the whole household. He grinned at the poverty, the pretence, the meanness of the people, as they knelt before him and did him homage. The father and mother trembling brought the girls up for punishment, and, piteously smiling, received their own boxes on the ear in presence of their children (10:155).[9]

We will briefly examine the Twysdens again later, but this passage epitomizes their role in the novel.

If the disgrace and discomfort visited upon a commonplace hypocrite and cheat, presented in the low-keyed tone of a man of the world, comprises the central experience of punishment in Volume One of *Philip,* that experience is still more complicated in Volume Two. The basic template of this novel casts Philip

Firmin in the role of the man fallen among thieves, but it must also be acknowledged that he and his friends often exacerbate his situation. Philip suffers two
great losses in Volume One of the novel (he scarcely notices the passing of his
mother) that are not the results of his own behavior. The first is his father's de-
falcation and the consequent loss of Philip's fortune, a misfortune that he bears
with remarkable *sangfroid*. The second is the romantic loss of his cousin Agnes
Twysden to a rival suitor, an event that produces a more powerful effect on the
young man. His reactions to these personal disasters show Philip to be a right-
minded man in Thackeray's world—he values human affection, truth, and honesty and he is indifferent to material comforts when they are taken away. But his
good attributes are related to his faults. If he is affectionate, he is also quickly
aroused to indignation and anger; if he is honest and truthful, he is also inclined
to rude and blunt speech. What he lacks most of all is tact in all of its varieties.

Volume Two begins with a description of Mrs. General Baynes' growing dislike for Philip and an emphasis upon his rude and direct behavior. His friends,
including Pendennis, caution him about his planned marriage to Charlotte
Baynes—the young couple would have a palsied income and Philip would acquire a rebarbative mother-in-law. His friends also urge Philip to cultivate Lord
Ringwood, who could assist him to some good employment if he chose. Philip
follows this latter advice, but as luck will have it, he attends upon his influential
relative on a day when the old man is suffering an attack of gout. He berates
Philip for his engagement to a poor girl, who, he supposes, is marrying Philip in
anticipation of money from Lord Ringwood himself. The exchange becomes
heated, and the two proud and headstrong relatives separate in anger. The outlook is not good for Philip, since "all the world knew what a man Lord Ringwood was—how arbitrary, how revengeful, how cruel!" (11:37). There is no
opportunity to test the extent of that cruelty, however, because Lord Ringwood
dies suddenly soon after. It turns out that he has left nothing for Philip in his will,
and so the young man's expectations in that direction are squelched.

An interesting thing happens in the narration at this point. Pendennis, who
was a principal instigator of Philip's visit to Lord Ringwood, now passes a severe
judgment on himself. Learning from lawyer Bradgate that Lord Ringwood had
arranged a handsome legacy in the will that he apparently destroyed after Philip's untimely visit, Pendennis blames himself. "And who sent Philip to see his
relative in that unlucky fit of gout? Who was so worldly wise—so Twysden-like,
to counsel Philip to flattery and submission? But for that advice he might be
wealthy now; he might be happy; he might be ready to marry his young sweet-
heart" (11:43). The story did not require that Pendennis be the unfortunate ora-
cle that sent Philip to an evil fate, but this fault in Pendennis helps to put the
narrative itself in a different perspective. One who plans to tell the unvarnished
truth about others must needs have a clear appreciation of the strengths and
weaknesses of his or her own character. Pendennis must not appear so free from
faults himself that he seems condescending toward his subject. Pendennis is not a

hagiographer, as he states in the very next chapter. "The describer and biographer of my friend Philip Firmin has tried to extenuate nothing; and, I hope, has set down naught in malice" (11:52). He has not disguised Philip's bad points, for example, and certainly has not minimized his rudeness. "He was often haughty and arrogant: he was impatient of old stories: he was intolerant of commonplaces" (11:52). But if Philip was no hero and had his faults like all of us, Pendennis included, then why does Pendennis suppose the story of his life is worth telling? Philip, as far as the narrative goes, achieves no great aim in life. He has no profession and never gets beyond hack writing. He is not a successful novelist like Pendennis, or an artist like J. J. Ridley. Then why should we be interested in his life?

The answer seems to be that we should not. We are interested instead in the adventures of an individual who moves through a certain kind of society, and in what it takes—morally, not financially—to survive in that society. Hence, once more, the parabolic design underlying Philip's "adventures," surely some of the blandest "adventures" ever recorded for a "hero" in fiction. And because Thackeray has this purpose in mind with his novel, he has Pendennis pause again to assure us that all will be well, and that he is not employing the usual novelistic tricks of secrecy and suspense. "I hope Philip and his wife will be Darby and Joan to the end. I tell you they are married; and don't want to make any mysteries about the business. I disdain that sort of artifice" (11:55). *That* kind of artifice, yes—but there are other kinds.

Pendennis warns us that we are now approaching the bad part of this history but comforts us by saying that it will be short. Pendennis might better have said this was *one* bad part of Philip's history, but what he is specifically referring to here is Philip's temporary separation from Charlotte. Typically, this agonizing episode is precipitated by one of Philip's own impulsive acts. Shabby as his old clothes are, Philip nonetheless decides to attend Lord Estridge's party for the respectable English families in Paris. Ringwood Twysden and his dancing partner collide with Philip and spoil his clothes to such an extent that he decides he is no longer presentable. As he is leaving, he overhears young Twysden boasting that he intentionally caused the collision; Philip kicks his relative into an illuminated fountain where he is scalded by burning oil and cut by fractured glass. Charlotte's parents use this "lamentable fracas" as an excuse for dissolving the engagement between the two young people. Thus Volume Two promptly imitates Volume One by depriving Philip of a fortune (but now partly through his own crustiness), and of his love object (but now through his own anti-social behavior). Also, whereas in Volume One Philip was mainly passive as a moral agent, in Volume Two he has become active, as his revenge upon Ringwood Twysden signifies.

Philip is unlike most of Thackeray's male protagonists, who are, like those of Dickens, reluctant to take judgment into their own hands. But I believe Philip is consciously made to differ from the Dobbinses, Pendennises, Clive Newcomes,

Henry Esmonds, and even Denis Duvals. He lacks their finer attributes and he lacks their patience. He is like us, for aren't we, too, impatient of old stories, easily bored by self-important acquaintances, and quick to seek punishment for those who intentionally do us harm? So yes, it would be better to show some tact in attending to the old anecdotes, and not yawn at those next to us at table, and hold our hand (and our foot) when we feel the impulse to deal out summary justice, but we are not all made that way. If Esmond was Thackeray's chief presentation of a good man—and despite Juliet McMaster's argument, I think he is—then Philip is his chief presentation of the ordinary man, and *that* is why his story is worth telling. In *Vanity Fair* people play out their roles in that worldly bazaar, but *Philip* takes place on the road from Jerusalem to Jericho. And it is not by chance that Pendennis is the narrator of this age-old narrative, for he too had his trials when he was young and thus understands that in human society, help for the victims of its thieves is likely to come from those who have themselves encountered misfortune on the way. As Pendennis remarks, when Madam Smolenski, the kindly lodgings-keeper, aids the separated young lovers by serving as a go-between, "The Samaritan who rescues you, most likely, has been robbed and has bled in his day, and it is a wounded arm that bandages yours when bleeding" (11:97).

Up until now, *Philip* has had little to say about forgiveness, except that Philip forgives his father's crime against him just as the Little Sister forgave the Doctor's crime against her. But now a complex pattern dealing with forgiveness develops. General Baynes, a good though henpecked man, allows his wife to involve him in the scheme to end Charlotte's engagement to Philip. Stubbornly he adheres to his position, though both of his old military friends, Colonel Bunch and Major MacWhirter, argue that he is behaving ignobly. Finally, after the threat of a duel and the loss of his friends, General Baynes is convinced of his error and changes his ground, much to his wife's chagrin. The night of the General's repentance neither of Charlotte's parents can sleep. "Baulked revenge and hungry disappointment, I think, are keeping the old woman awake," says Pendennis. The "old man is awake, because he is awake to the shabbiness of his own conduct" (11:135). There is no doubt here that the implied author, through Pendennis, is passing judgment on the Bayneses. Pendennis almost gloats, remarking of the General, "He is wrung with remorse, and shame and pity. Well, I am glad of it" (11:136). He is glad not out of a desire for revenge, but because to feel remorse is to make the first step toward a new course of behavior.

The very next day the General shows his new colors. He takes Emily MacWhirter out to buy her a bonnet—a symbol of his gratitude for her standing by Charlotte, while pointedly ignoring his own wife. There follows a reconciliation between father and daughter. "He would never do anything to give her pain, never! She had been his good girl, and his blessing, all his life! Ah! that is a prettier little picture to imagine—that repentant man, and his child clinging to him—than the tableau overhead, viz., Mrs. Baynes looking at her old bonnet" (11:141).

Charlotte's "soft tremulous smiles and twinkling dew-drops of compassion and forgiveness" for her father are replaced by flashing glances when her mother comes to her (11:141). Mrs. Baynes has not repented for her behavior and she is not forgiven, but she realizes she is beaten.

Charlotte travels to Tours in the care of the MacWhirters and the courtship continues by mail. Meanwhile, the General remains cool to his wife, who has caused him to besmirch his honor. He becomes ill and blames the illness on his wife, "and at other times said it was a just punishment for his wicked conduct in breaking his word to Philip and Charlotte" (11:165). The General may seem like an incidental figure, but this episode is significant in the moral structure of Thackeray's novel, and for this reason he employs a deathbed scene (a strong weapon in the Victorian novelist's arsenal) to engrave its meaning on the reader's memory. Charlotte returns to Paris to be with her failing parent. On his deathbed the General blesses Charlotte and Philip.

> The poor man laid the hands of the young people together, and his own upon them. The suffering to which he had put his daughter seemed to be the crime which specially affected him. He thanked Heaven he was able to see he was wrong. He whispered to his little maid a prayer for pardon in one or two words, which caused poor Charlotte to sink on her knees and cover his fevered hand with tears and kisses. Out of all her heart she forgave him. She had felt that the parent she loved and was accustomed to honour had been mercenary and cruel. It had wounded her pure heart to be obliged to think that her father could be other than generous, and just, and good. That he should humble himself before her, smote her with the keenest pang of tender commiseration. I do not care to pursue this last scene. Let us close the door as the children kneel by the sufferer's bedside, and to the old man's petition for forgiveness, and to the young girl's sobbing vows of love and fondness, say a reverent Amen. (11:165–66)

The General has repented and is forgiven, but his widow considers herself the injured party by Charlotte and Philip, "and thus neither side forgave the other" (11:171). Charlotte, we are told, "could be resolutely unforgiving" (11:170). Later, after Charlotte and Philip are married, the bride writes to the Pendennises, revealing, in a somewhat confused passage, how strong her emotions on this subject still are. "I bear no malice. I will do no injury. But I can never forgive: never! I can forgive Mamma, who made my husband so unhappy; but can I love her again?" (11:214–15).

If it is clearly the case that forgiveness is best and that in most of Thackeray's writing this message comes through clearly, why does he not insist on it from his good characters here? When Laura considers the additional suffering Dr. Firmin is occasioning for Philip, she urges him, " 'Be generous: be forgiving: be noble: be Christian! Don't be cynical, and imitating—you know whom!' " (11:173). She means Pendennis. Laura is frequently taken to be Thackeray's spokesperson for good sentiments, and so it is reasonable to consider that she here offers advice that he would endorse.[10] But it is also necessary to keep in mind another mode of thinking about forgiveness in nineteenth-century England. As we noted in chapter 1, one view asserted that real forgiveness had to follow upon repentance. Ruskin, for example, argued that the repentant sinner is then reinstated in the same moral position he or she held before the offense. Others argued that human beings might pardon, but only God could forgive. Perhaps the crucial point is that forgiveness is not required of a good Christian when repentance is lacking. We may turn the other cheek and offer meekness in return for injury, but that does not necessarily mean that we have *forgiven* the injury.

As so often in Thackeray, there are several ways to view this issue. The implied author of *Philip* clearly approves General Baynes' repentance and Charlotte's forgiveness of him—a sequence presented as a set piece and evoking the far more memorable fall, repentance, forgiveness, and death of Colonel Newcome. So forgiving the repentant sinner is good. Similarly, when the new Lord Ringwood, to whom the Twysdens have systematically calumniated Philip, learns from Mr. Tregarvan, Philip's patron, that Philip has not only forgiven his father but assisted him financially, he is deeply impressed and decides to foster Philip's acquaintance. From this point of view, forgiving can be a tactical social move, whether profoundly felt or simply a means of establishing a good reputation. Philip, of course, is sincere. But forgiveness may also be a handicap if it encourages the offender in his improprieties. Pendennis is appalled that Philip is prepared to acknowledge a forged bill that Doctor Firmin has drawn on his name. But Laura, true to form, takes Philip's side. "She was very much moved at his announcement that he would forgive his father this once at least, and endeavour to cover his sin." Using the standard intimidation, Laura says, " 'As you hope to be forgiven yourself, dear Philip, I am sure you are doing right' " (11:292).

But simple forgiveness may not always be the answer when the sinner is not only unrepentant, but entangled in a web of affairs that will nourish continued sinning. Accordingly, the implied author here employs a moral agent who is willing to get her hands dirty to do good. Doctor Firmin's forged bill reaches England in the hands of the disreputable Reverend Tufton Hunt. Realizing that Hunt means harm to Philip, Caroline Brandon lies to him, saying she is now on unfriendly terms with the Firmins. Caroline realizes that Hunt is "all intent on drink, on vanity, on revenge" and so she acts to prevent him, stunning him with chloroform and then burning the bill that he has shown her (11:302). Though Pendennis is "not about to endeavor to excuse" her for telling these "fibs," he also does not condemn her (11:291). The morally righteous and kindly Dr. Goodenough openly admires her for this conduct. When Hunt returns, claiming he has been robbed, the police officer he calls to his assistance does not believe him, and later a magistrate throws out Hunt's charges when Philip honestly testifies that he never signed the bill.

The Little Sister's illegal actions—starting with lies (not the "fibs" that Pendennis calls them) and progressing to drugging and theft—accomplish at least two good ends. They prevent Hunt from getting money from Philip and they end Dr. Firmin's depredations upon his son. Although Philip was prepared to spare his father by honoring the false bill, after the bill is destroyed he can safely send a signal by openly testifying that he did not sign it. The Doctor gets the message.

But another interesting narrative wrinkle arises out of the moral complications of this incident. Most of the good characters are powerless to shield Philip from the injury he is unwilling to spare himself at his father's expense. Caroline Brandon can and does spare him. Her impulse is to prevent an act of cruelty and revenge, not to punish Hunt, though she has every reason to punish the man who engineered her false marriage to Firmin. The *effect* of her action is to deal Hunt a punishing blow, but its *intent* is to shield the man she sees as her son. The implied author thus keeps Caroline's motives pure while he satisfies the moral sense that wants this wretched blackmailer to get what he deserves.

Laura's advice may generally be trusted as the best. We have heard this advice from Thackeray himself and from his various agents: If you hope for forgiveness yourself, try to forgive those who trespass against you. But unlike Dickens, who carefully keeps his paragons and their closest allies free from crude retributive behavior, Thackeray, in his relenting style, allows exceptions. If evil is to be held in check, perhaps it is necessary sometimes to forestall it by action and to forgive afterward, if that is possible. And perhaps this is why Philip, a good but imperfect character, is allowed to punish directly as most of Thackeray's adult heroes are not. He is one of the few good adults who has the same license to strike out that Thackeray grants to his schoolboy champions. Thus, when Philip kicks Ringwood Twysden into the fountain, Colonel Bunch, Major MacWhirter, and Doctor Martin all agree that such an action is consistent with a man's honor, given the provocation. Similarly, Philip kicks Hunt out of Caroline's house when he becomes offensive, and later the usually pacific Pendennis exclaims of the action, "Never was kicking more righteously administered than that which Philip once bestowed on this miscreant" (11:287).

Philip seems consciously to reduce to a very low level of intensity the significance Thackeray has attributed to punishment and forgiveness in most of his fiction. In this regard it approaches the less moralistic early writings, which used the crude device of narrative punishment because so many of them were satirical and had specific targets in mind. There is direct satire in *Philip*, too, as we shall see. But first it is worth commenting on a motif in Thackeray's mature fiction that is profoundly related to the subject of punishment and forgiveness. I have already referred to Hayden White's observation that records of events, once they move from annal and chronicle to narrated history, inevitably become freighted with some form of morality.[11] Because the narrative is now going somewhere, an endpoint or destination becomes necessary. Knowing the destination determines how the narrative must be assembled to explain the arrival at that particular destination. Depending upon the perspective of the narrator, the nature of the narrative may differ, even if the destination remains the same. Thus the Egyptians and the Israelites would be likely to tell different stories about the deliverance of the Jews, though both might agree that Moses and his followers left Egypt. Thackeray has a strong awareness of this insight, and more than once admits that if someone else told the story he is telling, that narrator might produce a very different account, even to the point where moral judgments, and hence worth and worthlessness, and hence punishment, reward, or pardon, might be reversed. But there is a peculiar new touch to the expression of this attitude in *Philip*.

Near the end of the novel, Pendennis is bringing Philip's bad days to a close in preparation for "The Realms of Bliss" (the title of chapter 23 of the second volume) that are to come. Having noted that there were some people Philip could not bring himself to forgive, Pendennis adds a remark on his own effort. "People there are in our history who do not seem to me to have kindly hearts at all; and yet perhaps, if a biography could be written from their point of view, some other novelist might show how Philip and *his* biographer were a pair of selfish worldlings unworthy of credit: how Uncle and Aunt Twysden were most exemplary people, and so forth" (11:349). The odd feature of this passage is that the terms *history, biography,* and *novelist* are used to refer to the text and its producer. I have commented earlier on Thackeray's scepticism about the accuracy of history, but here it seems clear that any kind of narrative record, whether factual accounts of ancient history, biographies of contemporaries, or fictional tales of past or present times, all share the indeterminacy caused by the existence of a narrator who cannot tell all the truth because he or she, even with the best intentions, cannot escape his or her ingrained manner of apprehending experience, or his or her particular prejudices.

In this novel Thackeray seems to be resisting his own predilections. An interesting instance of this is Agnes Twysden. Agnes obviously behaves badly by encouraging Philip's affections and then throwing him over for the wealthy Woolcomb. She commits one of the most serious treasons in Thackeray's catalog—she sells herself on the marriage market—prostitutes herself. She deserves to be punished. Laura reasonably argues that Agnes was brought up among mercenary people and learned the lesson from her own parents. This was the very argument Pendennis offered to modify judgment on Ethel Newcome, who was also putting herself on the block, ticketed for sale. But Pendennis will not accept this argument now, contending that there is no reason to stop with the Twysdens when blame could be assigned all the way back to William the Conqueror. Laura replies that human sin began at the beginning, and hopes that poor Agnes will find refuge from it and learn to repent. But Pendennis is adamant. "She knew quite well to whom she was selling herself, and for what" (11:329). Nor does he pity her later questionable career spent among "fogeys, rattling bachelors, and doubtful ladies," where she is unhappy—not because she is separated from her children or her family, whom she never loved, but because she is losing her looks

(11:330). Her choice has led Agnes to a purgatorial existence, according to Pendennis, and through his judgment the implied author provides us with a narrative punishment for this sinful woman. He does something similar with Woolcomb, the other party to this miserable marriage. "Did he not spend a great part of his fortune for the possession of this cold wife?" (11:330).

And yet the unpleasant people in the novel, seen from a slightly different perspective, go unpunished. After all, Agnes lives on in comfort if not in social respectability, and Woolcomb, though disappointed in his marriage, increases in power, successfully defeating a better man for a parliamentary seat. And the off-putting Philip Ringwood continues his inexplicable social successes. Even Mrs. Baynes, the dragon of Philip's story, may have a story of her own to tell.

> I hope he [Philip] has revenged himself by presenting coals of fire to his wife's relations. But to this day, when he is enjoying good health and competence, it is not safe to mention mothers-in-law in his presence. He fumes, shouts, and rages against them, as if all were like his; and his, I have been told, is a lady perfectly well satisfied with herself and her conduct in this world; and as for the next——but our story does not dare to point so far. It only interests itself about a little clique of people here below—their griefs, their trials, their weaknesses, their kindly hearts. (11:349)

As though to underscore the equality of the wicked and the good before fate— we are not talking here about the continuation of the tale into the next world— the implied author gives the news of the Little Sister's death by a fever caught from one of her patients, just a page from the account of Dr. Firmin's successful marriage and sudden death by fever soon after. The Grim Reaper cuts the tender career of the needy as surely as that of the selfish exploiter.

Philip is a novel that emphasizes disclosure, the unstinting presentation of whatever information is required for the narrative.[12] We are to have no surprises, no unexpected twists of fate, no novelist's tricks. But if that is so, why does the climax of the story turn upon one of the most shopworn of novelistic conventions—the discovery of a will? And why should this disclosure be brought about by Philip's low political trick against Woolcomb? With obvious racial prejudice, Philip employs a negro to drive a cart with the famous abolitionist sentence "Am I not a man and a brother" (here rendered "brudder") painted on it. This ploy leads to the overturning of Lord Ringwood's chariot, in which Woolcomb is riding, thus revealing the will of the late lord that previously had lain unnoticed in a deep doorwell of the carriage. Why, we might ask, should the implied author reward Philip for such an unsavory trick? But we must recall that Thackeray was something of a racist himself and might very well have seen Philip's joke as a good move in a political world for which he had little respect in any case.[13] So a good consequence may come to Philip whether he has misbehaved or not. The implicit message, of course, is an important one—our behavior should not be governed by our expectations of reward or fear of punishment, but should follow from principles of love, charity, and fairness.

The use of the discovered will *is* novelistic, but that only reminds us at the very end of the narrative that we have, in fact, been reading a novel. Looking back, we can also recall that Pendennis told us that, although Philip would pass through a brief bad period of suffering, he would end up happily married and prosperous at the end. But he did not reveal that there would be two kinds of hardship—the near loss of Charlotte and his financial sufferings. After all, however, the story is based on a parable that Thackeray and Pendennis could expect their readers to know. The trajectory of the tale is foreknown, but the manner in which Pendennis glances back and leaps proleptically forward determines the way we receive and interpret the information he provides, making it all concentrate on the consequences for the victim of the thieves. But what story would it be if we followed that Samaritan home and heard *him* recount the tale?

Narratives cannot help but preach—or let us say transmit—moral lessons—or let us say preferences. And Thackeray recognizes this very well. He is also pretty certain that those who read the novel will seek to find in it a confirmation of their preferences. Very likely the telling of the tale will change nothing. The thieves will continue to steal and the Samaritan to give aid; just as in *The Newcomes,* the creatures of fable will continually reenact their roles. But if this is so, why does the business of serious fabling go on? One answer might follow from J. Hillis Miller's argument in *The Ethics of Reading,* that a text is an inexact translation of the law it seeks to express. Any reader who creates a text to comment on that original text comments, in another form of faulty translation, on the law behind it instead, hence producing an endless and fruitless attempt to express the law behind the need to express.[14] Put another way, life compels us to formulate our experience in narratives, and any specific narrative—history, biography, fiction—is not so much an effort to teach an audience or alter its behavior as it is an inescapable expression of the need to reattempt a definition of existence. But some forms of writing—notably scientific expository texts—do set out to teach, and have had demonstrable consequences for human behavior. These expository texts, however, share with narratives the necessity of organizing language into a comprehensible pattern, largely through the use of repetitions, contrasts, likenesses, and differences. Similes, analogies, and exemplifications are necessary and helpful in discussing physics. The most succinct form of scientific discourse is the formula, and even when expanded, scientific discourse aims at leanness. But narratives do not. With increasing frequency, from history to biography to fiction, narratives not only do not court succinctness; they depend upon redundancy. Utilizing the contributions of information theory, we might say that the information of a narrative text is enhanced by its redundancy. Its *message* is more likely to be transmitted successfully if it is conveyed in a number of cooperating ways, with repetitions of key codes or symbols—in their semiotic sense only. Some of those repetitions might even appear in the form of apparent contradictions, though their purpose is to reinforce the "ground" message.[15]

In much fiction, and certainly in the works of Dickens and Thackeray, something like this repetition is happening. In *Philip*, I believe Thackeray was actually trying to convey a notion of this sort. Perhaps no single lesson that can be epitomized in a maxim—the literary equivalent of a scientific formula—can be conveyed in any significant way. I have suggested that the sentence "Judge not lest ye be judged" might serve as a good portal announcement above the gates to Thackeray's fiction. But many other similarly terse commonplaces might equally apply. In *Philip*, though forgiving remains a righteous act and punishment an appropriate means of correcting and controlling mischief, a broader sentiment seems to prevail, by which we are encouraged to recognize the density and multifariousness of human existence, and, in a forgiving mood, allow that there is room for such diversity. That is why the narrative balances and reiterates past and present as well as the careers of "good" and "bad" characters, perhaps most simply and symbolically in Dr. Firmin, the scamp turned honored medical doctor, and Caroline Brandon, his early romantic victim turned helpful and humble nurse. The former treats his son miserably, the second is devoted to him, but both must deal in their different ways with the threats against him—one negatively and one positively. Yet, at the end, both are leveled by the same kind of disease.

The narrative is extremely flexible in its treatment of the many characters, but its central character, Philip Firmin, has a rigorous binary outlook. He is for or against. Like a computer with its extremely complex pattern of yes/no responses, this rigor makes for efficiency. Philip uses physical punishment when certain of a wrong; he refuses to forgive when he retains a sense of injury. But along with this either/or mentality there is a reluctance to condemn. Philip is "slow in appreciating roguery, or recognising that there is meanness and double-dealing in the world," but when he learns that Tartuffe is a humbug and Bufo is a toady, he "becomes as absurdly indignant and mistrustful as before he was admiring and confiding." Pendennis tells us this, and then apostrophizes his friend with some familiar Thackerayan wisdom: "Ah, Philip! Tartuffe has a number of good respectable qualities; and Bufo, though an underground odious animal, may have a precious jewel in his head. 'Tis you are cynical. *I* see the good qualities in these rascals whom you spurn. I see. I shrug my shoulders. I smile: and you call me cynic" (11:105).

A strict either/or stand is useful insofar as it simplifies life and makes for easier, if less compassionate, responses to moral crises. But the more expansive middle way that Pendennis assumes, though it makes decisions and actions more difficult in the midst of moral dilemmas, ultimately serves one best, for it permits an intense degree of self-examination that cannot, to Thackeray's mind, be available to the truly censorious. If *Philip* may be said to have a somewhat different message from the earlier novels, it is probably that there is room in this world for both Pendennises and Philips, that those who suspend judgment and those who judge may live together amicably, provided they are fundamentally good-hearted. Thackeray had always shown his good characters to be flawed in some way, and many of his bad characters to have good traits. In *Philip*, he extends this view to suggest that even good dull folks who live according to a simplistic moral code can be at home with the "cynically" alert if both are capable of valuing some high human quality such as love. In Thackeray's uncompleted last novel, we see the extent to which he was willing to extend forgiveness for even the most wicked behavior.

NOTES

1. Deborah A. Thomas calls attention to the fact that "the hypocritical Dr. Firmin never fully pays the penalty for his misdeeds" (*Thackeray and Slavery* [Athens, OH: Ohio University Press, 1993], 173). She also cites the Roundabout Paper "De Finibus," in which Thackeray confessed that he originally intended to drown Dr. Firmin but instead let him live to have an opportunity to repent, unlikely as that was (187). Subsequent references appear in the text.

2. Juliet McMaster, *Thackeray: The Major Novels* (Toronto: University of Toronto Press, 1971), 187.

3. Frank Kermode, *The Genesis of Secrecy: On the Interpretation of Narrative* (Cambridge: Harvard University Press, 1979), 77.

4. *The Works of William Makepeace Thackeray*, 26 vols. (Philadelphia: J. B. Lippincott Company, 1901), 10, 177.

5. *The Letters and Private Papers of William Makepeace Thackeray, Volume 3: 1852-1856*, ed. Gordon N. Ray (Cambridge: Harvard University Press, 1946), 67.

6. Peter Rabinowitz, *Before Reading: Narrative Conventions and the Politics of Interpretation* (Ithaca, NY: Cornell University Press, 1987), 58.

7. Robert A. Colby, *Thackeray's Canvass of Humanity: An Author and His Public* (Columbus: Ohio State University Press, 1979), 440.

8. Benjamin Disraeli, *Coningsby, Or The New Generation*. ed. Thom Braun (New York: Penguin Books, 1989), 138.

9. In "Funeral Baked Meats: Thackeray's Last Novel," Juliet McMaster shows how consistently Thackeray employs violent and punitive metaphors in *Philip* (*Studies in the Novel* 13, nos. 1–2 [Spring-Summer 1981], 133–55). Subsequent references appear in the text.

10. Thackeray's dislike of Laura is referred to in *Interviews and Recollections*, ed. Philip Collins, 2 vols., (New York: St. Martin's Press, 1983), 2:215. But this assertion must be taken with a grain of salt, since Thackeray might have been teasing. Here is the passage: "He told Miss Hennell that he did not like 'dearest Laura' and that he made his women without character, or else so bad, because that was as he knew them." See Ina Ferris' "The Demystification of Laura Pendennis" (*Studies in the Novel* 13, nos. 1–2 [Spring-Summer 1981], 122–32, for a recent critical discussion of Laura's faults.

11. Hayden White, "The Value of Narrativity in the Representation of Reality," *Critical Inquiry* 7, no. 1 (Autumn 1980), 5–28.

12. Juliet McMaster keenly observes that Thackeray is using autobiographical materials from his earlier years for Philip's career and from his mature years in depicting Pendennis. In doing so, he is himself engaging in self-exposure twice over and is understandably lenient ("Baked Meats," 151ff.).

13. See Deborah A. Thomas' thorough examination of Thackeray's attitudes toward race, especially chapter 8 on *Philip*.

14. J. Hillis Miller, *The Ethics of Reading: Kant, de Man, Eliot, Trollope, James, and Benjamin* (New York: Columbia University Press, 1987), 120.

15. Jeremy Campbell, *Grammatical Man: Information, Entropy, Language, and Life* (New York: Simon and Schuster, Inc., 1983), 68ff.

TWENTY-SIX

Roundabout Papers and Denis Duval

BY HIS LAST YEARS Thackeray had decidedly mellowed, though he still now and then flashed out with humorous or serious judgments. *The Roundabout Papers* and *Denis Duval* reveal a man interested in fostering the gentler emotions while tempering the impulse to condemn and punish apparent evil-doers. Two of *The Roundabout Papers* illustrate this lenient mood by treating childhood experiences. In "On Being Found Out," Thackeray recalls an incident at school where having boys put their hand into a bag of soot was designed as a means of establishing guilt for some infraction. The technique did not work; it merely blackened a hand of each boy. This incident leads Thackeray to imagine what a dreadful world it would be if all guilty persons were found out, since most of us are guilty of something. This sentiment is often expressed in his writings, but it is carried further here as Thackeray observes that even serious crimes such as murder are not necessarily discovered. He offers instances of how guilty persons inadvertently reveal their own crimes and vanities, and ends the piece by cautioning the reader not to foster the illusion that he is as noble a figure as his wife and children suppose him to be. "Put away that monstrous conceit," he concludes, "and be thankful that *they* have not found you out."[1] This essay condenses, in a relaxed manner, Thackeray's abiding concern with being found out, and his insistence that since we all have something to hide, we should therefore agree upon a community of reticence and reserved judgment. Typically, it moves from a dramatized example, to an exposition of the subject, and finally to an implication of the reader. And reader complicity is essential to Thackeray's purpose. In "On Two Roundabout Papers Which I Intended to Write," he intimates that each of us has an inclination and susceptibility to antisocial behavior, using the recent Northumberland Street shooting as an occasion to ponder the unutterable thoughts and impulses we all conceal.

461

Is there some Northumberland Street chamber in your heart and mine, friend: close to the every-day street of life: visited by daily friends: visited by people on business; in which affairs are transacted; jokes are uttered; wine is drunk; through which people come and go; wives and children pass; and in which murder sits unseen until the terrible moment when he rises up and kills? (22:157–58).

But if we are all potentially sinners, a single transgression does not doom us. In "Tunbridge Toys," Thackeray recounts how as a child he spent fourpence of some money he was carrying in trust for his parents. Overcome by remorse, he immediately confesses to his parents, who are quite understanding. "I had confessed; I had been prodigal; I had been taken back to my parents' arms again" (22: 64).[2] This brief example of lapse and forgiveness suggests that such stories as the Idle Apprentice, in which a boy who commits one offense finds himself on the downward slope to crime, are foolish exaggerations. The sense that we are all capable of erring should make us sympathetic to others who err, even to downright criminals. Thackeray, as always, is intensely curious about such outlaws. In "On a Medal of George the Fourth" he wonders about the difference between ordinary people and rogues. What a queer exciting life a rogue's must be, he thinks. "Is conscious guilt a source of unmixed pain to the bosom which harbours it? Has not your criminal, on the contrary an excitement, an enjoyment within quite unknown to you and me who never did anything wrong in our lives?" (22: 328). Telling the story of a footman suspected of stealing his mistress's diamonds, Thackeray wonders what the thief's later career has been like.

I wonder has John prospered in life subsequently? If he is innocent, he does not interest me in the least. The interest of the case lies in John's behavior supposing him to be guilty. Imagine the smiling face, the daily service, the orderly performance of duty, whilst within John is suffering pangs lest discovery should overtake him. Every bell of the door which he is obliged to open may bring a police-officer. The accomplices may peach. What an exciting life John's must have been for a while. And now, years and years after, when pursuit has long ceased, and detection is impossible, does he ever revert to the little transaction? Is it possible those diamonds cost a thousand pounds? What a rogue the fence must have been who only gave him so and so! (22:330)

He concludes this essay with the familiar assertion that, although there are numerous shams of appearance and of the heart abroad, we should be chiefly concerned with our own moral condition. "Ah, friend! may our coin, battered, and clipped and defaced though it be, be proved to be Sterling Silver on the day of the Great Assay" (22:331).

Another motive for being understanding about the offenses of others surfaces in the wry "On a Pear Tree." Thackeray discovers that thieves have climbed his wall and stolen pears from his tree, an event that disturbs his peace of mind because he is now suspicious of his fellow man, not knowing who has purloined the fruit. He wonders if the thieves will ever be discovered, then considers his own fate. "If I, for my part, were to try and get up the smallest tree, on the darkest night, in the most remote orchard, I wager any money I should be found out—be caught by the leg in a man-trap, or have Towler fastening on me. I always am found out; have been; shall be. It's my luck" (22:275). Part of Thackeray's compassion for others is his own comic certainty that he could never himself get away with a crime. Thoughts about crime lead him to recall having dined in the house once owned by the financier Sadlier, who ended his own life on Hampstead Heath, and about other offenders and their fates, some of whom he knew. These gloomy thoughts are occasioned not only by the theft of his pears, it turns out, but also by an article in the *Saturday Review* about a man he knew and whom he had often seen elegantly dressed at social affairs. "So attired, he stood but yesterday in court; and to-day he sits over a bowl of prison cocoa, with a shaved head, and in a felon's jerkin" (22:280). He imagines how miserable this man must have been with the knowledge of his crimes gnawing at him while others considered him a happy man. Thackeray ends the essay with a sort of prayer (just as he had referred to it as a "sermon" at the beginning): "Ah! when I ask this day for my daily bread, I pray not to be led into temptation, and to be delivered from evil" (22:280).

Thackeray takes a long view when he laments the human tendency to believe ill of acquaintances. "An acquaintance grilled, scored, devilled, and served with mustard and cayenne pepper, excites the appetite; whereas a slice of cold friend with currant jelly is but a sickly unrelishing meat" (22:132). Ultimately this behavior is insignificant, since although people will continue to gossip and spread lies, none of that talk will matter much one hundred years hence. Thackeray cannot treat other sorts of injuries so cavalierly. A woman asks Mr. Roundabout why he always attacks a certain class of persons in his novels. He tells his interrogator the source of his anger, then admits his inability to forget the injury. "If I live half as long as Tithonus, that crack across my heart can never be cured. There are wrongs and griefs that *can't* be mended. It is all very well of you, my dear Mrs. G., to say that this spirit is unchristian, and that we ought to forgive and forget, and so forth. How can I forget at will? How forgive?" (22:12). Thus, although Thackeray prefers that we not be too judgmental and recommends clemency toward those who slip, he cannot unthinkingly recommend forgiveness in all cases, no matter how admirable it is as an ultimate aim.

This tendency toward lenity is evident in Thackeray's professional life as well. In "De Juventute," Thackeray remembers having been punished for reading a novel when he was supposed to be doing his Greek and Latin, but he himself, in "On A Lazy Idle Boy," the first of the Roundabout Papers, warns against spoiling one's appetite by consuming too much fiction too early. As in other aspects of life, so with reading, Excesses will bring their own consequences. An unwise diet of reading will punish us with troubled digestion and a ruined palate. Novelists, he explains, take the jellies of fiction but eat the roast beef of fact as well. Thackeray places his profession in a moral context, insisting that what he produces is not hurtful unless taken in excess; as editor of *The Cornhill Magazine,* he promises to provide a balanced diet of fiction and fact, for he wants the magazine to be one that readers can dip into with pleasure (22:13). In "Small Beer Chronicle," Thackeray says that he used to be happy to thong a literary enemy, but that he has grown peaceable in old age. This admission comes near the end of the essay, which was prompted by a *Saturday Review* writer's criticism of his pretensions to philosophy. All claret would be port if it could be is the theme of his sermon. Thackeray discusses the human tendency to pretend to be what we are not, and gently reminds the *Saturday Review* writer that he, too, is arrogating to himself the role of instructor. Elsewhere, after giving samples of how he has been criticized in the press, he admonishes literary critics to be responsible. "In the little court where you are paid to sit as judge, as critic, you owe it to your employers, to your conscience, to the honour of your calling, to deliver just sentences; and you shall have to answer to Heaven for your dealings, as surely as my Lord Chief Justice on the Bench" (22:58). Thackeray himself had a bad conscience about his early burlesques, especially his rough treatment of Bulwer-Lytton.

Although Thackeray had come to view novel writing as a trade requiring moral responsibility, he occasionally had to defend his own practice as a novelist. In "Thorns in the Cushion," Thackeray describes letters he receives complaining about his fiction; for example, his misrepresentation of ballet dancers. He admits that "In the little history of 'Lovel the Widower' I described, and brought to condign punishment, a certain wretch of a ballet-dancer, who lived splendidly for a while on ill-gotten gains, had an accident, and lost her beauty, and died poor, deserted, ugly, and every way odious" (22:50). But he adds that he also pictured ballet dancers behaving decently. This playful allusion to his punishment of a character, however, implies an underlying seriousness, for Thackeray seldom let a character get away without any punishment at all, though he was generally quite lenient. *The Roundabout Papers* and *Denis Duval* indicate that near the end of his life he had become even more interested in leniency, and this increased mildness makes a difference in the structure and characterization in his last, unfinished narrative.

In "Notes on Denis Duval," Leslie Stephen suggested that La Motte's betrayal by his smuggling and spying confederate Lütterloh was to be the focus of the novel. "It is not improbable," he says, "that from this narrative of a trial for high treason in 1781 the whole story radiated" (26:346). It would not be at all surprising, given Thackeray's tendency toward forgiveness and compassion in his later years, that he should base his narrative on an excruciating conflict between forgiveness on the one hand and violent retribution on the other.

From early in the narrative, Duval, who tells his story in the first person, alternately reduces and intensifies the kind of suspense designed to keep a reader reading, achieving both effects through brief proleptic passages. At the end of the very first chapter, in explaining who Agnes de Sauverne is, Duval reveals that "today her name is Agnes Duval, and she sits at her work-table hard by," adding that all his worthy achievements were done in trying to deserve this woman (24:209). Thus, at the very outset of the narrative, we know that whatever ordeals Denis and Agnes may endure, ultimately they will sail into safe harbor together. This is a device Thackeray used in his later novels, particularly *The Newcomes* and *The Adventures of Philip*, both narrated by Pendennis. But if Thackeray so benevolently lets his readers know immediately that his hero and his beloved will be happily united, as the convention of Victorian fiction requires, how can he sustain interest in Duval's tale? Partly, of course, by a sequence of interesting incidents skillfully rendered, but also by foregrounding the theme of transgression against an established background of virtue, sincerity, and happiness. That theme is traced chiefly in the career of Baron De la Motte. The use of adventure and dramatic incident in *Duval* is unlike most of Thackeray's later fiction and signals a more determined purpose in treating his themes, including those of punishment and forgiveness.

De la Motte first appears in chapter 2, which recounts the story of Agnes' parents, culminating in the flight of her mother, Clarisse de Sauverne, with De la Motte, from her husband, who is returning from war in Corsica. Clarisse has long disliked her husband and, although she does not commit adultery, she is unfaithful to him in her heart, loving De la Motte instead.[3] In passing, Duval explains that De la Motte would much later discuss these events "at a supreme moment of his life," perhaps after his trial when he awaits sentencing and execution (24:217). Recounting Clarisse's behavior, Duval emphasizes her error rather than her evil, and concludes of the two offenders, "these poor people are both gone to their account. Both suffered a fearful punishment. I will not describe their follies, and don't care to be Monsieur Figaro, and hold the ladder and lantern, while the Count scales Rosina's window. Poor frightened erring soul! She suffered an awful penalty for what, no doubt, was a great wrong" (24:222).

In this glance forward to the punishment of the offending Clarisse and De la Motte, an appropriate scheme of retribution is fixed in place as solidly as the virtuous hero's reward of a virtuous wife. In the first two chapters the moral design of the book stands fully revealed, and is even enhanced by Duval's frequent references to Agnes' presence while he writes. All that is lacking is the filling out of the design. But it is precisely in this filling out that Thackeray will achieve his most interesting effects. One might almost imagine him declaring to his audience: Here is the plot you want from me; now that you know the outcome, watch me take you there. Another way of viewing Thackeray's enterprise here is with the narratologically useful terms story and plot, or *fabula* and *sjuzet*. The implied author in Duval has the narrator provide us with a familiar story, or *fabula,* from the genre of romance, but the elaboration of plot, or *sjuzet,* through the narrator's telling strains in the direction of realist fiction. Similarly, though the story implies an almost melodramatic structuring of moral worth and blame, the plot complicates that simplicity into a world where absolute judgments are discouraged. This is a technique developed and refined later by such masters as Thomas Hardy and Joseph Conrad, where the conflicting demands of different genres within their novels subvert easy moral judgments.

Although we are offered the illusion that we are reading a familiar kind of story (now in the sense of tale or narrative) with a predictable outcome, in fact we do not know its ending. We know that Duval will win his Agnes, but we must wait a long while to learn De la Motte's fate. We know that he will be punished, but not how. Moreover, as the narrative continues and Duval offers more and more proleptic hints concerning De la Motte's fate, it becomes increasingly unclear for what sins he will ultimately pay. It is even likely that the moral outlawry by which the early chapters of the novel position us to revile the perpetrators—De la Motte's spiriting of Clarisse away from her husband—will ultimately stand as a virtuous act worthy of respect by a man otherwise deserving punishment for his economic and political rulebreaking.

When De la Motte "rescues" Clarisse, he takes her to her sister, Ursule Duval, in England. Count de Sauverne first summons De la Motte back to France for a duel, and when he refuses, the Count follows to England, catches a glimpse of his daughter, and then dies in a duel with his erstwhile friend. "Assuredly," Duval apostrophizes, "the guilt of that blood was on thy head Francis de la Motte" (24:254). De la Motte's motives, though complicated, were generous when he acted to liberate Clarisse from a situation that had become repulsive to her, and which Duval does not extenuate in his narrative. But generous or not, De la Motte's actions generate dire consequences for which he remains responsible. If there will later be a grand punishment for De la Motte, there is an immediate one as well, for by killing Clarisse's husband, he is, as he himself says, separated from her forever "as hopelessly as though one or the other were dead" (24:254). De la Motte is a Byronic figure, grand but flawed, capable of great generosity but also of great error. Finding him both appealing and repellent, Duval partially excuses De la Motte as a doomed man. "And so indeed there was a *Cain mark,* as it were, on this unhappy man. He *did* bring wreck and ruin on those who loved him. He was a lost soul, I somehow think, whose tortures had begun already. Predestined to evil, to crime, to gloom; but now and again someone took pity on this poor wretch, and amongst those who pitied him was my stern mother" (24:254–55).

Early in the novel Denis describes his mother as a violent woman, "jealous, hot, and domineering, but generous and knowing how to forgive" (24:205). In these qualities she is the opposite of Denis' cringing, mean, and vindictive grandfather. His mother can endorse the lucrative smuggling trade in which the family (and a good portion of the community) engages, but can also discontinue her involvement when the opportunity arises to make a gentleman of young Denis. If her character is morally ambiguous, she nonetheless tends to behave in a manner that accords with common sense and self-interest. But forgiveness goes beyond self-interest. By pitying De la Motte, she demonstrates the deeper humanity that is the energetic source both for her imperious judgments upon others and for her willingness to acknowledge mortal weakness. Taking this milder note from his mother, Denis, a more equable person altogether—though still capable of violence, as his youthful implementation of a pistol against a highwayman (Joseph Weston in disguise) indicates—tells us in another proleptic digression that he would ultimately forgive De la Motte himself. "A bad man no doubt this was; and yet not utterly wicked: a great criminal who paid an awful penalty. Let us be humble, who have erred too; and thankful, if we have a hope that we have found mercy" (24:259). Denis similarly extends compassion—no forgiveness is necessary—to poor Clarisse.

> Oh, pitiful was thy lot in this world, poor, guiltless, harmless lady! In thy brief years, how little happiness! For they marriage portion only gloom, and terror, and submission, and captivity. The awful Will above us ruled it so. Poor frightened spirit! it has woke under serener skies now, and passed out of reach of our terrors, and temptations, and troubles. (24:260)

I have already mentioned some deviations in the narrative that Duval allows himself. Chiefly these involve leaps forward, often indicating the consequences of behavior. At one point Duval admits the "zig-zag" nature of his storytelling and excuses it by saying, " 'Tis the privilege of old age to be garrulous, and its happiness to remember early days," though he says that, looking back, he feels as huntsmen do when they "look at the gaps and ditches over which they have leapt, and wonder how they are alive" (24:260). The whole novel is pervaded by this sense of its narrator securely established in safety and comfort, reflecting benevolently on pleasures and dangers past. But the zig-zag of the narrative is not simply garrulity; it is the implied author's way of linking together, more and more tightly, actions and their consequences, frequently with implied or explicit punishment and forgiveness. Some of these I have noted but there are several others. For example, Susy Rudge and her father, Denis' landlords when he is at school, falsely charge him with theft. This brings immediate punishment to the Rudges in the form of a beating by Mrs. Duval, but Duval glances forward to explain that, when he was found innocent of the charge and suspicion fell on the Rudges as liars, the schoolboys took to calling the two Ananias and Sapphira, causing their business to fall off. Duval says that he will presently tell "what a penalty they (and some others) had to pay for their wickedness; and of an act of contrition on poor Miss Sukey's part, whom, I am sure, I heartily forgave" (24: 317). Chapter 8 is littered with this device. In it Duval says he will later tell how bitterly De la Motte was to rue his friendship with Lieutenant Lütterloh, and also of the awful payment Lütterloh would make for his treachery. He also notes that his own grandfather would later pay a penalty for remaining involved with the smuggling trade.

The episode of the Rudges is interesting in the way it differs from the main narrative. In the story of De la Motte, huge issues are at stake politically, financially, and morally. By contrast, the Rudges are mean and trivial. Bad as he is, De la Motte reveals an important positive trait in Thackeray's scheme of things. He is kind to children. The Rudges provide a limited and simple moral drama that more forcefully sets off the complications of the larger narrative. The carefully orchestrated narrative punishment of the Rudges, extending from physical chastisement to the disclosure of their own seamy crimes to economic hardship, is not necessary to the story of Denis' adventures, but useful as that form of redundancy that reestablishes the moral ground upon which the whole narrative rides, by observing it from a slightly different perspective.

Though the Rudges exhibit a base and trivial mode of treachery, the plot involving De la Motte presents a major vehicle for that same theme in Lütterloh. We know from Thackeray's notes that Lütterloh would give evidence against De la Motte, who would be hanged, drawn, and quartered for treason, and that Lütterloh would drown in a foundered ship. De la Motte's punishment is different in kind from that of Lütterloh and implies a moral order in experience that, if it cannot be asserted, may be supposed. De la Motte is betrayed by his associate into the hands of the law and is executed for his crimes. Legal justice has its way. But the slimey Lütterloh suffers a more surprising fate, one that has nothing to do with human justice, but which suggests the operation of some providential dispensation. De la Motte's punishment for economic and political crimes takes place within the limits of human institutional justice. He has broken laws and he must pay. Since this kind of punishment is relative and depends upon the power of a prevailing code to enforce itself, it may also be considered nonmoral. But Lütterloh's fate occurs beyond the range of human retribution. The peculiar accident that takes his life allows for the operation of a moral power that transcends human judgment. How delighted Thackeray must have been to discover in a historical account such a splendid contrast of modes of punishment—the routinely human and the potentially divine. Equally convenient was the fact that both victims were clearly sinners. But De la Motte provided Thackeray the opportunity to balance this panorama of punishment with a display of charity.

Since De la Motte's career was taken from a true event, looking forward to the end of that career has the quality of tracing a predestined tale. Duval's frequent glances forward reinforce the sense of a moral teleology. Time and again we are reminded that good persons are rewarded and the wicked punished, but we are encouraged to remember that even the notably evil may have fine qualities. Despite his many sins, De la Motte did love and assist Clarisse—acting as a sort of corrupt Caponsacchi—and he did provide for Agnes' care and upbringing. Leslie Stephen shrewdly noted in "The Writings of W. M. Thackeray," that Thackeray "seldom loses his temper with his characters, and he evidently looked at this problem with his usual calmness. In several of his pictures we have the curious study of a villain seen from within" (26:388). But Thackeray could be thus calm and show his villains from within because he was so conscious of the fallible nature of even the best among us. How tireless he is in repeating the observation that we all would be more lenient toward rogues if we only considered what we would deserve were our private thoughts and actions to be found out. In his last novel he seems to have wanted to show that even those with the least guilty consciences can show compassion, that forgiveness and pardon can be the product not only of fellow feeling in guilt, but also of an imagination capable of picturing, without participating in, such a soiled conscience. But beyond examining the nature of human sympathy for even some of the worst among us, Thackeray seems to have wanted to emphasize that, for those who travel the perilous journey of life and reach virtue and safety at the end, it is important to extend forgiveness from that advantageous position to all who have failed to complete the journey.

NOTES

1. *The Works of William Makepeace Thackeray,* 26 vols. Philadelphia: J. B. Lippincott Company, 1901), 22:125. Subsequent references appear in the text.

2. Richard W. Oram examines the significance of memory in *The Roundabout Papers* in "'Just a Little Turn of the Circle': Time Memory, and Repetition in Thackeray's *Roundabout Papers,*" in *William Makepeace Thackeray,* ed. Harold Bloom (New York: Chelsea House Publishers, 1987), 169–78. Of the "Tunbridge Toys" essay, Oram says that memory serves a morally regenerating purpose, something that regularly happens in Dickens' work as well. "Even though the twelve-year-old's guilty feelings choked him all the way home, the painful experience has been transformed into something intensely valuable for the adult" (174).

3. De la Motte makes this assertion of Clarisse's physical chastity, but there are suggestions to the contrary. See, for example, 22:254 of *Works.*

Conclusion

I HAVE ARGUED that there is a profound relationship between the moral values shared by an author and his or her audience and the manner in which narration takes place. I have been concerned with two major novelists of the nineteenth century in England, but my argument can easily be extended to other writers of that time and beyond. To a certain degree nineteenth-century British fiction was an overdeveloped and redundant version of the moral fable, the parable, or the fairy tale. Its narrative events are elaborated upon an armature of moral prerequisites. For most of the century these strictures are rarely violated. Both Dickens and Thackeray disliked moral fables but loved biblical parables and fairy tales because, whereas the former drummed their moral lessons into their readers (as in *Sanford and Merton*), the latter were less explicit about the narrative's moral and more concerned that the story be enticing enough to convey that moral, even unconsciously if necessary. Bruno Bettelheim draws a distinction between fables, which are always moral, and fairy tales, which are moral but not explicitly so. He says that children's primitive sense of justice is gratified by the destruction of those who have done something really bad. Hence the suffering of the grasshopper in "The Grasshopper and the Ant" seems unjust, whereas it is fully appropriate that the carnivorous wolf of "The Three Little Pigs" should himself be eaten.[1] "It is not that the evildoer is punished at the story's end which makes immersing oneself in fairy stories an experience in moral education, although this is part of it," Bettelheim writes. "In fairy tales, as in life, punishment or fear of it is only a limited deterrent to crime. The conviction that crime does not pay is a much more effective deterrent, and that is why in fairy tales the bad person always loses out" (91). And it is even better if this losing out has the symmetry of poetic justice, as with the eater eaten in "The Three Little Pigs," or with the wicked servant in "The Goose Girl," who volunteers advice on how a person should be punished and promptly receives that punishment herself. "Adults," say Bettelheim, "often think that the cruel punishment of an evil person in fairy tales upsets and scares children unnecessarily. Quite the opposite is true: such retribution reassures the child that the punishment fits the crime" (141). As we saw in chapter 2, there was a marked change in children's literature in England

470

during the nineteenth century, and that movement was in the direction of greater lenity. Fundamentally, however, the same moral lessons were retained. What Bettelheim says of fairy tales applies to children's literature of this period in general: "The message is that evil intentions are the evil person's own undoing" (141). Dickens applied this same principle in his narratives, as did Thackeray to a lesser degree, and they shared this inclination with most of their contemporaries.

Although punishment and forgiveness as well as praise and blame had been important in literature of the eighteenth century, there is a characteristic difference in the Victorian period. The supposed author of the preface to *Moll Flanders* declares outright that intelligent "Readers will be much more pleas'd with the Moral than the Fable" of the narrative to follow.[2] The preface also states that after their legal punishment Moll and her husband returned from transportation to America and established themselves comfortably in England, and he admits that Moll, as she grew older, "was not so extraordinary a Penitent as she was at first; it seems only that indeed she always spoke with abhorence of her former Life, and of every Part of it" (6). These statements may be taken at their face value or dismissed as a necessary cover for telling the story of a decidedly fallen woman. Nonetheless, in the narrative itself Moll admits her own faults—her vanity and pride, for example, which contribute to her original lapse from virtue. At the same time Moll excuses some of her behavior by declaring that a woman's lot in her society was not an easy one. But while excusing herself in one direction she can blame herself in another. Speaking of her life as a thief, she says, "as Poverty brought me into the Mire, so Avarice kept me in it" (158). Only after she is imprisoned does Moll repent, though she realizes that this repentance is hollow, coming only after she is prevented from sinning further. Subsequently she becomes a true penitent through the ministrations of the prison chaplain, and soon after learns that she has been reprieved from a death sentence. By the end of the novel, she has fallen into the habit of crediting Providence with the wise disposition of events.

There is very little forgiveness in this novel, little demonstration of functional punishment within the narrative, and no narrative punishments. The whole narrative might easily be read as an elaborate example of therapeutic punishment. Moreover, there are no heroes and villains to be contrasted with one another and thus forceful or attenuated forms of melodrama are lacking. Defoe's moral world may resemble that of Dickens, but it has as many points of difference as of resemblance.

Joseph Andrews does have heroes and villains. Parson Adams is the genuinely good man and Joseph Andrews is an unblemished youth. Part of the fun of the novel lies in the improbability of Joseph's utter goodness and the scrapes that the good parson gets into despite his goodness. Fielding declares his purpose to be the discovery of "Affectation."[3] Given an account of imprisonment for debt, the genial Adams responds with a reference to the Lord's Prayer: "And as surely as we

do not forgive others their Debts when they are unable to pay them; so surely
shall we ourselves be unforgiven, when we are in no condition of paying" (171).
Though Adams is speaking literally of money debts, the wider implication of the
Lord's Prayer is surely intended. Young Joseph, hero that he is, says that if he
encountered the thieves who robbed and beat him he would like to attack them
and kill them. The Reverend Barnabas tries to evoke the expected Christian
response.

> "Doubtless," answered *Barnabas,* "it is lawful to kill a Thief: but can
> you say, you forgive them as a Christian ought?" Joseph desired to
> know what that Forgiveness was. "That is," answered *Barnabas,* "to
> forgive them as—as—it is to forgive them as—in short, it is to forgive
> them as a Christian." *Joseph* reply'd, "he forgave them as much as he
> could." "Well, well," said *Barnabas,* "that will do." (47–48)

Unlike Dickens' model heroes, Joseph is free to use physical force to punish rascals like the Captain, though it might be argued that he is, like Nicholas Nickleby, not yet mature in his virtue. Fielding has Adams urge Joseph to accept his
misfortunes as a form of therapeutic punishment. "'You are a Man, and consequently a Sinner; and this may be a Punishment to you for your Sins; indeed in
this Sense it may be esteemed as a Good, yea the greatest Good, which satisfies
the Anger of Heaven, and averts that Wrath which cannot continue without our
Destruction'" (207). But this proffering of human suffering as a providential benefit is later undercut as a message in the text when Adams himself cannot so
accept his own suffering—the imagined death of his beloved child. On the
whole, then, though closer to the Victorian mode than *Moll Flanders, Joseph Andrews* remains less concerned with the distribution of punishment and forgiveness
than with bringing good characters the rewards they deserve.

David Morse acutely observes that Oliver Goldsmith's *The Vicar of Wakefield*
might be considered the first Victorian novel, for it is with this simple tale that a
characteristic moral pattern becomes clearly established.[4] Ironically, the novel
depends heavily upon an instance of unjust imprisonment, and injustice and unearned suffering are central throughout the tale, as are repentance and forgiveness. Generally, however, forgiveness is far less prominent in eighteenth-century
fiction than it becomes in Victorian literature. At the end of the century Jane
Austen is still chiefly concerned with punishment and reward in *Mansfield Park,*
handing most of it out in the last chapter, which begins, "Let other pens dwell on
guilt and misery. I quit such odious subjects as soon as I can, impatient to restore
everybody, not greatly in fault themselves, to tolerable comfort, and to have
done with all the rest."[5] Maria Rushworth, née Bertram, and Henry Crawford
are the chief offenders as adulterers. But when Henry postpones marriage to
Maria once she is divorced, their relationship sours, rendering "her temper so
bad, and her feelings for him so like hatred as to make them for a while each

other's punishment and then induce a voluntary separation" (362). Maria is forced to retire into the company of her unappealing and now-humbled Aunt Norris. Things are somewhat different for Henry Crawford, but he suffers the natural punishment for his deeds.

> That punishment, the public punishment of disgrace, should in a just measure attend *his* share of the offence, is, we know, not one of the barriers, which society gives to virtue. In this world, the penalty is less equal than could be wished; but without presuming to look forward to a juster appointment hereafter, we may fairly consider a man of sense like Henry Crawford, to be providing for himself no small portion of vexation and regret—vexation that must rise sometimes to self-reproach, and regret to wretchedness—in having so requited hospitality, so injured family peace, so forfeited his best, most estimable and endeared acquaintance, and so lost the woman whom he had rationally, as well as passionately loved. (366)

Meanwhile, the persevering, virtuous characters Edmund Bertram and Fanny Price are allowed to marry and prosper. But there is very little talk about forgiveness. That was to be the hallmark of Victorian literature.

William Allingham tells of his grandmother listening to the Waverly novels being read aloud and exclaiming about the villainous characters: "They ought to have hanged him." Allingham comments, "From this it may be guessed that the modern scruples about capital punishment had never intruded on her mind."[6] The grandmother was a product of her times, times, as chapter 3 indicates, that were far more inclined to employ strict punishment than to favor rehabilitation and mercy. Allingham was himself a product of the later social atmosphere pervaded by a more lenient spirit. In his diary he wrote: "To Session Court: girl convicted of stealing a purse and sentenced to seven years' transportation; she removed shriekingly violent. It seems a severe sentence" (44).

The heroes and heroines of Victorian literature not only must keep out of trouble themselves; they have the additional obligation of having to endure the wickedness of others without actively and directly punishing them. Eighteenth-century heroes and heroines had to preserve their own virtue but they did not have to extend themselves to their opponents and enemies. In Disraeli's *Coningsby,* the eponymous hero is tempted to gain revenge on those who have acted against him by standing for Parliament as his grandfather, Lord Monmouth, suggests, despite his objection to the peer's politics. He decides instead to abide by his principles, thereby jeopardizing his relationship with his powerful relative. Later, when Coningsby is at the lowest point in his career, the wealthy industrialist Millbank supports him for Parliament with no strings attached, merely because he admires the young man's character. Coningsby can now congratulate himself for having chosen the higher path.

He dared not contemplate the ultimate result of all these wonderful changes. Enough for him, that when all seemed dark, he was about to be returned to Parliament by the father of Edith, and his vanquished rival who was to bite the dust before him was the author of all his misfortunes. Love, Vengeance, Justice, the glorious pride of having acted rightly, the triumphant sense of complete and absolute success, here were chaotic materials from which order was at length evolved; and all subsided in an overwhelming feeling of gratitude to that Providence that had so signally protected him.[7]

Providence sees to it that the good need not actively seek revenge but will be rewarded for preserving their own virtue and reaching out to their fellow human beings. It doesn't hurt, though, to see your enemy cast down in your own moment of triumph.

But human beings are not born appreciating the merits of forgiveness, whatever the case may be regarding the impulse to punish. Young Jane Eyre, when abused by John Reed, strikes back. She has a long way to go as a Victorian heroine, but she travels the course. Years later, when John Reed is dead from dissipations, Jane revisits the Reed household to find Eliza grown severly and punitively religious and Georgiana self-indulgent, all for lack of true feeling, Jane reflects. Mrs. Reed now confesses that she has not treated Jane as though she were her own child and that she has told Jane's wealthy relative in Madeira that Jane is dead. Jane now tries to comfort her dying aunt: "'If you could but be persuaded to think no more of it, aunt, and to regard me with kindness and forgiveness.'"[8] Of course the irony is that, as in so many Victorian novels, the plea for forgiveness is aimed in the wrong direction. The aunt insists that Jane has a bad disposition, to which Jane replies that she is passionate but not vindictive and could have responded with love if any had been shown to her. Though Aunt Reed cannot change, Jane has, and she says to the expiring woman, "'Love me, then, or hate me, as you will,' I said at last; 'you have my full and free forgiveness; ask now for God's; and be at peace'" (210–11). This is the necessary and signifying gesture proving that Jane is now a fully mature Victorian heroine.

Jane has a great deal left to endure, but except for a moment of passionate temptation, she is secure in her moral strength. But Rochester is not, and his suffering constitutes one of the most spectacular and memorable instances of narrative punishment in English literature. The mad wife who symbolizes his sensuous nature sets fire to the house that signifies his power and pride. Both are destroyed, and he is left a broken man. But this grand narrative punishment is also one of the most notable examples of therapeutic punishment, for now Rochester realizes that Providence has been at work to punish his guilt for trying to sully his innocent flower. "'*His* chastisements are mighty; and one smote me which has humbled me forever. . . . I began to see and acknowledge the hand of God in my doom'" (393). Once capable of this perception, Rochester is capable of rehabilitation as well. Jane, coming to him now as an equal, is the agent of that rehabilitation. Because of his suffering and redemption there is no need for further forgiveness.

There often surfaces some resistance to this obligatory forgiveness in morally endorsed characters. In *Wuthering Heights,* Nelly Dean makes the conventional observation that God punishes and we forgive.[9] But Isabella, who has endured marriage to Heathcliff, has far less of the expected Christian spirit. She says to Nelly of her husband, " 'On only one condition can I hope to forgive him. It is, if I may take an eye for an eye, a tooth for a tooth; for every wrench of agony, return a wrench, reduce him to my level' " (149). Of course this is not forgiveness at all, but the most elementary form of retribution, its very opposite. But Isabella's is not the spirit that informs Brontë's novel. If forgiveness does not so clearly prevail here as in *Jane Eyre,* it is nonetheless the preferable mode. Even the passionate Catherine, when she knows herself to be dying, says to Heathcliff, " 'I forgive you. Forgive me!' " (135). The more compassionate next generation, exemplified by Catherine and Hareton, exhibits the appropriately forgiving behavior that matures to love.

Women are often associated with forgiving natures in Victorian literature. So the prince seeks Ida's forgiveness for his intrusion upon her realm in Tennyson's *The Princess* (1847), but Ida realizes that "I want forgiveness too," and this self-recognition is the first step toward her escape from pride into a fruitful humility.[10] In the *Idylls of the King,* the monumental gesture of forgiveness comes from Arthur and is directed at the humbled Guinevere. " 'Lo! I forgive thee, as Eternal God / Forgives: do thou for thine own soul the rest' " (*Tennyson,* 3:543).

Often in novels of this period even a repentant character—often a woman—though forgiven, must still suffer some form of punishment, as with Little Em'ly in *David Copperfield.* But more extended instances occur in Mrs. Gaskell's *Ruth* and Mrs. Henry Wood's *East Lynne.* In both novels a spirit of forgiveness prevails, but narrative punishment is nonetheless exerted in the form of an early death. In Rhoda Broughton's *Not Wisely But Too Well,* sexual excess short of actual transgression occasions self-punishment as well as narrative punishment. Such punishments are not limited to women. In G. A. Lawrence's *Guy Livingstone* (1857), the eponymous protagonist is forgiven by his beloved Constance for his sexual lapses, but he must nonetheless lose her and atone unto death. The pattern is ubiquitous in the literature of the period, not merely because it fulfilled readerly expectations, but because those expectations were rooted in a moral creed taken to be true in its essentials, whether those essentials were acted upon in daily life or not.

Some writers, while ostensibly supporting the prevailing Christian ideology, slyly undermined many Christian conventions. Wilkie Collins does this often. In *Man and Wife* he can be especially cutting about the values of punishment and forgiveness. For one, his narrator comes to the defense of Anne Silvester, a woman who has strayed from the moral path. In Mrs. Gaskell's *Ruth,* and many another such story, the fallen woman is partially excused for the pain she has brought herself.

> Has she escaped, without suffering for it?
> Look at her as she stands there, tortured by the knowledge of her own secret—the hideous secret which she is hiding from the innocent girl, whom she loves with a sister's love. Look at her, bowed down under a humiliation which is unutterable in words. . . . Is there no atoning suffering to be seen here?[11]

In her farewell note to Blanche, Anne Silvester writes, "Forgive me, and forget me," thus asserting the conventional treatment of the socially unredeemed sinner (114). Later Anne says she has suffered for her sin and now wishes to behave in such a way that her readers will be able to forgive her (143ff.). Accordingly, the innocent Blanche later asks Anne and her husband to forgive her, believing that she has done them wrong (195). Granted, these are positive and conventional approaches to the theme of Christian forgiveness. The standard punitive conventions are present as well; for example, Lady Lundie thinks in terms of the money/morality trope we have examined. She says of Blanche, "I owe her an atonement," when what she really intends is malice (170). And when she receives no response to her request from Sir Patrick, she "entered that incident on her mental register of debts owed by her brother-in-law—to be paid, with interest, when the day of reckoning came" (173). This is all part of the usual equipment of the Victorian novel. In Collins' story, however, there is a strong tinge of irony associated with all of this conduct. He makes use of the strong convention of the melodramatic confession scene, as in the case of the murderess Hester Dethridge after her career of silence. "The sense of a coming punishment had hung over me. And the punishment had come. I had waited for the judgment of an Avenging Providence. And the judgment was pronounced. With pious David I could now say, Thy fierce wrath goeth over me; thy terrors have cut me off" (227). But it is clear that this pathetic figure has constructed her own providence and her own punishment, something that would become standard practice in the fiction at the end of the century.

Collins goes still further in his assessment of the underlying framework of conscience and morality upon which the Victorian moral pattern I have been describing depended. At one point the narrator of *Man and Wife* asks of his despicable character Geoffrey Delamyn, "Why should he feel remorse? All remorse springs, more or less directly, from the action of two sentiments, which are neither of them inbred in the natural man." These are respect for self and for others. In exalted form the first is love of God, the second love of man. I repent of bad actions, the narrator adds, "because there has been a sense put into me which tells me that I have sinned against Myself, and sinned against You. No such sense as that exists among the instincts of the natural man" (92). If these feelings are not innate in man, then perhaps neither are an established conviction of right and wrong. We are coined not by God but by the social structure, and many of us will thus appear as counterfeit currency. To stress that the Christian ethic is as much a social product as any other, Collins has Delamyn ape the role of a good Christian. He says to the wife who displeases him, "I don't hate you. I'm a good Christian. I owe it to you that I'm cut out of my father's will. I forgive you that. I owe it to you that I've lost the chance of marrying a woman with ten thousand a year. I forgive you that. I'm not a man who does things by halves. I said it should be my endeavor to make you a good husband. I said it was my wish to make it up. Well! I am as good as my word. And what's the consequence? I am insulted" (211). Meanwhile, Geoffrey is planning to murder Anne! This and other Collins texts thus stand in a middle ground, between fiction accepting the basic Christian pattern of morality entirely and those which will later reject it. Collins is content to exploit the conventions of this morality while subverting any belief in its authority.

I do not mean to insist that authors and readers throughout the Victorian period were constantly alert to Christian articles of faith as they wrote and read. Although the majority of the educated classes were trained in one or another form of Christian belief, a great many of these people were not serious practitioners. Of course, as the century neared its close, more and more intellectuals were declaring themselves free from traditional faiths. But that does not mean that these persons necessarily freed themselves from an ethic that remained rooted in the Christian faith. There is a strong trace of this ethic in the writings of George Eliot. Whether drawn directly from Christianity or not, such moral essentials as retribution for misconduct, self-renunciation, and mercy or forgiveness remain important in her work. There is, for example, an extensive language of punishment and retribution in *Daniel Deronda*. A. O. J. Cockshut calls attention to the prevalence of poetic justice in Eliot's fiction. Her characters, he says, get what they deserve.[12] One thinks of some extreme cases, such as the improbably poetic retribution of Tito's death in *Romola* (1863). Herman Melville, at about this same time in America, could play out the whole Christian paradigm with obvious imagery and intensified episodes of punishment and forgiveness in his superb fable of justice and innocence, *Billy Budd*. The Christian scheme had become nearly secularized in Thackeray's fiction; it soon became mainly so for serious writers. When Dickens entitled a chapter of *Dombey and Son* "Retribution," it carried the full weight of moral and even religious meaning. Years later, when Trollope used the same title for a chapter of *The Prime Minister* (1876), it signified only the consequences of Glencora's rash encouragement of Ferdinand Lopez's political ambitions, which include a virtual blackmail letter and embarrassment for her husband, the duke.

If one of Dickens' favorite devices was to have his scamps and outlaws pervert and invert Christian institutions and values so that his narratives could exterminate or disempower the offenders and right the values, one of the devices used by late-century writers was to parody or reinterpret the Christian story itself, in works such as Wilde's *Salome* (1896) and Wells' *The Island of Dr. Moreau* (1896). But, far more subtly, what signals the collapse of the "Victorian novel" and the Victorian worldview is the diminished role of forgiveness in serious literature. As early as Thomas Hardy, it is clear that good folks will not necessarily be rewarded and bad folks will not necessarily be punished. Both will suffer. A typical example is the end of *The Woodlanders* (1887), where a "good" woman and a "bad" man reunite for what is likely to be an uncomfortable marriage while a true loving heart is left bereft and ignored. The many episodes involving forgiveness or the lack of it in *The Return of the Native* (1878) and *The Mayor of Caster-bridge* (1886) count for almost nothing in the narrative structure of the novels. In *Tess of the d'Urbervilles*, when Tess, like her husband, has confessed to a sexual fault before marriage, she asks of him the forgiveness she has easily extended to him and he responds, " 'O Tess, forgiveness does not apply to the case.' "[13] Much later when they have both forgiven one another, the forgiveness means nothing in any grand terms; Tess is already doomed and Angel can offer no hope of a reconcilation in an afterlife. And in *Jude the Obscure* (1895), forgiveness itself and the self-renunciation that often accompanies it become obscene in Sue and problematic in Phillotson and Jude. This novel also closes with what might be read as an anti-prayer from Scripture, designed to erase the entire code upon which the morality of the Victorian novel was constructed.

The clear sign of genuine modernity comes, however, with the outright refusal to endorse the punishment/forgiveness paradigm. Joseph Conrad's first novel, *Almayer's Folly* (1895), ends with a determined refusal to forgive. More pointedly, in *Lord Jim* (1900), when Jim has decided, after the model of romance that commands his imagination, to sacrifice his life for honor's sake, Jewel, his beloved, protests: " 'You are false!' she screamed out after Jim. 'Forgive me,' he cried. 'Never! Never!' she called back.[14] Jewel marks a definitive moment when the illusions of moral romance are canceled by the realism of a cruel existence. This movement away from a morality rooted in a nonhuman power intensifies as the twentieth century proceeds, and assumes an aggressive but optimistic form in the Existentialist movement. John Fowles openly allied himself with Existentialism, and some of his assertions in *The Aristos* (revised 1970) are pertinent here. Dismissing the debt-credit language of Christian discourse, Fowles declares, "There is no redemption, no remission; a sin has no price. It cannot be bought back till time itself is bought back."[15] Of the legacy of "sin" and "crime" that Western culture inherits from Christianity and Greco-Roman law, he says, "They disseminate a shared myth: that an evil deed can be paid for. In one case by penance and remorse; in the other, by accepting punishment" (162). Justice cannot rest on an economic model. "In a truly just world, culpability would clearly be a scientific, not a moral calculation" (161). Many of the splendid moments in Victorian narratives depend upon the reversal of an imprudent or wicked course of conduct. Suddenly the wayward woman feels her womanly heart moved again by an act of charity or the sight of a fellow human in need. Or the immature man discovers his selfishness and reverses his pattern of behavior. Or the cruel parent suddenly yields to the warm irradiation of love. But how many Nancys, Marthas, Martin Chuzzlewits, and Dombeys are there? If Victorian fiction assumed the power of free will to revise the story of one's life under the guiding authorship of Providence, as the nineteenth century progressed a growing sense that free will, what there might be of it, had little power to rescript the narratives human beings were doomed to act out. By the mid-twentieth century there can be no escape from the past. Again Fowles writes, "Existentialism says, in short, that if I commit an evil then I must live with it for the rest of my life; and that the only way I can live with it is by accepting that it is always present in me. Nothing, no remorse, no punishment, can efface it; and therefore each new evil I do is not a relapse, a replacement, but an addition. Nothing cleans the slate; it can become only dirtier" (163). To compensate his characters for the world into which he scripts them Fowles at least struggles to keep them as free as possible, teaching them in *The Magus* (1965) to become the author of their own theater, where no external powers are watching, or, in *A Maggot* (1985), liberating them beyond authorial control into a time (and place) beyond the telling.

The narrator of Margaret Atwood's *The Handmaid's Tale* (1985), which is set in a future far less pleasant than the one hinted at in *A Maggot*, interestingly couples the complexity of constructing a "true" narrative with the complex nature of such an apparently simple act as forgiveness.

> When I get out of here, if I'm ever able to set this down, in any form, even in the form of one voice to another, it will be a reconstruction then too, at yet another remove. It's impossible to say a thing exactly the way it was, because what you say can never be exact, you always have to leave something out, there are too many parts, sides, crosscurrents, nuances; too many gestures, which could mean this or that, too many shapes which can never be fully described, too many flavors, in the air or on the tongue, half-colors, too many. But if you happen to be a man, sometime in the future, and you've made it this far, please remember: you will never be subject to the temptation or feeling you must forgive, a man, as a woman. It's difficult to resist, believe me. But remember that forgiveness too is a power. To beg for it is a power, and to withhold or bestow it is a power, perhaps the greatest.[16]

Atwood, Dickens, and Thackeray understand the artifice of narration and the subtlety of forgiveness in their own ways. Atwood's parody of religious paternalism offers a fable that actively excludes a non-human power or design. Dickens and Thackeray, with very different degrees of confidence, built their narratives as imitations of a vaster story. Edwin Muir explains this difference in "The Decline of the Novel." "To the novelist fifty or a hundred years ago," he says, "life obediently fell into the mould of a story; to the novelist to-day it refuses to do so."[17] The modern novel is like a sentence that sets out confidently but which remains hanging in the air. "This is another way of saying that the contemporary novelist has an imaginative grasp of origins but not ends" (173). Muir goes on to argue that life must always stop short of meaning if we seek its meaning merely in itself. "To seek its meaning in itself is to seek its meaning in time; and the conception of life which prevails to-day is a conception of life purely in time. The contemporary novel is a story of time against a background of time. The traditional novel is a story of time against a permanent pattern" (176). Life is a complete story when seen against the background of eternity. I would add that it was not merely the eternal, but some eternal set of values which gave that story meaning for the Victorians, and which no longer prevails today. Whatever ideology might be found to underlie modern literature there can be little doubt that a self-affirming set of moral values did serve as a foundation for the great majority of literary texts of nineteenth-century England. That foundation, because it was trusted, determined to a very great extent the way narratives could be imagined, constructed, and transmitted.

NOTES

1. Bruno Bettelheim, *The Uses of Enchantment: The Meaning and Importance of Fairy Tales* (New York: Vintage Books, 1977), 44–45. Subsequent references appear in the text.

2. Daniel Defoe, *Moll Flanders,* ed. Edward Kelly (New York: W. W. Norton and Company, 1973), 4. Subsequent references appear in the text.

3. Henry Fielding, *Joseph Andrews with Shamela and Related Writings,* ed. Homer Goldberg (New York: W. W. Norton and Co., 1987), 7. Subsequent references appear in the text.

4. David Morse, *High Victorian Culture* (New York: New York University Press, 1993), 125.

5. Jane Austen, *Mansfield Park* (New York: New American Library, 1979), 359. Subsequent references appear in the text.

6. William Allingham, *Diary,* ed. H. Allingham and D. Radford (Harmondsworth: Penguin Books Ltd., 1985), 11. Subsequent references appear in the text.

7. Benjamin Disraeli, *Coningsby,* or *The New Generation,* ed. Thom Braun (London and New York: Penguin Books, 1983), 488.

8. Charlotte Brontë, *Jane Eyre,* ed. Richard J. Dunn (New York: W. W. Norton and Co., 1971), 210. Subsequent references appear in the text.

9. Emily Brontë, *Wuthering Heights,* ed. William A. Sale, Jr. (New York: W. W. Norton and Co., 1972), 57.

10. *The Poems of Tennyson,* ed. Christopher Ricks, 3 vols. (London: Longman, 1987), 2:275ff. Subsequent references appear in the text.

11. Wilkie Collins, *Man and Wife* (New York: Dover Publications, Inc., 1983), 32–33.

12. A. O. J. Cockshut, *The Unbelievers: English Agnostic Thought 1840-1890* (London: Collins, 1964), 52ff.

13. Thomas Hardy, *Tess of the d'Urbervilles,* ed. Scott Elledge (New York: W. W. Norton and Co., 1991), 179.

14. Joseph Conrad, *Lord Jim,* ed. Thomas C. Moser (New York: W. W. Norton and Co., 1968), 251.

15. John Fowles, *The Aristos* (New York: New American Library, 1970), 107. Subsequent references appear in the text.

16. Margaret Atwood, *The Handmaid's Tale* (New York: Fawcett Crest, 1985), 173–74.

17. Edwin Muir, "The Decline of the Novel," *Religion and Modern Literature: Essays in Theory and Criticism,* ed. G. B. Tennyson and Edward E. Ericson, Jr. (Grand Rapids, MI: William B. Eerdmans Publishing Co., 1975), 173. Subsequent references appear in the text.

Bibliography

Adshead, Joseph. *Prisons and Prisoners*. London: Longman, Brown, Green, and Longman, 1845.

à Kempis, Thomas. *Of the Imitation of Christ*. London: Oxford University Press, 1947.

Allingham, William. *A Diary, 1824–1889,* ed. H. Allingham and D. Radford. New York: Penguin Books, 1985.

Altick, Richard. *The Shows of London*. Cambridge: The Belknap Press of Harvard University Press, 1978.

———. *The Presence of the Present: Topics of the Day in the Victorian Novel*. Columbus: Ohio State University Press, 1991.

Andersen, Olive. *Suicide in Victorian and Edwardian England*. Oxford: Clarendon Press, 1987.

Arnold, Thomas. *The Miscellaneous Works*. New York: D. Appleton & Co., 1846.

———. *Thomas Arnold on Education: A Selection from His Writings,* intro. T. W. Bamford. Cambridge: Cambridge University Press, 1970.

Arthur, H. W. *Administrative Justice and Legal Pluralism in Nineteenth-Century England*. Toronto: University of Toronto Press, 1985.

Ashforth, David. "The Urban Poor Law" in *The New Poor Law in the Nineteenth Century,* ed. Derek Fraser. New York: St. Martin's Press, 1976, 128–48.

Atwood, Margaret. *The Handmaid's Tale*. New York: Fawcett Crest, 1985.

Auden, W. H. *The Collected Poems of W. H. Auden*. New York: Random House, 1945.

Austen, Jane. *Mansfield Park*. New York: New American Library, 1979.

Avery, Gillian. *Nineteenth-Century Children: Heroes and Heroines in English Children's Stories 1780–1900*. London: Hodder and Stoughton, 1965.

Axton, William F. *Circle of Fire: Dickens' Vision and Style and the Popular Victorian Theatre*. Lexington: University of Kentucky Press, 1956.

Bal, Mieke. *Narratology: Introduction to the Theory of Narrative,* trans. Christine van Boheemen. Toronto: University of Toronto Press, 1985.

Ballantine, Mr. Serjeant. *Some Experiences of a Barrister's Life*. New York: Henry Holt and Co., 1882.

Barnard, Robert, "Imagery and Theme in *Hard Times*," *Hard Times*, ed. George Ford and Sylvère Monod. New York: W. W. Norton and Co., 1990, 2nd ed., 367–79.

Barnes, Albert. *The Atonement, in its Relations to Law and Moral Government*. Philadelphia: Parry & McMillan, 1860.

Barty-King, Hugh. *The Worst Poverty: A History of Debt and Debtors*. Wolfeboro Falls, NH: Alan Sutton Publishing Inc., 1991.

Bender, John. *Imagining the Penitentiary: Fiction and the Architecture of Mind in Eighteenth-Century England*. Chicago: The University of Chicago Press, 1987.

Bettelheim, Bruno. *The Uses of Enchantment: The Meaning and Importance of Fairy Tales*. New York: Vintage Books, 1977.

Booth, Alison. "Little Dorrit and Dorothea Brooke: Interpreting the Heroines of History," *Nineteenth-Century Fiction* 41, no. 2 (September 1986), 190–216.

Brandon, S. G. F. *The Judgment of the Dead: An Historical and Comparative Study of the Idea of a Post-Mortem Judgment in the Major Religions*. London: Weidenfeld and Nicolson, 1967.

Bratton, J. S. *The Impact of Victorian Children's Fiction*. Totowa, NJ: Barnes & Noble Books, 1981.

Brooks, Peter. *The Melodramatic Imagination: Balzac, Henry James, Melodrama, and the Mode of Excess*. New York: Columbia University Press, 1985.

Brontë, Charlotte. *Jane Eyre*, ed. Richard J. Dunn. New York: W. W. Norton and Co., 1971.

Brontë, Emily. *Wuthering Heights*, ed. William A. Sale, Jr. New York: W. W. Norton and Co., 1972.

Bruner, Jerome. *On Knowing: Essays for the Left Hand*, expanded edition. Cambridge: The Belknap Press of Harvard University Press, 1982.

Bushnell, Horace. *Forgiveness and Law Grounded in Principles Interpreted by Human Analogies*. Hicksville, New York: The Regina Press, 1975. Reprint Edition with a New Introduction.

Butler, Joseph. *The Works of the Right Reverend Father in God Joseph Butler, D.C.L., Late Lord Bishop of Durham*, with Preface by Samuel Halifax, D.D., Late Lord Bishop of Gloucester 2 vols. Oxford: The Clarendon Press, 1874.

Butler, Marilyn. *Romantics, Rebels and Reactionaries: English Literature and its Background 1760–1830*. Oxford: Oxford University Press, 1981.

Butt, John and Kathleen Tillotson. *Dickens at Work*. London: Methuen and Co., 1963.

———. *Pope, Dickens and Others: Essays and Addresses*. Edinburgh: Edinburgh University Press, 1969.

Byrd, Max. "'Reading' in *Great Expectations*," *PMLA* 91, no. 2 (March 1976), 259–65.

Campbell, Jeremy. *Grammatical Man: Information, Entropy, Language, and Life*. New York: Simon and Schuster, Inc., 1983.

Carey, John. *Here Comes Dickens: The Imagination of a Novelist.* New York: Schocken Books, 1974.

_____. *Thackeray: Prodigal Genius.* London: Faber & Faber, 1977.

Carlisle, Janice. "*Little Dorrit:* Necessary Fictions," *Studies in the Novel* 7, no. 2 (Summer 1975), 195–213.

_____. *The Sense of an Audience: Dickens, Thackeray, and George Eliot at Mid-Century.* Athens: University of Georgia Press, 1981.

Carlyle, Thomas. *Past and Present,* ed. Richard D. Altick. Boston: Houghton Mifflin Co., 1965.

_____. *The Works of Thomas Carlyle,* 30 vols. New York: Charles Scribner's Sons, 1898.

Cazamian, Louis. *The Social Novel in England 1830–1850: Dickens, Disraeli, Mrs. Gaskell, Kingsley,* trans. Martin Fido. London: Routledge and Kegan Paul, 1973.

Chase, Karen. *Eros and Psyche: The Representation of Personality in Charlotte Bronte, Charles Dickens, and George Eliot.* New York: Methuen, 1984.

Chatman, Seymour. *Coming to Terms: The Rhetoric of Narrative in Fiction and Film.* Ithaca: Cornell University Press, 1990.

Chesterton, G. K. *Appreciations and Criticisms of the Works of Charles Dickens.* New York: E. P. Dutton and Co., 1911.

_____. *Charles Dickens,* intro. Steven Marcus. New York: Schocken Books, 1965.

Chittick, Kathryn, "Dickens and Parliamentary Reporting in the 1830s," *Victorian Periodicals Review* 21, no. 4 (Winter 1988), 151–60.

Christensen, Torben, D.D. *The Divine Order: A Study in F. D. Maurice's Theology.* Leiden: E. J. Brill, 1973.

Christmas, Peter. "*Little Dorrit:* The End of Good and Evil," *Dickens Studies Annual* 6, ed. Robert B. Partlow, Jr. Carbondale: Southern Illinois University Press, 1977, 134–53.

Church, R. W. *Human Life and Its Conditions: Sermons Preached Before the University of Oxford in 1876–1878 with Three Ordination Sermons.* London: Macmillan and Co., 1878.

Clark, Robert. "Riddling the Family Firm: The Sexual Economy in *Dombey and Son,*" in *ELH* 51 (1984), 69–84.

Cockshut, A. O. J. *The Imagination of Charles Dickens.* New York: New York University Press, 1962.

_____. *The Unbelievers: English Agnostic Thought 1840–1890.* London: Collins, 1964.

Colby, Robert A. *Thackeray's Canvass of Humanity: An Author and His Public.* Columbus: Ohio State University Press, 1979.

Collins, Philip. *Dickens and Crime.* Bloomington: Indiana University Press, 1968.

Collins, Philip, ed. *Thackeray: Interviews and Recollections,* 2 vols. New York: St. Martin's Press, 1983.

Collins, Wilkie. *Man and Wife.* New York: Dover Publications, Inc., 1983.

Conrad, Joseph. *Lord Jim,* ed. Thomas C. Moser. New York: W. W. Norton and

Co., 1968.

Coolidge, Archibald C., Jr. *Charles Dickens as a Serial Novelist.* Ames: Iowa University Press, 1967.

Cox, Edward W. *The Principles of Punishment, as Applied in the Adminstration of Criminal Law, by Judges and Magistrates.* New York and London: Garland Publishing, Inc., 1984.

Cross, Nigel. *The Common Writer: Life in Nineteenth-Century Grub Street.* Cambridge: Cambridge University Press, 1985.

Crowther, M.A. *The Workhouse System 1834–1929: The History of an English Social Institution.* Athens, Georgia: The University of Georgia Press, 1981.

Cummings, John. *The Daily Life; or Precepts and Prescriptions for Christian Living.* Boston: John P. Jewett and Co., 1855.

Dale, R. W. *Christian Doctrine: A Series of Discourses.* New York: A.C. Armstrong and Son, 1895.

Damrosch, Leopold, Jr. *God's Plot and Man's Stories: Studies in the Fictional Imagination from Milton to Fielding.* Chicago: University of Chicago Press, 1985.

Davis, Earle. *The Flint and the Flame: The Artistry of Charles Dickens.* Columbia: The University of Missouri Press, 1963.

Davis, Lennard. *Resisting Novels: Ideology and Fiction.* New York: Methuen, 1987.

Day, Thomas. *The History of Sandford and Merton.* London: Darton and Hodge, n.d.

Defoe, Daniel. *Moll Flanders,* ed. Edward Kelly. New York: W. W. Norton and Company, 1973.

DiBattista, Maria. "The Triumph of Clytemnestra: The Charades in *Vanity Fair," William Makepeace Thackeray,* ed. Harold Bloom. New York: Chelsea House Publishers, 1987.

Dickens, Charles. "Curious Missprint in the *Edinburgh Review," Household Words* (August 1 1857), 97–100.

———. *The Life of Our Lord. Written for His Children During the Years 1846 to 1849.* New York: Simon and Schuster, 1934.

———. *The Oxford Illustrated Dickens.* Oxford: Oxford University Press, various dates.

———. *The Speeches of Charles Dickens. A Complete Edition,* ed. K. J. Fielding. Atlantic Highlands, NJ: Harvester Wheatsheaf, 1988.

Disraeli, Benjamin. *Coningsby, Or the New Generation,* ed. Thom Braun. New York: Penguin, 1989.

Donzelot, Jacques. *The Policing of Families,* trans. Robert Hurley. New York: Pantheon Books, 1979.

Duckworth, Alistair M. "Little Dorrit and the Question of Closure," *Nineteenth-Century Fiction* 33, no. 1 (June 1978), 110–30.

Duff, R. A. *Trials and Punishments.* Cambridge: Cambridge University Press, 1986.

Duke, Francis, "Pauper Education" in *The New Poor Law in the Nineteenth Century,* ed. Derek Fraser. New York: St. Martin's Press, 1976, 67–86.

Dyson, A. E. *The Inimitable Dickens: A Reading of the Novels.* New York: St. Martin's Press, Inc., 1970.

———. "An Irony Against Heroes," *Thackeray:* Vanity Fair: *A Casebook,* ed. Arthur Pollard. London: The Macmillan Press Ltd., 1978.

Eastlake, Elizabeth. "Children's Literature," *Quarterly Review* 71 (December 1842), 54–83.

Edgeworth, Maria and Richard Lovell Edgeworth. *Practical Education,* 2 vols., intro. Gina Luria. New York: Garland Publishing Inc., 1974.

Edsall, Nicholas C. *The Anti-Poor Law Movement 1834–44.* Totowa, New Jersey: Rowman & Littlefield, Inc., 1971.

Emsley, Clive. *Crime and Society in England, 1750–1900.* London: Longman, 1987.

Ewing, A. C. *The Morality of Punishment with Some Suggestions for a General Theory of Ethics.* Montclair, NJ: Patterson Smith, 1970.

Fasick, Laura. "Thackeray's Treatment of Writing and Painting," *Nineteenth-Century Literature* 47, no. 1 (June 1992), 72–90.

Feinberg, Monica L. "Reading Curiosity: Does Dick's Shop Deliver?" in *Dickens Quarterly* 7, no. 1 (March 1990), 200–11.

Ferris, Ina. "The Demystification of Laura Pendennis," *Studies in the Novel* 13, Nos. 1–2 (Spring-Summer 1981), 122–32.

———. *William Makepeace Thackeray.* Boston: Twayne Publishers, 1983.

Fielding, Henry. *Joseph Andrews with Shamela and Related Writings,* ed. Homer Goldberg. New York: W. W. Norton and Co., 1987.

Fielding, K. J. *Charles Dickens: A Critical Introduction.* Boston: Houghton Mifflin Co., 1965.

Flinn, M. W. "Medical Services under the New Poor Law" in *The New Poor Law in the Nineteenth Century,* ed. Derek Fraser. New York: St. Martin's Press, 1976, 45–65.

Flint, Kate. *Dickens.* Brighton: The Harvester Press, 1986.

Ford, George H. *Dickens and His Readers: Aspects of Novel-Criticism Since 1836.* New York: W. W. Norton and Company, 1965.

Forster, John. *The Life of Charles Dickens.* London: Chapman and Hall, 1893.

Forsythe, William James. *The Reform of Prisoners 1830–1900.* London: Croom Helm Ltd., 1987.

Foucault, Michel, trans. Alan Sheridan. *Discipline and Punish: The Birth of the Prison.* New York: Random House, 1979.

Fowles, John. *The Aristos.* New York: New American Library, 1970.

Frank, Lawrence. *Charles Dickens and the Romantic Self.* Lincoln: University of Nebraska Press, 1984.

Fraser, Derek, ed. *The New Poor Law in the Nineteenth Century.* New York: St. Martin's Press, 1976.

———. "The Poor Law as Political Institution," in *The New Poor Law in the Nineteenth Century,* ed. Derek Fraser. New York: St. Martin's Press, 1976, 111–27.

Friedman, Stanley. "The Motif of Reading in *Our Mutual Friend,*" *Nineteenth-Century Fiction* 28, no. 1 (June 1973), 38–61.

Garis, Robert. *The Dickens Theatre: A Reassessment of the Novels.* Oxford: Oxford University Press, 1965.

Garrett, Peter K. *The Victorian Multiplot Novel: Studies in Dialogical Form.* New Haven: Yale University Press, 1980.

Garson, Marjorie, "Henry Esmond's Love of Children," *Nineteenth-Century Fiction* 36, no. 4 (March 1982), 387–406.

Gatty, Margaret Scott. *Parables From Nature.* London: J. M. Dent, n. d.

Gibbs, J. F. *Crime, Punishment and Deterrence.* Amsterdam: Elsevier, 1975.

Ginsberg, Michal Peled. "The Case against Plot in *Bleak House* and *Our Mutual Friend,*" *ELH* 59 (1992), 175–95.

Gissing, George. *Charles Dickens: A Critical Study.* New York: Dodd, Mead and Co., 1924.

Gladstone, William Ewart. *Correspondence on Church and Religion,* 2 vols., selected and arranged by D.C. Lathbury. New York; The Mcmillan Company, 1910.

Glancy, Ruth F. "Dickens and Christmas: His Framed-Tale Themes," *Nineteenth-Century Fiction* 35, no. 1 (June 1980), 53–72.

Greg, William Rathbone. *The Creed of Christendom: Its Foundations Contrasted With Its Superstructure.* Toronto: Rose-Belford Publishing Co., 1878.

Hagan, John H. Jr. "The Poor Labyrinth: The Theme of Social Injustice in Dickens's *Great Expectations,*" *Critical Essays on Charles Dickens's* Great Expectations, ed. Michael Cotsell. Boston: G. K. Hall, 1990, 56–62.

Hardy, Barbara. *The Moral Art of Dickens.* New York: Oxford University Press, 1970.

Hardy, Thomas. *Tess of the d'Urbervilles,* ed. Scott Elledge. New York: W. W. Norton and Co., 1991.

Hart, H. L. A. *Punishment and Responsibility: Essays in the Philosophy of Law.* New York: Oxford University Press, 1968.

Hay, Douglas and Francis Snyder, ed. *Policing and Prosecution in Britain 1750–1850.* Oxford: Clarendon Press, 1989.

Hill, Nancy Klenk. "*Dombey and Son:* Parable for the Age," in *Dickens Quarterly* 8, no. 4 (December 1991), 169–78.

Hilton, Boyd. *The Age of Atonement: The Influence of Evangelicalism on Social and Economic Thought, 1795–1865.* Oxford: Clarendon Press, 1988.

Hinton, James. *Man and His Dwelling Place. An Essay Toward the Interpretation of Nature.* New York: D. Appleton and Co., 1872.

———. *The Mystery of Pain. A Book for the Sorrowful.* New York: Mitchell Kennerley, 1914.

———. *Philosophy and Religion: Selections from the Manuscripts of the Late James Hinton,* ed. Caroline Haddon. London: Kegan Paul, Trench and Co., 1881.

Hornback, Bert G. *"Noah's Arkitecture" A Study in Dickens's Mythology.* Athens: Ohio University Press, 1972.

Horton, Susan R. *Interpreting Interpreting: Interpreting Dickens's Dombey.* Baltimore: The Johns Hopkins University Press, 1979.

———. *The Reader in the Dickens World: Style and Response.* Pittsburgh: University of Pittsburgh Press, 1981.

Howarth, Patrick. *Play Up and Play the Game: The Heroes of Popular Fiction*. London: Methuen, 1973.

Hoyles, J. Arthur. *Punishment in the Bible*. London: Epworth Press, 1986.

Hughes, Robert. *The Fatal Shore: The Epic of Australia's Founding*. New York: Vintage Books, 1986.

Humphrey, Frances A. *Dean Stanley with the Children*. Boston: D. Lothrop and Company, 1884.

Hutter, Albert D. "Crime and Fantasy in Great Expectations," *Critical Essays on Charles Dickens's* Great Expectations, ed. Michael Cotsell. Boston: G. K. Hall, 1990, 93–121.

Ignatieff, Michael. *A Just Measure of Pain: The Penitentiary in the Industrial Revolution 1750–1850*. New York: Columbia University Press, 1978.

Iser, Wolfgang. *The Implied Reader: Patterns of Communication in Prose Fiction from Bunyan to Beckett*. Baltimore: The Johns Hopkins University Press, 1974.

————. *The Act of Reading: A Theory of Aesthetic Response*. Baltimore: The Johns Hopkins University Press, 1978.

Jackson, Arlene. "Reward, Punishment, and the Conclusion of *Dombey and Son*," in *Dickens Studies Annual* 7, ed. Robert B. Partlow, Jr. Carbondale: Southern Illinois University Press, 1978, 103–27.

Jackson, T. A. *Charles Dickens: The Progress of a Radical*. New York: International Publishers, 1938.

Jaffe, Audrey. *Vanishing Points: Dickens, Narrative, and the Subject of Omniscience*. Berkeley: University of California Press, 1991.

James, Louis, "Tom Brown's Imperialist Sons," *Victorian Studies* 18 (1973), 89–99.

Jann, Rosemary. *The Art and Science of Victorian History*. Columbus: Ohio State University Press, 1985.

Jay, Elizabeth. *The Religion of the Heart: Anglican Evangelicalism and the Nineteenth-Century Novel*. Oxford: The Clarendon Press, 1979.

Jeaffreson, J. Cordy. *Novels and Novelists, from Elizabeth to Victoria*, 2 vols. London: Hurst and Blackett, Publishers, 1858.

Johns, Bennett G. "Children's Fiction," *Quarterly Review*, vol. 122 (January 1867), 55–89.

Johnson, Edgar. *Charles Dickens: His Tragedy and Triumph: A Biography*, 2 vols. Boston: Little, Brown and Co., 1952.

Johnson, E. D. H. *Charles Dickens: An Introduction to His Novels*. New York: Random House, 1969.

Johnston, William. *England As It Is, Political, Social, and Industrial, in the Middle of the Nineteenth Century*, 2 vols. London: John Murray, 1851.

Joseph, Gerhard. "The Labyrinth and the Library: A View from the Temple in *Martin Chuzzlewit*," *Dickens Studies Annual* 15 (1986), 1–22.

Kaufmann, Walter. *Without Guilt and Justice: From Decidophobia to Autonomy*. New York: Delta Books, 1975.

Kermode, Frank. *The Genesis of Secrecy: On the Interpretation of Narrative.* Cambridge: Harvard University Press, 1979.

Kincaid, James. *Dickens and the Rhetoric of Laughter.* Oxford: The Clarendon Press, 1971.

_____. "All the Wickedness in the World is Print: Dickens and Subversive Interpretation," *Victorian Literature and Society,* ed. James R. Kincaid and Albert J. Kuhn. Columbus: Ohio State University Press, 1984.

Kingsley, Charles. *The Works of Charles Kingsley.* Hildesheim: Georg Olms Verlagsbuchhandlung, 1969.

_____. *The Water-babies,* illustrated by Linley Sambourne [as originally published by Macmillan & Co., Ltd; London, 1863] Ann Arbor: University Microfilms, Inc., 1966.

Kleinig, John. *Punishment and Desert.* The Hague: Martinus Nijhoff, 1973.

Knoepflmacher, U. C. *Laughter and Despair: Readings in Ten Novels of the Victorian Era.* Berkeley: University of California Press, 1971.

Kucich, John. *Excess and Restraint in the Novels of Charles Dickens.* Athens: The University of Georgia Press, 1981.

Lambert, Mark. *Dickens and the Suspended Quotation.* New Haven: Yale University Press, 1981.

Lankford, William T. "'The Parish Boy's Progress': The Evolving Form of *Oliver Twist,*" *PMLA* 93, no. 1 (January 1978), 20–32.

Larson, Janet. *Dickens and the Broken Scripture.* Athens: The University of Georgia Press, 1985.

Lea, Sydney. *The Floating Candles.* Urbana: University of Illinois Press, 1982.

Leavis, F. R. and Q. D. *Dickens the Novelist.* Harmondsworth: Penguin Books, 1972.

Levine, George. *The Realist Imagination: English Fiction from Frankenstein to Lady Chatterley.* Chicago: The University of Chicago Press, 1981.

Lindberg, John. "Individual Conscience and Social Injustice in *Great Expectations,*" *Assessing* Great Expectations, ed. Richard Lettis and William E. Morris. San Francisco: Chandler Publishing Co., 1960, 186–93.

Lodge, David. *Language of Fiction: Essays in Criticism and Verbal Analysis of the English Novel.* New York: Columbia University Press, 1966.

Loofbourow, John. *Thackeray and the Form of Fiction.* Princeton: Princeton University Press, 1964.

Lucas, John. *The Melancholy Man: A Study of Dickens's Novels.* London: Methuen and Co., Ltd., 1970.

Mack, Edward C. *Public Schools and British Opinion 1780–1860.* New York: Columbia University Press, 1939.

_____. *Public Schools and British Opinion Since 1860.* New York: Columbia University Press, 1941.

Mackenzie, Mary Margaret. *Plato and Punishment.* Berkeley: University of California Press, 1981.

Malone, Cynthia Northcutt. "The Fixed Eye and the Rolling Eye: Surveillance and Discipline in *Hard Times*," *Studies in the Novel* 21, no. 1 (Spring 1989), 14–26.

Manning, Sylvia. *Dickens as Satirist*. New Haven: Yale University Press, 1971.

————. "*David Copperfield* and Scheherazada: The Necessity of Narrative," *Studies in the Novel* 14, no. 4 (Winter 1982), 327–36

Marcus, Steven. *Dickens: From Pickwick to Dombey*. New York: Basic Books, Inc., 1965.

Marryat, Captain Frederick. *Mr. Midshipman Easy*, intro. David Hannay. London: Macmillan and Co., Ltd., 1932.

Massey, Gerald. *The Poetical Works of Gerald Massey*. London: Routledge, Warne, and Routledge, 1864.

Matthew, H. C. G. *Gladstone: 1809–1874*. New York: Oxford University Press, 1988.

Maurice, Frederick Denison. *Theological Essays*. New York: Redfield, 1984.

Maxwell, Richard. *The Mysteries of Paris and London*. Charlottesville: University Press of Virginia, 1992.

McCarron, Robert M. "Folly and Wisdom: Three Dickensian Wise Fools," *Dickens Studies Annual* 6 (1977), 40–56.

McCrum, Michael. *Thomas Arnold Head Master: A Reassessment*. Oxford: Oxford University Press, 1989.

McMaster, Juliet. *Thackeray: The Major Novels*. Toronto and Buffalo: University of Toronto Press, 1971.

————. "Funeral Baked Meats: Thackeray's Last Novel," *Studies in the Novel* 13, nos. 1–2 (Spring-Summer 1981), 133–55.

Metz, Nancy Aycock. "The Artistic Reclamation of Waste in *Our Mutual Friend*," *Nineteenth-Century Fiction* 34, no. 1 (June 1979), 59–72.

Mill, John Stuart. *Collected Works of John Stuart Mill*, 32 vols. Toronto: University of Toronto Press, 1969.

Miller, D. A. *The Novel and the Police*. Berkeley: University of California Press, 1988.

Miller, J. Hillis. *Charles Dickens: The World of His Novels*. Cambridge: Harvard University Press, 1965.

————. *Fiction and Repetition: Seven English Novels*. Cambridge: Harvard University Press, 1982.

————. *The Ethics of Reading: Kant, de Man, Eliot, Trollope, James, and Benjamin*. New York: Columbia University Press, 1987.

Moberly, Sir Walter. *The Ethics of Punishment*. Hamden, CT: Archon Books, 1968.

Monod, Sylvère. *Martin Chuzzlewit*. London: George Allen and Unwin, 1985.

Moretti, Franco. *Signs Taken For Wonders: Essays in the Sociology of Literary Forms*, trans. Susan Fischer, David Forgacs, and David Miller. London: Verso, 1988.

Morse, David. *High Victorian Culture*. New York: New York University Press, 1993.

Mortimer, Favell Lee. *The Peep of Day; Or, A Series of the Earliest Religious Instruction the Infant Mind is Capable of Receiving; with Verses Illustrative of the Subjects.* Boston: American Tract Society, n.d.

Moynahan, Julian, "The Hero's Guilt: The Case of *Great Expectations,*" *Critical Essays on Charles Dickens's* Great Expectations, ed. Michael Cotsell. Boston: G. K. Hall and Co., 1990, 73–86.

Muir, Edwin. "The Decline of the Novel," *Religion and Modern Literature: Essays in Theory and Criticism,* ed. G. B. Tennyson and Edward E. Ericson, Jr. Grand Rapids, MI: William B. Eerdmans Publishing Co., 1975.

Mundhenk, Rosemary. "The Education of the Reader in *Our Mutual Friend,*" *Nineteenth-Century Fiction* 34, no. 1 (June 1979), 41–58.

Munsche, P. B. *Gentlemen and Poachers: The English Game Laws 1671–1831.* Cambridge: Cambridge University Press, 1981.

Murphy, Jeffrie G. and Jean Hampton. *Forgiveness and Mercy.* Cambridge: Cambridge University Press, 1988.

Needham, Gwendolyn B. "The Undisciplined Heart of David Copperfield," *Nineteenth-Century Fiction* 9 (1954), 81–107.

Nelson, Claudia. *Boys will be Girls: The Feminine Ethic and British Children's Fiction, 1857–1917.* New Brunswick: Rutgers University Press, 1991.

Neuburg, Victor E. *The Penny Histories: a study of chapbooks for young readers over two centuries.* New York: Harcourt, Brace & World, Inc., 1968.

Newcomb, Mildred. *The Imagined World of Charles Dickens.* Columbus: Ohio State University Press, 1989.

Nietzsche, Friedrich. *On The Genealogy of Morals,* trans. Walter Kaufmann and R. J. Hollindale. New York; Vintage Books, 1969.

Oram, Richard W. "'Just a Little Turn of the Circle': Time, Memory, and Repetition in Thackeray's *Roundabout Papers,*" *William Makepeace Thackeray,* ed. Harold Bloom. New York: Chelsea House Publishers, 1987, 169–78.

Partlow, Robert B. "The Moving I: A Study of Point of View in *Great Expectations,*" *Assessing* Great Expectations, ed. Richard Lettis and William E. Morris. San Francisco: Chandler Publishing Co., 1960, 194–201.

Pearson, Audrey C. "Brain Fever in Nineteenth-Century Literature: Fact and Fiction," *Victorian Studies,* 19, no. 4 (June 1976), 445–64.

Pearson, Gabriel. "The Old Curiosity Shop," in *Dickens and the Twentieth Century,* ed. John Gross and Gabriel Pearson. Toronto: University of Toronto Press, 1962, 77–90.

Peltason, Timothy. "Esther's Will," *ELH* 59 (1992), 671–91.

Phelan, James. *Reading People, Reading Plots.* Chicago: University of Chicago Press, 1989.

Plint, Thomas. *Crime in England, Its Relation, Character, and Extent as developed from 1801 to 1848.* London: Charles Gilpin, 1851.

Polhemus, Robert. *Comic Faith: The Great Tradition from Austen to Joyce.* Chicago: University of Chicago Press, 1980.

Proctor, Adelaide Anne. *The Complete Poetical Works,* intro. Charles Dickens. New York: Thomas Y. Crowell & Co., n.d.

Pusey, Edward Bouverie. *Sermons for the Church's Seasons from Advent to Trinity.* New York: E.P. Dutton & Co., 1883.

Pykett, Lyn. "*Dombey and Son:* A Sentimental Family Romance," in *Studies in the Novel* 19, no. 2 (Spring 1987), 16–30.

Rabinowitz, Peter J. *Before Reading: Narrative Conventions and the Politics of Interpretation.* Ithaca: Cornell University Press, 1987.

Rawlins, Jack P. *Thackeray's Novels: A Fiction That Is True.* Berkeley: University of California Press, 1974.

——. "Great Expiations: Dickens and the Betrayal of the Child," *Critical Essays on Charles Dickens's* Great Expectations, ed. Michael Cotsell. Boston: G. K. Hall, 1990, 168–81.

Rawls, John. *A Theory of Justice.* Cambridge: The Belknap Press of Harvard University Press, 1971.

Ray, Gordon N. *Thackeray: The Uses of Adversity 1811–1846.* London: Oxford University Press, 1955.

——. *Thackeray: The Age of Wisdom 1847–1863.* London: Oxford University Press, 1958.

——. "*Vanity Fair:* One Version of the Novelist's Responsibility," *Thackeray: Vanity Fair: A Casebook,* ed. Arthur Pollard. London: The Macmillan Press Ltd., 1978.

Reed, John R. *Old School Ties: The Public Schools in British Literature.* Syracuse: Syracuse University Press, 1964.

——. "Confinement and Character in Dickens' Novels," *Dickens Studies Annual 1* (Carbondale: Southern Illinois University Press, 1970, 41–54.

——. *Victorian Conventions.* Athens: Ohio University Press, 1975.

——. "A Friend to Mammon: Speculation in Victorian Literature," *Victorian Studies* 27, no. 2 (Winter 1984), 179–202.

——. *Victorian Will.* Athens: Ohio University Press, 1989.

——. "Paying Up: The Last Judgment and Forgiveness of Debts," *Victorian Literature and Culture,* 20, ed. John Maynard and Adrienne Auslander Munich. New York: AMS Press, 1993, 55–68.

Richardson, Ruth. *Death, Dissection and the Destitute.* New York: Penguin, 1989.

Rignall, J. M. "Dickens and the Catastrophic Continuum of History in *A Tale of Two Cities,*" *ELH* 51, no. 3 (Fall 1984), 575–87.

Rimmon-Kenan, Shlomith. *Narrative Fiction: Contemporary Poetics.* London: Methuen, 1986.

Roberts, Helene E. "'The Sentiment of Reality': Thackeray's Art Criticism," *Studies in the Novel* 13, nos. 1–2 (Spring-Summer 1981), 21–39.

Robertson, Frederick W. *Sermons on St. Paul's Epistles to the Corinthians: Delivered at Trinity Chapel,* Brighton. Boston: Ticknor and Fields, 1866.

——. "The Human Race" and Other Sermons Preached At Cheltenham, Oxford, and Brighton. New York: Harper & Brothers, 1881.

_____. *Sermons On Bible Subjects.* London: J.M. Dent & Co., 1906.

Robson, John M. "Crime in *Our Mutual Friend,*" *Rough Justice: Essays on Crime in Literature,* ed. M. L. Friedland. Toronto: University of Toronto Press, 1991, 114–36.

Rose, Lionel. *The Massacre of the Innocents: Infanticide in Britain 1800–1939.* London: Routledge & Kegan Paul, 1986.

Rowell, Geoffrey. *Hell and the Victorians: A study of the nineteenth-century theological controversies concerning eternal punishment and the future life.* Oxford: Clarendon Press, 1974.

Rudé, George. *Criminal and Victim: Crime and Society in Early Nineteenth-Century England.* Oxford: Clarendon Press, 1985.

Ruskin, John. *The Winnington Letters: John Ruskin's Correspondence with Margaret Alexis Bell and the Children at Winnington Hall,* ed. Van Akin Burd. Cambridge: The Belknap Press of Harvard University Press, 1969.

Samuels, Allen. Hard Times: *An Introduction to the Variety of Criticism.* London: Macmillan, 1992.

Sanders, Andrew. *The Companion to* A Tale of Two Cities. London: Unwin Hyman, 1988.

Scarry, Elaine. "*Henry Esmond:* The Rookery at Castlewood," *Literary Monographs 7: Thackeray, Hawthorne and Melville, and Dreiser.* Madison: The University of Wisconsin Press, 1975, 3–43.

_____. *The Body in Pain: The Making and Unmaking of the World.* New York: Oxford University Press, 1985.

Schlicke, Paul. *Dickens and Popular Entertainment.* London: Allen & Unwin, 1985.

Schwarzbach, F. S. *Dickens and the City.* London: The Athlone Press, 1979.

Shattock, Joanne. *Politics and Reviewers:* The Edinburgh *and* The Quarterly *in the Early Victorian Age.* Leicester: Leicester University Press, 1989.

Shelston, Alan, ed. *Charles Dickens:* Dombey and Son *and* Little Dorrit: *A Casebook.* London: Macmillan Publishers, Ltd., 1985.

Sherwood, Mary. *The History of the Fairchild Family,* preface by Barry Westburg. New York: Garland Publishing, Inc., 1977.

Showalter, Elaine. "Guilt, Authority, and the Shadows of *Little Dorrit,*" *Nineteenth-Century Fiction* 34, no. 2 (June 1979), 20–40.

Siegle, Robert. *The Politics of Reflexivity: Narrative and the Constitutive Poetics of Culture.* Baltimore and London: The Johns Hopkins University Press, 1986.

Sinha, Susanta Kuman. "Authorial Voice in Thackeray: A Reconsideration," *English Studies* 3 (June 1983), 233–46.

Smith, Grahame. *Dickens, Money, and Society.* Berkeley: The University of California Press, 1968.

Smith, K. J. M. *James Fitzjames Stephen: Portrait of a Victorian Rationalist.* Cambridge: Cambridge University Press, 1988.

Sorenson, Gerald C. "Beginning and Ending: *The Virginians* as a Sequel," *Studies in the Novel* 13, nos. 1–2 (Spring-Summer 1981), 109–21.

Splitter, Randolph. "Guilt and the Trappings of Melodrama in *Little Dorrit,*"

Dickens Studies Annual 6, ed. by Robert B. Partlow, Jr. Carbondale: Southern Illinois University Press, 1977, 119–33.

Spurgeon, Charles Haddon. *Sermons, Sixth Series.* New York: Sheldon and Co., 1865.

Stange, G. Robert. "Expectations Well Lost: Dickens's Fable for His Time," *Critical Essays on Charles Dickens's* Great Expectations, ed. Michael Cotsell. Boston: G. K. Hall and Co., 1990, 63–72.

Stanley, Arthur Penrhyn. *Addresses and Sermons Delivered at St. Andrew's in 1872, 1875 and 1877.* London: Macmillan and Co., 1877.

Steele, Richard. *The Christian Hero,* ed. Rae Blanchard. New York: Octagon Books, 1977. Full title: *The Christian Hero: an Argument Proving that no Principles but those of Religon are Sufficient to make a Great Man* [London: 1710, 3rd ed.]

Steig, Michael. *Dickens and Phiz.* Bloomington: Indiana University Press, 1978.

Stephen, James Fitzjames. "The Criminal Law and the Detection of Crime," *The Cornhill Magazine* 2 (December 1860), 697–708.

——. *Liberty, Equality, Fraternity.* London: Smith, Elder, and Co., 1873.

Stewart, Garrett. *Dickens and the Trials of the Imagination.* Cambridge: Harvard University Press, 1974.

——. *Death Sentences: Styles of Dying in British Fiction.* Cambridge: Harvard University Press, 1984.

Stone, Harry. *Dickens and the Invisible World: Fairy Tales, Fantasy, and Novel-Making.* Bloomington: Indiana University Press, 1979.

——, ed. *Dickens' Working Notes for His Novels.* Chicago: The University of Chicago Press, 1987.

Storey, Graham. *Charles Dickens:* Bleak House. Cambridge: Cambridge University Press, 1987.

Sucksmith, Harvey Peter. *The Narrative Art of Charles Dickens: The Rhetoric of Sympathy and Irony in His Novels.* Oxford: Clarendon Press, 1970.

Sudrann, Jean. "The Philosopher's Property: Thackeray and the Use of Time," *Victorian Studies* 10, no. 4 (June 1967), 359–88.

Suleiman, Susan Rubin. *Authoritarian Fictions: The Ideological Novel as a Literary Genre.* New York: Columbia University Press, 1983.

Swinburne, Algernon Charles. *Charles Dickens.* London: Chatto and Windus, 1913.

Tambling, Jeremy. "Prison Bound: Dickens and Foucault," *Critical Essays on Charles Dickens's* Great Expectations, ed. Michael Cotsell. Boston: G. K. Hall, 1990, 182–97.

Taylor, Jenny Bourne. *In the Secret Theatre of Home: Wilkie Collins, Sensation Narrative, and Nineteenth-Century Psychology.* London: Routledge, 1988.

Ten, C. L. *Crime, Guilt and Punishment.* Oxford: Clarendon Press, 1987.

Tennyson, Alfred, Lord. *The Poems of Tennyson,* 3 vols., ed. Christopher Ricks. London: Longman, 1987.

Tennyson, Hallam. *Alfred Lord Tennyson: A Memoir,* 2 vols. New York: The Macmillan Co., 1905.

Terry, R. C. *Victorian Popular Fiction, 1860–80.* Atlantic Highlands, NJ: Humanities Press, 1983.

Thackeray, William Makepeace. *The Works of William Makepeace Thackeray,* 26 vols. Philadelphia: J. B. Lippincott Company, 1901.

_____. *The Letters and Private Papers of William Makepeace Thackeray,* ed. Gordon N. Ray, 4 vols. Cambridge: Harvard University Press, 1945–46.

_____. *Contributions to the* Morning Chronicle, ed Gordon N. Ray. Urbana: University of Illinois Press, 1955.

Thomas, Deborah A. *Dickens and the Short Story.* Philadelphia: University of Pennsylvania Press, 1982.

_____. *Thackeray and Slavery.* Athens: Ohio University Press, 1993.

Thompson, F. M. L. *The Rise of Respectable Society: A Social History of Victorian Britain 1830–1900.* Cambridge: Harvard University Press, 1988.

Thornton, Henry. *Family Prayers: To Which Is Added, A Family Commentary Upon The Sermon On The Mount.* 3rd American Edition. New York: Swords, Stanford, & Co., 1837.

Tillotson, Geoffrey and Donald Hawes, ed. *Thackeray: The Critical Heritage.* New York: Barnes & Noble Inc., 1968.

Tillotson, Kathleen. *Novels of the Eighteen-Forties.* London: Oxford University Press, 1961.

Trollope, Anthony. *An Autobiography,* intro. Bradford Allen Booth. Berkeley: University of California Press, 1947.

Trollope, Mrs. [Frances]. *The Vicar of Wrexhill.* London: Richard Bentley, 1840. Standard Novels, No. LXXVIII. New York: AMS Press, 1975.

Tupper, Martin. *Proverbial Philosophy: In Four Series.* London: E. Moxon, Son & Co., n.d.

Turner, E. S. *Boys Will Be Boys.* London: Michael Joseph, 1957.

Van Ghent, Dorothy. *The English Novel: Form and Function.* New York: Holt, Rinehart and Winston, Inc., 1953.

Vargish, Thomas. *Newman: The Contemplation of Mind.* Oxford: Clarendon Press, 1970.

_____. *The Providential Aesthetic in Victorian Fiction.* Charlottesville: University Press of Virginia, 1985.

Vogel, Jane. *Allegory in Dickens.* University, AL: The University of Alabama Press, 1977.

von Hirsch, A. *Doing Justice: The Choice of Punishments: Report of the Committee for the Study of Incarceration.* New York: Hill and Wang, 1976.

Walder, Dennis. *Dickens and Religion.* London: George Allen & Unwin, 1981.

Walker, Nigel. *Punishment, Danger and Stigma.* Oxford: Basil Blackwell, 1980.

_____. *Why Punish?* Oxford: Oxford University Press, 1991.

Warton, The Rev. John. *Death-Bed Scenes, and Pastoral Conversations.* Fourth edition in three volumes. London: John Murray, 1830.

Weber, Max. *The Protestant Ethic and the Spirit of Capitalism,* trans. Talbot Parsons. New York: Scribners, 1958.

Weiss, Barbara. *The Hell of the English: Bankruptcy and the Victorian Novel.* Lewisburg: Bucknell University Press, 1986.

Wells, H. G. *The Island of Dr. Moreau.* New York: Penguin, 1988.

Welsh, Alexander. *From Copyright to Copperfield: The Identity of Dickens.* Cambridge: Harvard University Press, 1987.

Westburg, Barry. *The Confessional Fictions of Charles Dickens.* DeKalb: Northern Illinois University Press, 1977.

Wheeler, Michael. *Death and the Future Life in Victorian Literature and Theology.* Cambridge: Cambridge University Press, 1990.

White, Hayden. "The Value of Narrativity in the Representation of Reality," *Critical Inquiry* 7, no. 1 (Autumn 1980), 5–28.

Whitehill, Sharon. "Jonas Chuzzlewit: Archetype of the Self-Destroyer," *Dickens Studies Newsletter* 9 (1978), 70–73.

Wiener, Martin J. *Reconstructing the Criminal: Culture, Law, and Policy in England, 1830–1914.* Cambridge: Cambridge University Press, 1990.

Wood, Allen W. *Kant's Moral Religion.* Ithaca: Cornell University Press, 1970.

Worth, George. *Dickensian Melodrama: A Reading of the Novels.* Lawrence: The University of Kansas Press, 1978.

Yonge, Charlotte. "Children's Literature of the Last Century," *Macmillan's Magazine* 20, (July 1869), 229–37; (August 1869), 302–10; (September 1869), 448–56.

INDEX

This index includes the names of nineteenth-century figures and of modern critics and writers but does not include the names of editors. I have selectively included titles of nineteenth-century books and poems, but have not included titles of modern critical texts. I have tried to include appropriate references to selected subjects, but have not listed regularly recurring subjects such as punishment, forgiveness, and so on, except where they are treated as subjects in themselves. Similarly references to Christ and Christianity are too numerous to list. Names and titles that appear primarily in notes are also included.

A Note about the Author

John R. Reed is Distinguished Professor of English at Wayne State University. Books by Dr. Reed previously published by Ohio University Press include *Perception and Design in Tennyson's Idylls of the King* (1970), *Victorian Conventions* (1975), *The Natural History of H. G. Wells* (1982), *Decadent Style* (1985), and *Victorian Will* (1989).